W9-BZT-584

Oracle PL/SQL Developer's Workbook

Oracle PL/SQL Developer's Workbook

Steven Feuerstein
with Andrew Odewahn

O'REILLY®

Beijing · Cambridge · Farnham · Köln · Paris · Sebastopol · Taipei · Tokyo

Oracle PL/SQL Developer's Workbook
by Steven Feuerstein with Andrew Odewahn

Copyright © 2000 O'Reilly & Associates, Inc. All rights reserved.
Printed in the United States of America.

Published by O'Reilly & Associates, Inc., 101 Morris Street, Sebastopol, CA 95472.

Editor: Deborah Russell

Production Editor: Mary Anne Weeks Mayo

Cover Designer: Edie Freedman

Printing History:

May 2000:   First Edition.

Nutshell Handbook, the Nutshell Handbook logo, and the O'Reilly logo are registered trademarks of O'Reilly & Associates, Inc. The association between the image of a stag beetle and the topic of Oracle PL/SQL is a trademark of O'Reilly & Associates, Inc. Oracle® and all Oracle-based trademarks and logos are trademarks or registered trademarks of Oracle Corporation, Inc. in the United States and other countries. O'Reilly & Associates, Inc. is independent of Oracle Corporation. Java™ and all Java-based trademarks and logos are trademarks or registered trademarks of Sun Microsystems, Inc. in the United States and other countries. O'Reilly & Associates, Inc. is independent of Sun Microsystems.

Many of the designations used by manufacturers and sellers to distinguish their products are claimed as trademarks. Where those designations appear in this book, and O'Reilly & Associates, Inc. was aware of a trademark claim, the designations have been printed in caps or initial caps. While every precaution has been taken in the preparation of this book, the publisher assumes no responsibility for errors or omissions, or for damages resulting from the use of the information contained herein.

CIP data can be found at *http://www.oreilly.com/catalog/ordevworkbook*.

ISBN: 1-56592-674-9
[M]

In memory of the hundreds of thousands of children who have been killed by the U.S.-led embargo of Iraq, and in honor of the many U.S. citizens, especially members of Voices in the Wilderness, who have worked to end that embargo

—Steven Feuerstein

Table of Contents

Preface

When I first started writing about the Oracle PL/SQL language back in 1994, there were precious few resources on the language besides Oracle's documentation. Six years later, the situation has changed radically. Not only does O'Reilly & Associates offer four full-length texts and two quick references on PL/SQL, but other publishers have also focused their attention on this important database programming language for Oracle developers.

Given this state of affairs, you might then reasonably ask: what need does the *Oracle PL/SQL Developer's Workbook* fill that thousands of other pages of writings on PL/SQL do not manage to meet?

One concern I have about texts on computer software is that reading a book is inherently a passive activity. You read, and you attempt to absorb information from another, more experienced (you hope) developer. Now, it is true that the act of engaging with the material is not entirely passive. Yet it is also true that until you actually try to write some code or solve some problem with the language, you will not really have tested or integrated your newfound knowledge.

The object of this workbook is to provide you with an active learning experience with PL/SQL. While you could simply read the workbook as you might read my first text, *Oracle PL/SQL Programming*, the book you are holding has been designed to engage you actively, to provoke a response, to get you solving problems immediately with the techniques at hand.

It is my hope that through your use of this workbook you will deepen your understanding of, and facility with, the PL/SQL language. Consequently, you will move more rapidly along the learning curve and join the ever-growing ranks of PL/SQL experts.

Structure of the Developer's Workbook

The *Oracle PL/SQL Developer's Workbook* is divided into two parts: problems and solutions. I separated the two so that you could concentrate on the problem and come up with your own solution, instead of allowing your eyes to wander over the page and—gosh!—coming across my solution. This design should also make the book more useful in a classroom environment.

Within each part of the book, chapters are grouped into categories as follows:

Chapters 1 through 5 contain exercises testing your mastery of *language fundamentals*:

1. *Declaring Variables and Naming Elements*
2. *Loops*
3. *Conditional and Sequential Control*
4. *Exception Handling*
5. *Records*

Chapters 6 through 9 contain exercises in the area of *data structures*:

6. *Index-by Tables*
7. *Nested Tables*
8. *Variable Arrays*
9. *Object Technology*

Chapters 10 through 13 cover *database interaction:*

10. *Cursors*
11. *DML and Transaction Management*
12. *Cursor Variables*
13. *Native Dynamic SQL*

Chapters 14 through 17 test your expertise in *program construction:*

14. *Procedures, Functions, and Blocks*
15. *Packages*
16. *Triggers*
17. *Calling Functions in SQL*

Chapters 18 through 25 focus on *built-in functionality:*

18. *Character Functions*
19. *Date Functions*

20. *Conversion, Numeric, and Miscellaneous Functions*

21. *DBMS_SQL Built-in Package*

22. *DBMS_PIPE Built-in Package*

23. *DBMS_OUTPUT Built-in Package*

24. *UTL_FILE Built-in Package*

25. *DBMS_JOB Built-in Package*

Chapters 26 through 30 include the following *miscellaneous topics*:

26. *Using Java with PL/SQL*

27. *External Programs*

28. *PL/SQL Web Development*

29. *Tuning PL/SQL*

30. *PL/SQL for DBAs*

Within each chapter, exercises are organized by level of expertise as follows:

Beginner

Problems in this section assume very little prior experience with the PL/SQL language and can be used to increase your familiarity with the basic functionality of the language.

Intermediate

You have been working with PL/SQL for a while and feel comfortable with finding your way around the built-in functions, cursor FOR loops, etc. The problems in this category will stretch your comfort level, confirm your knowledge, and take you in new directions.

Expert

Do you have a few minutes to spare to meet a challenge? The problems in this category often require that you apply your knowledge in new and creative ways. Some will take a fair amount of effort, but I hope you will then be able to apply the resulting code to your development environment.

In all cases, I have made an effort to design problems that engage and entertain you. I have always felt that programming can be (almost obsessively) fun to do and extremely satisfying.

About the Oracle PL/SQL Series

This workbook is not a self-contained teaching tool. In this book I assume that you have read about the PL/SQL features that are the subject of each chapter before you attempt that chapter's exercises. For PL/SQL background information, see the following books (all published by O'Reilly):

Oracle PL/SQL Programming
> The "bible" of PL/SQL development. Describes all the basic language features, including modular programming.

Oracle PL/SQL Programming Guide to Oracle8i Features
> A companion to *Oracle PL/SQL Programming*. Describes the new PL/SQL features added in the Oracle8i release.

Oracle Built-in Packages
> Describes all the built-in packages and contains many examples of how to use them most effectively in your PL/SQL programs.

Advanced Oracle PL/SQL Programming with Packages
> Explains how you can write your own packages and dramatically improve your PL/SQL programs by doing so.

In addition, two pocket references (*Oracle PL/SQL Language Pocket Reference* and *Oracle PL/SQL Built-ins Pocket Reference*) provide compact summaries of the PL/SQL core language and built-in functions and packages.

About the Examples

This book contains many examples, some short and some quite long. For everything but the simplest examples, you'll find the code shown in the book on the O'Reilly web site (*www.oreilly.com/catalog/ordevworkbook*). You'll also find additional examples on the book's web page that were too long to be included in the hard copy. I've included this code to give you a jump-start on writing your own Oracle8i PL/SQL code and to keep you from having to type many pages of PL/SQL statements from printed text.

The examples are provided in two ways:

- The Companion Utilities Reference for the *Oracle PL/SQL Developer's Workbook*, an online tool developed by RevealNet, Inc., gives you point-and-click access to all source code developed for this book. You can use this software in any Microsoft Windows environment (95, 98, NT 4.0, 2000).

- A simple ZIP file contains the code for all examples. You may prefer this format if you are working in a non-Windows environment or have limited memory or bandwidth.

Throughout the book, web icons (see the "Conventions Used in This Book" section) indicate that a code example shown or mentioned in the text is included on the web page.

I'll try to keep the code up to date, incorporating corrections to any errors that are discovered, as well as improvements suggested by readers. For an updated version of the examples, the O'Reilly site.

Conventions Used in This Book

The following conventions are used in this book:

Italic
> Used for file and directory names and URLs, and for the first mention of new terms under discussion.

Constant width
> Used for code examples.

Constant width bold
> In some code examples, highlights the statements being discussed (e.g., when a change occurs).

Constant width italic
> In some code examples, indicates an element (e.g., a filename) that you supply.

UPPERCASE
> In code examples, indicates PL/SQL keywords.

lowercase
> In code examples, indicates user-defined items like variables and parameters.

Punctuation
> In code examples, enter exactly as shown.

Indentation
> In code examples, helps to show structure (but is not required).

-- In code examples, begins a single-line comment, which extends to the end of a line.

/* and */
> In code examples, these characters delimit a multiline comment, which can extend from one line to another.

. In code examples and related discussions, periods qualify a reference by separating an object name from a component name. For example, dot notation is used to select fields in a record and to specify declarations within a package.

The web icon indicates that the code example described or shown in the text appears on the book's web page.

Indicates a tip, suggestion, or general note. For example, I'll tell you if you need to use a particular Oracle version or if an operation requires certain privileges.

Indicates a warning or caution. For example, I'll tell you if Oracle does not behave as you'd expect or if a particular operation has a negative impact on performance.

Comments and Questions

Please address comments and questions concerning this book to the publisher:

> O'Reilly & Associates, Inc.
> 101 Morris Street
> Sebastopol, CA 95472
> (800) 998-9938 (in the United States or Canada)
> (707) 829-0515 (international or local)
> (707) 829-0104 (fax)

You can also send messages electronically. To be put on the mailing list or request a catalog, send email to:

> *info@oreilly.com*

To ask technical questions or comment on the book, send email to:

> *bookquestions@oreilly.com*

We have a web site for this book, where we'll list examples and errata, and you'll also find a discussion of how you can help keep this book up to date at:

> *http://www.oreilly.com/catalog/ordevworkbook*

For more information about this book and others, see the O'Reilly web site:

> *http://www.oreilly.com*

Acknowledgments

I realized a while ago (around the time I completed my second book) that I was having way too much fun (and not nearly enough time) writing about PL/SQL to keep it all to myself. I wanted (and needed) to share the multitude of opportunities with the friends I have made around the world through my writing and through the PL/SQL Pipeline, an absolutely fantastic online, noncommercial community for PL/SQL developers (*http://www.revealnet.com/plsql-pipeline*). And that is what I have done with this book.

I have shared the opportunity, the excitement, and the agony of writing the material for this book with a number of excellent Oracle technologists: Darryl Hurley, Dwayne King, Vadim Loevski, Jim Lopatosky, Chuck Sisk, and Vladimir Trusevich. I feel particularly indebted to Darryl Hurley, who contributed many hours of effort—and many pages of problems—to this book. I've asked each of these contributors to share with you a brief biography:

- **Darryl Hurley** is a database developer for Mobile Data Solutions, Inc. (*http:// www.mdsi-advantex.com*) in Richmond, BC, Canada. What little free time he has is taken up loving Vanessa or doing something sports-related (occasionally both at the same time) and hoping to turn out just like his parents. He can be reached at *dhurley@mdsi.bc.ca* or *implestrat@yahoo.com*.

- **Dwayne King**, founder and principal of KRIDAN Consulting (*http://www. kridan-consulting.com*) has been working with Oracle for seven years. Specializing in server-side programming and database administration, he has also developed and taught classes in PL/SQL. Based in Ottawa, he has worked on projects across Canada and overseas.

- **Vadim Loevski** has been developing Oracle applications for the last nine years. He currently works as Senior Application Specialist at Quest Software and is part of the team developing SQL Navigator, a tool for PL/SQL developers.

- **Jim Lopatosky** is an inhouse consultant for the Maine state government, specializing in Oracle database administration. His material has appeared in *Oracle Professional*, RevealNet, UKOUG's *Oracle Scene* and other sources. He also presents regularly at Oracle conferences.

- **Chuck Sisk** is a developer and consultant and lives with his wife Stephanie in Western Springs, Illinois. He can be reached at *csisk@enteract.com*.

- **Vladimir Trusevich**'s technical accomplishments range from creating DB2-PL/I mainframe applications for MVS/ESA for IBM branches in Europe to Oracle server/applications tuning. For the last six years, he has focused on Oracle client/server development, including database design, Dev/Des2K applications development, PL/SQL backend design, and database tuning/administration.

Chris Racicot and Tushar Gadhia, my dedicated friends at Oracle, also assisted me greatly by keeping me current with the state of PL/SQL. Tom White, Steve Hilker, and the rest of the RevealNet crew once again pitched in—the primary evidence of which is the fine Knowledge Base software that will make it a pleasure for you to examine the many files that come with this book. At an entirely different level of involvement and thanks, Andrew Odewahn stepped in towards the end of this process to provide crucial energy and effort to complete the book. Andrew, I couldn't have it done it without you!

In addition to my contributors, a number of PL/SQL developers provided some awesome technical reviews; others contributed individual problem-solution couplets or simply shared their expertise. My heartfelt thanks, therefore, to Eva Blinder, Solomon Yakobson, John Beresniewicz, Steve Cosner, Joe Testa, Rudresh (Tubby) Rana, Dick Bolz, Bill Pribyl, Nitin Ghagare, Susan Kleinfelter, and countless Pipeliners who contributed time and brain power to share their expertise. Incorporating this input was made much easier by the contributions of Bob Amen and Mary Jane Caswell-Stephenson of O'Reilly, who set up an online collaboration system (via their WebBoard product) to use during the development of the book. Sure, there might still be some errors in the text, but don't blame them! Blame me, and let me know about any errors, of course, so I can fix them as soon as possible.

Many thanks to the production team at O'Reilly, who again turned out an excellent book. And then there is the preproduction team: Steve Abrams, who worked under severe time pressure to get the files into production; Michael Blanding, who at an earlier stage helped figure out the best format for the workbook; and primarily my editor, Deborah Russell. You'd think that after a while she wouldn't answer her phone, scared silly that it would be Steven the Obsessive PL/SQL Author with yet another idea for yet another PL/SQL book. To her credit, Deborah has answered all my calls and responded to each and every email, and in between all of that correspondence once again transformed a massive amount of marginally coherent information into what I believe will be an extremely useful text. Hey, Debby, I'll be getting in touch with you soon about four more books I'd like you to publish!

It is Sunday, March 26, 2000, 8:00 A.M. I sit in my smallish backyard, feel the sun on my face, listen to the birds come back to this world in force, watch flowers pushing out of the ground to meet spring...and I find myself needing to acknowledge and thank my readers. Besides the pleasure of my family (and the burning desire to help realize true equality and justice in this most imperfect world), I realize that nothing is more important to me than knowing that my writings have had a positive impact on others. I had no idea when I started writing my seemingly endless stream of words on PL/SQL that I would strike as deep a chord as it seems

I have. It is often the case that when I train a group of developers or give a presentation at a conference, attendees ask for autographs or even to have their pictures taken with me. I am told on a recurring basis that my advice and techniques have had a job- and sometimes life-changing impact. I am more than a little embarrassed and bewildered by all of this, but how I feel about it is actually rather unimportant. What is absolutely crucial is that I respect and understand the responsibility I have to my readers and the debt I owe to all of you.

I

Problems

1

Declaring Variables and Naming Elements

Variables allow you to store and manipulate data—such as column values, counters, or calculations—inside your PL/SQL programs. There are two types of variables: *scalar*, which are made up of a single value, and *composite*, which are made up of multiple pieces (a record, for example, is represented with a composite variable). Whether composite or scalar, every variable has a name (also called an identifier), a datatype (such as NUMBER or VARCHAR2), and a value. This chapter tests your ability to work with these most basic PL/SQL elements.

Beginner

1-1. Which of the following identifiers are valid, which are invalid, and why?

    a. `my_variable2`

    b. `my-variable2`

    c. `my^variable`

    d. `MyVariable`

    e. `my_variable_for_many_many_of_usages`

    f. `123myvariable`

    g. `"123myvariable"`

1-2. Which of the following blocks will compile, and which will fail to compile? Why?

    a.
```
DECLARE
    lastdate DATE;
    lastDate NUMBER;
BEGIN
    NULL;
END;
```

    b.
```
DECLARE
    lastdate DATE := sysdate;
```

```
      lastDate NUMBER := 50;
   BEGIN
     dbms_output.put_line(lastdate);
     dbms_output.put_line(lastDate);
   END;
```

1-3. Declare a date variable with an initial value of SYSDATE (show both valid formats).

1-4. Declare a local variable to have the same datatype as the last_name column in the employee table.

1-5. Explain what is wrong with each of the following declarations:

```
DECLARE
   INTEGER year_count;
   VARCHAR2(100) company_name, employee_name;
   delimiters VARCHAR2;
   curr_year CONSTANT INTEGER;
   invalid_date EXCEPTION := VALUE_ERROR;
```

1-6. What datatype is most appropriate to store the following data items?

```
'This is a test'
Values from 1 to 10
5.987
'This is a test    '
A string that is always nine characters long
January 10, 2000
A binary file
TRUE or FALSE
The internal identifier of a row in a table
```

Intermediate

1-7. Declare a local variable to have the same datatype as the dollar_amount variable in the types package.

1-8. Which of the following statements about the DATE datatype are true?

   a. The maximum (latest) date allowed in a date variable is January 1, 4712.

   b. The earliest date allowed in a date variable is January 1, 4712 BC (or BCE).

   c. A date variable contains both date and time information.

   d. A date variable records the time down to the nearest hundredth of a second.

   e. The DATE datatype stores only those numbers of digits for the year you specify when you assign a value to the variable.

1-9. Declare a local variable to have the same datatype as the dollar_amount_t SUBTYPE in the types package.

1-10. Explain what is wrong with the following anchored declaration:

```
DECLARE
   dollar_amt CONSTANT NUMBER (20, 2) := 0;
   other_dollar_amt dollar_amt%TYPE;
```

1-11. Explain what is wrong with the following SUBTYPE declaration:

```
DECLARE
   SUBTYPE small_number IS NUMBER (3);
```

1-12. What error is raised when you try to execute this block of code? What is the problem?

```
DECLARE
   your_choice SIGNTYPE := 2;
BEGIN
   NULL;
END;
```

1-13. Which of the following statements describe accurately how the "anchoring" of a variable's datatype to a data structure improves the maintainability of that code?

    a. To anchor, you have to use %TYPE or %ROWTYPE, which involves more typing and that means you have more time to think about what you are typing and can get it right.

    b. If you anchor against a table or column in a table, when that table changes, your compiled code will be marked invalid. After recompilation, your code automatically reflects the latest structure in the table.

    c. When you anchor against a PL/SQL variable, you make sure to define your type of data only once and then reuse that definition. So if the definition changes, you have to change your code in only one place.

1-14. Name at least three different objects to which you could anchor a variable.

1-15. What datatype would you expect a function of the name "is_value_in_list" to return?

Expert

1-16. Why does this code compile?

```
DECLARE
   sysdate NUMBER;
BEGIN
   sysdate := 1;
END;
```

But this code does not?

```
DECLARE
   then NUMBER;
BEGIN
   then := 1;
END;
```

1-17. How can you get around this restriction and declare SUBTYPEs which are, in effect, constrained? To be specific, I want to declare a subtype called primary_key_t that limits the size of any variable declared with that type to NUMBER(6).

1-18. The NULL value in Oracle is handled differently from other values. One could even say that there is no such thing as a "NULL value." (NULL means "indeterminate.") Name three rules that apply to NULLs when doing comparisons.

1-19. What special operators does Oracle provide for dealing with NULLs?

2

Loops

PL/SQL has four basic looping (or iterative) structures: the simple loop, the FOR loop, the cursor-based FOR loop, and the WHILE loop; these repeatedly execute a block of code. There are three things to worry about when designing a loop:

- How (or whether) the loop terminates
- When the test for termination takes place
- Whether the type of loop is suited to the particular task at hand

If you know the number of times a loop must execute (for example, to process the months in a year), you can be reasonably confident that a FOR loop is the best structure. If you don't know the number in advance (for example, the number of records in a table), you're probably better off using a WHILE loop. This chapter tests your ability to make these kinds of decisions.

Beginner

2-1. What are the different kinds of loops available in PL/SQL?

2-2. How do you stop a simple loop from continuing?

2-3. Why is the following form of a simple loop called an *infinite loop*?

```
DECLARE
    myDate DATE;
BEGIN
    LOOP
        myDate := SYSDATE;
    END LOOP;
END;
```

2-4. How many times does the body of the following loop execute?

```
FOR year_index IN 1990 .. 1999
LOOP
   calc_sales (year_index);
END LOOP;
```

2-5. Rewrite the following loop so that you do not use a loop at all:

```
FOR i IN 1 .. 2
LOOP
   IF i = 1
   THEN
      give_bonus (president_id, 2000000);

   ELSIF i = 2
   THEN
      give_bonus (ceo_id, 5000000);
   END IF;
END LOOP;
```

2-6. How many times are the first_year and last_year functions executed in the following loop?

```
FOR yearnum IN
   first_year (company_id => 1056) ..
   last_year (company_id => 1056)
LOOP
   show_sales (1056);
END LOOP;
```

Intermediate

2-7. How would you emulate a REPEAT UNTIL loop in PL/SQL?

2-8. How many times does the body of the following loop execute?

```
FOR year_index IN REVERSE 1999 .. 1990
LOOP
   calc_sales (year_index);
END LOOP;
```

2-9. Select the type of loop (FOR, WHILE, simple) appropriate to implement the following requirement: for each of 20 years in the loan processing cycle, calculate the outstanding loan balance for the specified customer. If the customer is a preferred vendor, stop the calculations after 12 years.

2-10. Select the type of loop (FOR, WHILE, simple) appropriate to implement the following requirement: display the name and address of each employee returned by the following query:

```
SELECT name, address FROM employee;
```

2-11. Select the type of loop (FOR, WHILE, simple) appropriate to implement this requirement: scan through the list of employees in the PL/SQL table, keeping a count of all salaries greater than $50,000. Don't even start the scan, though, if the table is empty, or if today is a Saturday, or if the first employee in the PL/SQL table is the president of the company.

2-12. What is the problem with (or area for improvement in) the following loop? How would you change the loop to improve it?

```
FOR i IN 1 .. total_count
LOOP
   calc_totals (i);
   IF i > 75
   THEN
      EXIT;
   END IF;
END LOOP;
```

2-13. What is the problem with (or area for improvement in) the following loop? How would you change the loop to improve it?

```
OPEN emp_cur;
FETCH emp_cur INTO emp_rec;
WHILE emp_cur%FOUND
LOOP
   calc_totals (emp_rec.salary);
   FETCH emp_cur INTO emp_rec;
   EXIT WHEN emp_rec.salary > 100000;
END LOOP;
CLOSE emp_cur;
```

2-14. What is the problem with (or area for improvement in) the following loop? How would you change the loop to improve it?

```
FOR a_counter IN lo_val .. hi_val
LOOP
   IF a_counter > lo_val * 2
   THEN
      hi_val := lo_val;
   END IF;
END LOOP;
```

2-15. What is the problem with (or area for improvement in) the following loop? How would you change the loop to improve it?

```
DECLARE
   CURSOR emp_cur IS SELECT ... ;
   emp_rec emp_cur%ROWTYPE;
BEGIN
   OPEN emp_cur;
   LOOP
      FETCH emp_cur INTO emp_rec;
      EXIT WHEN emp_cur%NOTFOUND;
      calc_totals (emp_rec.salary);
   END LOOP;
   CLOSE emp_cur;
END;
```

2-16. What is the problem with (or area for improvement in) the following loop? How would you change the loop to improve it?

```
no_more_data := FALSE;
WHILE no_more_data
LOOP
    read_next_line (text);
    no_more_data := text IS NULL;
    EXIT WHEN no_more_data;
END LOOP;
```

2-17. What is the problem with (or area for improvement in) the following loop? How would you change the loop to improve it?

```
FOR month_index IN 1 .. 12
LOOP
    UPDATE monthly_sales
        SET pct_of_sales = 100
     WHERE company_id = 10006
        AND month_number = month_index;
END LOOP;
```

2-18. What is the problem with (or area for improvement in) the following loop? How would you change the loop to improve it?

```
DECLARE
    CURSOR emp_cur IS SELECT ... ;
    emp_rec emp_cur%ROWTYPE;
BEGIN
    FOR emp_rec IN emp_cur
    LOOP
        calc_totals (emp_rec.salary);
    END LOOP;

    IF emp_rec.salary < 10000
    THEN
        DBMS_OUTPUT.PUT_LINE ('Give ''em a raise!');
    END IF;

    CLOSE emp_cur;
END;
```

2-19. What is the problem with (or area for improvement in) the following loop? How would you change the loop to improve it?

```
DECLARE
    CURSOR checked_out_cur IS
        SELECT pet_id, name, checkout_date
          FROM occupancy
         WHERE checkout_date IS NOT NULL;
BEGIN
    FOR checked_out_rec IN checked_out_cur
    LOOP
        INSERT INTO occupancy_history (
            pet_id,
            name,
            checkout_date)
```

```
        VALUES (
            checked_out_rec.pet_id,
            checked_out_rec.name,
            checked_out_rec.checkout_date);
    END LOOP;
END;
```

2-20. Suppose that you run a cursor FOR loop to display the names of all CEOs who in 1998 received millions of dollars in stock and cash in exchange for selling off their company and laying off at least 1,000 employees:

```
DECLARE
    CURSOR nasties_cur
    IS
        SELECT ceo_name || ' of ' || company_name of_the_year
          FROM merged_companies
         WHERE TO_CHAR (merger_date, 'YYYY') = '1998'
           AND layoffs >= 1000;
BEGIN
    FOR the_man IN nasties_cur
    LOOP
        DBMS_OUTPUT.PUT_LINE (the_man.of_the_year);
    END LOOP;
END;
```

Now suppose that you need to show when you are done, the total number of nasties displayed in the report. How can you do that?

2-21. The emp table contains 14 rows. Why does this program not produce any output when it completes?

```
DECLARE
    counter PLS_INTEGER;
    CURSOR emp_cur IS SELECT * FROM emp;
BEGIN
    FOR emp_rec IN emp_cur
    LOOP
        give_raise (emp_rec.empno, 10000);
        counter := counter + 1;
    END LOOP;

    IF counter > 0
    THEN
        DBMS_OUTPUT.PUT_LINE (
            'Raises Given to ' || counter || ' employees.');
    END IF;
END;
```

Expert

2-22. This block uses a FOR loop that has one way in, but two ways out:

```
FOR yearnum IN 1 .. years_in
LOOP
    show_profits (yearnum);
```

```
       IF yearnum > 10
       THEN
           EXIT;
       END IF;
END LOOP;
```

Which of the following loops provides a revised implementation of that FOR loop that has just one way in and one way out and that is logically equivalent to the original?

a.
```
FOR yearnum IN 1 .. 11
   LOOP
       show_profits (yearnum);
   END LOOP;
```

b.
```
FOR yearnum IN 1 .. 10
   LOOP
       show_profits (yearnum);
   END LOOP;
```

c.
```
FOR yearnum IN 1 .. LEAST (years_in, 11)
   LOOP
       show_profits (yearnum);
   END LOOP;
```

d.
```
FOR yearnum IN 1 .. LEAST (years_in, 11)
   LOOP
       show_profits (yearnum);
       EXIT WHEN yearnum > years_in;
   END LOOP;
```

2-23. How many times does the following WHILE loop execute?

```
DECLARE
    end_of_analysis BOOLEAN := FALSE;

    CURSOR analysis_cursor
        IS SELECT ...; /* Something that returns a few rows. */

    analysis_rec analysis_cursor%ROWTYPE;

    next_analysis_step NUMBER;

    PROCEDURE get_next_record (step_out OUT NUMBER) IS
    BEGIN
       FETCH analysis_cursor INTO analysis_rec;
       IF analysis_rec.status = 'FINAL'
       THEN
          step_out := 1;
       ELSE
          step_out := 0;
       END IF;
    END;

BEGIN
    OPEN analysis_cursor;
    WHILE NOT end_of_analysis
    LOOP
```

```
        get_next_record (next_analysis_step);
        IF analysis_cursor%NOTFOUND AND
           next_analysis_step IS NULL
        THEN
           end_of_analysis := TRUE;
        ELSE
           perform_analysis;
        END IF;
     END LOOP;
END;
```

2-24. Select the type of loop (FOR, WHILE, simple) appropriate to implement the following requirement: set the status of each company to closed for each company whose ID is defined as a row number in a PL/SQL table of integers.

2-25. Write a piece of code that prints all the numbers between 1 and 100 evenly divisible by 3. For an extra challenge, don't use the MOD function.

2-26. Write your own version of the Oracle POWER function. This function should accept two parameters: a base number and an integer exponent to which that number should be raised.

3

Conditional and Sequential Logic

Without conditional and sequential control statements, our programs would march inexorably from the first statement to the last, unable to respond to a variety of changing circumstances. The IF-THEN, IF-THEN-ELSE, and IF-ELSIF-ELSE conditional statements allow you to execute a block of code only when a specific condition occurs (for example, you might want to call the alert_management procedure only if profits are less than zero). The GOTO statement, a sequential control command, allows you to unconditionally jump, or branch, to another section in the code. While it's certainly true that the much-reviled GOTO can lead to "spaghetti code," remember that this lowly statement, along with the IF statement, is the hidden foundation of the iterative constructs we explored in the previous chapter and the exceptions we'll explore in the next. This chapter tests your ability to use conditional and sequential statements to direct your program's flow.

Beginner

3-1. Why doesn't the following code compile?

```
BEGIN
   IF SYSDATE > TO_DATE ('01-JAN-1999', 'DD-MON-YYYY')
   THEN
      DBMS_OUTPUT.PUT_LINE ('1999 Already!');
   ENDIF;
END;
```

3-2. Why doesn't the following code compile?

```
BEGIN
   IF SYSDATE > TO_DATE ('01-JAN-1999', 'DD-MON-YYYY')
   THEN
      DBMS_OUTPUT.PUT_LINE ('1999 Already!');
   ELSEIF SYSDATE < TO_DATE ('01-JAN-1888', 'DD-MON-YYYY')
   THEN
```

```
        DBMS_OUTPUT.PUT_LINE ('Living in the past.');
      END IF;
   END;
```

3-3. Why doesn't the following code compile?

```
BEGIN
   IF SYSDATE > TO_DATE ('01-JAN-1999', 'DD-MON-YYYY')
   THEN
      DBMS_OUTPUT.PUT_LINE ('1999 Already!');
   ELSE
   THEN
      DBMS_OUTPUT.PUT_LINE ('Living in the past.');
   END IF;
END;
```

3-4. Rewrite the following IF statement to get rid of unnecessary nested IFs:

```
IF salary < 10000
THEN
   bonus := 2000;
ELSE
   IF salary < 20000
   THEN
      bonus := 1500;
   ELSE
      IF salary < 40000
      THEN
         bonus := 1000;
      ELSE
         bonus := 500;
      END IF;
   END IF;
END IF;
```

3-5. Consider the following IF statement:

```
BEGIN
   IF sneezes_per_hour > 50
   THEN
      contact_hmo_service_rep;
      request_authorization;
      sneeze_wetly_into_phone;
   ELSE
      sorry_you_are_not_that_sick;
   END IF;
```

If sneezes_per_hour are set to NULL, does any of this code execute?

3-6. How can you tell PL/SQL to move from one line directly and unconditionally to another line of code?

3-7. What do you "go to" with a GOTO statement?

3-8. How do you tell the PL/SQL runtime engine you want to do nothing?

3-9. Which of the following statements describe valid usages for the NULL; statement?

a. Document to anyone reading your code that you *did* think about a certain branching of logic, and you definitely *don't* want to do anything.

b. Assign the value of NULL to a variable.

c. Ignore a specific (or any) exception that was raised in your code.

d. Provide a location in your code to which you can GOTO.

e. You're unsure what's supposed to happen next in your code, and NULL is an indeterminate value, so NULL; is an indeterminate statement.

f. Build "stubs" for programs so that they compile with a valid header and nothing else.

Intermediate

3-10. Rewrite the following IF statements so that you do not use an IF statement to set the value of no_revenue:

```
DECLARE
    total_sales NUMBER :=
        sales_for_year (company_id=>1056, yearnum=>1998);
    no_revenue BOOLEAN;
BEGIN
    IF total_sales <= 0
    THEN
        no_revenue := TRUE;

    ELSIF total_sales > 0
    THEN
        no_revenue := FALSE;
    END IF;
END;
```

3-11. Can you rewrite the following IF statements so that you do not use an IF statement to set the value of no_revenue?

```
DECLARE
    total_sales NUMBER :=
        sales_for_year (company_id=>1056, yearnum=>1998);
    no_revenue BOOLEAN;
BEGIN
    IF total_sales <= 0
    THEN
        no_revenue := TRUE;
    ELSE
        no_revenue := FALSE;
    END IF;
END;
```

3-12. Which procedure is never executed in this IF statement?

```
IF (order_date > SYSDATE) AND order_total >= min_order_total
THEN
    fill_order (order_id, 'HIGH PRIORITY');
ELSIF (order_date < SYSDATE) OR (order_date = SYSDATE)
THEN
    fill_order (order_id, 'LOW PRIORITY');
ELSIF order_date <= SYSDATE AND order_total < min_order_total
THEN
    queue_order_for_addtl_parts (order_id);
ELSIF order_total = 0
THEN
    disp_message (' No items have been placed in this order!');
END IF;
```

3-13. What is the difference in logic between these two IF statements? Why do you think it might be advantageous to use the form on the right?

```
IF potholes_after_storm > 1000          IF potholes_after_storm > 1000
THEN                                     THEN
    mayor_not_reelected;                     mayor_not_reelected;
END IF;                                  ELSE
                                             NULL;
                                         END IF;
```

3-14. Why doesn't the following code compile?

```
BEGIN
    IF presidents_lie
    THEN
        GOTO big_surprise;

    ELSIF ceos_don't_care
    THEN
        <<big_surprise>>
        hold_them_accountable;
    END IF;
END;
```

3-15. Which of the following is not a restriction on the GOTO statement?

a. Cannot branch from one section of an IF statement to another (from the IF/THEN section to the ELSE section is illegal)

b. Cannot branch into or out of a subprogram (BEGIN-END boundaries)

c. Cannot branch from the exception section to the executable section of a PL/SQL block

d. Cannot have more than one GOTO to the same label

e. Cannot branch from the executable section to the exception section of a PL/SQL block

Expert

3-16. Does PL/SQL offer a CASE statement?

3-17. How can you emulate a CASE statement in PL/SQL?

3-18. DECODE offers an implementation of inline conditional logic; you can build an expression that contains an IF statement inside it. DECODE is not available in PL/SQL without executing a SELECT. How can you emulate DECODE (i.e., build a function that acts like DECODE) in native PL/SQL functionality?

4

Exception Handling

Unlike politicians, who can resort to tired phrases like "Mistakes were made," PL/SQL developers must make sure their programs behave responsibly in the face of the unpredictable. For example, a database server can run out of memory; a user can attempt to insert a duplicate value for a primary key; a SELECT...INTO clause can return too many rows. You can use exception handlers to trap, or handle, these exceptions.

There are two steps to handling an exception:

1. Define the conditions that represent exceptions; you can supplement the extensive Oracle-supplied set (for example, DUP_VAL_ON_INDEX) by creating exceptions of your own (for example, PROFIT_TOO_LOW), by associating unnamed exceptions with your own names (via the EXCEPTION_INIT pragma), or even by defining your own unnamed exceptions.

2. Create an exception handling section in your code, where you associate a subset of named exceptions with corresponding blocks of code called *handlers*.

When an exception occurs (whether it's generated by the system or you use the RAISE command to create it), program control immediately branches to the handler associated with that exception. If there is no handler for that particular exception (or no exception section at all), you have an *unhandled exception*, in which case the program terminates immediately and returns the error to the original caller. This chapter tests your ability to define your own named exceptions, create an exception section in your code, and understand how exceptions propagate from one block to the next.

Beginner

4-1. Which of the following functions can you call to retrieve a text description of the most recent error that has occurred?

    a. SHOWERR

    b. SQLERRM

    c. SQL_ERROR_MESSAGE

4-2. Change the following block so that it traps a NO_DATA_FOUND exception and displays a description of the current error:

```
DECLARE
    my_flavor ice_cream.fav_flavor%TYPE;
BEGIN
    SELECT fav_flavor
      INTO my_flavor
      FROM ice_cream
     WHERE name = USER;
    DBMS_OUTPUT.PUT_LINE
        ('I love ' || my_flavor || '!');
END;
```

4-3. What are the two attributes of (pieces of information associated with) every exception? What third attribute is optional?

4-4. Which of the following named exceptions are defined by PL/SQL?

    a. DATA_NOT_FOUND

    b. VALUE_ERROR

    c. NO_DATA_FOUND

    d. DIVIDE_BY_ZERO

    e. INVALID_NUMBER

    f. TOO_MANY_ROWS

    g. DUP_KEY_IN_INDEX

    h. CURSOR_OPEN

    i. VALUE_TOO_LARGE

4-5. What is the only error that has two different error numbers?

4-6. Where are the predefined, named exceptions defined?

4-7. What is the error code and the error message of a user-defined exception?

4-8. What are the only two positive error numbers used by Oracle?

4-9. What does it mean for an exception to go "unhandled"?

4-10. Do you have to supply an exception section in your programs and blocks of code?

4-11. What special exception handler can you provide that will trap any error that is raised in a block of code?

4-12. What do you see on your screen (a message delivered via DBMS_OUT-PUT, or an unhandled exception, or perhaps nothing at all) when you execute this block?

```
DECLARE
   my_dream VARCHAR2(5);
BEGIN
   my_dream := 'JUSTICE';
END;
```

4-13. What do you see on your screen (a message delivered via DBMS_OUT-PUT, or an unhandled exception, or perhaps nothing at all) when you execute this block?

```
DECLARE
   my_dream VARCHAR2(5);
BEGIN
   BEGIN
      my_dream := 'JUSTICE';
   EXCEPTION
      WHEN VALUE_ERROR
      THEN
         DBMS_OUTPUT.PUT_LINE  ('Inner block');
   END;
   DBMS_OUTPUT.PUT_LINE ('Dream deferred...');
END;
```

4-14. What do you see on your screen (a message delivered via DBMS_OUT-PUT, or an unhandled exception, or perhaps nothing at all) when you execute this block?

```
DECLARE
   my_dream VARCHAR2(10) := 'JUSTICE';
BEGIN
   DECLARE
      reality VARCHAR2(3) := 'MILLIONS STARVE';
   BEGIN
      my_dream := 'PEACE';
   EXCEPTION
      WHEN VALUE_ERROR
      THEN
         DBMS_OUTPUT.PUT_LINE  ('Inner block');
   END;
EXCEPTION
   WHEN VALUE_ERROR
      THEN DBMS_OUTPUT.PUT_LINE  ('Outer block');
END;
```

4-15. In each of the following examples, there is an error that prevents compilation. What's wrong with each sample?

    a.
```
EXCEPTION
   WHEN ANY THEN
```

    b.
```
EXCEPTION
   WHEN VALUE_ERROR AND NO_DATA_FOUND THEN
```

```
c. EXCEPTION
      WHEN OTHERS THEN
         NULL;
      WHEN VALUE_ERROR THEN
         NULL;
d. BEGIN
      do_stuff;
   WHEN OTHERS
   THEN
      NULL;

   END;
e. BEGIN
      ...
   EXCEPTION
     WHEN -1403 THEN
        NULL;
   END;
```

4-16. How can you reraise the current exception from within an exception handler clause? Why would you want to do so?

4-17. You write the following block of code, declaring your own local exception and handling it as well. Under what circumstances is the exception raised?

```
FUNCTION big_name (name_in IN VARCHAR2)
   RETURN VARCHAR2
IS
  no_name EXCEPTION;
  name_in_caps VARCHAR2(100);
BEGIN
  name_in_caps := UPPER (name_in);

  RETURN (name_in_caps);
EXCEPTION
  WHEN no_name THEN
     DBMS_OUTPUT.PUT_LINE ('You must supply a name');
END;
```

4-18. The following code was written by your coworker Kristopher, who is conveniently on vacation, when you are asked to enhance the code. The users want a specialized message displayed when an invalid value is supplied for the sex parameter:

```
FUNCTION build_name (name_in IN VARCHAR2, sex_in IN VARCHAR2)
RETURN VARCHAR2 IS
  name_out VARCHAR2(100);
BEGIN
  IF first_char = 'M' THEN
    name_out := 'Mr. ' || name_in;

  ELSIF first_char = 'F' THEN
    name_out := 'Mrs. ' || name_in;
```

```
        END IF;
          RETURN (name_out);
        END;
```

Add the code necessary to display the text "A valid sex must be provided" whenever the parameter sex_in is neither "M" nor "F".

4-19. Employee SMITH currently earns a salary of $800, and ALLEN earns a sal-
ary of $1,600. What will the salaries be for SMITH and ALLEN after the fol-
lowing anonymous block of code executes:

```
BEGIN
  UPDATE EMP SET sal = sal * 2 where ename = 'SMITH';

  RAISE VALUE_ERROR;

  UPDATE EMP SET sal = sal * 2 where ename = 'ALLEN';
EXCEPTION
  WHEN OTHERS THEN
    DBMS_OUTPUT.PUT_LINE ('We had an error');
END;
```

4-20. The following anonymous block of code is executed directly from
SQL*Plus by the user SCOTT. What will the salaries be for SMITH and
ALLEN be after its execution?

```
BEGIN
  UPDATE EMP SET sal = sal * 2 where ename = 'SMITH';
  RAISE VALUE_ERROR;
  UPDATE EMP SET sal = sal * 2 where ename = 'ALLEN';
END;
/
```

Intermediate

4-21. When an exception is raised in a block of code, a number of actions
occur. Organize the following actions in the correct order, and identify
those that do not occur:

> Control is passed to the exception section, if it exists.
> Oracle goes to the package STANDARD to determine how to handle
>   the error.
> The executable section terminates immediately.
> If there is no match and no WHEN OTHERS clause, propagate the
>   exception out to the enclosing block.
> If after executing handler code, an exception is raised (or reraised),
>   propagate the exception out to the enclosing block.
> If there is no match for the error, check for a WHEN OTHERS section
>   and execute that handler code.
> If after executing handler code, an exception is raised (or reraised),
>   and there is no enclosing block, propagate the exception out to the
>   calling environment.

Oracle logs the exception to the alert log for the database.

If there is an exception section, find a match for the error and execute that handler code.

4-22. The built-in RAISE_APPLICATION_ERROR accepts three parameters: the error number to be used, the text of the error message, and whether or not to clear the error stack. List all the restrictions on each of these parameters.

4-23. The built-in RAISE_APPLICATION_ERROR can programmatically signal an error condition. Identify which of the following calls to RAISE_APPLICATION_ERROR are valid, and which are not. For those that are not valid, explain the problem:

a. `RAISE_APPLICATION_ERROR (20001, 'Invalid employee number!');`

b. `RAISE_APPLICATION_ERROR ('Invalid Social Security Number.');`

c. `RAISE_APPLICATION_ERROR (NO_DATA_FOUND);`

d. `RAISE_APPLICATION_ERROR (-20023, 'Date must not be in the future');`

e. `RAISE_APPLICATION_ERROR (-21001, 'Invalid date.');`

f. `RAISE_APPLICATION_ERROR (-20002, 'Invalid product code.', 'TRUE');`

g. `RAISE_APPLICATION_ERROR (-20002, 'Invalid product code.', FALSE);`

4-24. True or false? After you call RAISE_APPLICATION_ERROR to raise an application-specific error, you can call the APPLICATION_ERROR_CODE and APPLICATION_ERROR_MESSAGE functions to retrieve the error number and string passed to RAISE_APPLICATION_ERROR.

4-25. While talking with your boss, you mention casually how you think you could improve upon the current calc_commission function that was written by your predecessor. "If I were to write it," you say, "I would make it more flexible and more bulletproof." "What a great idea," says your boss, "by the end of today, trap the condition when an employee has no sales (or negative sales), and display a custom message."

```
FUNCTION calc_commission (sales_in IN NUMBER)
   RETURN NUMBER
IS
   commission NUMBER(5,2) := 0;
BEGIN
   RETURN (sales_in * 0.1);
END;
```

4-26. The following function accepts a first and last name and returns a formatted version of the name:

```
FUNCTION format_name (
   surname_in IN VARCHAR2,
   given_name_in IN VARCHAR2)
RETURN VARCHAR2 IS
   no_surname EXCEPTION;
   no_given_name EXCEPTION;
```

```
  formatted_name VARCHAR2(100);
BEGIN
  IF surname_in IS NULL THEN raise no_surname;

  ELSIF given_name_in IS NULL THEN raise no_given_name;

  ELSE
    formatted_name :=
      surname_in || ', ' ||
      SUBSTR (given_name_in, 1, 1);
  END IF;

  RETURN (formatted_name);
EXCEPTION
  WHEN OTHERS THEN
    RAISE_APPLICATION_ERROR
      (-20001, 'Invalid name supplied.');
END;
```

How does the output differ when the surname is not supplied, as opposed to when the given name is not supplied?

4-27. How would you change the program in 4-26 to take advantage of the locally defined exceptions?

4-28. Which of the following code segments trap the exception raised and provide the most information about the error that occurred? What is the difference between the two code blocks, and which provides greater control?

```
DECLARE
  bad_data EXCEPTION;
BEGIN
  RAISE bad_data;
EXCEPTION
  WHEN bad_data THEN
    DBMS_OUTPUT.PUT_LINE ('data was bad: ' || SQLCODE);
END;

DECLARE
  bad_data EXCEPTION;
BEGIN
  RAISE bad_data;
EXCEPTION
  WHEN OTHERS THEN
    DBMS_OUTPUT.PUT_LINE ('data was bad: ' || SQLCODE);
END;
```

4-29. Your manager has been so impressed with the previous improvements you made to the calc_commission function that he is just brimming with new ideas to improve it. In fact, he has already promised these improvements to his boss, and she expects them for the release going out tomorrow morning. One new requirement is that the function should optionally accept a second parameter, representing the amount of commission to be applied. Another is that the commission should be specified as a percentage (0 to 100), and that the condition of negative or zero sales should be handled as a custom exception. If the rate is not supplied, assume 10% commission. The same message should be displayed in the sales error condition.

Given the current version of the following calc_commission function, make the appropriate changes to satisfy the new requirements:

```
FUNCTION calc_commission (sales_in IN NUMBER)
   RETURN NUMBER
IS
   commission NUMBER(5,2) := 0;
BEGIN
   IF sales_in <= 0 THEN
     RAISE_APPLICATION_ERROR (-20001, 'Pull your own weight');
   ELSE
     RETURN (sales_in * 0.1);
   END IF;
END;
```

4-30. Laxmi of Technical Support at your company calls; a user has reported that the following program is failing. It "just suddenly stopped working," and it works for some clients but not others:

```
FUNCTION is_overdue (due_date IN DATE, paid_date IN DATE)
   RETURN BOOLEAN
IS
   days_between NUMBER(2) := due_date - paid_date;
BEGIN
   RETURN days_between > 30;
EXCEPTION
   WHEN OTHERS THEN
     DBMS_OUTPUT.PUT_LINE
        ('Error in is_overdue; Check input data.');
END;
```

You are sure this module is being executed, but the error message is never displayed. Instead, when an error occurs, it goes unhandled, and the user sees this incomprehensible "dump":

```
SQL> DECLARE
  2      gotAproblem BOOLEAN;
  3   BEGIN
  4      gotAproblem := is_overdue (SYSDATE+400, SYSDATE);
  5   END;
  6   /
DECLARE
*
ERROR at line 1:
ORA-06502: PL/SQL: numeric or value error:
   number precision too large
```

Why isn't the exception section trapping the error? Why is the error intermittent? How can you fix this program?

4-31. Your friend Jennifer comes to you at 4:45 on Friday (as usual) and asks you to look at the following code:

```
BEGIN

  BEGIN
    ...
    RAISE NO_DATA_FOUND;
    ...
  EXCEPTION
    WHEN VALUE_ERROR THEN
      DBMS_OUTPUT.PUT_LINE ('Value Error Alert!');
    WHEN OTHERS THEN
      DBMS_OUTPUT.PUT_LINE ('Other Alert!');
  END;

  IF SQLCODE != 0 THEN
    DBMS_OUTPUT.PUT_LINE ('We ran into some problems');
  END IF;

END;
```

Jennifer can't figure out why her second debug statement ("We ran into some problems") is never being displayed. No matter what exception is raised, all she sees is:

```
Other Alert!
```

Why is she not seeing her second debug statement?

4-32. Joe arrives on your doorstep with a puzzled look. "I keep getting this ORA-12154 error and have no idea what it is and what causes it." What is the easiest way of obtaining a description of the Oracle error message?

4-33. Under what circumstances might a NO_DATA_FOUND exception be raised?

4-34. Consider the following program:

```
/* Filename on web page: whodidthat.sql */
CREATE OR REPLACE PROCEDURE who_did_that (
    emp_in IN emp.empno%TYPE)
IS
   v_ename emp.ename%TYPE;

   line VARCHAR2(1023);
   fid UTL_FILE.FILE_TYPE;

   list_of_numbers PLVtab.number_table;
BEGIN
   SELECT ename INTO v_ename
     FROM emp
    WHERE empno = emp_in;

   DBMS_OUTPUT.PUT_LINE (v_ename);
```

```
      fid := UTL_FILE.FOPEN ('c:\temp', 'notme.sql', 'R');
      UTL_FILE.GET_LINE (fid, line);
      UTL_FILE.GET_LINE (fid, line);

      IF list_of_numbers (100) > 0
      THEN
          DBMS_OUTPUT.PUT_LINE ('Positive value at row 100');
      END IF;

EXCEPTION
   WHEN NO_DATA_FOUND
   THEN
       DBMS_OUTPUT.PUT_LINE ('Who did that?');
END who_did_that;
/
```

This program could raise the NO_DATA_FOUND exception in one of
three ways, yet the exception section can't tell us "who did that"—which
part of the code caused the problem. Rewrite this procedure so that the
exception section contains three different handlers for each potential
cause of this error.

4-35. What do you see on your screen (a message delivered via DBMS_OUT-
PUT, or an unhandled exception, or no error at all) when you execute the
following code segments?

```
DECLARE
    string_of_5_chars VARCHAR2(5);
BEGIN
    BEGIN
        string_of_5_chars := 'Daniel';
    EXCEPTION
       WHEN VALUE_ERROR
       THEN
           RAISE NO_DATA_FOUND;

       WHEN NO_DATA_FOUND
       THEN
           DBMS_OUTPUT.PUT_LINE  ('Inner block');
    END;
EXCEPTION
   WHEN NO_DATA_FOUND
   THEN
       DBMS_OUTPUT.PUT_LINE  ('Outer block');
END;
```

4-36. Suppose that you execute the following code segments:

```
DECLARE
   counter INTEGER;
BEGIN
   DBMS_OUTPUT.PUT('Starting test, ');

   BEGIN
     SELECT * INTO counter
```

```
        FROM dual
        WHERE 1 = 2;

        DBMS_OUTPUT.PUT('found data, ');
     EXCEPTION
        WHEN NO_DATA_FOUND THEN
           DBMS_OUTPUT.PUT('No data in inner block, ');
           RAISE;
     END;

     DBMS_OUTPUT.PUT_LINE ('Finished test.');
  EXCEPTION
     WHEN NO_DATA_FOUND THEN
        DBMS_OUTPUT.PUT_LINE ('No data in outer block');

     WHEN OTHERS THEN
        DBMS_OUTPUT.PUT_LINE ('Caught OTHER exception');
  END;
```

What do you see on your screen?

a. Starting test, found data, Finished test

b. Starting test, No data in inner block, Finished test

c. Starting test, No data in inner block, No data in outer block

d. Starting test, No data in inner block, Caught OTHER exception

e. Starting test, No data in inner block, No data in outer block, Finished
   test

Expert

4-37. Rewrite the following PL/SQL block so that it allows each of the following SQL DML statements to execute, even if any of the others fail:

```
BEGIN
   UPDATE emp SET empno = 100 WHERE empno > 5000;
   DELETE FROM dept WHERE deptno = 10;
   DELETE FROM emp WHERE deptno = 10;
END;
```

4-38. Write a PL/SQL block that handles by name the following Oracle error:

```
ORA-01014: ORACLE shutdown in progress.
```

The exception handler should display an appropriate message and then
reraise the exception.

4-39. Which of the following uses of the EXCEPTION_INIT pragma are valid,
which are invalid, and why?

a. ```
   DECLARE
      bad_date EXCEPTION;
      PRAGMA EXCEPTION_INIT (bad_date, -1843);
   ```

b. ```
   DECLARE
      bad_date EXCEPTION;
      PRAGMA EXCEPTION_INIT (bad_date, 1843);
   ```

c. DECLARE
```
    bad_date EXCEPTION;
    PRAGMA EXCEPTION_INIT (-1843, bad_date);
```
d. DECLARE
```
    bad_date EXCEPTION;
    err_num PLS_INTEGER := -1843;
    PRAGMA EXCEPTION_INIT (bad_date, err_num);
```
e. DECLARE
```
    bad_date EXCEPTION;
    PRAGMA EXCEPTION_INIT (bad_date, ORA-01843);
```
f. DECLARE
```
    bad_date EXCEPTION;
    PRAGMA EXCEPTION_INIT (bad_date, -01843);
```

4-40. What shows up on your screen when you run the following block of code in your execution environment as a top-level PL/SQL block? Explain the behavior.

```
DECLARE
    d VARCHAR2(1);
    no_data_found EXCEPTION;
BEGIN
    SELECT dummy INTO d FROM dual WHERE 1=2;

    IF d IS NULL
    THEN
        RAISE no_data_found;
    END IF;
EXCEPTION
    WHEN no_data_found
    THEN
        DBMS_OUTPUT.PUT_LINE ('Trapped the error!?');
END;
```

4-41. Change the code in 4-40 so that a NO_DATA_FOUND exception is trapped and handled. If you want to play around with various possible solutions, check out this code in *myndf.sql* on this book's web page.

4-42. First, compile the valerr package as shown here (can you imagine a more poorly named function?):

```
/* Filename on web page: valerr.pkg */
CREATE OR REPLACE PACKAGE valerr
IS
    FUNCTION get RETURN VARCHAR2;
END valerr;
/
CREATE OR REPLACE PACKAGE BODY valerr
IS
    v VARCHAR2(1) := 'ABC';

    FUNCTION get RETURN VARCHAR2
    IS
    BEGIN
```

```
        RETURN v;
    END;
BEGIN
   DBMS_OUTPUT.PUT_LINE ('Before I show you v...');

EXCEPTION
   WHEN OTHERS
   THEN
      DBMS_OUTPUT.PUT_LINE ('Trapped the error!');

END valerr;
/
```

Then call DBMS_OUTPUT.PUT_LINE to display the value returned by the valerr.get function as follows:

```
SQL> EXEC DBMS_OUTPUT.PUT_LINE ('Value of v is ' || valerr.get);
```

What information is displayed on the screen? What is displayed if you execute the same line of code a second time?

4-43. You are working on a program that requires exclusive access to data in the EMP table. You attempt to lock the rows using a SELECT FOR UPDATE. If you cannot immediately acquire the lock, you should simply print a message to try again later. If you do acquire the lock, print the name of each employee using a loop.

4-44. While helping a friend time his new program, you decide to calculate the elapsed time from executing the code as follows (note that you are better off using DBMS_UTILITY.GET_TIME instead of SYSDATE):

```
DECLARE
   start_time DATE;
   end_time DATE;
BEGIN
   start_time := SYSDATE;
   DBMS_OUTPUT.PUT_LINE ('Filler code...');
   end_time := SYSDATE;
   DBMS_OUTPUT.PUT_LINE (end_time - start_time);
END;
```

When you execute this block, you receive the following output, but you can successfully execute the new procedure on its own:

```
*
ERROR at line 1:
ORA-00604: error occurred at recursive SQL level 1
ORA-01422: exact fetch returns more than requested number of rows
ORA-06512: at "SYS.STANDARD", line 1027
```

What could be the problem?

4-45. Just about the most important information you can obtain about an error is the line number on which the error is raised. Which of the following statements accurately describes ways to obtain this information?

    a. Call the DBMS_UTILITY.FORMAT_ERROR_STACK to obtain the error stack, including the line numbers on which errors occurred.

    b. Examine the contents returned by SQLERRM to view the line number and program name in which the error originated.

    c. Let the error go unhandled and then view the error stack displayed in standard output (your screen, a web page, etc.).

4-46. You have been asked to record all errors that occur in your application so they can be examined later. Identify all the different forms your error log can take inside a PL/SQL environment.

4-47. You have decided to write your error information to a database table. You create a procedure to write to the log as follows:

```
/* Filename on web page: log.sql */
CREATE OR REPLACE PACKAGE logpkg
IS
    PROCEDURE putline
        (code_in IN INTEGER, text_in IN VARCHAR2);
END;
/

CREATE OR REPLACE PACKAGE BODY logpkg
IS
    CURSOR sess IS
        SELECT MACHINE, PROGRAM
          FROM V$SESSION
          WHERE AUDSID = USERENV('SESSIONID');
    rec sess%ROWTYPE;

    PROCEDURE putline (
        code_in IN INTEGER,
        text_in IN VARCHAR2)
    IS
    BEGIN
        INSERT INTO logtab VALUES (code_in, text_in, SYSDATE,
            USER, SYSDATE,
            USER, rec.machine, rec.program);
    END;
BEGIN
    OPEN sess; FETCH sess INTO rec; CLOSE sess;
END;
/
```

You then test the log mechanism as follows:

```
SQL> DECLARE
  2      myval NUMBER;
  3  BEGIN
  4      myval := 'abc';
  5  EXCEPTION
  6      WHEN OTHERS
  7      THEN
```

```
 8          logpkg.putline (SQLCODE, SQLERRM);
 9          RAISE;
10   END;
11   /
DECLARE
*
ERROR at line 1:
ORA-06502: PL/SQL: numeric or value error
ORA-06512: at line 9
```

But there is nothing in your log!

```
SQL> SELECT count(*) FROM logtab;

 COUNT(*)
---------
        0
```

Why didn't the log package insert a row into the log table?

4-48. Associate the type of error log in the first list with the characteristics in the second list:

Type of error log:

1. Database table
2. Database pipe
3. Operating system file
4. Standard output (screen)
5. Index-by table

Characteristics:

a. COMMIT and ROLLBACK do not affect I/O to this log.

b. You won't see information written to the log unless you take special action.

c. There is a built-in limit to the volume of error data that can be written to the log.

d. Entries written to the log become a part of the logical transaction of the application.

e. Only someone connected to the current session can see output sent to the log, and then only when the program has stopped executing.

f. The new AUTONOMOUS_TRANSACTION pragma in Oracle8*i* Release 8.1 allows you to write to this log and save the entry, without affecting the application's transaction.

g. An attempt to send error data to this log can cause your program to *block* or be stopped.

4-49. Write a procedure that raises any error number passed to it, whether it be an Oracle error number (like ORA-01855), an application-specific error (in the −20,XXX range), or your own positive error numbers. (Perhaps you did not want to be constrained by the 1,000 error numbers Oracle offers. You noticed, instead, that the only positive numbers used for error handling are 1 and 100, leaving an awful lot for you.)

5

Records

A *record*, a construct structurally and conceptually similar to a row in a database table, is a named collection of elements. Each element, or field, has its own name, datatype, and value. The record itself doesn't have a value; it's simply a named pointer to the collection of fields. One of the main advantages of records is their ability to simplify your code by grouping disparate elements into a logical unit. For example, rather than passing five parameters to a procedure, you can pass just one record that contains five fields. This chapter tests your ability to define a record's structure, create and use record variables, and set and retrieve values for a record's fields.

Beginner

5-1. Which of the following statements about a PL/SQL record are true, and which are false?

a. A record is a scalar datatype.

b. A record is a composite datatype, because more than one piece of information can be associated with the record.

c. A record contains a recording of a sound for storage in the Oracle database.

d. You can define a record that has the same structure of a cursor, table, or tablespace.

e. You can define a record to hold any combination of valid PL/SQL scalar data structures.

5-2. Which of the following lines of code demonstrate the correct method for referencing a string field named "favorite_flavor" in a record named "ice_cream"?

    a. ice_cream (favorite_flavor)

    b. ice_cream-favorite_flavor

    c. ice_cream.favorite_flavor

    d. favorite_flavor.ice_cream

5-3. Declare a record that has the same structure as the table called CEO.

5-4. Which of the following statements about a table-based record are true, and which are false?

    a. A table-based record contains a field for every nonnumeric column in the table.

    b. You can define a table-based record with either the %TYPE or %ROWTYPE attributes.

    c. Each field in a table-based record must have the same name and type as its corresponding column in the database table.

    d. You can define a table-based record based on a database table or view.

    e. When you declare a table-based record, you can use column aliases to change the names of the record's fields.

    f. Extensive use of table-based records slows down your application, because the engine has to look up the table structure in the data dictionary.

    g. The datatype of a field in a table-based record can be any valid PL/SQL datatype.

5-5. Which of the following statements about a cursor-based record are true, and which are false?

    a. A cursor-based record can be declared based on an implicit cursor (SELECT INTO), explicit cursor, or REF CURSOR.

    b. Each field in a cursor-based record must have the same name and type as its corresponding expression in the cursor.

    c. You cannot declare a record based on a cursor that is defined on a query with a join.

    d. When you declare a record based on a cursor, you can use column aliases to set the names of the record's fields.

    e. You must always provide a column alias for an expression if you want to declare a record based on that cursor.

    f. The datatype of a field in a cursor-based record can be any valid PL/SQL datatype.

5-6. True or false? The only valid way to fill a table-based record is by fetching a row from the table directly into that record. Similarly, you can only use a cursor-based record to hold a row of data retrieved from its "cursor of origin."

5-7. Which of the following record definitions are valid, and which are invalid (assume that the referenced tables exist and contain the named columns)?

a. `emp_rec emp%ROWTYPE;`

b.
```
CURSOR  order_item_cur IS
   SELECT  order_id,
           item_id,
           amt
     FROM  order_items;

order_item_rec order_item_cur%TYPE;
```

c.
```
TYPE customer_rec_type IS RECORD (
    customer_id customer.id%TYPE,
    customer_name customer.customer_name%TYPE
);

curr_customer_rec customer_rec_type%ROWTYPE;
```

d.
```
CURSOR employee_cur IS
   SELECT *
     FROM emp;

employee_rec employee_cur%ROWTYPE;
```

Intermediate

5-8. A programmer-defined record is based on a record "type" you define within your code. Which of the following statements represent valid reasons for working with a programmer-defined record?

a. You want a field in your record to be of type Boolean or some other datatype that is available in PL/SQL, but not in SQL.

b. You want to write PL/SQL code that is independent of Oracle so it can be ported easily to other database vendor products such as SQL Server.

c. The structure of the record you need, while consisting solely of SQL datatypes, does not match any table or cursor defined in your system.

d. You don't trust your table structures because the DBAs change them without notice, causing your programs to break.

e. You want to avoid repetitive definitions of data structures by using nested records.

5-9. Which of these statements about programmer-defined records are true, and which are false?

    a. The programmer-defined record gives the programmer tremendous flexibility and complete control over the number, names, and datatypes of fields in a record. It allows the creation of records that have nothing to do with either a table or cursor.

    b. You can declare fields to be NOT NULL, leaving it to the PL/SQL run-time engine to enforce your data integrity.

    c. A programmer-defined record can have as its field an index-by table, a programmer-defined subtype, another PL/SQL record type, or an object type.

    d. Working with programmer-defined records always involves two steps. First, define the record TYPE (which you must do if that TYPE is not already defined elsewhere, such as in a package specification), and then declare one or more records based on that TYPE.

    e. You can declare as many records as you like against a single record TYPE.

5-10. Declare a programmer-defined record that has exactly the same structure as the following query:

```
SELECT cookie,
       ice_cream
  FROM favorite_snacks;
```

5-11. Declare a programmer-defined record TYPE, along with a record based on that type, for these three pieces of information:

- A customer_id with datatype NUMBER(5). This field may not be NULL and has a default/initial value of 0.

- A customer_name with the same datatype as column customer_name in the customer table.

- A flag prefers_nonsmoking_fl of BOOLEAN datatype.

5-12. Write a PL/SQL block that:

- Declares a record based on the last_name, hire_date, and salary columns in the employee table.

- Assigns the value of "Feuerstein" to the last_name field, SYSDATE to the hire_date field, and 1000000 to the salary field of the record (hey, it's my book, right?)

- Displays to the screen the three fields of the record.

5-13. A phone number is made up of these components:

> Area code
> Prefix
> Number

Each tobacco-industry lobbyist has six numbers at which she or he can be reached:

> Home phone
> Office phone
> Cell phone
> Fax
> Bathroom phone
> Bathroom fax

Now create nested programmer-defined record TYPEs to support this description.

5-14. Declare a record based on the tobacco lobbyist record type. Assign the value '800SMOKENOW' to that lobbyist's bathroom phone.

5-15. Which of the following "aggregate" or record-level operations are supported by PL/SQL?

> a. Assign one record to another
>
> b. Subtract one record from another
>
> c. Compare two different records for equality
>
> d. Pass a record as an argument to a procedure
>
> e. Assign a record the value of NULL

5-16. Will the following code compile without error?

```
DECLARE
    childlabor sweatshops%ROWTYPE;

    CURSOR bigprofits_cur
    IS
        SELECT * FROM sweatshops;

    bigprofits bigprofits_cur%ROWTYPE;
BEGIN
    bigprofits := childlabor;
END;
```

5-17. Will the following code compile without error?

```
DECLARE
    CURSOR bigprofits_cur
    IS
        SELECT sells_to, daily_wage FROM sweatshops;
    bigprofits bigprofits_cur%ROWTYPE;
```

```
    RECORD childlabor_rec_type IS TYPE (
        sells_to      sweatshops.sells_to%TYPE,
        daily_wage    sweatshops.daily_wage%TYPE
        );
    childlabor    childlabor_rec_type;
BEGIN
    bigprofits := childlabor;
END;
```

5-18. Will the following code compile without error?

```
DECLARE
    CURSOR profitable_internet_stocks
    IS
        SELECT SUM (share_price)
          FROM NASDAQ
         WHERE profits > 0
           AND sector = 'INTERNET';
    few_and_far_in_between profitable_internet_stocks%ROWTYPE;
BEGIN
    OPEN profitable_internet_stocks;
    FETCH profitable_internet_stocks INTO few_and_far_in_between;
    DBMS_OUTPUT.PUT_LINE ('We found some!');
    DBMS_OUTPUT.PUT_LINE (
        'Total share prices are: ' || SUM (share_price));
END;
```

5-19. I have a table named sweatshops, and I declare two different records based on that table as follows:

```
DECLARE
    childlabor sweatshops%ROWTYPE;
    bigprofits sweatshops%ROWTYPE;
```

Which of the following statements are valid, and which will fail (assume that all field names and program calls are correct)?

a. `IF childlabor = bigprofits THEN ...`

b. `IF childlabor.wages = bigprofits.wages THEN ...`

c. `bigprofits :=`
   `analyze_sneaker_subcontractor_policies (childlabor);`

d. `INSERT INTO sweatshops VALUES (bigprofits);`

5-20. How would you implement a record equality check for these two records?

```
DECLARE
    CURSOR tasty
    IS
        SELECT ice cream,
               cookie
          FROM favorite_snacks;

    steven_preferences_so_tasty%ROWTYPE;
    veva_preferences_so_tasty%ROWTYPE;
BEGIN
```

5-21. Given this index-by table type definition (a table of employee ID numbers):

```
TYPE empno_table_type IS TABLE OF emp.empno%TYPE
    INDEX BY BINARY_INTEGER;
```

Declare a programmer-defined record TYPE, along with a record based on that type, for these pieces of information:

Column	Definition
deptno	NUMBER(5),
dept_name	Same datatype as column dept_name in the dept table
total_salary	NOT NULL, with datatype NUMBER and DEFAULT values of zero
emp_table	A index-by table of employee numbers

5-22. Write the header for a function called better_uses that accepts as its only parameter a record with the same structure as the corporate_welfare table and returns through its RETURN clause a record with the same structure as the quality_childcare table.

Expert

5-23. The following procedure header has a long list of parameters, making it difficult to use (you have to declare many variables, remember the order or names of the parameters, etc.). Rewrite the header to fix this problem.

```
CREATE OR REPLACE PROCEDURE
insert_lobbyist_contact
(
p_home_area_code_in         VARCHAR2,
p_home_prefix_in            VARCHAR2,
p_home_phone_number_in      VARCHAR2,
p_office_area_code_in       VARCHAR2,
p_office_prefix_in          VARCHAR2,
p_office_phone_number_in    VARCHAR2,
p_cell_area_code_in         VARCHAR2,
p_cell_prefix_in            VARCHAR2,
p_cell_phone_number_in      VARCHAR2,
p_fax_area_code_in          VARCHAR2,
p_fax_prefix_in             VARCHAR2,
p_fax_phone_number_in       VARCHAR2,
p_bath_phone_area_code_in   VARCHAR2,
p_bath_phone_prefix_in      VARCHAR2,
p_bath_phone_number_in      VARCHAR2,
p_bath_fax_area_code_in     VARCHAR2,
p_bath_fax_prefix_in        VARCHAR2,
p_bath_fax_number_in        VARCHAR2
);
```

5-24. Why does the following declaration section fail to compile (assume that all database objects are referenced correctly)?

```
DECLARE
    /*  Table Type - table of employee numbers  */
    TYPE empno_table_type IS TABLE OF emp.empno%TYPE
        INDEX BY BINARY_INTEGER;

    /*
    || Record Type - department information
    || with table of employees
    */
    TYPE dept_rec_type IS RECORD (
        deptno        NUMBER(5),
        dept_name     dept.dname%TYPE,
        total_salary  NUMBER NOT NULL := 0,
        emp_table     empno_table_type
        );

    /*  Table Type - table of departments  */
    TYPE dept_table_type IS TABLE OF dept_rec_type
        INDEX BY BINARY_INTEGER;
```

5-25. What is wrong with this code? How would you improve it?

```
DECLARE
    CURSOR so_tasty
    IS
        SELECT ice_cream,
               cookie
          FROM favorite_snacks;

    v_ice_cream   ice_cream%favorite_snacks;
    v_cookie      cookie%favorite_snacks;
BEGIN
    OPEN so_tasty;
    FETCH so_tasty INTO v_ice_cream, v_cookie;
END;
/
```

6

Index-by Tables

Oracle8 introduced the term *collection* to describe three new datatypes: index-by tables, nested tables, and variable arrays. These collections are quite similar and are really just conceptual riffs on the old PL/SQL table. We'll examine each of these new types in the next three chapters.

The *index-by table* (or the structure formerly known as a *PL/SQL table*) is PL/SQL's answer to an array. Like an array, an index-by table consists of homogeneous elements (meaning that all the elements have the same datatype) that are indexed by an integer (hence the name index-by table). Unlike arrays in other languages, PL/SQL index-by tables are one-dimensional, sparse (meaning that there can be "gaps" between elements), and unconstrained (meaning that the number of elements can grow). This chapter tests your understanding of these extremely useful structures.

Beginner

6-1. What two steps are required before you can work with an index-by table?

6-2. Can index-by tables be declared with indexes other than BINARY_INTE-GERs?

6-3. Consider this definition of an index-by table TYPE:

```
DECLARE
    TYPE number_tabtype IS TABLE OF NUMBER
        INDEX BY BINARY_INTEGER;
```

Which of the following index-by table declarations is valid?

  a. `number_tabtype salary_list;`

  b. `salaries, commissions number_tabtype;`

  c. `acres_clearcut number_tabtype;`

6-4. Consider this definition of an index-by table TYPE and table:

```
DECLARE
    TYPE number_tabtype IS TABLE OF NUMBER
        INDEX BY BINARY_INTEGER;
    acres_clearcut number_tabtype;
```

Which of the following assignments is valid?

```
a. acres_clearcut.15 := 1000000;

b. acres_clearcut(15) := 1000000;

c. acres_clearcut (15, 1000000);

d. acres_clearcut.ASSIGN (15, 1000000);
```

6-5. True or false?

a. Index-by tables are capable of handling only a single dimension of information.

b. Different rows in an index-by table can hold different types of information. Row 1, for example, might contain another index-by table, while row 2 contains a string.

c. Index-by tables can be stored in the database as columns in a table.

6-6. What types of data can be stored in index-by tables?

6-7. What is the difference between an index-by table and a PL/SQL table?

6-8. True or false?

a. There are no upper or lower bounds on the integer values you can use as row numbers.

b. Row numbers must be positive.

c. You must always specify a row number as an integer.

6-9. True or false?

a. When first declared, an index-by table contains no defined rows.

b. The default value for a row in an index-by table is NULL.

c. Each row in an index-by table contains the same type of data.

d. If you try to access (read) a row in a table that is not yet defined, PL/SQL raises the VALUE_ERROR exception.

6-10. How many elements does an index-by table contain when it is created?

6-11. Can an index-by table element be set back to undefined once you have assigned it a value?

6-12. What error is raised when you execute the following PL/SQL code:

```
DECLARE
    TYPE names_type IS TABLE OF VARCHAR2(100)
        INDEX BY BINARY_INTEGER;
    all_my_cousins names_type;
```

```
BEGIN
   all_my_cousins (POWER (2, 32)) := 'George Washington';
END;
/
```

6-13. True or false?

   a. Once you have defined a table TYPE, you can declare more than one index-by table from that TYPE.

   b. The table TYPE and all tables declared from that type must be defined in the same PL/SQL block or scope.

   c. Since BINARY_INTEGER is the only valid index type for an index-by table, you can omit the INDEX BY clause.

Intermediate

6-14. Consider the following table declarations:

```
-- table of numbers
TYPE number_table_type IS TABLE OF number
   INDEX BY BINARY_INTEGER;
number_table number_table_type;

-- table of empnos
TYPE empno_table_type IS TABLE OF employee.employee_id%TYPE
   INDEX BY BINARY_INTEGER;
empno_table empno_table_type;

-- table of employee table rows
TYPE employee_table_type IS TABLE of employee%ROWTYPE
   INDEX BY BINARY_INTEGER;
employee_table employee_table_type;

-- table of records of employee numbers
TYPE employee_record IS RECORD
   (empno employee.employee_id%TYPE );
TYPE employee_record_table_type IS TABLE OF employee_record
   INDEX BY BINARY_INTEGER;
employee_record_table employee_record_table_type;
```

Complete the following chart by supplying the command that assigns the value "100" to element number 100. For the tables of records, assign the value to the empno field.

Table Name	Syntax
Number_table	
Empno_table	
Employee_table	
Employee_record_table	

6-15. Oracle offers a set of "methods" (different in syntax usage from functions) to help you work with collections. Identify the method associated with each description:

   a. Returns TRUE if an element has been defined or FALSE if it has not.

   b. Returns the number of elements in an index-by table. It is 0 when the table is initially defined.

   c. Returns the number of the first element in the index-by table. It returns NULL if no elements are defined.

   d. Returns the number of the last element in the index-by table. It returns NULL if no elements are defined.

   e. Returns the number of the next lowest element to the one specified. If there are no lower elements it returns NULL. It also returns NULL if no elements are defined.

   f. Returns the number of the next highest element to the one specified. If there are no higher elements, it returns NULL. It also returns NULL if no elements are defined.

   g. Removes (undefines) elements in the index-by table.

6-16. What can you do to ensure that index-by table elements are never set to NULL?

6-17. Write a block to retrieve employee numbers from the employee table and put them into an index-by table sequentially, starting with row 0.

6-18. Write a block to retrieve employee last names from the employee table and put them into an index-by table nonsequentially, using the employee ID number as the index-by table row. Why would you want to use the employee ID number as the row number?

6-19. Nesting index-by table methods, an often underutilized feature, is some-times required to solve complex problems. Here is a simple example of nested calls to index-by table methods. What will the output look like?

```
DECLARE
   TYPE number_table_type IS TABLE OF number
      INDEX BY BINARY_INTEGER;
   number_table number_table_type;
   v_element PLS_INTEGER;

BEGIN
   number_table(1)   := 3;
   number_table(2)   := 2;
   number_table(3)   := 1;
   v_element := number_table.PRIOR
      (number_table.NEXT(number_table.FIRST));
   DBMS_OUTPUT.PUT_LINE(
      'Element ' || v_element || ' ' ||
      'Value '   || number_table(v_element));
END;
```

6-20. What are the two ways to delete all entries from an index-by table?

6-21. What is the output of the following block?

```
DECLARE
   TYPE a_table_type IS TABLE OF VARCHAR2(30)
      INDEX BY BINARY_INTEGER;
   a_table a_table_type;

BEGIN
   IF a_table IS NULL THEN
      DBMS_OUTPUT.PUT_LINE('The table is NULL?');
   ELSE
      DBMS_OUTPUT.PUT_LINE('The table is NOT NULL!');
   END IF;
END;
```

6-22. Rewrite the following code into a single line:

```
IF the_table.FIRST IS NULL /* table is empty */
THEN
   the_table(1) := 2067;
ELSE
   the_table(the_table.LAST + 1) := 2067;
END IF;
```

Expert

6-23. My son keeps track of every year's favorite birthday presents in a database table. To display the contents of that table, he loads them into an index-by table, using the year as the row number:

```
/* Filename on web page: presents.sql */
CREATE TABLE birthday (
   party_date DATE,
   fav_present VARCHAR2(100));

INSERT INTO birthday VALUES
   ('01-OCT-92', 'TEENAGE MUTANT NINJA TURTLE');
INSERT INTO birthday VALUES
   ('01-OCT-98', 'GAMEBOY POKEMON');

DECLARE
   TYPE name_tt IS TABLE OF birthday.fav_present%TYPE
      INDEX BY BINARY_INTEGER;
   the_best name_tt;
BEGIN
   FOR rec IN (
      SELECT TO_NUMBER (TO_CHAR (party_date, 'YYYY')) indx,
             fav_present
        FROM birthday)
   LOOP
      the_best (rec.indx) := rec.fav_present;
   END LOOP;
```

That's all well and good, but what he really wants to do is display those favorite presents and savor the moments of his recent past. The following loops demonstrate different ways he could see this information. Which is the best approach to take and what is wrong with each of the others?

a.
```
FOR indx IN the_best.FIRST .. the_best.LAST
LOOP
   DBMS_OUTPUT.PUT_LINE (the_best(indx));
END LOOP;
```

b.
```
IF the_best.COUNT > 0
THEN
    FOR indx IN the_best.FIRST .. the_best.LAST
    LOOP
       DBMS_OUTPUT.PUT_LINE (the_best(indx));
    END LOOP;
END IF;
```

c.
```
IF the_best.COUNT > 0
THEN
    FOR indx IN the_best.FIRST .. the_best.LAST
    LOOP
       IF the_best.EXISTS (indx)
       THEN
          DBMS_OUTPUT.PUT_LINE (the_best(indx));
       END IF;
    END LOOP;
END IF;
```

d.
```
/* assume indx is declared as PLS_INTEGER */
indx := the_best.FIRST;
LOOP
   EXIT WHEN indx IS NULL;
   DBMS_OUTPUT.PUT_LINE (the_best(indx));
   indx := the_best.NEXT (indx);
END LOOP;
```

6-24. The salary_grouping package creates a matrix grouping of employees and salary ranges. The package is used as follows:

```
DECLARE
   v_range salary_grouping.v_range_type;
BEGIN
   v_range(1) :=  20000;
   v_range(2) :=  30000;
   v_range(3) :=  75000;
   v_range(4) := 100000;
   v_range(5) := 125000;
   salary_grouping.build_range(v_range);
   salary_grouping.show_range(v_range);
END;
```

This example produces the following output, showing that three employees make more than \$30,000 and less than or equal to \$75,000, and two employees make more than \$75,000 and less than or equal to \$100,000:

```
20000  30000  75000 100000 125000
0      0      3      2      0
```

Here is a sample header for the package:

```
CREATE OR REPLACE PACKAGE salary_grouping
IS
   /* Type and table to store the salary groupings */
   TYPE v_range_type IS TABLE OF NUMBER
      INDEX BY BINARY_INTEGER;
   v_range_table v_range_type;

   /* Calculate the groupings  */
   PROCEDURE build_range ( p_range IN OUT v_range_type );

   /* Procedure to display the calculated groupings */
   PROCEDURE show_range ( p_range IN v_range_type );

   -- the number of categories defined
   v_num_categories PLS_INTEGER;
   -- the longest category (for display)
   v_maxlen        PLS_INTEGER;

END salary_grouping;
```

Write the code for the package body.

6-25. Wouldn't it be great to sort the contents of an index-by table? Here is the specification of such a package for sorting VARCHAR2(30) index-by tables:

```
CREATE OR REPLACE PACKAGE sort_routines
IS
   -- global types for sorting
   TYPE v_vc230_array_type IS TABLE OF VARCHAR2(30)
      INDEX BY BINARY_INTEGER;

   /* Overloaded sort procedures */
   PROCEDURE sort_table(
      p_array IN OUT v_vc230_array_type,
      p_duplicates BOOLEAN := FALSE );

END sort_routines;
```

The p_duplicates flag denotes whether duplicate values are to be included in the sorted array or not; the default is that duplicates are to be left out of the sorted version of the table.

Write the code for the package body.

6-26. Index-by tables can support bidirectional cursors that allow navigation forward and backward through rows in a table (Oracle does not support true bidirectional cursor access, at least up through Oracle8*i* Release 8.1).

Here is a package header that implements simplified bidirectional cursor capabilities for the employee table:

```
CREATE OR REPLACE PACKAGE employee_cursor IS
   -- record of the employee table declared
   -- globally for all to see
```

```
TYPE employee_record IS RECORD (
    empno       employee.empno%TYPE,
    empname     employee.empname%TYPE,
    empsalary   employee.empsalary%TYPE );

-- load the employee records into memory
FUNCTION load_rows RETURN PLS_INTEGER;

-- function to move to the next row
FUNCTION next_row RETURN BOOLEAN;

-- function to move to the previous row
FUNCTION prev_row RETURN BOOLEAN;

-- function to get the values for the current row
FUNCTION get_row RETURN employee_record;

-- function to go to a specific row
FUNCTION go_row ( p_row PLS_INTEGER ) RETURN BOOLEAN;

END employee_cursor;
```

Here is an example of using this package:

```
DECLARE
  v_num_employees PLS_INTEGER;
  v_employee employee_cursor.employee_record;

BEGIN
  -- load the employees into memory
  v_num_employees := employee_cursor.load_rows;

  -- display the first employee
  IF v_num_employees > 0 THEN
    v_employee := employee_cursor.get_row;
    DBMS_OUTPUT.PUT_LINE(v_employee.empno);
  END IF;

  -- loop through the rest and display them
  LOOP
    EXIT WHEN NOT employee_cursor.next_row;
    v_employee := employee_cursor.get_row;
    DBMS_OUTPUT.PUT_LINE(v_employee.empno);
  END LOOP;

  -- wait a minute, who was that second one again?
  IF employee_cursor.go_row(2) THEN
    v_employee := employee_cursor.get_row;
    DBMS_OUTPUT.PUT_LINE(v_employee.empno);
  END IF;

END;
```

Write the code for the package body.

7

Nested Tables

In addition to simply renaming PL/SQL tables to index-by tables in Oracle8, Oracle introduced two new collection datatypes: nested arrays and variable arrays. While conceptually similar to index-by tables, the two new collection types are usable in SQL statements (for example, you can insert multiple rows of a collection into a table via Oracle 8*i* Release 8.1's bulk collection operators) and may be stored as columns in a database table. This chapter tests your understanding of *nested tables*, the first of the new collection types. Specifically, it examines your ability to create a nested table type, store the array in a "store table," add and delete elements, and traverse each element.

Beginner

7-1. What SQL syntax is introduced in Oracle8 to create nested table types?

7-2. True or false?

    a. Nested table types can be used as datatypes for columns in Oracle tables.

    b. There is no limit to the number of rows that can be stored in a nested table type.

    c. Different rows in a nested table type can contain different types of information. Row 1, for example, might contain numeric data while Row 2 contains a string.

    d. Nested table types are stored in the database.

    e. Nested table types can be created based only on Oracle's native datatypes such as VARCHAR2 and NUMBER.

7-3. Fixit Later is the System Architect at Simplistic Procurement Systems, and he has executed the following DDL to create a new system:

```
SQL> CREATE TYPE detail_t AS OBJECT ( detail_no PLS_INTEGER,
  2                                    detail_desc VARCHAR2(30),
  3                                    detail_price NUMBER );
  4  /

Type created.

SQL> CREATE TYPE order_detail_t AS TABLE OF detail_t;
  2  /

Type created.

SQL> CREATE TABLE orders
  2  (order_no     PLS_INTEGER,
  3   order_desc   VARCHAR2(30),
  4   order_details order_detail_t )
  5  NESTED TABLE order_details STORE AS order_detail_store;

Table created.
```

Answer the following questions about Mr. Later's design:

a. How many nested table types were created?

b. What is the name of the outer table?

c. What is the name of the store table?

d. What is the structure of the store table?

7-4. Knowitall Andthensome has been given the task of creating data structures to record questions and answers for a series of tests given to students. The name of each test, as well as the questions and correct answers, must be stored. How might this be done using a nested table?

7-5. Which of the following statements regarding the use of nested table types as nested tables are true and which are false?

a. A nested table type cannot be the only column in a table>

b. Tables can only contain one nested table type.

7-6. How do you declare a variable for a nested table type?

7-7. What is a default constructor?

7-8. Declare and initialize to NULL a variable for each of the following datatypes:

```
CREATE TYPE a_blob_t IS TABLE OF BLOB;
/
CREATE TYPE a_number_t IS TABLE OF NUMBER(10);
/
CREATE TYPE a_detail_t IS OBJECT ( detail_no     NUMBER(10),
                                   some_blobs    a_blob_t,
                                   some_numbers a_number_t );
/
```

7-9. True or false?

    a. Nested tables are stored in the database; index-by tables are not.

    b. Index-by tables are persistent between logins.

    c. Nested tables are homogeneous, and index-by tables are heterogeneous.

    d. Index-by tables are not as sparse as nested tables.

Intermediate

7-10. When these commands are executed in SQL*Plus or a similar interface, what is the output?

```
CREATE TYPE temperature_t AS TABLE OF NUMBER;
/

CREATE TABLE hourly_temperatures
(temperature_date DATE,
 temperatures temperature_t)
NESTED TABLE temperatures STORE AS temperature_store;

SELECT COUNT(*)
  FROM hourly_temperatures
/

SELECT COUNT(*)
  FROM temperature_store
/
```

7-11. Assuming the same types and declarations shown in 7-10, what happens when a user issues the following SELECT statement?

```
SELECT COUNT(*)
  FROM temperature_store
/
```

7-12. Knowitall Andthensome passed his MCSE exam by answering question number 1 as 10, question 2 as 20, question 3 as 30, question 4 as 40, and question 5 as 50. Given the following type definitions, create a single SQL statement that inserts Knowitall's responses into the student_answers table:

```
CREATE TYPE answer_t AS OBJECT ( question_no NUMBER(10),
                                 answer_no   NUMBER(10));

CREATE TYPE answer_list_t AS TABLE OF answer_t;

CREATE TABLE student_answers (
    student_id INTEGER,
    exam_date DATE,
    exam_id INTEGER,
    student_answer_values answer_list_t)
NESTED TABLE student_answer_values
STORE AS student_answer_store;
```

7-13. Now that there is an entry in the student_answers, what syntax is required to query all fields in the student_answers table? All fields in the nested table?

7-14. Continuing with the student_answers example, what SQL syntax is required to add another answer?

7-15. What is the SQL syntax to delete the entry just added?

7-16. An Oracle error is lurking within this code snippet. Can you spot and fix it?

```
BEGIN
   /*
    || Insert an exam entry
   */
   INSERT INTO student_answers
      (student_id,
       exam_date,
       exam_id,
       student_answer_values)
   VALUES
      (100,
       SYSDATE,
       100,
       NULL);
   /*
    || Insert a single answer for the entry just created
   */
   INSERT INTO THE ( SELECT student_answer_values
                       FROM student_answers
                      WHERE student_id = 100
                        AND TRUNC(exam_date) = TRUNC(SYSDATE)
                        AND exam_id = 100 )
   VALUES (answer_t(1,10));
END;
```

7-17. Identify each of the following nested table methods:

a. Returns TRUE if an element has been defined or FALSE if it has not.

b. Returns the number of elements a nested table contains. It is 0 when the table is initially defined.

c. Always returns NULL for nested tables.

d. Returns the number of the first element in the nested table. It returns NULL if no elements are defined.

e. Returns the number of the last element in the nested table. It returns NULL if no elements are defined.

f. Returns the number of the next lowest element to the one specified. If there are no lower elements, it returns NULL. It also returns NULL if no elements are defined.

g. Returns the number of the next highest element to the one specified. If there are no higher elements, it returns NULL. It also returns NULL if no elements are defined.

h. Removes (undefines) elements in the nested table. However, it leaves a placeholder behind.

i. Creates new placeholders on the end of the nested table. These place-holders can then be assigned values.

j. Removes elements from the end of nested tables and leaves no place-holder behind.

7-18. True or false (assume x is a nested table variable)?

a. NVL(x.LAST,0) will always be equal to NVL(x.COUNT,0).

b. x.FIRST will always be 1 or NULL.

c. NVL(x.LAST,0) may not be equal to NVL(x.COUNT,0).

d. x.LIMIT will always be NULL.

7-19. Supply the missing datatype for v_answers:

```
DECLARE
    -- cursor to finally get some answers
    CURSOR curs_get_answers IS
        SELECT student_answer_values
            FROM student_answers;
    v_answers <data type required>;

BEGIN
    -- I want some answers!
    OPEN curs_get_answers;
    FETCH curs_get_answers INTO v_answers;
    CLOSE curs_get_answers;

    -- display the last value if the first
    -- exists?
    IF v_answers.EXISTS(v_answers.FIRST) THEN
        DBMS_OUTPUT.PUT_LINE(v_answers.LAST);
    END IF;

    -- add an element
    v_answers.EXTEND;
END;
```

7-20. This code does not execute because of an error lurking within. What line causes the failure and why?

```
DECLARE
    v_answers_a answer_list_t := answer_list_t();
    v_answers_b answer_list_t := answer_list_t();
    v_answers_c answer_list_t;
    v_answers_d answer_list_t := answer_list_t();

BEGIN
```

```
v_answers_a.EXTEND;
v_answers_a(1) := answer_t(1,10);

v_answers_b.EXTEND;
v_answers_b(1) := answer_t(1,10);

v_answers_c.EXTEND;
v_answers_c(1) := answer_t(1,10);

v_answers_d.EXTEND;
v_answers_d(1) := answer_t(1,10);
END;
```

7-21. What line in this code causes an Oracle error?

```
DECLARE
  -- declare a collection with no null
  -- answers allowed
  v_no_null_answers answer_list_t NOT NULL;

BEGIN
  -- add an answer
  v_no_null_answers.EXTEND;
  v_no_null_answers(1) := answer_t(1,10);

  -- add a NULL answer
  v_no_null_answers.EXTEND;
  v_no_null_answers(2) := NULL;
END;
```

7-22. What can be done to ensure that no NULL values are inserted into a user-defined type?

7-23. Other than programmatic validation, how can you ensure that entries in a nested table are unique within their corresponding outer-table record?

7-24. What is the output from this block?

```
DECLARE
  /*
    || Simple program to demonstrate the
    || interaction of EXTEND, TRIM and DELETE
  */
  v_answers answer_list_t := answer_list_t();
  v_element PLS_INTEGER;

BEGIN
  v_answers.EXTEND;-- line 1
  v_answers(1) := answer_t(1,10);-- line 2
  v_answers.EXTEND(3);-- line 3
  v_answers.EXTEND(10,1);-- line 4

  v_answers.DELETE(1,3);-- line 5
  v_answers.DELETE(7);-- line 6
```

```
v_answers.TRIM(2);-- line 7
v_answers.TRIM; -- line 8

DBMS_OUTPUT.PUT_LINE('First Element Is     ' ||
    v_answers.FIRST);
DBMS_OUTPUT.PUT_LINE('Last Element Is      ' ||
    v_answers.LAST);
DBMS_OUTPUT.PUT_LINE('Count Of Elements Is ' ||
    v_answers.COUNT);

v_element := v_answers.FIRST;
LOOP
  EXIT WHEN v_element IS NULL;
  DBMS_OUTPUT.PUT_LINE(
    'Element ' || v_element ||
    ' = ' || v_answers(v_element).question_no);
  v_element := v_answers.NEXT(v_element);
END LOOP;

END;
```

7-25. An Oracle error arises from within this block. What error message is displayed, and what line causes the error?

```
DECLARE
  v_answers answer_list_t := answer_list_t();  -- line 1

BEGIN
  v_answers.EXTEND(10);             -- line 2
  v_answers.DELETE(1,99);           -- line 3
  v_answers.TRIM(11);               -- line 4
END;
```

7-26. What is the output of this block?

```
DECLARE
  v_answers answer_list_t := answer_list_t();
BEGIN
  v_answers.EXTEND(10);-- line 1
  v_answers.DELETE(4,5);-- line 2
  v_answers.TRIM(v_answers.COUNT);-- line 3
  DBMS_OUTPUT.PUT_LINE('Remaining Elements = ' ||
    v_answers.COUNT);
END;
```

7-27. Using the test_answers and student_answers tables created in previous exercises, write a function to calculate the percentage of questions a particular student got correct for a particular test on a particular day. Use the following function header:

```
CREATE OR REPLACE FUNCTION calculate_score (
    p_student_id student_answers.student_id%TYPE,
    p_test_id test_answers.test_id%TYPE,
    p_exam_date DATE)
    RETURN NUMBER
```

7-28. Write a function that returns TRUE if duplicate answers are found within a passed answer list. Use the following function header:

```
CREATE OR REPLACE FUNCTION duplicates_exist (
    p_answer_list answer_list_t)
    RETURN BOOLEAN
```

7-29. Supply an argument to the DBMS_OUTPUT.PUT_LINE function that raises the "ORA-06533: Subscript beyond count" error:

```
DECLARE
    v_answers answer_list_t := answer_list_t();
BEGIN
    DBMS_OUTPUT.PUT_LINE(<your answer here>);
END;
```

7-30. What are nested table locators and in what situations should they be used?

7-31. How are nested table locators implemented?

7-32. How can PL/SQL determine if a nested table is returning a locator?

Expert

7-33. The questions in this section refer to the following tables and types, which implement a rudimentary purchase-order system. The ORDERS table stores a sequential order number along with a short description. The lines of the purchase order are stored in the nested table column ORDER_DETAIL. The TAX_CODES column records the tax codes that apply to the purchase order.

Write a SQL script to create the following structures:

```
SQL> DESCRIBE orders;
 Name                             Null?    Type
 -------------------------------- -------- ----
 ORDER_NO                         NOT NULL NUMBER
 ORDER_DESC                                VARCHAR2(30)
 ORDER_DETAIL                              ORDER_DETAIL_T
 TAX_CODES                                 TAX_CODE_T

SQL> DESCRIBE order_detail_t;
 order_detail_t TABLE OF DETAIL_T
 Name                             Null?    Type
 -------------------------------- -------- ----
 DETAIL_NO                                 NUMBER
 DETAIL_DESC                               VARCHAR2(30)
 DETAIL_PRICE                              NUMBER

SQL> DESCRIBE detail_t;
 Name                             Null?    Type
 -------------------------------- -------- ----
 DETAIL_NO                                 NUMBER
 DETAIL_DESC                               VARCHAR2(30)
 DETAIL_PRICE                              NUMBER
```

```
SQL> DESCRIBE tax_code_t;
 tax_code_t TABLE OF TAX_CODE_DETAIL_T
 Name                             Null?     Type
 -----------------------------    --------  ----
    TAX_CODE                                VARCHAR2(10)


SQL> DESCRIBE tax_code_detail_t;
 Name                             Null?     Type
 -----------------------------    --------  ----
    TAX_CODE                                VARCHAR2(10)


SQL> DESCRIBE order_detail;
 Name                             Null?     Type
 -----------------------------    --------  ----
    DETAIL_NO                               NUMBER
    DETAIL_DESC                             VARCHAR2(30)
    DETAIL_PRICE                            NUMBER


SQL> DESCRIBE order_tax_codes;
 Name                             Null?     Type
 -----------------------------    --------  ----
    TAX_CODE                                VARCHAR2(10)
```

7-34. Now that we have the data structures for our system, we can create a manage_orders package to encapsulate the required DML operations. The next several exercises ask you to implement the package's various procedures and functions. In this first exercise, write a function called create_order. The function should use the next sequential order_no to create an new entry in the order; the entry should have a blank description and no detail lines. If the p_default_taxes parameter is TRUE, insert two tax codes for the order, GST and PST (eh!). Otherwise do not include any tax codes. Use the following function header:

```
FUNCTION create_order (
    p_default_taxes BOOLEAN := FALSE)
RETURN NUMBER;
```

7-35. Next, add an update_order procedure to change an order's description. Use the following header:

```
PROCEDURE update_order (
    p_order_no ORDERS.ORDER_NO%TYPE,
    p_new_desc ORDERS.ORDER_DESC%TYPE );
```

7-36. Next, add an add_details procedure to insert one or more order details for the specified order. Make sure that detail_no is unique within the details being added as well as within the order. Use the following header:

```
PROCEDURE add_details (
    p_order_no    ORDERS.ORDER_NO%TYPE,
    p_new_detail ORDER_DETAIL_T );
```

7-37. Next, add a get_details function, which queries and returns all detail lines for the specified order. Use the following header:

```
FUNCTION get_details (
    p_order_no ORDERS.ORDER_NO%TYPE )
RETURN ORDER_DETAIL_T;
```

7-38. Next, assume that there are only two tax codes available, PST and GST, and both are charged as 7% of every line. Add a function to calculate the total cost of an order by adding up the price of each line and adding any applicable taxes. Use the following header:

```
FUNCTION calculate_cost (
    p_order_no ORDERS.ORDER_NO%TYPE )
RETURN NUMBER;
```

7-39. Finally, write a PL/SQL block to demonstrate the use of the new package by inserting a new order with multiple lines and then calculate its cost.

8

Variable Arrays

Variable arrays (VARRAYs) are the third collection type introduced in Oracle8. Unlike index-by tables or nested arrays, VARRAYs are bounded, meaning they contain a fixed number of elements. This chapter tests (among other things) your ability to define a VARRAY, store a VARRAY in a database table, and add new elements to a VARRAY.

Beginner

8-1. What is a variable array?

8-2. Where can you use variable arrays?

8-3. How do you define variable arrays for use in the database?

8-4. What is a bounded array?

8-5. What SQL syntax do you use to create a variable array column inside a database table?

8-6. What syntax do you use to define a variable array as a PL/SQL variable?

8-7. For what datatypes can you create variable arrays?

8-8. What data dictionary views are available to see which variable arrays exist?

8-9. How can you display the structure of a variable array?

Intermediate

8-10. How can you create and use default constructors for variable arrays?

8-11. What is the result of running this block?

```
DECLARE
  TYPE v_single_element_type IS VARRAY(1) OF VARCHAR2(1);
  v_single_element_array v_single_element_type;

BEGIN
  v_single_element_array := v_single_element_type(1,2);
END;
```

8-12. Identify the variable array methods that have the following characteristics:

a. Returns TRUE if an element has been defined or FALSE if it has not.

b. Returns the number of elements a virtual array contains. It is 0 when the array is initially defined.

c. Returns the upper bound specified for the virtual array.

d. Returns the number of the first element in the variable array. It returns NULL if no elements are defined. Because variable arrays are never sparse and their order is tightly maintained, this function never returns anything other than NULL or 1.

e. Returns the number of the last element in the variable array. It returns NULL if no elements are defined.

f. Returns the number of the next lowest element to the one specified. If there are no lower elements, it returns NULL. It also returns NULL if no elements are defined. Because variable arrays are never sparse and their order is maintained, the value returned is always sequential.

g. Returns the number of the next highest element to the one specified. If there are no higher elements, it returns NULL. It also returns NULL if no elements are defined. Because variable arrays are never sparse and their order is maintained, the value returned is always sequential.

h. Removes (undefines) elements in the variable array. Because variable arrays are dense, this function can only remove all elements.

i. Creates a new placeholder on the end of the variable array. This placeholder can then be assigned a value.

j. Removes elements from the end of variable arrays.

8-13. True or false (assume x is a variable array)?

a. NVL(x.LAST,0) will always be equal to NVL(x.COUNT,0).

b. x.FIRST will always be 1 or NULL.

c. NVL(x.LAST,0) may not be equal to NVL(x.COUNT,0).

d. x.LIMIT will always be NULL.

8-14. Give the commands to set the first element of each of the following VARRAY variables to 100:

```
DECLARE
   TYPE v_numbers_type IS VARRAY(10) OF NUMBER(10);
   v_numbers v_numbers_type := v_numbers_type();

   TYPE v_emp_row_type IS VARRAY(10) OF emp%ROWTYPE;
   v_emp_row v_emp_row_type := v_emp_row_type();

   TYPE v_emp_record_type IS RECORD (
      empno       emp.empno%TYPE,
      empname     emp.empname%TYPE,
      empsalary emp.empsalary%TYPE );

   TYPE v_emp_record_varray IS VARRAY(10) OF v_emp_record_type;
   v_emp_record v_emp_record_varray := v_emp_record_varray();
```

8-15. This code raises an Oracle error at runtime. What error is raised and why?

```
DECLARE
   -- cursor to select employee records
   CURSOR curs_get_emps IS
   SELECT *
     FROM employee;

   -- variable array based on the cursor
   TYPE v_employee_rec IS VARRAY(10) OF curs_get_emps%ROWTYPE;

BEGIN
   -- fetch an employee record
   OPEN curs_get_emps;
   FETCH curs_get_emps INTO
      v_employee_rec(curs_get_emps%ROWCOUNT);
   CLOSE curs_get_emps;

END;
```

8-16. Attempting to run this code produces a rather tiresome Oracle error. What line causes the error and what is the error?

```
DECLARE
   TYPE v_varray IS VARRAY(100) OF VARCHAR2(30);
   v_varray_a v_varray := v_varray();-- line 1
   v_varray_b v_varray := v_varray();-- line 2
   v_varray_c v_varray;-- line 3
   v_varray_d v_varray := v_varray();-- line 4
   v_varray_e v_varray := v_varray();-- line 5

BEGIN
   v_varray_a.EXTEND;
   v_varray_b.EXTEND;
   v_varray_c.EXTEND;
   v_varray_d.EXTEND;
   v_varray_e.EXTEND;

END;
```

8-17. If x is a variable array, is the following looping method safe from Oracle errors?

```
FOR counter IN x.COUNT LOOP
  DBMS_OUTPUT.PUT_LINE(counter);
END LOOP;
```

8-18. There is a rather glaring logic error in the following declarations and code. What Oracle error does the code raise?

```
CREATE TYPE dwarf_t AS OBJECT ( name VARCHAR2(30) );
/
CREATE TYPE seven_dwarves_t AS VARRAY(6) OF dwarf_t;
/
DECLARE
  v_local_dwarf_list      seven_dwarves_t := seven_dwarves_t( );
  v_local_dwarf           dwarf_t;

  PROCEDURE add_dwarf (name_in IN VARCHAR2) IS
  BEGIN
      v_local_dwarf := dwarf_t(name_in);
      v_local_dwarf_list.EXTEND;
      v_local_dwarf_list(NVL(v_local_dwarf_list.LAST,0)) :=
          v_local_dwarf;
  END;
BEGIN
  add_dwarf ('Happy');
  add_dwarf ('Bashful');
  add_dwarf ('Sneezy');
  add_dwarf ('Doc');
  add_dwarf ('Grumpy');
  add_dwarf ('Dopey');
  add_dwarf ('Sleepy');
END;
```

8-19. This code snippet simply performs a loop 10 times and places the loop counter into a variable array. Which methods can be used to ensure that elements are loaded sequentially with sequential numbers?

```
DECLARE
    TYPE v_local_array_t IS VARRAY(10) OF NUMBER;
    v_local_array v_local_array_t := v_local_array_t();

BEGIN
  FOR counter IN 1..10 LOOP
    v_local_array.EXTEND;
    v_local_array(v_local_array.<method>) := counter;
  END LOOP;
END;
```

8-20. What SQL commands create these structures?

```
SQL> DESC top_ten
Name                              Null?     Type
-------------------------------   --------  ----
TOP_TEN_NAME                                VARCHAR2(100)
TOP_TEN_VALUES                              TOP_TEN_T
```

```
SQL> DESC top_ten_t
 top_ten_t VARRAY(10) OF LIST_T
 Name                                  Null?    Type
 ------------------------------------- -------- ----
 LIST_VALUE                                     VARCHAR2(100)


SQL> DESC list_t
 Name                                  Null?    Type
 ------------------------------------- -------- ----
 LIST_VALUE                                     VARCHAR2(100)
```

8-21. Write a PL/SQL block to insert the 10 most misspelled PL/SQL keywords into a variable array.

8-22. What happens when you use the nested table THE operator on a VARRAY, as shown in the following example?

```
SQL> SELECT *
  2    FROM THE ( SELECT top_ten_values
  3                 FROM top_ten )
  4   WHERE top_ten_name = 'Misspelled PL/SQL Keywords';
```

8-23. What can you do to avoid the error created in 8-22?

8-24. How can you ensure that the top 10 list values are always returned in the correct order (to maintain a semblance of suspense during presentation)?

8-25. What syntax would you use to query those in the top 10 list that contain underscores?

8-26. Selecting the top_ten_values column from the top_ten table returns the values encapsulated within the top_ten_t constructor (a variable array):

```
SQL> SELECT top_ten_values
  2    FROM top_ten;


TOP_TEN_VALUES(LIST_VALUE)
----------------------------------------
TOP_TEN_T(LIST_T('ELSIF'), LIST_T('END I
F'), LIST_T('PRAGMA'), LIST_T('EXCEPTION
'), LIST_T('BINARY_INTEGER'), LIST_T('EX
CEPTION_INIT'), LIST_T('PLS_INTEGER'), L
IST_T('SET_SQL_TRACE_IN_SESSION'), LIST_
T('PUT_LINE'), LIST_T('EXECUTE_AND_FETCH
'))
```

Write a function called top_ten_caster that returns the values encapsulated within a TOP_TEN_NESTED_T constructor (a nested table type). Here is an example of using the function:

```
SQL> SELECT top_ten_caster(top_ten_values)
  2    FROM top_ten;


TOP_TEN_CASTER(TOP_TEN_VALUES)(LIST_VALUE)
-------------------------------------------
```

```
TOP_TEN_NESTED_T(LIST_T('ELSIF'), LIST_T('END
 IF'), LIST_T('PRAGMA'), LIST_T('EXCEPTION'),
 LIST_T('BINARY_INTEGER'), LIST_T('EXCEPTION_
 INIT'), LIST_T('PLS_INTEGER'), LIST_T('SET_SQ
 L_TRACE_IN_SESSION'), LIST_T('PUT_LINE'), LIS
 T_T('EXECUTE_AND_FETCH'))
```

8-27. What Oracle error does the following statement raise and why?

```
UPDATE THE ( SELECT CAST ( top_ten_values AS top_ten_nested_t )
               FROM top_ten
               WHERE top_ten_name = 'Misspelled PL/SQL Keywords')
SET list_value = 'BIT_XOR'
WHERE list_value = 'PRAGMA';
```

8-28. Here is a PL/SQL block that performs the update attempted in 8-27. Some of the code has been removed; (indicated by brackets < >) after all, these are exercises. Add the missing code and change it into a procedure with three parameters: the top 10 list name, the entry to replace, and the entry to replace it with:

```
DECLARE
  /*
   || This block changes the top ten entry
   || of PRAGMA to BIT_XOR for the list titled
   || Misspelled PL/SQL Keywords
  */

  -- cursor to get top ten entries for update
  CURSOR curs_get_top_ten IS
  SELECT top_ten_values
    FROM top_ten
   WHERE top_ten_name = 'Misspelled PL/SQL Keywords'
  FOR UPDATE of top_ten_values;
  v_top_ten <variable type>;

BEGIN
  -- get all ten entries at once!
  OPEN curs_get_top_ten;
  FETCH curs_get_top_ten INTO v_top_ten;

  -- if the entries exist...
  IF curs_get_top_ten%FOUND THEN

    -- for every one of the top ten entries...
    FOR counter IN 1..<loop boundary> LOOP

      -- if the entry is PRAGMA then change it to BIT_XOR
      IF <array element> = 'PRAGMA' THEN
        <array element> := 'BIT_XOR';
      END IF;

    END LOOP;  -- every top ten entry
```

```
     -- perform the update
     UPDATE top_ten
     SET top_ten_values = v_top_ten
     WHERE CURRENT OF curs_get_top_ten;

  END IF;  -- the entries exist

  CLOSE curs_get_top_ten;

END;
```

8-29. True or false (assume x is a variable array)?

    a. The number of rows removed by x.DELETE can be less than x. COUNT.

    b. The number of rows removed by x.DELETE will always equal x. COUNT.

    c. The number of rows removed by x.TRIM can be less than x.COUNT.

    d. The number of rows removed by x.TRIM will always equal x.COUNT.

    e. x.TRIM can change the value returned by x.FIRST.

8-30. What is the output of this code block?

```
DECLARE
   TYPE v_local_array_t IS VARRAY(10) OF NUMBER;
   v_local_array v_local_array_t := v_local_array_t();

BEGIN
  FOR counter IN 1..10 LOOP
    v_local_array.EXTEND;
    v_local_array(v_local_array.LAST) := counter;
  END LOOP;

  v_local_array.TRIM;
  v_local_array.TRIM(2);

  FOR counter IN 1..v_local_array.COUNT LOOP
    DBMS_OUTPUT.PUT_LINE('element ' || counter ||
                         ' = ' || v_local_array(counter));
  END LOOP;

END;
```

8-31. Write a procedure to allow rows to be deleted from the variable array top_ten_t (similar to the behavior for nested tables). Use the following header:

```
/*
|| This procedure removes elements from p_list.
|| If p_start_del and p_end_del are NULL then
|| all elements are removed.
|| If p_start_del is NOT NULL and p_end_del is NULL
|| then p_start_del element is a goner.
```

```
|| If neither are NULL then the elements between
|| p_start_del and p_end_del are removed
|| inclusively
*/
CREATE OR REPLACE PROCEDURE del_top_ten (
    p_list        IN  OUT top_ten_t,
    p_start_del   PLS_INTEGER := NULL,
    p_end_del     PLS_INTEGER := NULL );
```

8-32. Indicate whether the following calls to the EXTEND method are valid or invalid:

　　a. a_varray.EXTEND;

　　b. a_varray.EXTEND(2);

　　c. a_varray.EXTEND(-1);

　　d. a_varray.EXTEND(2,1);

Expert

8-33. All the questions in this section refer to the tables and user-defined datatypes (UDTs) for a rudimentary purchase order system. The orders table stores a sequential order number along with a short description. The lines of the purchase order are stored in the nested table column order_detail. The tax_codes column records the tax codes that apply to the purchase order.

As the first exercise in this section, write a SQL script to create the following structures:

```
SQL> DESC orders
 Name                            Null?     Type
 ------------------------------- --------- ----
 ORDER_NO                        NOT NULL  NUMBER
 ORDER_DESC                                VARCHAR2(30)
 ORDER_DETAIL                              ORDER_DETAIL_T
 TAX_CODES                                 TAX_CODE_T


SQL> DESC order_detail_t
 order_detail_t VARRAY(10) OF DETAIL_T
 Name                            Null?     Type
 ------------------------------- --------- ----
 DETAIL_NO                                 NUMBER
 DETAIL_DESC                               VARCHAR2(30)
 DETAIL_PRICE                              NUMBER


SQL> DESC order_detail_nt
 order_detail_nt TABLE OF DETAIL_T
 Name                            Null?     Type
 ------------------------------- --------- ----
```

```
               DETAIL_NO                                      NUMBER
               DETAIL_DESC                                    VARCHAR2(30)
               DETAIL_PRICE                                   NUMBER

SQL> DESC detail_t
 Name                                      Null?      Type
 ---------------------------------------- --------   ----
 DETAIL_NO                                            NUMBER
 DETAIL_DESC                                          VARCHAR2(30)
 DETAIL_PRICE                                         NUMBER

SQL> DESC tax_code_t
 tax_code_t VARRAY(2) OF TAX_CODE_DETAIL_T
 Name                                      Null?      Type
 ---------------------------------------- --------   ----
 TAX_CODE                                             VARCHAR2(10)

SQL> DESC tax_code_detail_t
 Name                                      Null?      Type
 ---------------------------------------- --------   ----
 TAX_CODE                                             VARCHAR2(10)
```

8-34. Why were order_detail_t (a variable array) and order_detail_nt (a nested table type) created?

8-35. Now that we've created the data structures for our purchase order system, we need to create a manage_orders package to encapsulate the DML performed on the orders table and detail lines. We'll write several procedures and functions, each in a separate exercise.

First, write a function called create_order, which performs the following tasks:

- Gets the next sequential order_no.
- Creates an entry in the orders table using the order_no from the previous step with a blank description and no detail lines.
- If the p_default_taxes parameter is TRUE, inserts two tax codes for the order, GST and PST (eh!). Otherwise do not include any tax codes.

Use the following header:

```
FUNCTION create_order (
    p_default_taxes BOOLEAN := FALSE )
RETURN NUMBER;
```

8-36. Next, add a procedure called update_order, which changes the description of the order. Use the following header:

```
PROCEDURE update_order (
    p_order_no ORDERS.ORDER_NO%TYPE,
    p_new_desc ORDERS.ORDER_DESC%TYPE );
```

8-37. Next, add a procedure called add_details, which inserts one or more order details for the specified order; make sure that detail_no is unique within the details being added as well as within the order. Use the following header:

```
PROCEDURE add_details (
    p_order_no    ORDERS.ORDER_NO%TYPE,
    p_new_detail ORDER_DETAIL_T );
```

8-38. Next, add a function called get_details, which queries and returns all detail lines for the specified order. Use the following header:

```
-- query all details
FUNCTION get_details (
    p_order_no ORDERS.ORDER_NO%TYPE )
RETURN ORDER_DETAIL_T;
```

8-39. Next, write a function called calculate_cost, which calculates the total cost of an order by adding up the price of each line and adding any applicable taxes. Assume that there are only two tax codes available (PST and GST) and that both are charged as 7% of every detail line. Use the following header:

```
FUNCTION calculate_cost (
    p_order_no ORDERS.ORDER_NO%TYPE )
RETURN NUMBER;
```

8-40. Next, write a procedure called delete_detail, which deletes a single detail line from a purchase order. Use the following header:

```
PROCEDURE delete_detail (
    p_order_no       ORDERS.ORDER_NO%TYPE,
    p_detail_no      NUMBER,
    p_num_deleted OUT PLS_INTEGER );
```

8-41. Finally, write a PL/SQL block to demonstrate the use of the new package by inserting a multiline order and then calculating its cost.

9

Object Technology

Oracle8 ushered us into the brave new world of object-oriented programming... almost. Since Oracle is, after all, a relational database, much of the object technology introduced in the Oracle8 (as well as the Oracle8*i*) release is a hybrid between true object data and relational data. The CREATE TYPE command, for example, looks suspiciously like a familiar record or table, with the exception that you can now include methods (procedures and functions) that act on the object's attributes (columns and fields). This chapter tests your understanding of object types and your ability to apply object-oriented principles when designing a data structure.

Beginner

9-1. True or false? An *object type*:

a. Is a database construct created via the CREATE TYPE statement.

b. Defines a data structure with attributes, each having a single datatype.

c. Defines legal methods or operations on the object's attributes.

d. Is a template only and holds no actual data.

9-2. True or false? An object type can serve as the datatype of:

a. Each of the rows in a table.

b. A column in a table.

c. A PL/SQL variable.

d. A PL/SQL module's IN, OUT, or RETURN parameter.

e. A index-by table, nested table, or VARRAY.

f. A "field" in a PL/SQL record variable.

9-3. A *constructor* is a special method that creates an instance of an object from an object type. True or false? A constructor:

  a. Has the same name as its object type.

  b. Is a function rather than a procedure.

  c. Returns an instance of its object type.

  d. Has one parameter per attribute of the object type.

  e. Is available "by default" for each object type.

  f. Has an analogous "destructor" method for deletion of an object.

9-4. Which of the following statements correctly describes how to specify the source code for an object's method(s)?

  a. In an object body that is separate from the *object specification*—much like a package specification and its separate package body:

```
CREATE OR REPLACE TYPE BODY CD_t
AS
    MEMBER FUNCTION set_title  (title_in IN VARCHAR2)
    RETURN CD_t
    IS
        the_cd CD_t := SELF;
    BEGIN
        IF title_in IS NOT NULL
        THEN
            the_cd.title := title_in;
        END IF;
        RETURN the_cd;
    END set_title;
END;
```

  b. In a standalone procedure or function:

```
CREATE OR REPLACE FUNCTION set_title (title_in IN VARCHAR2)
RETURN CD_t
AS MEMBER OF CD_t
IS
    the_cd CD_t := SELF;
BEGIN
    IF title_in IS NOT NULL
    THEN
        the_cd.title := title_in;
    END IF;
    RETURN the_cd;
END set_title;
```

9-5. Which of the following statements about object methods are true, and which are false?

  a. Object methods can be declared as STATIC, indicating they do not operate on a particular object.

  b. STATIC object methods were introduced with the release of Oracle8*i*.

    c. Non-STATIC object methods operate within the context of a specific object instance.

    d. Non-STATIC object methods have an implied parameter called SELF.

9-6. True or false? SELF can be included as a parameter in the parameter list of an object method.

9-7. Suppose that we have an *object table* of compact discs:

```
CREATE TABLE compact_discs OF CD_t;
```

Which of the following examples retrieves an object row into an object variable?

    a. Use the OBJECT operator to SELECT from the object table:

```
DECLARE
    the_cd    CD_t;

    CURSOR CD_cur IS
        SELECT OBJECT(cd)
          FROM compact_discs cd
         WHERE id = 100;
BEGIN
    OPEN  CD_cur;
    FETCH CD_cur INTO the_cd;
END;
```

    b. Use the VALUE operator to SELECT from the object table:

```
DECLARE
    the_cd    CD_t;

    CURSOR CD_cur IS
        SELECT VALUE (cd)
          FROM compact_discs cd
         WHERE id = 100;

BEGIN
    OPEN  CD_cur;
    FETCH CD_cur INTO the_cd;
END;
```

9-8. Each row in an object table is automatically assigned an Object Identifier (OID) by Oracle. True or false? The OID:

    a. Is a 16-byte RAW value

    b. Uniquely identifies an object in the database

    c. Resides in a "hidden" column in the object table

    d. Has a value that cannot be "seen" by the user

9-9. Which of the following types of objects have an OID?

    a. Column objects

    b. Transient objects stored in PL/SQL variables

    c. Nested objects, for example, the previous nested table of lost CDs named lost_cd_tab

9-10. A REF is a *reference* to a row object in an object table. REFs are the basis of relationships between objects and allow "object joins." True or false?

    a. A REF points at a row object. It encapsulates the row object's OID.

    b. REFs are used like a foreign key.

    c. The keyword REF can modify a datatype, indicating a *pointer* to an object.

    d. The REF operator accepts a table alias and returns a pointer to a row object that is constructed from the row object's OID.

    e. A REF can point to a column object.

9-11. Suppose that item 1 of CD order 10000 in the cd_order_items table points to the Beatles' *White Album* CD object in the compact_discs table (see the solution for 9-10 for the associated code). What is the result produced by the following SQL statement? Can you delete a compact disc if there is an order pointing to it?

```
DELETE FROM compact_discs
WHERE artist = 'Beatles'
AND   title = 'White Album';
```

9-12. Here is one way of joining a CD from the cd_order_items table to its definition in the compact_discs table:

```
SELECT items.item_id, cd.artist, cd.title
  FROM cd_order_items items, compact_discs cd
 WHERE items.cd_ref = REF (cd)
   AND items.order_id = 10000;
```

What is another way of expressing this join using *object navigation*?

9-13. DEREF is the "de-reference" operator. Given a REF, it returns the referenced object. DEREF is the logical inverse of REF. It "un-does" the REF:

```
DECLARE
   the_cd CD_t;
BEGIN
   SELECT DEREF(cd_ref)
     INTO the_cd
     FROM cd_order_items
    WHERE order_id = 10000
      AND item_id = 1;

   DBMS_OUTPUT.PUT_LINE('Artist: ' || the_cd.artist);
END;
```

What is produced by the code segment?

9-14. Suppose you have a table of music fans and their favorite CDs. Note that favorite_cd is a column object, not a REF:

```
SQL> DESC fan_favorites;

Name            Null?    Type
-------------- -------- --------------------
MUSIC_FAN_NAME           VARCHAR2(60)
FAVORITE_CD              CD_T
```

What happens when you try to ORDER BY an object?

```
SELECT music_fan_name,
       favorite_cd
  FROM fan_favorites
 ORDER BY favorite_cd;
```

9-15. Oracle must be told how to compare objects of the same type. This allows objects to be ORDERed, for example.

The MAP and ORDER methods allow Oracle to compare objects of the same type. MAP translates an object into a scalar value Oracle can use for comparison. ORDER compares two objects. Either MAP or ORDER may be used for an object type, but not both.

You might specify a MAP method for our CD object type as follows:

```
CREATE TYPE CD_t AS OBJECT (
    id    INTEGER,
    title VARCHAR2(60),
    artist VARCHAR2(60),

       MEMBER FUNCTION set_title  (title_in IN VARCHAR2)
       RETURN CD_t,

    MAP MEMBER FUNCTION compare RETURN VARCHAR2
);
```

Give an example of the contents found in the object body for the MAP method "compare."

Intermediate

9-16. True or false?

    a. With the release of the Oracle Objects option, the USER_OBJECTS view became available in the data dictionary.

    b. An entry for each object type is found in the USER_OBJECTS view.

    c. An entry for each object instance is found in the USER_OBJECTS view.

9-17. True or false? A constructor:

    a. Can be modified by a developer.

    b. Can be called in SQL or PL/SQL.

    c. Accepts attributes in named notation or positional notation.

9-18. What is wrong with the following object type definition?

```
CREATE TYPE CD_t AS OBJECT (
    id              INTEGER,
    title           VARCHAR2(60) := 'Greatest Hits',
    artist          VARCHAR2(60),
    label           VARCHAR2(60),
    MEMBER FUNCTION
        set_title (title_in    IN VARCHAR2)
            RETURN CD_t,
    MEMBER FUNCTION
        set_artist (artist_in   IN VARCHAR2)
            RETURN CD_t,
    MEMBER FUNCTION
        set_label (label_in     IN VARCHAR2)
            RETURN CD_t
);
```

9-19. What is wrong with the following object type definition?

```
CREATE TYPE CD_t AS OBJECT (
    id               INTEGER,
    title            VARCHAR2(60),
    artist           VARCHAR2(60),
    label            VARCHAR2(60),
    classification   VARCHAR2(60),

    MEMBER FUNCTION  set_title (title_in    IN VARCHAR2)
        RETURN CD_t;
    MEMBER FUNCTION  set_artist (artist_in   IN VARCHAR2)
        RETURN CD_t;
);
```

9-20. True or false? An object method:

a. Can be implemented in PL/SQL.

b. Can be implemented via an external procedure, such as a procedure written in the C language.

c. Can be implemented in Java.

9-21. What happens when you forget to FETCH something as an object, as shown next? How can you fix the problem?

```
DECLARE
    the_cd    CD_t;

    CURSOR   cd_cur
    IS
    SELECT *
      FROM compact_discs cd
     WHERE id = 100;

BEGIN
    OPEN cd_cur;
    FETCH cd_cur INTO the_cd;
    CLOSE cd_cur;
```

```
        DBMS_OUTPUT.PUT_LINE (the_cd.id || ' ' || the_cd.title);
    END;
```

9-22. True or false?

    a. OIDs arc *immutable*: if you want to change the value of an OID, you must delete the object and recreate it.

    b. Oracle automatically creates a unique index on an object table's hidden OID column.

    c. As with ROWIDs, OID values are lost and recreated anew when an object table is exported and then imported.

9-23. What output is generated by the following code segment?

```
DECLARE
    new_cd CD_t;
BEGIN
    IF new_cd IS NULL
    THEN
        DBMS_OUTPUT.PUT_LINE ('New CD is NULL');

        IF new_cd.title IS NULL
        THEN
            DBMS_OUTPUT.PUT_LINE ('New CD Title is NULL');
        ELSE
            DBMS_OUTPUT.PUT_LINE ('New CD Title is NOT NULL');
        END IF;

    ELSE
        DBMS_OUTPUT.PUT_LINE ('New CD is NOT NULL');
    END IF;

END;
```

9-24. What is wrong with the following code segment?

```
DECLARE
    new_cd    CD_t;
BEGIN
    new_cd.id := 75000;
    new_cd.artist := 'Grateful Dead';
    new_cd.title := 'Live in Branson';
END;
```

9-25. Given a REF, the UTL_REF package allows the following operations on the referenced object:

- Lock
- Retrieve
- Update
- Delete

This is possible (without UTL_REF's knowing the table name) where the referenced object resides. This allows programs to be "blind" to the table where an object is stored.

Write a code segment that locks and updates the title of the *White Album* CD object.

Expert

9-26. Which of the following statements accurately describe an object view and its capabilities?

   a. An object view is any SQL view found in the ALL_OBJECTS data dictionary view.

   b. An object view is a view that presents data stored in relational tables as an object.

   c. You can use an object view to navigate using REFs rather than joins.

   d. Object views can help you circumvent "schema evolution" problems that arise when working with the object layer of the Oracle RDBMS.

   e. If you decide to use object views, you can no longer make direct references to relational tables in your application.

9-27. Object views allow us to layer an object-like approach onto existing (non-object) relational tables. Let's apply object views to our compact disc example. Suppose that our compact_discs table is no longer an object table, but instead a relational table:

```
/* Filename on web page: objview.sql */
CREATE TABLE compact_discs (
    ID      INTEGER NOT NULL,
    title   VARCHAR2(60),
    artist  VARCHAR2(60),
    label   VARCHAR2(60),
    PRIMARY KEY (ID)
);

INSERT INTO compact_discs VALUES
    (100, 'White Album', 'Beatles', 'Apple');
```

We would then have a second table of keywords that are related to a compact_disc:

```
CREATE TABLE cd_keywords (
    cd_id      INTEGER NOT NULL REFERENCES compact_discs (id),
    keyword    VARCHAR2(60) NOT NULL,
    PRIMARY KEY (cd_id, keyword)
);

INSERT INTO cd_keywords VALUES (100, 'Lennon');
INSERT INTO cd_keywords VALUES (100, 'McCartney');
```

What you want to do now is create a CD object (actually an object view) that has CD attributes and a collection of its related keywords.

Given these two definitions (collection and object type):

```
CREATE TYPE cd_keyword_tab_t AS TABLE OF VARCHAR2(60);

CREATE TYPE CD_t AS OBJECT (
    id          INTEGER,
    title       VARCHAR2(60),
    artist      VARCHAR2(60),
    label       VARCHAR2(60),
    keywords    cd_keyword_tab_t,
    MAP MEMBER FUNCTION compare RETURN VARCHAR2
);
```

What is the definition of an object view that returns objects of type CD_t?

9-28. The following creation and drop of an object type succeeds:

```
CREATE TYPE temp_t AS OBJECT (
    name VARCHAR2(1000),
    hobbies VARCHAR2(1000));
/

DROP TYPE temp_t;
```

But after creating a table of objects based on this type, the next attempt to drop the type fails:

```
CREATE TYPE temp_t AS OBJECT (
    name VARCHAR2(1000),
    hobbies VARCHAR2(1000));
/

CREATE TABLE temp_tab OF temp_t;

DROP TYPE temp_t;
```

Why can't you drop the object type as shown above, and how do you get around this problem?

10

Cursors

In one form or another, every SQL statement in your PL/SQL program is associated with either an implicit or an explicit cursor. You can think of a *cursor* as a pointer into the result set of a SQL statement; its job is to allow you to access and manipulate the data inside the set. This chapter tests your ability to define cursors for use in you PL/SQL programs, to process the data within a cursor, and to create maintainable and efficient cursor definitions.

Beginner

10-1. What does it mean to be an *implicit cursor* in a PL/SQL program? Which of the following SQL statements are implicit cursors?

```
a. BEGIN
      UPDATE preferences
         SET ice_cream_flavor = 'CHOCOLATE'
       WHERE name = 'STEVEN';
```

```
b. DECLARE
      CURSOR around_the_house_jobs_cur
      IS
          SELECT job, frequencey
            FROM adolescent_workload
           WHERE name = 'ELI';
```

```
c. DECLARE
      next_key employee.employee_id%TYPE;
   BEGIN
      SELECT employee_seq.NEXTVAL
        INTO next_key
        FROM dual;
```

```
d. SQL> ALTER TABLE ceo_compensation MODIFY options NUMBER;
```

```
e. FOR indx IN 1 .. 12
   LOOP
```

```
        DELETE FROM ceo_compensation
          WHERE layoffs > 1000 * indx
            AND options > 100000;
      END LOOP;
```

10-2. What does it mean to be an *explicit cursor* in a PL/SQL program?

10-3. What predefined exceptions can be raised when a block executes an implicit cursor?

10-4. How many times does the Oracle SQL engine attempt to fetch a row from the employee table in this block (assume that a row exists for employee_id = 150667)?

```
DECLARE
   my_reward NUMBER;
 BEGIN
    SELECT salary
      INTO my_reward
      FROM employee
     WHERE employee_id = 150667;
END;
```

10-5. What are the possible and predictable exceptions that could occur when this block is run? How can you change this code to trap the errors (or avoid them altogether)?

```
DECLARE
   v_name VARCHAR2(30);
 BEGIN
    SELECT last_name
      INTO v_name
      FROM employee;
END;
```

Intermediate

10-6. Which of the following strings are valid cursor attributes (which means they are "attached" as a suffix to the name of the cursor)?

   a. %ROWNUM
   b. %FOUND
   c. %TOO_MANY_ROWS
   d. %NO_DATA_FOUND
   e. %NOTFOUND
   f. %ROWCOUNT
   g. %ISCLOSED
   h. %ISOPENED
   i. %ISOPEN

10-7. Which of the following uses of cursor attributes are valid? If they are not valid, what is the problem? Assume that the following cursor is declared in the same block when referenced in the problems:

```
CURSOR possibly_in_danger_cur IS
   SELECT status
     FROM genetically_modified_foods
    WHERE product = 'CORN'
      AND animal = 'MONARCH BUTTERFLY';
```

a.
```
BEGIN
     IF possibly_in_danger_cur%FOUND
     THEN
        OPEN possibly_in_danger_cur;
```

b.
```
BEGIN
     UPDATE jobs_to_mexico
        SET total_count = 10000000
      WHERE nafta_status = 'IN FORCE';
     DBMS_OUTPUT.PUT_LINE (SQL%ROWCOUNT);
```

c.
```
BEGIN
     FOR big_loss IN possibly_in_danger_cur
     LOOP
        IF possibly_in_danger_cur%ROWCOUNT
        THEN
            ...
```

d.
```
BEGIN
     OPEN possibly_in_danger_cur;
     FETCH possibly_in_danger_cur INTO I_am_sad;
     IF I_am_sad%FOUND
     THEN
```

e.
```
FOR indx IN 1 .. 12
   LOOP
      DELETE FROM genetically_modified_foods
       WHERE product = 'CORN';
      DBMS_OUTPUT.PUT_LINE (
         'All gone:  ' || genetically_modified_foods%ROWCOUNT);
      END LOOP;
```

10-8. What is wrong with the following code? Will you eventually run out of open cursors in the session if you execute this program, say, 100,000 times?

```
CREATE OR REPLACE FUNCTION totalsales (year_in IN INTEGER)
   RETURN NUMBER
IS
   CURSOR sales_cur IS SELECT SUM (amt) FROM ...;
   total NUMBER;
BEGIN
   OPEN sales_cur;
   FETCH sales_cur INTO total;
   RETURN total;
   CLOSE sales_cur;
END;
```

10-9. Which employee will become more and more loyal to the company when this function is run for everyone at year's end?

```
CREATE OR REPLACE FUNCTION increment_salary (
   employee_id employee.employee_id%TYPE)
```

```
      RETURN BOOLEAN
/*
|| Give the applicable employee a 10% Raise
*/
IS
   -- cursor to get the employees current salary
   CURSOR curs_get_curr_sal (
      employee_id employee.employee_id%TYPE)
   IS
      SELECT salary FROM employee
       WHERE employee_id = employee_id
         FOR UPDATE OF salary;
   v_curr_sal   employee.salary%TYPE;
   v_ret_val    BOOLEAN := FALSE;   -- return value

BEGIN
   /*
   || Query the employee's current salary and increment it by 10%
   */
   OPEN curs_get_curr_sal (employee_id);
   FETCH curs_get_curr_sal INTO v_curr_sal;
   IF curs_get_curr_sal%found
   THEN
      UPDATE employee SET salary = salary +  (salary / 10)
       WHERE CURRENT OF curs_get_curr_sal;
      v_ret_val := TRUE;
   END IF;
   CLOSE curs_get_curr_sal;

      Return TRUE if update was successful, FALSE if not
   RETURN  (v_ret_val);
END;
```

10-10. What is the output of the following code snippet, assuming there is an employee whose ID is 7566?

```
DECLARE
   v_name employee.last_name%TYPE;

   PROCEDURE bpl (str IN VARCHAR2, bool IN BOOLEAN) IS
   BEGIN
      IF bool THEN DBMS_OUTPUT.PUT_LINE (str || '-TRUE');
      ELSIF NOT bool THEN DBMS_OUTPUT.PUT_LINE (str || '-FALSE');
      ELSE DBMS_OUTPUT.PUT_LINE (str || '-NULL');
      END IF;
   END;

BEGIN
   SELECT last_name INTO v_name FROM employee
    WHERE employee_id = 7566;

   bpl ('%FOUND', SQL%FOUND);
   bpl ('%NOTFOUND', SQL%NOTFOUND);
   bpl ('%ISOPEN', SQL%ISOPEN);
```

```
    DBMS_OUTPUT.PUT_LINE ('%ROWCOUNT-' || SQL%ROWCOUNT);
END;
/
```

10-11. What is required in this code snippet to validate that indeed no rows were returned?

```
DECLARE
   CURSOR curs_failure IS
      SELECT null
        FROM employee
        WHERE 1 = 2;
   v_dummy VARCHAR2(1);
BEGIN
   OPEN curs_failure;
   FETCH curs_failure INTO v_dummy;
   CLOSE curs_failure;
END;
```

10-12. Write a function that uses a cursor to find the total of the three highest salaries in the employee table using the following cursor:

```
CURSOR curs_get_salary IS
   SELECT salary
     FROM employee
   ORDER BY salary desc;
```

10-13. Given the following cursor declaration:

```
CURSOR curs_get_emps IS
   SELECT employee_id, last_name, salary
     FROM employee;
```

Which of the following approaches is preferable from the standpoint of maintainability and robustness?

a.
```
   v_employee_id  employee.employee_id%TYPE;
   v_name  employee.last_name%TYPE;
   v_salary employee.salary%TYPE;
   BEGIN
     OPEN curs_get_emps;
     FETCH curs_get_emps INTO v_employee_id, v_last_name, v_salary;
```

b.
```
   v_emprec curs_get_emps%ROWTYPE;
   BEGIN
     OPEN curs_get_emps;
     FETCH curs_get_emps INTO v_emprec;
```

10-14. What do you see in your session when the following procedure is executed (the employee table has 32 rows; the person with the lowest salary is named MURRAY)?

```
CREATE OR REPLACE PROCEDURE show_lots
IS
   CURSOR by_sal_cur IS
      SELECT last_name
        FROM employee
        ORDER BY salary DESC;
   rec by_sal_cur%ROWTYPE;
```

```
BEGIN
    OPEN by_sal_cur;
    FOR rows IN 1 .. 10000
    LOOP
        FETCH by_sal_cur INTO rec;
    END LOOP;
    DBMS_OUTPUT.PUT_LINE (by_sal_cur%ROWCOUNT);
    DBMS_OUTPUT.PUT_LINE (rec.last_name);
    CLOSE by_sal_cur;
END;
/
```

10-15. Which statement can be removed from the following block of code without changing the behavior or effect of the code?

```
DECLARE
    CURSOR brought_to_you_by_unions
    IS
        SELECT weekends, forty_hour_weeks, overtime_pay
            FROM business_practices;
    social_benefits brought_to_you_by_unions%ROWTYPE;
BEGIN
    OPEN brought_to_you_by_unions;
    FETCH brought_to_you_by_unions INTO social_benefits;
    CLOSE brought_to_you_by_unions;
END;
/
```

10-16. Rewrite the following program to reduce code volume to an absolute minimum (without changing the names of the elements):

```
/* Filename on web page: unions.sql */
DECLARE
    CURSOR brought_to_you_by_unions
    IS
        SELECT weekends, forty_hour_weeks, overtime_pay
            FROM business_practices;
    social_benefits brought_to_you_by_unions%ROWTYPE;
BEGIN
    OPEN brought_to_you_by_unions;
    LOOP
        FETCH brought_to_you_by_unions INTO social_benefits;
        EXIT WHEN brought_to_you_by_unions%NOTFOUND;
        calculate_impact (social_benefits);
    END LOOP;
    CLOSE brought_to_you_by_unions;
END;
```

10-17. Modify the script in the *unions.sql* file (see 10-16) so that (1) it uses a cursor FOR loop, and (2) after all rows have been processed, the block displays how many rows were fetched. Does the following implementation do the trick?

```
/* Filename on web page: unions.sql */
DECLARE
    CURSOR brought_to_you_by_unions
```

```
        IS
            SELECT weekends, forty_hour_weeks, overtime_pay
              FROM business_practices;
     BEGIN
        FOR social_benefits IN brought_to_you_by_unions
        LOOP
            calculate_impact (social_benefits);
        END LOOP;
        DBMS_OUTPUT.PUT_LINE (
            'Calculated impact of ' || brought_to_you_by_unions%ROWCOUNT
            || ' benefits brought about by unions.');
     END;
```

Expert

10-18. What is the output from the following code snippet?

```
BEGIN
   UPDATE employee SET salary = salary;
   FOR v_rec IN ( SELECT employee_id FROM employee )
   LOOP
     IF SQL%ISOPEN THEN
       DBMS_OUTPUT.PUT_LINE('TRUE - ' || SQL%ROWCOUNT);
     ELSE
       DBMS_OUTPUT.PUT_LINE('FALSE - ' || SQL%ROWCOUNT);
     END IF;
   END LOOP;
END;
/
```

10-19. What is the output from the following code snippet?

```
DECLARE
     CURSOR cur IS SELECT employee_id FROM employee;
BEGIN
   FOR rec IN cur
   LOOP
     IF cur%ROWCOUNT = 1
     THEN
        IF cur%ISOPEN THEN
          DBMS_OUTPUT.PUT_LINE('TRUE');
        ELSE
          DBMS_OUTPUT.PUT_LINE('FALSE');
        END IF;
     END IF;
   END LOOP;
END;
```

10-20. How would you change the following block of code to make better use of the FOR UPDATE clause and also improve the program's performance?

```
DECLARE
   CURSOR upd_all_cur
      IS SELECT * FROM employee FOR UPDATE;
```

```
BEGIN
   /*
   || Double everyone's commisson
   */
   FOR rec IN upd_all_cur
   LOOP
      IF rec.commission IS NOT NULL
      THEN
         UPDATE employee
            SET commission = commission * 2
          WHERE employee_id = rec.employee_id;
      END IF;
   END LOOP;
END;
```

10-21. Which row in the employee table is locked when this block is executed?

```
DECLARE
   CURSOR upd_of_sal_cur
   IS
      SELECT * FROM employee FOR UPDATE OF salary;
BEGIN
   FOR rec IN upd_of_sal_cur
   LOOP
      IF rec.commission IS NOT NULL
      THEN
         UPDATE employee
            SET commission = commission * 2
          WHERE CURRENT OF upd_of_sal_cur;
      END IF;
   END LOOP;
END;
```

10-22. Suppose you create the following package; it contains three cursors (door_number_one, door_number_two and door_number_three) that have the same query but are not identical in the way they are defined in the package:

```
CREATE OR REPLACE PACKAGE lets_make_a_deal
AS
   CURSOR door_number_one IS
      SELECT useless_information
        FROM consumer_products
       WHERE the_price = 'YOUR BEST GUESS';

   PROCEDURE open_door_number_two;

   PROCEDURE open_door_number_three;

END lets_make_a_deal;
/
CREATE OR REPLACE PACKAGE BODY lets_make_a_deal
AS
  CURSOR door_number_two IS
     SELECT useless_information
```

```
        FROM consumer_products
      WHERE the_price = 'YOUR BEST GUESS';

    PROCEDURE open_door_number_two
    IS
    BEGIN
      OPEN door_number_two;
    END;

    PROCEDURE open_door_number_three
    IS
      CURSOR door_number_three IS
        SELECT useless_information
          FROM consumer_products
         WHERE the_price = 'YOUR BEST GUESS';
    BEGIN
      OPEN door_number_three;
    END;
END lets_make_a_deal;
/
```

Suppose you then want to execute the following block, which defines yet a fourth door (cursor):

```
DECLARE
    CURSOR door_number_four IS
      SELECT useless_information
        FROM consumer_products
       WHERE the_price = 'YOUR BEST GUESS';
BEGIN
    OPEN lets_make_a_deal.door_number_one;
    lets_make_a_deal.open_door_number_two;
    lets_make_a_deal.open_door_number_three;
    OPEN door_number_four;
END;
/
```

When you run this block the first time, what happens? What happens if you run it a second time in the same session?

10-23. What two structures can make up a valid cursor return clause in a package specification?

10-24. Rewrite the following to maximize code reuse and improve performance:

```
/* Filename on web page: jobinfo.sql */
CREATE OR REPLACE PROCEDURE show_jobs
IS
    CURSOR around_the_house_jobs_cur
    IS
        SELECT job
          FROM adolescent_workload
         WHERE name = 'ELI';
BEGIN
    FOR rec IN around_the_house_jobs_cur
    LOOP
```

```
            DBMS_OUTPUT.PUT_LINE (rec.job);
        END LOOP;
    END;
    /
    CREATE OR REPLACE FUNCTION job_for (name_in IN VARCHAR2) RETURN VARCHAR2
    IS
        CURSOR around_the_house_jobs_cur
        IS
            SELECT job FROM adolescent_workload
              WHERE name = name_in;
         retval adolescent_workload.job%type;
    BEGIN
        OPEN around_the_house_jobs_cur;
        FETCH around_the_house_jobs_cur INTO retval;
        RETURN retval;
    END;
    /
```

10-25. (Oracle8*i* only) The following function retrieves all employees for a given department, returning them in the form of a nested table. Each row is fetched individually and placed in the nested table (see the *bulksel.sql* file for the statements that create the various types).

```
/* Filename on web page: bulksel.sql */
CREATE OR REPLACE FUNCTION get_a_mess_o_emps80
    (deptno_in IN dept.deptno%TYPE)
RETURN emplist_t
IS
    emplist emplist_t := emplist_t();
    oneEmp emp_t;

    CURSOR ecur IS
        SELECT emp_t(empno, ename, hiredate)
          FROM emp2
          WHERE deptno = deptno_in;
    counter PLS_INTEGER := 1;
BEGIN
    OPEN ecur;
    LOOP
        FETCH ecur INTO oneEmp;
        EXIT WHEN ecur%NOTFOUND;
        emplist.EXTEND;
        emplist(counter) := oneEmp;
        counter := counter + 1;
    END LOOP;
    CLOSE ecur;
    RETURN emplist;
END;
/
```

Rewrite this function using new capabilities in Oracle8*i* to improve the performance of this multirow select.

11

DML and Transaction Management

You can embed any of the Data Manipulation Language statements—such as INSERTs, UPDATEs, DELETEs, and SELECTs—inside your PL/SQL programs. You can also combine these statements into an "all or nothing" unit of work called a *transaction*. The basic idea is that once you begin an operation (for example, once you delete all the employees from a table), you must complete an entire set of operations before any changes are committed, or saved, to the database. If anything interrupts the logical flow (for example, a database error), the entire transaction is rolled back to its starting point. Oracle provides a number of commands that allow you to manage transactions, such as COMMIT, ROLLBACK, SAVEPOINT, and SET TRANSACTION. This chapter tests your ability to use these and other statements to precisely control transactions inside PL/SQL.

 DML (Data Manipulation Language) refers to those statements in SQL that allow you to manipulate or modify the contents of your data. DDL (Data Definition Language) statements (such as CREATE TABLE), on the other hand, modify the definition of your data structures, rather than their contents.

Beginner

11-1. What SQL statements do you execute to make changes to the contents of tables? Which of these statements are allowed in PL/SQL?

11-2. Which of the following statements are true, and which are false?

a. When a PL/SQL block finishes execution, it always saves any changes made in that block.

   b. Even when an exception is raised in a PL/SQL block, any DML
   changes made in that block are preserved.

   c. You can insert only one row with each INSERT statement within
   PL/SQL.

11-3. Are DELETE, UPDATE, and INSERT statements considered implicit or
   explicit cursors?

11-4. How can you tell how many rows you updated, inserted, or deleted in
   your program?

11-5. What PL/SQL statement(s) are used to save any changes in your session?

11-6. What PL/SQL statement(s) are used to erase any changes in your session?

11-7. Which of the following statements are valid, and which are invalid?

   a. `COMMIT;`

   b. `COMMIT 'NY transaction';`

   c. `COMMIT WHEN mycount > 1000;`

   d. `ROLLBACK;`

   e. `ROLLBACK TO 'last_change';`

   f. `ROLLBACK TO my_savepoint;`

   g. `DBMS_STANDARD.ROLLBACK_SV ('last_change');`

   h. `ROLLBACK 'LA transaction';`

   i. `DBMS_STANDARD.COMMIT;`

11-8. Write a procedure that cuts the compensation of all employees who are
   CEOs (job_ID = 1) by 90%, increases the salaries of all hourly workers
   (job_id = 1000) by 30%, and commits those changes. Include an exception section that issues a rollback if any error occurs.

11-9. Write a block of code that gives everyone in the employee table a raise of
   10%. If more than 10 employees are updated, roll back the change.

Intermediate

11-10. Suppose that you want to erase only some of your session's changes but
   retain others for saving. How can you do this?

11-11. Write an exception section that traps any error, rolls back any changes to
   the last log savepoint, inserts a row into a log table and then sets a new
   log savepoint.

11-12. What happens if you try to roll back to a savepoint that has not been set
   in your session?

11-13. How can you make sure you never get an exception when you issue a
   ROLLBACK TO command?

11-14. The following block executes a series of INSERT statements:

```
BEGIN
   FOR yearnum IN 1 .. 10
   LOOP
      SAVEPOINT start_of_loop;
      INSERT INTO emp (ename, deptno, empno)
         VALUES ('Steven' || yearnum, 10, yearnum);
   END LOOP;
   ROLLBACK TO start_of_loop;
END;
```

When this block finishes executing, how many savepoints have been set, how many savepoints are "active" (can be rolled back to), and how many rows have been inserted into the emp table (assuming that the data being inserted is valid)?

11-15. What number is displayed on the screen for "rows deleted" when the following code is executed (assume that the employee table has 1,435 rows and that the department table has 25 rows)?

```
CREATE OR REPLACE merge_and_purge_departments
IS
BEGIN
   DELETE FROM department;
END;
/

BEGIN
   DELETE FROM employee;
   merge_and_purge_departments;
   DBMS_OUTPUT.PUT_LINE ('Rows deleted = ' || SQL%ROWCOUNT);
END;
/
```

11-16. Suppose that you have a complex, long-running process that issues a series of queries, each of which might take half an hour to execute. You want to make sure each query's view of the database is consistent. In other words, if the first query starts at 10:00 A.M. and the second query starts at 10:30 A.M., you want the process to ignore any changes to database tables that might have taken place in between. What PL/SQL statement enforces this consistent image of the database?

11-17. How do you end a read-only transaction in your session?

11-18. What is wrong with the following block?

```
DECLARE
   v_sal10    REAL;
   v_sal20    REAL;
   v_sal30    REAL;
BEGIN
   SELECT SUM(salary) INTO v_sal10 FROM employee
    WHERE department_id = 10;
```

```
SET TRANSACTION READ ONLY;

SELECT SUM(salary) INTO v_sal20 FROM employee
 WHERE department_id = 20;

COMMIT;
END;
```

11-19. Which of the following statements about SET TRANSACTION READ ONLY are not true?

a. The SELECT INTO, OPEN, FETCH, CLOSE, COMMIT, and ROLLBACK statements are allowed in a read-only transaction.

b. SELECT FOR UPDATE statements are allowed in read-only transactions.

c. You cannot issue a LOCK TABLE statement in a read-only transaction.

d. If your connection to Oracle sets the transaction to READ ONLY and issues a query against the employee table, no other users can modify the employee table until you commit or roll back.

11-20. What SELECT clause does PL/SQL offer that allows you to issue exclusive row locks on rows you are querying? How does this behavior differ from the default locking behavior?

11-21. Write a block that executes a cursor retrieving all columns for each row in the employee table, issues an exclusive row lock on all those rows, and increases the salary of each employee by 50%. Write the UPDATE statement so that the WHERE clause does not need to reference any columns in the table to properly identify the current row.

11-22. Consider the following query:

```
DECLARE
    CURSOR dept_emp_names_cur
    IS
        SELECT ename, dname
          FROM emp, dept
         WHERE emp.deptno = dept.deptno
           AND job = 'MANAGER'
           FOR UPDATE OF ename, sal NOWAIT;
```

Which of these tables will have locks applied to them?

11-23. Which of the following statements about the FOR UPDATE clause are true, and which are false?

a. Locks are placed on rows identified by the query as those rows are fetched.

b. If more than half the rows in a table are locked with FOR UPDATE, the entire table is locked.

c. If you specify a column in the FOR UPDATE OF clause, that column must be listed in the SELECT list.

d. You can request that your query wait for a specified number of seconds to obtain the necessary locks.

e. You can COMMIT or ROLLBACK at any time during the fetching of records from a FOR UPDATE cursor.

11-24. You are building applications in Oracle 8.0 or above. Rewrite this procedure so that only one SQL statement implements the same functionality:

```
PROCEDURE update_salary (emp_id NUMBER)
IS
   name     VARCHAR2(15);
   new_sal NUMBER;
BEGIN
   UPDATE emp SET sal = sal * 1.1
      WHERE empno = emp_id;

   SELECT ename, sal INTO name, new_sal
     FROM emp
    WHERE empno = emp_id;

   DBMS_OUTPUT.PUT_LINE (
      name || ' given a raise to ' || new_sal);
END;
```

Expert

11-25. Here is a typical use of the SAVEPOINT statement:

```
BEGIN
   SAVEPOINT start_process;
   INSERT INTO ...;
   DELETE FROM ...;
```

In this example the savepoint, start_process, is an "undeclared identifier." It is a name that is, essentially, hard-coded into your application. How can you specify a savepoint as a variable or string literal, instead of this hard-coded value?

11-26. What are all the different ways you can set a savepoint in your program?

11-27. What are all the different ways you can roll back your transaction in PL/SQL?

11-28. What is wrong with the following block of code?

```
BEGIN
   DBMS_STANDARD.SAVEPOINT ('start_process');
   ROLLBACK TO start_process;
END;
```

11-29. As a rule, the transactions in my database are short and frequent, so by default I use a set of small rollback segments. Occasionally, I need to run batch programs that:

- Need to commit changes during the process

- Require much larger than normal rollback segments

At the start of my job, I change the rollback segment for my long-running transaction. I then commit intermittently as shown:

```
DECLARE
    CURSOR my_million_row_cursor IS SELECT ...;
    ctr PLS_INTEGER := 1;
BEGIN
    DBMS_TRANSACTION.USE_ROLLBACK_SEGMENT ('big_rb');
    FOR every_rec IN my_million_row_cursor
    LOOP
        make_the_changes (every_rec);
        IF ctr > 10000
        THEN
            COMMIT;
            ctr := 1;
        ELSE
            ct := ctr + 1;
        END IF;
    END LOOP;
END;
```

Yet I still get the following error:

```
rollback segment too small
```

Assuming my rollback segment is big enough, what am I doing wrong?

11-30. What are the different ways you can set the rollback segment for your current transaction?

11-31. If you are using Oracle8*i*, what new feature is available that allows you to save or roll back your changes in one PL/SQL block without affecting the transactions?

11-32. What statement do you add to your programs or blocks to allow them to commit or roll back within their own transaction space?

11-33. Define a procedure so that it deletes all the rows from the employee table in its own transaction space, not affecting the transaction of any session that calls it.

11-34. Which of the following can be defined as an autonomous transaction?

   a. Top-level (not nested) anonymous PL/SQL blocks

   b. Nested anonymous PL/SQL blocks

   c. Local, standalone, and packaged functions and procedures

   d. Methods of a SQL object type

   e. Database triggers

11-35. Which statements can be placed in a database trigger set up as an anonymous transaction that otherwise are not allowed in a trigger?

11-36. Suppose you create a package with 20 procedures and functions. You want each one to execute as an autonomous transaction. You can define the package specification as follows:

```
CREATE OR REPLACE PACKAGE all_auton
IS
    PRAGMA AUTONOMOUS_TRANSACTION;

    PROCEDURE auton1 ...;
    PROCEDURE auton1 ...;
    ...
    FUNCTION auton20 ...;
END;
/
```

Why doesn't this code compile?

11-37. If a program is an autonomous transaction, then, by default, any changes that occur in that program are visible to the main or outer transaction. If you don't want the effect of the DELETE in the following procedure to be visible to calling programs, how would you change the procedure?

```
CREATE OR REPLACE PROCEDURE del_emps (deptno_in IN emp.deptno%TYPE)
IS
    PRAGMA AUTONOMOUS_TRANSACTION;
BEGIN
    DELETE FROM emp WHERE deptno = deptno_in;
    COMMIT;
END;
```

11-38. If you create a procedure to delete all the rows of the emp table and establish it as an autonomous transaction as follows:

```
CREATE OR REPLACE PROCEDURE del_emps
IS
    PRAGMA AUTONOMOUS_TRANSACTION;
BEGIN
    DELETE FROM emp;
END;
/
```

And you then use it inside a procedure that is the "main" transaction:

```
CREATE OR REPLACE PROCEDURE del_emps2
IS
    n NUMBER;
BEGIN
    SELECT COUNT(*) INTO n FROM emp;
    p.l (n);
    del_emps;
    SELECT COUNT(*) INTO n FROM emp;
    p.l (n);
END;
/
```

What do you see when you run del_emps2?

11-39. Which of the following statements about autonomous transactions are true, and which are false?

    a. If an autonomous transaction attempts to access a resource held by the main transaction (which cannot resume until the autonomous routine exits), a deadlock can occur.

    b. Only one COMMIT or ROLLBACK is permitted in an autonomous transaction.

    c. A rollback in the main transaction causes a rollback in the autonomous transaction.

    d. You can decide if you want changes in your autonomous transaction to be visible to the main transaction.

    e. Parallel queries are not allowed in an autonomous transaction.

11-40. Oracle does not support SELECT FOR UPDATE WAIT *n* SECONDS (you either WAIT or you NOWAIT). Emulate a WAIT *n* SECONDS capability for the following cursor:

```
CURSOR emp_cur IS SELECT ename, rowid FROM emp;
```

and for this UPDATE statement:

```
UPDATE emp SET sal = sal + 1000 WHERE ROWID = emp_rec.rowid;
```

12

Cursor Variables

Cursor variables, first available in PL/SQL Version 2.3, are reference pointers to a cursor's result set. The main advantage of a cursor variable is that it allows us to easily pass the result of a query among different PL/SQL blocks, such as procedures or functions. This chapter tests your ability to define and use cursor variables in your applications.

Beginner

12-1. Which of the following statements describe a cursor variable?

    a. A SELECT statement whose WHERE clause can be varied each time the query is opened in a PL/SQL program.

    b. A pointer to the result set of a cursor (a SELECT statement that has been opened in a PL/SQL program).

    c. An explicit cursor declared in the specification of a package.

12-2. What are the two steps you must take to declare a cursor variable?

12-3. Which of the following declarations of REF CURSOR types are valid, and which are invalid?

    a. `TYPE my_type IS REF CURSOR;`

    b. `TYPE empdept_t IS REF CURSOR JOINED emp, dept;`

    c. `TYPE living_wage_t IS REF CURSOR RETURN (SELECT salary FROM employee);`

    d. `TYPE all_orders_cvt IS REF CURSOR RETURN orders%ROWTYPE;`

12-4. Given the following definitions of the table and REF CURSOR:

```
CREATE TABLE environmental_disaster (
    company_responsible VARCHAR2(100),
    occurred_on DATE;
);

DECLARE
    TYPE disasters_cvt IS REF CURSOR RETURN environmental_disaster%ROWTYPE;
```

Which of the declarations of cursor variables are valid, and which are invalid?

    a. `exxon_valdez disasters_cvt;`

    b. `union_carbide_in_bhopal disasters_cvt%ROWTYPE;`

    c. `love_canal environmental_disaster%ROWTYPE;`

12-5. Write a block of code that declares a REF CURSOR with the same structure as the employee table and also declares two cursor variables based on that REF CURSOR.

12-6. Of the following cursor operations, which are the same for cursor variables and hardcoded (explicit) cursors, and which are different?

    a. Open the cursor

    b. Close the cursor

    c. Fetch from the cursor

    d. Check cursor attributes

Intermediate

12-7. Write a block of code that uses a strong REF CURSOR to retrieve all the rows from the employee table and calls the double_salary program for each employee as shown:

```
PROCEDURE double_salary (
    id_in IN employee.employee_id%TYPE,
    sal_in IN employee.salary%TYPE);
```

12-8. Given the following data element definitions:

```
CREATE TABLE funny_democracy (
    work_on_election_day DATE,
    only_two_parties NUMBER
    );

DECLARE
    TYPE very_funny_t IS RECORD (
        first_tuesday DATE,
        dems_and_repubs NUMBER := 2);

    TYPE ours_cvt IS REF CURSOR RETURN funny_democracy%ROWTYPE;
    the_finest_cv ours_cvt;
```

Which of the following record declarations can validly be used to hold a row fetched from the_finest_cv cursor variable?

   a. `one_employee funny_democracy%ROWTYPE;`

   b. `one_employee ours_cvt%ROWTYPE;`

   c. `one_employee ours_cvt;`

   d. `one_employee the_finest_cv;`

   e. `one_employee very_funny_t;`

   f. `one_employee very_funny_t%ROWTYPE;`

   g. `one_employee the_finest_cv%ROWTYPE;`

12-9. Which of the following statements correctly identify the differences between strong and weak REF CURSORs?

   a. You can use a weak REF CURSOR to declare cursor variables that can fetch rows from any SQL statement.

   b. A strong REF CURSOR offers stronger performance and should be used whenever possible to improve program efficiency.

   c. Using weak REF CURSORs means you have to deal more often with runtime errors, as opposed to compile-time errors with strong REF CURSORs.

   d. You must close a cursor variable based on a strong REF CURSOR twice because it persists (strongly) past the first close.

   e. A cursor variable based on a strong REF CURSOR fetches data only into a record whose structure is compatible with the RETURN clause in the REF CURSOR.

12-10. Which of the following scenarios calls for the use of cursor variables?

   a. Various application components, including an Oracle Forms application and several stored procedures, all need to work with the same result set.

   b. The columns to be queried and the table from which they are to be queried are not known until runtime.

   c. You have six different queries, all exactly the same except for a different ORDER BY clause. You need to write a program to display the data retrieved from each query.

   d. You need to reduce your network traffic between client and server Oracle programs when obtaining and manipulating information from the database.

   e. You want to let the user supply the WHERE clause to apply to an otherwise standardized query.

12-11. None of the following blocks compile. Explain the problems.

a.
```
CREATE OR REPLACE PACKAGE all_my_sql
IS
    TYPE one_ref_cur IS REF CURSOR;
    one_cv one_ref_cur;
```

b.
```
DECLARE
    TYPE one_ref_cur IS REF CURSOR;
    one_cv one_ref_cur;
BEGIN
    OPEN one_cv FOR 'SELECT * FROM employee';
```

c.
```
DECLARE
    TYPE one_ref_cur IS REF CURSOR;
    one_cv one_ref_cur;
BEGIN
    OPEN one_cv FOR SELECT * FROM employee FOR UPDATE;
```

d.
```
DECLARE
    TYPE one_ref_cur IS REF CURSOR;
    one_cv one_ref_cur;
BEGIN
    /* Initialize the cursor variable. */
    one_cv := NULL;
```

12-12. Which of the following blocks raise a ROWTYPE_MISMATCH error? Does the error occur at compile time or runtime?

a.
```
CREATE OR REPLACE PROCEDURE do_stuff
IS
    TYPE one_ref_cur IS REF CURSOR;
    one_cv one_ref_cur;
    one_rec department%ROWTYPE;
BEGIN
    OPEN one_cv FOR SELECT * FROM employee;
    FETCH one_cv INTO one_rec;
```

b.
```
CREATE OR REPLACE PROCEDURE do_stuff
IS
    TYPE one_ref_cur IS REF CURSOR RETURN department%ROWTYPE;
    one_cv one_ref_cur;
    one_rec one_cv%ROWTYPE;
BEGIN
    OPEN one_cv FOR SELECT * FROM employee;
    FETCH one_cv INTO one_rec;
```

c.
```
CREATE TABLE airplane_food (
    digestibility INTEGER,
    nutritional_value INTEGER
    );

CREATE OR REPLACE PROCEDURE do_stuff
IS
    TYPE one_ref_cur IS REF CURSOR RETURN airplane_food%ROWTYPE;
    one_cv one_ref_cur;
    one_rec one_cv%ROWTYPE;
BEGIN
    OPEN one_cv FOR SELECT salary, commission FROM employee;
    FETCH one_cv INTO one_rec;
```

12-13. The next four problems use the following four queries against the employee table:

/* Filename on web page: 4queries.sql */

a. SELECT last_name, salary FROM employee ORDER BY salary;

b. SELECT last_name, salary FROM employee ORDER BY salary DESC;

c. SELECT last_name, department_id FROM employee ORDER BY department_id;

d. SELECT first_name || ' ' || last_name, salary
       FROM employee ORDER BY last_name;

You want to build a function that returns a strong REF CURSOR-based cursor variable that points to a result set from any one of these four queries. What PL/SQL data structures need to be defined in order to write this function? Where can these structures be defined?

12-14. Suppose you want to create a single package specification to contain all the elements described in 12-13's solution for: programmer-defined record type, REF CURSOR, and function. You want the function to accept a single integer argument (the query number as defined earlier) and return a cursor variable pointing to one of these four queries. Write the specification for that package, providing named constants for each of the query numbers.

12-15. Implement the open function for the empinfo package.

12-16. Add a procedure to the empinfo package that displays all the rows fetched by each different query.

Expert

12-17. Suppose you define a package with a procedure that opens a cursor variable as shown:

```
CREATE OR REPLACE PACKAGE dizmee
AS
    TYPE swallow_florida_cvt IS
       REF CURSOR RETURN hickey_grouse%ROWTYPE;
    PROCEDURE open_wide (yum_cv swallow_florida_cvt);
END dizmee;
/
CREATE OR REPLACE PACKAGE BODY dizmee
AS
    PROCEDURE open_wide (yum_cv swallow_florida_cvt)
    IS
    BEGIN
       OPEN yum_cv FOR SELECT * FROM hickey_grouse;
    END open_wide;
END dizmee;
/
```

Why does the package body fail to compile?

12-18. None of the following blocks compile. Explain the problems.

a. DECLARE
```
    TYPE one_ref_cur IS REF CURSOR;
    one_cv one_ref_cur;
BEGIN
    OPEN one_cv FOR SELECT * FROM employee;
    display_employees@hong_kong_office (one_cv);
```

b. DECLARE
```
    TYPE one_ref_cur IS REF CURSOR;
    first_cv one_ref_cur;
    second_cv one_ref_cur;
BEGIN
    OPEN first_cv FOR SELECT * FROM employee;
    second_cv := first_cv;
    IF first_cv != second_cv THEN
```

c. DECLARE
```
    TYPE one_ref_cur IS REF CURSOR;
    TYPE list_of_cvs IS TABLE OF one_ref_cur;
BEGIN
    OPEN one_cv FOR SELECT * FROM employee FOR UPDATE;
```

d. DECLARE
```
    TYPE emp_cvt IS REF CURSOR RETURN emp%ROWTYPE;
    TYPE tmp_cvt IS REF CURSOR RETURN emp%ROWTYPE;
    PROCEDURE open_emp_cv (
        emp_cv IN OUT emp_cvt, tmp_cv IN OUT tmp_cvt)
    IS
    BEGIN
        emp_cv := tmp_cv;
    END;
```

12-19. Which of the following declarations allows you to work with REF CUR-SORs in SQL*Plus?

a. SQL> VARIABLE cv REFCURSOR

b. SQL> VARIABLE cv REF CURSOR

c. SQL> VARIABLE cv CUR VARIABLE

12-20. The following scenario is used for this question and the next. Suppose you are building a repository of information about crimes against humanity. You've identified three types of people involved in such crimes:

People	Description
Direct combatants	People who performed the crime.
Indirect enablers	People who were in a position to stop the crime, but were not directly involved.
Noninnocent bystanders	People who let the crime occur without speaking out.

Given the nature of the information that needs to be tracked about these individuals, you have created a different table for each grouping. You also have defined a central person table; partial table definitions (all you need for the exercise) follow:

```
/* Filename on web page: cah.pkg */
CREATE TABLE person (
    name VARCHAR2(200),
    cah_type INTEGER
);

CREATE TABLE direct_combatant (
    incident VARCHAR2(200),
    name VARCHAR2(200),
    description VARCHAR2(2000),
    main_weapon VARCHAR2(1000),
    ...
);

CREATE TABLE indirect_enabler (
    incident VARCHAR2(200),
    name VARCHAR2(200),
    description VARCHAR2(2000),
    enabling_method VARCHAR2(1000),
    ...
);

CREATE TABLE noninnocent_bystander (
    incident VARCHAR2(200),
    name VARCHAR2(200),
    description VARCHAR2(2000),
    what_they_did_instead VARCHAR2(1000),
    ...
);
```

where the cah_type indicates the type of person: 1 for direct combatant, 2 for indirect enabler, and 3 for noninnocent bystander.

Create a package specification containing a procedure that accepts the name of a person and returns a cursor variable that allows you to find the information about that person from the appropriate table.

12-21. Now build the package body for the cah package, in other words, the implementation of the identify_person procedure. If the name supplied to the procedure is not found in the person table, make sure you return an invalid cursor.

13

Native Dynamic SQL

Ever since Oracle 7.1, PL/SQL developers have been able to use the built-in DBMS_SQL package to execute dynamic SQL and PL/SQL. This means that at run-time, you can construct the query, the DELETE or CREATE TABLE statement, or even the PL/SQL block as a string and then execute it. Dynamic SQL comes in extremely handy when you are building ad-hoc query systems, when you need to execute DDL inside PL/SQL, and just generally when you don't know in advance exactly what you need to do or what the user will want to do. Dynamic SQL is a frequent requirement in web-based applications.

The problem with DBMS_SQL is that it's a complicated package; it has a number of restrictions (such as not recognizing and working with new Oracle8 datatypes); and it's relatively slow. So our dear friends at PL/SQL Central in Redwood Shores took pity on us all and reimplemented dynamic SQL directly in the PL/SQL 8.1 language itself. This feature, called *native dynamic SQL* (NDS), is available only in Oracle8*i*.

Beginner

13-1. What are the two statements added to the PL/SQL language to implement native dynamic SQL?

13-2. Write an anonymous block that drops the employee table.

13-3. Write a procedure that drops whichever table you pass to the procedure.

13-4. Write a function that returns the number of rows in the specified table.

Intermediate

13-5. Enhance your table count function (see the "Beginner" section) that returns the number of rows in the specified table to add an optional WHERE clause. The user should not have to include the WHERE keyword, but if he does, the function interprets and constructs the request properly.

13-6. Write a procedure that drops whatever object you specify (table, view, object type, etc.).

13-7. Why can't the dropit procedure be implemented as follows?

```
CREATE OR REPLACE PROCEDURE dropit (
    ittype IN VARCHAR2, itname IN VARCHAR2)
IS
BEGIN
    EXECUTE IMMEDIATE 'drop :type :name'
        USING ittype, itname;
END;
/
```

13-8. Build a generic procedure to execute any DDL statement. Specify that this program "run as invoker" and not as the definer.

13-9. Use your solution to 13-8 to create a procedure that creates an index of the specified name for the specified table and columns.

13-10. In Illinois, 11 men have been released from Death Row (as of March 1999) after having finally been proven innocent (one man spent over 17 years there). Which of the following two programs that remove innocent men from Death Row will run more efficiently? Why?

```
a. CREATE OR REPLACE PROCEDURE release_innocents_in_illinois
   IS
      TYPE names_t IS TABLE OF VARCHAR2(100);
      innocent names_t := names_t (
         'WILLIAMS', 'JIMMERSON', 'LAWSON', 'GAUGER',
         'BURROWS', 'CRUZ', 'TILLIS', 'COBB',
         'HERNANDEZ', 'PORTER', 'SMITH');
   BEGIN
      FOR indx IN innocent.FIRST .. innocent.LAST
      LOOP
         EXECUTE IMMEDIATE
            'DELETE FROM death_row WHERE name = ' || innocent(indx);
      END LOOP;
   END;
   /
b. CREATE OR REPLACE PROCEDURE release_innocents_in_illinois
   IS
      TYPE names_t IS TABLE OF VARCHAR2(100);
      innocent names_t := names_t (
         'WILLIAMS', 'JIMMERSON', 'LAWSON', 'GAUGER',
```

```
                    'BURROWS','CRUZ', 'TILLIS', 'COBB',
                    'HERNANDEZ', 'PORTER', 'SMITH');
          BEGIN
             FOR indx IN innocent.FIRST .. innocent.LAST
             LOOP
                EXECUTE IMMEDIATE
                   'DELETE FROM death_row WHERE name = :so_sorry'
                   USING innocent(indx);
             END LOOP;
          END;
          /
```

13-11. The following procedure deletes rows from any table specified by the WHERE condition:

```
CREATE OR REPLACE PROCEDURE delete_from (
   table_name IN VARCHAR2, condition IN VARCHAR2)
AS
BEGIN
   EXECUTE IMMEDIATE
      'DELETE FROM ' || table_name || ' WHERE ' || condition;
END;
```

Change this procedure to a function that returns the number of rows that were deleted.

13-12. To fetch a single row of information using NDS, use this statement:

```
EXECUTE IMMEDIATE sql_string INTO record_or_variable_list
```

If you want to fetch multiple rows of information, what kind of cursor construct do you need to use?

13-13. Write a procedure to display each of the last names of employees in the employee table allowing the user to specify a dynamic WHERE clause.

13-14. Write a generic program to execute any PL/SQL procedure with a single IN numeric argument. In other words, if you have a show_total_sales procedure that accepts as a single argument the year number, you'd call it dynamically as follows:

```
SQL> exec runplsql ('show_total_sales', 1998);
```

13-15. Write a generic program to execute any PL/SQL procedure that has a single IN numeric argument and two VARCHAR2 OUT arguments. Suppose, for example, you have a procedure named "special_friend" that accepts the year number and returns the name of the company that gave you (a member of Congress) the largest "soft money" contribution in that year, along with name of that company's lobbying firm. You could then call it dynamically as follows:

```
DECLARE
   my_pal VARCHAR2(100);
   his_lobbyist VARCHAR2(100);
BEGIN
```

```
    runplsql (
      'special_friend', 1998, my_pal, his_lobbyist);

    DBMS_OUTPUT.PUT_LINE (
      'Send ' || my_pal || ' chocolates, ' ||
      ' and set up a power lunch with ' || his_lobbyist);
END;
```

13-16. Suppose you work for an insurance company. A policy has many different line items, and each line item has its own procedure for processing the data (a single IN string) and returning (through an OUT argument) a numeric value rating that information for premium pricing purposes.

The current implementation of the "master processing" procedure looks like this:

```
CREATE OR REPLACE PROCEDURE master_line_processor (
    line_in IN INTEGER,
    data_in IN VARCHAR2,
    rating_out OUT NUMBER)
IS
BEGIN
    IF line_in = 1
    THEN
        process_line_1 (data_in, rating_out);
    ELSIF line_in = 2
    THEN
        process_line_2 (data_in, rating_out);
    ...
    ELSIF line_in = 20456
    THEN
        process_line_20456 (data_in, rating_out);
    END IF;
END;
```

Unfortunately, there are lots of different line items; this procedure is long, cumbersome, and slow. It is also very hard to maintain. Rewrite the procedure using NDS to correct all of those deficiencies.

13-17. Given the insurance company scenario from 13-16, what is the output of the following procedure if the acct_balance table has 10 entries for account 10 and 20 entries for account 20?

```
DECLARE
   TYPE v_curs_type IS REF CURSOR;
   v_curs          v_curs_type;
   v_balance_entries PLS_INTEGER;
   v_acct          PLS_INTEGER := 10;
BEGIN
   OPEN v_curs FOR 'SELECT COUNT(*) '     ||
                   ' FROM acct_balance ' ||
                   ' WHERE acct = :acct'
        USING v_acct;
   LOOP
     v_acct := 20;
```

```
        FETCH v_curs INTO v_balance_entries;
        EXIT WHEN v_curs%NOTFOUND;
        DBMS_OUTPUT.PUT_LINE('entries = ' || v_balance_entries);
      END LOOP;
      CLOSE v_curs;
    END;
```

Expert

13-18. Suppose you want to pass the same value repeatedly in a dynamic SQL statement. Here is an example of such a string:

```
sql_stmt := 'INSERT INTO old_growth VALUES (:x, :x, :y, :x)';
```

Which of the following EXECUTE IMMEDIATE statements correctly handle this situation?

```
EXECUTE IMMEDIATE sql_stmt USING a, a, b, a;
EXECUTE IMMEDIATE sql_stmt USING a, b;
```

13-19. Write a function that returns the value stored in the data element specified by name. In other words, if you have a variable last_date in the profits package, your function retrieves its value as follows:

```
got_it := value_in ('profits.last_date');
```

13-20. Why won't the following use of the value_in function (see 13-19) work?

```
DECLARE
   n NUMBER := 100;
BEGIN
   IF value_in ('n') = 100
   THEN
```

13-21. Suppose that you want to pass the same value repeatedly in a dynamic PL/SQL statement. Here is an example of such a string:

```
sql_stmt := 'BEGIN show_min_compensation (:x, :x, :y, :x); END;';
```

Which of the following EXECUTE IMMEDIATE statements correctly handles the situation in 13-20?

```
EXECUTE IMMEDIATE sql_stmt USING a, a, b, a;
EXECUTE IMMEDIATE sql_stmt USING a, b;
```

13-22. Suppose you want to pass a NULL value to a dynamic SQL statement through the USING clause. What happens when you try to execute the following statement?

```
BEGIN
   EXECUTE IMMEDIATE
      'UPDATE employee SET salary = :x
         WHERE fire_date IS NOT NULL' USING NULL;
END;
```

13-23. How can you transform the following statement so that you can pass a NULL value for the salary?

```
BEGIN
    EXECUTE IMMEDIATE
        'UPDATE employee SET salary = :x
            WHERE fire_date IS NOT NULL' USING NULL;
END;
```

13-24. What are all the problems with the following program, which is intended to display the names of all CEOs in the compensation table who have received large bonuses after laying off at least 1,000 of their own employees? Rewrite this program so that it works properly.

```
DECLARE
    TYPE execute_action_t IS REF CURSOR RETURN employee%ROWTYPE;
    ceo_cv execute_action_t;
    v_minbonus REAL := 1000000;
BEGIN
    OPEN ceo_cv FOR
        'SELECT CEO FROM compensation
            WHERE layoffs > 1000
                AND bonus > :minbonus';
    FOR rec IN ceo_cv
    LOOP
        DBMS_OUTPUT.PUT_LINE (rec.ceo);
    END LOOP;
END;
```

13-25. Write a function that executes a group function for any table, any column and a specified WHERE clause. Here is the header:

```
FUNCTION grpval (
    tab IN VARCHAR2,
    col IN VARCHAR2,
    grpfunc IN VARCHAR2,
    whr IN VARCHAR2)
RETURN VARCHAR2;
```

And here is a example of applying this function:

```
SQL> EXEC p.l(grpval ('employee', 'salary', 'sum'))
60700
```

14

Procedures, Functions, and Blocks

Procedures and functions are the heart and soul of most PL/SQL programs. A *procedure* is a named group of instructions—a *block*—that performs a specific task. A *function* is similar in structure to a procedure, but it returns a value (called, fittingly enough, a return value) to the block that called it. Both procedures and functions are examples of named blocks; you can also create unnamed—or anonymous—blocks of instructions.

The term "block" is a very apt description, since these groups of instructions literally form the building blocks you can use—and reuse—to create sophisticated applications. This chapter tests your ability to create a procedure or function, define parameters, and analyze a function's design.

Beginner

14-1. What is the difference between a procedure and function?

14-2. What are the four sections in a procedure or function? Which of these sections are optional, and which are required?

14-3. What statement do you use to return a value from within a function? Can you use this same statement in a procedure?

14-4. Write a procedure that displays "hello world!" on your monitor.

14-5. Write a function that returns the string "hello world!"

14-6. How many RETURNs can you place in your function?

14-7. Which of the following function headers are valid, and which cause compile errors?

```
a. FUNCTION deptname (id_in IN department.department_id%TYPE)
      RETURN VARCHAR2
```

   b. FUNCTION deptname (id_in IN NUMBER) RETURN VARCHAR2(100)

   c. FUNCTION 2topsellers (for_this_dept IN INTEGER) RETURN INTEGER

   d. FUNCTION better_sales (revenue_in IN NUMBER(10,2)) RETURN BOOLEAN

14-8. What are the different parameter modes available in PL/SQL?

14-9. Can you provide default values for parameters?

Intermediate

14-10. Are parameters in PL/SQL passed by value or by reference?

14-11. How many RETURNs should the executable section of a function contain?

14-12. Should you include RETURNs in your function's exception section?

14-13. Should the following function have an exception section? If so, what should it handle?

```
CREATE OR REPLACE FUNCTION deptname (
    id_in IN department.department_id%TYPE
    )
    RETURN VARCHAR2
IS
    retval department.name%TYPE;
BEGIN
    SELECT name
      INTO retval
      FROM department
     WHERE department_id = id_in;

    RETURN retval;
END deptname;
/
```

14-14. What are the restrictions on setting default values for parameters?

14-15. What advantage is there to providing default values for parameters?

14-16. Suppose that five years ago, a developer wrote a procedure with the following header:

```
PROCEDURE calc_totals (
    department_id_in IN department.department_id%TYPE)
```

There are many calls to this procedure in a variety of production applications. A new requirement has now been requested by users to be able to calculate totals per department and also for sections within departments. How would you change the header of calc_totals so that:

- Developers can pass in the section ID in addition to the department ID.

- Existing calls to calc_totals will remain valid.

14-17. Can you skip over parameters when you call a procedure or function?

14-18. Given the header for the calc_profit procedure:

```
PROCEDURE calc_profit
   (company_id_in IN NUMBER,
    profit_out OUT NUMBER
    fiscal_year_in IN NUMBER,
    profit_type_in IN VARCHAR2 := 'NET_PROFITS',
    division_in IN VARCHAR2 := 'ALL_DIVISIONS')
```

Which of the following calls are valid:

a. `calc_profit(1005, profit_level, 1995, 'ALL', 'FINANCE');`

b. `calc_profit(new_company, profit_level);`

c. `calc_profit(company_id_in=>32,fiscal_year_in=>1995,profit_out=>big_number);`

d. `calc_profit(company_id_in => 32, fiscal_year_in => 1995, profit_out => 1000);`

14-19. Suppose that I have the following procedure header:

```
PROCEDURE calc_totals (
   id_in IN department.department_id%TYPE,
   total_type_in IN VARCHAR2 := 'ALLREV',
   quarter_in IN INTEGER DEFAULT 1,
   currency_in IN VARCHAR2
   )
```

and I want to call calc_totals, specifying values for only the first, third, and fourth arguments, relying on the default value for the second argument. Which of the following calls to calc_totals meet that requirement?

a. `calc_totals (1056,,2,'EURO');`

b. `calc_totals (1056,NULL,2,'EURO');`

c. `calc_totals (1056, quarter_in => 2, 'EURO');`

d. `calc_totals (quarter_in => 2, id_in => 1056, currency_in => 'EURO');`

e. `calc_totals (quarter => 2, id => 1056, currency =>'EURO');`

f. `calc_totals (quarter_in => 2, id_in => 1056, currency_in = > 'EURO');`

14-20. What does it mean to overload a procedure?

14-21. In what parts of PL/SQL code can you overload a program?

14-22. Identify changes you would make to improve the structure, performance, and functionality of the following program. Rewrite the function to incorporate your improvements.

```
FUNCTION status_desc (status_cd_in IN VARCHAR2) RETURN VARCHAR2
IS
BEGIN
   IF    status_cd_in = 'C' THEN RETURN 'CLOSED';
   ELSIF status_cd_in = 'O' THEN RETURN 'OPEN';
   ELSIF status_cd_in = 'A' THEN RETURN 'ACTIVE';
   ELSIF status_cd_in = 'I' THEN RETURN 'INACTIVE';
   END IF;
END;
```

Expert

14-23. Suppose that five years ago, a developer wrote a packaged procedure with the following header:

```
PACKAGE calc
IS
    PROCEDURE totals (
        department_id_in IN department.department_id%TYPE);
END calc;
```

There are many calls to this procedure (stored in the server database) in a variety of production applications written in Oracle Forms. Client-side Oracle Forms PL/SQL code does not recognize default values in parameters lists of stored code. A new requirement has now been requested by users to be able to calculate totals per department and also for sections within departments. How would you change the implementation of the calc package to satisfy these requirements?

14-24. Improve the following procedure:

```
PROCEDURE calc_percentages (total_in IN NUMBER)
IS
BEGIN
    food_sales_stg :=
        TO_CHAR ((sales.food_sales / total_in)  * 100, '$999,999');
    service_sales_stg :=
        TO_CHAR ((sales.service_sales / total_in) * 100, '$999,999');
    toy_sales_stg :=
        TO_CHAR ((sales.toy_sales / total_in)  * 100, '$999,999');
END;
```

14-25. Improve the structure, performance, and functionality of the following function:

```
FUNCTION company_name (
    company_id_in IN company.company_id%TYPE,
    industry_type_out OUT VARCHAR2
    )
    RETURN VARCHAR2
IS
    cname company.company_id%TYPE;
    found_it EXCEPTION;
BEGIN
    SELECT name, industry_type
      INTO cname, industry_type_out
      FROM company
     WHERE company_id = company_id_in;
    RAISE found_it;
EXCEPTION
    WHEN found_it THEN RETURN cname;
END;
```

14-26. The remainder of this chapter is a case study of a function published by Oracle Corporation in its Oracle Forms documentation. Now, I don't mean to pick on Oracle Corporation. In fact, I find that in general their documentation—including their sample code fragments—is outstanding and improved beyond words over earlier manuals. To show just how far they've come, we'll look at a function in the *Oracle Forms Reference Manual*, Volume 1.

The manual presents a function called Is_Value_In_List, which returns the row number of the specified value if it is found in the record group (or "list"). Here is the Oracle Corporation-suggested implementation for such a function (reproduced as is, but without the comments):

```
/* Filename on web page: isvalinlis.sql */
FUNCTION Is_Value_In_List( the_value VARCHAR2,
              the_rg_name VARCHAR2,
              the_rg_column VARCHAR2)
RETURN NUMBER IS
   the_rowcount    NUMBER;
   rg_id           RECORDGROUP;
   gc_id           GROUPCOLUMN;
   col_val         VARCHAR2(80);
   Exit_Function   EXCEPTION;
BEGIN
   rg_id := Find_Group( the_rg_name );

   If Id_Null(rg_id) THEN
      Message ('Record Group '||the_rg_name||' does not exist.');
      RAISE Exit_Function;
   END IF;

   gc_id := Find_Column( the_rg_name||'.'||the_rg_column );
   If Id_Null(gc_id) THEN
      Message ('Column '||the_rg_column||' does not exist.');
      RAISE Exit_Function;
   END IF;
   the_rowcount := Get_Group_Row_Count( rg_id );
   FOR j IN 1..the_rowcount LOOP
      col_val := Get_Group_Char_Cell( gc_id, j );
      IF UPPER(col_val) = UPPER(the_value) THEN
         RETURN j;
      END IF;
   END LOOP;
   RAISE Exit_Function;

EXCEPTION
   WHEN Exit_Function THEN
      RETURN 0;
END;
```

Here's how you would use the function in another program:

```
IF Is_Value_In_List ('hello', 'word_group', 'name') > 0
THEN
   MESSAGE ('they said hello already');
END IF;
```

As the first question in the case study, critique this usage. Do you find the module name particularly descriptive or appropriate? To help you answer this question, begin by expressing the condition in the IF statement as an English sentence.

14-27. Rewrite the function header so that its name more accurately reflects what it returns. Provide an example of how it would be used in another program, and apply the "sentence" test.

14-28. The function uses exceptions in several inappropriate ways. Explain how.

14-29. What's the effect of the RETURN statement inside the FOR loop?

14-30. How could you redesign the function so that it has only one RETURN statement?

14-31. The Is_Value_In_List function works properly, yet has a serious long-term problem. Identify the problem.

14-32. You have been asked to rewrite Is_Value_In_List. Provide an outline, in pseudo-code, of your algorithm.

14-33. Rewrite the Is_Value_In_List function. Be sure to address the problems you identified in earlier questions.

14-34. Rewrite the function so that it returns a Boolean value, and provide an example of how it would be used in another program. Express the function's usage in a sentence. Is this any better?

15

Packages

A *package* is a named collection of procedures, functions, and data structures. A package has two parts: a *specification*, which lists its publicly available elements, and a *body*, which contains the actual implementations for the procedures and functions listed in the specification (the body can also contain private procedures, functions, and data structures that are available only within the package itself). This chapter tests your ability to define your own packages, create packaged data structures such as cursors, and use packages to encapsulate, or hide, the implementation details (e.g., data structures) of your programs.

Beginner

15-1. Is it possible to execute a package?

15-2. If I want to call a procedure named "calc_totals" in the "financial_pkg" package, how would I write the code?

15-3. What are the exceptions to the dot-notation rule for packaged elements? In other words, when don't you need to qualify a package element with its package name?

15-4. List all the packages referenced in the following piece of code, and say what types of packaged elements are used:

```
DECLARE
   v_new_pet pet.pet_id%TYPE;
   v_last_appointment DATE;
BEGIN
   IF pets_r_us.max_pets_in_facility >
        TO_NUMBER (v_current_count)
   THEN
     /* Add another pet ... */
   ELSE
```

```
            DBMS_OUTPUT.PUT_LINE ('Facility is full');
        END IF;
EXCEPTION
    WHEN pets_r_us.pet_is_sick
    THEN
        ...
    WHEN NO_DATA_FOUND
    THEN
        RAISE_APPLICATION_ERROR (
            -20555, 'Pet not found');
END;
```

15-5. Write a package specification that contains a DATE variable that retains its value (i.e., persists) for the duration of your session.

15-6. Write a package that allows a developer to read and write the value of a DATE package variable through "get and set" programs.

15-7. Which of the following cursor declarations, which appear in a package specification called empdata, are valid?

a. CURSOR allrows IS SELECT * FROM employee;

b. CURSOR onerow (pk_in IN employee.employee_id%TYPE)
        RETURN employee%ROWTYPE;

15-8. Why would you want to hide the SELECT statement of a packaged cursor inside the package body?

15-9. Does every package need to have both a specification and a body?

15-10. For which of the following package specifications is a package body required or not required?

a. PACKAGE pkg1
    IS
        employee_too_young EXCEPTION;
        minimum_salary NUMBER;
    END pkg1;

b. PACKAGE pkg2
    IS
        employee_too_young EXCEPTION;
        minimum_salary NUMBER;
        FUNCTION performance_evaluation_score (
            employee_id_in IN employee.employee_id%TYPE)
            RETURN INTEGER;
    END pkg2;

c. PACKAGE pkg3
    IS
        employee_too_young EXCEPTION;
        minimum_salary NUMBER;
        CURSOR allrows IS SELECT * FROM employee;
    END pkg3;

d. PACKAGE pkg4
    IS

```
       employee_too_young EXCEPTION;
       minimum_salary NUMBER;
       CURSOR allrows RETURN employee%ROWTYPE;
  END pkg4;
```

15-11. The following code snippet contains a hardcoded value (the maximum date allowed in the application). Rewrite this code to take advantage of a global, named constant that hides the value, and implement that named constant. How can you implement this constant so that if the value for the maximum date changes, you don't have to recompile programs that contain a reference to the constant?

```
IF v_date > TO_DATE ('31-DEC-2010', 'DD-MON-YYYY')
```

15-12. Is it possible to design a package so that the first time a session tries to use anything in the package (run a program, reference a variable, use a TYPE), code is run to initialize the package?

Intermediate

15-13. The DBMS_UTILITY.GET_TIME function returns the number of hundredths of seconds that have elapsed since a point in time in the past. You can use this function to calculate the elapsed time of your program's execution. Here is the kind of script you might write to figure out how long it takes to run calc_totals:

```
DECLARE
    time_before BINARY_INTEGER;
    time_after BINARY_INTEGER;
BEGIN
    time_before := DBMS_UTILITY.GET_TIME;
    calc_totals;
    time_after := DBMS_UTILITY.GET_TIME;
    p.1 (time_after - time_before);
END;
```

Create a package that allows you to rewrite the above block of code as follows:

```
BEGIN
    timer.capture;
    calc_totals;
    timer.show_elapsed;
END;
```

so the code displays the following form of output:

```
Elapsed time: 2.43 seconds
```

15-14. This package specification doesn't compile. What is the problem?

```
CREATE OR REPLACE PACKAGE curvar
IS
    TYPE cv_t IS REF CURSOR RETURN employee%ROWTYPE;
    emp_cv cv_t;
```

```
END curvar;
/
```

15-15. (For Oracle Developer users only) Consider the following package specification defined in the database:

```
CREATE OR REPLACE PACKAGE emp_rules
IS
    latest_birthday DATE;
    emp_too_young EXCEPTION;
    FUNCTION too_young (birthdate_in IN DATE) RETURN BOOLEAN;
END curvar;
/
```

Which of the following client-side blocks (defined in Oracle Reports or Oracle Forms, for example) don't compile?

a.
```
BEGIN
    IF emp_rules.latest_birthday > ADD_MONTHS (SYSDATE, -216)
        THEN
            MESSAGE ('Employees must be at least 18 years old.');
        END IF;
    END;
```

b.
```
BEGIN
        IF emp_rules.too_young (:empblock.birthdate) >
            ADD_MONTHS (SYSDATE, -216)
        THEN
            MESSAGE ('Employees must be at least 18 years old.');
        END IF;
    END;
```

c.
```
BEGIN
        IF emp_rules.too_young (:empblock.birthdate) >
            ADD_MONTHS (SYSDATE, -216)
        THEN
            RAISE emp_rules.emp_too_young;
        END IF;
    END;
```

15-16. Modify the following package so that whenever a program attempts to change the value of mydate, the program displays (on the screen) the current value, the new value, and the execution call stack so that you can see what program is attempting the change. Also, make sure that the new date is never set into the future.

```
CREATE OR REPLACE PACKAGE sessval
IS
    PROCEDURE set_mydate (date_in IN DATE);
    FUNCTION mydate RETURN DATE;
END sessval;
/
CREATE OR REPLACE PACKAGE BODY sessval
IS
    g_mydate DATE;

    PROCEDURE set_mydate (date_in IN DATE)
```

```
   IS
   BEGIN
      g_mydate := date_in;
   END;

   FUNCTION mydate RETURN DATE
   IS
   BEGIN
      RETURN g_mydate;
   END;
END sessval;
/
```

15-17. Enhance the following package so that you only see the trace output when requested. As an added wrinkle, you are not allowed to change the definition of set_mydate.

```
/* Filename on web page: sessval1.pkg */
CREATE OR REPLACE PACKAGE sessval
IS
   PROCEDURE set_mydate( date_in IN DATE );

   FUNCTION mydate RETURN DATE;
END sessval;
/
CREATE OR REPLACE PACKAGE BODY sessval
IS
   g_mydate DATE;

   PROCEDURE set_mydate( date_in IN DATE) IS
   BEGIN
      IF    date_in IS NULL
         OR date_in > SYSDATE
      THEN
         DBMS_OUTPUT.put_line (
            'Sessval.mydate cannot be set into the future.'
         );
      ELSE
         DBMS_OUTPUT.put_line (
            'Current value of sessval.mydate: ' ||
            g_mydate
         );
         DBMS_OUTPUT.put_line (
            'New value of sessval.mydate: ' ||
            date_in
         );
         DBMS_OUTPUT.put_line (
            DBMS_UTILITY.format_call_stack
         );
         g_mydate := date_in;
      END IF;
   END;

   FUNCTION mydate RETURN DATE IS
   BEGIN
```

```
        RETURN g_mydate;
    END;
END sessval;
/
```

15-18. The following package allows you to display the elapsed time of program execution using DBMS_OUTPUT.PUT_LINE. What if you want to use this utility in an environment that does not easily integrate with DBMS_OUTPUT and uses some other mechanism to display information? Modify the timer package so that you can retrieve the elapsed time without having to display it:

```
/* Filename on web page: timer.pkg */
CREATE OR REPLACE PACKAGE timer
IS
    PROCEDURE capture;
    PROCEDURE show_elapsed;
END timer;
/

CREATE OR REPLACE PACKAGE BODY timer
IS
    last_timing INTEGER := NULL;

    PROCEDURE capture
    IS
    BEGIN
      last_timing := DBMS_UTILITY.GET_TIME;
    END;

    PROCEDURE show_elapsed
    IS
    BEGIN
      DBMS_OUTPUT.PUT_LINE (
        'Elapsed time: ' ||
        (DBMS_UTILITY.GET_TIME - last_timing)/100);
    END;

END timer;
/
```

15-19. Write a package that calculates and displays a person's age. The user should be able to provide his or her date of birth as a date, a number, or a string.

15-20. The DBMS_OUTPUT.PUT_LINE procedure allows PL/SQL developers to print output from their programs on the screen (standard output). There are a number of problems associated with the package, including the following:

- The command itself, DBMS_OUTPUT.PUT_LINE, requires way too much typing.
- It is not overloaded for Boolean values.

- If you try to display a string with more than 255 characters, it raises an exception.
- If your buffer size is set too low (the default in SQL*Plus is 2000 bytes; the maximum is 1 million bytes), it raises an exception.

Create a package to corrects these problems.

15-21. Can you declare the same data structure in a package specification and its package body?

Expert

15-22. Suppose you define the following package:

```
/* Filename on web page onecur.sql */
CREATE OR REPLACE PACKAGE onecur
IS
    CURSOR onerow (
        id_in IN employee.employee_id%TYPE)
    IS
        SELECT * FROM employee
         WHERE employee_id = id_in;
END onecur;
/
```

You then create the following procedure, procA:

```
CREATE OR REPLACE PROCEDURE procA
IS
BEGIN
    OPEN onecur.allrows (1005);
END procA;
/
```

Next, you create the procedure procB:

```
CREATE OR REPLACE PROCEDURE procB
IS
BEGIN
    OPEN onecur.allrows (2356);
    procA;
END procB;
/
```

What happens when you execute procB?

15-23. Rewrite the package in 15-22 so that it provides procedures to open and close the cursor, ensuring that a user never receives a "cursor already open" error when opening the cursor and never receives an "invalid cursor" error when closing the cursor.

15-24. Every time you reference the USER function to retrieve the currently connected username, you do a SELECT FROM dual. On a 300-MHz laptop, 10,000 consecutive calls to USER take approximately 2.5 seconds to complete. While this is not a long time, it's not exactly fast either. How could you modify the loop so that the USER function is called only once?

15-25. The following package won't compile because it's too big: proc1 contains 20 KB of source code, and proc2 contains 22 KB. How can you redefine this code so that the call interface remains the same, but you can still call toobig.proc1 and toobig.proc2 to get your work done?

```
/* Filename on web page: splitpkg.pkg */
CREATE OR REPLACE PACKAGE toobig
IS
    PROCEDURE proc1;
    PROCEDURE proc2;
END;
/
CREATE OR REPLACE PACKAGE BODY toobig
IS
    PROCEDURE proc1
    IS
    BEGIN
       /* lots of code */
       NULL;
    END;

    PROCEDURE proc2
    IS
    BEGIN
       /* lots more code */
       NULL;
    END;
END;
/
```

15-26. Does the following package specification contain a valid implementation of overloading? Specifically, does the package specification compile? If so, can you actually run either of the programs successfully?

```
/* Filename on web page: sales.pkg */
CREATE OR REPLACE PACKAGE salespkg
IS
    PROCEDURE calc_total (zone_in IN VARCHAR2);
    PROCEDURE calc_total (reg_in IN VARCHAR2);
END salespkg;
/
```

15-27. Suppose you want more flexibility than DBMS_OUTPUT can provide for your tracing and debugging needs. For example, in some circumstances, you want to see the output from your program while it is still running; most of the time, though, you're quite content with output to the screen. You also want to see the execution call stack when your trace program is called to see where you are in the process. Create a package that offers a replacement for the built-in procedure, DBMS_OUTPUT.PUT_LINE, with the options mentioned. Build a body to fit the following specification for such a package:

```
/* Filename on web page: watch.pkg */
CREATE OR REPLACE PACKAGE watch
IS
    /* Direct output to the screen; the default. */
    PROCEDURE toscreen;

    /* Direct output to a pipe so it can be viewed even
       while the program is still running. */
    PROCEDURE topipe;

    /* Watch a specific action; the replacement for the
       DBMS_OUTPUT.PUT_LINE procedure. */
    PROCEDURE action (prog IN VARCHAR2, val IN VARCHAR2);

    /* Show the contents of the database pipe. */
    PROCEDURE show;
END;
```

15-28. When you want to execute a SQL statement constructed at runtime (dynamic SQL), you must call the DBMS_SQL.EXECUTE function. If your SQL statement is an INSERT, UPDATE, or DELETE, this function returns the number of rows modified by the statement. Otherwise, the return value is ignored. This means that if you execute a query or a DDL statement or a PL/SQL block—anything except a DML statement—you must declare a variable to hold a return value and then not use it, as shown:

```
DECLARE
    cur INTEGER := DBMS_SQL.OPEN_CURSOR;
    feedback INTEGER;
BEGIN
    DBMS_SQL.PARSE (cur, 'TRUNCATE TABLE employee', DBMS_SQL.NATIVE);
    feedback := DBMS_SQL.EXECUTE (cur);
    DBMS_SQL.CLOSE (cur);
END;
```

Do what Oracle should have done: create a package that offers an implementation of the EXECUTE program that allows developers to avoid the need to declare a "feedback" variable unless they are executing DML.

15-29. Suppose that you have set up a database table to store standard user configuration information. These configuration values are changed only when users are off the system; they do not change during an active session. Here is the definition of the table:

```
/* Filename on web page: usrcnfg.ins */
CREATE TABLE user_config (
    username VARCHAR2(30),
    cubicle# VARCHAR2(20),
    max_coffee_breaks INTEGER
    );
```

Furthermore, suppose you use this package to retrieve this information:

```
/* Filename on web page: usrcnfg1.pkg */
CREATE OR REPLACE PACKAGE userconfig
IS
   FUNCTION cubicle# RETURN VARCHAR2;
   FUNCTION max_coffee_breaks RETURN INTEGER;
END userconfig;
/
CREATE OR REPLACE PACKAGE BODY userconfig
IS
   FUNCTION cubicle# RETURN VARCHAR2
   IS
      retval user_config.cubicle#%TYPE;
   BEGIN
      SELECT user_config.cubicle#
        INTO retval
        FROM user_config
        WHERE username = USER;
      RETURN retval;
   EXCEPTION
      WHEN NO_DATA_FOUND
      THEN
         RETURN 'SECURITY DESK';
   END;

   FUNCTION max_coffee_breaks RETURN INTEGER
   IS
      retval user_config.max_coffee_breaks%TYPE;
   BEGIN
      SELECT user_config.max_coffee_breaks
        INTO retval
        FROM user_config
        WHERE username = USER;
      RETURN retval;
   EXCEPTION
      WHEN NO_DATA_FOUND
      THEN
         RETURN 0;
   END;
END userconfig;
/
```

What are the problems with the design of this package? How would you change the package to improve its performance? As you design your changes, remember that only the package body should change, so that existing calls to the usrcnfg package aren't affected.

15-30. As a general rule, when you define data structures in a package, but not within any procedure or function of the package, this data persists for your entire session. What feature in Oracle8*i* Release 8.1 allows you to have your package data treated like "local" data (i.e., to discard memory and reinstantiate data structures with each block execution)?

16

Triggers

A *trigger* is a special PL/SQL procedure that fires, or executes, in response to a specific triggering event. For example, you might write a trigger to enforce a business rule on INSERT statements on a particular table, maintain referential integrity in a distributed database, or track user logons. A trigger has three parts:

- A header line that defines the triggering event
- An optional WHEN clause that restricts the trigger's firing to a specific condition (for example, the trigger fires only when salary is greater than $50,000)
- The actual trigger code itself

This chapter tests your ability to define triggers for a variety of events, work with correlation variables (special pseudo-column names that represent things like the old and new values of a column), and use triggers to implement business logic.

Beginner

16-1. What is a trigger?

16-2. For which of the following events can you create a trigger?

    a. An INSERT, UPDATE, or DELETE statement on a specific object

    b. An execution of a specific procedure

    c. A user logon (or logoff)

    d. A DDL statement, such as DROP or ALTER, on a specific object

16-3. What is one of the main differences between the execution of a trigger and the execution of a stored procedure?

16-4. What are the two modes a trigger can have?

16-5. Which of the following terms describes the situation in which the execution of one trigger results in the execution of another, or possibly more, different triggers?

    a. Trigger torrent

    b. Cascading triggers

    c. Chain reaction

    d. Interlock

    e. Recursive nesting

16-6. What is the difference between a statement-level trigger and a row-level trigger?

16-7. What clause makes a trigger fire only when a specific condition is true?

16-8. Which of the following triggers populates the employee_id column of the employee table with the next employee_seq sequence value?

```
a. CREATE OR REPLACE TRIGGER employee_ins_t1
      BEFORE INSERT
      ON employee
      FOR EACH ROW
   BEGIN
      INSERT INTO employee (employee_id)
         VALUES (employee_seq.nextval);
   END;
b. CREATE OR REPLACE TRIGGER employee_ins_t1
      BEFORE INSERT
      ON employee
      FOR EACH ROW
   BEGIN
      SELECT employee_seq.nextval
        INTO :new.employee_id
        FROM dual;
   END;
```

16-9. Which of these special "pseudo" records are allowed inside a trigger?

    a. :NEW

    b. :CURRENT

    c. :OLDEST

    d. :PARENT

    e. :OLD

    f. :NEWEST

    g. :RECORD

16-10. What system privileges are required to create a trigger?

16-11. What is the difference between the ALTER ANY TRIGGER privilege and the CREATE ANY TRIGGER privilege?

16-12. Why does the following trigger generate a "ORA-00920: invalid relational operator" error?

```
CREATE OR REPLACE TRIGGER emp_before_ins_t
   BEFORE INSERT
   ON employee
   FOR EACH ROW
   WHEN (:NEW.mgr is null)
BEGIN
   IF (:NEW.sal > 800)
   THEN
      :NEW.sal := 850;
   END IF;
END;
```

16-13. How can you view a trigger's compilation errors?

16-14. How many different ways can you recompile a trigger?

16-15. Why might you want to omit the OR REPLACE clause when you first create a trigger?

16-16. Which of the following statements are correct, and which are incorrect?

   a. A user can create a trigger in any database schema if she has the CREATE ANY TRIGGER privilege.

   b. A user can create a trigger in any database schema (with the exception of SYS) if she has the CREATE ANY TRIGGER privilege.

   c. Triggers can trap only DML events such as INSERT, DELETE, and UPDATE.

16-17. True or false? You can define a trigger for:

   a. Any schema-level object

   b. A table

   c. A view

   d. Any nested table

   e. The entire database or a user schema

16-18. Examine the following trigger:

```
CREATE OR REPLACE TRIGGER upd_employee_commision
FOR EACH ROW
BEGIN
   <<Trigger logic>>
END;
```

Which of the following statements must you add to the trigger definition to make sure this trigger executes only after updating the comm column of the emp table?

   a. `AFTER UPDATE(comm) ON emp`

   b. `AFTER UPDATE ON emp`

   c. AFTER UPDATE OF comm ON emp

   d. AFTER comm UPDATE ON emp

16-19. Examine the following trigger:

```
CREATE OR REPLACE TRIGGER insert_employee
  AFTER INSERT ON emp
BEGIN
   <<Trigger logic>>
END;
```

Which of the following statements must you add to the trigger definition to make sure it executes only once for each INSERT operation on the emp table?

   a. FOR EVERY ROW

   b. WHEN (new.sal IS NULL)

   c. FOR EACH ROW

   d. No modifications are necessary

16-20. Why does the following trigger fails when it's executed?

```
CREATE OR REPLACE TRIGGER ins_emp_summary
   AFTER INSERT
   ON emp
BEGIN
   INSERT INTO emp_summary (empno, period, ytd_salary)
        VALUES (:new.empno, SYSDATE, :new.sal);
END;
```

16-21. What is a mutating table?

Intermediate

16-22. What happens when the following trigger executes?

```
CREATE OR REPLACE TRIGGER employee_ins_t1
   BEFORE UPDATE
   ON employee
   FOR EACH ROW
DECLARE
   cur    PLS_INTEGER    := DBMS_SQL.open_cursor;
   fdbk   PLS_INTEGER;
   stmt   VARCHAR2(2000);
BEGIN
   stmt := 'BEGIN IF :old.' ||
           emp_pkg.col_name ||
           '= ' ||
           emp_pkg.col_value ||
           '''' ||
           ' THEN  :new.salary := :new.salary * 2; ' ||
           ' END IF;' ||
           ' END; ';
   DBMS_SQL.parse (cur, sql_stmt, DBMS_SQL.native);
   fdbk := DBMS_SQL.execute (cur);
END;
```

16-23. Provide a template for a trigger that raises an error when a client application violates a business rule (e.g., a trigger that raises an error if a user attempts to delete a row from the employee table).

16-24. You want to issue DML statements or execute PL/SQL stored programs inside a trigger. Which of the following describes how you must grant the necessary privileges on the underlying object?

    a. Privileges on the underlying object must be granted through the database roles.

    b. Privileges on the underlying object must be granted directly from the user who owns the object.

    c. Privileges can be granted either through database roles or directly from the user who owns the object.

16-25. Indicate whether the following triggers are valid or invalid (a valid procedure both compiles and executes without error):

    a.
```
CREATE OR REPLACE TRIGGER emp_audit_trg
    BEFORE INSERT OR UPDATE
    ON employee
    FOR EACH ROW
BEGIN
    IF (inserting)
    THEN
        INSERT INTO employee_audit
            VALUES (:new.empno, USER, 'Inserting a row into table_a');
    ELSE
        INSERT INTO employee_audit
            VALUES (:new.empno, USER, 'Updating a row in table_a');
    END IF;
    COMMIT;
END;
```

    b.
```
CREATE OR REPLACE TRIGGER format_table_trig
    AFTER INSERT
    ON format_table
    FOR EACH ROW
    WHEN (new.tablecode = 3334)
DECLARE
    seq_sql        VARCHAR(200);
    cursor_handle  INTEGER;
    execute_ddl    INTEGER;
BEGIN
    seq_sql := 'CREATE SEQUENCE ' ||
                SUBSTR (:new.table_id, 1, 21) ||
                '_SEQ START WITH 0 INCREMENT BY 1 MINVALUE 0';
    cursor_handle := DBMS_SQL.open_cursor;
    DBMS_SQL.parse (cursor_handle, seq_sql, DBMS_SQL.native);
    execute_ddl := DBMS_SQL.execute (cursor_handle);
    DBMS_SQL.close_cursor (cursor_handle);
END;
```

```
C. CREATE OR REPLACE TRIGGER set_scott_on_logon
     AFTER logon
     ON SCHEMA
   DECLARE
     seq_sql        VARCHAR(200) := 'alter package emp_pkg compile';
     cursor_handle  INTEGER      := DBMS_SQL.open_cursor;
     execute_ddl    INTEGER;
   BEGIN
     DBMS_SQL.parse (cursor_handle, seq_sql, DBMS_SQL.native);
     execute_ddl := DBMS_SQL.execute (cursor_handle);
     DBMS_SQL.close_cursor (cursor_handle);
   END;
```

16-26. DDL and transaction control statements such as ROLLBACK, COMMIT, and SAVEPOINT are not allowed in the body of a trigger. Can you circumvent this restriction by calling a stored procedure, which does contain the statement, in the trigger's body?

16-27. Sometimes, depending on the context of the application being constructed, you need to implement logic that requires explicit (or implicit) transaction control. For example, suppose you want to create a sequence when a user inserts a row into a table. How would you perform this function in Oracle8*i*? In previous versions of Oracle?

16-28. True or false (note that number 32 really is a magical number for triggers!)?

   a. The trigger body cannot contain more than 32 lines of PL/SQL code.

   b. The size of a trigger cannot be more than 32K.

   c. Oracle allows up to 32 triggers to cascade at any one time.

   d. LONG or LONG RAW column can be referenced in a SQL statement within a trigger only if they can be converted into a constrained datatype. The maximum length for these datatypes can be up to 32K.

16-29. Sometimes you need to enable or disable triggers when you perform certain tasks, such as loading data or reorganizing a table. Write a script that enables or disables all triggers for the user who runs it.

Expert

16-30. If you create several triggers of the same type for the same table, in what order do the triggers fire?

16-31. Optimize the performance of the following trigger and explain how this technique can minimize the number of times the trigger fires:

```
CREATE OR REPLACE TRIGGER employee_ins_t1
    AFTER UPDATE OR DELETE OR INSERT
    ON employee
    FOR EACH ROW
BEGIN
```

```
      IF (UPDATING) THEN
        IF :old.sal <> :new.sal THEN
          Employee_pkg.update_emp (:new.employee_id, :new.sal);
        END IF;
      END IF;
    END;
```

16-32. An HR system has an employee table that holds a row for each employee within the company. Each record in the table has a manager field, (mgr), that holds the ID for the employee's manager. Write a trigger so that when a manager record is deleted, the mgr field of that manager's employees is set to NULL. In other words, implement the following SQL statement:

```
WHEN AN EMPLOYEE IS DELETED,
  UPDATE employee SET
    mgr = null
  WHERE
    mgr = employee id of the deleted employee
```

16-33. Due to a runtime error, an AFTER LOGON trigger in your database has become invalid. As a consequence, all users receive the following error when trying to connect to the database:

```
ORA-04098: trigger 'ON_LOGON' is invalid and failed re-validation
```

How can you fix the problem?

16-34. What are the possible implications of using the pseudo-column names :OLD and :NEW in the following trigger, which uses autonomous transactions?

```
/* Filename on web page: iris_emp_trig */
CREATE OR REPLACE TRIGGER ins_emp
    AFTER INSERT
    ON emp
 FOR EACH ROW
DECLARE
    PRAGMA AUTONOMOUS_TRANSACTION;
    vsal    NUMBER;
BEGIN
    SELECT SUM (sal)
      INTO vsal
      FROM emp e
     WHERE e.deptno = :new.deptno;

    BEGIN
       INSERT INTO dept_history
           VALUES (:new.deptno, vsal);
    EXCEPTION
       WHEN DUP_VAL_ON_INDEX
       THEN
          UPDATE dept_history
             SET sal = vsal
           WHERE deptno = :new.deptno;
    END;

    COMMIT;
END;
```

16-35. Suppose that the procedures called by the following triggers are recompiled. What happens at the next execution of each trigger?

```
CREATE OR REPLACE TRIGGER loc_proc_trigger
   BEFORE UPDATE
   ON bonus
   FOR EACH ROW
BEGIN
   update_bonus;
END;
/

CREATE OR REPLACE TRIGGER rem_proc_trigger
   BEFORE UPDATE
   ON bonus
   FOR EACH ROW
BEGIN
   update_bonus@rdb;
END;
/
```

17

Calling Functions in SQL

As we've seen, you can use functions to compute and return a value for a set of input parameters. For example, you can write a lookup function that returns an employee name for a given primary key. What many developers don't realize is that you can (within certain limits) use these functions in SQL statements, allowing you to considerably simplify complex statements. For example, you could replace messy and error-prone DECODE statements with a simple function call or eliminate complex outer-joins or subqueries with a lookup function.

This chapter describes the features that allow PL/SQL developers to embed calls to their own functions inside SQL statements and tests your ability to use these functions in SQL.

 Prior to Oracle 8.1, if you wanted to call—directly or indirectly—package-based functions and procedures from within an SQL statement, it was necessary to provide RESTRICT_REFERENCE pragmas in the package specification. A number of exercises in this chapter cover this topic. As of Oracle 8.1, you're no longer required to provide the pragmas; the PL/SQL runtime engine figures it out by itself.

Beginner

17-1. Can you call a PL/SQL function from within a SQL statement?

17-2. Can your own function act like a SQL group function (SUM, MIN, MAX, etc.) in a SQL statement?

17-3. The following query contains a redundant formula to compute the total compensation of an employee (salary + commission):

```
SELECT ename, sal + NVL (comm, 0)
  FROM emp
 WHERE sal + NVL (comm, 0) > 1000;
```

Rewrite this query so that it instead calls a function to calculate the total compensation.

17-4. Which of the following statements regarding the execution of functions in SQL are true, and which are false?

a. The function can only have IN parameters; OUT and IN OUT modes are not allowed.

b. The datatypes of the parameters and the RETURN clause of the function can be any valid PL/SQL datatype.

c. The function must have the same name as the table in the FROM clause of a query in which the function is run.

d. A function defined in an Oracle Forms or Oracle Reports module can be called inside a query that is also defined in that module.

e. You can only use a user-defined function within a query; UPDATEs, INSERTs, and DELETEs must consist of "pure" SQL.

17-5. Can you call a PL/SQL procedure from within a SQL statement?

Intermediate

17-6. When you want to call a packaged function (a function defined in the specification of a package) from within an SQL statement, what statement do you need to add to that specification? What is it for?

17-7. What are the four different purity levels you can attempt to assert about a function?

17-8. Add the necessary code to this package specification to assert all four purity levels for the total function:

```
CREATE OR REPLACE PACKAGE comp
IS
   FUNCTION total
      (sal_in IN NUMBER,
       comm_in IN NUMBER := NULL)
      RETURN NUMBER;
END;
/
```

17-9. What is the minimum required purity level for a packaged function to be callable inside SQL?

17-10. Under what circumstances do you need to assert the WNPS purity level for a packaged function or procedure?

17-11. Which purity levels can you assert about the following function if you define it inside a package?

```
FUNCTION betwnstr
    (str IN VARCHAR2, startat IN INTEGER, endat IN INTEGER := NULL)
    RETURN VARCHAR2
IS
BEGIN
    RETURN SUBSTR (str, startat, endat-startat+1);
END;
```

17-12. Which purity levels can you assert about the following function?

```
FUNCTION ename_from (empno_in IN emp.empno%TYPE)
    RETURN emp.ename%TYPE
IS
    retval emp.ename%TYPE;
BEGIN
    SELECT ename INTO retval
      FROM emp WHERE empno = empno_in;
    RETURN retval;
END;
```

17-13. Suppose that you define the following package in the database:

```
PACKAGE who_is_paying_whom
IS
    too_low CONSTANT NUMBER := 15000; /* This is above minimum wage! */
    my_salary CONSTANT NUMBER := too_low;
    ceo_salary NUMBER := too_low * 250;
END;
```

Which purity levels can you assert about the following functions?

    a.
```
   FUNCTION betwnstr
       (str IN VARCHAR2, startat IN INTEGER, endat IN INTEGER := NULL)
       RETURN VARCHAR2
   IS
   BEGIN
       IF who_is_paying_whom.my_salary < 20000
          THEN i_am_a_wage_slave; END IF;
       RETURN SUBSTR (str, startat, endat-startat+1);
   END;
```

    b.
```
   FUNCTION betwnstr
       (str IN VARCHAR2, startat IN INTEGER, endat IN INTEGER := NULL)
       RETURN VARCHAR2
   IS
   BEGIN
       IF who_is_paying_whom.my_salary <
          who_is_paying_whom.ceo_salary / 50
       THEN
          who_is_paying_whom.ceo_salary := 0; /* Greedy bum! */
       END IF;

       RETURN SUBSTR (str, startat, endat-startat+1);
   END;
```

17-14. Suppose you define a package specification as follows:

```
CREATE OR REPLACE PACKAGE comp
IS
    FUNCTION total
        (sal_in IN NUMBER, comm_in IN NUMBER := NULL)
        RETURN NUMBER;

    FUNCTION total (emp_in IN emp.empno%TYPE)
        RETURN NUMBER;

    PRAGMA RESTRICT_REFERENCES (total, WNDS, WNPS, RNDS, RNPS);
END;
/
```

You also create the body and get no compile errors. But when you try to use your function in a SELECT statement (prior to Oracle 8.1) as shown here, you get this error:

```
SQL> SELECT ename, comp.total (sal, comm) total
  2    FROM emp
  3    WHERE comp.total (sal, comm) > 0;
SELECT ename, comp.total (sal, comm) total
                *
ERROR at line 1:
ORA-06571: Function TOTAL does not guarantee not to update database
```

Why does this error occur?

17-15. Suppose you wrote a query to implement this requirement:

"If a person has been hired within the last 30 days, display "JUST HIRED". Otherwise, if that person's last evaluation took place at least 10 days ago, display "NEEDS REVIEW"; otherwise, display "UP TO DATE".

You used DECODE as follows:

```
SELECT ename,
       DECODE (
          GREATEST (
             SYSDATE - 30,
             hire_date
          ),
          SYSDATE - 30,
             DECODE (
                LEAST (
                   SYSDATE - 10,
                   eval_date
                ),
                eval_date, 'NEEDS REVIEW',
                'UP TO DATE'
             ),
          'JUST HIRED'
       ) status
  FROM emp;
```

Rewrite this query so that it does not use DECODE.

Expert

17-16. Which purity levels can you assert about the following function?

```
FUNCTION ename_from (empno_in IN emp.empno%TYPE)
   RETURN emp.ename%TYPE
IS
   retval emp.ename%TYPE;
BEGIN
   DBMS_OUTPUT.PUT_LINE ('Getting name for ' || empno_in);
   SELECT ename INTO retval
     FROM emp WHERE empno = empno_in;
   RETURN retval;
END;
```

17-17. Build a function that can be called from within a SQL statement that provides a DBMS_OUTPUT trace of each row returned by a query, showing the table name and the ROWID.

17-18. Build a function that can be called from within a SQL statement that provides a DBMS_PIPE trace of each row returned by a query, showing the table name and the ROWID. Why might you use DBMS_PIPE, rather than DBMS_OUTPUT?

17-19. In Oracle 8.0 and earlier, suppose you define your total compensation as follows:

```
CREATE OR REPLACE FUNCTION totcomp
   (sal_in IN PLS_INTEGER,
    comm_in IN NUMBER :- NULL)
   RETURN NUMBER
IS
BEGIN
   DELETE FROM emp;
   RETURN (sal_in + NVL (comm_in, 0));
END;
/
```

What happens when you execute this INSERT statement?

```
insert into emp (empno) values (totcomp(100,200));
```

And what behavior do you see when you take these same steps in Oracle 8.1?

17-20. Implement the following request in "straight SQL" and then using PL/SQL functions:

"Show me the name and salary of the employee with the highest salary in each department, along with the total salary for each department."

17-21. Suppose you want to call your PL/SQL function in both the SELECT list and the WHERE clause. Here is an example:

```
SELECT my_function (col1)
  FROM table1
 WHERE my_function (col1) > 3;
```

If table1 has 100 rows in it and the WHERE clause filters out 50 of those rows, my_function is called 150 times.

Rewrite this statement using new SQL features available in Oracle8 to reduce the number of executions of my_function.

18

Character Functions

The character functions allow you manipulate VARCHAR2, CHAR, and RAW variables. For example, there are character functions to concatenate (join) two strings, return a string in all uppercase, extract a substring from another string, or trim leading or trailing blanks. This chapter tests your ability to work with the individual character functions, as well as your ability to perform complex string manipulations by combining the atomic character functions.

Beginner

18-1. What are the two different ways you can concatenate strings together?

18-2. What function can you use to find the location of a substring in a string?

18-3. What functions can you use to substitute a character or pattern in a string?

18-4. What function can you use to find how many characters a string contains?

18-5. What is the output of the following?
```
SQL> EXEC DBMS_OUTPUT.PUT_LINE(LENGTH(1 * 100));
```

18-6. Update the last_name column in the employee table to uppercase. Only update the rows where the last_name is not already uppercased.

18-7. What functions can you use to change the case (upper, lower) of a string?

18-8. Write a block that displays the middle three characters of this string:
```
BRUSHLOTS
```

18-9. What functions can you use to pad a string?

18-10. Change the string "this is a headline" into "This Is A Headline" using a character function.

18-11. Write a PL/SQL block that shows the names of all employees in the employee table whose last names contain the letter "e".

18-12. Write a PL/SQL block that displays the location of the second letter "e" found in the string (my name was *made* for the character function I have in mind):

```
Steven Feuerstein
```

18-13. Write a PL/SQL block that displays the location of the third letter "e" from the end of the string:

```
Steven Feuerstein
```

18-14. Remove all the leading zeros from the my_formatted_number VARCHAR2 variable.

18-15. Left-pad a string containing a number so that the resulting string always has a length of 15.

18-16. Replace all occurrences of the letter "e" with the letter "z" in the following string:

```
Steven Feuerstein
```

18-17. Remove all occurrences of the letter "e" in the following string:

```
Steven Feuerstein
```

18-18. Replace all occurrences of "YY" with "RR" in the following string:

```
DECLARE
   mystr VARCHAR2(200) :=
      'IF TO_DATE (my_date_str, ''MM-DD-YY'') > SYSDATE';
```

18-19. Replace all occurrences (regardless of case) of "YY" with "RR" in the following string:

```
DECLARE
   mystr VARCHAR2(200) :=
   'IF TO_DATE (my_date_str, ''MM-DD-YY'') >
         TO_DATE (your_date_str, ''mmddyy'')';
```

18-20. Create a string of 80 hyphens to use as a border line in a report.

Intermediate

18-21. What string is displayed on the screen when this code is executed?

```
/* Filename on web page: sefx.sql */
DECLARE
   hollywood VARCHAR2(100) :=
      'Sound effects BAM!ARGH!BAM!HAM!';
BEGIN
   DBMS_OUTPUT.PUT_LINE (RTRIM (hollywood, 'BAM!ARGH!'));
END;
```

18-22. What string is displayed on the screen when this code is executed?

```
BEGIN
   DBMS_OUTPUT.PUT_LINE (RTRIM ('ABCDEF', 'ABCDE'));
END;
```

18-23. Write a function to display the character set location or number for a specified character.

18-24. Write a function to determine whether two different strings "sound" the same.

18-25. Write a function that gives a name to (and makes accessible via that name) the newline character. Do the same for the tab character.

18-26. Write a PL/SQL block that replaces all occurrences (regardless of case) of "YY" with "RR" in the following string:

```
IF TO_DATE (my_date_str, 'MM-DD-YY') > TO_DATE (your_date_str, 'mmddyy')
```

18-27. Write a function that strips all numeric digits from the specified string and returns what is left.

18-28. Consider the following call to SUBSTR:

```
SUBSTR ('Sunny February in Chicago', -10, 3)
-- ruler 12345678901234567890012345
-- ruler 54321098765432109087654321
```

Which of the following substrings does this function return?

```
in
y i
i y
```

18-29. Consider the following call to INSTR:

```
INSTR ( 'Sandy February in East Chicago', 'a', -15, 2)
-- ruler 12345678901234567890001234567890
-- ruler 09876543210987654321009087654321
```

Which of the following locations does this function return?

```
12
2
28
```

18-30. Which character functions do not return NULL even if you pass them one or more NULL arguments?

18-31. Write a PL/SQL block that displays that portion of the string:

```
Steven Feuerstein
```

that lies between the second and fourth letter "e".

18-32. What formula should be used to obtain that part of a string that starts on character *n* and ends on character *m* (greater than *n*)?

18-33. Write a function called betwnstr that returns theat portion of a string between the specified start and end locations in the string (end >= start).

18-34. Write a PL/SQL block that finds all rows in the USER_SOURCE data dictionary view (containing source code for programs you have stored under your schema) whose "text" column contains at least one occurrence of the string "YY" (regardless of case). Display the name of the program ("name" column) and the potentially problematic text.

18-35. Write a function that accepts a single string and returns a string that has replaced all occurrences of the single quotes with two single quotes. This is a handy function when you want the string after evaluation to still contain a single quote (often an issue when writing dynamic SQL).

18-36. Remove all leading repetitions of "abc" from the string:

abcabccccccI LOVE CHILIabc

18-37. True or false?

   a. The SOUNDEX value always begins with the first letter in the input string.

   b. SOUNDEX uses only the first two consonants in the string to generate the return value.

   c. Only consonants are used to compute the numeric portion of the SOUNDEX value. Except for a possible leading vowel, all vowels are ignored.

   d. SOUNDEX is not case-sensitive. Both uppercase and lowercase letters return the same SOUNDEX value.

   e. The SOUNDEX function is used by the FBI to identify potential terrorists during airport passport checks.

   f. The letter Y is considered a consonant for purposes of SOUNDEX's analysis.

18-38. The REPLACE function in Oracle's STANDARD package makes extensive use of recursion as you can see from its source displayed here (as coded by the lovely and talented folks at Oracle):

```
FUNCTION REPLACE (srcstr VARCHAR2, oldsub VARCHAR2, newsub VARCHAR2 := NULL)
   RETURN VARCHAR2
IS
   brk BINARY_INTEGER;
BEGIN
   IF srcstr IS NULL
   THEN
      RETURN srcstr;    -- NULL
   ELSE
      brk := INSTR (srcstr, oldsub);
      IF brk > 0
      THEN
         RETURN (SUBSTR (srcstr,
               1,
               brk - 1
```

```
                    ) ||
                    newsub ||
                    REPLACE (SUBSTR (srcstr, brk + LENGTH (oldsub)),
                    oldsub,
                    newsub
                    )
                        );
        ELSE
            RETURN srcstr;
        END IF;
    END IF;
END;
```

Write a function called rplc that does the same thing REPLACE does without using recursion.

18-39. Pretend or forget that the standard INSTR function searches backwards if the third argument (starting position) is negative, and write a function to do it. Here is an example call to the function:

```
SQL> EXEC DBMS_OUTPUT.PUT_LINE(rinstr('Hairball and Crumbhead','r',30,1));
15
```

18-40. Write a function that generates a "ruler" as shown here:

```
SQL> BEGIN
        DBMS_OUTPUT.PUT_LINE (rulerstr (25));
    END;
    /

1234567890123456789012345
```

Expert

18-41. Write a function that left-pads the integer component and right-pads the decimal component of a string containing a number in a balanced way to return a string of a specified length and the decimal point (if it is present) located at the center position. For example, the string "23091958.47" with a specified length of 30 is changed to:

```
-- ruler 123456789012345678901234567890
        00000023091958.470000000000000
```

Here is the skeleton specification of the function:

```
CREATE OR REPLACE FUNCTION center_number ( p_num_to_center VARCHAR2,
                                           p_total_length  INT := 30 )
                    RETURN VARCHAR2 IS

 v_ret_val VARCHAR2(2000); -- return value

BEGIN

  RETURN(v_ret_val);

END;
```

18-42. Write a function called betwnstr that returns the portion of a string that lies between specified start and end locations in the string, where (1) both start and end locations can be negative and (2) end can be less than start.

18-43. Write a function called betwnstr that returns the portion of a string that lies between specified start and end substrings, as in:

```
FUNCTION betwnstr (
    str IN VARCHAR2, start_str IN VARCHAR2, end_str IN VARCHAR2 := NULL)
    RETURN VARCHAR2;
```

If end_str is NULL, return everything starting from the start_str's location.

18-44. Write a function to trim patterns, not individual characters, from the beginning of a string.

18-45. Write a function that returns the location of the specified letter in a string that is closest to another specified letter, as in:

```
FUNCTION closest_loc (str IN VARCHAR2, findit IN VARCHAR, closeto IN
VARCHAR2)
    RETURN INTEGER
```

18-46. Enhance the "ruler" function (see the *rulerstr.sf* file on the book's web page) to accept a second argument indicating the starting number in the rule. If the starting number is negative, reverse the order of the numbers in the ruler. Here are some examples of desired behavior:

```
SQL> EXEC DBMS_OUTPUT.PUT_LINE (rulerstr (25, 5))
56789012345678901234567890123456789
SQL> EXEC DBMS_OUTPUT.PUT_LINE (rulerstr (25, -5))
67890123456789012345678901234567890
SQL> EXEC DBMS_OUTPUT.PUT_LINE (rulerstr (25, 0))
012345678901234567890123456789801234
SQL> EXEC DBMS_OUTPUT.PUT_LINE (rulerstr (25, 10))
0123456789012345678901234
SQL> EXEC DBMS_OUTPUT.PUT_LINE (rulerstr (25))
1234567890123456789012345
SQL> EXEC DBMS_OUTPUT.PUT_LINE (rulerstr (25, 11))
1234567890123456789012345
```

18-47. Write a package containing a function that returns an index-by table of integers containing the ASCII codes for each character in the specified string.

19

Date Functions

Almost all business applications require dates in one form or another. Often, you have to store the date an order was entered, generate a quarterly sales report, or compute the number of days a bill has gone unpaid. Dates are deceptively complex: they come in dozens of formats, have sophisticated arithmetic rules (quick, what's May 21, 1994 from February 29, 2000?), and, in general, give most developers fits. Fortunately, Oracle has provided a set of functions that make the job much easier. This chapter tests your ability to work with dates in PL/SQL, covering topics such as converting a formatted string into a DATE variable or performing date arithmetic.

Beginner

19-1. What function can you use to move a date forward by six months?

19-2. Write a procedure to display the current date and time so the information looks like this:

```
January 17th, 1999 13:05:44
```

19-3. What function can you use to find the date of the last day in the month for a specified date?

19-4. What function can you use to wipe clean the time component of a date variable?

19-5. Write a line of code that transforms today's date to the first date in the current quarter.

19-6. Write a line of code that calculates the number of whole months between start_date and end_date.

19-7. Write a line of code that moves a date back 18 years.

19-8. What is the default time in a variable declared as type DATE?

19-9. Write a function that returns the number of days left in the current month.

Intermediate

19-10. If you want to know the date of the first Monday in the current month, what function(s) can you use?

19-11. Your server is located in London, but your client-side programs are doing their job in Chicago. Write a function that translates the time component of SYSDATE in the server to the time zone of your users.

19-12. Write a function that returns the first day in the month that contains a specified date.

19-13. Write a line of code that returns the date/timestamp for 9 A.M. on the first day in the twenty-fifth year of the current century.

19-14. "Thirty days hath September..." and if you keep singing, you'll be reminded that January and March both have 31 days. Given that startling new information, what dates are displayed by the following code that moves a date forward by one month using ADD_MONTHS?

```
/* Filename on web page: lastday.sql */
DECLARE
    PROCEDURE forward_1_month (dt IN VARCHAR2) IS
    BEGIN
        DBMS_OUTPUT.PUT_LINE (
            dt || ' -> ' || ADD_MONTHS (dt, 1));
    END;
BEGIN
    forward_1_month ('30-JAN-99');
    forward_1_month ('27-FEB-99');
    forward_1_month ('31-JAN-99');
    forward_1_month ('28-FEB-99');
END;
/
```

Try to figure it out by walking through the code before executing the file!

19-15. Which of the following statements accurately describe the behavior of ADD_MONTHS concerning the last day in the month (in the sentences below, ODT is the original date, and RDT is the resulting date):

a. If ODT is the last day of the month and the resulting month has more days than the original month, RDT is set to the same day number as the original in the resulting month. Otherwise, if ODT is the last day of the month, RDT is the last day of the resulting month.

b. If ODT is the last day of the month or if the resulting month has fewer days than the day component of ODT, RDT is the last day of the resulting month.

c. If ODT is the last day of the month, ADD_MONTHS of 1 sets RDT to the first day of the next month, while a value of −1 sets RDT to the last day of the previous month.

Hint: see 19-14 and its solution.

19-16. Write a database trigger so that before any new employee is inserted into the database, the time that the employee was hired (stored in the hire_date) column is rounded to the nearest hour.

Expert

19-17. Write a function that returns the date of the nearest day named to the specified date, as in:

```
FUNCTION nearestday (
   yourdate IN DATE,
   dayname  IN VARCHAR2)
RETURN DATE;
```

19-18. Write a function to return the number of business days (defined in this exercise as all days that are not Saturdays and Sundays) between two dates. Here is the header:

```
FUNCTION bizdays_between (
   start_date IN DATE, end_date IN DATE)
   RETURN INTEGER;
```

19-19. Enhance the "business days between" function to also subtract from total the number of holidays stored in the following table:

```
CREATE TABLE holiday (dt DATE);
```

19-20. Write a function that returns the *n*th named day in the month in which the specified date is located. Here is the header for such a function:

```
FUNCTION nthday (
   yourdate IN DATE,
   dayname  IN VARCHAR2,
   nthday   IN INTEGER)
RETURN DATE;
```

and here is the expected behavior:

```
SQL> EXEC DBMS_OUTPUT.PUT_LINE(nthday(SYSDATE,'monday',1))
February 1, 1999 00:00:00
SQL> EXEC DBMS_OUTPUT.PUT_LINE(nthday(SYSDATE,'monday',2))
February 8, 1999 00:00:00
SQL> EXEC DBMS_OUTPUT.PUT_LINE(nthday(SYSDATE,'monday',3))
February 15, 1999 00:00:00
SQL> EXEC DBMS_OUTPUT.PUT_LINE(nthday(SYSDATE+30,'monday',5))
March 29, 1999 00:00:00
```

19-21. I discovered recently (March 1999) that the documented maximum allowable date in PL/SQL had changed from the long-standing December 31, 4712. How did I discover this? A visitor to the PL/SQL Pipeline found that he could work with dates well beyond this "limit." He wondered what the actual limit was. Rather than try to find this information in the possibly outdated Oracle documentation, write a PL/SQL block that verifies the maximum date supported in your version of PL/SQL.

19-22. Write an alternative to ADD_MONTHS so the date returned is always on the same day of the month, unless the original day number does not appear in the new month, in which case the last day of the month is returned.

19-23. Oracle does a great job implementing powerful database technology—most of the time. One area where they fall a bit flat, though, concerns the conversion of strings to dates. Amazingly enough, the powerful Oracle RDBMS can understand only a one-date format for conversion purposes. The default format has been "DD-MON-YY" (with obvious Y2K consequences); you can change it, but you're still stuck with only one. That means the following script will blow up, even though anybody with a modicum of intelligence knows what I "mean":

```
/* Filename on web page: dates.sql */
BEGIN
    DBMS_OUTPUT.PUT_LINE (TO_DATE ('1/1'));
    DBMS_OUTPUT.PUT_LINE (TO_DATE ('6/1996'));
    DBMS_OUTPUT.PUT_LINE (TO_DATE ('12-APR-09'));
    DBMS_OUTPUT.PUT_LINE (TO_DATE ('19991205'));
    DBMS_OUTPUT.PUT_LINE (TO_DATE ('1/1/1'));
END;
/
```

Write a replacement for TO_DATE so that this script runs without an error:

```
BEGIN
    DBMS_OUTPUT.PUT_LINE (dt.from_string ('1/1'));
    DBMS_OUTPUT.PUT_LINE (dt.from_string ('6/1996'));
    DBMS_OUTPUT.PUT_LINE (dt.from_string ('12-APR-09'));
    DBMS_OUTPUT.PUT_LINE (dt.from_string ('19991205'));
    DBMS_OUTPUT.PUT_LINE (dt.from_string ('1/1/1'));
END;
/
```

In other words, you don't have to specify a format mask. The program figures out automatically how to convert the string to a date.

Hint: there's a reason for putting the from_string function inside the dt package!

Conversion, Numeric, and Miscellaneous Functions

This chapter tests your ability to work with a grab-bag assortment of functions to compute mathematical equations you studied (and probably have forgotten!) in high school, convert data from one format to another, and perform miscellaneous operations such as fetching environment variables.

Beginner

20-1. What are the only two built-in PL/SQL functions that allow you to pass in a variable number of arguments?

20-2. Complete the following code snippet:

```
/* Print each character in a string */
CREATE OR REPLACE PROCEDURE nvl_test (i_val IN VARCHAR2 DEFAULT NULL)
IS
    str_len NUMBER := <your code here>;
BEGIN
    FOR i IN 1 .. str_len
    LOOP
        DBMS_OUTPUT.put_line (UPPER (SUBSTR (i_val, i, 1)));
    END LOOP;
END;
```

20-3. Complete the following code snippet:

```
/* Set the name of the currently connected user */
BEGIN
    v_user := <your code here>;
```

20-4. What function can you use to obtain a unique identifier for your session?

20-5. What function can you use to convert a ROWID value to a string?

20-6. Complete the following code snippet; the function should return a string consisting of today's date formatted to a four-digit year:

```
CREATE OR REPLACE FUNCTION four_digit_today
   RETURN VARCHAR2
IS
BEGIN
   RETURN <your code here>;
END;
```

20-7. What year number is returned by the following statement?

```
DBMS_OUTPUT.PUT_LINE (TO_CHAR
   (TO_DATE ('10-JAN-19', 'DD-MON-RR'), 'YYYY')_)
```

20-8. To which PL/SQL package do numeric functions (CEIL, COS, EXP, etc.) belong?

    a. DBMS_MATH

    b. DBMS_NUMERIC

    c. DBMS_LOB

    d. DBMS_REAL

    e. None of the above

20-9. What numeric function computes the absolute value of a number?

20-10. What function finds the whole number nearest to a specified number?

    a. FLOOR

    b. CEILING

    c. MOD

    d. ROUND

    e. LOG

Intermediate

20-11. Write a function that returns TRUE if a number is odd.

20-12. Which function returns the error message associated with a particular Oracle error number?

    a. GET_ERROR_MESSAGE

    b. ORA_MSG

    c. ORA_ERROR

    d. SQLERRM

    e. SQLCODE

20-13. Write an exception section to display the current error code and its associated error message.

20-14. Provide the format mask that prints the date "21-MAY-94" in the following formats:

Desired Date	Required Format
May 21, 1994	
05/21/94	
The 21st of May, 1994	
Quarter 2	
Week 21	
Week 3 in Month 05	
The 3rd week in May	

20-15. Suppose you need to add a new value to the "end" of your PL/SQL or index-by table. In other words, if the last row used is 10, you want to put your next value in row 11. Here is one way to do it:

```
IF names_list.LAST IS NULL
THEN
    names_list( 1) := next_name;
ELSE
    names_list (names_list.LAST + 1) := next_name;
END IF;
```

Rewrite the code so that you can do the assignment in a single line.

20-16. Write a function that returns TRUE if the specified string is a valid number, FALSE if it is not. In other words, "123" and "–1e15" are valid numbers, while "123abc" is not.

20-17. What is the output of this program?

```
DECLARE
    v_number NUMBER (10) := ABS (-99);
BEGIN
    IF v_number > -1
    THEN
        DBMS_OUTPUT.put_line ('It''s positive');
    ELSE
        DBMS_OUTPUT.put_line ('It''s negative');
    END IF;
END;
```

20-18. What condition must be added to this code so it displays only every third row?

```
DECLARE
    CURSOR curs_get_numbers IS
    SELECT *
        FROM a_bunch_of_numbers;
BEGIN
    FOR v_number_rec IN curs_get_numbers LOOP
        IF <condition> THEN
            DBMS_OUTPUT.put_line(v_number_rec.number_col1);
        END IF;
    END LOOP;
END;
```

20-19. Suppose you have a table called expenses that contains a column called expense_date and a column called amount. Provide a code snippet to show how you could use the date conversion functions to populate an index-by table with quarterly expense totals.

20-20. What is the output from this code?

```
BEGIN
    FOR number_value IN 1112..1116 LOOP
        FOR round_value IN -2..2 LOOP
            DBMS_OUTPUT.PUT(ROUND(number_value / 100,round_value) || ' ');
        END LOOP;
        DBMS_OUTPUT.PUT_LINE(' ');
    END LOOP;
END;
```

Expert

20-21. How should the format mask be changed in this call to TO_CHAR so that all extra spaces and padded zeros are removed?

```
TO_CHAR (SYSDATE, 'Month DD, YYYY')
```

20-22. What format mask element could you use to validate a date (i.e., raise an exception if a date uses a four-digit year)?

20-23. The built-in TO_DATE function—just like the underlying database itself—can understand only one date format: either the default for the database instance or the "override" format provided in the call to TO_DATE. For example, if the default date mask is MM/DD/YYYY, these calls to TO_DATE work fine:

```
TO_DATE ('1/7/1999')
TO_DATE ('01-07-1999')
TO_DATE ('Jan-19-99', 'MON-DD-RR')
```

But these calls to TO_DATE raise errors:

```
TO_DATE ('Jan-19-99')
TO_DATE ('1999-1-1')
```

Write a replacement smarter version of TO_DATE; the function should accept a single string argument and, if it represents a supported date format, return a date. Your function should support (at minimum) the following date formats:

> MM/DD
> M/DD/YY
> MM/DD/YYYY
> DD-MON
> MON DD, YYYY
> MONTH DD, YYYY

DD-MON-YY

DD-MON-YYYY

MON-DD-YYYY

20-24. Assume that the following data is in a table called a_bunch_of_numbers:

```
number_col1 number_col2
1            99
2            98
3            97
...          ...
100          0
```

Write a query to retrieve rows where the difference between the two columns is less than or equal to 25.

20-25. Professor Twoplus Two needs a function to generate a specific set of numbers for his experiments. He has identified this requirement:

Given a number of length n, return a set of numbers with the last digits sequentially changed to zero. For example, given 1111, return three numbers 1110, 1100, and 1000.

The header for the packaged function is as follows:

```
CREATE OR REPLACE PACKAGE number_manipulation AS

   -- globally declare a collection type
   TYPE v_num_table_type IS TABLE OF NUMBER
      INDEX BY BINARY_INTEGER;

   -- function to generated set of trial numbers
   FUNCTION GEN_TRIAL ( p_number NUMBER )
      RETURN v_num_table_type;

   -- test function; should print out the trial numbers
   PROCEDURE test (i_val IN NUMBER);

END number_manipulation;
```

Write the package body.

20-26. Assuming that the number_col2 column in the table a_bunch_of_numbers contains all whole numbers between 1 and 100, write a query to find the numbers with square roots equal to whole numbers (1, 4, 9, etc.). Use only numeric functions.

21

DBMS_SQL Built-in Package

DBMS_SQL is probably the most flexible and powerful (and potentially danger-ous!) of the built-in packages. By giving you the ability to construct and execute SQL and PL/SQL statements and commands on the fly, DBMS_SQL makes a wide range of applications possible. For example, you can use the package to write your own web-based version of SQL*Plus by allowing users to enter a variety of DML and DDL commands into a browser, or you can build a self-modifying pro-gram that adds or drops PL/SQL components as they are needed. This chapter tests your understanding of this remarkably useful built-in package.

Figure 21-1 shows the flow of DBMS-SQL execution.

Beginner

21-1. What does "dynamic SQL" mean?

21-2. What does "dynamic PL/SQL" mean?

21-3. What are the four different methods of dynamic SQL?

21-4. What is a "placeholder" in a dynamic SQL string?

21-5. What DBMS_SQL program can you use to open a dynamic cursor?

21-6. What DBMS_SQL program can you use to close a dynamic cursor?

21-7. What DBMS_SQL program can you use to parse a dynamic SQL string?

21-8. What DBMS_SQL programs can you use to execute a dynamic cursor?

21-9. What DBMS_SQL programs can you use to fetch rows from a dynamic cursor?

21-10. What DBMS_SQL programs can you use to extract values from columns and variables in a dynamic cursor?

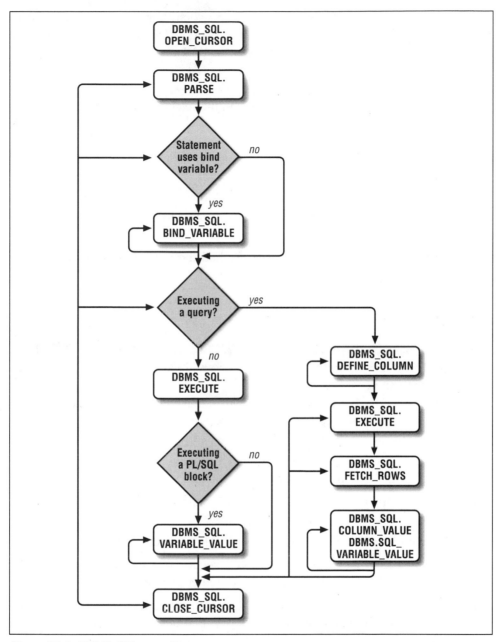

Figure 21-1. DBMS_SQL execution

21-11. How can you include values stored in variables in your own program in the string you are constructing for dynamic execution?

21-12. Put the following steps in the order in which they must be performed to execute a dynamic DML statement (UPDATE, INSERT, DELETE); identify which steps are not needed for dynamic DML.

> Close the cursor.
> Bind any variables into placeholders.
> Extract the value from a column in the fetched row.
> Execute the cursor.
> Define the type of the columns.
> Open the cursor.
> Fetch a row.
> Parse the SQL statement string.

21-13. Write a program to create an index using DBMS_SQL; allow a user to specify the index name, table name, and column name(s).

21-14. How can you tell when you have fetched the last row from a query using DBMS_SQL?

Intermediate

21-15. List each step required to fetch multiple rows from a dynamic SQL query string, and include the name of the DBMS_SQL program or programs that implement those steps.

21-16. When you fetch past the last row with static SQL, you do not get an error; the request is simply ignored. What happens in DBMS_SQL if you try to fetch after the last row was fetched?

21-17. Which program in DBMS_SQL offers similar behavior to the implicit SELECT INTO static query in PL/SQL?

21-18. What happens if DBMS_SQL.EXECUTE_AND_FETCH finds more than one row matching the query's WHERE clause?

21-19. Do you have to call DBMS_SQL.EXECUTE to execute a DDL statement?

21-20. If you call DBMS_SQL.EXECUTE to execute a DDL statement right after you parsed it, is the DDL statement executed twice?

21-21. Does the name of the placeholder in a SQL string need to match the name of the variable that is bound to the placeholder? In other words, will the following code cause a problem?

```
DECLARE
    the_year INTEGER := 1999;
BEGIN
    DBMS_SQL.PARSE (cur,
        'UPDATE laptop SET mhz = 500 WHERE yearnum = :my_year',
        DBMS_SQL.NATIVE);
```

```
        DBMS_SQL.BIND_VARIABLE (cur, 'my_year', the_year);
        ...
     END;
```

21-22. How can you tell if a variable contains a pointer to a valid and open DBMS_SQL cursor?

21-23. Why won't the following block compile in an Oracle Forms or Oracle Reports application module?

```
DECLARE
   cur INTEGER := DBMS_SQL.OPEN_CURSOR;
   rec employee%ROWTYPE;
   fdbk INTEGER;
BEGIN
   DBMS_SQL.PARSE (
      cur,
      'SELECT employee_id, last_name FROM employee ',
      DBMS_SQL.NATIVE);
END;
```

21-24. What is wrong with the following parse call?

```
DECLARE
   cur INTEGER := DBMS_SQL.OPEN_CURSOR;
   rec employee%ROWTYPE;
   fdbk INTEGER;
BEGIN
   DBMS_SQL.PARSE (
      cur,
      'SELECT employee_id, last_name FROM employee ',
      1);
END;
```

21-25. Rewrite the following code to use bind variables instead of concatenation. Can you get rid of all the concatenation? Explain.

```
/* Filename on web page: concat.sp */
CREATE OR REPLACE PROCEDURE updnumval
/* Updates the value of the named columns in all rows
   where employee was hired between start_in and end_in. */
   (col_in IN VARCHAR2,
    start_in IN DATE,
    end_in IN DATE,
    val_in IN NUMBER)
IS
   cur PLS_INTEGER := DBMS_SQL.OPEN_CURSOR;
   fdbk PLS_INTEGER;
BEGIN
   DBMS_SQL.PARSE (cur,
      'UPDATE emp SET ' || col_in || ' = ' || val_in ||
      ' WHERE hiredate BETWEEN ' ||
      ' TO_DATE (''' || TO_CHAR (start_in)  || ''')' ||
      ' AND ' ||
      ' TO_DATE (''' || TO_CHAR (end_in)  || ''')' ,
      DBMS_SQL.NATIVE);
```

```
    fdbk := DBMS_SQL.EXECUTE (cur);
    DBMS_OUTPUT.PUT_LINE ('Rows updated: ' || TO_CHAR (fdbk));
    DBMS_SQL.CLOSE_CURSOR (cur);
END;
/
```

21-26. In most cases, you can choose between concatenation and binding to include your own variable data in a dynamically constructed SQL string. Why would you choose one method over another?

21-27. The following block contains unnecessary code. Which lines can be removed without changing the logical functionality, and perhaps improve the performance a little bit?

```
DECLARE
    cur PLS_INTEGER := DBMS_SQL.OPEN_CURSOR;
BEGIN
    DBMS_SQL.PARSE (cur,
        'SELECT ename FROM emp',
        DBMS_SQL.NATIVE);

    ... execute and fetch ...

    DBMS_SQL.CLOSE_CURSOR (cur);
    cur := DBMS_SQL.OPEN_CURSOR;
    DBMS_SQL.PARSE (cur,
        'UPDATE emp SET sal = sal * 3',
        DBMS_SQL.NATIVE);

    ... execute the update ...

    DBMS_SQL.CLOSE_CURSOR (cur);
END;
```

21-28. How many companies are in the internet_startups table after the following script executes?

```
CREATE TABLE internet_startups (
    name VARCHAR2,
    profit NUMBER);

INSERT INTO internet_startups VALUES (''paperclips4all', -100000;
INSERT INTO internet_startups VALUES ('mytoeclippings.com', -250000000);
COMMIT;

DECLARE
    cur PLS_INTEGER := DBMS_SQL.OPEN_CURSOR;
BEGIN
    DELETE FROM internet_startups;

    DBMS_SQL.PARSE (cur, 'DROP TABLE common_sense', DBMS_SQL.NATIVE);
    ROLLBACK;
    DBMS_SQL.CLOSE_CURSOR (cur);
END;
```

21-29. Here is an exercise from the "real world." I encountered the following procedure, which consists of nothing more than a seemingly endless IF statement, at an insurance company. The program was often too large to even compile! How can you use DBMS_SQL to reduce significantly the code volume in the program?

```
PROCEDURE process_lineitem (line_in IN INTEGER)
IS
BEGIN
   IF line_in = 1
     THEN
        process_line1;

   ELSIF line_in = 2
     THEN
        process_line2;
   ...
   ELSIF line_in = 277
     THEN
        process_line277;
   ...
   ELSIF line_in = 2045
   THEN
        process_line2045;
   END IF;
END;
```

21-30. Which program can you use to extract a value (say, an OUT argument) from a dynamically constructed and executed PL/SQL block?

21-31. Write a program to update any numeric column in the employee table, where the user specifies the column name, new value, and a variable WHERE clause.

21-32. What is wrong with this code?

```
CREATE OR REPLACE PACKAGE BODY employee_pkg
IS
    TYPE list_tabtype IS TABLE OF advertisers.name
        INDEX BY BINARY_INTEGER;

    PROCEDURE make_it_safe (
       list IN list_tabtype
       )
    IS
       list_row PLS_INTEGER := list.FIRST;
       cursor_id PLS_INTEGER;
       exec_stat PLS_INTEGER;
    BEGIN
       LOOP
          EXIT WHEN list_row IS NULL;
          cursor_id := DBMS_SQL.OPEN_CURSOR;
```

```
                    DBMS_SQL.PARSE(
                        cursor_id,
                        'DELETE negativity
                           FROM media_coverage
                           WHERE company_mentioned =  ' || list(list_row),
                        DBMS_SQL.NATIVE);

                    exec_stat := DBMS_SQL.EXECUTE(cursor_id);
                    list_row := list.NEXT (list_row);
                END LOOP;
                DBMS_SQL.CLOSE_CURSOR(cursor_id);
            END make_it_safe;
        END employee_pkg;
```

21-33. What is the scope of a DBMS_SQL cursor? To help you answer that question, in the following block of code, how many cursors (static or dynamic) are opened? How many are closed?

```
DECLARE
    cursor_id PLS_INTEGER := DBMS_SQL.OPEN_CURSOR;
    CURSOR all_employees IS
        SELECT * FROM employee;
    emp_rec all_employees%ROWTYPE;

BEGIN
    OPEN all_employees;
    FETCH all_employees INTO emp_rec;
    OPEN department_pkg.all_departments;
    cursor_id := DBMS_SQL.OPEN_CURSOR;

    DBMS_SQL.PARSE (
        cursor_id,
        'DROP TABLE employee',
        DBMS_SQL.NATIVE);
END;
```

21-34. Write a procedure to display the last_name and employee_id columns for each row in the employee table identified by a WHERE clause that is passed in as an argument.

21-35. What happens if you try to close an already closed dynamic SQL cursor? How can you keep that from happening?

21-36. When the following block of code is run, the following error occurs.

```
DECLARE
    cur PLS_INTEGER := DBMS_SQL.OPEN_CURSOR;
BEGIN
    DBMS_SQL.PARSE (cur,
        'SELECT ename FROM emp WHER deptno = 10',
        DBMS_SQL.NATIVE);
END;

DECLARE
    *
```

```
ERROR at line 1:
ORA-00933: SQL command not properly ended
ORA-06512: at "SYS.DBMS_SYS_SQL", line 491
ORA-06512: at "SYS.DBMS_SQL", line 32
```

It is very difficult to understand from the resulting unhandled exception the cause of the problem (picture this block embedded in a sizable application filled with lots of dynamic SQL; how could you find the troublemaker?). How can you change the block to improve your ability to debug the dynamic SQL?

21-37. How can you find out what type of SQL statement was last executed by DBMS_SQL in your session?

21-38. Which DBMS_SQL program tells you how many rows have been fetched from a dynamic SQL cursor?

21-39. Write a "run DDL" program that executes (or tries to execute) any DDL statement passed to it.

21-40. Suppose that the "run DDL" program requested in 21-39 was stored in a central code repository schema, "ALLCODE" (which has the standard CONNECT and RESOURCE privileges assigned to it), and that EXECUTE authority was granted to all users as follows:

```
GRANT EXECUTE ON runDDL TO PUBLIC;
```

I then connect to SCOTT. I create a table without any trouble using the CREATE TABLE command in SQL*Plus. But then I need to do the same thing inside a stored procedure, so I use runDDL:

```
CREATE OR REPLACE myproc
IS
BEGIN
   /* Create a "temporary" table. */
   allcode.runDDL ('CREATE TABLE temp (temp VARCHAR2(2000))');
   ... do temporary things with it ...
END;
/
```

This procedure compiles without any errors, but when I try to run myproc in SCOTT, I get this error:

```
SQL> EXEC allcode.runddl (
   'CREATE TABLE scott.newtemp (mycol DATE)');
```

```
ORA-01031: insufficient privileges
```

Why do I get this error? I seemed to have sufficient privileges to create a table in my SCOTT schema.

21-41. Write a function that returns the number of rows in the specified table. Here is the header for the procedure:

```
FUNCTION tabcount (
   sch IN VARCHAR2,
```

```
      tab IN VARCHAR2)
      RETURN INTEGER;
```

21-42. Enhance the tabcount function to allow the user to supply an optional and dynamic WHERE clause.

Expert

21-43. Which of the following actions cannot be performed with DBMS_SQL in a stored procedure:

     a. Create a table by selecting rows from another existing table.

     b. Set a role by executing the ALTER SESSION SET ROLE DDL statement.

     c. Create a new user.

     d. Set the value of a column to NULL for all rows.

     e. Declare a cursor variable based on a REF CURSOR type and retrieve that variable's value.

     f. Truncate a table.

     g. Connect to another database session with the CONNECT statement.

21-44. Write a program that accepts the name of a global variable defined in a package specification and a value, and assigns that value to the variable.

21-45. Now that you've built a dynamic assignment program, let's use it to modify the value of a local variable. In the following block, for example, You want to fill up a PL/SQL table with a variety of strings:

```
DECLARE
    TYPE str_t IS TABLE OF VARCHAR2(100) INDEX BY BINARY_INTEGER;
    greetings str_t;
BEGIN
    FOR yearnum IN 1 .. 10
    LOOP
        assign (
            ' Welcome to Year ' || TO_CHAR (yearnum),
            'greetings(' || TO_CHAR(yearnum) || ')');
    END LOOP;
END;
```

But when you run this code, you get the following error:

```
PLS-00201: identifier 'GREETINGS' must be declared
```

Why can't it recognize the greetings table, even though it is declared right in the block?

21-46. 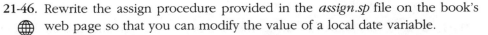 Rewrite the assign procedure provided in the *assign.sp* file on the book's web page so that you can modify the value of a local date variable.

21-47. What programs are available in DBMS_SQL to transfer a LONG value (with more than 32 KB) from a database table to a PL/SQL data structure?

21-48. Write a program that transfers a LONG value from any column in any database table to an index-by table.

21-49. You have a SQL query string that was generated by a frontend application, and it is enormous—about 40 KB. How can you parse this query with DBMS_SQL?

21-50. Which Oracle8 DBMS_SQL program can you call to get information about the various columns associated with a dynamic SQL query?

21-51. Use the DBMS_SQL.DESCRIBE_COLUMNS procedure to build a generic utility that displays the column information for any cursor passed to it.

21-52. You create two procedures that make sure all employees are earning at least the minimum salary. First, there's an update_salary procedure:

```
/* Filename on web page: nocount.sp */
CREATE OR REPLACE PROCEDURE update_salary (
    empid_in IN INTEGER, newsal_in IN NUMBER)
IS
    updcur INTEGER := DBMS_SQL.OPEN_CURSOR;
    fdbk INTEGER;
BEGIN
    DBMS_SQL.PARSE (updcur,
        'UPDATE employee SET salary = GREATEST (:minsal, salary)
          WHERE employee_id = :empid',
        DBMS_SQL.NATIVE);
    DBMS_SQL.BIND_VARIABLE (updcur, 'empid', empid_in);
    DBMS_SQL.BIND_VARIABLE (updcur, 'minsal', newsal_in);
    fdbk := DBMS_SQL.EXECUTE (updcur);
    DBMS_SQL.CLOSE_CURSOR (updcur);
END;
/
```

Then there's the ensure_minsal procedure, which identifies a set of employee records through a dynamic WHERE clause, and then calls update_salary:

```
/* Filename on web page: nocount.sp */
CREATE OR REPLACE PROCEDURE ensure_minsal (
    minsal_in IN NUMBER, where_in IN VARCHAR2 := NULL)
IS
    cur INTEGER := DBMS_SQL.OPEN_CURSOR;
    rec employee%ROWTYPE;
    fdbk INTEGER;
BEGIN
    DBMS_SQL.PARSE (cur,
        'SELECT employee_id, salary FROM employee
          WHERE ' || NVL (where_in, '1=1'),
        DBMS_SQL.NATIVE);

    DBMS_SQL.DEFINE_COLUMN (cur, 1, 1);
    DBMS_SQL.DEFINE_COLUMN (cur, 2, 1);
```

```
      fdbk := DBMS_SQL.EXECUTE (cur);
      LOOP
         /* Exit when number of rows fetched is > 10 or
            we are done. */
         EXIT WHEN DBMS_SQL.LAST_ROW_COUNT > 10 OR
                  DBMS_SQL.FETCH_ROWS (cur) = 0;

         /* Get column information */
         DBMS_SQL.COLUMN_VALUE (cur, 1, rec.employee_id);
         DBMS_SQL.COLUMN_VALUE (cur, 2, rec.salary);

         /* Get everyone to the minimum */
         update_salary (rec.employee_id, minsal_in);
         DBMS_OUTPUT.PUT_LINE ('Updated salary for ' ||
            rec.employee_id);
      END LOOP;

      DBMS_SQL.CLOSE_CURSOR (cur);
END;
/
```

Notice that there's a "break" in the code: you don't want to update the salary for more than 10 employees with each execution of the program:

```
EXIT WHEN DBMS_SQL.LAST_ROW_COUNT > 10 OR
          DBMS_SQL.FETCH_ROWS (cur) = 0;
```

When you run this program, however, it updates all the rows in the employee table; it doesn't stop after 10. Why is that? And how can you fix the program so that it stops after 10 rows processed?

21-53. What new features have been added to DBMS_SQL in Oracle8 to speed up the performance of processing multiple rows of information?

21-54. Write a program to perform a bulk update of salaries for employees, providing one list or table of employee names and another table of salaries.

21-55. Write a program to query and display the last_name and hire_date of all rows in the employee table specified by a WHERE clause supplied as an argument to the procedure. Use bulk binding so that you only need to fetch a single time.

21-56. Write a single function that can return the aggregate value for the specified function (MIN, MAX, AVG, SUM, COUNT) for any given table, column, and WHERE clause.

22

DBMS_PIPE Built-in Package

A *pipe* is a named communication channel that allows different database sessions to communicate. The basic logic of pipe-based applications is fairly straightforward (it's illustrated in Figure 22-1):

1. Program A creates a pipe and assigns it a name (it creates the data structure in the middle box in the figure).

2. Program B packs, or loads, a message into a private buffer, which it then sends out over the pipe (left side of the figure).

3. Program C, which is monitoring the pipe, sees the new message arrive and unpacks it into a private buffer; program C then processes the message it received from program B (right side of the figure).

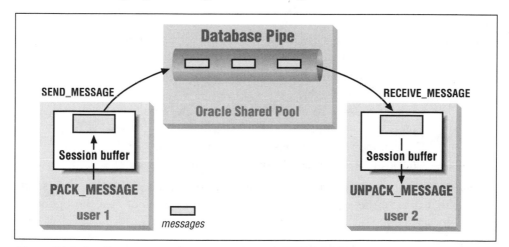

Figure 22-1. Sending messages between sessions via DBMS_PIPE

The advantage of pipes is that they allow programs A, B, and C (as well as D, E, and F) to communicate independently across different sessions outside of their respective transactions. Without pipes (or the Advanced Queuing package, Oracle's asynchronous messaging package), we might resort to message tables to achieve this sort of intersession communication. Program B would INSERT and then COMMIT—possibly interfering with the current transaction—a message into the table, and program C would SELECT the new message. The pipe eliminates the COMMIT and, since it resides in memory, is much faster than physically writing messages to (and reading messages from) a table.

This chapter tests your ability to use DBMS_PIPE, the built-in package for developing pipe-based applications.

Beginner

22-1. Do you have to issue a COMMIT in your program to send or receive messages via database pipes?

22-2. Place the following steps involved in sending a message through a publicly accessible pipe in the proper order. Remove any steps that are not required.

> Send the message.
> Check to make sure the pipe exists.
> Pack data into the message buffer.
> Check the status of the send operation.
> Convert all numeric and date information to VARCHAR2 before
>   packing it into the message buffer.
> Create the pipe.

22-3. Place the following steps involved in receiving a message in the proper order. Remove any steps that are not required.

> Check to make sure the pipe exists.
> Receive the message.
> Send a "message received" confirmation message back on the same
>   pipe.
> Unpack individual packets of data from the message buffer.
> Check the status of the receive operation.

22-4. Write a procedure that accepts the name of a pipe and a date and sends that date to the pipe, waiting no more than one minute for the operation to succeed.

22-5. Write a function that accepts the name of a pipe and returns the single string that is the next message in that pipe (an assumption of the program, not a necessity). Don't wait more than 10 seconds to receive the message.

22-6. Which of the following are valid applications for DBMS_PIPE:

    a. Build a home-grown debugger that allows you to watch what is happening in your program before the program completes.

    b. Schedule jobs to run at certain times during the day.

    c. Communicate with the underlying operating system of the database server (run shell scripts in Unix, for example).

    d. Store sensitive information retained during database instance "downtime" for maintenance.

    e. Instead of running three independent jobs in sequence, run them all simultaneously.

    f. Whenever a new row is inserted successfully into a table, send out a message to the DBA.

    g. Coordinate the transaction activity in three distributed databases.

22-7. What DBMS_PIPE program can you call to remove a pipe from shared memory?

22-8. What DBMS_PIPE program can you call to remove all messages from a specified pipe?

Intermediate

22-9. What is the maximum length of a pipe name?

22-10. Which of the following statements are true, and which are false?

    a. A DBMS_PIPE message consists of a single VARCHAR2 string.

    b. The maximum size of a pipe is 2 GB.

    c. The maximum size of a message is 4 KB.

    d. The default wait time for a send or receive operation is 1,000 days (86,400,000 seconds).

    e. You can send a LONG value through a database pipe.

    f. If a database pipe is "private," you must provide a password to read/write the contents of the pipe.

    g. Once you read a message from a pipe, that information is removed from the pipe.

    h. Each session maintains a separate message buffer for each of its pipes.

22-11. Write a block of code to create a private pipe named "national_security" with an initial size of 2 MB.

22-12. Why might you want to call DBMS_PIPE.RESET_BUFFER before packing your message for sending?

22-13. You send a message to a pipe as follows:

```
DECLARE
    stat INTEGER;
BEGIN
    DBMS_PIPE.PACK_MESSAGE (SYSDATE);
    stat := DBMS_PIPE.SEND_MESSAGE ('when');
END;
```

But when you try to read the contents of the pipe with the following block, you get an error. What are you doing wrong?

```
DECLARE
    stat INTEGER;
BEGIN
    stat := DBMS_PIPE.RECEIVE_MESSAGE ('when');
    DBMS_PIPE.UNPACK_MESSAGE (stat);
END;
```

22-14. Write a block of code that sets up an infinite loop to receive a single numeric value from a pipe named "production"; specify that you are willing to wait up to 10 minutes for a message to appear in the pipe. If the message is not received successfully, display an error message. Otherwise, call the analyze_production procedure and pass the number to it.

22-15. Write a function that creates a private pipe with a name that is unique across all sessions in the database and returns that name. Then test that pipe by sending and receiving the current date/time as the message.

22-16. Use a FOR loop to pack SYSDATE and the nine days after that into a message and send it to the "future" pipe.

22-17. Write a function that reads a message from the "impeachment" pipe (waiting no more than 30 days) and then unpacks three pieces of information from the message in this order: the date on which President Clinton's trial for impeachment began in the Senate, the number of millions of tax dollars spent on the impeachment trial, and the name of the U.S. Representative (a.k.a., "house manager") who headed up the prosecution at the trial. Return this information in a programmer-defined record.

22-18. Write a block of code that reads all the messages from the "encrypted_fbi_files" pipe and, for each message, unpacks the single RAW value, converts it to hexadecimal format, and then displays the hex data.

Expert

22-19. Write a package that manages communication through a private pipe named "invasions". Each message in the pipe contains the information as specified by the following query:

```
SELECT country, date_of_invasion, people_killed
  FROM invasions
 WHERE (invader IN ('USA', 'CHINA', 'GERMANY', 'SOVIET UNION')
   AND date_of_invasion > '01-JAN-1900';
```

Features of this package should include the following:

- The user never specifies or knows the name of the pipe; it is hidden to avoid any spelling mistakes and to ensure consistency.
- It create the pipe automatically when a session tries to use the pipe.
- The list is a long one (including, for example, Grenada, Poland, Nicaragua, Vietnam, Chile, France, Tibet, Norway, El Salvador, and Iraq), so set the initial pipe size to at least 2 MB.
- It waits up to 10 seconds to get or send the information.

Here is the package specification; you write the body:

```
/* Filename on web page: invasions.pkg */
CREATE OR REPLACE PACKAGE invasion
IS
    TYPE inv_rectype IS RECORD (
       country IN invasions.country%TYPE,
       date_of_invasion invasions.date_of_invasion%TYPE,
       people_killed invasions.people_killed%TYPE
       );

    PROCEDURE sendinfo (
       country IN VARCHAR2,
       date_of_invasion DATE,
       people_killed NUMBER
       );

    PROCEDURE sendinfo (rec IN inv_rectype);

    FUNCTION nextinfo RETURN inv_rectype;
END;
/
```

22-20. How can you can obtain a list of all the currently defined database pipes to which you have access?

22-21. Write a "pipe maintenance" package containing one procedure to purge the contents of those accessible pipes specified by the string parameter and another procedure to remove any accessible pipe whose name is like a specified string. Here is the package specification; you write the body:

```
/* Filename on web page: pipemnt.pkg */
CREATE OR REPLACE PACKAGE pipemaint
/* Original version by John Beresniewicz */
AS
    PROCEDURE purge_pipes (nm IN VARCHAR2);
    PROCEDURE remove_pipes (nm IN VARCHAR2);
END pipemaint;
/
```

22-22. Write a procedure that forwards a message from one pipe to another without unpacking and repacking the message contents.

22-23. The following scenario applies to this problem and the rest of the problems in this chapter.

These exercises are drawn from the research into DBMS_PIPE as performed by John Beresniewicz and published in *Oracle Built-in Packages*.

Most of the time when you work with database pipes you know the structure of the packets in the message. It may be composed of three dates and a string, or a number, a string, and a raw. What if you want or need to work under more generic circumstances. Specifically, what if you don't know the structure of the message?

Let's explore the kind of code you need to write to handle this situation. When we are done, you will have (let's hope) built a package that contains programs allowing you to:

- Dump the contents of your message buffer (containing the message from any pipe) into an index-by table.

- Retrieve the message that contains a specified string or other value from the specified pipe (a kind of "INSTR" for pipes).

But let's take it a step at a time. If you don't know in advance how many packets and the datatypes of those packets in a pipe's message, then:

a. What DBMS_PIPE program can be used to get that information?

b. Use that program to build a function that returns the date in the next packet of your session's message buffer or NULL if the next packet is not of date type.

c. What PL/SQL data structure can be used to hold the individual packets of information when you unpack them?

22-24. Write a procedure that unpacks the session's message buffer into an index-by table with the structure you defined in 22-23. Here is the header for that procedure (to be defined inside the dbpipe package, or whatever your package is called):

```
CREATE OR REPLACE PACKAGE dbpipe
IS
    ... definition of message_tbltype as shown earlier ...

    PROCEDURE unpack_to_tbl (tbl_out IN OUT message_tbltype);
END;
/
```

22-25. Now let's see how that generic unpack program might be put to use. Write a function to perform an "INSTR" type of action on the contents of a database pipe. This function accepts a pipe name, the nth packet in which to search, and the value (string, date, or number) for which you are looking. The function then returns all the packets for the message that contains the value. Here are the headers for the function (again, defined within the dbpipe package for reasons that should be clear):

```
CREATE OR REPLACE dbpipe
IS
    ... all the other stuff already covered ...

    FUNCTION msgwith (
        pipename IN VARCHAR2,
        nthpacket IN INTEGER,
        matchon IN VARCHAR2)
    RETURN message_tbltype;

    FUNCTION msgwith (
        pipename IN VARCHAR2,
        nthpacket IN INTEGER,
        matchon IN DATE)
    RETURN message_tbltype;

    FUNCTION msgwith (
        pipename IN VARCHAR2,
        nthpacket IN INTEGER,
        matchon IN NUMBER)
    RETURN message_tbltype;
END;
```

They are overloaded so that you can pass a string, date, or number and have it do the appropriate search. You can add your own overloadings for RAW and ROWID!

23

DBMS_OUTPUT
Built-in Package

This chapter tests your understanding of DBMS_OUTPUT, the built-in package that allows you to display messages to your session's standard output device.

Beginner

23-1. Before developers had DBMS_OUTPUT, how did they obtain information about the activity that had taken place inside their code?

23-2. DBMS_OUTPUT has a buffer or memory area defined inside the package that holds the data you want displayed until the time comes to "flush" it to the screen. What is the maximum size of the buffer for any single PL/SQL block execution? What are the different types of information you can put in the buffer?

23-3. Write a "Hello World" procedure that puts into the DBMS_OUTPUT buffer (and eventually displays on the screen) the string "hello world" followed by a newline character.

23-4. How do you enable output from the DBMS_OUTPUT package?

23-5. How do you enable DBMS_OUTPUT in your SQL*Plus session?

23-6. How can you flush the DBMS_OUTPUT buffer and turn off output from this package?

23-7. What is the default size of the DBMS_OUTPUT buffer in SQL*Plus?

23-8. How do you minimize the chance of hitting the buffer overflow error when working with DBMS_OUTPUT in SQL*Plus?

23-9. Write a procedure to display the current date and time on two different lines.

23-10. Write a procedure to display the last_name and salary of each person in the employee table.

Intermediate

23-11. Explain the output displayed in the following session in SQL*Plus:

```
SQL> SET SERVEROUTPUT ON
SQL> EXEC DBMS_OUTPUT.PUT_LINE (
    '    Where oh where did my spaces go?');
Where oh where did my spaces go?
```

23-12. Enable DBMS_OUTPUT in your SQL*Plus session with a buffer size of 500,000 bytes, request that leading spaces and blank lines not be ignored, and also request that output from the package be wrapped at the SQL*Plus line length.

23-13. What variation of the SET SERVEROUTPUT statement allows you to display the DBMS_OUTPUT buffer within the SQL*Plus line length, but doesn't break words?

23-14. What variation of the SET SERVEROUTPUT statement allows you to display the DBMS_OUTPUT buffer, but truncates any text that exceeds the SQL*Plus line length?

23-15. What do you see on the screen when you execute this block, and why do you see it?

```
DECLARE
    oracle_consultant_egosize INTEGER := 10000000;
    ego_too_big BOOLEAN;
BEGIN
    ego_too_big := oracle_consultant_egosize > 500;
    DBMS_OUTPUT.PUT_LINE (ego_too_big);
END;
```

23-16. What do you see on the screen when you execute this block, and why do you see it?

```
BEGIN
    DBMS_OUTPUT.PUT_LINE (
        RPAD (USER, 2000, ' is connected as ' || USER);
END;
```

23-17. Suppose you are working in an environment that does not automatically flush the DBMS_OUTPUT buffer to the screen. What DBMS_OUTPUT program can you use to extract that data into your own data structure?

23-18. Write a procedure that extends DBMS_OUTPUT.PUT_LINE functionality to the Boolean datatype.

23-19. Explain the following behavior in SQL*Plus:

```
SQL> SET SERVEROUTPUT ON SIZE 1000000
SQL> EXEC DBMS_OUTPUT.PUT_LINE (SYSDATE);
20-JAN-99
```

```
SQL> CONNECT SCOTT/TIGER
Connected
SQL> EXEC DBMS_OUTPUT.PUT_LINE (SYSDATE);
SQL>
```

In other words: you "SET SERVEROUTPUT ON," but the second time
DBMS_OUTPUT.PUT_LINE is called, it doesn't display anything. Why not?

Expert

23-20. Write a procedure called println that allows a developer to display with
DBMS_OUTPUT.PUT_LINE strings containing up to 32,767 bytes (32K, the
maximum size of a VARCHAR2 variable in PL/SQL).

23-21. Enhance the procedure in 23-20 to automatically expand the DBMS_OUT-
PUT buffer size to the maximum if a call to DBMS_OUTPUT.PUT_LINE
causes the current buffer size to be exceeded.

23-22. Create a package based on the println procedure so that you can instead
call print.ln and pass a particular type of value (string, date, number, or
Boolean) and see the results. Here is the specification for that package:

```
CREATE OR REPLACE PACKAGE print
IS
    PROCEDURE ln (val IN VARCHAR2);
    PROCEDURE ln (val IN DATE);
    PROCEDURE ln (val IN NUMBER);
    PROCEDURE ln (val IN BOOLEAN);
END print;
/
```

23-23. Why does the PRAGMA RESTRICT_REFERENCES for DBMS_OUTPUT.
PUT_LINE assert only WNDS and RNDS?

23-24. As of Oracle 7.3.4 and Oracle 8.0.4, you can now call DBMS_OUTPUT
and DBMS_PIPE from within functions, which are then called from within
SQL. This allows you to build a trace feature into your SQL. The following function, for example, uses DBMS_OUTPUT.PUT_LINE to display the
ROWID of each row touched by a query:

```
/* Filename on web page: traceit.sf */
CREATE OR REPLACE FUNCTION traceit (
    tab IN VARCHAR2,
    rowid_in IN ROWID)
    RETURN INTEGER
IS
BEGIN
    DBMS_OUTPUT.PUT_LINE (
      tab ||
      '-' ||
      ROWIDTOCHAR (rowid_in));
```

```
    RETURN 0;
END;
/
```

This function returns a "dummy" value of zero; it has to be a function to
be callable directly in SQL, but its return value is irrelevant. You can then
use this function inside a query as follows, directly in SQL*Plus:

```
SQL> SELECT ename, traceit ('emp', ROWID) FROM emp;
```

If you run this query on the standard demo emp table, you see this:

```
ENAME       TRACEIT('EMP',ROWID)
---------- --------------------
SMITH                        0
ALLEN                        0
WARD                         0
JONES                        0
MARTIN                       0
BLAKE                        0
CLARK                        0
SCOTT                        0
KING                         0
TURNER                       0
ADAMS                        0
JAMES                        0
FORD                         0
MILLER                       0
```

Well, that's odd...where is the trace information?

23-25. What is the first row used in the PL/SQL table populated by a call to
DBMS_OUTPUT.GET_LINES?

23-26. Suppose that you need to display more than 1 million bytes of information through DBMS_OUTPUT. Build a mechanism in PL/SQL for buffering
as much as 50 MB of information in your session without raising any
exceptions.

23-27. Suppose you take the following steps:

1. You open two different SQL*Plus sessions connected to SCOTT and
SET SERVEROUTPUT on in both.

2. In session A, you compile the xbuff package shown in 23-26.

3. In session B, you run the *xbuff.tst* script.

4. In session A, you recompile the xbuff package.

5. In session B, you then take the steps shown next and get the displayed behavior:

```
SQL> EXEC DBMS_OUTPUT.PUT_LINE (SYSDATE);
10-MAR-99
SQL> @xbuff.tst
ERROR at line 1:
ORA-04068: existing state of packages has been discarded
```

```
ORA-04061: existing state of package "SCOTT.XBUFF" has been invalidated
ORA-04065: not executed, altered or dropped package "SCOTT.XBUFF"
ORA-06508: PL/SQL: could not find program unit being called
SQL> EXEC DBMS_OUTPUT.PUT_LINE (SYSDATE);
SQL>
```

Explain the following:

- Why do you get the error?

- Why does the second call to DBMS_OUTPUT.PUT_LINE display absolutely nothing?

24

UTL_FILE Built-in Package

The UTL_FILE package, available in PL/SQL Version 2.3 and later, allows PL/SQL programs to read and write operating-system files. For example, you can use PL/SQL to create text-based reports that you can send as an email or view over the Web. This chapter tests your ability to establish file and directory privileges and use UTL_FILE to read and write operating-system files.

Beginner

24-1. Before using UTL_FILE in your PL/SQL programs, what changes do you have to make to your instance parameter initialization file (your *INIT.ORA* file)? Can you read and/or write files in any directory on your database server?

24-2. Suppose you want to enable read/write access on these three directories:

```
/tmp
/app/datafiles
/app/datafiles/q1
```

Which of the following sets of entries in the initialization file will successfully enable those directories?

a. `utl_file_dir = /tmp;/app/datafiles;/app/datafiles/q1`

b. `utl_file_dir = /tmp`
   `utl_file_dir = /app/datafiles/*`

c. `utl_file_dir = /tmp`
   `utl_file_dir = /app/datafiles`
   `utl_file_dir = /app/datafiles/q1`

d. `utl_file_dir = '/tmp'`
   `utl_file_dir = '/app/datafiles'`
   `utl_file_dir = '/app/datafiles/q1'`

```
e. utl_file_dir = /tmp/
   utl_file_dir = /app/datafiles/
   utl_file_dir = /app/datafiles/q1/
```

24-3. How can you specify that you want to read/write in any directory on the server? Under what circumstances would you use this setting?

24-4. How can you specify that you want to read/write in the current directory for your session, regardless of that particularly location?

24-5. Can you read and write files on your client-side computer with UTL_FILE?

24-6. What is the maximum-sized line you can read/write using UTL_FILE?

24-7. Which of the following exceptions are defined in UTL_FILE or raised by UTL_FILE, and which are not?

    a. UTL_FILE.INVALID_PATH

    b. NO_DATA_FOUND

    c. TOO_MANY_ROWS

    d. UTL_FILE.FILE_ALREADY_OPEN

    e. UTL_FILE.INVALID_OPERATION

24-8. To open a file, you call UTL_FILE.FOPEN. Which of the following uses of this program are valid, and which are invalid?

```
a. BEGIN
       UTL_FILE.FOPEN (
           'c:\temp\lotsa_data.txt', 'READ');
b. DECLARE
       myfile INTEGER;
   BEGIN
       myfile := UTL_FILE.FOPEN (
           'c:\temp\lotsa_data.txt', 'READWRITE');
c. DECLARE
       myfile UTL_FILE.FILE_TYPE;
   BEGIN
       myfile := UTL_FILE.FOPEN (
           'c:\temp', 'lotsa_data.txt', 'R');
d. DECLARE
       fname VARCHAR2(100) := 'lotsa_data.txt';
       myfile UTL_FILE.FILE_TYPE := UTL_FILE.FOPEN (
           'c:\temp', fname, 'R');
   BEGIN
```

24-9. Write a procedure that opens a file to read it (specified by location and name) and returns (through IN/OUT parameters) the handle to the file and a status flag indicating whether the file was opened successfully.

24-10. How can you close all files that are open in your session? Why might you want to do this?

24-11. What are the differences between UTL_FILE.PUT, UTL_FILE.PUTF, UTL_FILE.PUT_LINE, and UTL_FILE.NEW_LINE?

24-12. What program do you call to read the next line in a file?

Intermediate

24-13. Which of the following actions are not possible with UTL_FILE?

    a. Read sequentially the contents of a server-side file.

    b. Append text to the end of an existing file.

    c. Read from a "random" location in a file.

    d. Delete a file.

    e. Create a new file and write text to it.

    f. Copy a file.

    g. Move a file to a different location.

    h. Change the access privileges on a file.

    i. Obtain the number of bytes in a file without reading the entire file.

24-14. What is displayed in your SQL*Plus session when the following program is run (assume that UTL_FILE has the necessary privileges to read the file)?

```
DECLARE
    fid UTL_FILE.FILE_TYPE :=
        UTL_FILE.FOPEN ('/tmp', 'twolines.txt', 'R');
    line VARCHAR2(2000);
BEGIN
    LOOP
        UTL_FILE.GET_LINE (fid, line);
        DBMS_OUTPUT.PUT_LINE (line);
    END LOOP;
END;
```

Here are the contents of the data file that is read:

```
I am not a very large file, really I consist
of nothing more than two lines.
```

24-15. Write a procedure to display the contents of the specified file to standard output (usually your screen). Make sure you don't leave a file open if an error occurs.

24-16. What is wrong with the following code?

```
CREATE TYPE string_list_t IS TABLE OF VARCHAR2(255);
/

1 CREATE OR REPLACE PROGRAM nest2file (file IN VARCHAR2,
2     list IN string_list_t%TYPE)
3 /* Move contents of nested table to file. */
4 IS
5     fid UTL_FILE.FILE_TYPE := UTL_FILE.FOPEN (file, 'R');
```

```
 6    line VARCHAR2(100);
 7    linenum INTEGER;
 8 BEGIN
 9    FOR linenum IN list.LAST .. list.FIRST
10    LOOP
11       line := list(linenum);
12       UTL_FILE.WRITE_LINE (line);
13       EXIT WHEN linenum = list.FIRST;
14    END LOOP;
15 END;
16 /
```

24-17. Rewrite the awfully written program in 24-16 to get rid of its problems.

24-18. Write a procedure to transfer the last_name, hire_date, and salary for each row of the employee table to the specified file, using commas to delimit each column's data.

24-19. When you write a file using UTL_FILE, is that file owned by your user process or by the Oracle process?

24-20. Write a procedure that uses a single call to a UTL_FILE "put" procedure to write the following text to a file:

```
"Freedom's just another word
for working on your ***"
-- Dave Lippman
```

where *** is a string that is provided through the parameter list of the procedure, whose header is:

```
PROCEDURE what_is_freedom (
   fid IN UTL_FILE.FILE_TYPE,
   it_is IN VARCHAR2);
```

24-21. How can you determine whether a file is already open?

24-22. What is the maximum number of files you can have open in a single Oracle session?

24-23. How many different ways can you use UTL_FILE programs to insert into a file the string "I LUV ORACLE" followed by a newline character?

24-24. Write a procedure that returns the next line of an already-opened file and also returns a Boolean flag indicating whether you have reached the end-of-file. Is there any advantage to using this procedure rather than the built-in UTL_FILE.GET_LINE?

24-25. If you try to append to a file with a call to FOPEN as follows:

```
   fid := UTL_FILE.FOPEN (mydir, myfile, 'A');
```

and the file does not exist, what happens?

24-26. Write a substitute for (or encapsulation of) FOPEN that allows developers to not have to worry about whether they are appending to an existing file or a new file.

24-27. What happens if you try to close a file that has already been closed?

24-28. There are times when a developer might like to create a file to use as a flag indicating that a certain action is taking place—or not taking place. Write a program that creates a file with the specified location and name, but that does not require the user to declare a FILE_TYPE record and perform each of the necessary steps himself.

Expert

24-29. What information is displayed on the screen when you run this code (assume that you have UTL_FILE privileges on the *c:\temp* directory):

```
DECLARE
    fid UTL_FILE.FILE_TYPE :=
        UTL_FILE.FOPEN ('c:\temp', 'new.txt', 'W');
    line VARCHAR2(2000);
BEGIN
    fid.id := NULL;
    IF UTL_FILE.IS_OPEN (fid)
    THEN
        DBMS_OUTPUT.PUT_LINE ('Seems open to me...');
    ELSE
        DBMS_OUTPUT.PUT_LINE ('Who closed my file?');
    END IF;
END;
/
```

24-30. Create a procedure that allows you to write lines of arbitrary length (even exceeding the maximum allowed in UTL_FILE) to a file.

24-31. Write an INSTR-like function for UTL_FILE. It should implement the following header:

```
CREATE OR REPLACE FUNCTION infile
    (loc_in IN VARCHAR2,
     file_in IN VARCHAR2,
     text_in IN VARCHAR2,
     occurrence_in IN INTEGER := 1,
     start_line_in IN INTEGER := 1,
     end_line_in IN INTEGER := 0,
     ignore_case_in IN BOOLEAN := TRUE)
RETURN INTEGER;
```

In other words, find the *n*th occurrence of the string text_in between lines start_line_in and end_line_in, either matching or ignoring case. Assume that the following rules are obeyed to simplify your solution:

* The file always contains text.
* The number of occurrences is positive.
* The starting line is not negative.
* The ending line is greater than the starting line.

24-32. Let's take a look at error handling with the UTL_FILE package. I created this procedure (as well as *fileplay2.sp*) to play around with files:

```
/* Filename on web page: fileplay.sp */
CREATE OR REPLACE PROCEDURE play_with_files
    (loc_in IN VARCHAR2,
     file_in IN VARCHAR2,
     mode_in IN VARCHAR2,
     mixed_up IN BOOLEAN := FALSE)
IS
    fID UTL_FILE.FILE_TYPE;
    line VARCHAR2(32767) := 'fun stuff!';
BEGIN
    IF mixed_up AND mode_in = 'R'
    THEN
        fID := UTL_FILE.FOPEN (loc_in, file_in, 'W');
    ELSIF mixed_up
    THEN
        fID := NULL;
    ELSE
        fID := UTL_FILE.FOPEN (loc_in, file_in, mode_in);
    END IF;

    IF mode_in = 'R'
    THEN
        UTL_FILE.GET_LINE (fid, line);
        DBMS_OUTPUT.PUT_LINE (
            'Read from ' || file_in || ' in ' || loc_in);
    ELSE
        UTL_FILE.PUT_LINE (fid, line);
        DBMS_OUTPUT.PUT_LINE (
            'Wrote to ' || file_in || ' in ' || loc_in);
    END IF;

    UTL_FILE.FCLOSE (fid);
END;
/
```

As you can see, it lets me either write to a file or read from a file. If I specify that I want things "mixed up," the program tries to write to a read-only file or sets the file handle to NULL. Then I set up the following script to exercise my play_with_files procedure:

```
/* Filename on web page: fileplay.tst */
SET FEEDBACK OFF
EXEC fcreate ('c:\temp', 'newfile.txt');
EXEC play_with_files ('c:\temp', 'newfile.txt', 'R');
EXEC play_with_files ('c:\nosuchdir', 'new.txt', 'R');
EXEC play_with_files ('c:\nosuchdir', 'new.txt', 'X');
EXEC play_with_files ('c:\temp', 'nosuchfile.txt', 'R');
EXEC play_with_files ('c:\temp', 'nosuchfile.txt', 'A');
EXEC play_with_files (
    'c:\temp', 'nosuchfile.txt', 'R', mixed_up => TRUE);
```

```
EXEC play_with_files (
    'c:\temp', 'nosuchfile.txt', 'W', mixed_up => TRUE);
EXEC UTL_FILE.FCLOSE_ALL;
HOST DEL c:\temp\nosuchfile.txt
HOST DEL c:\temp\new.txt
```

The fcreate procedure creates a new file (see the *fcreate.sp* file on the book's web page). There is no directory named *nosuchdir* and no file named *nosuchfile.txt*. Here is the somewhat abbreviated output from running this script:

```
SQL> @fileplay.tst
ORA-01403: no data found
ORA-06510: PL/SQL: unhandled user-defined exception
ORA-06510: PL/SQL: unhandled user-defined exception
ORA-06510: PL/SQL: unhandled user-defined exception
Wrote to nosuchfile.txt in c:\temp
ORA-06510: PL/SQL: unhandled user-defined exception
ORA-06510: PL/SQL: unhandled user-defined exception
```

Not too informative, is it? If I try to read past the end of a file (in this case, read the first line of an empty file), UTL_FILE raises NO_DATA_FOUND. I also find that in Oracle 8.1, if I append to a nonexistent file, I no longer get an error; the script wrote to *nosuchfile.txt* successfully. But once I get past those conclusions, I can determine little else from the output.

Why do I keep seeing the same error message, even though it seems as if I am encountering different errors?

24-33. How can you obtain more meaningful error information from UTL_FILE-dependent programs? Specifically, how could I change the play_with_files procedure to see precisely which error was raised by my "foolin' around"?

24-34. Implement the concept of a path for UTL_FILE by creating the package body for this specification:

```
/* Filename on web page: filepath.pkg */
CREATE OR REPLACE PACKAGE fileIO
IS
    c_delim CHAR(1) := ';';

    PROCEDURE setpath (str IN VARCHAR2);
    FUNCTION path RETURN VARCHAR2;

    FUNCTION open (file IN VARCHAR2) RETURN UTL_FILE.FILE_TYPE;
END;
/
```

where the c_delim constant "publicizes" the delimiter to be used in parsing the path string, setpath sets the path to a list of delimited directories, path returns the current path, and open opens.

24-35. You can use UTL_FILE is to write error information to a file; with files, you don't have to worry about ROLLBACKs erasing your log entries. Write a package that allows a developer to:

- Specify the location and name of the error log file, which are maintained as global values in the package and for the session.

- Write the error code, error message, and program name to the file (with the current date, time, and user supplied by the logging program).

- The components of the line written to the file are separated by a vertical bar, defined as a constant in the package specification.

- See each line after it is written to the log, even though the file is not yet closed.

- Close the log at user request.

Here is the specification for the package; you write the body:

```
/* Filename on web page: flog.pkg */
CREATE OR REPLACE PACKAGE flog /* File LOG */
IS

    delim CONSTANT CHAR(1) := '|';
    PROCEDURE setfile (loc IN VARCHAR2, file IN VARCHAR2);
    PROCEDURE put_line (
        prog IN VARCHAR2, code IN INTEGER, msg IN VARCHAR2);
    PROCEDURE close;
END flog;
/
```

Don't forget to open for append and catch the error if the file does not yet exist. And when and how often should you open and close the file?

25

DBMS_JOB Built-in Package

The DBMS_JOB package allows you to schedule PL/SQL routines, or *jobs*, to run periodically based on intervals you define. Each job has an associated job ID, a next execution date, an interval function that computes the next execution date, and a flag indicating whether the job is broken. This chapter tests your ability to use the DBMS_JOB package to submit new jobs to the job queue, change a job's execution parameters (for instance, how often it runs), and remove a job from the queue.

Beginner

25-1. Why do you need the DBMS_JOB built-in package?

25-2. Which three *INIT.ORA* parameters do you (or your DBA) need to set before using the DBMS_JOB package?

25-3. What happens when JOB_QUEUE_PROCESSES = 1, and you submit two long-running jobs that execute at the same time?

25-4. Is it possible to execute two instance of the same job by two different SNP background processes in parallel mode?

25-5. What are the two DBMS_JOB procedures that submit jobs? What are their parameters?

25-6. What is the difference between the DBMS_JOB.SUBMIT and DBMS_JOB. ISUBMIT procedures?

25-7. You submit this job, but it doesn't execute immediately. Why?

```
SQL> EXEC (33, 'calc_totals;', SYSDATE, 'SYSDATE + 1'); DBMS_JOB.ISUBMIT
PL/SQL procedure successfully completed.
```

25-8. Why does the following job never execute?

```
DBMS_JOB.ISUBMIT (
        job => 33,
        what => 'NULL;',
        next_date => NULL,
        interval => 'SYSDATE + 1'
      );
```

25-9. What is wrong with this call to ISUBMIT?

```
DBMS_JOB.ISUBMIT (
        job => 33,
        what => 'foo',
        next_date => SYSDATE,
        interval => 'SYSDATE + 1'
      );
```

25-10. If you submit the previous job (#33) with next_date equal to 1:00 P.M., is the start time the same one year later? How might you specify an exact starting time?

25-11. Assume that you need to correct the "foo" procedures mentioned in the what parameter for Job 33. How can you temporarily stop the job while you correct foo?

25-12. Other than setting Job 33's broken flag to true after fixing the foo procedure, is there a way to move the job's status from broken to nonbroken?

25-13. How can you submit a job and have it run exactly once?

25-14. How can you cause a job to execute, regardless of the current next execution date? What possible side effect could that have on the next execution date?

25-15. Which views provide information about all submitted jobs?

25-16. Write a script to show the status (broken or not, how many failures, etc.) of all jobs in the queue.

25-17. Write a script to show information about currently running jobs.

25-18. What's wrong with this call to DBMS_JOB?

```
DBMS_JOB.ISUBMIT (
        job => 35,
        what => ' delete from CONFIDENTIAL_DOCS;',
        interval => 'NEXT_BUSINESS_DAY (SYSDATE) + 1/24'
      );
```

25-19. What DBMS_JOB procedures can you use to change the execution parameters for a job that already exists?

25-20. Assume that you have two procedures: LFF for loading data from a file and PRR to calculate some statistic about the data. How can you schedule the procedures so that PRR starts right after LFF finishes?

25-21. How can you jump a job to the head of the job queue?

25-22. How can you remove a job from the job queue?

25-23. How can you export your job to move it into another database?

Intermediate

25-24. How does the job scheduler handle a job that terminates abnormally?

25-25. Put the following steps of the SNP execution process in order:

   Start database session with job owner's username.

   Execute PL/SQL mentioned in "what" parameter.

   If there are no errors, update next_date.

   If block fails, increment failures number, and set next execution date
      to one minute later if it's the first failure, double interval otherwise.

   Calculate next execution date using interval's formula.

   Alter session NLS settings to match those settings that were in effect
      when the job was originally submitted.

25-26. How do you capture the error message associated with a job failure?

25-27. How can you check to see if a job is currently running?

25-28. How can you check to see how long a currently running job has been
   executing?

25-29. What date functions can you use inside the interval string?

25-30. What interval value can you use to execute a job every hour?

25-31. What interval value can you use to execute a job every minute?

25-32. What interval value can you use to execute a job every second?

25-33. What interval value can you use to execute a job every day at 11 A.M.?

25-34. What interval value can you use to execute a job every Friday at 9 P.M.
   (i.e., 21:00)?

25-35. What interval value can you use to execute a job every Saturday and Sunday at 6 A.M.?

25-36. What interval value can you use to execute a job at 11 P.M. of the last day
   of every month?

25-37. How can you retrieve the values of the job, next_date, and broken_flag
   parameters inside the job's procedure?

25-38. Create a job called users_dump that dumps information from the V$SES-
   SION view into a log file. You want to use users_dump to make sure
   employees aren't working too much. Consequently, users_dump should

start hourly on the weekend and every nonworking hour (i.e., before 8:00 A.M. and after 6:00 P.M.) during the work week.

Expert

25-39. You have a job (#47) that has been running an incredibly long time, and you want to stop it. How can you do this?

25-40. Write a procedure called run_job that simplifies the process of submitting a job that runs at a predefined time for a specific day. For example, the program makes it easy to submit a job that runs every Monday and Friday at 11:00 P.M. The procedure should accept a job number (like ISUBMIT), the job, an initial execution date, a single start time, and a string representing the days on which the job is to run. This last string should accept a comma-delimited list of ordinal days of the week (i.e., 0=Sunday, 1=Monday,...6=Saturday). If the user does not specify a set of days, the job should be scheduled to run every day of the week. Use the following header:

```
CREATE OR REPLACE PROCEDURE run_job (
    job IN VARCHAR2,
    job_text VARCHAR2 DEFAULT 'begin NULL; end;',
    next_date DATE DEFAULT SYSDATE,
    extime VARCHAR2 DEFAULT '13',
    exdays VARCHAR2 DEFAULT NULL
)
```

25-41. Why is the next_date parameter declared differently in the SUBMIT and ISUBMIT procedures?

26

Using Java with PL/SQL

One of Oracle8*i*'s major new features is the ability to store and execute Java programs inside the database, giving Oracle developers another server-side development language (the first language, of course, is PL/SQL). These *Java stored procedures* (JSPs) open up a whole new realm of potential applications. For example, developers can use the Java networking classes to allow their database applications to communicate directly with network applications, such as a web server, on other computers.

Fortunately for us, Oracle has made PL/SQL and Java interoperable, allowing PL/SQL developers to call JSPs and Java developers to call PL/SQL stored procedures. This chapter tests your ability to define PL/SQL wrappers that allow you to call JSPs within PL/SQL.

Beginner

26-1. Oracle8*i*'s Java Virtual Machine is called:

    a. SunSpot

    b. Nova

    c. Aurora

    d. Prometheus

    e. Zeus

26-2. True or false?

    a. Java performance stinks because you have to download an applet across the network.

    b. You must know Java to take advantage of it in Oracle8*i*.

  c. You can call Java-stored procedures from a variety of clients, including SQL, PL/SQL, Java applets, Pro*C, Visual Basic, and Oracle Forms.

  d. Except for its ugly syntax, Java is just like PL/SQL.

  e. Java has hundreds of built-in classes to use in your PL/SQL programs.

  f. Java is a replacement for PL/SQL.

  g. Java, like PL/SQL, is a proprietary language controlled by Oracle.

  h. You can run your Java programs on a variety of platforms with very little effort.

  i. Java programs, such as C or C++ programs, are compiled into binary executables.

  j. The Java language is case-sensitive (i.e., the variable names junk, Junk, and JUNK are different.)

26-3. Java programs that are compiled and stored in the database are called:

  a. Internal Java

  b. Java stored procedures

  c. Oracle Jclass files

  d. External procedures

  e. HotJava

26-4. PL/SQL procedures and functions are most similar to Java:

  a. Classes

  b. Variables

  c. Enterprise JavaBeans

  d. Methods

  e. Objects

26-5. What kind of file is created when you compile a Java program?

  a. *.src*

  b. *.exe*

  c. *.obj*

  d. *.class*

  e. *.jvm*

26-6. Which of the following establishes a logical correspondence between a Java method and a PL/SQL procedure or function (standalone or packaged) or a member method of a SQL object type:

  a. Call specification (call spec)

  b. External definition

    c. Remote method invoker

    d. IDL definition

    e. CORBA object

26-7. Consider the following Java program:

```
public class xxx {
   public static void doit () {
       System.out.println("Hello World!!!");
   }
}
```

The missing element (denoted by *xxx*) is the:

    a. Filename

    b. Class name

    c. Procedure name

    d. Method name

    e. Package name

26-8. Consider the following Java program:

```
public class helloWorld {
   public static void xxx () {
       System.out.println("Hello World!!!");
   }
}
```

The missing element (denoted by *xxx*) is the:

    a. Filename

    b. Class name

    c. Procedure name

    d. Method name

    e. Package name

26-9. Consider the following Java program:

```
public class simpleJava {
   public static void printIt (xxx s) {
      System.out.println (s);
   }
}
```

The missing element (denoted by *xxx*) is the:

    a. Parameter name

    b. Parameter datatype

    c. Call spec

    d. Object name

    e. Modifier

26-10. Consider the following Java program:

```
public class simpleMath {

   public static xxx fact ( int N ) {
      int retVal = N;
      for (int i=(N-1); i > 0; i--) {
         retVal = retVal * i;
      }
      return retVal;
   }
}
```

The missing element (denoted by **xxx**) is the:

a. Method parameter name

b. Class datatype

c. Call spec

d. Object return type

e. Method return type

26-11. Suppose that you have compiled the following Java program and loaded it into the database:

```
public class simpleMath {

   public static xxx fact ( int N ) {
      int retVal = N;
      for (int i=(N-1); i > 0; i--) {
         retVal = retVal * i;
      }
      return retVal;
   }
}
```

Which of the following commands allows you to call the Java program from within PL/SQL to calculate a factorial?

a. CREATE OR REPLACE FUNCTION factorial (n NUMBER) RETURN NUMBER
AS LANGUAGE JAVA
NAME 'fact.simpleMath(int) return int';

b. retVal := CALL_JAVA(NAME 'simpleMath.fact(' || N || ') return int');

c. CREATE OR REPLACE PROCEDURE factorial (n NUMBER, f OUT NUMBER)
AS JAVA CLASS
NAME 'simpleMath.fact(int) return int';

d. CREATE OR REPLACE FUNCTION factorial (n NUMBER) RETURN NUMBER
AS LANGUAGE JAVA
NAME 'simpleMath.fact(int) return int';

e. CREATE OR REPLACE FUNCTION factorial (n NUMBER) RETURN NUMBER
AS LANGUAGE JAVA
NAME 'simpleMath.fact';

Intermediate

26-12. Put the following steps for accessing a Java class from PL/SQL in order:

Grant the necessary privileges on the PL/SQL wrappers.

Use *javac* (or an Integrated Development Environment such as JDeveloper) to compile the Java code.

Write PL/SQL wrappers to publish the class' methods.

Call the PL/SQL wrapper programs.

Use *loadjava* to load the class into the database.

26-13. Show the operating system commands that load the following class into the SCOTT (password TIGER) schema:

```
public class helloWorld {
   public static void doit () {
       System.out.println("Hello World!!!");
   }
}
```

26-14. Show the Oracle8*i* DDL command that loads the following class into the database:

```
public class helloWorld {
   public static void doit () {
       System.out.println("Hello World!!!");
   }
}
```

26-15. What clause must you include in a function or procedure header to create a call spec for a Java method?

a. PARALLEL_ENABLE

b. LANGUAGE JAVA

c. JAVA SPEC

d. AUTHID USER

e. DETERMINISTIC

26-16. What is the Java equivalent of the command SET SERVEROUTPUT ON?

26-17. To publish a *void* Java method, you should use a PL/SQL:

a. Function

b. Blob

c. Procedure

d. Index-by table

e. External procedure

26-18. For each PL/SQL datatype in the left column, provide a corresponding Java datatype (there are many possible answers):

PL/SQL Datatype	Java Equivalent
VARCHAR2	
DATE	
NUMBER (integer)	
NUMBER (real)	
ROWID	
OBJECT	
RAW	

26-19. Write a call spec for the following Java class:

```
public class OutputTest {
  public static void printIt (String s) {
     System.out.println (s);
  }
}
```

26-20. Write a call spec for the following Java method:

```
public class Fibonacci {
  public static int fib (int n) {
    if (n == 1 || n == 2)
      return 1;
    else
      return fib(n - 1) + fib(n - 2);
  }
}
```

26-21. The following Java program is saved in a file called *test.java*. What happens when you try to use javac to compile it?

```
public class helloWorld {
  public static void doit () {
     System.out.println("Hello World!!!");
  }
}
```

Expert

26-22. Describe what happens when the call spec specified for the following class is created and executed:

```
public class helloWorld {
  public static void doit () {
     System.out.println("Hello World!!!");
  }
}
```

```
-- Call spec used for the class
CREATE OR REPLACE PROCEDURE my_hello
AS LANGUAGE JAVA
NAME 'helloWorld.doIt()';
```

26-23. Describe what happens when the call spec specified for the following class is created and executed:

```
public class helloWorld {
   public void doit () {
       System.out.println("Hello World!!!");
   }
}
```

```
-- Call spec used for the class
CREATE OR REPLACE PROCEDURE my_hello
AS LANGUAGE JAVA
NAME 'helloWorld.doit()';
```

26-24. Write a query to display information about the Java objects in a user schema.

26-25. Write a procedure to print the source code for a Java-stored procedure (assuming, of course, that the source has been loaded).

26-26. Write a call spec for the following Java class:

```
public class NumberTest{
  public static void smallestFirst (int[] a, int[] b) {
     int tmp = a[0];
     if (a[0] > b[0]) {
        a[0] = b[0];
        b[0] = tmp;
     }
   }
}
```

26-27. Complete the following call spec:

```
CREATE OR REPLACE FUNCTION wages (e Employee) RETURN NUMBER
AS LANGUAGE JAVA
NAME 'Paymaster.wages( xxx ) return BigDecimal';
```

26-28. You have been asked to design a PL/SQL interface for a subset of the methods in a Java file-manipulation class. Specifically, you are to write two functions and one procedure: a function that deletes a given file and returns a Boolean flag indicating whether the delete succeeded; a function that returns a file's size; and a procedure that uses an OUT parameter, based on a index-by table type, to return the names of all the files in a given directory. Base your procedure on the following Java class:

```
import java.io.File;

public class JFile {
```

```
public static int tVal () { return 1; };  // True Value
public static int fVal () { return 0; };  // False Value
public static String listDelimiter () { return "|"; };  // File Delimiter

// Return the length of the file
public static long length (String fileName) {
   File myFile = new File (fileName);
   return myFile.length();
   }

// Delete a file
public static int delete (String fileName) {
   File myFile = new File (fileName);
   boolean retval = myFile.delete();
   if (retval) return tVal(); else return fVal();
   }

// Return a list of file names delimited by "|"
public static String dirContents (String dir) {
   File myDir = new File (dir);
   String[] filesList = myDir.list();
   String contents = new String();
   for (int i = 0; i < filesList.length; i++)
      contents = contents + listDelimiter() + filesList[i];
   return contents;
   }

/*
|| Lots more classes...
*/
}
```

Write a specification for your package.

26-29. The Jfile class defined in 26-28 uses three "get" methods—tval(), fval(), and listDelimiter()—to represent (respectively) the Boolean TRUE value, the Boolean FALSE value, and the delimiter character used by the dirContents method. As a first step in implementing your file package, develop a method to retrieve and use these same values in your PL/SQL program.

26-30. Implement the function to delete a file; remember that it must return a Boolean value.

26-31. Implement the function to retrieve a file's size.

26-32. Implement the procedure to populate an index-by table with the contents of a directory.

26-33. Before you start using the package, you have to set up the appropriate permissions. What new role do you need to grant to a schema to allow it to read or write a file? What new role do you need to create a file? What *INIT.ORA* parameter do you need to modify to control the directories in which you can perform file operations?

27

External Procedures

As powerful as PL/SQL is, there are simply some things it cannot do because it's locked inside the database. For example, there are many occasions where you might want to send an email (in an alert, for instance), perform some really complex mathematical functions (for example, an encryption system), or even just invoke a C library function. Fortunately, Oracle8 has a way to supplement the base PL/SQL language by allowing you to make calls to external libraries written in other languages, such as C. This chapter tests your understanding of this very advanced topic.

Beginner

27-1. What is an external procedure in Oracle?

27-2. Where can an external procedure be called in PL/SQL?

27-3. True or false?

    a. Interprocess communication using external procedures requires about the same amount of complexity as using database pipes.

    b. The programmer can pass information to an external procedure, but the external program cannot yet pass information back.

    c. External procedures can be used as functions in SQL.

    d. While the most common language for external procedures is C, the code for an external procedure can be written in any language that can be compiled into a C-callable format.

    e. External procedures must be procedures; functions are not allowed.

    f. All that is required to execute an external procedure is the library itself and a PL/SQL wrapper.

g. One *extproc* process is started per database.

h. Oracle can call not only shared libraries, but any executable program.

i. A CREATE LIBRARY statement needs to be issued only once for each external library, not for each routine used inside the library.

j. Oracle raises an error if a CREATE LIBRARY statement references an external library that doesn't exist.

27-4. How are external procedures defined for use in the database?

27-5. How are external shared libraries generally identified in a Windows environment? In a Unix environment?

27-6. What privilege must be granted to each user who wishes to create a PL/SQL library?

27-7. Do external processes take part in a database transaction? What exactly does this mean?

27-8. Before the introduction of external procedures in Oracle8, explain how a programmer could execute or establish communications with an operating-system program. What disadvantages did this have?

27-9. What data dictionary views are available to see what libraries currently exist in the system?

27-10. Are there any restrictions on what types of operating system programs can be called?

27-11. How do you determine whether a call to an external program should be mapped to a PL/SQL function or procedure?

27-12. Place the following chain of events in the order in which they occur when an external procedure is called:

> PL/SQL looks for a special listener process that is running in the background.
> The code in the library returns the result back to PL/SQL.
> A PL/SQL application calls a special PL/SQL module body.
> The listener process spawns a program called *extproc* that loads the external library.

27-13. Your colleague has created a library for you with an assortment of tools to use in your new system. He has provided you with a DLL (dynamic link library) *APPUTIL.DLL* in the directory *C:\MYAPP\UTIL*. Inside this library there is a function you wish to use, named generate_password, that takes no parameters but returns a string. What is the statement required to create the library necessary to access this function?

27-14. Suppose that the DLL mentioned in 27-13 has been changed so that the generate_password function now takes a parameter (password length).

What do you need to change in the declaration of the PL/SQL wrapper for this external procedure?

27-15. The following declaration for an external procedure works only if the module in the external library is also named COLLECT_DATA:

```
CREATE OR REPLACE FUNCTION COLLECT_DATA
RETURN PLS_INTEGER IS EXTERNAL
LIBRARY UTIL_LIB
LANGUAGE C;
```

What do you need to change in the declaration if the name of the function in the library is either not in all uppercase or not the same as the function declared?

27-16. For each of the following CREATE LIBRARY statements, state whether they are valid or invalid and, if invalid, why:

    a. `CREATE LIBRARY libc_1 AS '/lib/libc.so'`
    b. `CREATE LIBRARY libc_1 AS '/LIB/LIBC.SO'`
    c. `CREATE LIBRARY UNIX_operating_system_c_library AS '/lib/libc.so'`
    d. `CREATE LIBRARY libc_1 FOR '/lib/libc.so'`
    e. `CREATE LIBRARY libc_1 AS /lib/libc.so`

27-17. How can a library be removed from the system?

27-18. Suppose that you have created an external shared library, the Oracle library, and a package containing all of the PL/SQL wrapper functions. You have given several people the appropriate privileges to access this package. Now Sue has irked you by misusing one of the functions in your external shared library. What is the easiest way to prevent Sue from accessing these functions further?

27-19. Since external procedures are not written in PL/SQL, the datatypes used are not the same. Assuming that you are calling an external procedure written in C, complete the following table:

External Datatype	PL/SQL Datatype
int	
char * (string)	
double	
float	

Intermediate

27-20. What are some of the similarities and differences between native PL/SQL procedures and external procedures?

27-21. How does being able to access external procedures overcome some of the shortcomings of the PL/SQL language?

27-22. What steps are necessary to create and call an external procedure?

27-23. Are there any disadvantages with the current implementation of external procedures?

27-24. When attempting to call an external procedure you just wrote, you receive the following error:

```
ORA-28575: unable to open RPC connection to external procedure agent
```

What could be causing this error, and how can you fix it?

27-25. What does the BY REFERENCE option do in the PARAMETERS clause?

27-26. How does the concept of dynamic linking make the current implementation of external procedures more efficient?

27-27. What advantages are there to placing PL/SQL wrapper procedures inside a package instead of creating them as standalone program units?

27-28. You are about to drop a library you believe is not being used by any users. How can you ensure that the library is not referenced by any existing database code before you remove the library?

27-29. This problem has a larger scope than most others in this book. It's a case study involving the following situation:

You would like to provide a facility to other programmers to log debugging messages to an operating system file. Your colleague (who is a C programmer) has written a Unix shared library (*/usr/local/bin/debug.sl*), that contains a procedure log_text that writes the string passed to it in an OS file.

Describe the necessary steps and provide any PL/SQL code needed to implement this functionality.

Expert

27-30. The DBA for your site has added the required entries in the *LISTENER. ORA* and *TNSNAMES.ORA* files, but you are still not able to communicate with your external procedures. Is there anything else that you or your DBA should check to ensure that the new information is active?

27-31. Here is another extensive case study for you to develop involving sending email from a Unix server:

Suppose that you currently work for the company Widgets R Us and are involved in building a long-awaited, brand-new automated system. One of the services this new system will offer to customers is that they can be notified by email of any new products being produced by your company. Your System Architect has done a wonderful job and has produced a perfectly normalized model, which has an entity that contains high-level information about all the products currently offered by the company (products table). For the sake of this example, assume that email addresses of the clients who wish notification are contained in a table called clients_to_notify.

Describe all the tasks needed to implement the email notification component of the system using external procedures, and write the necessary PL/SQL code.

27-32. *extproc* is currently implemented by Oracle as a single-threaded process. As a developer, what concerns would you have if, in future releases, Oracle decided to implement external procedures in a multithreaded manner?

27-33. Can external program calls be debugged?

28

PL/SQL Web Development

While the Oracle database doesn't currently support web access directly (there is talk, though, of building an HTTP listener), there are a number of Oracle tools, such as Oracle Application Server (OAS) and WebDB, that allow you to build web applications using PL/SQL. This chapter tests your understanding of how to use the tools provided with these add-on systems (particularly the OWA packages) to develop web systems.

Beginner

28-1. An HTML document is most similar to:

    a. A report created using Oracle reports

    b. A report created using Crystal Reports

    c. A file created using WordPerfect

    d. A screen layout created using ISPF

    e. A Java class file

28-2. An HTML form is most similar to:

    a. A form created using Oracle Forms

    b. A form created using Powerbuilder

    c. A form created using Microsoft Access

    d. A form created using the Java Swing classes

    e. None of the above

28-3. In which of the following products/languages can you use PL/SQL for web development?

    a. OAS

    b. WebDB

    c. Java

    d. Oracle Forms

    e. All of the above

28-4. What kinds of web content can you generate directly with the PL/SQL toolkit?

    a. HTML

    b. XML

    c. Delimited text files

    d. JavaScript

    e. All of the above

28-5. Detail the major architectural components in a PL/SQL-based web system.

28-6. What does the HTTP listener component do?

28-7. What does the PL/SQL gateway do?

28-8. What is the PL/SQL toolkit? List its packages.

28-9. Which toolkit package contains procedures to print syntactically correct HTML into a buffer? Which of these procedures is most similar to DBMS_OUTPUT.PUT_LINE? Use this procedure to write a program that displays "Hello, World" in a user's browser.

28-10. What OWA_UTIL procedure can create a dynamic list of values (LOV) to use in an HTML form? Give an example that creates a drop-down LOV of the departments in the SCOTT.DEPT table.

28-11. What OWA_UTIL procedure can you use to change a PL/SQL resource's MIME header? Under what circumstances might you want to do this?

28-12. What OWA_UTIL command can you use to set a cookie on a user's browser?

28-13. What function in the OWA_OPT_LOCK package can you use to compute a checksum on a record? How would you use this value?

28-14. Use the MATCH function in OWA_PATTERN to determine if the string S is a floating number.

28-15. What are the three ways you can call a PL/SQL procedure from a web browser?

28-16. What is the general structure of a URL that calls a PL/SQL procedure? Briefly describe the function of each part of the URL.

28-17. How can you use the query string section of a URL to pass parameters to a PL/SQL procedure?

28-18. The characters in a query string must be encoded so they are transmitted properly across the Web. The encoding process is fairly simple: all non-alphanumeric characters in the value must be converted to a percent sign (%) followed by the original character's hexadecimal equivalent. There are two exceptions to this rule: the underscore character is left alone and the space character is converted to a plus (+). Develop an algorithm to encode a value.

28-19. Use your algorithm (when necessary) to complete the following table:

Character	ASCII Value	Encoded Value
The digit 9	48	
The letter A	65	
	32	
Ampersand (&)	38	
Forward slash (/)	47	
Right curly brace (})	125	

28-20. How can you use an HTML form to call a PL/SQL procedure?

28-21. Write a procedure that formats the rows of the SCOTT.EMP table into an HTML table. It should show all rows in the table unless the user passes a specific job category. (Don't use OWA_UTIL for this exercise!)

28-22. Provide an HTML snippet that creates two hyperlinks to the show_emps procedure. The first link should show all analysts, and the second should show all clerks.

28-23. Provide an HTML snippet that lets a user call show_emps using a drop-down of job categories. The list should contain only the analyst and clerk jobs.

28-24. In the previous two exercises, you manually created lists of job categories. What might have been a better approach?

28-25. A procedure has the following specification:

```
PROCEDURE foo (
    i_emp_no IN VARCHAR2 DEFAULT NULL,
    i_lname IN VARCHAR2 DEFAULT NULL )
```

A developer is trying, unsuccessfully, to call the procedure using the following HTML snippet. What's the problem?

```
<form action=foo>
    Employee Number:<input name=i_emp_num value="125"><p>
    Employee Name:<input name=i_lname><p>
</form>
```

Intermediate

28-26. Given what you know about how procedures are called from the Web, what calling notation (positional or named) do you think the PL/SQL gateway uses to actually perform the call? Discuss the implications the calling format has on your web development effort.

28-27. Under what circumstances can you call a procedure from the Web using just its name and parameters (i.e., when can you omit the server, port, and virtual schema mappings)?

28-28. A developer has written the following program:

```
PROCEDURE val_test (i_val in number default 0) IS
  BEGIN
      HTP.PRINT('The value is: ' || i_val );
  EXCEPTION
    WHEN OTHERS THEN
        HTP.PRINT ('Invalid number');
  END;
```

What happens when the following hyperlink is used to call the procedure?

```
http://myserver/virtual_schema_mapping/val_test?i_val=four
```

28-29. Discuss three ways to maintain state in a PL/SQL web application.

28-30. A consulting company is developing a simple system to help its employees prepare for visits to client sites. The basic idea is that each consultant gets an online schedule of all the clients they are going to see. The schedule also contains a hyperlink to each company's home page so that the consultant can easily do some basic research.

You have been asked to write an HTML interface based on a view named onsite_schedule. It has the following columns:

```
Name                             Null?     Type
-------------------------------- --------  ----
SALESMAN_ID                                NUMBER
VISIT_DATE                                 DATE
COMPANY_NAME                               VARCHAR2(50)
COMPANY_URL                                VARCHAR2(200)
```

What single PL/SQL toolkit procedure can you use to create this interface?

 Use the *onsite.sql* file provided on this book's web page to create the onsite_schedule table with example data.

28-31. A guestbook is a simple application that allows web browsers to leave basic information about themselves—name, email address, and a few comments—as well as to read comments from other visitors.

Write a PL/SQL package to implement a guestbook. The system should have two screens. The first screen displays a list of all visitors to the site, the date they visited, and their comments. It should also have a button labeled "Sign the Guestbook!!!" Figure 28-1 shows a sample.

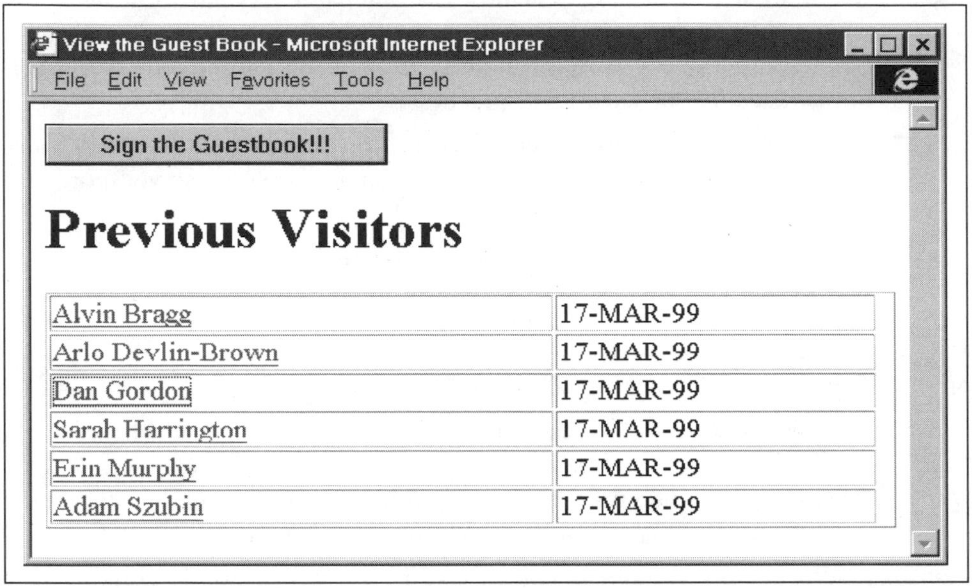

Figure 28-1. Sample guestbook

Clicking this button takes you to the second screen, a form where you can enter your name, email address, and a comment. Submitting the form saves the entry and returns you to the original screen. (For extra credit, design the first screen so that clicking on the visitor's name automatically kicks you into a preaddressed email message.)

28-32. A programmer is writing a system to manage "to do" lists. Part of the program builds a list of hyperlinks (defined as relative URLs) that passes a date (defined as a VARCHAR2 string in "DD-MON-YYYY" format) to another part of the system. What is wrong with the following implementation for this program?

```
Qstr := 'create_to_do_form?i_date=';
Qstr : q_str || tbl_rec.todo_date ;
HTP.ANCHOR (
   Curl => qstr,
   Ctext => 'Enter an item for ' || tbl_rec.todo_date );
```

Expert

28-33. In 28-32, you correctly encoded a parameter's value because you already knew its format. This is usually not the case. Write a general function that can encode *any* string into CGI (Common Gateway Interface) format. Test your function using the value "The date {05/21/1994}". It should return the string "the+date+%7B05%2F21% 2F1994%7D".

28-34. Your company uses an online system that allows employees to fill out expense reports, which are stored in a table. At the end of each month, there are usually several thousand records. On May 1st, the Payables department asks you to write a system to monitor employee expenses, and you dutifully comply by writing a PL/SQL procedure. Everything works fine. On May 21st, you start receiving complaints that the system is "slow," and the next week you receive a call that it has blown up entirely, displaying the message "Internal Error." What might be happening, and how can you fix the problem?

28-35. A programmer has written the following procedure:

```
CREATE OR REPLACE PROCEDURE foo AS
    x NUMBER DEFAULT 1;
  BEGIN
    LOOP
      EXIT WHEN x = 0;
      x := x + 1;
      IF x > 100 THEN
        x := 1;
      END IF;
    END LOOP;
    HTP.PRINT('All done!');
END;
```

When the programmer calls it from the Web, the browser simply hangs and never returns the expected output. He presses the "Stop" button and rechecks the code. After finding the bug that caused the program to hang, he attempts to recompile the procedure. This time, the compiler itself hangs for several minutes. Eventually, it returns the error "ORA-XXX: Could not lock procedure."

What was the original error in the program? Why did the compiler subsequently lock up? What must the programmer do to fix the problem?

28-36. A table that holds the messages in a web-based threaded discussion list is defined as follows:

```
Name                            Null?     Type
------------------------------- --------  ----
MSG_ID                          NOT NULL  NUMBER
MSG_PARENT                                NUMBER
MSG_AUTHOR                                VARCHAR2(20)
MSG_SUBJECT                               VARCHAR2(200)
MSG_BODY                                  VARCHAR2(2000)
DATE_CREATED                              DATE
```

Write a recursive procedure that uses the HTML ordered list tags (<ol>) to create a hierarchical list of message subjects. Each list item should include an anchor tag based on the message's subject line, author, and date submitted. Your procedure should accept a parameter for the "root" message of the list. The anchor tag should link back to your procedure, passing a new message id for the selected link. Figure 28-2 shows an example:.

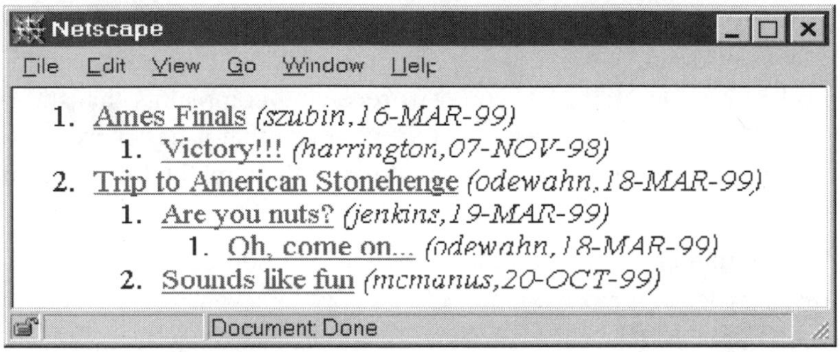

Figure 28-2. Using anchor tags

Use the *messages.sql* file provided on this book's web page to create the messages table with sample data.

29

Tuning PL/SQL

Contrary to the opinion of C programmers everywhere, tuning is not simply a matter of eking the last bit of performance out of a program by condensing a five-line sequence of commands down to one super-dense statement. Instead, tuning is more a state of mind: good performance is a natural consequence of clean, well-designed programs. It is not an afterthought. If you've been using what you've learned from this book, particularly about packages, in your PL/SQL code, you're well on your way to developing high-performance PL/SQL programs.

Having said all that, there's still a lot you can do to improve your PL/SQL programs. Once of the most interesting aspects of PL/SQL tuning stems from the fact that PL/SQL, unlike C or COBOL, lives and executes inside the database. Consequently, you must carefully manage how your programs move in and out of memory, and how they interact with competing processes. On a less esoteric front, you must also make sure that your programs don't do unnecessary work and that they effectively use algorithms, SQL, and data structures. This chapter tests your ability to apply these concepts.

Beginner

29-1. True or false?

    a. A fast program is as important as a correct one.

    b. Shorter programs (in terms of lines of code) are faster than longer programs.

    c. You can't optimize a program without first identifying performance bottlenecks.

    d. Performance is the most important aspect of high-quality software.

    e. Tuning is part of the testing process.

    f. Tuning PL/SQL is the same as tuning other languages (i.e., C, Java).

    g. PL/SQL tuning is the process of tuning the SQL statements contained in the PL/SQL code.

    h. The only way to tune a PL/SQL program is to build performance-related logging functions into an application (i.e., commands to report the amount of time spent inside an application).

    i. It's the DBA's responsibility to tune applications.

29-2. Which of the following is a technique for storing frequently used values in memory so they can be accessed quickly?

    1. Globalization

    2. Pinning

    3. Caching

    4. "Get and set"

    5. Hashing

29-3. What's the first thing you should do when writing a program such as a string or date function from scratch?

29-4. What's the difference between an algorithm and a program?

29-5. You need a persistent (i.e., extending across PL/SQL program unit calls) high-performance data-caching mechanism. Which of the following should you use, and which is optimal?

    1. Database tables

    2. PL/SQL packages

    3. Operating system files

    4. Database schemas

    5. DBMS_JOB

29-6. Match the following tuning tools to their proper description.

Tool:

    1. DBMS_APPLICATION_INFO

    2. TKPROF

    3. DBMS_PROFILER

    4. SQL*Lab

    5. PL/Vision

Description:

    a. Third-party tool for analyzing SQL statements

    b. Oracle8*i* built-in package used to gather performance statistics

    c. Packages built by Revealnet to help implement PL/SQL best practices

d. Built-in package that provides procedures that "register" the execution status of Oracle code

e. Oracle operating system utility that provides useful tuning information

29-7. Upon execution, PL/SQL programs are compiled and loaded into which of the following areas of memory?

a. CGA

b. UGA

c. UPI

d. SGA

e. RMI

29-8. A PL/SQL program's session data (i.e., variables, data structures, etc.) are loaded into which of the following areas of memory?

a. CGA

b. UGA

c. UPI

d. SGA

e. RMI

29-9. Which of the following packages keeps, or *pins*, a package in memory until the instance is shut down?

a. DBMS_PIN_PACKAGE

b. DBMS_APPLICATION_INFO

c. DBMS_KEEP

d. DBMS_SHARED_POOL

e. DBMS_SESSION

29-10. Improve the performance of the following procedure:

```
PROCEDURE process_data (nm_in IN VARCHAR2) IS
BEGIN
   FOR rec IN pkgd.cur
   LOOP
      process_rec (UPPER (nm_in), rec.total_production);
   END LOOP;
END;
```

29-11. Improve the performance of the following code:

```
DECLARE
   my_value INTEGER NOT NULL := 0;
BEGIN
   IF my_value > 0 THEN ...
END;
```

29-12. Improve the following procedure, which reassigns employees to a new department and then deletes the original department:

```
CREATE OR REPLACE PROCEDURE drop_dept
   (deptno_in IN NUMBER, reassign_deptno_in IN NUMBER)
IS
   temp_emp_count  NUMBER;
BEGIN
   -- Do we have any employees in this department to transfer?
   SELECT COUNT(*)
     INTO temp_emp_count
     FROM emp WHERE deptno = deptno_in;

   -- Reassign any employees
   IF temp_emp_count >0
   THEN
      UPDATE emp
         SET deptno = reassign_deptno_in
       WHERE deptno = deptno_in;
   END IF;

   DELETE FROM dept WHERE deptno = deptno_in;
   COMMIT;
END drop_dept;
```

Intermediate

29-13. What is the most efficient integer datatype for numbers in the 2^{31} range?

   a. NUMBER

   b. BINARY_INTEGER

   c. PLS_INTEGER

   d. INT

   e. POSITIVE

29-14. Explain why Snippet (a) is superior to Snippet (b):

```
   a. PROCEDURE exec_line_proc (line IN INTEGER)
      IS
      BEGIN
         IF line = 1 THEN exec_line1; END IF;
         IF line = 2 THEN exec_line2; END IF;
         IF line = 3 THEN exec_line3; END IF;
         ...
         IF line = 2045 THEN exec_line2045; END IF;
      END;
   b. PROCEDURE exec_line_proc (line IN INTEGER)
      IS
      BEGIN
         IF indx = 1 THEN exec_line1;
         ELSIF indx = 2 THEN exec_line2;
         ELSIF indx = 3 THEN exec_line3;
         ...
```

```
            ELSIF indx = 2045 THEN exec_line2045;
            END IF;
        END;
```

29-15. Explain why Trigger (a) is better than Trigger (b):

```
a. CREATE OR REPLACE TRIGGER check_raise
        AFTER UPDATE OF salary, commission
        ON employee FOR EACH ROW
    WHEN (NVL (OLD.salary, -1) != NVL (NEW.salary, -1) OR
        NVL (OLD.commission, -1) != NVL (NEW.commission, -1))
    BEGIN
        compensation_pkg.alert(old.emp_id);
    END;

b. CREATE OR REPLACE TRIGGER check_raise
        AFTER UPDATE
        ON employee
        FOR EACH ROW
    BEGIN
        IF    NVL (old.salary, -1) != NVL (new.salary, -1)
            OR NVL (old.commission, -1) != NVL (new.commission, -1)
        THEN
            compensation_pkg.alert(old.emp_id);
        END IF;
    END;
```

29-16. Improve the performance of the following code (assume that process_employee_history has been optimized):

```
DECLARE
    CURSOR emp_cur
    IS
        SELECT last_name, TO_CHAR (SYSDATE, 'MM/DD/YYYY') today
            FROM employee;
BEGIN
    FOR rec IN emp_cur
    LOOP
        IF LENGTH (rec.last_name) > 20
        THEN
            rec.last_name := SUBSTR (rec.last_name, 20);
        END IF;
        process_employee_history (rec.last_name, rec.today);
    END LOOP;
END;
```

29-17. Improve the performance of the following cursor definition:

```
DECLARE
    CURSOR marketing_cur IS
        SELECT last_name FROM employee
         WHERE department_id = 20;
BEGIN
    OPEN marketing_cur;
```

29-18. Improve the performance of the following PL/SQL snippet:

```
FOR rec IN (SELECT ename, sal FROM emp)
LOOP
```

```
         UPDATE emp SET sal = rec.sal * 1.01
           WHERE ename = rec.ename;
       END LOOP;
```

29-19. Redesign the following query:

```
SELECT 'Top employee in ' || department_id || ' is ' ||
          E.last_name || ', ' || E.first_name str
   FROM employee E
  WHERE E.salary = (SELECT MAX (salary) FROM employee E2
                  WHERE E2.department_id = E.department_id)
```

29-20. Write a package that caches the value of the USER function for later retrieval.

29-21. Given a primary key, write a lookup function that retrieves the name column from a table called company. If the name has already been retrieved from the company table during a previous execution, the function should return the name from a local cache. If not, the function should perform the database fetch, cache the results, and then return the ID. (Hint: you must use a package.)

29-22. How many distinct SQL statements (and PL/SQL blocks) are parsed when this code is run?

```
SELECT ename, sal
  FROM emp
 WHERE deptno = 10 and ename LIKE 'S%';

SELECT ename, sal FROM emp
   WHERE deptno = 10 AND ename LIKE 'S%';

DECLARE
    rec emp%rowtype;
    v_dept INTEGER := 10;
    v_name VARCHAR2(100) := 'S%';
BEGIN
    FOR rec IN (
       SELECT ename, sal
         FROM EMP
        where deptno = 10 AND ename LIKE 'S%')
    LOOP
       NULL;
    END LOOP;

    FOR rec IN (select ename, sal
    FROM
    emp WHERE deptno = 10 AND ename LIKE 'S%')
    LOOP
       NULL;
    END LOOP;
END;
```

29-23. Improve the performance of the following program:

```
BEGIN
    INSERT INTO UnionBuster VALUES (ub_seq.NEXTVAL, 'Prison', 5);
    SELECT ub_id, hourly_wage INTO v_latest_bustID, v_hard_to_beat
      FROM UnionBuster
     WHERE labor_type = 'Prison';
END;
```

29-24. Assuming that the cursor in the following example includes SELECT FOR UPDATE, improve the following loop:

```
LOOP
    FETCH cur INTO rec;
    EXIT WHEN cur%NOTFOUND;

    UPDATE employee SET last_name = UPPER (last_name)
      WHERE employee_id = rec.employee_id;
END LOOP;
```

29-25. Improve the performance of the following code snippet:

```
CREATE TYPE dlist_t AS TABLE OF INTEGER;

PROCEDURE whack_emps_by_dept (deptlist dlist_t)
IS
BEGIN
    FOR aDept IN deptlist.FIRST..deptlist.LAST
    LOOP
        DELETE emp WHERE deptno = deptlist(aDept);
    END LOOP;
END;
```

29-26. Complete the following function by creating a SQL statement that uses the Oracle8*i* BULK COLLECT clause to populate these collection variables:

```
/* Filename on web page: bulkcol.sf */
CREATE OR REPLACE FUNCTION get_a_mess_o_emps
    (deptno_in IN dept.depno%TYPE)
RETURN emplist_t
IS
    emplist emplist_t := emplist_t();
    TYPE numTab IS TABLE OF NUMBER;
    TYPE charTab IS TABLE OF VARCHAR2(12);
    TYPE dateTab IS TABLE OF DATE;
    enos numTab;
    names charTab;
    hdates dateTab;
BEGIN

    <your SQL statement here>

    emplist.EXTEND(enos.COUNT);
    FOR i IN enos.FIRST..enos.LAST
    LOOP
        emplist(i) := emp_t(enos(i),
            names(i), hiredates(i));
```

```
     END LOOP;
       RETURN emplist;
   END;
```

29-27. Write a SQL script that shows the sizes of a user's database objects. The
       script should display only those objects whose code size (in KB) is larger
       than a user-supplied value.

Expert

29-28. Match the following V$ views to their proper description:

   View:

   1. V$ROWCACHE

   2. V$LIBRARYCACHE

   3. V$SQLAREA

   4. V$DB_OBJECT_CACHE

   Description:

   a. Contains the number of times an element has been loaded into the
      SGA, its number of executions, whether it has been pinned, and
      whether it has been referenced but not loaded

   b. Contains object access cache "hits and misses"

   c. Contains statistics on the shared SQL area, one row per string

   d. Contains data dictionary cache "hits and misses"

29-29. The following program creates an index-by table holding a schedule of
       lease payments. The payment for each year is calculated as the sum of
       lease amounts for the remaining years. In other words, the total lease for
       year 10 consists of the lease amounts (fixed and variable) for years 10
       through 20. Assuming that the functions pv_of_fixed and pv_of_variable
       are defined elsewhere, can you improve the program?

```
/* Filename on web page: presvalue.sp */
/* Construct present value lease schedule over 20 years. */
PROCEDURE build_lease_schedule
IS
    /* Temporary variable to hold lease accumulation. */
    pv_total_lease NUMBER (9);
BEGIN
    fixed_count := 0;
    var_count := 0;

    FOR year_count IN 1 .. 20
    LOOP
       /* Reset the lease amount for this year. */
       pv_total_lease := 0;
```

```
         /*
         || Build the PV based on the remaining years
         || plus the fixed and variable amounts.
         */
         FOR year_count2 IN year_count .. 20
         LOOP
            /* Add annual total lease amount to cummulative. */
            pv_total_lease :=
               pv_total_lease +
               pv_of_fixed (year_count2) +
               pv_of_variable (year_count2);
         END LOOP;

         /* Add the annual PV to the table. */
         pv_table (year_count) :=
            pv_total_lease;
      END LOOP;
   END;
```

29-30. Rewrite the following procedure so that the big_string and big_list variables consume memory and CPU resources only when the IF condition is met (hint: think anonymous block...)?

```
PROCEDURE always_do_everything
   (...)
IS
   big_string VARCHAR2 (32767) :=
      ten_minute_lookup (...);
   big_list
      list_types.big_strings_tt;
BEGIN
   IF <condition>
   THEN
      use_big_string (big_string);
      Process_big_list (big_list);
   ELSE
      /* Nothing big
         going on here */
      ...
   END IF;
END;
```

29-31. Sometimes, particularly in batch jobs, you want to disable a table's triggers and perform some bulk operation. Using native dynamic SQL, write a generic procedure that accepts the name of a table and a trigger status. The procedure should set each of the table's triggers to the passed status.

29-32. You can use DBMS_JOB to approximate multithreading. For example, suppose you have a procedure called calc_comp that computes the compensation for a given job (i.e., clerk, vice president, or programmer) and stores it in a table. Show how you might use DBMS_JOB to calculate each job's compensation in parallel.

29-33. Continuing with 29-32, suppose that the compensation at each level is the sum of the compensations of the previous levels (i.e., the vice president makes as much as programmer and clerk combined). Does this affect your ability to parallelize calc_comp?

29-34. Suppose a PL/SQL program contains the SQL statements a and b, in that order. What effect, if any, does the difference between the two (logically equivalent) statements have on the program's performance?

```
a. UPDATE ceo_compensation
      SET stock_options = 1000000,
          salary = salary * 2.0
    WHERE layoffs > 10000;
```

```
b. UPDATE ceo_compensation
      SET stock_options = 1000000,
          salary = salary * 2
    WHERE layoffs > 10000;
```

29-35. Write a SQL script to show the table and view dependencies for all the procedures, functions, and packages.

29-36. Suppose you a have a collection table called emp, a collection of department IDs (defined as a dlist_t type), and a collection of employee IDs (defined as an enolist_t type). Write a function that deletes all the employees of a passed collection of departments. The function should return a collection of the ids of the employees who were deleted. (Hint: use the bulk collection operations FORALL and RETURNING.)

29-37. Improve the performance of the following procedure:

```
CREATE OR REPLACE PROCEDURE insert_many_emps
IS
    cur INTEGER := DBMS_SQL.open_cursor;
    rows_inserted INTEGER;

BEGIN
    DBMS_SQL.parse (cur,
        'INSERT INTO emp (empno, deptno, ename)
           VALUES (:empno, :deptno, :ename)',
        DBMS_SQL.native);

    FOR rowind IN 1 .. 1000
    LOOP
       DBMS_SQL.bind_variable (cur, 'empno', rowind);
       DBMS_SQL.bind_variable (cur, 'deptno', 40);
       DBMS_SQL.bind_variable (cur, 'ename', 'Steven' || rowind);
       rows_inserted := DBMS_SQL.execute (cur);
    END LOOP;

    DBMS_SQL.close_cursor (cur);
END;
```

29-38. What happens to real memory when you run the following script in an Oracle 7.3 database?

```
DECLARE
    TYPE big_type IS TABLE OF VARCHAR2(32767)
        INDEX BY BINARY_INTEGER;
    big big_type;
BEGIN
    DBMS_OUTPUT.enable;
    FOR i IN 1 .. 32767
    LOOP
        big (i) := NULL;
    END LOOP;
END;
```

29-39. Pass-by-value, the default method for passing IN OUT parameters in PL/SQL, works as follows. When an actual value is passed to a procedure or function, its value is copied into the formal parameter as a local variable. The procedure or function makes its changes and, when the code terminates, copies the new values back to the actual parameter. Under what circumstances does the pass-by-value method create a memory-related performance problem? What two methods can you use to mitigate this problem? What are some potential pitfalls of these two methods?

30

PL/SQL for DBAs

This chapter, meant specifically for DBAs, tests your ability to use the base PL/SQL language, as well as an assortment of built-in packages, to simplify and automate a variety of database maintenance tasks.

Beginner

30-1. How can database parameters (from the *INIT.ORA* file) be examined from within PL/SQL?

30-2. Write a function that accepts the name of a database parameter and returns its value.

30-3. Database administrators usually have a collection of many scripts they've written. Unfortunately, each new version of Oracle wreaks havoc with these scripts. One solution is to have a set of scripts for each version of the database. Another solution is to build a database version check into each script. Oracle8 includes a built-in to determine the database version for you. What is the name of the utility? Use it in an example.

30-4. Suppose you need to write a script that depends on using a particular version of Oracle (you'll do one thing for Oracle7 and another for Oracle8). Write a procedure to display the version of the database for either Oracle7 or Oracle8.

30-5. What Oracle built-in package maintains the SHARED_POOL portion of the System Global Area (SGA)?

30-6. What command do you use to pin the DBMS_SHARED_POOL package in the shared pool?

30-7. What attribute of PL/SQL packages allows them to be written by a DBA (accessing DBA objects) and then to be successfully executed by non-DBAs (with no access to DBA objects)?

Intermediate

30-8. One of a DBA's tasks is to ensure that Oracle's cost-based optimizer is using up-to-date statistics. Luckily, this task can be automated using a combination of two of Oracle's built-in packages, DBMS_JOB and DBMS_UTILITY.

Write a procedure that analyzes a specific schema to create statistics for the cost-based optimizer. This procedure will be submitted hourly by DBMS_JOB. At 1:00 A.M. and 2:00 A.M., perform a complete analysis; otherwise, do it only for the indexes.

30-9. Oracle8 introduced partitioned tables and indexes that are both a DBA's dream and a DBA's nightmare. They are a dream because they distribute system I/O and allow maintenance to be performed without causing all data to be unavailable. They can be nightmarish if they are used to perform business logic, as in the following exercise where no account transactions can be entered for a given month until after the 20th day of the previous month.

Suppose that a table called account_trx is created and partitioned as shown here:

```
CREATE TABLE account_trx
(account_no NUMBER,
 trx_amt    NUMBER,
 trx_date   DATE)
PARTITION BY RANGE (trx_date)
(PARTITION trx_199812 VALUES LESS THAN (to_date('01-JAN-1999',
                                        'DD-MON-YYYY')),
  PARTITION trx_199901 VALUES LESS THAN (to_date('01-FEB-1999',
                                        'DD-MON-YYYY')),
  PARTITION trx_199902 VALUES LESS THAN (to_date('01-MAR-1999',
                                        'DD-MON-YYYY')))
/
```

Write a procedure that sets up a job to run on the 20th of each month to create the partition for that month's data.

Expert

30-10. How would you execute the ALTER SYSTEM and ALTER DATABASE commands in PL/SQL prior to Oracle8?

30-11. Oracle8 introduced a built-in package that allows DDL statements to be executed dynamically, while eliminating much of the coding that goes with DBMS_SQL. What is it? Use it in an example to coalesce a tablespace (note that we are not referring to Native Dynamic SQL).

30-12. Working with the built-in discovered in 30-11, let's look at a couple of scripts that assist the DBA. The examples use a cursor to retrieve information from the Oracle catalog and then issue DDL statements to perform a task.

Part of a DBA's job is to be proactive and look for problems before they occur. One problem that can crop up is corrupt data blocks that require an object to be recovered. Because this is a repetitive task that should be done periodically, it's nice to have a script that automatically analyzes all your objects for you.

First, develop a CURSOR statement that identifies all the tables and clusters that need to be examined for a given schema.

30-13. Next, write a procedure that uses the cursor created in 30-12 and automatically analyzes all the objects, searching for corrupt blocks.

30-14. Here is another example of issuing object-level DDL statements based on information retrieved from a cursor. This procedure works on indexes.

Indexes are strange beasts. Unlike tables, their space cannot be reused, and in an update- or delete-intensive environment, much of the space can end up wasted. It is wise to periodically rebuild or recreate the indexes. Because of the periodic and repetitive nature of this task, let's write a procedure that does the work for us.

First, develop a CURSOR statement that identifies all the indexes and their tablespaces for a given schema where the index is in more than one extent. These will be the ones to rebuild.

30-15. Next, finish the procedure by taking this cursor and using the EXEC_DDL_ STATEMENT built-in to rebuild the index.

30-16. Within PL/SQL, how can you determine if you're working in a Parallel Server environment?

30-17. One of the key performance factors for a database is the performance of the database buffer cache. But above and beyond the usual hit ratio calculations, it's sometimes nice to know exactly what is in the cache at any given time.

The DBBC package is intended to be an API into the database buffer cache. It lists the contents of the cache by object and lets you prune what is displayed by object owner, object type, and number of buffers used.

Here is the initial package header along with a skeleton package body to show the query used:

```
* Filename on web page: dbbc2/sql */
CREATE OR REPLACE PACKAGE dbbc AS
  PROCEDURE show;
END dbbc;
/

CREATE OR REPLACE PACKAGE BODY dbbc AS

  /*<<<<<<<<<<<<<<<<<<<<<<<<<<<<<<<<<<<<<<>>>>>>>>>>>>>>>>>>>>>>>>>>>>>>>>*/
  PROCEDURE show IS
  /*<<<<<<<<<<<<<<<<<<<<<<<<<<<<<<<<<<<<<<>>>>>>>>>>>>>>>>>>>>>>>>>>>>>>>>*/
    -- Get the object ID and the number of buffers it is using
    CURSOR curs_get_counts IS
    select obj,
           count(*) num_buffers
      from x$bh
    group by obj
    order by count(*) desc;

    -- Get pertinent information about the object
    CURSOR curs_get_obj ( cp_object_id NUMBER ) IS
    select owner,
           object_name,
           object_type
      from dba_objects
     where object_id = cp_object_id;
    v_obj_rec      curs_get_obj%ROWTYPE;

  BEGIN
    NULL;
  END show;

END dbbc;
/
```

Write the show procedure so it displays the contents of the cache.

30-18. Add procedures to allow the display to be limited by object owner, object type, and number of buffers used.

30-19. Oracle maintains a vast array of statistics to allow a DBA to tune and maintain a database. The problem is that the statistics' values at a given point in time are not always as important as their trends over time. This exercise creates a package to quickly and easily capture a set of Oracle system statistics over a period of time.

Write a package that is an API to the V$SYSSTAT table. It should allow a list of statistics (e.g., physical reads, consistent gets) to be tracked for a specified period of time at regular intervals.

Here is the package header:

```
/* Filename on web page: stats.pkg */
CREATE OR REPLACE PACKAGE stats AS

   /*
      || This package tracks a set of user specified
      || system statistics from V$SYSSTAT. The length of
      || interval and number of iterations can also be specified
      ||
      || Requires : SELECT ANY TABLE
      ||            EXECUTE ON DBMS_LOCK
      ||
      || 04-FEB-1999 DRH Started
   */

   -- add a stat to the list to record
   PROCEDURE add_stat ( p_statname v$statname.name%TYPE );

   -- show the list of stats being recorded
   PROCEDURE show_stats;

   -- record stats; perform p_iterations with a break of
   -- p_wait-seconds in between
   PROCEDURE record_stats ( p_iterations INT := 1,
                            p_wait_seconds INT := 0 );

   -- display what was recorded
   PROCEDURE show_record;

END stats;
```

And here is example output:

```
SQL> EXEC stats.add_stat('physical reads');

PL/SQL procedure successfully completed.

SQL> EXEC stats.record_stats(10,10);

PL/SQL procedure successfully completed.

SQL> EXEC stats.show_record;
physical reads
19990316 08:24:54 30750980
19990316 08:25:04 30751199
19990316 08:25:14 30751420
19990316 08:25:24 30751640
19990316 08:25:34 30751872
19990316 08:25:44 30752151
19990316 08:25:54 30752360
19990316 08:26:04 30752567
19990316 08:26:14 30752723
19990316 08:26:24 30752944
Total Time   170 seconds.
Total Change 1964
```

30-20. Constraints are a valuable commodity in Oracle during day-to-day operations. However, they can occasionally get in the way when debugging or
fixing data. If a table has many constraints, it can be tedious to disable
and then reenable them. It would be nice to automate this enabling and
disabling on a per-table basis. Hey, that sounds like a good exercise.

The constraint_manager package automates the enabling, disabling, defer-
ring, and undeferring of constraints for a table. The package header is displayed here:

```
CREATE OR REPLACE PACKAGE constraint_manager AS
    /*
     || This package automates the deferring, undeferring,
     || enabling and disabling of constraints for a table.
     ||
     || 15-FEB-2000 DRH Coded for workbook
    */

    -- defer deferrable constraints
    PROCEDURE defer ( p_owner dba_constraints.owner%TYPE,
                      p_table dba_constraints.table_name%TYPE );

    -- undefer deferrable constraints
    PROCEDURE immediate ( p_owner dba_constraints.owner%TYPE,
                          p_table dba_constraints.table_name%TYPE );

    -- enable all constraints
    PROCEDURE enable ( p_owner dba_constraints.owner%TYPE,
                       p_table dba_constraints.table_name%TYPE );

    -- disable all constraints
    PROCEDURE disable ( p_owner dba_constraints.owner%TYPE,
                        p_table dba_constraints.table_name%TYPE );

END constraint_manager;
```

Write a package body to perform the appropriate tasks.

30-21. Nothing is worse than deleting a large number of rows from a table and
then watching the process die because of rollback segment problems. To
avoid such problems, create a procedure to delete records from a table in
bunches. The procedure will have four arguments: the owner of the table,
the table name, the number of records to delete at one time (default to
100), and a Boolean to indicate whether a commit should take place after
each deletion. Here's the skeleton of the procedure:

```
CREATE OR REPLACE PROCEDURE incremental_del
                ( p_owner       dba_tables.owner%TYPE,
                  p_table       dba_tables.table_name%TYPE,
                  p_rows_to_del INT := 100,
                  p_commit      BOOLEAN := FALSE ) IS
```

```
BEGIN
   IF p_commit THEN
      commit;
   END IF;

END;
```

30-22. Now back to partitions. Beyond the obvious performance and maintenance gains, partitions are handy because they can be reorganized easily.
Like most DBAs, I seldom have a lot of time (or patience) for doing things
more than once, so I always attempt to automate them. Hence the following exercise.

The PARTITION_MANAGER package allows restructuring of a table's partitions. It contains the following procedures:

LOAD
   Loads the table's partition information into memory (a PL/SQL table)

SHOW
   Displays the table's old and new partition information

CHANGE_NAME
   Modifies the partition name in memory

CHANGE_TABLESPACE
   Modifies the new tablespace for a partition in memory

CHANGE_HIGH
   Modifies the new high value for a partition in memory

CHANGE_PART
   Adds a new partition or changes new attributes of an existing one

REPARTITION
   Changes a table's partition structure from old to new values

Here is the package header:

```
CREATE OR REPLACE PACKAGE partition_manager IS
   /*
      || This package allows the automated reconstruction of
      || table and index partitions.
      ||
      || 08-FEB-2000 DRH Began slimmed-down version for workbook
   */

   -- load tables partition info
   PROCEDURE load ( p_owner dba_tables.owner%TYPE,
                    p_table dba_tables.table_name%TYPE );

   -- show tables partition info
   PROCEDURE show;

   -- procedures to allow changes to the name, tablespace, high value
   -- or all of the above
```

```
        PROCEDURE change_name       (
             p_element         INT,
             p_new_name        dba_tab_partitions.partition_name%TYPE );
        PROCEDURE change_tablespace (
             p_element         INT,
             p_new_tablespace  dba_tab_partitions.tablespace_name%TYPE );
        PROCEDURE change_high       (
             p_element         INT,
             p_new_high        dba_tab_partitions.high_value%TYPE );
        PROCEDURE change_part       (
             p_element         INT,
             p_new_name        dba_tab_partitions.partition_name%TYPE,
             p_new_high        dba_tab_partitions.high_value%TYPE,
   p_new_tablespace dba_tab_partitions.tablespace_name%TYPE );

        -- procedure that attempts the repartitioning
        PROCEDURE repartition;

   END partition_manager;
```

Here is an example of using the package to change the high value of the second partition to 30 and adding a third partition with a high value of MAXVALUE.

```
SQL> EXEC partition_manager.load('dhurley','demo');

PL/SQL procedure successfully completed.

SQL> EXEC partition_manager.change_high(2,'30');

PL/SQL procedure successfully completed.

SQL> EXEC partition_manager.change_part(3,'P3','MAXVALUE','USERS');

PL/SQL procedure successfully completed.

SQL> EXEC partition_manager.show;
```

| # | ---- Existing | | | ---- New | | | |
	Name	High	Tablespace	Name	High	Tablespace	Num Rows
1	P1	10	USERS	P1	10	USERS	0
2	P2	15	USERS	P2	30	USERS	0
3				P3	MAXVALUE	USERS	

```
PL/SQL procedure successfully completed.

SQL> EXEC partition_manager.repartition;

PL/SQL procedure successfully completed.

SQL> EXEC partition_manager.show;
```

```
-     ---- Existing                              ---- New
#     Name   High       Tablespace   Name   High       Tablespace   Num Rows
1     P1     10         USERS        P1     10         USERS        0
2     P2     30         USERS        P2     30         USERS        0
3     P3     MAXVALUE   USERS        P3     MAXVALUE   USERS        0

PL/SQL procedure successfully completed.
```

Write the package body.

30-23. Log switches have a huge effect on system performance and recovery. Sometimes, you need to ensure that they happen at regular intervals.

The log_switch procedure runs in the background by DBMS_JOB to ensure that log switches happen at least once every hour. The procedure doesn't perform a log switch if a natural one has occurred less than 60 minutes before the procedure is invoked. Write the procedure.

30-24. Estimating table sizes is often cumbersome. One way to accomplish this task is to use test data information to determine the average row length. Armed with this information and an estimated number of rows, it's fairly easy to estimate table sizes. In the next set of exercises, we'll try building a procedure that estimates the storage required for a table.

Initially, you need to do a little thinking. You need to decide what pieces of information are needed, what input you want to receive from the user, and what assumptions you'll make on your own.

Minimally, the user has to provide the schema and table names, as well as the number of rows estimated for the table. There is no way we can guess at those. It's also helpful to know the PCTFREE setting, which determines how much space is left in each Oracle block for updates. When estimating table sizes, it is important to allow space for rows to be updated, as the data will change.

You also need to know how much to allow for overhead, such as block headers, segment headers, and the like. Many DBAs have come up with elaborate calculations to accurately compute (to the byte) what overhead will be incurred. While this is nice, it is (in my opinion) overkill for an estimate. A simple fudge factor will suffice. Quite often, a 3% fluff factor comes close to the exact calculations. I use a 10% factor, just to be sure.

Write a CREATE PROCEDURE stub and declarative section for a procedure called estimate_tabsize that receives as input the schema, table, number of rows, and PCTFREE settings. The PCTFREE has a default value of 30. The procedure has an outgoing variable that is the initial extent. In the declarative section, define a constant for the overhead fudge factor at 10%.

30-25. Before the actual estimation procedure is put together, you need to create a few other procedures and functions. For example, you need a function that returns the average row length for a given table. Sounds as simple as getting information from the DBA_TABLES view, right? Well, yes to a point. As it turns out, that information is added to the view only when the table is analyzed. Therefore, you also have to determine whether or not the table has been analyzed.

This is the first step: write a function that returns TRUE or FALSE, depending on whether or not the table has been analyzed.

30-26. Next, you need to decide what to do if there are no statistics, meaning that the column DBA_TABLES.AVG_ROW_LEN is NULL. One possibility is to analyze the table, generating the statistics for the procedure to use. Another is to end with an error message. Use the first approach.

Write a procedure that calls the table_is_analyzed function, Then determines whether or not the table has been analyzed, and if it hasn't, analyzes the table. In this procedure, utilize an Oracle built-in that analyzes a specific object, as opposed to a whole schema or database.

30-27. Once the table has been analyzed, it's time to do the dirty work: bring the data together and perform the calculation. Write an execution section of a procedure that calls the ensure_table_analyzed procedure, gets the average row length, makes the calculation, and returns the initial extent size. It utilizes the stub previously worked out that creates the procedure called estimate_tabsize.

30-28. Put the entire procedure together.

30-29. One of the key components of Oracle's recovery facilities is redo logs. These logs store before and after images of all transactions that occur in the database including rollback segments. During instance recovery, the statements in these logs are reapplied to bring the database up-to-date. Redo logs can be archived to provide for point-in-time recovery. Oracle has obviously been able to read the contents of the redo logs for many years; in Oracle 8.1.5, Oracle is finally allowing the logs to be read by users. Actually they are allowing users to *mine* them; hence the capability is referred to as a Log Miner.

What two PL/SQL packages provide Log Miner functionality?

30-30. Once a log mining session is begun, is it kept in sync with changes occurring in the database?

30-31. Write a procedure to load the current online redo log files into Log Miner. Two queries are required to find the redo logs to load:

```
/* Get the redo log group numbers */
SELECT group#
  FROM v$log;
```

```
/* get redo log group members */
SELECT member
  FROM v$logfile
 WHERE group# = n;
```

30-32. Once redo log files have been loaded into Log Miner, take a *snapshot* of them to view their contents. Update the procedure written in 30-31 to include a call to START_LOGMNR. This procedure can be called with a range of dates/times or a range of System Change Numbers (SCNs). Use the SCNs in this example. The first SCN for each online redo log group is retrieved from the V$LOG table using this query:

```
SELECT first_change#
  FROM v$log
 WHERE group# = 1;
```

To retrieve the current SCN for the whole database, use this query:

```
SELECT checkpoint_change#
  FROM v$database;
```

Use these two queries to determine the range of SCNs to use in the call to START_LOGMNR.

30-33. Once Log Miner is loaded and started, there are several "V$" views that contain information. The following table contains a list of these views, some real and some not so real. Decide which ones are real and enter a brief description of their contents:

View Name	Description
V$LOGMNR_CONTENTS	
V$LOG_CABIN	
V$LOGMNR_DICTIONARY	
V$LOGMAJOR	
V$LOGMNR_LOGS	
V$LOGGER	
V$LOGMNR_PARAMETERS	

30-34. As shown, the redo logs contain cryptic information in their native format:

```
SQL> SELECT username,
  2          operation,
  3          sql_redo,
  4          sql_undo
  5     FROM v$logmnr_contents;
```

```
USERNAME                          OPERATION
------------------------------ --------------------------------
SQL_REDO
---------------------------------------------------------------------
SQL_UNDO
---------------------------------------------------------------------

DEPLOYER                          DELETE
delete from UNKNOWN.Objn:47172 where ROWID = 'AAALhEAACAAAKOCAAB'
```

Delete from unknown? Objn? 47172? This is clearly only readable by Oracle's internal programs. What can be done to make this information readable by humans?

30-35. Write a package to simplify the usage for Log Miner. Your package should encapsulate the following logic:

- Loading the current and archived redo logs
- Starting and stopping the Log Miner process

30-36. True or false?

   a. Once a dictionary file is created in a Log Miner session, it is automatically kept up-to-date with all changes to database structure (table, views, etc.).

   b. Once a Log Miner session is started (START_LOGMNR), all users can see the contents of the related V$ tables.

   c. Once a Log Miner session is started (START_LOGMNR), it is kept up-to-date with all data manipulation.

30-37. As mentioned earlier, Oracle's cost-based optimizer (CBO) has long been an integral part of application performance and tuning. There are many ways to use the optimizer effectively in applications, such as setting initialization parameters or including optimizer hints in application code. However, it is rendered useless if the database statistics in the database are not kept up-to-date. The task of keeping the statistics up-to-date usually falls to the DBA, who dutifully writes scripts to analyze all the key tables and indexes at regular intervals. This task is all the more complicated because the DBA has to keep up with database structure changes, and may need to use dynamic SQL, which can be pretty tricky. Oracle 8.1.5 introduces a PL/SQL API called DBMS_STATS to the netherworld of statistics gathering.

OK, enough with the long-winded introduction; let's do some exercises. But first, consult the Oracle documentation for a thorough explanation of the CBO, statistics, and performance tuning before adding anything to your applications.

What SQL command creates statistics for database objects?

30-38. Explain why the ANALYZE command can't be used in PL/SQL as in this snippet:

```
BEGIN
  ANALYZE TABLE x COMPUTE STATISTICS;
END;
```

30-39. Beside the syntactical requirements, why else is it be necessary to use PL/SQL to gather statistics for an application?

30-40. Above and beyond ease of use, what are two key benefits of using the DBMS_STATS package instead of the SQL ANALYZE command?

30-41. Match the SQL ANALYZE commands in the first list below with their corresponding DBMS_STATS calls in the second list.

SQL ANALYZE commands:

1. `ANALYZE TABLE x COMPUTE STATISTICS;`
2. `ANALYZE INDEX x COMPUTE STATISTICS;`
3. `ANALYZE TABLE x ESTIMATE STATISTICS SAMPLE 10 PERCENT;`
4. `ANALYZE TABLE x COMPUTE STATISTICS FOR ALL INDEXED COLUMNS;`
5. `ANALYZE TABLE x DELETE STATISTICS;`

DBMS_STATS calls:

a. `DBMS_STATS.GATHER_TABLE_STATS(USER,'x',ESTIMATE_PERCENT=>10);`
b. `DBMS_STATS.GATHER_TABLE_STATS(USER,'x');`
c. `DBMS_STATS.GATHER_TABLE_STATS(USER,'x',METHOD_OPT=>'FOR ALL INDEXED COLUMNS');`
d. `DBMS_STATS.GATHER_INDEX_STATS(USER,'y');`
e. `DBMS_STATS.DELETE_TABLE_STATS(USER,'x');`

30-42. What procedure in DMBS_STATS can be used to analyze a whole database? (Note that this is similar to using the DBMS_UTILITY.ANALYZE_DATABASE procedure.)

30-43. What procedure in DBMS_STATS analyzes a whole schema? (Note that this is similar to using the DBMS_UTILITY.ANALYZE_SCHEMA procedure.)

30-44. Write a procedure that uses DBMS_STATS to generate statistics for a table. Here is an outline:

```
CREATE OR REPLACE PROCEDURE analyze_table
                    ( p_owner  VARCHAR2,
                      p_table  VARCHAR2 ) IS
  /*
  || Gather statistics for the table identified
  || by p_owner and p_table.
  ||
  || Requires : ANALYZE ANY privilege
  */
BEGIN
  ...
END;
```

30-45. What attribute of a table must be set so that Oracle can track when its statistics become stale?

30-46. Write a procedure to generate statistics for all stale objects in a user's schema and output a list of objects analyzed. The following is a shell of the procedure:

```
CREATE OR REPLACE PROCEDURE analyze_schema
                ( p_owner  VARCHAR2 ) IS
BEGIN
   ...
END;
```

30-47. The DBMS_STATS package allows you to store statistics in tables other than the data dictionary. What procedures maintain these tables?

30-48. Change the analyze_table procedure written in 30-44 to store the gathered statistics in a table called my_stats owned by a user called stats_god.

30-49. The DBMS_STATS package contains many procedures that essentially perform the same function but have differing input sources and output destinations. This can be confusing if you don't understand the basic concept of how these procedures are named. Match the procedure names in the first list with their functionality in the second.

Procedure names that begin with:

   1. SET
   2. GET
   3. DELETE
   4. EXPORT
   5. IMPORT
   6. GATHER

Have the functionality:

   a. Explicitly set statistics in a local statistics table or the data dictionary
   b. Retrieve statistics from a local statistics table or the data dictionary
   c. Remove statistics from a local statistics table or the data dictionary
   d. Transfer statistics into a local statistics table from the data dictionary
   e. Transfer statistics from a local statistics table into the data dictionary
   f. Gather statistics and/or transfer them into a local statistics table or the data dictionary

Note that there are also procedures to create and manipulate the internal representations of statistics.

30-50. Earlier in this chapter, we coded a procedure that generates statistics for a specific schema. Let's take the next step and build a package that uses

DBMS_STATS to analyze all schemas. What, analyze *every* schema!? Are you nuts? Do you have any idea how long that will take? Why, yes I do, and I also know that the time to perform this analysis can be drastically reduced via the DBMS_STATS package and its ability to detect stale statistics. First, let's set up some control tables.

The admin_log table records status messages when the procedure is run:

```
CREATE TABLE admin_log
(admin_name    VARCHAR2(30),
 admin_message VARCHAR2(100),
 admin_date    DATE );
```

Since you don't want to gather statistics for all users, you build a table to store the ones that, deep down, you really want to succeed:

```
CREATE TABLE users_we_care_about
(username VARCHAR2(30) NOT NULL PRIMARY KEY);
```

The package will be submitted every hour via DBMS_JOB. Therefore, you want to control the exact type of statistics gathered. This table does that:

```
CREATE TABLE stats_control
(username        VARCHAR2(30) NOT NULL,
 stats_type      VARCHAR2(30) NOT NULL
    CONSTRAINT valid_stats_type CHECK ( stats_type IN ('COMPUTE ALL') ),
 minimum_hour    INT NOT NULL
    CONSTRAINT valid_min_hour CHECK ( minimum_hour BETWEEN 0 AND 23 ),
 maximum_hour    INT NOT NULL
    CONSTRAINT valid_max_hour CHECK ( maximum_hour BETWEEN 0 AND 23 ),
 gather_stale    VARCHAR2(3) DEFAULT 'YES' NOT NULL
    CONSTRAINT gather_stale_yes_no CHECK ( gather_stale IN ( 'YES','NO' ) ),
 gather_empty    VARCHAR2(3) DEFAULT 'NO' NOT NULL
    CONSTRAINT gather_empty_yes_no CHECK ( gather_empty IN ( 'YES','NO' ) ),
 bypass_gather   VARCHAR2(3) DEFAULT 'NO' NOT NULL
    CONSTRAINT bypass_gather_yes_no CHECK ( bypass_gather IN ( 'YES','NO') ),
 indexes_only    VARCHAR2(3) DEFAULT 'NO' NOT NULL
    CONSTRAINT indexes_only_yes_no CHECK ( indexes_only IN ( 'YES','NO' ) ),
 last_run        DATE
);
```

Here are the rules that apply to the stats_control table:

- Full statistic "computes" are always performed. Bonus points are given for implementing estimation.
- If gather_stale is set to YES, stale statistics are gathered.
- If gather_empty is set to YES, empty statistics are gathered.
- If bypass_gather is set to YES, all statistics are gathered for all objects, regardless of whether their statistics are empty or stale.
- If indexes_only is set to YES, statistics are gathered only for indexes.
- Setting bypass_gather to YES overrides any settings of gather_stale, gather_empty and indexes_only.

By now you may be wondering why anyone would bother coding encapsulation on top of an Oracle built-in package. After all, the built-in itself encapsulates some core functionality, and that should more than suffice, right? The answer is a resounding "Well, sort of." There are many reasons to build packages that encapsulate a built-in:

- To provide successive runs of procedures or functions with different variables
- To provide trapping of built-in specific error messages so they can be formatted or ignored
- To provide formatting of rows in interface tables
- To allow for nonexisting interface tables

Let's use the handy-dandy built-in package DBMS_OLAP to demonstrate these points.

First, a few important points about DBMS_OLAP. Introduced in Oracle 8.1.5, it provides an API to Oracle's Summary Advisor (DBMS_OLAP is actually a synonym for DBMS_SUMMARY). The Summary Advisor provides evaluation and recommendation functions for data warehouse structures such as materialized views and dimensions. Consult the Oracle documentation for a thorough discussion of these topics.

Now for the first exercise—providing successive runs of procedures. Let's start by building a package with one procedure, DBMS_OLAP.ESTIMATE_SUMMARY_SIZE, which uses DBMS_OUTPUT to display the results on the screen. By the way, the ESTIMATE_SUMMARY_SIZE procedure provides estimates of the size of materialized views for SQL statements.

Here is a possible package header and body:

```
CREATE OR REPLACE PACKAGE olapper AS
   PROCEDURE do_estimates ( p_stmnt VARCHAR2 );
END olapper;

CREATE OR REPLACE PACKAGE BODY olapper AS
   /*-----------------------------------------------*/
   PROCEDURE do_estimates ( p_stmnt VARCHAR2 ) IS
   /*-----------------------------------------------*/
     v_num_rows  NUMBER;
     v_num_bytes NUMBER;
   BEGIN
     DBMS_OLAP.ESTIMATE_SUMMARY_SIZE( stmt_id       => 'OLAPPER',
                                      select_clause => p_stmnt,
                                      num_rows      => v_num_rows,
                                      num_bytes     => v_num_bytes );
     DBMS_OUTPUT.PUT_LINE('A Materialized View for the statement : ');
     DBMS_OUTPUT.PUT_LINE(CHR(9) || p_stmnt);
     DBMS_OUTPUT.PUT_LINE(CHR(9) || 'Is estimated to require '
        || v_num_rows || ' rows ' ||
                               ' and ' || v_num_bytes || ' bytes.');
```

```
END do_estimates;
END olapper;
```

Already we can display the output from these calls in a formatted way that is better than the built-in itself provided.

If you don't already have materialized views or dimensions in your database, use the OLAP_DATA.SQL script to create some.

In this exercise, augment the olapper package by allowing the entry of multiple SQL statements that are stored in memory and then executed successively by the do_estimates procedure.

30-51. The DBMS_OLAP package relies heavily on other Oracle utilities, including the EXPLAIN PLAN table. As a matter of fact, calls to the package just created fail miserably if the plan table does not exist. It also ends abruptly if the SQL passed to it is invalid. This segues nicely into the next point about encapsulation; trapping errors. Add an exception handler to the procedure to handle the exceptions I've noted.

30-52. The last two benefits of encapsulation concern interface tables. First off, simply querying these tables does not easily provide any kind of formatted results Second, sometimes they do not exist!

Two procedures within DBMS_OLAP fall into this category:

EVALUATE_UTILIZATION

Evaluates the utilization of existing materialized views based on either a hypothetical workload or Oracle Trace results. The results of this procedure are stored in a table called MVIEW$_EVALUATIONS created by the first procedure call.

RECOMMEND_SUMMARIES

Provides possible new materialized views to improve performance. Again, this can be based on a hypothetical workload or Oracle Trace results; the results are stored in an interface table, MVIEW$_RECOMMENDATION, created by the first procedure call.

In this exercise, augment the package you are building with calls to these procedures as well as procedures to display their output using DBMS_OUTPUT. Remember that the package may get created before the interface tables exist.

II

Solutions

Declaring Variables and Naming Elements

Beginner

1-1. The following variables are valid or invalid for these reasons:

    a. Valid. `my_variable2` starts with a letter, is less than 31 characters in length, and contains only letters, digits, and $, #, or _.

    b. Invalid. `my-variable2` may not contain a dash.

    c. Invalid. `my^variable` contains an illegal character, ^.

    d. Valid. `MyVariable` starts with a letter, is less than 31 characters in length, and contains only letters, digits, and $, #, or _.

    e. Invalid. `my_variable_for_many_many_of_usages` contains more than 30 characters.

    f. Invalid. `123myvariable` cannot start with a number.

    g. Valid. `"123myvariable"` is surrounded by double quotes. If you surround an identifier with double quotes (very different from two consecutive single quotes), then all rules about identifiers are suspended *except* for the maximum length of 30 characters.

1-2. Oddly enough, (a) compiles, while (b) fails with the following error message:

`PLS-00371: at most one declaration for 'LASTDATE' is permitted`

PL/SQL is a case-insensitive language (except for the contents of literal strings). Therefore, in both cases you are trying to declare two variables with the same name, which is not allowed. It turns out, however, that the compiler will not reject the duplicate declarations unless you actually try to use one of the variables!

1-3. Here is an example that demonstrates these two formats and shows that the same value is assigned:

```
DECLARE
   myDate DATE := SYSDATE;
   yourDate DATE DEFAULT SYSDATE;
BEGIN
   DBMS_OUTPUT.PUT_LINE
      ('The date value in myDate is '||mydate);
   DBMS_OUTPUT.PUT_LINE
      ('The date value in yourDate is '||yourdate);
END;
/
The date value in myDate is 29-OCT-99
The date value in yourDate is 29-OCT-99
```

1-4.
```
DECLARE
   my_name employee.last_name%TYPE;
```

1-5. These declarations are invalid for the following reasons:

Invalid Code	Problem	Valid Code
`INTEGER year_count;`	The datatype must come after the identifier.	`year_count INTEGER;`
`VARCHAR2(100) company_name, employee_name;`	The datatype must come after the identifier, *and* you can declare only one variable per logical statement.	`company_name VARCHAR2(100); employee_name VARCHAR2(100);`
`delimiters VARCHAR2;`	You must provide a constraint (maximum number of characters) for a VARCHAR2 declaration unless you are declaring a parameter.	`delimiters VARCHAR2(100);`
`curr_year CONSTANT INTEGER;`	If you declare a variable to be a constant, you must provide a default value.	`curr_year CONSTANT INTEGER := TO_NUMBER (TO_CHAR (SYSDATE, 'YYYY'));`
`invalid_date EXCEPTION := VALUE_ERROR;`	You can declare your own exceptions, but they cannot be given default or initial values.	`invalid_date EXCEPTION;`

1-6. These are the most appropriate datatypes for these data items:

Data Item	Datatype
a. 'This is a test'	VARCHAR2 or CHAR
b. Values from 1 to 10	PLS_INTEGER (best performance), INTEGER, BINARY_INTEGER, NATURAL, POSITIVE
c. 5.987	NUMBER
d. 'This is a test '	CHAR;. you need a fixed-length declaration to preserve the spaces
e. A string that is always nine characters long	CHAR
f. January 10, 2000	DATE
g. A binary file	BFILE (in Oracle8); prior to Oracle8, LONG or LONG RAW
h. TRUE or FALSE	BOOLEAN
i. The internal identifier of a row in a table	ROWID

Intermediate

1-7. Use the %TYPE anchoring attribute against a PL/SQL variable, just as you would anchor to the column of a table:

```
CREATE OR REPLACE PACKAGE types
IS
 dollar_amount NUMBER(20,2);
END;
/
DECLARE
   my_dollars types.dollar_amount%TYPE;
BEGIN
   ...
END;
```

1-8. The statements about the DATE datatype are:

a. Both true and false. Prior to Oracle 7.3, the maximum date was January 1, 4712. In later versions of Oracle, the maximum date has now been set to December 31, 9999.

b. True

c. True. The Oracle DATE is really a date-time data structure.

d. False. A date variable records the time down only to the nearest second.

e. False. No matter how you specify the date value, the internal format always uses a four-digit year.

1-9. The thing to remember when using a SUBTYPE is that you do not include a %TYPE anchoring attribute. A subtype already is a type. Here is the solution:

```
CREATE OR REPLACE PACKAGE types
IS
   SUBTYPE dollar_amount_t IS NUMBER;
END;
/
DECLARE
   my_dollars types.dollar_amount_t;
BEGIN
   ...
END;
```

1-10. You can't anchor (use %TYPE) against a CONSTANT; it must be a variable.

1-11. Unlike the folks who wrote the PL/SQL language, we developers are not allowed to "constrain" our own SUBTYPEs. In other words, after the IS keyword you cannot supply a datatype declaration that limits the size or length explicitly. Note that this restriction is relaxed in Oracle8*i*.

1-12. You receive this error:

```
ORA-06502: PL/SQL: numeric or value error
```

because a variable assigned the type SIGNTYPE can have only one of three values: −1, 1, or NULL.

1-13. Statements (b) and (c) both describe the value of anchoring.

1-14. You can anchor to a table, a view, a column in a table or view, a cursor, or a scalar PL/SQL variable.

1-15. One would hope that this function returns a BOOLEAN, as in:

```
FUNCTION is_value_in_list (list IN VARCHAR2, value IN VARCHAR2)
   RETURN BOOLEAN;
```

Oracle Forms documentation for the GET_GROUP_CHAR_CELL function unfortunately offers an example program named is_value_in_list that returns a number. If you name programs inaccurately, developers will have a much harder time understanding and using those programs.

Expert

1-16. THEN is a reserved word; the PL/SQL compiler refuses to interpret it as a variable name. SYSDATE, on the other hand, is not a reserved word. Rather, it is a function declared in the STANDARD package, one of the two default packages of PL/SQL. You could write that block in an even more confusing manner, just to drive home the difference between "your" sysdate variable and the STANDARD's SYSDATE function:

```
DECLARE
   sysdate DATE;
BEGIN
   sysdate := sysdate;
   DBMS_OUTPUT.PUT_LINE ('Date is ' || sysdate);
   sysdate := STANDARD.SYSDATE;
   DBMS_OUTPUT.PUT_LINE ('Date is ' || sysdate);
END;
```

You will see this output:

```
Date is
Date is 24-JAN-99
```

As explained in 1-11, we developers are not allowed to constrain our own SUBTYPEs. In other words, you cannot supply after the IS keyword a datatype declaration that limits the size or length explicitly. Check out *$ORACLE_HOME/RdbmsNN/admin/standard.sql* (the file that creates the PL/SQL STANDARD package) for examples of constrained SUBTYPEs.

1-17. The following block of code raises a VALUE_ERROR exception when executed. It demonstrates the technique of constraining a SUBTYPE:

```
DECLARE
   primary_key NUMBER(6);
   SUBTYPE primary_key_t IS primary_key%TYPE;
   mypky primary_key_t;
BEGIN
   mypky := 11111111;
END;
```

What you've done is a sleight-of-hand maneuver. You want the SUBTYPE declaration to look like this:

```
SUBTYPE primary_key_t IS NUMBER(6);
```

But that code will be rejected by the compiler. Instead, you must declare a variable with the appropriate constraint and then reference that variable with a %TYPE in your SUBTYPE statement. The subtype then inherits the constraint.

1-18. Here are three rules to keep in mind when working with NULLs:

- For all operators except for concatenation (the || symbol), if a value in an expression is NULL, that expression evaluates to NULL.

- NULL is never equal or not equal to another value.

- NULL is never TRUE or FALSE.

1-19. These operators allow you to work with NULLs in a structured way:

NVL

> Converts a NULL to another specified value, as in:

```
myValue := NVL (yourValue, 'WHOOPS');
```

IS NULL and IS NOT NULL

> You can use this syntax to check specifically to see if a variable's value is NULL or NOT NULL.

2

Loops

Beginner

2-1. There are four kinds of PL/SQL loops:

a. Simple or infinite loop:

```
LOOP
   ...
END LOOP;
```

b. Numeric FOR loop:

```
FOR loop_index IN [REVERSE] low_value .. high_value
LOOP
   ...
END LOOP;
```

c. Cursor FOR loop:

```
FOR loop_index IN cursor_name
LOOP
   ...
END LOOP;
```

or:

```
FOR loop_index IN (SELECT ...)
LOOP
   ...
END LOOP;
```

d. WHILE loop:

```
WHILE condition
LOOP
   ...
END LOOP;
```

2-2. You can stop the execution of a simple loop in at least three ways:

a. Issue an EXIT or EXIT WHEN statement:

```
LOOP
    lotsa-code
    EXIT WHEN salary_count > 10000;
END LOOP;
```

b. Raise an exception:

```
LOOP
    lotsa-code
    RAISE VALUE_ERROR;
END LOOP;
```

c. Use the GOTO command:

```
LOOP
    lotsa-code
    GOTO <<outa_here>>
END LOOP;
<<outa_here>>
NULL;
```

2-3. The loop does not contain an EXIT statement. It therefore never stops executing unless an exception is raised, which doesn't appear likely. It assigns SYSDATE to myDate an infinite number of times.

2-4. This loop executes 10 times, unless calc_sales raises an exception for one of the years between 1990 and 1999.

2-5. This is an example of a *phony loop*. It wasn't needed in the least, and the IF statements were needed only because the loop was used. You can simply write this code to get the job done. (Whether or not they deserve it. That's not up to you; you just write the code.)

```
give_bonus (president_id, 2000000);
give_bonus (ceo_id, 5000000);
```

2-6. Each function is run a single time; the low and high values in a numeric FOR loop range are evaluated once, before the loop body is executed even a single time.

Intermediate

2-7. A REPEAT UNTIL loop executes its body and then checks to see if the condition for stopping execution is TRUE. You can implement a REPEAT UNTIL loop with the simple loop as follows:

```
LOOP
    ...
    EXIT WHEN <condition>;
END LOOP;
```

2-8. This loop does not execute even once. When you use the REVERSE keyword, the year_index moves from highest to lowest value (the reverse of the normal order). However, the low value of the range must still be first, as shown here:

```
FOR year_index IN REVERSE 1990 .. 1999
LOOP
   calc_sales (year_index);
END LOOP;
```

2-9. At first glance, you might think that a FOR loop would make the most sense ("for each..."). A FOR loop would be a mistake in this context, however, because there is also a *conditional exit* (under certain conditions, stop after 12 years). You should use a FOR loop only when you are going to iterate unconditionally through every value between the low- and high-range limits. Instead, use a simple or WHILE loop to satisfy this requirement.

2-10. Since there is no conditional exit described in this requirement, you should use the cursor FOR loop.

2-11. Use the WHILE loop, since there are conditions under which you do not want the loop body to execute even a single time.

2-12. Do not use a generic loop index name (i); it makes the code less readable, and it looks unprofessional. In addition, the conditional EXIT from the FOR loop should be removed. Instead, use a FOR loop that iterates as follows:

```
FOR i IN 1 .. LEAST (76, total_count)
LOOP
   calc_totals (i);
END LOOP;
```

2-13. This loop relies on two different FETCH statements, so there is some redundant code. What's the big deal? What if the condition becomes a bit more complex? What if after fetching, you need to execute a few functions to transform the data before calculating totals? Then you have to do all that in both places.

In addition, there are two different termination conditions in two places in the loop (WHILE condition and EXIT WHEN clause). You should not EXIT from inside a WHILE loop. You should instead rely on the loop boundary condition. You are much better off using a simple loop and just a single FETCH inside the loop, as shown here:

```
OPEN emp_cur;
LOOP
   FETCH emp_cur INTO emp_rec;
   EXIT WHEN
      emp_cur%NOTFOUND OR
      emp_rec.salary > 100000;
   calc_totals (emp_rec.salary);
END LOOP;
CLOSE emp_cur;
```

You should not use a cursor FOR loop in this case, since there is a conditional exit (salary > 100000). Use a cursor FOR loop only if you are going to retrieve and process unconditionally each row identified by the cursor.

2-14. This loop's body changes the value of its high range value, which is considered bad programming practice. Never attempt to change the values used in the range scheme. Doing so will not actually affect the execution of the loop, since the range scheme is evaluated only once, at the time the loop begins. It will, however, cause lots of confusion Andes code will be difficult to maintain.

2-15. This code fetches each and every record from the cursor, without any conditional exits from the simple loop. Therefore, you should use a cursor FOR loop instead to reduce code volume:

```
DECLARE
    CURSOR emp_cur IS SELECT ... ;
BEGIN
    FOR emp_rec IN emp_cur
    LOOP
        calc_totals (emp_rec.salary);
    END LOOP;
END;
```

2-16. You have one way in to the loop, but two ways out (the WHILE condition and the EXIT WHEN statement). In this simple example, this doesn't seem to be a crucial flaw. However, your programs are much more complicated. If you allow multiple exits from a loop (or a function, for that matter) your code will be harder to debug and maintain.

Avoid the use of EXIT or EXIT WHEN inside a WHILE loop. You should rely only on changes in the loop boundary condition to cause the loop to terminate execution.

There is a related problem in this code: the two different logical checks are actually directly opposed to each other. One (WHILE condition) terminates the loop when no_more_data is FALSE; the second (EXIT WHEN) terminates the loop when no_more_data is TRUE. This is the kind of trouble you run into when you write (or think you are writing) the same thing twice (or more). Do everything you can to avoid code redundancy!

2-17. You should not use a PL/SQL loop at all; nothing is gained by performing 12 separate updates since you don't have an exception handler around the UPDATE. For better performance, employ straight SQL as shown here:

```
UPDATE monthly_sales
    SET pct_of_sales = 100
  WHERE company_id = 10006
    AND month_number BETWEEN 1 AND 12;
```

2-18. First, this loop raises an error. The cursor FOR loop closes the loop automatically when it is done. The final "manual" close causes an error.

Second, the code declared a record named emp_rec with the clear intention that it be used inside the FOR loop and then in the subsequent IF statement. In reality, the emp_rec in the FOR loop is a different record from that defined in the declaration section.

As a direct consequence, the reference to emp_rec.salary after the loop now references the still-null record declared in the block, not the record filled inside the loop (which has by this time terminated and erased that record).

Never try to declare the FOR loop index. It won't have the intended effect. A FOR loop, whether integer or cursor, always implicitly declares its own loop index.

2-19. You should not use a PL/SQL loop at all; nothing is gained by performing the separate inserts since you don't have an exception handler around the INSERT. For better performance, employ straight SQL as follows:

```
INSERT INTO occupancy_history (pet_id, name, checkout_date)
   SELECT pet_id, name, checkout_date
     FROM occupancy
    WHERE checkout_date IS NOT NULL;
```

2-20. The challenge here is that since you have used a cursor FOR loop, you cannot take advantage of the %ROWCOUNT attribute with something like this:

```
FOR the_man IN nasties_cur
LOOP
   DBMS_OUTPUT.PUT_LINE (the_man.of_the_year);
END LOOP;
DBMS_OUTPUT.PUT_LINE (nasties_cur%ROWCOUNT);
```

The cursor is closed; that last line raises an error. Instead, you must put code inside the FOR loop to keep track of any information you want to retain after the loop is done. Here is one possible implementation:

```
DECLARE
   counter PLS_INTEGER;
   CURSOR nasties_cur
   IS
      SELECT ceo_name || ' of ' || company_name of_the_year
        FROM merged_companies
       WHERE TO_CHAR (merger_date, 'YYYY') = '1998'
         AND layoffs >= 1000;
BEGIN
   FOR the_man IN nasties_cur
   LOOP
      DBMS_OUTPUT.PUT_LINE (the_man.of_the_year);
      counter := nasties_cur%ROWCOUNT;
   END LOOP;
   DBMS_OUTPUT.PUT_LINE (counter);
END;
```

2-21. The value of counter is the default NULL when the cursor is opened, and the loop starts its work. The assignment of counter + 1 to counter merely assigns NULL again and again to counter. So after the loop has completed, counter is still NULL, and therefore, not > 0.

Expert

2-22. The first two rewrites (a and b) have just one way out, but they do not accurately reflect the processing that took place in the original. What if years_in is 3? Rewrite (d) correctly stops the loop from continuing if year-num exceeds the value of years_in, but it still has two ways out (with the addition of the EXIT WHEN statement). Rewrite (c) is the only one that is both logically equivalent and well-structured (one way in, one way out).

2-23. It executes an infinite number of times; this is an infinite WHILE loop. The local module called inside the loop never returns NULL for step_out, so next_analysis_step is never NULL. The analysis_cursor%NOTFOUND attribute returns TRUE, but no exception is raised even though you are fetching past the end of the result set. Thus, the loop never terminates.

2-24. At first glance, you might think it best to use the numeric FOR loop, as shown here:

```
PACKAGE BODY company_pkg
IS
    TYPE ids_tabtype IS TABLE OF INTEGER
        INDEX BY BINARY_INTEGER;

    PROCEDURE close_all (company_ids IN ids_tabtype) IS
    BEGIN
        FOR id_ind IN company_ids.FIRST .. company_ids.LAST
        LOOP
            UPDATE company SET status = 'C'
            WHERE company_id = company_ids(id_ind);
        END LOOP;
    END;
END;
```

The problem with this code is that it assumes the company_ids table is filled from first to last row. But the row numbers are company ID numbers, and there is a good chance they are not sequentially defined (at least those companies slotted to be closed).

Consequently, you are always better off using a simple loop and the FIRST and NEXT table methods to traverse the table:

```
PACKAGE BODY company_pkg
IS
    TYPE ids_tabtype IS TABLE OF INTEGER
        INDEX BY BINARY_INTEGER;
```

```
     PROCEDURE close_all (company_ids IN ids_tabtype)
     IS
         id_ind PLS_INTEGER := company_ids.FIRST;
     BEGIN
        LOOP
           EXIT WHEN id_ind IS NULL;
           UPDATE company SET status = 'C'
            WHERE company_id = company_ids(id_ind);
           id_ind := company_ids.NEXT (id_ind);
        END LOOP;
     END;
 END;
```

2-25. Here are the solutions:

```
   a. BEGIN
         FOR indx in 1..100
         LOOP
           IF MOD (indx,3) = 0
           THEN
              DBMS_OUTPUT.PUT_LINE (indx);
           END IF;
         END LOOP;
      END;
```

```
   b. DECLARE
         indx INTEGER := 3;
      BEGIN
        WHILE indx < 100
        LOOP
          DBMS_OUTPUT.PUT_LINE (indx);
          indx := indx + 3;
        END LOOP;
      END;
```

2-26. Here is a suggested version of the Oracle POWER function:

```
CREATE OR REPLACE FUNCTION my_power (
   base IN NUMBER,
   exponent IN INTEGER)
   RETURN  number
IS
  ret_val NUMBER := base;
BEGIN
  IF exponent = 0 THEN
    ret_val := 1;

  ELSE
    FOR i in 1..(exponent-1)
    LOOP
      ret_val := ret_val * base;
    END LOOP;
  END IF;

  RETURN ret_val;
END;
```

3

Conditional and Sequential Logic

Beginner

3-1. A classic typo in the world of PL/SQL: the "END" is glommed together with the "IF". You need a space in between:

```
END IF;
```

3-2. Another classic typo in the world of PL/SQL: when you write an ELSE-IF clause, you must drop the "E" at the end of "ELSE", as in:

```
ELSIF
```

3-3. Yet another classic typo in the world of PL/SQL: when you write an ELSE clause, you do not provide a THEN after the ELSE. Just the ELSE, ma'am.

3-4. It's always a good idea to minimize the levels of nested IFs (and loops as well). In this case, you can take advantage of the ELSIF clause as follows:

```
IF salary < 10000
THEN
   bonus := 2000;
ELSIF salary < 20000
THEN
   bonus := 1500;
ELSIF salary < 40000
THEN
   bonus := 1000;
ELSE
   bonus := 500;
END IF;
```

I hope you will agree that this code is more readable!

3-5. Yes, the sorry_you_are_not_that_sick procedure executes. The ELSE statements executes if previous IF and ELSIF clauses all evaluate to FALSE or NULL.

3-6. You can use the GOTO command, or you can RAISE an exception.

3-7. You have to go to a *label*. A label in PL/SQL is an identifier (maximum of 30 characters, starts with a letter, etc.) that is surrounded by pairs of angle brackets, as shown here:

```
BEGIN
    GOTO skip_two_lines;
    democrats;
    republicans;

    <<skip_two_lines>>
    try_the_new_party;
```

In this block of code, you never get to the Democrats and the Republicans (as if they can be avoided). Instead, you skip right to the New Party. If that interests you, check it out at *www.newparty.org*.

3-8. Use the NULL; statement, as in:

```
BEGIN
    NULL;
END;
/
```

3-9. The following usages are:

   a. Valid. Suppose you were writing an application to analyze the need to "reform" the Social Security system. The requirements say that we must use the Social Security surplus to fund the Pentagon if the surplus is less than $100 billion. You could write this:

```
IF social_security_surplus < 100,000,000,000
THEN
    use_the_surplus_for_weapons;
END IF;
```

   but then a person maintaining your code might say, "Hey, George forgot to code the ELSE clause. I'd better do something quick," which may be precisely the wrong thing to do. If, on the other hand, you write your code like this:

```
IF social_security_surplus > 100,000,000,000
THEN
    /* Don't fix it; it's not broken! */
    NULL;
ELSE
    use_the_surplus_for_weapons;
END IF;
```

   then it is self-documenting: you thought about the ELSE clause, and you don't want anything to be changed in the Social Security system.

   b. Invalid. The NULL; statement is not the same as a NULL value.

   c. Valid. Here is the "I don't care" exception handler:

```
EXCEPTION
    WHEN OTHERS THEN NULL;
```

d. Valid usage. If you use the GOTO statement, you have to go to a label, and there must be an executable statement following the label. The code shown next will not even compile:

```
BEGIN
    IF total_salary > 1000000
    THEN
        GOTO better_to_share;
    END IF;
    <<better_to_share>>
END;
```

Often you don't want to do anything after you have gone to some escape location, so you would simply write:

```
BEGIN
    ...
    <<better_to_share>>
    NULL;
END;
```

e. Invalid. If you're not sure what is supposed to happen next in your code, you need to figure it out; don't put a "placeholder" in your code with the NULL; statement.

f. Valid. Here, for example, is a procedure stub that compiles and can even be referenced in other compilable program units.

```
CREATE PROCEDURE calc_total (company_in IN INTEGER) IS
BEGIN
    NULL;
END;
```

Intermediate

3-10. You can rewrite this block of code as follows:

```
DECLARE
    total_sales NUMBER :=
        sales_for_year (company_id=>1056, yearnum=>1998);
    no_revenue BOOLEAN;
BEGIN
    no_revenue := total_sales <= 0;
END;
```

You do not need an IF statement in situations where you assign the value to a Boolean variable. Instead, you can assign the expression that would have appeared in the IF statement, directly to the Boolean. Note that if total_sales is set to NULL, no_revenue is set to NULL in both cases.

3-11. In this case, you can't quite obtain the same behavior by replacing the IF statement with a direct assignment. You might consider the following statement:

```
no_revenue := total_sales <= 0;
```

But you run into trouble if total_sales is NULL. The original code would have set no_revenue to FALSE if total_sales was NULL, since it would cause the ELSE clause to execute. If you replace it with a single line assignment, no_revenue is set to NULL instead of FALSE.

3-12. The queue_order_for_addtl_parts procedure is never executed, regardless of the values for order_date, order_total, and min_order_total. For this procedure to run, order_date must be less than or equal to SYSDATE. If this is the case, the second condition would also be TRUE, and then fill_order is run for "LOW PRIORITY". When working with IF-ELSIF statements, it is extremely important that you make sure the Boolean expressions are mutually exclusive.

3-13. There is no difference logically between these two statements. The only difference is the addition of a NULL ELSE clause. It executes if potholes_after_storm is 1,000 or less, or NULL, but it won't have any effect.

Why include the ELSE NULL? It is a way of self-documenting in the code this message from the author: "I considered the "otherwise" condition and decided nothing should happen." That way someone doesn't come along later and say, "Gee! Steven forgot the ELSE clause. Hmmm, looks to me like the mayor should get reelected if there are only 999 potholes." And that could well be an incorrect assumption.

3-14. You receive the following error:

```
PLS-00375: illegal GOTO statement;
        this GOTO cannot branch to label 'BIG_SURPRISE'
```

There are a number of restrictions on the use of GOTO. In this case, you see that you cannot "escape" from within one IF-ELSIF clause and go to another clause within that statement.

3-15. Only the fourth selection (d) is not a valid restriction. You can have more than one GOTO going to the same label, as in:

```
BEGIN
   IF presidents_lie
   THEN
      GOTO big_surprise;

   ELSIF ceos_don't_care
   THEN
      GOTO big_surprise;
   END IF;
   <<big_surprise>>
   get_cynical;
END;
```

Expert

3-16. No. The IF statement is the only native PL/SQL conditional syntax.

3-17. There are two basic possibilities:

- Use the SQL DECODE function inside a SELECT FROM dual (or other table with just one row). Here is a demonstration of the DECODE solution:

```
eypBEGIN
    SELECT DECODE (friend_type,
                   'B', 'BEST',
                   'K', 'BACKSTABBING',
                   'C', 'CLOSE',
                   'L', 'LIKE A BROTHER',
                   'ACQUAINTANCE')
      INTO friend_descrip
      FROM dual;
```

- Structure the IF statement to look and act as much like a CASE statement as possible. Here is an example of an IF statement posing as a CASE statement:

```
BEGIN
    IF    friend_type    -  'B'
       THEN friend_descrip =  'BEST'
          ;
    ELSIF friend_type    =  'K'
       THEN friend_descrip =  'BACKSTABBING'
          ;
    ELSIF friend_type    =  'C'
       THEN friend_descrip =  'CLOSE'
          ;
    ELSIF friend_type    =  'L'
       THEN friend_descrip =  'LIKE A BROTHER';
          ;
    ELSE                    'ACQUAINTANCE';
    END IF;
```

3-18. Here is a function that implements an inline IF-ELSE statement, returning one of two strings:

```
CREATE OR REPLACE FUNCTION ifelse
    (bool_in IN BOOLEAN, tval_in IN VARCHAR2, fval_in IN VARCHAR2)
     RETURN VARCHAR2
IS
BEGIN
    IF bool_in
    THEN
       RETURN tval_in;
    ELSE
       RETURN fval_in;
    END IF;
END;
/
```

And here is an example of the ifelse function put to use:

```
BEGIN
    emp_status :=
        ifelse (
            hiredate > ADD_MONTHS (SYSDATE, -216),
            'TOO YOUNG',
            'OLD ENOUGH');
```

This example is equivalent to this code:

```
BEGIN
    IF hiredate > ADD_MONTHS (SYSDATE, -216)
    THEN
        emp_status := 'TOO YOUNG';
    ELSE
        emp_status := 'OLD ENOUGH';
    END IF;
```

If you like this technique (it comes in especially handy when you want to, say, concatenate different strings together but not to include a delimiter or space if the next string is NULL, and not write a tiresome sequence of IF statements), you could overload ifelse inside a package to accept and return different datatypes.

4

Exception Handling

Beginner

4-1. The built-in SQLERRM (b) displays the error text associated with a particular error. If it is used without any arguments, it returns a description of the most recently raised error. If an error code is provided, it returns the description of that error, as illustrated here:

```
SQL> EXEC DBMS_OUTPUT.PUT_LINE (SQLERRM (-1855))
ORA-01855: AM/A.M. or PM/P.M. required
```

4-2. To solve this problem, you need to:

- Add an exception section to the end of the block.
- Include a handler for the NO_DATA_FOUND exception.
- Call the SQLERRM function to retrieve the error message.

Here is the modified block:

```
DECLARE
    my_flavor ice_cream.fav_flavor%TYPE;
BEGIN
    SELECT fav_flavor
      INTO my_flavor
      FROM ice_cream
     WHERE name = USER;
    DBMS_OUTPUT.PUT_LINE
        ('I love ' || my_flavor || '!');
EXCEPTION
    WHEN NO_DATA_FOUND
    THEN
        DBMS_OUTPUT.PUT_LINE (SQLERRM);
END;
```

4-3. Each exception has associated with it an error number and an error description or message. An optional attribute is the *name* of an exception; not all exceptions have a name.

4-4. These exceptions are predefined by Oracle in the STANDARD package: VALUE_ERROR, NO_DATA_FOUND, INVALID_NUMBER, TOO_MANY_ ROWS.

These identifiers do not name predefined exceptions: DATA_NOT_ FOUND (should be NO_DATA_FOUND), DIVIDE_BY_ZERO (should be ZERO_DIVIDE), DUP_KEY_IN_INDEX (should be DUP_VAL_ON_INDEX), CURSOR_OPEN (should be CURSOR_ALREADY_OPEN), and VALUE_ TOO_LARGE (should be VALUE_ERROR).

4-5. The NO_DATA_FOUND exception is represented by two different error numbers in Oracle: −1403 and 100. The use of 100 dates back to conformance with a very early ANSI SQL standard.

4-6. The predefined exceptions are defined in the Oracle-supplied package STANDARD. This package is one of the two default packages of PL/SQL (the other is DBMS_STANDARD); this means you don't have to qualify references to elements in STANDARD with the name of the package.

Here are some of the definitions of exceptions from STANDARD:

```
LOGIN_DENIED exception;
    pragma EXCEPTION_INIT(LOGIN_DENIED, '-1017');

NO_DATA_FOUND exception;
    pragma EXCEPTION_INIT(NO_DATA_FOUND, 100);

ZERO_DIVIDE exception;
    pragma EXCEPTION_INIT(ZERO_DIVIDE, '-1476');

INVALID_NUMBER exception;
    pragma EXCEPTION_INIT(INVALID_NUMBER, '-1722');
```

You can look at the code for STANDARD. It is contained in the *standard. sql* file located in the *RdbmsNN\Admin* subdirectory, where *NN* is the version number (or not present in the new Oracle8*i* directory structure. Check with your DBA to get read-only access to this file. You can learn lots about PL/SQL by studying it.

Oracle PL/SQL offers a number of predefined, named exceptions in the STANDARD package (NO_DATA_FOUND, for example). You can also create your own "user-defined exceptions." Write a block of code that defines an exception named balance_too_low and then raises that exception:

```
DECLARE
   balance_too_low EXCEPTION;
BEGIN
   RAISE balance_too_low;
```

4-7. The previous information can be obtained by running a simple anonymous block such as the following:

```
DECLARE
    big_problem EXCEPTION;
BEGIN
    RAISE big_problem;
EXCEPTION
    WHEN OTHERS
    THEN
        DBMS_OUTPUT.PUT_LINE ('error code = '||SQLCODE);
        DBMS_OUTPUT.PUT_LINE ('error message = '||SQLERRM);
END;
```

When this block of code is run, you can see that the error code—for any and every user-defined exception—is "1", and the error message is "User-Defined Exception".

4-8. Generally, Oracle error numbers are negative. There are two, ahem, exceptions:

100 The error number for NO_DATA_FOUND (also known as –1403)

1 The error number for any and all user-defined exceptions

4-9. An exception is said to go "unhandled" when neither the block that it was raised in, nor any of the enclosing blocks contain an exception handler for the exception raised (or a WHEN_OTHERS handler). In this case, the exception propagates to the calling environment without being handled and stops that host program from executing.

4-10. The exception section of a PL/SQL block is optional; the only section of a PL/SQL block that is mandatory is the execution section (i.e., the text between BEGIN and END). If you do not include an exception section, all exceptions raised in the block propagate to the enclosing block, if any.

4-11. The exception block can trap exceptions by name or by using a catch-all handler named OTHERS. If the WHEN OTHERS handler is declared, it must be the last one specified in the exception block. Any exception raised in the block (and not trapped by some other exception handler) is then trapped by the OTHERS handler. Here is an example:

```
EXCEPTION
    WHEN OTHERS
    THEN
        log_error (SQLCODE);
END;
```

4-12. You get an unhandled exception. This example raises a VALUE_ERROR, since you are trying to assign a seven-character string to a variable with a maximum length of five (there never has been much room for justice in our world). Since there is no exception section, the error goes unhandled, and you will see one of the following error messages onscreen (at least in SQL*Plus).

In Oracle8*i* release 8.1, you see this error message:

```
ORA-06502: PL/SQL: numeric or value error:
   character string buffer too small
```

Prior to Oracle 8.1, you see this message:

```
ORA-06502: PL/SQL: numeric or value error
```

4-13. This block displays the following text when executed:

```
Inner block
Dream deferred...
```

The VALUE_ERROR exception raised by assigning the string "Justice" to the variable (maximum length 5), is trapped by the exception handler in the inner block, which displays the message. Control is then passed to the outer block, and since no error was propagated, PL/SQL simply continues executing the next statement in that block.

4-14. This example displays the message "Outer block". The initial value assigned to reality causes a VALUE_ERROR exception to be raised. Since we have not yet reached the execution section of the code, it is not trapped by the exception block of the inner block. The exception section only traps exceptions raised in the execution section of that block. Therefore, the exception propagates out to the exception handler for the outer block, where it is handled explicitly.

4-15. Here are the error conditions:

a. There is no predefined exception ANY. Unless the user has predefined the exception named "ANY", the code fails to compile. The developer most likely meant:

```
WHEN OTHERS THEN
```

b. You could write something like this:

```
WHEN VALUE_ERROR OR NO_DATA_FOUND
```

but you cannot combine multiple exceptions in a WHEN clause with AND. There can only be one exception raised at any given point; thus the AND operator makes no sense in this context.

c. In this example, the OTHERS exception handler is not the last exception handler. For PL/SQL to handle the exception properly, all errors you wish to handle must be specified before the WHEN OTHERS exception handler.

d. The keyword EXCEPTION is missing in this example. The keyword must be included to mark the end of the execution section and the beginning of the exception section.

e. You cannot specify an error number in a WHEN clause. You must use a named exception (either defined by PL/SQL in the STANDARD package or defined in your own code) or the OTHERS keyword.

4-16. The RAISE command can be used to raise any predefined or user-defined exception, as in:

```
RAISE NO_DATA_FOUND;
```

When you are within an exception section, you can issue an "unqualified" RAISE:

```
RAISE;
```

and PL/SQL reraises the current exception. This is useful in situations where you wish to perform certain activities when an exception is raised, such as logging error information, but also wish to propagate the exception to the calling block to stop further processing.

4-17. The no_name exception is never raised in this code. A programmer-defined exception can only be raised as a result of being explicitly named in a RAISE statement, as follows:

```
RAISE no_name;
```

The PL/SQL runtime engine raises predefined exceptions, such as NO_DATA_FOUND, and VALUE_ERROR, only when those errors are detected. The rest is up to you.

4-18. The following code satisfies the requirement. There are three changes necessary to handle the condition:

- The exception must be declared.

- The declared exception must be raised under the appropriate circumstances.

- The exception must be handled explicitly in the EXCEPTION section of the block.

```
FUNCTION build_name (name_in IN VARCHAR2, sex_in IN VARCHAR2)
RETURN VARCHAR2 IS
   exception unknown_sex;
   name_out VARCHAR2(100);
BEGIN
   IF first_char = 'M' THEN name_out := 'Mr. ' || name_in;
   ELSIF first_char = 'F' THEN name_out := 'Mrs. ' || name_in;
   ELSE
      RAISE unknown_sex
   END IF;
   RETURN (name_out);
EXCEPTION
   WHEN unknown_sex THEN
      DBMS_OUTPUT.PUT_LINE
         ('Unable to determine gender of individual!');
END;
```

4-19. When this block completes, the salaries of both SMITH and ALLEN will be $1,600. In other words, SMITH's salary has doubled, while ALLEN's remains the same. The first UPDATE executes successfully, but then an exception is raised, so the second UPDATE never occurs. The exception section traps the error with the WHEN OTHERS handler and displays a message. No exception propagates out of this block, and even if it did, the first UPDATE would remain (as long as the exception was handled at the calling block or above). Exceptions do not roll back DML statements unless the exception goes unhandled.

4-20. When this block completes, both salaries will remain unchanged. The first UPDATE statement executes successfully, but then an exception is raised, so the second UPDATE never occurs. Since there is no exception handler in this example, and this is the outermost block (recall that we are running this code from SQL*Plus), the exception goes unhandled and causes Oracle to perform a ROLLBACK implicitly. Therefore, all changes to the EMP table have been reversed, and the salaries are unchanged. When an unhandled exception is encountered, all DML statements since the last COMMIT or ROLLBACK are rolled back.

Intermediate

4-21. The steps listed in the problem are performed in the following order:

> The executable section terminates immediately.
>
> Control is passed to the exception section, if it exists.
>
> If there is an exception section, find a match for the error and then execute that handler code.
>
> If there is no match for the error, check for a WHEN OTHERS section and execute that handler code.
>
> If after executing handler code, an exception is raised (or re-raised), and there is no enclosing block, propagate the exception out to the calling environment.
>
> If after executing handler code, an exception is raised (or re-raised), propagate the exception out to the enclosing block.
>
> If there is no match and no WHEN OTHERS clause, propagate the exception out to the enclosing block.
>
> Oracle logs the exception to the alert log for the database.

The following steps are not performed by the database:

> Oracle goes to the package STANDARD to determine how to handle the error.

Oracle first checks to see if the code is being called from another block before propagating the exception to the calling environment. Oracle does not automatically log exceptions to the alert log for the instance. The alert log tracks physical database problems and abnormal conditions, and does not have anything to do with errors generated programmatically.

4-22. Here are the restrictions:

Parameter	Restrictions
Error Number	The number must be an integer or an integer expression returning a number in the range −20000 to −20999.
Error Message	The message text must be a character expression (literal or variable). The length of the string must be no longer than 2000 bytes in Oracle7 and no longer than 4000 bytes in Oracle8.
Keep Clear Stack	Must be a valid Boolean expression (TRUE, FALSE, or NULL).

4-23. The following calls are:

a. Invalid. The error number supplied is not in the range −20000 to −20999. These are the only values you may pass to this built-in procedure.

b. Invalid. A call to RAISE_APPLICATION_ERROR must have at least two arguments: the error number in the proper range and the error message.

c. Invalid. RAISE_APPLICATION_ERROR cannot be used to raise Oracle predefined exceptions.

d. Valid.

e. Invalid. The error number supplied is not in the range −20000 to −20999.

f. Invalid. The third parameter of RAISE_APPLICATION_ERROR, keep-errorstack, is type BOOLEAN, whereas the example is passing a string.

g. Valid.

4-24. False. When you call RAISE_APPLICATION_ERROR, it sets the values for the current error code and message inside your PL/SQL Program Global Area (memory reserved for your session). An enclosing block can then call the standard SQLCODE and SQLERRM functions to retrieve those values.

4-25. The custom message can be displayed using the built-in RAISE_APPLICATION_ERROR. An invalid value for sales_in has been defined as

zero or less. Therefore, you could satisfy the requirements by implementing the following code:

```
FUNCTION calc_commission (sales_in IN NUMBER)
   RETURN NUMBER
IS
  commission NUMBER(5,2) := 0;
BEGIN
  IF sales_in <= 0 THEN
     RAISE_APPLICATION_ERROR (-20001, 'Pull your own weight');
  ELSE
     RETURN (sales_in * 0.1);
  END IF;
END;
```

4-26. The code shown in the problem uses two programmer-defined exceptions to handle the possibility of either parameter not being supplied. If
either of these conditions is true, the appropriate exception is raised. Since
neither of the named exceptions is explicitly handled in the exception section, however, both are trapped by the WHEN OTHERS exception clause.

The behavior is therefore the same for both error conditions. If either of
the parameters is not supplied, the exception raised is trapped by the
WHEN OTHERS clause, causing the text "Invalid name supplied" to be
output. Only when both parameters are supplied is the formatted name
output.

4-27. The main advantage of declaring local exceptions in your code is to allow
you to exercise greater control over how errors are handled. By adding
explicit handlers to the exception section for each programmer-defined
exception, you can offer improved messages to the user explaining the
cause of the error.

Here is a new version of the exception section that does the job:

```
EXCEPTION
   WHEN no_surname THEN
      RAISE_APPLICATION_ERROR (-20001, 'No surname supplied.');
   WHEN no_given_name THEN
      RAISE_APPLICATION_ERROR (-20002, 'No given name supplied.');
   WHEN OTHERS THEN
      RAISE_APPLICATION_ERROR (-20003, 'Invalid name supplied.');
END;
```

4-28. Both blocks trap the exception successfully. The difference is that in the
second case, you cannot be sure what caused the exception or where it
was raised (or even that it was the bad_data exception that was raised).
The first block provides better control, since you know that a bad_data
exception must have been raised for this code to execute. This provides
the programmer with "context" information that would have otherwise
been lost with the WHEN OTHERS handler. Even though you include the

display of SQLCODE, you cannot tell what the error was, because all programmer-defined exceptions have the same number: 1.

If a user-defined exception is not handled explicitly in the block in which it is defined, there is a loss of information as the exception propagates outward to the enclosing blocks.

4-29. The custom message, as before, can be displayed by using the built-in RAISE_APPLICATION_ERROR. Two user-defined exceptions must be declared, one for signaling a bad commission rate and a second for signaling a bad sales figure.

An invalid value for rate is defined as anything outside the range 0 to 100. A simple IF...THEN statement can conditionally raise an exception for this scenario.

An invalid value for sales is defined as zero or less. A simple IF...THEN statement can conditionally raise an exception for this situation.

This code satisfies the requirements:

```
FUNCTION calc_commission (
    sales_in IN NUMBER,
    comm_rate_in IN NUMBER DEFAULT 10)
    RETURN NUMBER
IS
  bad_rate EXCEPTION;
  bad_sales EXCEPTION;
  commission NUMBER(5,2) := 0;
BEGIN
  IF rate_in not between 0 and 100 THEN
    raise bad_rate;
  END IF;

  IF sales_in <= 0 THEN
    raise_bad_sales;
  END IF;

  RETURN (sales_in * (rate_in / 100) );

EXCEPTION
  WHEN bad_sales THEN
    RAISE_APPLICATION_ERROR (-20001, 'Pull your own weight');

  WHEN bad_rate THEN
    RAISE_APPLICATION_ERROR (-20002, 'Invalid rate supplied');
END;
```

4-30. The key to solving this problem is to recall that the exception section in a block traps and potentially handles only errors that occur in the executable section of the block.

In this case, a VALUE_ERROR exception is raised in the *declaration* section of the code. This exception is never trapped by the exception section of this block but is always instead propagated to the calling block. This explains why the error message is not displayed upon failure.

The problem appears to be intermittent because only clients who are more than 99 days overdue cause the error to occur. Increasing the size of the days_between variable will alleviate the problem. Here is a recasting of the function:

```
/* Filename on web page: is_overdue.sf */
FUNCTION is_overdue (due_date IN DATE, paid_date IN DATE)
   RETURN BOOLEAN
IS
   days_between NUMBER; /* No more constraint on size. */
BEGIN
   /* Move assignment to executable section, so error
      is trappable. */
   days_between := due_date - paid_date;
   RETURN days_between > 30;
EXCEPTION
   WHEN OTHERS THEN
      DBMS_OUTPUT.PUT_LINE
         ('Error in is_overdue; Check input data.');
END;
```

4-31. SQLCODE returns the number of the current error. An error is raised in the inner block, but it is also trapped and handled. No error is propagated out to the enclosing block. Thus, when the PL/SQL engine encounters this line of code:

```
IF SQLCODE != 0 THEN
```

SQLCODE has already been reset to 0.

4-32. Use the built-in SQLERRM function; it doesn't only return the message associated with the current error. You can also pass it an error code and get the message associated with that code. You could use this code:

```
SQL> EXEC DBMS_OUTPUT.PUT_LINE (SQLERRM (-12154));
ORA-12154: TNS:could not resolve service name
```

4-33. A NO_DATA_FOUND exception is raised in any of these circumstances:

- A SELECT INTO finds no matching rows.
- Your code references an undefined row in a PL/SQL or index-by table.
- You read past the end of a file with UTL_FILE.GET_LINE.
- You read past the end of a BFILE with DBMS_LOB.READ.

4-34. The "trick" to solving this problem is to use programmer-defined exceptions and nested blocks that narrow the scope of propagation of the various NO_DATA_FOUND exception and then translate that "generic" error into a more specific, meaningful error. One implementation is shown in the *whodidthat2.sql* file. Here is a fragment:

```
/* Filename on web page: whodidthat2.sql */
. . .

   eof EXCEPTION;

BEGIN
   . . .

   BEGIN
      fid := UTL_FILE.FOPEN ('c:\temp', 'notme.sql', 'R');
      UTL_FILE.GET_LINE (fid, line);
   EXCEPTION
      WHEN NO_DATA_FOUND
      THEN
         RAISE eof;
   END;

EXCEPTION
   . . .

   WHEN eof
   THEN
      DBMS_OUTPUT.PUT_LINE ('Read past end of file');

END who_did_that;
/
```

4-35. This code displays the message "Outer block". The VALUE_ERROR exception is raised in the execution section of the inner block and is trapped by the inner block exception handler. A NO_DATA_FOUND exception is then raised and propagated to the outer block; it is not handled by the NO_DATA_FOUND handler in that same exception section. The explicitly raised exception is then handled by the exception section of the outer block.

4-36. The correct answer is (b). The inner query doesn't find any data, causing a NO_DATA_FOUND exception to be raised in the inner block. The text in the inner block is printed, and then the exception is re-raised. Since an exception name isn't specified explicitly, the last exception is raised again, causing a NO_DATA_FOUND exception to be raised in the outer block, where the text there is printed.

Expert

4-37. To allow each of the DML statements to execute, you must ensure that any exception raised by the statement is trapped and handled. This is done by enclosing each statement in its own anonymous block. Since you just want to keep on processing the DML statements, you can use the "I don't care" handler as shown here:

```
BEGIN
    BEGIN
        UPDATE emp SET empno = 100 WHERE empno > 5000;
    EXCEPTION WHEN OTHERS THEN NULL;
    END;

    BEGIN
        DELETE FROM dept WHERE deptno = 10;
    EXCEPTION WHEN OTHERS THEN NULL;
    END;

    BEGIN
        DELETE FROM emp WHERE deptno = 10;
    EXCEPTION WHEN OTHERS THEN NULL;
    END;
END;
```

4-38. To handle an exception (that is, an error code) by name, it must be assigned a name. In the STANDARD package Oracle assigns a name to a variety of error codes, such as ORA-01403 (NO_DATA_FOUND). ORA-01014 is not assigned a name, so you have to do it yourself—using the EXCEPTION_INIT pragma, as shown here:

```
DECLARE
    shutting_down EXCEPTION;
    PRAGMA EXCEPTION_INIT (shutting_down, -1014);
BEGIN
    ...
EXCEPTION
    WHEN shutting_down
    THEN
        DBMS_OUTPUT.PUT_LINE
            ('Cannot comply. System is shutting down!');
        RAISE;
END;
```

4-39. Examples (a) and (f) are valid usages of this pragma. To see what is wrong with the other declaration sections, run the *pragmaei.sql* script and examine the output:

```
SQL> @pragmaei

a. Just twelve months in a year...

b. DECLARE
   *
   ERROR at line 1:
   PLS-00701: illegal ORACLE error number 1843 for
       PRAGMA EXCEPTION_INIT

c.     PRAGMA EXCEPTION_INIT (-1843, bad_date);
                          *
   ERROR at line 3:
```

```
PLS-00124: name of exception expected for
    first arg in exception_init pragma
```
d. DECLARE
```
*
ERROR at line 1:
PLS-00702: second argument to PRAGMA EXCEPTION_INIT
    must be a numeric literal
```
e.   PRAGMA EXCEPTION_INIT (bad_date, ORA-01843);
```
                                       *
ERROR at line 3:
ORA-06550: line 3, column 40:
PLS-00103: Encountered the symbol "-" when expecting
    one of the following:) , => The symbol "," was
    substituted for "-" to continue.
```
f. Just twelve months in a year...

To sum up, here are the rules to follow when using the EXCEPTION_INIT pragma:

- You pass the exception name first, then the error number.

- The error number must be a negative integer, and it must be a literal, not a variable or an expression that evaluates to the number.

4-40. Execution of this block results in an unhandled exception:
```
DECLARE
*
ERROR at line 1:
ORA-01403: no data found
ORA-06512: at line 7
```

At first glance, this seems very surprising. Certainly, NO_DATA_FOUND was raised. No matter how many rows are in the dual table (and there can be more than one, so watch out for your assumptions!), 1 is never equal to 2 in the world of Oracle, so no rows are found. There is, in addition, a handler included specifically for that error. So why isn't NO_DATA_ FOUND being trapped?

The answer can be found in the declaration section. You've defined your own exception with the same name as the "default" or system exception. Within this block, then, any unqualified reference to NO_DATA_FOUND is resolved back to your exception and not the PL/SQL exception defined in the STANDARD package.

4-41. There are a number of ways to make sure that NO_DATA_FOUND is handled. These are each demonstrated in the *myndf2.sql* file.

- Don't declare your own exception with the same name. While it is possible and legal to declare variables, programs, etc., with the same names as code elements in the STANDARD package, I'd advise you to avoid this practice unless you have a clearly justified reason. So if you do not declare the exception with that name, the problems go away.

- Qualify your reference to NO_DATA_FOUND with its package name, "STANDARD", to make clear which NO_DATA_FOUND you mean.

- Avoid the implicit query. If you use an explicit cursor instead, you don't have to worry about raising NO_DATA_FOUND.

4-42. The first time you run this function in your session, you get this an unhandled exception:

```
SQL> EXEC DBMS_OUTPUT.PUT_LINE  ('Value of v is ' || valerr.get);
BEGIN DBMS_OUTPUT.PUT_LINE  (valerr.get); END;


*
ERROR at line 1:
ORA-06502: PL/SQL: numeric or value error:
  character string buffer too small
```

But when this function is called again in the same session, it shows the value of v (NULL):

```
SQL> EXEC DBMS_OUTPUT.PUT_LINE('Value of v is ' || valerr.get);
Value of v is
```

To explain this behavior, let's step through what is happening:

1. When you first call valerr.get, the newly compiled code is loaded into the SGA.

2. The package is then instantiated for the session. To do this, PL/SQL declares and initializes all variables and then runs the initialization section.

3. When the runtime engine tries to assign "abc" to v, it raises VALUE_ERROR, because the variable can hold only a single character.

4. There is an exception section for the package with a WHEN OTHERS clause. It would seem that this should trap the VALUE_ERROR exception. It does not, however, because that exception section applies only to operations performed in the initialization section itself, not in the "declaration section" of the package.

5. So, the error goes unhandled, and the initialization section is never executed.

6. The runtime engine does, on the other hand, consider the package to be initialized. As a result, the second time you execute valerr.get, it does not try to initialize the package again and simply returns the current value of v, which is NULL.

So if you ever find yourself in a situation in which the first time you run some code, you get an error, but you cannot reproduce it without reconnecting to Oracle, look for recent changes in a package-initialization process.

4-43. Hint: use the NOWAIT option with FOR UPDATE and declare your own exception for the Oracle error ORA-00054. Here is one possible solution:

```
/* Filename on web page: nolock.sql */
DECLARE
  no_lock EXCEPTION;
  pragma EXCEPTION_INIT(no_lock, -00054);
BEGIN
  FOR my_rec IN (SELECT * from EMP FOR UPDATE NOWAIT)
  LOOP
    DBMS_OUTPUT.PUT_LINE ('Employee: ' || my_rec.ename);
  END LOOP;
EXCEPTION
  WHEN no_lock THEN
    DBMS_OUTPUT.PUT_LINE ('Could not get lock.  Try again later');
END;
```

This solution can be tested using two separate SQL*Plus sessions. Run the code in the first session, and don't do a COMMIT or ROLLBACK. The names should be printed out for each employee. Run the code in a second session. The "try again" message should then appear. Go back to the first session and issue ROLLBACK. Then return to the second session and run the code. You should now see the employees.

One conclusion to draw from this exercise: you should consider adding a ROLLBACK or ROLLBACK TO *savepoint* statement in your exception to make sure all locks are cleared when an error occurs.

4-44. SYSDATE is a function implemented in the STANDARD package. If you look in *standard.sql*, you can view the implementation of this function:

```
function sysdate return date is
d date;
begin
   select sysdate into d from sys.dual;
   return d;
end;
```

Thus, if the SYS.dual table has more than one row, calling the SYSDATE function (and lots of other programs in the world of Oracle) raises the ORA-01422 error. This is, needless to say, a poor architecture for implementing the SYSDATE function.

Different versions of Oracle 8.x treat this condition differently. For example, Version 8.0.4 does not raise an error in this circumstance and returns the correct value. Version 8.0.5 though, displays the error shown in the previous question, as does Oracle8*i* Release 8.1.

Even with more than one row in dual, however, when you executed a query against that table in 8.1, it shows just a single row:

```
SQL> SELECT * FROM dual;

D
-
X

SQL> DELETE FROM dual WHERE dummy != 'X';

1 row deleted.
```

4-45. First, the "short version" of the answers:

 a. False. DBMS_UTILITY.FORMAT_ERROR_STACK will not give you the line number you need.

 b. False. SQLERRM does not contain error stack and line number information.

 c. True-False. An unhandled exception is your best bet.

Now, some elaboration: to some extent, the answer depends on which version of Oracle you are running. In general, if you let an exception go unhandled, a full error stack is displayed, including the line on which the original error was raise. In Oracle8*i* Release 8.1, however, there seems to be a bug, and that piece of information is left out.

DBMS_UTILITY.FORMAT_ERROR_STACK should return to you the full error stack in a formatted string. Prior to Oracle8, this function returned a totally worthless stack, barren of any line-number information. In Oracle8 and Oracle8*i*, the situation has improved, but it still looks as though the function returns line numbers for every error in the stack except the very first, original error.

 Try running the *disperr.tst* script to see what kind of behavior you get in your environment.

4-46. You could deploy an error log as any of the following:

Database table

 Perform an INSERT to populate the table with error information.

Operating system file

 In Oracle 7.3 and above, use UTL_FILE to write error information to a file.

Database pipe

 Use DBMS_PIPE to send error information to a pipe in the SGA. Another session can then extract that data and process it in "real time" (while the application is still running).

Standard output

Write error data to the screen using DBMS_OUTPUT.

In-memory collection

Write error information to an index-by or nested table in your own Program Global Area. When your application finishes, dump the in-memory data to a more persistent data source.

4-47. The log package did, in fact, write a row to the log table. After it completed that task, however, the calling block re-raised the exception, which came out unhandled. When SQL*Plus (and other host environments) detect an unhandled exception, an unqualified ROLLBACK occurs in your session. The entry to the log table is, therefore, rolled back, and there is no log to see.

4-48. Here are the error log types and characteristics:

1. Database table

   (b) You have to COMMIT in order to see the rows, at least from another session or while the code is still executing; (d) Your log INSERT is part of the overall transaction; (f) With autonomous transactions, you can write to the log and COMMIT without affecting the main or outer transaction.

2. Database pipe

   (a) Database pipes are not affected by database transaction activity; (g) If you attempt to write to a pipe and it is full, your program is blocked until space frees up in the pipe or you time out.

3. Operating system file

   (a) File I/O is not affected by database transaction activity); (b) Lines written to a file may not be visible unless you call UTL_FILE.FFLUSH to flush out the buffer to the disk file; (c) Sort of; there is no limit to the size of a file, but prior to Oracle 8.0.5, your line of error data could not exceed 1,023 bytes in length.

4. Standard output (screen)

   (a) Screen I/O is not affected by database transaction activity; (b) You must enable DBMS_OUTPUT, usually in SQL*Plus with a SET SERVEROUTPUT ON command); (c) Maximum amount of data allowed in DBMS_OUTPUT buffer is 1 million bytes; (e) No other session has access to your buffered DBMS_OUTPUT information.

5. Index-by table

   (a) Index-by tables are per-session data structures, whose content is not affected by database transaction activity); (b) You will have to write a program to display the contents of the index-by table or transfer it to another repository; (e) No other session has access to the data in your PGA.

4-49. You need to address these issues as you implement this procedure:

- If the error number is between −20,999 and −20,000, you must call RAISE_APPLICATION_ERROR.

- If the error number is negative and not in that range, you need to raise that error with the RAISE statement, which means you need an error name.

- You cannot use the EXCEPTION_INIT pragma for ORA-01403.

One possible implementation is shown in the *myraise.sp* file on the book's web page.

Here are examples of behavior of the myraise procedure:

```
SQL> EXEC myraise (-1855)
BEGIN myraise (-1855); END;

*
ERROR at line 1:
ORA-01855: AM/A.M. or PM/P.M. required
ORA-06512: at line 1
ORA-06512: at "SYS.DBMS_SYS_SQL", line 781
ORA-06512: at "SYS.DBMS_SQL", line 316

SQL> EXEC myraise (-20100, 'My error')
BEGIN myraise (-20100, 'My error'); END;

*
ERROR at line 1:
ORA-20100: My error

SQL> EXEC myraise (30400, 'Balance too low')
BEGIN myraise (30400, 'Balance too low'); END;

*
ERROR at line 1:
ORA-20000: 30400-Balance too low
```

So, if you want to use positive error numbers, simply parse the error message returned by SQLERRM to grab the custom error number and corresponding text.

5

Records

Beginner

5-1. The statements are:

    a. False. A record is not a scalar datatype, meaning that it contains only one piece of information. The whole point of a record is to contain multiple pieces of information: it is a *composite* datatype whose structure is much like a row in a database table.

    b. True.

    c. False. A record is not designed specifically to hold sounds, but you could (in Oracle8 and above) easily define a record with a LOB (large object) field that contains a sound file.

    d. False. It doesn't make any sense to define a record based on a tablespace. You can, on the other hand, define a record that resembles a row in a table or row fetched by a cursor.

    e. True.

5-2. Only the format shown in (c), called *dot notation*, can reference a field in a record. In general, you refer to an individual field in a record as *record_name.field_name*. You must always use the fully qualified name of a field when referencing that field.

5-3. To define a table-based record, use the %ROWTYPE declaration attribute:

```
DECLARE
    ceo_rec ceos%ROWTYPE;
```

5-4. The statements are:

    a. False. A table-based record takes its definition from the structure of a table: each field has the same name and datatype as each and every column in its associated table (not just the nonnumeric fields). To define a table-based record, declare it with the %ROWTYPE attribute (you can only use %TYPE with scalar variable declarations). Suppose the emp table is defined as follows:

```
CREATE TABLE emp (
    empno NUMBER,
    ename VARCHAR2(30),
    hiredate DATE
);
```

b. False. To define a record called emp_rec based on the emp table, issue this declaration:

```
DECLARE
    emp_rec emp%ROWTYPE;
```

c. True.

d. True.

e. False. The emp_rec then has three fields: empno, ename, and hire-date; each has the data type of its corresponding column in the emp table. You cannot change the names of the fields with column aliases unless you have declared a record based on a cursor.

f. False. The resolution of a <table>%ROWTYPE reference occurs at compile time and in no way affects the runtime performance of your code.

g. False. Only SQL datatypes are valid as datatypes for fields in a table-based record. You cannot, for example, have a Boolean field in a table-based record.

5-5. The statements are:

a. False. A cursor-based record takes its definition from the SELECT list of an explicit cursor or a REF CURSOR object (but you cannot %ROWTYPE against an implicit cursor). Any valid SELECT statement can be used as the basis of a cursor-based record (joins are certainly allowed!). Each field in the record has the same name and datatype as a column or aliased expression in that SELECT list. The %ROWTYPE attribute defines a cursor-based record, as in this example:

```
CURSOR emp_cur
IS
    SELECT empno, ename, TRUNC (hiredate, 'YYYY') hire_year
       FROM emp;
emp_rec     emp_cur%ROWTYPE;
```

b. True.

c. False. The emp_rec has three fields: empno, ename, and hire_year, each having the data type of its corresponding column or expression in the cursor's SELECT list. The TRUNC function in the SELECT list transforms hiredate to a year string, and the alias hire_year provides a descriptive name.

d. True.

e. False. The alias is required to access the transformed hire date with a record only if you wish to reference that field inside your PL/SQL code. The following block, for example, executes without error, even though the expression has no alias:

```
DECLARE
    CURSOR emp_cur
    IS
        SELECT empno,
               ename,
               TRUNC (hiredate, 'YYYY')
          FROM emp;
    emp_rec emp_cur%ROWTYPE;
BEGIN
    OPEN emp_cur;
    DBMS_OUTPUT.PUT_LINE (emp_rec.ename);
END;
/
```

f. False. Only SQL datatypes are valid as datatypes for fields in a cursor-based record. You cannot, for example, have a Boolean field in a cursor-based record.

5-6. False. Once you declare a record based on a table (or a cursor), that record is a variable data structure you can fill and manipulate independently of the "source" of that record. You might simply want to use a table-based record to more easily declare a set of variables. Without the use of %ROWTYPE, you would have to declare individual variables.

5-7. The record definitions are:

a. Valid. The table-based record is associated with the emp table.

b. Invalid. A cursor-based record should use the %ROWTYPE attribute, not %TYPE.

c. Invalid. The TYPE statement indicates that this is a "programmer-defined record" (see the "Intermediate" section for more information and problems/solutions on this topic). You do not use the %ROWTYPE attribute, because it already is a type.

d. Valid. You can use "SELECT *" with a cursor and cursor-based record. Because all columns are selected in the cursor definition, the employee_rec record has, in this case, the same structure as a table-based record.

Intermediate

5-8. The statements are:

    a. Valid. This reason, along with (c) and (e), is an excellent reason to define your own record TYPE and then declare records from that TYPE. With programmer-defined records, you can rely on any and all native PL/SQL datatypes. You are not restricted to the definitions of existing tables or cursors. And, in a record TYPE you can declare another record TYPE, or even a collection TYPE (index-by table, nested table, variable array).

    b. Invalid. Using programmer-defined records does not, on the other hand, result in PL/SQL code that is independent of Oracle and can be ported to SQL Server. PL/SQL is a language proprietary to Oracle.

    c. Valid.

    d. Invalid. This reason may reflect a real concern ("fear" may be a better word) in your development organization, but the solution to this problem is not an avoidance of the %ROWTYPE attribute. Perhaps a round of mud wrestling will do the trick.

    e. Valid.

5-9. All these statements are true. A programmer-defined record takes its definition from a TYPE statement in which each field in the record (its name and datatype) is defined explicitly (kind of like a CREATE TABLE statement inside PL/SQL). To declare a programmer-defined record:

- Use the TYPE statement to declare a record type: a general record structure that can be shared by multiple record instances.

- Use the record type as a basis for declarations of actual records having that structure.

Here is an example of both these steps:

```
DECLARE
   TYPE summer_fun_rt IS RECORD (
      favorite_ice_cream_flavor VARCHAR2(30),
      min_hours_in_pool NUMBER,
      name_of_sailboat VARCHAR2(100)
   );

   eli_holiday summer_fun_rt;
   dad_holiday summer_fun_rt;
BEGIN
   eli_holiday.favorite_ice_cream := 'MINT CHOC CHIP';
   ...
   dad_holiday.name_of_sailboat := 'NOT THE SAILING TYPE';
END;
```

Programmer-defined records allow fields to be declared with NOT NULL constraints, in which case a default value must be provided (using the DEFAULT or := syntax).

You can define record TYPEs with fields that are composite datatypes themselves. As an example of a programmer-defined record with a field that is a index-by table, suppose you have this index-by table definition (a table of employee id numbers):

```
DECLARE
    TYPE empno_table_type IS
        TABLE OF emp.empno%TYPE
        INDEX BY BINARY_INTEGER;
```

You can then declare a department record type that holds a collection of information about a department:

```
TYPE dept_rec_type IS RECORD (
    deptno          dept.deptno%TYPE,
    dept_name       dept.dept_name%TYPE,
    total_salary    NUMBER,
    emp_table       empno_table_type
);


dept_rec dept_rec_type;
```

The emp_table field in dept_rec is a PL/SQL table of employees assigned to a department.

5-10. To make sure the record TYPE reflects the columns exactly (and continues to do so with every recompile), use the %TYPE attribute as follows:

```
DECLARE
    TYPE favorite_snacks_query_rec_type  IS RECORD (
        cookie  favorite_snacks.cookie%TYPE,
        ice_cream favorite_snacks.ice_cream%TYPE
    );


favorite_snacks_query_rec favorite_snacks_query_rec_type;
```

5-11. Here is an appropriate type:

```
TYPE customer_rec_type IS RECORD (
    customer_id NUMBER(5) NOT NULL 0,
    customer_name customer.customer_name%TYPE,
    prefers_nonsmoking_fl BOOLEAN
    );


customer_rec customer_rec_type;
```

5-12. Here is such a block:

```
DECLARE
    TYPE employee_rec_type IS RECORD (
        last_name employee.last_name%TYPE,
        hire_date employee.hire_date%TYPE,
        salary    employee.salary%TYPE);
```

```
        employee_rec    employee_rec_type;
BEGIN
    employee_rec.last_name := 'Feuerstein';
    employee_rec.hire_date := SYSDATE;
    employee_rec.salary := 1000000;

    DBMS_OUTPUT.PUT_LINE
        ('Last Name: ' || employee_rec.last_name);
    DBMS_OUTPUT.PUT_LINE
        ('Hire Date: ' || employee_rec.hire_date);
    DBMS_OUTPUT.PUT_LINE
        ('Salary:    ' || employee_rec.salary);
END;
/
```

Of course, I'd really like to do something like this:

```
DBMS_OUTPUT.PUT_LINE (employee_rec);
```

But PL/SQL doesn't know how to dynamically determine the names of each field and display them in a reasonable way, so I have to do all the work!

5-13. Here is an appropriate programmer-defined record TYPE:

```
/* Filename on web page: file tobacco.sql */
DECLARE
    TYPE phone_num_rec_type IS RECORD (
        area_code           VARCHAR2(3),
        phone_prefix        VARCHAR2(3),
        phone_number        VARCHAR2(4)
    );

    TYPE lobbyist_contact_rec_type IS RECORD (
        home_phone      phone_num_rec_type,
        office_phone    phone_num_rec_type,
        cell_phone      phone_num_rec_type,
        fax_phone       phone_num_rec_type,
        bathroom_phone  phone_num_rec_type,
        bathroom_fax    phone_num_rec_type
    );
```

5-14. Here is such a record:

```
        lobbyist_rec    lobbyist_contact_rec_type;
BEGIN
    lobbyist_rec.bathroom_phone.area_code := '800';
    lobbyist_rec.bathroom_phone.phone_prefix := 'SMO;
    lobbyist_rec.bathroom_phone.phone_number := 'KENO';
    -- The 'W' is extra
END;
/
```

5-15. The operations are:

a. Supported. You can assign one record to another with the assignment operator as shown here:

```
prev_customer_rec := curr_customer_rec;
```

Each field in prev_customer_rec is set to the value of its corresponding field in curr_customer_rec. The two records must have the same structure (numbers of fields and same datatypes).

b. Not supported. You cannot subtract one record from another (what would that mean, anyway?). PL/SQL does not, sadly, allow you to compare two records with syntax like this:

```
IF rec1 = rec2 /* INVALID */
```

c. Not supported.

d. Supported. You can pass a record as an argument to a procedure as long as the parameter type is a record type of one sort or another (%ROWTYPE or programmer-defined record).

e. Supported. You can assign a value of NULL to a record (Oracle 7.3 and above). This action sets each field in the record to NULL.

5-16. Yes. Both childlabor and bigprofits have the structure of the sweatshops table, although childlabor is a table-based record, and bigprofits is a cursor-based record. The PL/SQL compiler allows aggregate assignments between records of the same structure (although in this example they have different record types).

5-17. Yes. Both childlabor and bigprofits have the structure of the bigprofits_cur cursor, although childlabor is a programmer-defined record, and bigprofits is a cursor-based record. The PL/SQL compiler allows aggregate assignments between records of the same structure (although in this example they have different record types).

5-18. No. SUM(share_price) is an SQL expression that transforms the share_price column within the profitable_internets_stocks cursor definition. An alias for SUM(share_price) is required in the cursor definition before you can access the transformed share_price with a record. The DBMS_OUTPUT.PUT_LINE statement that references SUM(share_price) will fail.

5-19. The statements are:

a. Invalid. You cannot do an "aggregate" comparison for record equality (or inequality). You can only perform aggregate assignments. If you want to compare records, you must always do so by comparing the records' individual fields.

b. Valid. You're comparing individual scalar values.

c. Valid. You're calling a function that accepts one record and returns another record. This is a form of an aggregate record assignment.

d. Invalid. Although greatly desired; you cannot perform an insert into all columns by simply specifying a record of the right structure. Oracle

Corporation is, by the way, considering enhancing PL/SQL to support this syntax for some 8.x release.

5-20. Your first inclination would be to write code like this:

```
IF   steven_preferences.ice_cream = veva_preferences.ice_cream
  AND steven_preferences.cookie = veva_preferences.cookie
THEN
```

The problem with this approach is that it does not take into account NULLs. You would generally expect that if both fields are NULL, you want to consider the fields to be "equal." But NULL is never equal to anything, even itself, so you will really want to write code like this:

```
IF   (steven_preferences.cookie =
          veva_preferences.cookie
    OR
    (steven_preferences.cookie  IS NULL AND
     veva_preferences.cookie IS NULL))
   AND
    (steven_preferences.ice_cream =
          veva_preferences.ice_cream
    OR
    (steven_preferences.ice_cream IS NULL AND
     veva_preferences.ice_cream IS NULL))
THEN
```

5-21. Here is a possible TYPE:

```
TYPE dept_rec_type IS RECORD (
   deptno          NUMBER(5),
   dept_name       dept.dname%TYPE,
   total_salary    NUMBER NOT NULL := 0,
   emp_table       empno_table_type
   );

dept_rec   dept_rec_type;
```

Note that the total_salary field must have an initial (DEFAULT) value due to its NOT NULL constraint.

5-22. Here is the header:

```
CREATE OR REPLACE FUNCTION better_uses (
   p_corporate_welfare_rec   corporate_welfare%ROWTYPE)
   RETURN quality_childcare%ROWTYPE;
```

Expert

5-23. Multiple steps are necessary. First of all, you want to move the procedure within a package, so that you can define and make available to the procedure's parameter list these required structures:

- A record type containing a single phone number
- A record type containing multiple phone numbers

So within the lobbying package, define a phone number record type:

```
/* Filename on web page: lobbying.pkg */
CREATE OR REPLACE PACKAGE lobbying
IS
   TYPE phone_num_rec_type IS RECORD (
   area_code      VARCHAR2(3),
   phone_prefix   VARCHAR2(3),
   phone_number   VARCHAR2(4)
   );
```

Then declare a lobbyist contact record type, which is a collection of phone-number records:

```
TYPE lobbyist_contact_rec_type IS RECORD (
   home_phone        phone_num_rec_type,
   office_phone      phone_num_rec_type,
   cell_phone        phone_num_rec_type,
   fax_phone         phone_num_rec_type,
   bathroom_phone    phone_num_rec_type,
   bathroom_fax      phone_num_rec_type
   );
```

Finally, declare the insert_lobbyist_contact procedure in terms of the lobbyist contact record type:

```
   PROCEDURE insert_lobbyist_contact (
      p_lobbyist_contact_rec_in lobbyist_contact_rec_type);
END lobbying;
```

5-24. When you create a PL/SQL table based on a record structure, that record can be composed only of scalar fields. A nested record type may not define a PL/SQL table type. Yet, in this example, dept_rec_type has a field that is not scalar; it contains a field which is a PL/SQL table.

5-25. The compiler will not understand the favorite_snacks syntax. To define a variable v_ice_cream of the same datatype as the cookie column in the favorite_snacks table, use the %TYPE attribute:

```
v_ice_cream favorite_snacks.cookie%TYPE;
```

To improve this code, use a cursor-based record to reduce the number of variables (i.e., v_ice_cream, v_cookie are no longer necessary) and to avoid specifying individual target variables in the FETCH statement:

```
DECLARE
CURSOR so_tasty
   IS
      SELECT cookie, ice_cream
        FROM favorite_snacks;

   so_tasty_rec    so_tasty%ROWTYPE;
BEGIN
   OPEN so_tasty;
   FETCH so_tasty INTO so_tasty_rec;
END;
/
```

6

Index-by Tables

Beginner

6-1. The first step is to define the type of table, and then declare actual index-by tables from that type. Here is the generic syntax for an index-by table type definition:

```
TYPE type_name IS TABLE OF datatype
   INDEX BY BINARY_INTEGER;
```

Once the type is defined, the next step is to declare an index-by table based on that type:

```
Mytab type_name;
```

6-2. No. Attempts to do so are greeted by the PL/SQL error:

```
PLS-00315: INDEX-BY TABLE declarations must currently use
   binary_integer indexes
```

6-3. The statements are:

    a. Invalid. In PL/SQL, the datatype must follow the variable.

    b. Invalid. You can only declare one variable per declaration.

    c. Valid. This example shows a correct declaration.

6-4. The statements are:

    a. Invalid. You cannot use a period to set the index.

    b. Valid. The row number is placed inside parentheses, directly after the name of the table. In general, elements in collections are identified using their unique BINARY_INTEGER index row numbers

    c. Invalid. Index-by tables are referenced like single-dimensional arrays.

    d. Invalid. There is no such thing as an ASSIGN operator.

6-5. The statements are:

    a. True. Oracle does not support multidimensional arrays with index-by tables.

    b. False. Each row in an index-by table must store the same structure of data, though that row can consist of a record with scalar fields.

    c. True. Index-by tables cannot be saved in the database. They are only available as variable data structures (stored in memory) within a PL/SQL block.

6-6. All standard Oracle datatypes can be stored in index-by tables. PL/SQL Version 2.3 (Oracle 7.3) introduced the ability to store PL/SQL records and anchored datatypes. The following examples demonstrate this flexibility:

```
DECLARE
   CURSOR curs_get_employees IS
      SELECT last_name, hire_date FROM employee;

   TYPE from_cursor_type IS TABLE OF curs_get_employees%ROWTYPE
      INDEX BY BINARY_INTEGER;

   from_cursor_table from_cursor_type;

   TYPE from_table_type IS TABLE OF employee%ROWTYPE
      INDEX BY BINARY_INTEGER;

   from_table from_table_type;

   TYPE record_type IS RECORD ( record_col1 NUMBER(10),
                                record_col2 NUMBER(10));

   TYPE from_record_type IS TABLE OF record_type
      INDEX BY BINARY_INTEGER;

   from_record_table from_record_type;
```

6-7. There is no difference. *Index-by table* is just the new name—as of Oracle8—for what were previously called *PL/SQL tables* in Oracle7. This name was introduced to better distinguish the index-by table (with its INDEX BY clause) from the nested table, whose declaration looks exactly the same, minus the INDEX BY clause.

6-8. The statements are all false.

    a. False. The limitation on row numbers is the same limitation on BINARY_INTEGER values: $-2^{31} + 1$ through $2^{31} - 1$ (about -2.4 billion to 2.4 billion).

    b. False. Row numbers can be positive, negative, or zero.

    c. False. You can specify a row number as a decimal value or even as a string. As long as PL/SQL can convert implicitly your value to an integer, your code compiles and executes.

Here are some examples:

```
SQL> DECLARE
  2     TYPE number_table_type IS TABLE OF NUMBER(10,2)
  3        INDEX BY BINARY_INTEGER;
  4     number_table            number_table_type;
  5  BEGIN
  6     number_table (1.4) := 1.4;
  7     number_table (1.6) := 1.6;
  8     number_table ('25' || '16') := 10000;
  9     DBMS_OUTPUT.PUT_LINE (number_table(1));
 10     DBMS_OUTPUT.PUT_LINE (number_table(2));
 11     DBMS_OUTPUT.PUT_LINE (number_table(2516));
 12  END;
 13  /


1.4
1.6
10000
```

Note that decimal values are rounded to the nearest integer, not truncated.

6-9. The statements are:

a. True. When first declared, an index-by table contains no defined rows. An index-by table is like a database table in this regard. Memory is allocated for rows only when data is assigned to the row (thereby defining it).

b. False. The default value for a row in an index-by table is not NULL; it is simply undefined.

c. True. Each row in an index-by table contains the same type of data. Index-by tables are *homogeneous*. The datatype used to define the table TYPE is the datatype found in each row of the index-by table, though that datatype may be a record containing more than one scalar value.

d. False. If you try to access (read) a row in a table that is not yet defined, PL/SQL raises the NO_DATA_FOUND exception.

6-10. Zero. An index-by table is empty when it's first declared. Unlike the elements in the arrays of other languages, the elements in an index-by table are initially unassigned. The unassigned nature of a row can prove troublesome and must be guarded against by using the EXISTS function, as shown here:

```
DECLARE
   TYPE number_table_type IS TABLE OF NUMBER(10)
      INDEX BY BINARY_INTEGER;
   number_table number_table_type;
BEGIN
   IF number_table.EXISTS(12345)
   THEN
```

```
        DBMS_OUTPUT.PUT_LINE('Element 12345 has been assigned');
     ELSE
        DBMS_OUTPUT.PUT_LINE
           ('Element 12345 has NOT been assigned');
     END IF;
  END;
```

6-11. Yes. You can use the DELETE function (available in Oracle 7.3 and above) to de-assign an element:

```
DECLARE
   TYPE number_table_type IS TABLE OF NUMBER(10)
      INDEX BY BINARY_INTEGER;
   number_table  number_table_type;
BEGIN
   number_table(-87654) := 22;

   IF number_table.EXISTS(-87654)
   THEN
      DBMS_OUTPUT.PUT_LINE('It exists!');
   END IF;

   number_table.DELETE(-87654);

   IF NOT number_table.EXISTS(-87654)
   THEN
      DBMS_OUTPUT.PUT_LINE('Where did it go?');
   END IF;
END;
```

6-12. The code raises the following error because the row number exceeds the BINARY_INTEGER limit of $2^{31} - 1$:

```
ORA-01426: numeric overflow
```

6-13. These statements are:

a. True. Once you define a table TYPE, you can declare more than one index-by table from that TYPE. This is, in fact, the preferred approach. A TYPE is a *template,* a generic structure from which actual tables are declared. Here is an example:

```
TYPE number_table_type IS TABLE OF NUMBER(10)
      INDEX BY BINARY_INTEGER;

   salaries      number_table_type;
   commissions   number_table_type;
```

b. False. The table TYPE and all tables declared from that type can be defined in different scopes. You can and should define your table TYPEs in package specifications so that they are "globally" available throughout your application. With this approach, you avoid redundant TYPE definitions. Here is an example:

```
CREATE PACKAGE my_types
   IS
      TYPE number_tt IS TABLE OF NUMBER(10)
```

```
        INDEX BY BINARY_INTEGER;
     TYPE date_tt IS TABLE OF DATE INDEX BY BINARY_INTEGER;
   END;
   /

   DECLARE
      birthdays my_types.date_tt;
      population_count my_types.number_tt;
   BEGIN
```

c. False. If you leave off the INDEX BY clause in your TYPE definition, you end up with a nested table, which has different properties from those of the index-by table.

Intermediate

6-14. The only complication comes into play when you assign a value to a field in a record:

Table Name	Syntax
Number_table	`number_table(100) := 100;`
Empno_table	`empno_table(100) := 100;`
Employee_table	`employee_table(100).empno := 100;`
Employee_record_table	`employee_record_table(100).empno := 100;`

6-15. Here are the methods:

    a. EXISTS

    b. COUNT

    c. FIRST

    d. LAST

    e. PRIOR

    f. NEXT

    g. DELETE

Prior to Oracle 7.3, these methods were not available, and you had to write code yourself to keep track of FIRST, LAST, etc. To see an example of the kind of code you had to write to do this, see the *lclmthd.sql* file on the book's web page.

6-16. You can specify NOT NULL for the collection type:

```
SQL> DECLARE
  2     TYPE a_table_type IS TABLE OF NUMBER(10) NOT NULL
  3        INDEX BY BINARY_INTEGER;
  4     a_table a_table_type;
  5  BEGIN
  6     a_table(-100) := -9876;
```

```
  7    a_table(-100) := NULL;  -- will fail!
  8  END;
  9  /
DECLARE
*
ERROR at line 1:
ORA-06502: PL/SQL: numeric or value error
```

 You can also use IS NULL to check values before assigning them to rows. This approach involves writing more code, but Oracle claims that it is more efficient than the declarative constraint NOT NULL.

6-17. First, declare a cursor to fetch the employee numbers:

```
DECLARE
   CURSOR curs_get_empnos IS
   SELECT employee_id
     FROM employee;
```

Then define a table TYPE and index-by table based on the employee ID number:

```
TYPE v_employee_table_type IS TABLE OF
   employee.employee_id%TYPE
   INDEX BY BINARY_INTEGER;
v_employee_table v_employee_table_type;
```

You can then use a cursor FOR loop to easily populate the index-by table. Rely on %ROWCOUNT to set the row number:

```
BEGIN
  FOR v_empno_rec IN curs_get_empnos
  LOOP
     v_employee_table(curs_get_empnos%ROWCOUNT-1) :=
        v_empno_rec.employee_id;
  END LOOP;
END;
```

A more generic approach to sequentially filling an index-by table from a specified row number is to use LAST:

```
BEGIN
  FOR v_empno_rec IN curs_get_empnos
  LOOP
     v_employee_table(NVL (v_employee_table.LAST, -1)+1) :=
        v_empno_rec.employee_id;
  END LOOP;
END;
```

6-18. First, declare a cursor to fetch the employee numbers:

```
DECLARE
   CURSOR names_cur IS
   SELECT employee_id, last_name
     FROM employee;
```

Then, define a table TYPE and index-by table based on the cursor (notice that this is a table of records):

```
TYPE names_tt IS TABLE OF names_cur%ROWTYPE
   INDEX BY BINARY_INTEGER;
emp_names names_tt;
```

You can then use a cursor FOR loop to easily populate the index-by table:

```
BEGIN
  FOR name_rec IN names_cur
  LOOP
      emp_names (name_rec.employee_id).last_name :=
          name_rec.last_name;
  END LOOP;
END;
```

If you have the employee ID number, you might want to use it as the row number to efficiently retrieve the employee last name from the index-by table.

6-19. This is what the output looks like:

```
Elemement 1 Value 3
```

The nested methods are evaluated from right to left. The FIRST method finds the initial element, the NEXT method moves to the second element, and the PRIOR method goes right back to element 1.

One cautionary note: be very sure of what is happening when nesting methods. If any of the nested calls return a NULL value, the following PL/SQL error is raised:

```
ORA-06502: PL/SQL: numeric or value error:
   NULL index table key value
```

6-20. You can use the DELETE method with no parameters as in:

```
a_table.DELETE;
```

You can also assign an empty table of the same type as in this example:

```
DECLARE
  CURSOR curs_get_empnos IS
      SELECT empno FROM employee;

  TYPE empno_table_type IS TABLE OF
      employee.employee_id%TYPE NOT NULL
      INDEX BY BINARY_INTEGER;
  v_empno_table        empno_table_type;
  v_empty_empno_table empno_table_type;

BEGIN
  FOR v_emp_rec IN curs_get_empnos LOOP
    v_empno_table(curs_get_empnos%ROWCOUNT) :=
        v_emp_rec.employee_id;
  END LOOP;
```

```
DBMS_OUTPUT.PUT_LINE ('Count After Loading = ' ||
   v_empno_table.COUNT);

v_empno_table := v_empty_empno_table;

DBMS_OUTPUT.PUT_LINE
   ('Count After Assigning Empty Table = ' ||
      v_empno_table.COUNT);
END;
```

The output of this example is:

```
Count After Loading = 32
Count After Assigning Empty Table = 0
```

The DELETE method is the preferred approach; prior to Oracle 7.3, assignment of an empty table was the only way to delete any/all rows from an index-by table.

6-21. You see this:

```
The table is NOT NULL!
```

Index-by tables do not have, as a whole, a NULL state. That applies only to nested tables and variable arrays.

6-22. Here is the rewrite:

```
the_table (NVL (the_table.FIRST, 0) + 1) := 2067;
```

Expert

6-23. The best way to scan the contents of an index-by table is shown in (d). Start with the first row in the table. If this returns NULL, the table is empty, and you stop immediately. Otherwise, display the present and then move on to the next defined row with the NEXT method. It is efficient, very readable, and doesn't raise NO_DATA_FOUND errors.

Now what is wrong with each of the other approaches?

a. Reliance on the numeric FOR loop in this first attempt has a big problem: if the table is empty, FIRST and LAST return NULL. You would like to think that a numeric FOR loop from NULL to NULL—NULL to anything for that matter—would simply not execute. Sadly, this is not the case. PL/SQL will try to run the body of the loop and immediately raise a VALUE_ERROR exception. Very difficult to track down!

b. You have placed the numeric FOR loop inside a conditional. As a result, you execute the FOR loop only when you know that there is something in the table. So you don't get the VALUE_ERROR exception. There is still a problem, however; You are assuming that the table is filled sequentially (i.e., there is a present for each year between first and last). This is always a dangerous assumption to make about an index-by table, and in this case it is a false assumption. The result? This loop raises the NO_DATA_FOUND exception.

c. Here you use the EXISTS operator to make sure you never raise the NO_DATA_FOUND exception. This loop displays correctly each of my son's favorite presents. The problem with this approach is that it is potentially very inefficient. What if the first row defined in the table is 1 and the second row 2,000,000 (unlikely in this scenario, but then this is a silly example, right?)? Your loop executes two million times, displaying data just twice.

6-24. The implementation for the package body is shown in the *salgrp.pkg* file on the book's web page.

6-25. The implementation for the package body is shown in the *sorts.pkg* file on the book's web page.

6-26. The implementation for the package body is shown in the *bidir.pkg* file on the book's web page.

7

Nested Tables

Beginner

7-1. The syntax for creating a nested table is similar to that for an index-by table:

```
TYPE type name IS TABLE OF element datatype [NOT NULL];
```

For example, here's the command to create a nested table type called a_simple_udt_t; its elements consist of numeric data, each with no more than 10 digits:

```
CREATE TYPE a_simple_udt_t IS TABLE OF NUMBER(10);
```

7-2. The statements are:

   a. True. Nested table types can indeed be used as datatypes for Oracle tables as in this DDL:

```
SQL> CREATE TABLE a_table (
  2      col1 number,
  3      col2 a_simple_udt_t )
  4    NESTED TABLE col2 STORE AS a_table_col2;

Table created.
```

   The NESTED TABLE clause specifies the name of the table used to store the data in the nested column.

   b. True. Whether a nested table type is used as a column in a table or in PL/SQL itself, there is no limit to the number of rows it can store.

   c. False. All rows in a nested table must contain the same type of data.

   d. True. Nested table types are stored in the database. To view information about the nested table types in a database including their structure, use the data dictionary views ALL_TYPES and ALL_TYPE_ATTRS.

e. False. Nested table types can be based on user-defined data types as well as Oracle's native data types. For example, you can create an object as:

```
SQL> CREATE TYPE an_object_t AS OBJECT (
  2      column_one VARCHAR2(30),
  3      column_two NUMBER(10,2) );

Type created.
```

And then create a nested table type based on the object as:

```
SQL> CREATE TYPE a_nested_table_t AS TABLE OF an_object_t;
  2  /

Type created.
```

7-3. The answers to the questions are:

a. One nested table type was created called order_detail_t.

b. The table that contains a nested table column is referred to as the *outer table*. In this case it is called orders.

c. The table that winds up containing the data from the nested table column is called the *store table*. In this example it is called order_detail_store.

d. The store table takes on the structure of the nested table type (order_detail_t), which, in turn, takes on the structure of the object (detail_t) to yield the following structure:

```
SQL> DESC order_detail_store
 Name                              Null?    Type
 --------------------------------- -------- ----
 DETAIL_NO                                  NUMBER(38)
 DETAIL_DESC                                VARCHAR2(30)
 DETAIL_PRICE                               NUMBER
```

7-4. Three commands get things rolling. The first creates an object with columns for the question number and the answer. Note that the question number is required to maintain ordering of the questions:

```
CREATE TYPE answer_t AS OBJECT ( question_no NUMBER(10),
                                 answer_no   NUMBER(10));
/
```

The object is then used to create a nested table type:

```
CREATE TYPE answer_list_t AS TABLE OF answer_t;
/
```

The nested table type is then used as a column datatype in the table that holds the test information:

```
CREATE TABLE test_answers
  ( test_ID  NUMBER,
    test_name VARCHAR2(30),
    answers  answer_list_t )
  NESTED TABLE answers STORE AS answers_store;
```

7-5. These statements are:

a. False. The following is perfectly valid:

```
SQL> CREATE TABLE list_1
  2  (a_list list_of_numbers)
  3  NESTED TABLE a_list STORE AS a_list_store;

Table created.
```

b. False. There is no limit to the number of nested table types used in a table:

```
SQL> CREATE TABLE list_1
  2  (a_list list_of_numbers,
  3   b_list list_of_numbers)
  4  NESTED TABLE a_list STORE AS a_list_store,
  5  NESTED TABLE b_list STORE AS b_list_store;

Table created.
```

7-6. You declare a nested table type variable in exactly the same manner as Oracle's native datatypes:

```
DECLARE
   -- assume LIST_OF_NUMBERS already created
   v_list_of_numbers list_of_numbers;
BEGIN
   NULL;
END;
```

7-7. A default constructor is the method used to directly manipulate a nested table and is automatically created when the type is created. It has the same name as the type and takes each field as an argument. For example, the previously created answer_t and answer_list_t have the following default constructors:

```
DECLARE
   /*
   || Define a local variable of answer_t and initialize it
   || to NULL with the default constructor
   */
   v_local_answers answer_list_t := answer_list_t();

BEGIN
   /*
   || Set the values in the local variable using the
   || default constructor again
   */
   v_local_answers := answer_list_t(answer_t(1,10),
                                    answer_t(2,20),
                                    answer_t(3,30));

END;
```

7-8. Here are the PL/SQL statements:

UDT	Declare and Initialize
A_blob_t	v_blob a_blob_t := a_blob_t();
A_number_t	v_number a_number_t := a_number_t();
A_detail_t	v_dtl_t a_detail_t := a_detail_t (NULL,a_blob_t(),a_number_t());

7-9. The statements are:

a. True. Nested tables are stored in the database, while index-by tables are stored in process memory.

b. False. Since index-by tables are stored in memory, they cannot remain when a user logs off. Their contents are lost when the user disconnects.

c. False. Both nested tables and index-by tables can contain data only of a single type. Of course, that datatype may be a composite datatype, made up of several components.

d. False. Nested tables are not as sparse as index-by tables (unless a lot of deletes are done).

Intermediate

7-10. The output is:

```
Type created.

No errors.

Table created.

  COUNT(*)
---------
        0

ERROR at line 2:
ORA-22812: cannot reference nested table column's storage table
```

7-11. An error is produced because store tables cannot be accessed directly. All access must be through the outer table (hourly_temperatures):

```
SQL> SELECT count(*) FROM temperature_store;
SELECT count(*) FROM temperature_store
                     *
ERROR at line 1:
ORA-22812: cannot reference nested table column's storage table
```

7-12. Here is the SQL syntax:

```
INSERT INTO student_answers (
    student_id,
    exam_date,
```

```
         exam_id,
         student_answer_values )
     VALUES   (
         1,
         SYSDATE,
         1,
         answer_list_t(
            answer_t(1,10),
            answer_t(2,20),
            answer_t(3,30),
            answer_t(4,40),
            answer_t(5,50))));
```

7-13. The query to show all fields is simple:

```
SQL> SET linesize 50
SQL> SELECT * FROM student_answers
  2  /

STUDENT_ID EXAM_DATE   EXAM_ID
---------- --------- ---------
STUDENT_ANSWER_VALUES(QUESTION_NO, ANSWER_NO)
-------------------------------------------------
        1 05-FEB-99          1
ANSWER_LIST_T(ANSWER_T(1, 10), ANSWER_T(2, 20), AN
SWER_T(3, 30), ANSWER_T(4, 40), ANSWER_T(5, 50))
```

The results however, leave something to be desired. This query returns the student_answer_values encapsulated within answer_list_t and answer_t.

In Oracle 8.0, the second query requires the THE operator (I'm not making this up) to translate the contents of the student_answer_values column into a table format:

```
SQL> SELECT *
  2     FROM THE ( SELECT student_answer_values
  3                   FROM student_answers );

QUESTION_NO ANSWER_NO
----------- ---------
          1        10
          2        20
          3        30
          4        40
          5        50
```

Oracle 8.1 performs this operation using the less-wordy TABLE operator:

```
SQL> SELECT av.*
  2     FROM student_answers sa,
  3          TABLE(sa.student_answer_values) av
```

7-14. To add another answer, use the following syntax:

```
SQL> INSERT INTO THE ( SELECT student_answer_values
  2                       FROM student_answers
  3                      WHERE student_id = 1
```

```
4                        AND TRUNC(exam_date) = TRUNC(SYSDATE) )
5   VALUES(answer_t(6,60));
```

```
1 row created.
```

The THE operator translates the student_answer_values column into a table format to become the target of the INSERT statement.

7-15. Use the following syntax to delete the entry:

```
SQL> DELETE THE ( SELECT student_answer_values
 2                 FROM student_answers
 3                WHERE student_id = 1
 4                  AND TRUNC(exam_date) = TRUNC(SYSDATE) )
 5   WHERE question_no = 6;
```

```
1 row deleted.
```

7-16. Because the first INSERT statement sets the nested table column to NULL, the second raises this pesky error:

```
ORA-22908: reference to NULL table value
```

The code must be changed as follows to avoid this:

```
/* Filename on web page: answers.sql */
BEGIN
  /*
  || Insert an exam entry. Note the use of
  || the default constructor to initialize
  || the nested table column.
  */
  INSERT INTO student_answers
    (student_id,
     exam_date,
     exam_id,
     student_answer_values)
  VALUES
    (100,
     SYSDATE,
     100,
     answer_list_t());
  /*
  || Insert a single answer for the entry just created
  */
  INSERT INTO THE ( SELECT student_answer_values
                      FROM student_answers
                     WHERE student_id = 100
                       AND TRUNC(exam_date) = TRUNC(SYSDATE)
                       AND exam_id = 100 )
  VALUES (answer_t(1,10));
END;
```

I recommend never setting table columns to NULL; doing so may produce seemingly untraceable errors. Instead, it's good standard practice to always use a nested table's default constructor to initialize.

7-17. Here are the methods associated with each description:

    a. EXISTS

    b. COUNT

    c. LIMIT

    d. FIRST

    e. LAST

    f. PRIOR

    g. NEXT

    h. DELETE

    i. EXTEND

    j. TRIM

7-18. The statements are:

    a. False. Nested tables are sparse, so the last element could be well beyond the count of elements.

    b. False. Because nested tables are sparse, the first element can be NULL or any number greater than zero.

    c. True. This is the inverse of the first statement (a).

    d. True. There is no upper bound for nested tables.

7-19. The v_answer variable must be declared as answer_list_t (the datatype of the student_answer_values column in the previous student_answers table) in order for the collection methods (EXISTS, FIRST, LAST, and EXTEND) to succeed. Declaring it as curs_get_answers%ROWTYPE satisfies the cursor, but not the unforgiving collection methods.

7-20. The offending line is v_answers_c.EXTEND, although it is not alone; the next line causes the same error. Both raise the Oracle error "ORA-06531: Reference to uninitialized collection", because, of course, they were not initialized as the others were. Use the default constructor to initialize all local variables declared using an object type.

7-21. Surprisingly, the declaration of v_no_null_answers raises this unexpected exception:

```
PLS-00218: a variable declared NOT NULL must have an
    initialization assignment
```

This can be avoided using the default constructor to initialize it:

```
v_no_null_answers answer_t NOT NULL := answer_t();
```

The line that sets element 2 to NULL causes no disruption at all.

7-22. Checks for NULL values must be done manually. However, it is possible to put a check constraint on the outer table to prevent a record with zero entries in the nested table:

```
SQL> ALTER TABLE test_answers
ADD CONSTRAINT no_null_answers CHECK (
    answers IS NOT NULL );

Table altered.
```

7-23. Oracle provides a pseudo-column, called NESTED_TABLE_ID, to identify the record in the outer table. Here's an example:

```
/* Filename on web page: snowflake.sql */
/*
  || Create a simple type to describe a snowflake
*/
CREATE TYPE snowflake_detail_t AS OBJECT (
    snowflake_id PLS_INTEGER,
    diameter     NUMBER,
    points       PLS_INTEGER );
/

/*
  || Create a nested table type for the snowflake
  || definition
*/
CREATE TYPE snowflake_t AS TABLE OF snowflake_detail_t
/

/*
  || Create a snowfall table
*/
CREATE TABLE snowfall
( snowfall_id INTEGER PRIMARY KEY,
  snowflake snowflake_t )
NESTED TABLE snowflake STORE AS snowflake_nt
/

/*
  || Slap a unique constraint on the nested table consisting
  || of the nested_table_id and the snowflake_id
*/
CREATE UNIQUE INDEX unique_snowflake
ON snowflake_nt ( nested_table_id, snowflake_id );

/*
  || These inserts will succeed
*/
INSERT INTO snowfall
VALUES(1,snowflake_t(snowflake_detail_t(1,10,10),
                     snowflake_detail_t(2,20,20)));
INSERT INTO snowfall
VALUES(2,snowflake_t(snowflake_detail_t(1,10,10),
                     snowflake_detail_t(2,20,20)));
```

```
/*
|| This insert violates the constraint
*/
INSERT INTO snowfall
VALUES(3,snowflake_t(snowflake_detail_t(1,10,10),
                     snowflake_detail_t(1,20,20)));
```

7-24. Here is the output:

```
First Element Is     4
Last Element Is      11
Count Of Elements Is 7
Element 4 =
Element 5 = 1
Element 6 = 1
Element 8 = 1
Element 9 = 1
Element 10 = 1
Element 11 = 1
```

The first element in the collection has an index of 4, a result of the following: one element was added, three elements were added, ten elements were added, elements one to three were removed. This last operation makes the fourth element become the first. Since lines seven and eight both remove elements from the end of the collection, this makes the last element the one with an index of 11 and the remaining number of elements 7.

All the remaining elements in the collection are displayed in the LOOP construct.

7-25. Line 4 raises the following Oracle error:

```
ORA-06533: Subscript beyond count
```

The error is raised when attempting to TRIM 11 elements from v_answers (which contains only 10). The DELETE method used in line 3 is far more forgiving and does not raise an error when trying to DELETE nonexistent elements.

7-26. Here is the output:

```
Remaining Elements = 2
```

The first command will create 10 rows in the v_answers collection; the second command will delete the values from elements 4 and 5.

Note that while elements 4 and 5 will no longer affect the COUNT of the collection, they are still considered when TRIMming elements from the collection. For example, the result of v_answers.COUNT is 8, but the effect of TRIMming eight elements from the collection still leaves 2 (elements with indexes 1 and 2).

7-27. The complete function is shown in the *calc.sf* file on the book's web ⊕ page.

7-28. The complete function is shown in the *duplicates.sf* file on the book's web
⊕   page.

7-29. Any statement that causes an element to be referenced that does not exist
      raises ORA-06533. A solution (but specific to this question) is to use:

```
DBMS_OUTPUT.PUT_LINE(v_answers(1).question_no);
```

The following code always raises the error:

```
DECLARE
    v_answers answer_list_t := answer_list_t();

BEGIN
  DBMS_OUTPUT.PUT_LINE
      (v_answers(NVL(v_answers.LAST,0) + 1).question_no);
END;
```

7-30. When a nested table column is queried it returns all records associated
      with the outer table record. This default behavior is very handy for simpli-
      fying coding logic, but it can wreak havoc with memory management if
      the nested table contains many rows for every parent.

      In Oracle 8.1, if a nested table is configured to return a locator when que-
      ried (using the RETURN AS LOCATOR syntax), it provides a locator to a
      copy of the nested table instead of a copy of the nested table itself. This
      avoids having to transport child rows for every parent. Thankfully, the
      DML syntax for nested tables does not change regardless of whether they
      return locators or values.

7-31. The return type of a nested table is specified at creation time, although it
      can be altered later. It is specified using the RETURN AS option, as shown:

```
CREATE TYPE a_locator_t AS TABLE OF VARCHAR2(30);
/

CREATE TABLE table_with_locators
( some_column INTEGER,
  locator_column a_locator_t )
NESTED TABLE locator_column STORE AS locator_column_nt
RETURN AS LOCATOR;
```

The other option is RETURN AS VALUE which is the default. Note that the
AS keyword can be left out, making RETURN LOCATOR and RETURN
VALUE usable as well.

7-32. The return type is determined using the aptly titled IS_LOCATOR function
      in the UTL_COLL package:

```
DECLARE

  CURSOR curs_get_loc IS
  SELECT locator_column
    FROM table_with_locators;
  v_locator a_locator_t;
```

```
BEGIN

  OPEN curs_get_loc;
  FETCH curs_get_loc INTO v_locator;
  CLOSE curs_get_loc;

  IF UTL_COLL.IS_LOCATOR(v_locator) THEN
    DBMS_OUTPUT.PUT_LINE('It is a locator!');
  ELSE
    DBMS_OUTPUT.PUT_LINE('It is not a locator!');
  END IF;

END;
/
```

Expert

7-33. Here is the script to create the necessary objects:

```
/* Filename on web page: manage_orders.sql */
/*
   Drop existing objects
*/
DROP TABLE orders;
DROP TYPE order_detail_t;
DROP TYPE detail_t;
DROP TYPE tax_code_t;
DROP TYPE tax_code_detail_t;

/*
   Create a tax code object and table
*/
CREATE TYPE tax_code_detail_t AS OBJECT(
   tax_code VARCHAR2 (10)
);
/

CREATE TYPE tax_code_t AS TABLE OF tax_code_detail_t;
/

/*
   Create a detail type and table
*/
CREATE TYPE detail_t AS OBJECT(
   detail_no NUMBER,
   detail_desc VARCHAR2 (30),
   detail_price NUMBER
);
/

CREATE TYPE order_detail_t AS TABLE OF detail_t;
/
```

```
/*
   Create an orders table with a nested table of details
   and tax codes
*/
CREATE TABLE orders
   (order_no    NUMBER NOT NULL PRIMARY KEY USING INDEX,
    order_desc VARCHAR2(30),
    order_detail    order_detail_t,
    tax_codes    tax_code_t)
   NESTED TABLE order_detail STORE AS order_detail,
   NESTED TABLE tax_codes STORE AS order_tax_codes
/
```

7-34. The code for the create_order function is in the *manage_orders.sql* file on the book's web page.

7-35. The code for the update_order procedure is in the *manage_orders.sql* file on the book's web page.

7-36. The code for the add_details procedure is in the *manage_orders.sql* file on the book's web page.

7-37. The get_details function is in the *manage_orders.sql* file on the book's web page.

7-38. The calculate_cost procedure is in the *manage_orders.sql* file on the book's web page.

7-39. Here's a SQL script to test the manage_orders package:

```
/* Filename on web page: manage_orders.tst */
DECLARE
   v_new_no    PLS_INTEGER := manage_orders.create_order(TRUE);
   v_new_detail  order_detail_t := order_detail_t();
   v_num_deleted PLS_INTEGER;

BEGIN
   manage_orders.update_order(v_new_no,'New Description');
   v_new_detail.EXTEND;
   v_new_detail(1) := detail_t(1,'Detail 1',100);
   v_new_detail.EXTEND;
   v_new_detail(2) := detail_t(2,'Detail 2',100);
   v_new_detail.EXTEND;
   v_new_detail(3) := detail_t(3,'Detail 3',100);
   v_new_detail.EXTEND;
   v_new_detail(4) := detail_t(4,'Detail 4',100);
   v_new_detail.EXTEND;
   v_new_detail(5) := detail_t(5,'Detail 5',100);
   manage_orders.add_details(v_new_no,v_new_detail);

   DBMS_OUTPUT.PUT_LINE('The cost is ' ||
      manage_orders.calculate_cost(v_new_no));

END;
```

Variable Arrays

Beginner

8-1. A variable array (VARRAY) is a collection type introduced in Oracle8. Variable arrays are similar to nested tables in that they are homogenous and indexed, but they're very different in that they are never sparse and always maintain their order.

8-2. You can use VARRAYs as variables in PL/SQL and as columns in database tables.

8-3. You define the structure of a VARRRAY using the CREATE TYPE command introduced in Oracle8. For example:

```
SQL> CREATE TYPE a_varray AS VARRAY(10) OF NUMBER;
  2  /

Type created.
```

8-4. Variable arrays can store only a finite number of rows, as defined in the declaration. This finite number is called their *limit* and is specified when they are created. In the previous example, a_varray is a bounded array having a limit of 10 elements.

8-5. It's actually quite simple; you specify the column datatype as the variable array, just as you would specify any other data type. For example, assuming that a_varray has been previously declared as a VARRAY type in the database, you can create a VARRAY column using this command:

```
SQL> CREATE TABLE a_table
  2  (col1    NUMBER,
  3   col2    a_varray );

Table created.
```

8-6. The syntax to define a VARRAY is similar to that used to define an index-by table, with the exception that the INDEX BY clause is omitted:

```
DECLARE
    TYPE x_t IS VARRAY(10) OF NUMBER;
    x x_t;

BEGIN
...
END;
```

8-7. Most of the standard Oracle datatypes are available:

```
SQL> CREATE TYPE a_number_array AS VARRAY(10) OF NUMBER(22);
  2  /

Type created.

SQL> CREATE TYPE a_varchar2_array AS VARRAY(10) OF VARCHAR2(30);
  2  /

Type created.
```

Types can also be created from other user-defined types:

```
SQL> CREATE TYPE answer_array AS VARRAY(10) OF answer_t;
  2  /

Type created.
```

In PL/SQL, you have the added capability of creating variable arrays of table rows:

```
DECLARE
    TYPE v_employee_array IS VARRAY(10) OF employee%ROWTYPE;

BEGIN
    NULL;
END;
```

8-8. The data dictionary views USER_TYPES, ALL_TYPES, and DBA_TYPES display a complete list of all variable arrays owned by the current user, available to the current user, and defined in the whole database, respectively. Only DBAs (or users with the DBA role) can use the DBA_TYPES table, which displays all user-defined types (not just variable arrays).

8-9. For variable arrays defined in the database, the standard SQL*Plus DESCRIBE command does the trick. Alternatively, if SQL*PLUS is unavailable, you can query the view USER_TYPE_ATTRS:

```
SQL> DESC a_varray
 a_varray VARRAY(10) OF NUMBER

SQL> DESC answer_array
 answer_array VARRAY(10) OF ANSWER_T
```

```
Name                              Null?    Type
--------------------------------- -------- ----
QUESTION_NO                                NUMBER(10)
ANSWER_NO                                  NUMBER(10)
```

Intermediate

8-10. Default constructors are created when the variable array is defined in PL/SQL or in the database. They can initialize the variable to a known state, as in the following examples:

```
DECLARE
  /*
  || define a variable based on a variable array from the
  || database and initialize it with its default constructor
  */
  v_a_varray a_varray := a_varray();

  /*
  || define a local variable array and then create a variable
  || based on it and initialize it with its default constructor
  */
  TYPE v_local_array_type IS VARRAY(10) OF NUMBER;
  v_local_array v_local_array_type := v_local_array_type();

BEGIN
  /*
  || Put 10 elements into each variable array
  */
  v_a_varray := a_varray(1,2,3,4,5,6,7,8,9,10);
  v_local_array := v_local_array_type(1,2,3,4,5,6,7,8,9,10);

END;
```

8-11. You'll see this error:

```
ORA-06532: Subscript outside of limit
```

This error occurs because you attempted to put two elements into a variable array with a limit of 1. Since VARRAYs are "bounded" (unlike index-by tables), attempting to assign a value to an element with a nonpositive index, or greater than the declared limit of the VARRAY, causes this error.

8-12. Here are the methods associated with each description:

    a. EXISTS

    b. COUNT

    c. LIMIT

    d. FIRST

    e. LAST

    f. PRIOR

  g. NEXT

  h. DELETE

  i. EXTEND

  j. TRIM

8-13. The statements are:

  a. True. Elements cannot be removed from the middle of a variable array; they can be removed only from the end using the TRIM method.

  b. True. Variable arrays cannot be sparse so the first element is always number 1 or NULL (undefined).

  c. False. This is the inverse of the first statement.

  d. False. The LIMIT method returns the variable array's upper bound.

8-14. Here is the syntax:

Variable Array	Syntax
v_numbers	`v_numbers(1) := 100;`
v_emp_row	`v_emp_row(1).empno := 100;`
v_emp_record	`v_emp_record(1).empno := 100;`

8-15. The FETCH statement raises the following error because variable arrays cannot be created based on cursor return row types:

```
PLS-00403: expression 'V_EMPLOYEE_REC' cannot be used as
    an INTO-target of a SELECT/FETCH statement
```

8-16. The v_array_c.EXTEND line raises the error:

```
ORA-06531: Reference to uninitialized collection
```

It does this because, of course, the collection is uninitialized. You can avoid this error by simply initializing the variable v_varray_c using the same technique as the others.

8-17. Yes. Because variable arrays are dense (i.e., each element in the VARRAY is defined), this method is safe from Oracle's NO_DATA_FOUND error. Conversely, when using index-by tables, you aren't always guaranteed that a given element will be defined (since it is a sparse data structure).

8-18. Through no fault of his own, the seventh dwarf Sleepy raises this error:

```
ORA-06532: Subscript outside of limit
```

The seven_dwarves_t variable array was erroneously created with an upper limit of 6. When the code attempts to add the seventh element (using EXTEND), it fails because this is larger than the limit defined in its declaration.

8-19. Both LAST and COUNT can be used because they are synonymous when applied to variable arrays. Both functions return the subscript of the last element in the VARRAY.

8-20. Here are the SQL commands:

```
CREATE TYPE list_t AS OBJECT ( list_value VARCHAR2(100) );
/

CREATE TYPE top_ten_t AS VARRAY(10) OF list_t;
/

CREATE TABLE top_ten
( top_ten_name VARCHAR2(100),
  top_ten_values top_ten_t )
/
```

8-21. Here is the appropriate PL/SQL block:

```
DECLARE
   -- declare and initialize a local top ten
   v_top_ten top_ten_t := top_ten_t();

BEGIN
   -- insert 10 entries
   v_top_ten.EXTEND;
   v_top_ten(1) := list_t('ELSIF');
   v_top_ten.EXTEND;
   v_top_ten(2) := list_t('END IF');
   v_top_ten.EXTEND;
   v_top_ten(3) :- list_t('PRAGMA');
   v_top_ten.EXTEND;
   v_top_ten(4) := list_t('EXCEPTION');
   v_top_ten.EXTEND;
   v_top_ten(5) := list_t('BINARY_INTEGER');
   v_top_ten.EXTEND;
   v_top_ten(6) := list_t('EXCEPTION_INIT');
   v_top_ten.EXTEND;
   v_top_ten(7) := list_t('PLS_INTEGER');
   v_top_ten.EXTEND;
   v_top_ten(8) := list_t('SET_SQL_TRACE_IN_SESSION');
   v_top_ten.EXTEND;
   v_top_ten(9) := list_t('PUT_LINE');
   v_top_ten.EXTEND;
   v_top_ten(10) := list_t('EXECUTE_AND_FETCH');

   -- insert the top 10 into the table
   INSERT INTO top_ten
   (top_ten_name,top_ten_values)
   VALUES('Misspelled PL/SQL Keywords',v_top_ten);

END;
```

8-22. This query is unceremoniously met with the following Oracle error:

```
ORA-22905: cannot access rows from a non-nested table item
```

This error occurs whenever an attempt is made to access rows of an item whose type is not a nested table type.

8-23. Even though Oracle can store variable arrays, it still needs to see them in a table format for DML. Variable array columns must be made to look like nested tables for row access. In true Hollywood fashion, the function to perform this task is called CAST. In Oracle 8.0, the top_ten_values column must be CAST as a nested table datatype with the same structure as the top_ten_t UDT. First, create the new nested table type:

```
CREATE TYPE top_ten_nested_t AS TABLE OF list_t;
/
```

Here is the query syntax and the results:

```
SQL> SELECT *
  2   FROM THE ( SELECT CAST(top_ten_values AS top_ten_nested_t)
  3                 FROM top_ten
  4     WHERE top_ten_name = 'Misspelled PL/SQL Keywords');


LIST_VALUE
--------------------------------------------------------------------
ELSIF
END IF
PRAGMA
EXCEPTION
BINARY_INTEGER
EXCEPTION_INIT
PLS_INTEGER
SET_SQL_TRACE_IN_SESSION
PUT_LINE
EXECUTE_AND_FETCH
```

Note also that the WHERE clause is inside the subquery. Thankfully Oracle 8.1 removes this restriction for queries by allowing the TABLE operator to perform the conversion on the fly:

```
SQL> SELECT ttv.*
  2    FROM top_ten tt,
  3         TABLE(tt.top_ten_values) ttv
  4   WHERE tt.top_ten_name = 'Misspelled PL/SQL Keywords';
```

8-24. Absolutely nothing. Variable arrays are very stingy about maintaining order (just as arrays in other programming languages are). Rows are returned in the order in which they were put in.

8-25. In Oracle 8.0 the syntax is:

```
SQL> SELECT *
  2    FROM THE ( SELECT CAST
  3       ( top_ten_values AS top_ten_nested_t )
  4             FROM top_ten
  5             WHERE top_ten_name =
  6     'Misspelled PL/SQL Keywords')
  5   WHERE INSTR(list_value,'_',1,1) > 0;
```

```
LIST_VALUE
---------------------------------------------------------
BINARY_INTEGER
EXCEPTION_INIT
PLS_INTEGER
SET_SQL_TRACE_IN_SESSION
PUT_LINE
EXECUTE_AND_FETCH
```

In Oracle 8.1 the syntax is:

```
SQL> SELECT ttv.*
  2    FROM top_ten tt,
  3         TABLE(tt.top_ten_values) ttv
  4   WHERE tt.top_ten_name = 'Misspelled PL/SQL Keywords'
  5     AND INSTR(ttv.list_value,'_',1,1) > 0;
```

8-26. Here is the appropriate function:

```
CREATE TYPE top_ten_nested_t AS TABLE OF list_t;
/

CREATE OR REPLACE FUNCTION top_ten_caster (
    p_top_ten top_ten_t )
RETURN top_ten_nested_t IS

   CURSOR curs_cast_it IS
   SELECT CAST ( p_top_ten AS top_ten_nested_t )
     FROM DUAL;
   v_ret_val top_ten_nested_t;

BEGIN
   OPEN curs_cast_it;
   FETCH curs_cast_it INTO v_ret_val;
   CLOSE curs_cast_it;
   RETURN(v_ret_val);
END;
```

8-27. Any attempts to use the CAST function on the right side of a SQL statement or the target of any DML quickly raises this error:

```
ORA-22906: cannot perform DML on expression or on nested table view column
```

This message is a little misleading because it is actually a variable array made to look like a nested table. Maybe that's what is meant by "nested table view column?"

8-28. Here is the complete procedure:

```
/* Filename on web page: change_top.sp */
CREATE OR REPLACE PROCEDURE change_top_ten
               ( p_list_name top_ten.top_ten_name%TYPE,
                 p_old       VARCHAR2,
                 p_new       VARCHAR2 ) IS
```

```
/*
   || This block changes the top ten entry
   || of p_old to p_new for the list titled
   || p_list_name
*/

-- cursor to get top ten entries for update
CURSOR curs_get_top_ten
      ( cp_list_name top_ten.top_ten_name%TYPE ) IS
SELECT top_ten_values
  FROM top_ten
 WHERE top_ten_name = cp_list_name
FOR UPDATE of top_ten_values;
v_top_ten top_ten_t;

BEGIN
  -- get all ten entries at once!
  OPEN curs_get_top_ten(p_list_name);
  FETCH curs_get_top_ten INTO v_top_ten;

  -- if the entries exist...
  IF curs_get_top_ten%FOUND THEN

     -- for every one of the top ten entries...
     FOR counter IN 1..v_top_ten.COUNT LOOP

        -- if the entry is PRAGMA then change it to BIT_XOR
        IF v_top_ten(counter).list_value = p_old THEN
          v_top_ten(counter).list_value := p_new;
        END IF;

     END LOOP;  -- every top ten entry

     -- perform the update
     UPDATE top_ten
     SET top_ten_values = v_top_ten
     WHERE CURRENT OF curs_get_top_ten;

  END IF;  -- the entries exist

  CLOSE curs_get_top_ten;

END change_top_ten;
```

8-29. These statements are:

   a. False. The DELETE method takes an "all or nothing" approach to variable arrays; hence, the number of rows deleted is always equal to the number of rows in the array.

   b. True. This is the inverse of the first statement.

   c. True. The TRIM method is far less autocratic about things and allows removal of a selection of rows.

   d. False. This is the inverse of the previous statement.

e. True. Although the TRIM method removes rows from the end of the array, it can be made to remove them all, which causes the FIRST method to return NULL.

8-30. The code block starts out by looping from 1 to 10, adding an element each time through, and assigning it the value of the loop counter. Next, it removes the last element in the list, and then again removes the last two elements. After this, the contents of the VARRAY are displayed by looping from 1 to the number of elements left in the VARRAY (seven at this time). So the output is:

```
element 1 = 1
element 2 = 2
element 3 = 3
element 4 = 4
element 5 = 5
element 6 = 6
element 7 = 7
```

8-31. Here is the complete procedure:

```
/* Filename on web page: del_top.sp */
/*
|| This procedure removes elements from p_list.
|| If p_start_del and p_end_del are NULL then
|| all elements are removed.
|| If p_start_del is NOT NULL and p_end_del is NULL
|| then p_start_del element is a goner.
|| If neither are NULL then the elements between
|| p_start_del and p_end_del are removed
|| inclusively
*/

CREATE OR REPLACE PROCEDURE del_top_ten (
    p_list       IN  OUT top_ten_t,
    p_start_del  PLS_INTEGER := NULL,
    p_end_del    PLS_INTEGER := NULL ) IS

  -- local top_ten
  v_local_ten top_ten_t := top_ten_t();

BEGIN
    -- trap invalid arguments
    IF p_end_del IS NOT NULL AND
      p_start_del IS NULL THEN
      RAISE_APPLICATION_ERROR(-20000,'ERROR : Invalid Arguments');
    END IF;

    -- if a start criteria was specified
    IF p_start_del IS NOT NULL THEN

      -- for every element in the list...
      FOR counter IN 1..p_list.COUNT LOOP
```

```
      /*
       || Transfer all but those to be deleted to the
       || local list
      */
      IF counter < p_start_del OR
        counter > NVL(p_end_del,p_start_del) THEN
       v_local_ten.EXTEND;
       v_local_ten(NVL(v_local_ten.LAST,0)) := p_list(counter);
      END IF;

    END LOOP;  -- every element in list

  END IF;  -- was start criteria specified

  -- transfer local list to parameter
  p_list := v_local_ten;

END;
```

8-32. The calls are:

    a. Valid. This example extends the VARRAY by one element.

    b. Valid. This example extends the VARRAY by two elements (specified by the optional parameter).

    c. Invalid. VARRAY subscripts must be positive.

    d. Valid. This example extends the VARRAY by two elements and initializes them to the current value of the first element in the VARRAY. This syntax is commonly used for collections where the declaration specifies that the elements are non-NULL.

Expert

8-33. Here is the script that can be used to create the tables and types for the purchase order system:

```
/* Filename on web page: vaexprt.sql */
/*
   Drop existing objects
*/
DROP TABLE orders;
DROP TYPE order_detail_nt;
DROP TYPE order_detail_t;
DROP TYPE detail_t;
DROP TYPE tax_code_t;
DROP TYPE tax_code_detail_t;

/*
   Create a tax code object and table
*/
CREATE TYPE tax_code_detail_t AS OBJECT (
   tax_code VARCHAR2(10));
/
```

```
CREATE TYPE tax_code_t AS VARRAY(2) OF tax_code_detail_t;
/

/*
   Create a detail type and table
*/
CREATE TYPE detail_t AS OBJECT
   (detail_noNUMBER,
    detail_descVARCHAR2(30),
    detail_price        NUMBER)
/

CREATE TYPE order_detail_t AS VARRAY(10) OF detail_t;
/

CREATE TYPE order_detail_nt AS TABLE OF detail_t;
/

/*
   Create an orders table with a variable array column for
   details and tax codes
*/
CREATE TABLE orders
   (order_noNUMBER NOT NULL PRIMARY KEY USING INDEX,
    order_descVARCHAR2(30),
    order_detail        order_detail_t,
    tax_codes           tax_code_t)
/
```

8-34. The variable array is used as the datatype of the column in the orders table while the nested table type is created in anticipation of future DML. It will be used in conjunction with the CAST function.

8-35. For this solution, see the *va_manage_orders.sql* file on the book's web page.

8-36. For this solution, see the *va_manage_orders.sql* file on the book's web page.

8-37. For this solution, see the *va_manage_orders.sql* file on the book's web page.

8-38. For this solution, see the *va_manage_orders.sql* file on the book's web page.

8-39. For this solution, see the *va_manage_orders.sql* file on the book's web page.

8-40. For this solution, see the *va_manage_orders.sql* file on the book's web page.

8-41. Here is the PL/SQL block to test the package:

```
/* Filename on web page: va_manage_orders.tst */
DECLARE
  v_new_no        PLS_INTEGER := manage_orders.create_order(TRUE);
  v_new_detail  order_detail_t := order_detail_t();
  v_num_deleted PLS_INTEGER;

BEGIN
  manage_orders.update_order(v_new_no,'New Description');
  v_new_detail.EXTEND;
  v_new_detail(1) := detail_t(1,'Detail 1',100);
  v_new_detail.EXTEND;
  v_new_detail(2) := detail_t(2,'Detail 2',100);
  v_new_detail.EXTEND;
  v_new_detail(3) := detail_t(3,'Detail 3',100);
  v_new_detail.EXTEND;
  v_new_detail(4) := detail_t(4,'Detail 3',100);
  manage_orders.add_details(v_new_no,v_new_detail);
  manage_orders.delete_detail(v_new_no,1,v_num_deleted);

  DBMS_OUTPUT.PUT_LINE('The cost is ' ||
     manage_orders.calculate_cost(v_new_no));

END;
```

Object Technology

Beginner

9-1. All these statements are (or can be) true:

Suppose you want to keep track of your compact disc collection. Before the Oracle Objects option was available, you could have created a record type and some related procedures:

```
TYPE CD_rec_type IS RECORD (
    id      INTEGER,
    title   VARCHAR2(60),
    artist  VARCHAR2(60),
    label   VARCHAR2(60)
);

PROCEDURE
set_cd_title
(cd_rec_in    IN OUT CD_rec_type,
 title_in     IN VARCHAR2)
IS ...

PROCEDURE
set_cd_artist
(cd_rec_in    IN OUT CD_rec_type,
 artist_in    IN VARCHAR2)
IS ...
```

With the Oracle Objects option you can bring together the data structure and its associated logic. You define an object type that encapsulates the CD data structure along with functions and procedures needed to manipulate the data.

a. This CREATE TYPE statement defines object type CD_t:

```
CREATE TYPE CD_t AS OBJECT (
    id      INTEGER,
```

```
title  VARCHAR2(60),
artist VARCHAR2(60),
label  VARCHAR2(60),
MEMBER FUNCTION
    set_title  (title_in    IN VARCHAR2)
        RETURN CD_t,
MEMBER FUNCTION
    set_artist (artist_in   IN VARCHAR2)
        RETURN CD_t,
MEMBER FUNCTION
    set_label (label_in     IN VARCHAR2)
        RETURN CD_t
);
```

b. CD_t is a data structure with attributes id, title, artist, and label, as well as methods set_title, set_artist and set_label. So CD_t defines both data (e.g., attributes ID, title) and behavior (e.g., methods set_title, set_artist).

c. Same as (b).

d. CD_t is also a template and can hold no data; it can be used simply to define object instances.

9-2. All these statements are true. But (e) has a restriction, explored later.

a. The following command:

```
CREATE TABLE compact_discs OF CD_t;
```

creates an object table called compact_discs. Each of its rows is an *instance* of object type CD_t:

```
SQL> DESCRIBE compact_discs;
```

Name	Null?	Type
ID		NUMBER(38)
TITLE		VARCHAR2(60)
ARTIST		VARCHAR2(60)
LABEL		VARCHAR2(60)

b. The following command:

```
CREATE TABLE cd_order_items (
    order_id        INTEGER,
    item_id         INTEGER,
    cd              CD_t);
```

creates a table with a column object called cd.

c. The following command:

```
DECLARE
    my_favorite_cd   CD_t;
```

creates a PL/SQL object variable of type CD_t.

d. The following command:

```
CREATE OR REPLACE FUNCTION
    get_cd ( id_in    IN INTEGER )
```

```
        RETURN CD_t
IS ...
```
creates a function that returns an object of type CD_t.

e. The following command:

```
CREATE TYPE cd_t_tab_t AS TABLE OF cd_t;
```
creates a nested table datatype that can define a collection of compact discs, and the declaration:

```
DECLARE
    lost_cd_tab   cd_t_tab_t;
```
creates a collection of lost compact discs. Note that the object type that defines the collection datatype cannot have collection attributes (e.g., TABLE, VARRAY) itself.

f. The following declaration:

```
DECLARE
    TYPE music_fan_rec_type IS RECORD (
       music_fan_name    VARCHAR2(50),
       favorite_cd       CD_t);
```
defines a PL/SQL record type with object field favorite_cd, while the declaration:

```
music_fan_rec   music_fan_rec_type;
```
creates a PL/SQL record with a CD object field.

9-3. All except the last statement (f) are true.

a. True. A constructor has the same name as its object type. For our CD_t object type, the constructor is CD_t.

b. True. The constructor is a function, not a procedure.

c. True. The constructor returns an instance of its object type. Constructor CD_t is a function that returns an instance of object type CD_t.

d. True. The constructor accepts one parameter per attribute (in order) and returns an instance of its object type with its attributes holding the input parameter values. The declaration is:

```
DECLARE
    my_favorite_cd   CD_t :=
       CD_t (1, 'Beatles', 'White Album', 'Apple');
```
uses the constructor CD_t to assign to object variable my_favorite_cd values for the Beatles' *White Album*.

Note that CD_t is used as both a datatype and a constructor function in one statement.

e. True. The constructor function is available by default once an object type has been created via the CREATE TYPE statement.

f. False. There is no "destructor" method analogous to the constructor method.

9-4. The statements are:

    a. True. The methods of an object type are implemented by creating the object type body, using syntax that is quite similar to that used for creating a package body. As with package bodies, object type bodies are optional. They are needed only if a method is part of the object specification.

    b. False. Object methods cannot be implemented outside the object type body.

9-5. All these statements are true:

    a. A STATIC method can be used for operations related to an object type, but that do not act on a specific object instance. For example, the STATIC function new_cd_id generates a new identifier:

```
CREATE TYPE CD_t AS OBJECT (
    id              INTEGER,
    title           VARCHAR2(60),
    ...
    MEMBER FUNCTION
        set_title (title_in    IN VARCHAR2)
            RETURN CD_t,
    ...
    STATIC FUNCTION
        new_cd_id
            RETURN INTEGER
);

CREATE TYPE BODY CD_t
AS
    MEMBER FUNCTION set_title (title_in    IN VARCHAR2)
    RETURN CD_t
    IS
    ...

    STATIC FUNCTION new_cd_id
    RETURN INTEGER
    IS
        v_return_value    INTEGER;
    BEGIN
        SELECT cd_id_seq.NEXTVAL
          INTO v_return_value
          FROM DUAL;

        RETURN v_return_value;
    END new_cd_id;

END;
```

    b. STATIC methods were not present in Oracle8 until the release of Oracle8*i*.

c. Non-STATIC object methods operate on a specific object instance. The object instance must already exist before the method can be invoked. For example, a CD's set_title method is invoked within the context of a specific CD:

```
DECLARE
    my_next_cd   CD_t := CD_t (10000, NULL, NULL, NULL);
BEGIN
    my_next_cd := my_next_cd.set_title ('Beatles in Nashville');
    my_next_cd := my_next_cd.set_artist ('Beatles');
    my_next_cd := my_next_cd.set_label ('Apple');
END;
```

CD instance my_next_cd is initialized via its constructor. We invoke its set_title function using object.method syntax. set_title returns an object of type CD_t, which is assigned to my_next_cd.

d. As shown in the previous example, a nonstatic method operates on a specific object instance. This object instance is an "implied parameter" of the method, which can be referenced using the keyword SELF. SELF acts as a preinitialized object variable. SELF is a way of referencing the object on which the method has been invoked.

```
CREATE OR REPLACE TYPE BODY CD_t
AS
    MEMBER FUNCTION set_title  (title_in    IN VARCHAR2)
    RETURN CD_t
    IS
        the_cd   CD_t := SELF;
    BEGIN
        IF title_in IS NOT NULL
        THEN
            the_cd.title := title_in;
        END IF;
        RETURN the_cd;
    END set_title;
```

In the set_title method, local object variable the_cd is set to SELF. The contents of the object on which set_title has been invoked are copied to local object variable the_cd.

9-6. True. For member functions, SELF has the default IN mode. For member procedures, SELF has the default IN OUT mode. So set_title could be expressed as follows:

```
CREATE OR REPLACE TYPE BODY CD_t
AS
    MEMBER FUNCTION set_title
    (SELF        IN CD_t,
    title_in    IN VARCHAR2)
    RETURN CD_t
    IS
        the_cd   CD_t := SELF;
    BEGIN
```

```
      IF title_in IS NOT NULL
      THEN
         the_cd.title := title_in;
      END IF;
      RETURN the_cd;
   END set_title;
```

9-7. The examples are:

    a. Invalid. There's no OBJECT operator in the SQL or PL/SQL languages.

    b. Valid. The VALUE operator returns an entire object from an object table.

Note that the object table is designated in the FROM clause by an alias (cd). This alias is the input to the VALUE operator. Because it requires a table alias, the VALUE operator can be used only with row (i.e., persistent) objects.

There is now a *transient* copy of the CD with ID = 100 in the object variable the_cd.

9-8. The statements are:

    a. True. The OID is a 16-byte RAW value.

    b. True. The OID uniquely identifies the object. No other object will have the same OID value. Note that the OID is unique not only within one object table but across all object tables.

    c. True. Oracle stores the OID in a column named SYS_NC_OID$. This column is "hidden" in that you cannot see it when you DESCRIBE the object table:

```
SQL> DESCRIBE compact_discs;

Name                  Null?    Type
--------------------- -------- --------------
ID                             NUMBER(38)
TITLE                          VARCHAR2(60)
ARTIST                         VARCHAR2(60)
LABEL                          VARCHAR2(60)
```

But you can SELECT the column from SQL*Plus:

```
SQL> SELECT SYS_NC_OID$ FROM compact_discs
        WHERE id = 100

SYS_NC_OID$
--------------------------------
1A84C0D43CDE11D385F5000000000000
```

    d. False. As shown previously in (c), you can see the OID value via a SELECT statement.

9-9. None of these types of objects are assigned an OID. The OID is created upon insertion into an object table. An OID can be referenced only in the context of a persistent object in an object table. Therefore, transient objects and nested objects, such as the lost compact discs collected in lost_cd_tab, will not have an OID.

Likewise, a column object does not have an OID. However its row will have some means of unique identification, which may be an OID associated with its row if the column object is a column in an object table.

9-10. The statements are:

a. True. REFs are constructed from, but are not identical to, OIDs.

b. True. Where you want to indicate a relationship with a particular CD (e.g., an order for a CD), you can use a REF to a CD row object. This is similar to a foreign key column in a table, which holds the primary key of a related record in a second table (e.g., the dept_no column in the emp table holds the primary key of an employee's department).

c. True. The keyword REF can modify a datatype, indicating a pointer to an object. For example:

```
DECLARE
    CD_ref    REF CD_t;
```

means that local variable CD_ref is not a CD object of type CD_t, but a pointer to a CD object. The following command:

```
CREATE TABLE cd_order_items
( order_id    INTEGER,
  item_id     INTEGER,
  cd_ref      REF CD_t );
```

creates a table with column cd_ref, which contains a pointer to a CD row object:

```
SQL> DESCRIBE cd_order_items;
```

Name	Null?	Type
ORDER_ID		NUMBER(38)
ITEM_ID		NUMBER(38)
CD_REF		REF OF CD_T

d. True. The REF operator accepts a table alias and returns a pointer to a row object that is constructed from the row object's OID. Consider the following:

```
DECLARE
    CD_ref    REF CD_t;

    CURSOR CD_ref_cur
    IS
    SELECT REF(cd)
      FROM compact_discs    cd
     WHERE title = 'White Album'
       AND artist = 'Beatles';
```

```
BEGIN
   OPEN  CD_ref_cur;
   FETCH cd_ref_cur INTO CD_ref;
   CLOSE CD_ref_cur;

   INSERT INTO cd_order_items (order_id, item_id, cd_ref)
      VALUES ( 10000, 1, CD_ref);
END;
```

In the cd_order_items table, Item 1 of CD orders 10,000 points to the Beatles' *White Album* in the compact_discs table.

   e. False. A REF is constructed from an OID. Column objects do not have OIDs. Therefore we cannot create a REF to a column object. Likewise, a REF cannot point to a transient object or a nested object.

9-11. The row in compact_discs holding the Beatles' *White Album* is deleted. However the REF to this compact disc is still present in the cd_order_items record. This is a *dangling REF*: a reference to a compact disc object that no longer exists. REFs can dangle. Foreign keys cannot. In designing an application using objects, some thought should be devoted to how dangling REFs can be prevented.

9-12. Here is another approach:

```
SELECT items.item_id,
       items.cd_ref.artist,
       items.cd_ref.title
  FROM cd_order_items  items
 WHERE items.order_id = 10000;

  ITEM_ID CD_REF.ARTIST CD_REF.TITLE
--------- ------------- -----------------
        1 Beatles       White Album
```

SQL gracefully allows you to navigate from a REF (cd_ref) to the referenced object without specifying a join to the referenced object table. This is cool!

9-13. This code segment returns the object:

```
Artist: Beatles
```

The REF in the cd_ref column of the cd_order_items table is passed to DEREF, which returns the referenced object. This CD object is placed into object variable the_cd.

Like the VALUE operator, DEREF returns the value of an object.

9-14. Before you can put objects in order (for example, to sort a CD object by title), you must first explicitly create a method that returns a value on which to base the sort. Until you create this mapping function, you'll receive the following error:

```
ORA-22950: cannot ORDER objects without MAP or ORDER method
```

9-15. Here is an example of how to create a MAP method to put objects in order:

```
CREATE OR REPLACE TYPE BODY CD_t
AS
    MEMBER FUNCTION set_title  (title_in IN VARCHAR2)
    RETURN CD_t
    IS

    MAP MEMBER FUNCTION compare RETURN VARCHAR2
    IS
    BEGIN
       RETURN (SELF.artist || SELF.title);
    END;

END;
```

With this MAP method in place, when Oracle needs to compare two CD objects, it uses the artist/title concatenation in a character comparison.

Intermediate

9-16. The statements are:

   a. False. This view lists "database objects" (as opposed to "object objects") owned by the user, such as tables, procedures, and packages. USER_OBJECTS has been around for quite some time. Now with the Objects option, its name will be confusing.

   b. True. An object type is a database construct, created with a CREATE TYPE statement, and therefore appears in the USER_OBJECTS view.

   c. False. An object instance, which can be a persistent row in an object table or held temporarily in a PL/SQL variable, does not have an entry in USER_OBJECTS. This is consistent with Oracle's treatment of other rows in (nonobject) tables and values held in (nonobject) PL/SQL variables.

9-17. The statements are:

   a. False. The constructor function cannot be modified.

   b. True. The constructor can be called in SQL or PL/SQL.

   c. True. Like other Oracle functions, the constructor can use named notation or positional notation:

```
DECLARE
    cd_to_avoid   CD_t;
BEGIN
    cd_to_avoid := CD_t (
        id => -1000000,
```

```
      artist => 'Garth Brooks',
      title => 'Salutes The Chipmunks',
      label => 'Nonesuch' );
```

Constructor CD_t is invoked using this named notation.

9-18. An object type attribute cannot have a DEFAULT value (e.g., 'Greatest Hits'). This means that a call to a constructor must supply a value—or the nonvalue NULL—for every attribute of the object type.

9-19. The syntax for creating an object type specification is a *comma-separated list* of attributes and methods; you do not use semicolons in the list, as you'd find in a package specification, after the member methods. To fix the problem in the type definition, you should replace the semicolons following the member functions with commas, except for the last member function, which should be followed by a right parenthesis that ends the type definition:

```
CREATE TYPE CD_t AS OBJECT (
    id                 INTEGER,
    title              VARCHAR2(60),
    artist             VARCHAR2(60),
    label              VARCHAR2(60),
    classification     VARCHAR2(60),
    MEMBER FUNCTION  set_title (title_in    IN VARCHAR2)
        RETURN CD_t,  -- Use a comma, NOT a semi-colon!
    MEMBER FUNCTION  set_artist (artist_in   IN VARCHAR2)
        RETURN CD_t
);
```

9-20. All these statements are true. However, (c) has a restriction: Oracle8*i* allows methods to be implemented in Java. Prior Oracle releases do not permit the use of Java as a language for method implementation.

9-21. You get a "type mismatch" error, as follows:

```
PLS-00386:
type mismatch found at 'THE_CD' between
FETCH cursor and INTO variables
```

To avoid this error, fetch using the VALUE operator:

```
CURSOR    cd_cur
IS
SELECT VALUE (cd)
   FROM compact_discs cd
  WHERE id = 100;
```

9-22. The statements are:

a. True. When you reinsert an object into an object table, Oracle assigns a new OID.

b. True. The hidden OID column of an object table automatically gets a unique index.

c. False. Unlike ROWIDs, OID values are preserved after export/import.

9-23. A newly declared object variable is NULL. The object itself is NULL, as well as its attributes. Therefore, the block of code displays the following lines:

```
New CD is NULL
New CD Title is NULL
```

9-24. There is no *initialization* of object new_cd. This raises the predefined exception ACCESS_INTO_NULL.

There are three ways to initialize an object:

- Use a constructor function
- Direct assignment from another (already initialized) object
- FETCH the contents of a row object into the object via the VALUE operator

9-25. Here is the code:

```
DECLARE
    the_cd_ref    REF CD_t;
    the_cd        CD_t;
BEGIN
   SELECT REF(cd)
     INTO the_cd_ref
     FROM compact_discs    cd
    WHERE artist = 'Beatles'
      AND title = 'White Album';

      -- Lock and retrieve the referenced object into the_cd
      UTL_REF.LOCK_OBJECT (the_cd_ref, the_cd);
      the_cd.title := 'Abbey Road';
      UTL_REF.UPDATE_OBJECT (the_cd_ref, the_cd);
END;

SQL> SELECT id, title
   2    FROM compact_discs
   3   WHERE artist = 'Beatles';

        ID TITLE
---------- --------------------------
       100 Abbey Road
```

Expert

9-26. The statements are:

a. False. ALL_OBJECTS shows you the list of all views (standard SQL and object views) accessible to your schema.

b. True. An object view is a view that presents data stored in relational tables as an object.

c. True. You can use an object view to navigate using REFs rather than joins; one of the nice features of the object layer is the ability to avoid complex and expensive joins. Object views allow you to do this with underlying relational tables.

d. True. Early versions of object support in Oracle make it difficult to change the definitions of object types. Object views offer ways to change table structures and object type definitions in existing systems.

e. False. One of the primary motivations for providing object views was to allow you to extend the design of a legacy database, implementing new features with objects, while retaining existing functionality.

9-27. Most of the definition of the object view is quite straightforward. It gets a bit tricky when you want to include the collection. To accomplish this, you must use the CAST and MULTISET operators to transform the child relational table to a collection column:

```
CREATE VIEW CD_object_vw
   OF CD_t
   WITH OBJECT OID (id)
AS
   SELECT cd.id,
          cd.title,
          cd.artist,
          cd.label,
          CAST (MULTISET
             (SELECT keyword
                FROM cd_keywords
               WHERE cd_keywords.cd_id = cd.id)
             AS cd_keyword_tab_t)
      FROM compact_discs cd
;
```

And here is a query that verifies the results:

```
SQL> SELECT artist, title, keywords
        FROM cd_object_vw;

ARTIST     TITLE       KEYWORDS
---------- ----------- ---------------------------------------
Beatles    White Album CD_KEYWORD_TAB_T('Lennon', 'McCartney')
```

9-28. If the object type is referenced in any other database element, such as a table, you cannot drop the object type with the standard DROP command. You get the following error:

```
ORA-02303: cannot drop or replace a type with type or table dependents
```

Instead, you must use the special FORCE option:

```
DROP TYPE temp_t FORCE;
```

This action makes all dependent elements invalid; you will have to recreate them.

10

Cursors

Beginner

10-1. An implicit cursor is a SQL statement whose associated cursor is implicitly (performed automatically by Oracle) opened, executed, and closed. The code snippets are:

   a. An example of an implicit cursor. Any INSERT, UPDATE, or DELETE is always an implicit cursor (you never open an UPDATE's cursor explicitly).

   b. An example of an explicit cursor.

   c. An example of an implicit cursor. A SELECT INTO is an implicit query to retrieve (you hope) a single row.

   d. A DDL (Data Definition Language) command executed in SQL*Plus. It is not a cursor inside a PL/SQL program.

   e. An example of an implicit cursor.

10-2. An *explicit cursor* is a SELECT statement that is declared explicitly in a declaration section (of an anonymous block, procedure, function, or package) with the CURSOR statement, as in the following:

```
DECLARE
   CURSOR my_cur
   IS
      SELECT * FROM employee;
```

10-3. If the implicit cursor is a SELECT INTO, the TOO_MANY_ROWS exception is raised when the cursor returns more than one row; NO_DATA_FOUND is raised if the query does not return any rows. If the cursor is an INSERT, it may also raise DUP_VAL_ON_INDEX. Finally, if the cursor contains expressions, it may also raise exceptions such as ZERO_DIVIDE and INVALID_NUMBER.

10-4. Even though this query returns at most one row, the SQL engine fetches or attempts to fetch twice: once to retrieve the row and then again to see if the TOO_MANY_ROWS exception should be raised.

10-5. The block could fail for any of the following reasons:

- There is more than the number of rows in the employee table, which raises the TOO_MANY_ROWS exception.

- There are no rows in the employee table, which raises the NO_DATA_FOUND exception.

- The last_name column of the employee table may have a maximum length greater than 30, which is hard-coded into the declaration of the v_name variable. If this block reads in a single employee's long name, a VALUE_ERROR exception is raised.

If you want to stick with an implicit query (SELECT INTO), change the code to this:

```
DECLARE
   v_name employee.last_name%TYPE;
BEGIN
   SELECT last_name
     INTO v_name
     FROM employee;
EXCEPTION
   WHEN NO_DATA_FOUND
   THEN
      DBMS_OUTPUT.PUT_LINE (
        'Quick, hire one person so my cursor will work!');

   WHEN TOO_MANY_ROWS
   THEN
      DBMS_OUTPUT.PUT_LINE (
        'Quick, fire somebody so my cursor will work!');
END;
```

Note that you do not have to include a handler for VALUE_ERROR. Instead, you can change the way you declare the variable, so that if and when the column size changes, this program adapts automatically to that new structure.

Intermediate

10-6. Choices (b), (e), (f), and (i) are all valid cursor attributes. They return the following information:

%*ROWCOUNT*

> Returns the number of rows processed by the cursor at that point (this number might reflect the number of rows fetched or the number of rows processed—that is, deleted, updated, or inserted).

%*ISOPEN*

> Is a Boolean attribute that returns TRUE when a cursor is open.

%*FOUND*

> Is a Boolean attribute that returns TRUE if the last fetch returned a row and FALSE if not.

%*NOTFOUND*

> Is a Boolean attribute that returns TRUE if the last fetch did not return a row and FALSE if it did.

For explicit cursors, they are specified as *cursor name%attribute*; for example, CURS_GET_EMPS%FOUND. For implicit cursors, they are specified as SQL%*attribute*; for example, SQL%NOTFOUND.

10-7. The usages are:

    a. Invalid. It raises an INVALID_CURSOR exception, since the cursor has not been opened, and you are checking the FOUND attribute.

    b. Valid.

    c. Invalid. You're referencing the %ROWCOUNT attribute as though it were a Boolean expression. It is, in fact, a numeric attribute.

    d. Invalid. You're applying the attribute to a record instead of the cursor.

    e. Invalid. You're applying the attribute to the table name rather the "SQL" keyword, as is necessary with implicit attributes.

10-8. You are executing the CLOSE after the RETURN statement, so in fact that CLOSE statement is *never* run. It would therefore seem that your cursor would remain open and you would run out of open cursors in your session. That is not, however, the case. Since your cursor is declared locally, it is automatically closed when the function returns its value. You can leave the CLOSE statement out entirely, and the function will work.

10-9. The loyal employee cannot be identified by this code alone. It might not even be the same one each time unless the same index is always used. The point is that the first employee returned by the query always receives the 10% raise regardless of which employee_id is passed to the function. The cursor parameter is ignored within the query that simply equates the employee_id column to the employee_id column that is true for all rows.

In an effort to appease the other angry employees (and disappoint a few ecstatic ones) the cursor should be changed to avoid the naming conflict between the parameter and the column.

Here is one possibility:

```
CURSOR curs_get_curr_sal (cp_employee_id employee.employee_id%TYPE )
IS
  SELECT salary
    FROM employee
   WHERE employee_id = cp_employee_id
  FOR UPDATE OF salary;
```

This clearly differentiates the cursor parameter from the table column.

10-10. The output is as follows:

```
%FOUND-TRUE
%NOTFOUND-FALSE
%ISOPEN-FALSE
%ROWCOUNT-1
```

These are the four attributes of implicit cursors.

10-11. The cursor attributes %FOUND and %NOTFOUND come in handy here. If a row is returned, the %FOUND is TRUE, and %NOTFOUND is FALSE. Conversely, %FOUND is FALSE and %NOTFOUND is TRUE when no rows are returned. Either one can be used in this case.

```
DECLARE
  CURSOR curs_failure IS
    SELECT null
      FROM employee
     WHERE 1 = 2;
  v_dummy VARCHAR2(1);
BEGIN
  OPEN curs_failure;
  FETCH curs_failure INTO v_dummy;

  IF curs_failure%NOTFOUND
  THEN
    DBMS_OUTPUT.put_line (
      'It is official. 1 ' ||
      'does not equal 2!' );
  ELSE
    DBMS_OUTPUT.put_line (
      'It is still official. ' ||
      '1 does not equal 2!' );
  END IF;

  CLOSE curs_failure;
END;
```

10-12. The %ROWCOUNT cursor attribute is incremented every time a row is returned by the cursor. It can be used to process a select number of rows from the query:

```
CREATE OR REPLACE FUNCTION three_highest RETURN NUMBER
IS
  -- Cursor to get the salaries in descending order
  CURSOR curs_get_salary IS
    SELECT NVL (salary, 0) salary
```

```
          FROM employee
        ORDER BY salary desc;
     v_salary_rec curs_get_salary%ROWTYPE;

     v_ret_val NUMBER := 0;

  BEGIN
     /*
        || Use the cursor to fetch rows and increment the
        || salary total. Stop after processing the third row.
     */
     OPEN curs_get_salary;
     LOOP
        FETCH curs_get_salary INTO v_salary_rec;
        EXIT WHEN curs_get_salary%NOTFOUND; -- Fewer than 3 rows?
        v_ret_val := v_ret_val + v_salary_rec.salary;
        EXIT WHEN curs_get_salary%ROWCOUNT = 3;
     END LOOP;

     CLOSE curs_get_salary;

     RETURN(v_ret_val);

  END three_highest;
```

10-13. You should always take the approach shown in (b): do not declare and fetch into individual variables. Instead, declare a record based on the cursor and fetch into the record. You can then reference whichever fields you need.

10-14. You see the following output:

```
32
MURRAY
```

This program does not raise a NO_DATA_FOUND error, even though it is fetching well beyond the end of the result set of this cursor. An explicit FETCH past the last row simply has no effect; the contents of the record (rec in this case) remains unchanged.

10-15. You can remove the CLOSE statement, and the code executes in exactly the same way—and the cursor closes. If you declare a cursor in a local block, its scope and visibility are restricted to this block (or procedure or function). When the block finishes executing, the memory associated with the cursor and any other local data structures is released.

10-16. Since you are fetching and processing each and every row identified by the cursor, you can use a cursor FOR loop and delete much of the code you previously wrote:

```
DECLARE
   CURSOR brought_to_you_by_unions
   IS
      SELECT weekends, forty_hour_weeks, overtime_pay
```

```
        FROM business_practices;
BEGIN
   FOR social_benefits IN brought_to_you_by_unions
   LOOP
      calculate_impact (social_benefits);
   END LOOP;
END;
```

10-17. The example shown in the problem most definitely does not do the trick. It, instead, raises the following error:

```
ORA-01001: invalid cursor
```

When you reference the %ROWCOUNT attribute, the cursor has already been opened, fetched from, and closed. That is the trade-off with a cursor FOR loop: it makes it easy to write the body of your loop, but outside of your loop, you are in the dark about what just happened. To obtain the count, you have to create a local variable and keep count yourself. Here is one implementation:

```
DECLARE
   CURSOR brought_to_you_by_unions
   IS
      SELECT weekends, forty_hour_weeks, overtime_pay
        FROM business_practices;
   v_count PLS_INTEGER;
BEGIN
   FOR social_benefits IN brought_to_you_by_unions
   LOOP
      calculate_impact (social_benefits);
      v_count := brought_to_you_by_unions%ROWCOUNT;
   END LOOP;
   DBMS_OUTPUT.PUT_LINE (
      'Calculated impact of ' || NVL (v_count, 0) -- in case of NOT FOUND
      || ' benefits brought about by unions.');
END;
```

Expert

10-18. The call to DBMS_OUTPUT.PUT_LINE shows the following:

```
FALSE - 32
```

for each row fetched (a total of 32 lines). How can this be? Here's a somewhat strange situation. You execute an implicit cursor (UPDATE), and then after that you open and process another cursor—the SELECT embedded in the cursor FOR loop.

Even though you have not declared a cursor by name for this SELECT, it is still not an implicit cursor; it is simply unnamed. Any reference, therefore, to the SQL% cursor attributes reflects the results of the UPDATE statement, not the query.

10-19. This block displays a single line of output:

TRUE

You are now using a declared, explicit cursor, so you can reference that cursor with these attributes. This block displays output only when you have fetched the first row, and the cursor is open (which is always the case inside the cursor FOR loop).

10-20. When you use the FOR UPDATE clause in a query, you can then specify:

WHERE CURRENT OF *cursor*

as the WHERE clause of DML statements inside the FOR loop. The run-time engine automagically updates/inserts/deletes the current row in the cursor's result set. You can also add a WHERE clause to minimize data queried back to the PL/SQL block and then rejected with the IF statement. Here is the rewrite:

```
DECLARE
    CURSOR upd_all_cur
        IS SELECT * FROM employee
            WHERE commission IS NOT NULL
            FOR UPDATE;
BEGIN
    FOR rec IN upd_all_cur
    LOOP
        UPDATE employee
            SET commission = commission * 2
        WHERE CURRENT OF upd_all_cur;
    END LOOP;
END;
```

 You should also see an improvement in program performance with this change. My tests (see the *wco_vs_pkey.sql* file on the book's web page) revealed these results:

```
SQL> @wco_vs_pkey 500
WHERE CURRENT OF Elapsed: 12.3 seconds.
BY PRIMARY KEY Elapsed: 14.52 seconds.
```

10-21. The block locks each and every row in the employee table, whether or not an UPDATE is actually performed on a particular row. Specifying the column name in the FOR UPDATE clause has an impact only if there are multiple tables specified in the FROM clause. In that situation, only tables whose columns are specified in the FOR UPDATE OF clause will have rows locked.

10-22. The first time you execute the block, all four cursors will be opened and no error occurs. The second time you run the block, you get this error:

ORA-06511: PL/SQL: cursor already open

when the block attempts to open door number one. Why does this happen? When the anonymous block terminates, doors number three and four are closed, while doors one and two remain open. Cursors door_number_ three and door_number_four are declared within a specific PL/SQL block (a procedure and an anonymous block, respectively). When that block closes, the cursors also close. Doors numbered one and two are declared at the package level (one in the package specification and one in the body), so their scope is the entire session. These cursors will not close until you close them explicitly, or you exit the session.

10-23. A database record (%ROWTYPE) or a programmer-defined record.

10-24. The best solution is to move all this related code into a single package, as shown here:

```
CREATE OR REPLACE PACKAGE jobinfo
IS
   FUNCTION job_for (name_in IN VARCHAR2) RETURN VARCHAR2;
   PROCEDURE show_jobs;
END jobinfo;
/
CREATE OR REPLACE PACKAGE BODY jobinfo
IS
   CURSOR around_the_house_jobs_cur (
      name_in IN adolescent_workload.name%TYPE)
   IS
       SELECT job
         FROM adolescent_workload
        WHERE name = name_in;

   PROCEDURE show_jobs IS
   BEGIN
      FOR rec IN around_the_house_jobs_cur ('ELI')
      LOOP
         DBMS_OUTPUT.PUT_LINE (rec.job);
      END LOOP;
   END;

   FUNCTION job_for (name_in IN VARCHAR2) RETURN VARCHAR2
   IS
      Retval adolescent_workload.job%type;
   BEGIN
      OPEN around_the_house_jobs_cur (name_in);
      FETCH around_the_house_jobs_cur INTO retval;
      CLOSE around_the_house_jobs_cur;
      RETURN retval;
   END;
END jobinfo;
/
```

In the original programs, there were two different cursors that were logically equivalent, but physically different. This led to excessive parsing of SQL statements. In this version, we have just one cursor, and it has been parameterized, so no matter what name is passed to it, the same pre-parsed SQL statement cached in the SGA is used.

Notice that you need to add the CLOSE statement to the function (in bold). When the cursor is defined inside the function, it's closed automatically when the function returns its data. Once you move the cursor to the package level, it stays open unless closed.

10-25. Oracle8*i* offers a new feature called *bulk collect* that allows you to request that all rows in a query be fetched in a single pass to the database, depositing the result set directly into the specified nested tables. Here is a rewrite of the original program utilizing that technique:

```
CREATE OR REPLACE FUNCTION get_a_mess_o_emps
    (deptno_in IN dept.deptno%TYPE)
RETURN emplist_t
IS
    emplist emplist_t := emplist_t();
    TYPE numTab IS TABLE OF NUMBER;
    TYPE charTab IS TABLE OF VARCHAR2(12);
    TYPE dateTab IS TABLE OF DATE;
    enos numTab;
    names charTab;
    hdates dateTab;
BEGIN
    SELECT empno, ename, hiredate
       BULK COLLECT INTO enos, names, hdates
       FROM emp1
     WHERE deptno = deptno_in;
    emplist.EXTEND(enos.COUNT);
    FOR i IN enos.FIRST..enos.LAST
    LOOP
       emplist(i) := emp_t(enos(i), names(i), hdates(i));
    END LOOP;
    RETURN emplist;
END;
/
```

11

DML and Transaction Management

Beginner

11-1. DELETE, UPDATE, and INSERT. You can execute any of these statements directly in a PL/SQL block. Here is an example of a block that removes all the rows from the employee table:

```
BEGIN
   DELETE FROM employee;
END;
/
```

11-2. Statements are:

a. False. DML changes made in a PL/SQL block are saved only when a COMMIT is executed in that session.

b. True. An exception doesn't cause a rollback of changes made unless that exception propagates unhandled out of the outermost block. Then the host environment usually (but not necessarily) issues a ROLLBACK.

c. False. The INSERT...INTO...SELECT FROM statement is valid in PL/SQL, so you can insert multiple rows with a single INSERT statement.

11-3. All the native DML statements in PL/SQL are *implicit* cursors. This means that the underlying SQL engine automatically and implicitly opens, executes, and closes the cursor containing your DML statement.

11-4. You can obtain this information by examining the value of the SQL%ROWCOUNT attribute. The following block illustrates this technique:

```
BEGIN
   DELETE FROM employee WHERE salary > 10000;
   DBMS_OUTPUT.PUT_LINE (
```

```
                      'We can now hire ' || SQL%ROWCOUNT ||
                      ' cheap, young college graduates!');
       END;
```

11-5. To save changes, issue a COMMIT command. You can do this with either of the following statements:

```
COMMIT;
DBMS_STANDARD.COMMIT;
```

11-6. To erase changes in your session, use the ROLLBACK command. You can do this as follows:

```
ROLLBACK;
DBMS_STANDARD.ROLLBACK;
```

11-7. The following statements are valid:

    a. `COMMIT;`

    b. `COMMIT 'NY transaction';`

    d. `ROLLBACK;`

    f. `ROLLBACK TO my_savepoint;`

    g. `DBMS_STANDARD.ROLLBACK_SV ('last_change');`

    i. `DBMS_STANDARD.COMMIT;`

In other words, you can specify a comment when you commit. You can use the native ROLLBACK command to a specified savepoint, but that savepoint name is not a literal string. It is an "undeclared identifier." If you want to roll back to a literal string (or variable value), you must call the DBMS_STANDARD.ROLLBACK_SV procedure.

The following statements are invalid:

    c. `COMMIT WHEN mycount > 1000;`

    e. `ROLLBACK TO 'last_change';`

    h. `ROLLBACK 'NY transaction';`

In other words, there is no WHEN clause for a COMMIT that allows a conditional save (though it seems like a nice idea, doesn't it?). You cannot ROLLBACK TO a literal value. You cannot provide a comment for the ROLLBACK; this feature is allowed only for a COMMIT and is used in two-phase commits (distributed transactions).

11-8. Here is a suggested procedure:

```
CREATE OR REPLACE PROCEDURE spread the wealth
IS
BEGIN
   UPDATE employee SET salary = salary * .1
    WHERE job_id = 1;

   UPDATE employee SET salary = salary * 1.30
    WHERE job_id = 1000;
```

```
    COMMIT;
EXCEPTION
    WHEN OTHERS
    THEN
        ROLLBACK;
END;
/
```

11-9. Here is a suggested block of code:

```
BEGIN
    UPDATE employee SET salary = salary * 1.10;

    IF SQL%ROWCOUNT > 10
    THEN
        ROLLBACK;
    END IF;
END;
/
```

Intermediate

11-10. PL/SQL offers the concept of a *savepoint* to allow you to roll back selectively, which is the same as saving selectively, when you think about it.

11-11. Here is a suggested exception section:

```
EXCEPTION
    WHEN OTHERS
    THEN
        myerr := SQLCODE;
        ROLLBACK to log_savepoint;
        INSERT INTO log VALUES (SYSDATE, USER, myerr);
        SAVEPOINT log_savepoint;
END;
```

11-12. You receive an error:

```
SQL>
  1   BEGIN
  2       ROLLBACK TO nonexistent_sp;
  3   END;
  4   /
BEGIN
*
ERROR at line 1:
ORA-01086: savepoint 'NONEXISTENT_SP' never established
```

11-13. There are two possible approaches:

- Maintain your own stack of savepoints issued in your session and check the savepoint name against this stack before you issue a ROLLBACK TO command. This is rather complicated.

- Build a PL/SQL block around your ROLLBACK TO command and trap the ORA-01086 error if it occurs.

Here is a block of code that demonstrates the second technique:

```
EXCEPTION
   WHEN OTHERS
   THEN
      BEGIN
         ROLLBACK to log_savepoint;
      EXCEPTION
         WHEN OTHERS
         THEN
            IF SQLCODE = -1086
            THEN
               /* Can't use savepoint, so roll all the way back. */
               ROLLBACK;
            ELSE
               /* Re-raise exeption. Who knows what went wrong! */
               RAISE;
            END IF;
      END;
END;
```

11-14. Ten savepoints were set, but only one savepoint is "active" at any time. A total of nine rows are inserted. If you issue a new savepoint with the same name as an "old" (previously set) savepoint, the new savepoint completely replaces any others with that same name. In this block of code, the same savepoint is set 10 times, so there is really just one savepoint to which you can roll back at any time. The ROLLBACK after the end of the loop rolls back the last INSERT, but leaves all others intact.

11-15. You will see:

```
Rows deleted = 25
```

when you run this code. Remember that the SQL%ROWCOUNT attribute returns the number of rows modified by the last UPDATE, INSERT, or DELETE in your session, regardless of the specific block in which the action took place.

11-16. PL/SQL provides the following statement:

```
SET TRANSACTION READ ONLY;
```

This indicate that all SQL operations refer to the same snapshot of the database.

11-17. By issuing a COMMIT or ROLLBACK.

11-18. This block raises the following error:

```
ORA-01453: SET TRANSACTION must be first statement of transaction
```

The SET TRANSACTION cannot come after any SQL statements in your session's transaction. You may want to perform a COMMIT or ROLLBACK before issuing SET TRANSACTION to be sure of this state.

11-19. The statements are:

    a. True.

    b. False. You cannot SELECT FOR UPDATE when you have specified a read-only transaction.

    c. False. You can request a lock of the entire table with LOCK TABLE.

    d. False. And if you do set up a read-only transaction in your session, it will not have any impact on other sessions.

11-20. You can use the FOR UPDATE clause in your query to request that exclusive row locks be issued on rows in the result set. The default behavior is that reading data never blocks another session from reading from and/or writing to that data.

11-21. Here is a suggested block:

```
DECLARE
   CURSOR cur IS SELECT * FROM employee FOR UPDATE;
BEGIN
   FOR emp_rec IN cur
   LOOP
      UPDATE employee SET salary = salary * 1.5
       WHERE CURRENT OF cur;
   END LOOP;
END;
```

The CURRENT OF syntax can be used only with a FOR UPDATE cursor. It automatically refers the UPDATE or DELETE to the most recently fetched row from the cursor. It allows you to avoid writing a WHERE clause that relies on primary keys or ROWID.

11-22. Only rows in the emp table will be locked. The FOR UPDATE clause lists only columns in the emp table, so no locks need be issued for dept.

11-23. None of these statements are true.

    a. False. Locks are placed on rows when the cursor is opened, not as each row is fetched. That is the only way to guarantee your requested, exclusive access to the data.

    b. False. Only those rows specified by the WHERE and FOR UPDATE OF clauses of the query are locked.

    c. False. In your FOR UPDATE OF clause, you can specify any column from any of the tables in your FROM clause; those columns do not need to be selected; they identify only tables whose rows are to be locked.

    d. False. You can specify NOWAIT so that your query immediately raises an error if it cannot obtain locks on the specified rows, or you can leave off the NOWAIT clause, which means that your session waits for an unlimited amount of time. You cannot specify a period of time to wait.

e. False. If you COMMIT or ROLLBACK while you are fetching records from a FOR UPDATE cursor, the next time you try to fetch a row, you receive an error. The FOR UPDATE clause obtains exclusive row locks. This means that all rows are locked when you open the cursor; they are unlocked when you commit the transaction.

11-24. You can combine this two-step process into a single UPDATE statement by taking advantage of the RETURNING clause:

```
PROCEDURE update_salary (emp_id NUMBER) IS
    name    VARCHAR2(15);
    new_sal NUMBER;
BEGIN
    UPDATE emp SET sal = sal * 1.1
        WHERE empno = emp_id
        RETURNING ename, sal INTO name, new_sal;
END;
```

Expert

11-25. You can either use dynamic SQL (DBMS_SQL prior to Oracle 8.1 or native dynamic SQL from 8.1 onwards) to execute a dynamic PL/SQL block. You can also take advantage of the SAVEPOINT procedure in the DBMS_STANDARD package as shown in this rewrite:

```
BEGIN
    DBMS_STANDARD.SAVEPOINT ('start_process');
    INSERT INTO ...;
    DELETE FROM ...;
```

11-26. You can set a savepoint in any of these ways:

- SAVEPOINT *savepoint;*
- DBMS_TRANSACTION.SAVEPOINT *savepoint;*
- DBMS_STANDARD.SAVEPOINT *savepoint;*
- Through the use of DBMS_SQL

11-27. You can roll back your transaction in PL/SQL in any of these ways:

- ROLLBACK;
- DBMS_TRANSACTION.ROLLBACK_SAVEPOINT *savepoint;*
- DBMS_STANDARD.ROLLBACK_SV *savepoint;*
- Dynamic SQL (DBMS_SQL or native dynamic SQL in Oracle 8.1)
- Unhandled exception

11-28. When you execute this code, you get the following error:

```
ORA-01086: savepoint 'START_PROCESS' never established
```

At first glance this doesn't make sense. You set the savepoint and then try to roll back to that savepoint. Unfortunately, Oracle doesn't consider them to be the *same* savepoint. If you are going to set a savepoint by using the DBMS_STANDARD.SAVEPOINT program, you must roll back *to* that savepoint by calling another DBMS_STANDARD program:

```
BEGIN
   DBMS_STANDARD.SAVEPOINT ('start_process');
   DBMS_STANDARD.ROLLBACK_SV ('start_process');
END;
```

11-29. Each time you issue a COMMIT in your session, the rollback segment is set back to the default for your session. You must, therefore, be careful to reset the current rollback segment back to the nondefault after each COMMIT (see the bold statement):

```
DECLARE
   CURSOR my_million_row_cursor IS SELECT ...;
   ctr PLS_INTEGER := 1;
BEGIN
   DBMS_TRANSACTION.USE_ROLLBACK_SEGMENT ('big_rb');
   FOR every_rec IN my_million_row_cursor
   LOOP
      make_the_changes (every_rec);
      IF ctr > 10000
      THEN
         COMMIT;
         DBMS_TRANSACTION.USE_ROLLBACK_SEGMENT ('big_rb');
         ctr := 1;
      ELSE
         ct := ctr + 1;
      END IF;
   END LOOP;
END;
```

11-30. You can set the rollback segment in any of these ways:

  • DBMS_SQL execution of the DDL statement

  • Native dynamic SQL execution of the DDL statement (Oracle 8.1 only)

  • DBMS_TRANSACTION.USE_ROLLBACK_SEGMENT

  • DBMS_STANDARD.SET_TRANSACTION_USE

11-31. Oracle has implemented *autonomous transactions* in Oracle8*i* Release 8.1. This feature allows you to save changes to the database in one procedure or PL/SQL block without saving changes to the "main" transaction in your session.

11-32. Add the following statement:

```
PRAGMA AUTONOMOUS_TRANSACTION;
```

11-33. Here's a suggested procedure:

```
CREATE OR REPLACE PROCEDURE del_emps
IS
   PRAGMA AUTONOMOUS_TRANSACTION;
```

```
BEGIN
   DELETE FROM employee;
   COMMIT;
END;
/
```

11-34. Everything except (b) can be defined as autonomous transactions.

11-35. You can place COMMIT and ROLLBACK inside a database trigger if it is an autonomous transaction.

11-36. You cannot apply AUTONOMOUS_TRANSACTION to an entire package. Instead, you have to include the pragma in each individual program.

11-37. You would add the line marked in bold:

```
CREATE OR REPLACE PROCEDURE del_emps (deptno_in IN emp.deptno%TYPE)
IS
   PRAGMA AUTONOMOUS_TRANSACTION;
BEGIN
   SET TRANSACTION ISOLATION LEVEL SERIALIZABLE;
   DELETE FROM emp WHERE deptno = deptno_in;
   COMMIT;
END;
```

11-38. You get an error:

```
ORA-06519: active autonomous transaction detected and rolled back
```

The problem with the del_emps procedure is that it's defined as an autonomous transaction, but the transaction isn't ended properly, with either a COMMIT or a ROLLBACK. This causes an error to be raised.

11-39. Statements are:

    a. True.

    b. False. You can have multiple COMMIT and/or ROLLBACK statements in your autonomous transaction.

    c. False. A rollback or commit in the main transaction will absolutely not affect the changes saved or rejected in your autonomous transaction; that is the whole point!

    d. True.

    e. True.

11-40. The best way to obtain this behavior is to try to open the cursor inside a loop. If the open attempt fails, go to sleep for a short amount of time and then try again, until you have used up the full wait time. Here is one possible implementation (the original idea was provided by Steve Cosner):

```
/* Filename on web page forupdwait.sql */
DECLARE
   waitsecs CONSTANT PLS_INTEGER := 10;
```

```
    CURSOR emp_cur IS SELECT ename, rowid FROM emp FOR UPDATE NOWAIT;
    emp_rec emp_cur%ROWTYPE;

    resource_busy EXCEPTION;
    PRAGMA EXCEPTION_INIT (resource_busy, -54);

    starttime PLS_INTEGER;
BEGIN
    starttime := DBMS_UTILITY.GET_TIME;
    LOOP
       BEGIN
          /* If open raises no errors, then exit the loop. */
          OPEN emp_cur;
          EXIT;
       EXCEPTION
          WHEN resource_busy
          THEN
             /* Wait no more than 10 seconds; DBMS_UTILITY.GET_TIME works
                in hundredths of seconds. */
             IF DBMS_UTILITY.GET_TIME - starttime < waitsecs / 100
             THEN
                /* Sleep for half a second, then try again. */
                DBMS_LOCK.SLEEP (.5);
             ELSE
                RAISE;
             END IF;
       END;
    END LOOP;

    /* Cursor has been opened successfully. Locks are acquired. */
    LOOP
       FETCH emp_cur INTO emp_rec;
       EXIT WHEN emp_cur%NOTFOUND;
       UPDATE emp SET sal = sal + 1000 WHERE ROWID = emp_rec.rowid;
    END LOOP;

    CLOSE emp_cur;
    COMMIT;
END;
```

12

Cursor Variables

Beginner

12-1. Statement (b) describes a cursor variable. Rather than pointing directly or in a hardcoded way to a result set, a cursor variable is a pointer to a work area in the System Global Area (SGA).

12-2. First, you must declare a cursor variable type, also known as a REF CURSOR. Then you declare a variable based on that cursor. The following is an example:

```
DECLARE
    TYPE emp_t IS REF CURSOR RETURN emp%ROWTYPE;
    emp_cv emp_t;
```

12-3. The declarations are:

    a. Valid. This format declares a type of REF CURSOR that is not tied to any specific format or result set; this is called a *weak* or *nonrestrictive* REF CURSOR.

    b. Invalid.

    c. Invalid.

    d. Valid. This format allows you to declare cursor variables that can fetch rows having the same format as the orders table; this is called a *strong* or *restrictive* REF CURSOR.

Statements (b) and (c) are invalid. After the REF CURSOR keywords, you either have simply a semicolon or a RETURN *rowtype* clause, where *rowtype* is either a %ROWTYPE definition or the name of a previously defined record type.

12-4. The declarations are:

    a. Valid. Only (a) is a valid cursor variable declaration based on the disasters_cvt REF CURSOR.

    b. Invalid. This declaration will fail to compile because of the %ROW-TYPE attribute. A REF CURSOR type is already a type; you don't need to %ROWTYPE it.

    c. Invalid. This declaration will compile, but it simply creates a record with the same structure as a row in the environmental_disaster table, not a cursor variable.

12-5. Here is a suggested block:

```
DECLARE
    TYPE emp_cvt IS REF CURSOR RETURN employee%ROWTYPE;
    developer emp_cvt;
    dba emp_cvt;
BEGIN
```

12-6. All cursor operations and cursor attributes work the same for cursor variables as for hardcoded or explicit cursors, *except* for the OPEN statement (a). When you open a cursor variable, you open it for a specific SELECT statement, as in:

```
OPEN my_cv FOR SELECT * FROM employee;
```

Intermediate

12-7. Here is one possible implementation:

```
DECLARE
    TYPE emp_cvt IS REF CURSOR RETURN employee%ROWTYPE;
    employees emp_cvt;
    one_employee employees%ROWTYPE;
BEGIN
    OPEN employees FOR SELECT * FROM employee;
    LOOP
        FETCH employees INTO one_employee;
        EXIT WHEN employees%NOTFOUND;
        double_salary (one_employee.employee_id, one_employee.salary);
    END LOOP;
    CLOSE employees;
END;
/
```

12-8. Here are the rules to keep in mind in solving this problem:

    a. The statement must be valid.

    b. The number and datatypes of the record being declared must be compatible with the record structure in the RETURN clause of the REF CURSOR statement.

The declarations are:

a. Valid. This statement (as well as (e) and (g)) declares records that can be used in FETCH statements against the_finest_cv cursor variable. This one declares a standard table-based record, exactly the same structure used in the REF CURSOR.

b. Invalid. Doesn't compile. You can't use %ROWTYPE against a REF CURSOR, only against a cursor variable.

c. Invalid. Doesn't compile. You can't declare a record of type REF CURSOR; you can only declare cursor variables based on REF CURSOR types.

d. Invalid. Doesn't compile. You need to add %ROWTYPE to this statement.

e. Valid. This statement relies on a programmer-defined record that has the same structure as the table, so that works just fine.

f. Invalid. Doesn't compile. You can't put a %ROWTYPE at the end of a record TYPE; it already is a type.

g. Valid. This statement demonstrates that you can declare a record from a cursor variable with %ROWTYPE, just as you can with a table or cursor.

12-9. Statements are:

a. Correct.

b. Correct.

c. Incorrect (weakly).

d. Incorrect (and downright silly).

e. Correct. When you close a cursor variable, it closes the underlying cursor object.

You should not expect to see any significant difference in runtime performance between cursor variables based on strong and weak REF CURSORs, though the PL/SQL runtime engine will be doing a little more work at runtime with weak REF CURSORs.

12-10. Statements (a), (b), and (e) are all "poster children" for the cursor variable feature:

a. Yes. Cursor variables allow you to "pass" result sets of queries between client and server programs, or between various server programs without actually passing the data. You just pass the pointer to the data. This reduces network traffic.

b. No. This one requires the use of dynamic SQL (the SQL string is not complete at compile time). You need to use the DBMS_SQL package to implement this scenario, since Method 4 dynamic SQL is requested.

     c. Yes. This is a perfect example of why you might use cursor variables to "hide" minor differences between queries and write a single block of code that works for all of the queries.

     d. Yes.

     e. No. This one also requires dynamic SQL; it can be implemented with DBMS_SQL or native dynamic SQL (if you are running Oracle 8.1).

12-11. The problems are:

     a. You cannot declare cursor variables in a package because they do not have persistent state.

     b. The SQL statement cannot be a literal string or a variable. It must be hardcoded or static at the time of program compilation. The OPEN FOR *string* syntax is used by native dynamic SQL.

     c. You cannot use FOR UPDATE inside a cursor variable's SELECT statement.

     d. You cannot assign the NULL value to a cursor variable.

12-12. The statement:

     a. Raises a ROWTYPE_MISMATCH error when the procedure is executed. You have requested that a record based on the department table receive a row from the employee table. When unhandled, this error displays as:

```
ORA-06504: PL/SQL: Return types of Result Set variables or query do not
match
```

       This error always rears its ugly head at runtime (a difficult point at which to debug one's code) when you rely on weak REF CURSORs.

     b. Fails to compile with this error:

```
PLS-00382: expression is of wrong type
```

       Once again, you have requested that a record based on the department table receive a row from the employee table. This time, however, the compiler can check for compatibility because you have used a strong REF CURSOR.

     c. Doesn't cause a mismatch error. The airplane_food table has two numeric columns, and your query selects two numeric columns from the employee table.

12-13. The function returns a cursor variable, so the RETURN clause of the function must reference a REF CURSOR type. The REF CURSOR type can be defined in the same package as the function (unless the function is to be "standalone"), or it can be declared in a separate package specification. Furthermore, since the REF CURSOR is based on a subset of the columns of the employee table, you also need to define a programmer-defined record type to reflect that two-field structure. Again, this needs to be defined in a package specification, either with the function or independent of it.

12-14. Here is one possible implementation of the package specification:

```
/* Filename on web page: empinfo.pkg */
PACKAGE empinfo
IS
    bysal CONSTANT INTEGER := 1;
    bysaldesc CONSTANT INTEGER := 2;
    bydept CONSTANT INTEGER := 3;
    byname CONSTANT INTEGER := 4;

    TYPE two_pieces_t IS RECORD (str VARCHAR2(100), num NUMBER);
    TYPE emp_cvt IS REF CURSOR RETURN two_pieces_t;
    FUNCTION open (query_number IN INTEGER) RETURN emp_cvt;
END;
```

Notice that you need to specify only that the record consists of one string and one number. You could have also relied on %TYPE declarations as follows:

```
TYPE two_pieces_t IS RECORD (
        str employee.last_name%TYPE, num employee.salary%TYPE);
```

12-15. Here is one possible implementation:

```
/* Filename on web page: empinfo.pkg */
CREATE OR REPLACE PACKAGE BODY empinfo
IS
    FUNCTION open (query_number IN INTEGER) RETURN emp_cvt
    IS
        retval emp cvt;
    BEGIN
        IF query_number = bysal
        THEN
            OPEN retval FOR
                SELECT last_name, salary FROM employee ORDER BY salary;
        ELSIF query_number = bysaldesc
        THEN
            OPEN retval FOR
                SELECT last_name, salary
                    FROM employee ORDER BY salary DESC;
        ELSIF query_number = bydept
        THEN
            OPEN retval FOR
                SELECT last_name, department_id
                    FROM employee ORDER BY department_id;
        ELSIF query_number = byname
        THEN
            OPEN retval FOR
                SELECT first_name || ' ' || last_name, salary
                    FROM employee ORDER BY last_name;
        END IF;
        RETURN retval;
```

```
        END;
END;
/
```

12-16. Here is one possible implementation:

```
PROCEDURE show (query_number IN INTEGER)
IS
    cv emp_cvt;
    rec cv%ROWTYPE;
BEGIN
    cv := open (query_number);
    LOOP
        FETCH cv INTO rec;
        EXIT WHEN cv%NOTFOUND;
        IF cv%ROWCOUNT = 1
        THEN
            DBMS_OUTPUT.PUT_LINE (RPAD ('-', 60, '-'));
            DBMS_OUTPUT.PUT_LINE ('Contents of Query ' || query_number);
            DBMS_OUTPUT.PUT_LINE (RPAD ('-', 60, '-'));
        END IF;
        DBMS_OUTPUT.PUT_LINE (RPAD (rec.str, 30) || rec.num);
    END LOOP;
    CLOSE cv;
END;
```

Expert

12-17. When you declare a cursor variable as the formal parameter of a subprogram that opens the cursor variable, you must specify the parameter to be of mode OUT or IN OUT. That way, the subprogram can pass an open cursor back to the caller.

12-18. Problems are:

> a. You cannot pass a cursor variable through the parameter list of a remote procedure call (RPC). The variable points to a result set in the current database instance.

> b. You cannot use comparison operators to test two or more different cursor variables for equality, inequality, or nullity (IS NULL or IS NOT NULL).

> c. You cannot use a REF CURSOR type to specify the element type of a collection (error PLS-00990). As a consequence, a cursor variable may not be an element in a nested table, index-by table, or VARRAY.

> d. Even through the two different REF CURSOR types have the same RETURN clause, they are considered different types; you cannot, therefore, assign tmp_cv to emp_cv.

12-19. The declaration in (a) defines a cursor variable in SQL*Plus of type REF CURSOR (weak). The following is an example of declaring and using such a variable:

```
SQL> VARIABLE bysal REFCURSOR
SQL> exec :bysal := empinfo.open (empinfo.bysal)
PL/SQL procedure successfully completed.
SQL>
```

12-20. Here is one possible implementation:

```
/* Filename on web page: cah.pkg */
CREATE OR REPLACE PACKAGE cah
AS
    TYPE tainted_person IS REF CURSOR;

    PROCEDURE identify_person (
        name IN VARCHAR2,
        info_out IN OUT tainted_person
        );
END cah;
/
```

The most important thing to remember here is that you need a weak REF CURSOR, since each of the table structures is different.

12-21. The following code is one possible implementation. Notice that a standard explicit cursor is used to first determine the type of involvement of the person in a crime against humanity. Once you have the type, you can use an IF statement to perform a SELECT from the appropriate table. If you don't find a match, make sure that the cursor variable you return to the calling program is closed.

```
/* Filename on web page: cah.pkg */
PROCEDURE identify_person (
    name IN VARCHAR2,
    info_out IN OUT tainted_person
    )
IS
    CURSOR cah_type_cur IS
        SELECT cah_type
          FROM person
         WHERE name = identify_person.name;

    v_type person.cah_type%TYPE;
BEGIN
    OPEN cah_type_cur;
    FETCH cah_type_cur INTO v_type;

    IF cah_type_cur%NOTFOUND
    THEN
        /* Close the CV if it is open to indicate that the
           name did not provide valid results. */
        IF info_out%ISOPEN THEN CLOSE info_out; END IF;
    ELSIF v_type = 1
```

```
    THEN
        OPEN info_out FOR SELECT * FROM direct_combatant
            WHERE name = identify_person.name;
    ELSIF v_type = 1
    THEN
        OPEN info_out FOR SELECT * FROM indirect_enabler
            WHERE name = identify_person.name;
    ELSIF v_type = 1
    THEN
        OPEN info_out FOR SELECT * FROM noninnocent_bystander
            WHERE name = identify_person.name;
    END IF;
    CLOSE cah_type_cur;
END identify_person;
```

13

Native Dynamic SQL

Beginner

13-1. Yes, that's right! Just two new statements:

```
EXECUTE IMMEDIATE SQL_string USING
OPEN cursor_variable FOR query_string USING
```

You use EXECUTE IMMEDIATE to, well, immediately execute the specified string with the bind variables specified in the USING clause.

You use the OPEN FOR statement to open a multiple row query. After that, use standard cursor variable FETCH operations to retrieve the data.

13-2. They can't make it much easier than this:

```
BEGIN
    EXECUTE IMMEDIATE 'drop table employee';
END;
/
```

13-3. Here is a suggested procedure:

```
CREATE OR REPLACE PROCEDURE drop_table (tab IN VARCHAR2)
IS
BEGIN
    EXECUTE IMMEDIATE 'drop table ' || tab;
END;
/
```

13-4. Here is a suggested function:

```
/* Filename on web page: tabcount81.sf */
CREATE OR REPLACE FUNCTION tabcount (nm IN VARCHAR2)
    RETURN PLS_INTEGER
IS
    retval PLS_INTEGER;
BEGIN
    EXECUTE IMMEDIATE 'SELECT COUNT(*) FROM ' || nm INTO retval;
```

```
        RETURN retval;
END;
/
```

Intermediate

13-5. Here is the enhanced table count function:

```
/* Filename on web page: tabcount81-2.sf */
CREATE OR REPLACE FUNCTION tabcount (
    nm IN VARCHAR2,
    whr IN VARCHAR2 := NULL)
    RETURN PLS_INTEGER
IS
    retval PLS_INTEGER;
    v_where VARCHAR2(2000) := whr;
BEGIN
    IF UPPER (whr) NOT LIKE 'WHERE %'
    THEN
        v_where := 'WHERE ' || v_where;
    END IF;

    EXECUTE IMMEDIATE
        'SELECT COUNT(*) FROM ' || nm || ' ' || v_where
        INTO retval;
    RETURN retval;
END;
/
```

13-6. Just construct the appropriate DDL statement, and the deed is done:

```
/* Filename on web page: dropit.sp */
CREATE OR REPLACE PROCEDURE dropit (
    ittype IN VARCHAR2, itname IN VARCHAR2)
IS
BEGIN
    EXECUTE IMMEDIATE 'drop ' || ittype || ' ' || itname;
END;
/
```

13-7. You cannot use placeholders for schema elements of the dynamic SQL statement. What is a schema element? It's the name of an element in your schema: table, column, view, object type, etc. If you have variable schema elements, you must use concatenation to incorporate that variable name into the SQL string.

13-8. Here is a generic procedure:

```
/* Filename on web page: runddl81.sp */
CREATE OR REPLACE PROCEDURE runddl (ddl_in in VARCHAR2)
    AUTHID CURRENT_USER
IS
BEGIN
    EXECUTE IMMEDIATE ddl_in;
END;
/
```

13-9. Here is a suggested modification:

```
/* Filename on web page: creind81.sp */
CREATE OR REPLACE PROCEDURE creindx
    (index_in IN VARCHAR2,
     tab_in IN VARCHAR2,
     col_in IN VARCHAR2)
IS
    DDL_statement VARCHAR2(200)
        := 'CREATE INDEX ' || index_in ||
        ' ON ' || tab_in ||
        ' ( ' || col_in || ')';
BEGIN
    runddl (DDL_statement);
END;
/
```

13-10. Implementation (b) runs more efficiently. It uses a bind variable and the USING clause, rather than an explicit concatenation of the name into the dynamic SQL string. If you use concatenation to add variable values to your SQL string, the SQL statement changes with each call to EXECUTE IMMEDIATE, requiring reparsing of the statement. If you use a place-holder (:so_sorry), the SQL statement does not change in each iteration of the loop, and it isn't reparsed.

13-11. You can use the same SQL%ROWCOUNT attribute for static, implicit cursors with native dynamic SQL cursors as well. Here is a recoding of that procedure:

```
CREATE OR REPLACE FUNCTION rows_deleted (
    table_name IN VARCHAR2,
    condition IN VARCHAR2)
RETURN INTEGER AS
BEGIN
    EXECUTE IMMEDIATE
        'DELETE FROM ' || table_name || ' WHERE ' || condition;
    RETURN SQL%ROWCOUNT;
END;
```

13-12. To fetch multiple rows of information, you need to declare a REF CURSOR type and a cursor variable based on that REF CURSOR. You can then fetch one or more rows from that cursor variable.

13-13. Here is a display procedure:

```
/* Filename on web page: showemps81.sp */
CREATE OR REPLACE PROCEDURE showemps81 (
    where_in IN VARCHAR2 := NULL)
IS
    TYPE cv_typ IS REF CURSOR;
    cv cv_typ;
    v_id employee.employee_id%TYPE;
    v_nm employee.last_name%TYPE;
BEGIN
```

```
      OPEN cv FOR
        'SELECT last_name FROM employee
          WHERE ' || NVL (where_in, '1=1');
      LOOP
        FETCH cv INTO v_nm;
        EXIT WHEN cv%NOTFOUND;
        DBMS_OUTPUT.PUT_LINE (v_nm);
      END LOOP;
      CLOSE cv;
   END;
   /
```

13-14. Don't forget that you have to execute the procedure invocation within a valid PL/SQL block. Use the USING clause to pass in the single argument value. Don't use concatenation.

```
CREATE OR REPLACE PROCEDURE runplsql (
   progname IN VARCHAR, singlevalue IN NUMBER)
IS
BEGIN
   EXECUTE IMMEDIATE
      'BEGIN ' || progname || '(:val); END;' USING singlevalue;
END;
```

13-15. Remember: when you are working with OUT or IN OUT arguments, you must specify those nondefault parameter modes in your USING clause:

```
CREATE OR REPLACE PROCEDURE runplsql (
   progname IN VARCHAR,
   inval IN NUMBER,
   outval1 OUT VARCHAR2,
   outval2 OUT VARCHAR2
   )
IS
BEGIN
   EXECUTE IMMEDIATE
      'BEGIN ' || progname || '(:val1, :val2, :val3); END;'
      USING inval, OUT outval1, OUT outval2;
END;
```

13-16. Here's the rewrite:

```
CREATE OR REPLACE PROCEDURE master_line_processor (
   line_in IN INTEGER,
   data_in IN VARCHAR2,
   rating_out OUT NUMBER)
IS
BEGIN
   EXECUTE IMMEDIATE
      'BEGIN process_line_' || line_in ||
         '(:indata, :outrating); END;'
      USING data_in, OUT rating_out;
END;
```

13-17. The procedure displays "entries = 10". Changing the value of the bind variable inside the loop does not have any effect because the cursor is only parsed when it's opened.

Expert

13-18. The first EXECUTE IMMEDIATE is the correct one. NDS associates placeholders in a SQL statement with bind arguments in the USING clause by position, not by name. Therefore, you must repeat the bind value for each appearance of the same placeholder in your string.

13-19. The implementation seems straightforward enough:

```
/* Filename on web page: value_in.sf */
CREATE OR REPLACE FUNCTION value_in (
    varname IN VARCHAR
    )
    RETURN VARCHAR2
IS
    retval VARCHAR2(2000);
BEGIN
    EXECUTE IMMEDIATE
      'BEGIN :val := ' || varname || '; END;'
      USING OUT retval;
    RETURN retval;
END;
/
```

You probably had to experiment, however, with a few approaches before you got it to work properly. I did. I tried this EXECUTE IMMEDIATE first:

```
EXECUTE IMMEDIATE
      'BEGIN :val := :varname; END;'
      USING OUT retval, varname;
```

But when I executed the function I got these results:

```
SQL> exec DBMS_OUTPUT.PUT_LINE (value_in('p.linelen'))
p.linelen
```

In other words, it did not evaluate what is in this case a function call. It simply treated it as a literal string. I realized that I needed to *concatenate* the variable name into the string so that it would be evaluated when the dynamic PL/SQL block was executed.

13-20. When this code is executed with the logic shown in the problem, you get this error:

```
PLS-00201: identifier 'N' must be declared
```

The problem is that when you execute a dynamic PL/SQL block, it executes in "global" scope. Within that string you can reference only data elements that are globally available, which means they are standalone functions or elements defined in a package specification.

13-21. The second EXECUTE IMMEDIATE is the correct one. When executing dynamic PL/SQL, NDS associates placeholders with bind arguments in the USING clause by name.

13-22. You receive the following error:

```
PLS-00457: in USING clause, expressions have to be of SQL types
```

The NULL value does not have a defined datatype; it is a value that can be assigned to a variable of any type.

13-23. Simply replace the direct reference to the NULL literal with a reference to an uninitialized variable (meaning that its value is NULL):

```
DECLARE
    nothing_for_you NUMBER;
BEGIN
    EXECUTE IMMEDIATE
        'UPDATE employee SET salary = :x
            WHERE fire_date IS NOT NULL' USING nothing_for_you;
END;
```

13-24. This is a technologically impaired piece of code. Here are the problems:

- You are selecting the CEO name only, but using a cursor variable whose REF CURSOR type is based on the employee table. That is sure to result in a ROWTYPE_MISMATCH error.

- A placeholder (:minbonus) is specified in the dynamic SQL string, but there is no USING clause to replace that placeholder with an actual value.

- You can't use a cursor FOR loop with the cursor variable. Use a simple or WHILE loop instead, with the fetches and closes necessary.

Here is a much cleaner version of the code:

```
/* Filename on web page: correctnds.sql */
DECLARE
    /* Just use a weak REF CURSOR. */
    TYPE execute_action_t IS REF CURSOR;
    ceo_cv execute_action_t;
    ceo_nm compensation.ceo%TYPE;
    v_minbonus REAL := 1000000;
BEGIN
    OPEN ceo_cv FOR
        'SELECT CEO FROM compensation
          WHERE layoffs > 1000
            AND bonus > :minbonus'
        USING v_minbonus; -- replace the placeholder

    /* Simple loop */
    LOOP
        FETCH ceo_cv INTO ceo_nm;
        EXIT WHEN ceo_cv%NOTFOUND;
        DBMS_OUTPUT.PUT_LINE (ceo_nm);
    END LOOP;
```

```
        CLOSE ceo_cv;
    END;
    /
```

13-25. Here is one possible implementation:

```
/* Filename on web page: grpval.sf */
CREATE OR REPLACE FUNCTION grpval (
    tab IN VARCHAR2,
    col IN VARCHAR2,
    grpfunc IN VARCHAR2,
    whr IN VARCHAR2 := NULL)
RETURN VARCHAR2
IS
    retval VARCHAR2(32767);
BEGIN
    EXECUTE IMMEDIATE
        'SELECT ' || grpfunc || '(' || col || ')
            FROM ' || tab || ' WHERE ' || NVL (whr, '1=1')
        INTO retval;

    RETURN retval;
END;
/
```

Clearly, this function always returns a string value. You then have to convert the string value to the appropriate native format (usually a number).

14

Procedures, Functions, and Blocks

Beginner

14-1. A procedure executes one or more statements and then terminates. A function executes one or more statements and then returns a result via the RETURN statement.

14-2. Procedures and functions are composed of the following four sections:

Section	Description	Optional or Required?
Header	The "signature" of the program: its name, parameter list (if any), and RETURN clause if a function	Required
Declaration	A series of declarations of data structures and TYPEs that exist only for the duration of the execution of the program	Optional; you do not have to declare any local data elements
Execution	One or more executable statements performed by the program	Required; both procedures and functions must have at least one executable statement to be valid
Exception	One or more exception handler clauses that trap and handle errors that occur in the executable section	Optional

14-3. Use the RETURN statement to return a value from a function. It has the following format:

```
RETURN expression;
```

where *expression* is a literal, variable, or complex expression whose datatype matches (or can be converted to) the datatype in the function's header's RETURN clause.

You can use RETURN inside a procedure, but you may not specify data to be returned. Instead you simply state:

```
RETURN;
```

The procedure immediately terminates and returns control to the enclosing block. You should avoid using RETURN in a procedure, however, because it leads to unstructured code that is hard to read and maintain.

14-4. The following procedure displays "hello world!" (remember to use the SET SERVEROUT ON command when you run the program from SQL*Plus):

```
CREATE OR REPLACE PROCEDURE hello_world
IS
BEGIN
   DBMS_OUTPUT.PUT_LINE ('hello world!');
END;
/
```

14-5. The following function returns "hello world!" as a string:

```
CREATE OR REPLACE FUNCTION RETURN VARCHAR2
IS
BEGIN
   RETURN 'hello world!';
END;
/
```

14-6. As many as you want. There is no limit on the number of RETURNs in a function. At most one, however, runs for any execution of the function. Structured coding methodology also recommends that you have just one RETURN statement in your executable section, so as to follow the precept "one way in, one way out."

14-7. The function headers are:

a. Valid. The declaration shows all the necessary components.

b. Invalid. You cannot constrain the return datatype of a function. This means that you can return VARCHAR2, but you cannot specify that the maximum size string returned by the function is 100 characters.

c. Invalid. The name of the function is invalid. A function name must start with a letter (a through z; the case is not significant).

d. Invalid. You cannot constrain the datatype of a parameter. This means that you can accept a number amount for revenue, but you cannot specify that the maximum size of that number is (10,2).

14-8. Yes; PL/SQL has three parameter modes:

IN

Only read the value of the argument

OUT

Only change the value of the argument

IN OUT

Read and write values in arguments

14-9. Yes. You can provide a default value in the parameter list using the DEFAULT keyword or the := assignment operator. Both techniques are shown here:

```
CREATE OR REPLACE PROCEDURE calc_totals (
    department_id_in IN department.department_id%TYPE,
    total_type_in IN VARCHAR2 := 'ALLREV',
    quarter_in IN INTEGER DEFAULT 1
    )
```

The total_type_in parameter has a default value of "ALLREV"; quarter_in has a default value of 1.

Intermediate

14-10. In all versions of PL/SQL before Oracle 8.1, IN parameters are passed by reference, while OUT and IN OUT parameters are passed by value.

14-11. You should try to have just one RETURN statement in the executable section of your functions, preferably the last line in the section. Think of the body of the function as a funnel, with all the other lines in the executable section narrowing down to a single RETURN statement at the end of the function. Here is a "template" for such a function:

```
CREATE OR REPLACE FUNCTION function_name RETURN datatype
IS
    retval datatype;
BEGIN
    ... Your code here...

    RETURN retval;

EXCEPTION
    WHEN OTHERS
    THEN
        RETURN NULL;
END function_name;
/
```

Why should you have only one RETURN statement? Multiple RETURN statements translate to multiple possible exit points from the function.

Such a structure makes it harder for developers to understand, debug, and maintain the code.

14-12. There is no one right or wrong answer to this question. Generally, you want to design your functions so that they are as reusable as possible, to avoid code redundancy and maintenance headaches. As a rule, a function is more useful if it does not allow exceptions to propagate out unhandled for predictable kinds of problems. So you should include an exception handler with a RETURN NULL;—or some other value that indicates something went wrong—for errors that might occur in the function. You could then allow other exceptions to go unhandled.

14-13. You should include an exception handler for NO_DATA_FOUND, since the department ID number passed in might not be valid (i.e., might not have a corresponding row in the database). In this case, you would probably simply want to return NULL, indicating clearly that no department for that ID was found (a department cannot have a NULL name). But what about TOO_MANY_ROWS? I would argue that in this case, you might want to *skip* an exception handler for that error. The reason? If you have more than one row, you have a serious data integrity problem: two rows with the same primary key. Rather than trap the error, just let the function pass it back out as an unhandled exception. Let the program that called the function figure out what it wants to do with that situation.

Here is the modified version of the deptname function with appropriate error handling:

```
CREATE OR REPLACE FUNCTION deptname (
    id_in IN department.department_id%TYPE
    )
    RETURN VARCHAR2
IS
    retval department.name%TYPE;
BEGIN
    SELECT name
      INTO retval
      FROM department
     WHERE department_id = id_in;

    RETURN retval;
EXCEPTION
    WHEN NO_DATA_FOUND
    THEN
        RETURN NULL;
END deptname;
/
```

14-14. The restrictions on default values for parameters are:

- You can only provide a default value for IN parameters. OUT and IN OUT parameters may not have default values.

- The default value can be a literal or an expression, but it cannot reference other parameters in the program.

14-15. When you provide a default value for a parameter, then if a developer calls that program and doesn't need to provide a value for the parameter, the default value is used in the body of the program. This process is identical to that employed by SQL. Suppose that when you create a table you supply a default value for a column. When you perform an INSERT on that table and do not specify a value for that column, the default value is used. This technique often comes in handy when you need to add new IN parameters to an existing program and do not want to invalidate existing calls to the program.

14-16. The key here is to make sure that you provide a default value for the new parameter (the section ID). Here is one possible implementation:

```
PROCEDURE calc_totals (
   department_id_in IN department.department_id%TYPE,
   section_id_in IN INTEGER DEFAULT NULL)
```

Since section_id_in is a trailing IN parameter with a default value, you do not have to provide a value for the parameter. This allows existing calls to calc_total to remain valid. NULL is a good choice for the default value, because it indicates that the section ID is not being used.

14-17. Yes, you can "skip" parameters in either of two ways:

- If the parameter is defined with mode IN, has a default value, and is a trailing parameter (at the end of the parameter list), you don't need to specify a value for the argument.
- You can use named notation (the => symbol) to explicitly associate a value with its parameter.

14-18. The calls are:

a. Valid. The call correctly uses the positional notation.

b. Invalid. You must supply a value for fiscal year, since it does not have a default value.

c. Valid. All three required parameters are present, even if they are not supplied in the original, positional order.

d. Invalid. The profit_out actual argument must be a variable; the procedure cannot return a value to a literal.

14-19. The calls that meet the requirement are:

a. Invalid. You cannot skip over an argument simply by indicating "no value" with contiguous commas. This is invalid syntax.

b. Invalid. This is a valid call to calc_totals, but it doesn't use the default value "ALLREV". Instead, total_type_in is set to NULL, which could well cause problems in the program.

c. Invalid. If you are going to mix positional and named notation in one parameter list, all the positional arguments must come before any named notational arguments. In other words, once you start using named notation, you must use it for the remainder of the parameter list.

d. Valid. The values are passed in out of order, but named notation is used throughout, allowing the default value of "ALLREV" to be used within the procedure.

e. Invalid. Named notation must properly name existing parameters in the parameter list. I have left off the "_in" suffix, and so this call won't compile.

f. Invalid. I inadvertently (oh, I admit it: I did it intentionally!) put a space between = and > in the last argument. The compiler no longer recognizes this as a named notation symbol.

14-20. *Overloading* is the process of defining, in a single declaration section, more than one program with the same name. Since the name is the same, the program's "signature" (name, parameter list, return TYPE) must differ in some other way, usually by the number and datatype of the parameters.

14-21. You can overload in three "locations" in PL/SQL code:

- The declaration section of an anonymous block.
- The declaration section of a named block (procedure or function).
- The specification and body of a PL/SQL package.

14-22. There are several possible problems with this function:

- Most seriously, if you pass it any value other than C, O, A, or I, you will get this runtime exception:

  ```
  ORA-06503: PL/SQL: Function returned without value
  ```

  This is an error you should never get from a function; it is evidence of very poor design and is related to the reliance on multiple RETURN statements in the function.

- There are lots of hardcoded values here; the only justification for this approach is that this function is essentially a "code lookup" that avoids the need for a database table containing the values.

- The user of the function has to know to uppercase his input to get the program to work properly. Is that really necessary or is it just an extra burden on the user?

Here is my reworking of the function:

```
FUNCTION status_desc (status_cd_in IN VARCHAR2) RETURN VARCHAR2
IS
   retval VARCHAR2(20);
   v_status_cd CHAR(1) := UPPER (status_cd_in);
```

```
BEGIN
    IF    v_status_cd = 'C' THEN retval := 'CLOSED';
    ELSIF v_status_cd = 'O' THEN retval := 'OPEN';
    ELSIF v_status_cd = 'A' THEN retval := 'ACTIVE';
    ELSIF v_status_cd = 'I' THEN retval := 'INACTIVE';
    END IF;
    RETURN retval;
EXCEPTION
    WHEN VALUE_ERROR THEN RETURN NULL;
END;
```

This new version:

- Relies on my standard template approach to functions, in which the last line of the executable section returns the "return value" variable. This way, there is just one RETURN, and you don't get the "Function returned without value" error.

- Transfers the parameter value to a local variable and uppercases it in the process. Now you can pass lowercase or uppercase values, and it works appropriately.

- Adds an exception section to trap values of status_cd_in that are too large.

Expert

14-23. You can't simply add a second argument with a default value in this case; the earlier calls to calc.totals in the Oracle Forms applications don't compile, because they haven't passed values for all the arguments. You must instead rely on overloading:

```
PACKAGE calc
IS
    PROCEDURE totals (
        department_id_in IN department.department_id%TYPE);

    PROCEDURE totals (
        department_id_in IN department.department_id%TYPE,
        section_id_in IN INTEGER);
END calc;
```

Inside an Oracle Forms application, a developer can now call calc.totals in one of two ways, as shown in these examples:

```
calc.totals (:emp.deptno);
calc.totals (my_dept_var, :sections.section_id);
```

Existing calls to calc.totals do not need to be changed; new calls to the calc.totals procedure providing a section will unambiguously be routed to the "second" implementation of the totals procedure.

14-24. To remove the redundancies, you can use a local procedure (defined in the declaration section) to centralize all common code elements:

```
PROCEDURE calc_percentages (total_in IN NUMBER)
IS
   FUNCTION formatted_pct   (val_in IN NUMBER)
      RETURN VARCHAR2 IS
   BEGIN
      RETURN TO_CHAR ((val_in/total_in) * 100, '$999,999');
   END;
BEGIN
   food_sales_stg := formatted_pct  (sales.food_sales);
   service_sales_stg := formatted_pct  (sales.service_sales);
   toy_sales_stg := formatted_pct  (sales.toy_sales);
END;
```

14-25. This is a poorly designed function for a number of reasons:

- The function returns two different pieces of information: the company name as the RETURN value and the industry type through the parameter list. You are much better off if you only return values from a function through the RETURN clause; never have OUT or IN OUT parameters in a function's parameter list. In this case, you can either change the function to a procedure or return a record containing both pieces of information.

- The exception handling mechanism is expected to return a value, rather than directly execute a RETURN. This is an abuse of exception handling—and is explored in much more detail in the next problem.

- There is no exception handling for errors that commonly arise with an implicit cursor (TOO_MANY_ROWS and NO_DATA_FOUND). You can fix this problem by adding handlers for one or both of those exceptions, or you can switch to an explicit cursor.

Here's one possible reworking of this function, correcting these problems:

```
/* Filename on web page: twovals.pkg */
CREATE OR REPLACE PACKAGE company_pkg
IS
   TYPE name_and_ind_rectype IS RECORD (
      );

      FUNCTION name_and_ind_type (
         company_id_in IN company.company_id%TYPE
         )
         RETURN name_and_ind_rectype;

END company_pkg;
/
CREATE OR REPLACE PACKAGE company_pkg
IS
   CURSOR twovals_cur (company_id_in IN company.company_id%TYPE)
   IS
      SELECT name, industry_type
        FROM company
       WHERE company_id = company_id_in;
```

```
FUNCTION name_and_ind_type (
    company_id_in IN company.company_id%TYPE
    )
    RETURN name_and_ind_rectype
IS
    retval name_and_ind_rectype;
BEGIN
    OPEN twovals_cur (company_id_in);
    FETCH twovals_cur INTO retval;
    RETURN retval;
END;
END company_pkg;
/
```

14-26. The function name is awkward. To see why, try to interpret its usage as an English sentence: "If is the value 'hello' is in the list 'word group' is greater than 0, then display the message." It doesn't quite flow properly as a sentence, does it? The reason for the awkwardness is that the function returns the row in which the value is found (RETURN INTEGER), not whether or not the value is in the list (which would RETURN BOOLEAN). The name confuses anyone who would use the module, because the name has a Boolean or TRUE-FALSE flavor, while the actual return value is the row number.

The best rule of thumb for naming a function is this: give it the name of the value that is being returned by the function. If you do this, you can include a call to the function in-line with its calling code and have it read smoothly and properly.

14-27. As shown in the listing, the Is_Value_In_List function returns a row number that contains a matching value. If that's what it does, then that's what the name should reflect. Let's change the name accordingly, try it in the code, and see how that reads:

```
FUNCTION matching_row(
    the_value VARCHAR2,
    the_rg_name VARCHAR2,
    the_rg_column VARCHAR2)
RETURN NUMBER;

IF matching_row ('hello', 'word_group', 'name') > 0
THEN
    MESSAGE ('They said hello already');
END IF;
```

In conversational English, this code now reads as follows: "If the *row* in the list 'word group' that contains a *match* for 'hello' is greater than 0, then display the message." That sentence can be readily understood. The function name describes precisely what it returns, and so it fits neatly within the code that calls it.

14-28. The function make three inappropriate uses of exceptions. The first problem is that the function uses the RAISE statement as a branching mechanism. The second is that the function misuses an exception (an error condition) as an outcome (a logical condition). The third misuse is that the exception name, Exit_Function, is simply too general.

Let's look at each misuse in turn.

First, the function inappropriately uses the RAISE statement as a control mechanism. The first two RAISEs occur when the user has passed an invalid record group name or column name. The exception transfers control to the exception section, and the handler RETURNs 0 from the function. This is a perfectly appropriate use of the exception and exception handler. The designer of this function has made certain that the function returns a value even if there is an error. The third use of the Exit_Function exception, however, occurs as the last statement in the executable section of the function. With just a quick read of the function, I would conclude that when the function runs to completion, the last thing it does is raise an exception! That is hardly a reasonable way to end a function. The last statement of a function's body should, as a matter of course, be a RETURN statement, since that is the whole point of the function.

Second, the function confuses an exception with an outcome. If the function reaches the last RAISE statement, then the value was not found in the record group. Consequently, the function should return a zero value. "Since the exception handler already returns zero," the author apparently reasoned, "I might as well just raise the exception and return the zero value." But is "value not found" an exception or just one of the possible outcomes of the function? I would argue for the latter. The value may or may not be in the group. You are calling the function to determine that fact. One of the reasons the author could end up blurring the distinction between exception and outcome is that the user-defined exception is named poorly. "Exit_Function" clearly does not describe an exception condition. Instead, it describes an action to be taken in response to certain conditions.

Third and finally, the exception name is simply too general and should be renamed to something more descriptive, for example:

```
invalid_name EXCEPTION;
```

The exception should be raised only when there is a serious problem with the record group or column name. If the author had used this name, it is less likely that he would have tried to RAISE invalid_name in order to handle the "value not in group" condition. In this case, the very name of the exception should have raised a red flag in the author's mind. If you find yourself naming structures in ways that are not appropriate to their normal use, stop for a moment and evaluate your motives. You may well find that you are, in effect, abusing the programming language. The result of such abuse is usually code that is harder to understand, debug, and maintain.

14-29. The effect of placing the RETURN statement inside the loop is to break out of the function as soon as a match is found. If you are going to use a FOR loop, then you should let the loop run to completion; there shouldn't be any reason to cut it short. If you know that you may want to bail out of the loop before you reach the limit, you should not use the FOR loop construct. You should use a WHILE loop with an appropriate condition or an infinite loop—with an EXIT statement.

14-30. The easiest way to eliminate multiple RETURNs is to set a variable (for example, ret_val) to the desired return value, and then RETURN that variable in the last statement in the program. This simple step makes a function easier to understand. For example, Is_Value_In_List has two RETURN statements—one inside the exception section and one inside the FOR loop. Ideally, a function should have only one RETURN in the executable section.

The first step in understanding a program is to identify its entry and exit points. The entry point of the function is always the first executable statement. The exit point(s) of a function are its RETURN statements or unhandled exceptions. So one of the most critical elements of a function's structure is the proper organization of its RETURNs. They should be easy to identify and should fit naturally into the logical flow of the program.

14-31. The Is_Value_In_List functions work properly; you get the right answer each and every time you use it. Unfortunately, the biggest challenge in programming isn't getting the code to work; rather, it's constructing the code so that it works today and can be easily modified so that it works tomorrow with the latest enhancements specified by your users. Is_Value_In_List simply doesn't meet this goal.

14-32. Is_Value_In_List has three distinct phases:

1. Validate and initialize

    a. Validate record group and column names. If invalid, return 0 (or raise error).

    b. Get number of records in group.

2. Find the matching record

    a. Scan the contents of the record group until a match is found.

3. Return the matching record number

    a. If no matches or no records to search, return 0.

    b. Else return the matching record.

14-33. Here is a rewrite of Is_Value_In_List that addresses the concerns raised in the previous questions:

```
/* Filename on web page: matchrow.sf */
FUNCTION matching_row (
    the_value VARCHAR2,
    the_rg_name VARCHAR2,
    the_rg_column VARCHAR2
    )
    RETURN INTEGER
IS
    rg_id          recordgroup;
    gc_id          groupcolumn;
    col_val        VARCHAR2(80);

    invalid_rgname EXCEPTION;

    the_rowcount   INTEGER;
    rownum         INTEGER;
    retval         INTEGER;
BEGIN
    rg_id := FIND_GROUP (the_rg_name);
    IF ID_NULL (rg_id)
    THEN
        MESSAGE (
            'Record Group ' || the_rg_name || ' does not exist.');
        RAISE invalid_rgname;
    END IF;

    gc_id := FIND_COLUMN (the_rg_name || '.' || the_rg_column);
    IF ID_NULL (gc_id)
    THEN
        MESSAGE ('Column ' || the_rg_column || ' does not exist.');
        RAISE invalid_rgname;
    END IF;

    rownum := 1;
    the_rowcount := get_group_row_count (rg_id);

    WHILE (retval IS NULL AND rownum < the_rowcount)
    LOOP
        col_val := get_group_char_cell (gc_id, j);
        IF UPPER (col_val) = UPPER (the_value)
        THEN
            retval := rownum;
        ELSE
            rownum := rownum + 1;
        END IF;
    END LOOP;

    RETURN retval;

EXCEPTION
    WHEN invalid_rgname
```

```
THEN
    RETURN 0;
END;
```

14-34. You can change the function to return a Boolean TRUE if the value is found, or FALSE if the value is not found in the record group. Here's the new header and an example:

```
FUNCTION Is_Value_In_List(
    the_value VARCHAR2,
    the_rg_name VARCHAR2,
    the_rg_column VARCHAR2)
RETURN BOOLEAN

IF Is_Value_In_List ('hello', 'word_group', 'name')
THEN
    MESSAGE ('they said hello already');
END IF;
```

Now you can read this code as follows: "If is the value 'hello' is in the list 'word group', then display the message." It still doesn't sound quite right; the "is" doesn't belong. Look at the module name. It still doesn't quite describe the return value. Instead, it reads as a partial sentence starting with "is". The most readable Boolean name for this function is simply: value_is_in_list. Then the code is:

```
IF value_is_in_list ('hello', 'word_group', 'name')
THEN
    MESSAGE ('they said hello already');
END IF;
```

And you can read the code as follows: "If the value 'hello' is in the list 'word group', then display the message." Now that is a grammatically correct sentence! Unfortunately, this rewrite no longer returns a row number: it returns a Boolean, which isn't much help if you actually want the row's location in the group. Back to the drawing board.

15

Packages

Beginner

15-1. No. You can't execute the package as a whole; it's simply a container for other PL/SQL elements. You can execute procedures and functions defined in the package specification, as well as reference data structures defined in a package specification (a constant, variable, exception, etc.).

15-2. You would use dot notation, in the form of *package.element*, as in:

```
financial_pkg.calc_totals (...);
```

15-3. You don't need to qualify a package element with its package name under these circumstances:

- You are currently writing code within that package's specification or body. This package is then the default scope. You can qualify with the package name if you want or leave it off.

- You are referencing an element in one of the two default packages in PL/SQL, STANDARD, and DBMS_STANDARD.

15-4. This table explains the use of the packaged elements in this code:

Package	Element	Element Type
STANDARD	DATE	Datatype
pets_r_us	max_pets_in_facility	Variable, constant, or function
STANDARD	TO_NUMBER	Function
STANDARD	>	Function
DBMS_OUTPUT	PUT_LINE	Procedure
pets_r_us	pet_is_sick	Exception
DBMS_STANDARD	RAISE_APPLICATION_ERROR	Procedure

The STANDARD package contains the definitions of many of the elements of the PL/SQL language, including datatypes, exceptions, and functions. DBMS_STANDARD contains database-related programs, including COMMIT, ROLLBACK, and RAISE_APPLICATION_ERROR. They are the defaults, so dot notation is not required.

15-5. Any data structure declared in a package specification persists throughout your session. Data structures declared in the body, but not contained in a procedure or function, also persist throughout the session; these datatypes, however, are called *private variables* because they are not directly accessible outside the package. To answer the original question, here is the definition of a "global" date variable:

```
CREATE OR REPLACE PACKAGE sessval
IS
    mydate DATE;
END sessval;
/
```

15-6. The following package uses a private package variable. You set and retrieve the value using accessor functions named "get" and "set":

```
/* Filename on web page: sessval1.pkg */
CREATE OR REPLACE PACKAGE sessval
IS
    PROCEDURE set_mydate (date_in IN DATE);
    FUNCTION mydate RETURN DATE;
END sessval;
/
CREATE OR REPLACE PACKAGE BODY sessval
IS
    g_mydate DATE;

    PROCEDURE set_mydate (date_in IN DATE)
    IS
    BEGIN
        g_mydate := date_in;
    END;

    FUNCTION mydate RETURN DATE
    IS
    BEGIN
        RETURN g_mydate;
    END;
END sessval;
/
```

Why would you hide the mydate variable behind these get and set procedures? If you define mydate in the package specification, any program that references the package (runs from a session with EXECUTE authority on the package) can directly read and write the variable. This means you cannot control the values placed in the variable, which can often lead to problems in development.

Get and set programs force users of the package to go through your programs to both read and write the variable. This then allows you to:

- Make sure that the value they set the variable to is valid

- Trace access to the variable, such as displaying a message each time a program tries to set the value

- Change the implementation of the variable without affecting applications that use the data

You can also use standard get and set prefixes as follows:

```
/* Filename on web page: sessval2.pkg */
CREATE OR REPLACE PACKAGE sessval
IS
    PROCEDURE set_mydate (date_in IN DATE);
    FUNCTION get_mydate RETURN DATE;
END sessval;
/
```

I like to leave off the "get," because functions by their very nature get information and return it to you. It is redundant and slightly less readable to include the get.

You can follow standard Java naming conventions for the get and set programs by rewriting the package as follows:

```
/* Filename on web page: sessval3.pkg */
CREATE OR REPLACE PACKAGE sessval
IS
    PROCEDURE setMydate (date_in IN DATE);
    FUNCTION getGydate RETURN DATE;
END sessval;
/
```

15-7. The cursors are:

  a. Valid. This is a standard cursor definition.

  b. Valid. When you define a cursor in a package specification, you can hide the SELECT statement inside the package body by specifying only the record structure of the row that is returned when you FETCH from that cursor.

15-8. There are two reasons to hide a cursor definition inside a package body:

- You don't want users to see the SELECT statement. Everybody thinks they can do it better than everybody else. So if you expose the query, *and* if developers have direct SELECT access to the underlying table(s), they might rewrite the query in ways that reduce performance, have errors, or simply introduce redundancy.

- If you change the query, you have to recompile only the package body and not the specification. As a result, all those programs that are dependent on the package aren't marked INVALID and don't have to be recompiled.

15-9. No. A package may only have a package specification. Under some circumstances a package body is not required.

15-10. For the package specifications shown, a package body is:

    a. Not required. pkg1 consists solely of complete declarations of data elements (an exception and a number).

    b. Required. pkg2 contains the header for a function; the body must contain that function's implementation.

    c. Not required. pkg3 includes the SELECT statement required by the cursor declaration.

    d. Required. pkg4 contains the header for a cursor, but not the definition; the body must contain that cursor's implementation (the SELECT statement).

15-11. Here is a new version of the line of code that gets rid of the hardcoded value:

```
IF v_date > constants.maxdate
```

Note that this solution also requires the following "constants" package that implements this global, named constant:

```
PACKAGE constants
IS
   maxdate CONSTANT DATE := TO_DATE ('31-DEC-2010', 'DD-MON-YYYY');
END constants;
```

The problem with this implementation is that if the date changes (say, to the year 2020), you must recompile the package specification. This action causes the status of all programs that reference the constants package to be set to INVALID, thereby requiring a recompile.

To get around this problem, store the value of the constant in the package body and provide access to the constant through a function call:

```
PACKAGE constants
IS
   FUNCTION maxdate RETURN DATE;
END constants;

PACKAGE BODY constants
IS
   g_maxdate CONSTANT DATE := TO_DATE ('31-DEC-2010', 'DD-MON-YYYY');

   FUNCTION maxdate RETURN DATE
      IS BEGIN RETURN g_maxdate; END;
END constants;
```

15-12. Yes, you can add an initialization section to a package. If after all of the declarations of elements in your package (variables, cursors, programs, etc.), you include a BEGIN statement and executable statements of code, that code runs once, and only once, in each session using the package. Here is an example of a simple initialization section:

```
PACKAGE BODY session_init
IS
    g_user VARCHAR2(100);

    PROCEDURE hello IS
    BEGIN
        DBMS_OUTPUT.PUT_LINE ('Hello ' || g_user || '!');
    END;
BEGIN
    g_user := USER;
END session_init;
```

You can tell that this package has an initialization section because the BEGIN is *not* contained within a procedure or function definition. Here is the sequence of events that takes place whenever a developer calls the session_init.hello procedure:

1. The partially compiled package code is loaded into memory.

2. All variables (g_user) are instantiated.

3. Default values (usually NULL) are assigned to all variables.

4. The initialization section executes (g_user is assigned to the current user).

Intermediate

15-13. This code allows you to deduce (and create) the package specification:

```
/* Filename on web page: timer.pkg */
CREATE OR REPLACE PACKAGE timer
IS
    PROCEDURE capture;
    PROCEDURE show_elapsed;
END timer;
/
```

To create the body, you need to not only define the two procedures but also create a global data structure to hold the "time before" you'll use to subtract from the "time after." Here is the complete package:

```
/* Filename on web page: timer.pkg */
CREATE OR REPLACE PACKAGE BODY timer
IS
    last_timing INTEGER := NULL;

    PROCEDURE capture IS
    BEGIN
```

```
      last_timing := DBMS_UTILITY.GET_TIME;
   END;

   PROCEDURE show_elapsed IS
   BEGIN
      DBMS_OUTPUT.PUT_LINE (
        'Elapsed time: ' ||
        (DBMS_UTILITY.GET_TIME - last_timing)/100);
   END;

END timer;
/
```

15-14. You cannot declare a cursor variable as part of a package; you can only declare a cursor variable within PL/SQL blocks.

15-15. For each of the examples, the block:

    a. Does not compile. Within Oracle Developer (at least through version 2.1), you can reference only stored packaged elements if the elements are functions or procedures. You can't reference constants, variables, TYPEs, or exceptions.

    b. Compiles. This block is fine.

    c. Does not compile. See explanation for (a).

15-16. Here is one possible way to add trace and validation capabilities to the sessval package:

```
/* Filename on web page: sessval4.pkg */
CREATE OR REPLACE PACKAGE sessval
IS
   PROCEDURE set_mydate (date_in IN DATE);
   FUNCTION mydate RETURN DATE;
END sessval;
/
CREATE OR REPLACE PACKAGE BODY sessval
IS
   g_mydate DATE;

   PROCEDURE set_mydate (date_in IN DATE)
   IS
   BEGIN
      IF date_in IS NULL OR date_in > SYSDATE
      THEN
         DBMS_OUTPUT.PUT_LINE (
            'Sessval.mydate cannot be set into the future.' );
      ELSE
         DBMS_OUTPUT.PUT_LINE (
            'Current value of sessval.mydate: ' || g_mydate );
         DBMS_OUTPUT.PUT_LINE (
            'New value of sessval.mydate: ' || date_in );
         DBMS_OUTPUT.PUT_LINE (
            DBMS_UTILITY.FORMAT_CALL_STACK );
         g_mydate := date_in;
```

```
        END IF;
    END;

    FUNCTION mydate RETURN DATE
    IS
    BEGIN
        RETURN g_mydate;
    END;
END sessval;
/
```

Here is sample output from the previous implementation:

```
SQL> EXEC sessval.set_mydate (sysdate+15)
Sessval.mydate cannot be set into the future.

PL/SQL procedure successfully completed.

SQL> EXEC sessval.set_mydate (sysdate-10)
Current value of sessval.mydate:
New value of sessval.mydate: 04-JAN-99
----- PL/SQL Call Stack -----
  object      line   object
  handle     number  name
  2a81c3c       20   package body SCOTT.SESSVAL
  2a4aea0        1   anonymous block
```

As you can see, the built-in function DBMS_UTILITY.FORMAT_CALL_ STACK returns a string containing the formatted (with embedded new line characters) execution call stack.

If you call this program from a stored procedure, that procedure's name then shows up in the call stack:

```
CREATE OR REPLACE PROCEDURE test_trace
IS
BEGIN
    sessval.set_mydate (
        NVL (sessval.mydate, SYSDATE) -100);
END;
/

SQL> EXEC test_trace
Current value of sessval.mydate:
New value of sessval.mydate: 06-OCT-98
----- PL/SQL Call Stack -----
  object      line   object
  handle     number  name
  2a81c3c       20   package body SCOTT.SESSVAL
  2a4a5c4        4   procedure SCOTT.TEST_TRACE
  2a31d2c        1   anonymous block

SQL> EXEC test_trace
Current value of sessval.mydate: 06-OCT-98
New value of sessval.mydate: 28-JUN-98
```

```
----- PL/SQL Call Stack -----
  object      line  object
  handle     number name
 2a81c3c        20  package body SCOTT.SESSVAL
 2a4a5c4         4  procedure SCOTT.TEST_TRACE
 2a31d2c         1  anonymous block
```

I call this built-in trace a "window" into a package, because it lets you look inside the package body and examine the values of otherwise-hidden data structures and activities.

15-17. The rationale for making the trace's output controllable is as follows. You don't want to see trace information when the application is running in production. It slows things down, confuses your users, and even raises errors (if, for example, the buffer overflows). Instead, you should build an on-off switch or toggle, so that you can turn on the output only when desired. Here is one possible implementation of such a toggle:

```
/* Filename on web page: sessval5.pkg */
CREATE OR REPLACE PACKAGE sessval
IS
   PROCEDURE set_mydate (date_in IN DATE);
   FUNCTION mydate RETURN DATE;

   -- Turn on the trace
   PROCEDURE trc;

   -- Turn off the trace
   PROCEDURE notrc;

   -- Show current status of the trace.
   FUNCTION tracing RETURN BOOLEAN;

END sessval;
/
CREATE OR REPLACE PACKAGE BODY sessval
IS
   g_mydate DATE;

   /* Implementation of the trace; by default, turned off.
      As you can see, it is very simple code. */
   g_trace BOOLEAN := FALSE;

   PROCEDURE trc IS BEGIN g_trace := TRUE; END;

   PROCEDURE notrc IS BEGIN g_trace := FALSE; END;

   FUNCTION tracing RETURN BOOLEAN IS BEGIN RETURN g_trace; END;

   PROCEDURE set_mydate (date_in IN DATE)
   IS
   BEGIN
      IF date_in IS NULL OR date_in > SYSDATE
```

```
       THEN
          DBMS_OUTPUT.PUT_LINE (
             'Sessval.mydate cannot be set into the future.'
             );
       ELSE
          /* Only show trace information if enabled. */
          IF tracing
          THEN
             DBMS_OUTPUT.PUT_LINE (
                'Current value of sessval.mydate: ' || g_mydate );
             DBMS_OUTPUT.PUT_LINE (
                'New value of sessval.mydate: ' || date_in );
             DBMS_OUTPUT.PUT_LINE (
                DBMS_UTILITY.FORMAT_CALL_STACK );
          END IF;
          g_mydate := date_in;
       END IF;
    END;

    FUNCTION mydate RETURN DATE
    IS
    BEGIN
       RETURN g_mydate;
    END;
END sessval;
/
```

As you can see from the following sequence, when you first call the test_ trace procedure, there is no output because the default setting for the trace is "off." Then you turn on trace and call test_trace again, at which point you see the trace information:

```
SQL> EXEC test_trace
SQL> EXEC sessval.trc
SQL> EXEC test_trace
Current value of sessval.mydate: 06-OCT-98
New value of sessval.mydate: 28-JUN-98
----- PL/SQL Call Stack -----
   object      line   object
   handle    number   name
   2a81c3c       31   package body SCOTT.SESSVAL
   2a4a5c4        4   procedure SCOTT.TEST_TRACE
   2a31d2c        1   anonymous block
```

15-18. One possible solution is to add a function named "elapsed" that returns the elapsed time. You can then direct the results of this function to the appropriate place (for example, in Oracle Forms to display the elapsed time using the MESSAGE utility):

```
/* Filename on web page: timer2.pkg */
CREATE OR REPLACE PACKAGE timer
IS
   PROCEDURE capture;
   FUNCTION elapsed RETURN INTEGER;
   PROCEDURE show_elapsed;
```

```
END timer;
/
CREATE OR REPLACE PACKAGE BODY timer
IS
    last_timing INTEGER := NULL;

    PROCEDURE capture
    IS
    BEGIN
      last_timing := DBMS_UTILITY.GET_TIME;
    END;

    FUNCTION elapsed RETURN INTEGER
    IS
    BEGIN
       RETURN (DBMS_UTILITY.GET_TIME - last_timing)/100;
    END;

    PROCEDURE show_elapsed
    IS
       v_timing INTEGER := elapsed;
    BEGIN
       DBMS_OUTPUT.PUT_LINE (
           'Elapsed time: ' || v_timing);
    END;

END timer;
/
```

15-19. Here is a package to calculate a person's age. Note how the private procedure showage eliminates the need for repetitive formatting code inside
each procedure:

```
/* Filename on web page: datecalc.pkg */
CREATE OR REPLACE PACKAGE datecalc
IS
    PROCEDURE showage (birthday_in IN DATE);
    PROCEDURE showage (birthday_in IN INTEGER);
    PROCEDURE showage (
       birthday_in IN VARCHAR2,
       mask_in IN VARCHAR2 := NULL);
END datecalc;
/

CREATE OR REPLACE PACKAGE BODY datecalc
IS
    FUNCTION datestring (date_in IN DATE) RETURN VARCHAR2
    IS
    BEGIN
      RETURN
         'You are ' ||
         ROUND (TO_NUMBER (SYSDATE - date_in)) ||
         ' days old.';
    END datestring;
```

```
   PROCEDURE showage (birthday_in IN DATE)
   IS
   BEGIN
      DBMS_OUTPUT.PUT_LINE (datestring (birthday_in));
   END showage;

   PROCEDURE showage (birthday_in IN INTEGER)
   IS
   BEGIN
      showage (TO_DATE (birthday_in, 'J'));
   END showage;

   PROCEDURE showage (
      birthday_in IN VARCHAR2,
      mask_in IN VARCHAR2 := NULL)
   IS
   BEGIN
      IF mask_in IS NULL
      THEN
         showage (TO_DATE (birthday_in));
      ELSE
         showage (TO_DATE (birthday_in, mask_in));
      END IF;
   END showage;
END datecalc;
/
```

15-20. There are a number of ways to solve this problem; PL/Vision's p package is a good example of a comprehensive and robust substitute for DBMS_OUTPUT. Here is a simpler version that handles the three obstacles listed in the problem:

```
/* Filename on web page: prt.pkg */
CREATE OR REPLACE PACKAGE prt
IS
   PROCEDURE ln (val IN VARCHAR2);
   PROCEDURE ln (val IN DATE);
   PROCEDURE ln (val IN NUMBER);
   PROCEDURE ln (val IN BOOLEAN);
END prt;
/
```

As you can see, the package specification adds an overloading for Boolean; otherwise it looks just like the DBMS_OUTPUT.PUT_LINE definitions (except that you only have to type prt.ln instead of DBMS_OUTPUT.PUT_LINE!). Let's now take a look at the package body. First, here are the implementations of the date, number, and Boolean overloadings:

```
   PROCEDURE ln (val IN DATE) IS
   BEGIN
      ln (TO_CHAR (val, 'MM/DD/YYYY HH24:MI:SS'));
   END;
```

```
PROCEDURE ln (val IN NUMBER) IS
BEGIN
   ln (TO_CHAR (val));
END;

PROCEDURE ln (val IN BOOLEAN) IS
BEGIN
   IF          val THEN ln ('TRUE');
   ELSIF NOT val THEN ln ('FALSE');
   ELSE                ln ('');
   END IF;
END;
```

As you can readily see, each of these overloadings of the ln procedure simply calls the VARCHAR2 overloading of ln. This way, all the special code required to get around the other problems with DBMS_OUTPUT (lines too long, buffer too small) can be written in one place and shared with all overloadings. A full implementation would, by the way, probably also allow a user to pass in his own date and number format masks. I leave this as an exercise for the reader.

The Boolean implementation is the most interesting. The IF and ELSIF clauses are straightforward "translations" from Boolean values to strings. But why pass an empty string for the ELSE clause, instead of just passing in the NULL literal?

Let's see what happens if you try to call DBMS_OUTPUT.PUT_LINE with a NULL argument:

```
SQL> EXEC DBMS_OUTPUT.PUT_LINE (NULL)
*
ERROR at line 1:
PLS-00307: too many declarations of 'PUT_LINE' match this call
```

The problem is that NULL does not have a datatype, and any datatype accepts NULL as a valid value. As a consequence, the PL/SQL compiler does not know which version of DBMS_OUTPUT.PUT_LINE to call.

If, on the other hand, you pass in an empty or NULL string, there is no confusion:

```
SQL> EXEC DBMS_OUTPUT.PUT_LINE ('')
SQL>
```

It simply displays nothing (or it ignores your request entirely, which is what happens in SQL*Plus if you SET SERVEROUTPUT ON and don't specify FORMAT WRAPPED as an option—available in Oracle 7.3 and above).

Finally, let's take a look at the most interesting part of this package body, the VARCHAR2 overloading of prt.ln:

```
PROCEDURE ln (val IN VARCHAR2)
IS
```

```
BEGIN
    /* Don't display lines longer than 80 characters;
       they are hard to read. */
    IF LENGTH (val) > 80
    THEN
       DBMS_OUTPUT.PUT_LINE (SUBSTR (val, 1, 80));
       ln (SUBSTR (val, 81));
    ELSE
       DBMS_OUTPUT.PUT_LINE (val);
    END IF;
EXCEPTION
    WHEN OTHERS
    THEN
       DBMS_OUTPUT.ENABLE (1000000);
       ln (val);
END;
```

This procedure uses recursion to handle (with a minimum of fuss) those long lines (defined here to be anything with more than 80 characters); it simply displays up to the first 80 characters and then calls prt.ln again to handle anything beyond it.

The procedure also includes an error handler that says, in effect: if anything goes wrong, assume that it's the error caused by a too-small buffer. So expand the size of the buffer and try again.

Now if only the PL/SQL development team would think of stuff like this, right?

15-21. You're not supposed to be able to declare the same data structure in a package specification and its package body, but at least in Oracle 8.0.5, the package body compiles. For example, the following code compiles fine:

```
CREATE OR REPLACE PACKAGE demo
AS
    global_x PLS_INTEGER := 20;
END;
/
CREATE OR REPLACE PACKAGE BODY demo
AS
    global_x PLS_INTEGER := 10;
END;
/
```

Expert

15-22. You get this unhandled exception:

```
ORA-06511: PL/SQL: cursor already open
```

When you declare a cursor in a package specification, it has global scope. One consequence is that you can open the cursor in one program, and it stays open even after that program terminates. And if you try to close a packaged cursor that has already been closed in another program, you get this error:

```
ORA-01001: invalid cursor
```

15-23. Here is one possible solution to this requirement:

```
/* Filename on web site: onecur.pkg */
CREATE OR REPLACE PACKAGE onecur
IS
    CURSOR onerow (
        employee_id_in IN employee.employee_id%TYPE)
    IS
        SELECT * FROM employee
         WHERE employee_id = employee_id_in;

    PROCEDURE open_onerow(
        employee_id_in IN employee.employee_id%TYPE,
        close_if_open IN BOOLEAN := TRUE
        );

    PROCEDURE close_onerow;

END onecur;
/
```

Before moving to the package body, let's review the procedures. The open procedure accepts the same parameters as the cursor, plus the close_if_open argument. If you pass TRUE (the default) for this argument, the program closes the cursor if it is already open. If you pass FALSE, it assumes that if the cursor is open, you just want to keep on fetching from the current location in the result set.

Here is the package body:

```
/* Filename on web page: onecur.pkg */
CREATE OR REPLACE PACKAGE BODY onecur
IS
    PROCEDURE open_onerow (
        employee_id_in IN employee.employee_id%TYPE,
        close_if_open IN BOOLEAN := TRUE
        )
    IS
        v_close BOOLEAN := NVL (close_if_open, TRUE);
        v_open BOOLEAN := TRUE;
    BEGIN
        IF onerow%ISOPEN AND v_close
        THEN
            CLOSE onerow;

        ELSIF onerow%ISOPEN AND NOT v_close
        THEN
            v_open := FALSE;
        END IF;
```

```
        IF v_open THEN
            OPEN onerow (employee_id_in);
        END IF;
    END;

    PROCEDURE close_onerow
    IS
    BEGIN
        IF onerow%ISOPEN
        THEN
            CLOSE onerow;
        END IF;
    END;
END onecur;
/
```

The open procedure simply steps through the different scenarios, and makes certain to attempt to open the cursor only if it is not already open. The close procedure doesn't try to close the cursor unless it is open.

15-24.   The simplest way to eliminate the 10,000 calls to "SELECT user from dual" is to replace the USER with a packaged function. The function returns the value of a variable that has been initialized by calling the USER function. For example:

```
CREATE OR REPLACE PACKAGE userinfo
IS
    FUNCTION name RETURN VARCHAR2;
END userinfo;
/
CREATE OR REPLACE PACKAGE BODY userinfo
IS
    g_name ALL_USERS.USERNAME%TYPE := USER;

    FUNCTION name RETURN VARCHAR2 IS BEGIN RETURN g_name; END;
END userinfo;
/
```

It takes less than 1/10 of a second to execute info.name 10,000 times on the same laptop. Any time you can improve the performance of anything in your application by an order of magnitude, do it, so long as you are not sacrificing maintainability and readability. See the *dualcost.sql* and *dualcost.tst* files for timing tests.

15-25.   The trick here is to split the toobig package into a shell of its former self. While the package specification must remain unchanged, you can change the body into something like this:

```
/* Filename on web page: splitpkg.pkg */
CREATE OR REPLACE PACKAGE BODY toobig
IS
    PROCEDURE proc1
```

```
      IS
      BEGIN
         not_toobig1.proc;
      END;

      PROCEDURE proc2
      IS
      BEGIN
         not_toobig2.proc;
      END;
END;
/
```

What have we here? Two new packages! Here is their skeletal implementation:

```
CREATE OR REPLACE PACKAGE not_toobig1
IS
   PROCEDURE proc;
END;
/
CREATE OR REPLACE PACKAGE BODY not_toobig1
IS
   PROCEDURE proc
   IS
   BEGIN
      /* Lots of code */
      NULL;
   END;
END;
/
CREATE OR REPLACE PACKAGE not_toobig2
IS
   PROCEDURE proc;
END;
/
CREATE OR REPLACE PACKAGE BODY not_toobig2
IS
   PROCEDURE proc
   IS
   BEGIN
      /* Lots more code */
      NULL;
   END;
END;
/
```

15-26. Yes, this is a valid overloading. The package compiles without any errors. Assuming you have written a body for this package, you might then try to run one of the calc_total implementations as follows:

```
salespkg.calc_total ('zone15');
```

In this case, you get this error:

```
PLS-00307: too many declarations of 'CALC_TOTAL' match this call
```

Do not, however, rush to judgment! The answer to the second part of this problem is: Yes! You can run either of these programs. You just have to use named notation:

```
salespkg.calc_total (zone_in => 'zone15');
```

While it's poor form to require a particular notation to execute a procedures, it's certainly possible.

15-27. The best way to implement this kind of package is to provide on-off switches or toggles that give the user of the package control over its behavior. The package specification has a toggle to direct the output to the screen or a pipe. When you direct output to a pipe, the contents of that pipe can be read even while the original program is still running; the watch.show procedure dumps the pipe contents for you. You can run this from the same session that calls watch.action or a different session.

I show the implementation of the body, broken up with explanations. See *watch.pkg* on the book's web site for the full implementation—and try it out!

First, the declarations:

```
/* Filename on web site: watch.pkg */
CREATE OR REPLACE PACKAGE BODY watch
IS
    c_pipe_name CONSTANT VARCHAR2(9) := 'watch$trc';

    c_screen CONSTANT INTEGER := 0;
    c_pipe   CONSTANT INTEGER := 1;

    g_target INTEGER := c_screen;
```

I put the pipe name in a constant so that it is not hardcoded in multiple places throughout the packages. The c_screen and c_pipe constants give names to the two types of output targets; the g_target global variable contains the currently selected target, the default being "to screen."

Now here is the implementation of the target toggle:

```
PROCEDURE toscreen IS
BEGIN
    g_target := c_screen;
    DBMS_OUTPUT.PUT_LINE (
        Watch output will be sent to screen.');
END;

PROCEDURE topipe IS
BEGIN
    g_target := c_pipe;
    DBMS_OUTPUT.PUT_LINE (
        Watch output will be sent to pipe.');
END;
```

As you can see, these programs do nothing more than set the target global variable and give feedback on the action.

Moving on to more complex code, here is the action procedure:

```
PROCEDURE action (prog IN VARCHAR2, val IN VARCHAR2)
IS
    stat INTEGER;
    msg VARCHAR2(32767);
BEGIN
    /* Put together string */
    msg :=
        ***WATCHing at: ' ||
        TO_CHAR (SYSDATE, 'MM/DD/YYYY HH24:MI:SS') ||
        CHR(10) || '   Context: ' || prog ||
        CHR(10) || '   Message: ' || val;

    IF g_target = c_screen
    THEN
        DBMS_OUTPUT.PUT_LINE (msg);

    ELSIF g_target = c_pipe
    THEN
        DBMS_PIPE.RESET_BUFFER;
        DBMS_PIPE.PACK_MESSAGE (msg);
        stat := DBMS_PIPE.SEND_MESSAGE (c_pipe_name, timeout => 0);
        IF stat != 0
        THEN
            DBMS_OUTPUT.PUT_LINE (
                'WATCH: failure to send information to pipe...');
        END IF;
    END IF;
END;
```

You construct the watch message, which includes the date-time stamp, the context (usually the program name), and the message. After that, pass that message out of the program, usually either DBMS_OUTPUT (if the current target is the screen) or DBMS_PIPE (if the current target is a pipe).

And, finally, here is the watch.show procedure:

```
PROCEDURE show
IS
    stat INTEGER;
    msg PLV.dbmaxvc2;
BEGIN
    DBMS_OUTPUT.PUT_LINE ('Contents of WATCH Trace:');
    LOOP
        stat := DBMS_PIPE.RECEIVE_MESSAGE (c_pipe_name, timeout => 0);
        EXIT WHEN stat != 0;
        DBMS_PIPE.UNPACK_MESSAGE (msg);
        DBMS_OUTPUT.PUT_LINE (msg);
    END LOOP;
  END;
END;
/
```

This procedure simply dumps the contents of the pipe until it is empty. You can run this as frequently as you like, to see what has happened since the last call to watch.show.

15-28. The trick here is to create two overloaded programs of your own version of EXECUTE: one procedure and one function:

```
/* Filename on web page: dynsql.pkg */
CREATE OR REPLACE PACKAGE dynsql
IS
   PROCEDURE execute (cur IN INTEGER);
   FUNCTION execute (cur IN INTEGER) RETURN INTEGER;
END dynsql;
/
CREATE OR REPLACE PACKAGE BODY dynsql
IS
   PROCEDURE execute (cur IN INTEGER)
   IS
      feedback INTEGER;
   BEGIN
      feedback := DBMS_SQL.EXECUTE (cur);
   END;

   FUNCTION execute (cur IN INTEGER) RETURN INTEGER
   IS
   BEGIN
      RETURN DBMS_SQL.EXECUTE (cur);
   END;

END dynsql;
/
```

If you use the procedure version, it declares the feedback variable, uses it, and ignores it, thereby saving you the trouble. If you want some feedback, call the function version. This is an example of using overloading to anticipate the different ways programmers will use your functionality, and then build to meet those needs.

15-29. From the standpoint of performance, the most important clue to the redesign lies in the statement: "These configuration values are only changed when users are off the system; they do not change during an active session." The userconfig package requeries the database table each time either the cubicle# or max_coffee_breaks is needed. This could amount to lots of unnecessary work over the course of application execution. A better approach takes advantage of the initialization section to query the values just once, the first time either of the functions is referenced in the session. These values can be stored in package data that persists for the entire session.

Another problem with the userconfig package lies with the NO_DATA_FOUND exception handlers. In both cases, the developer has hardcoded the default values (when the user is not found in the configuration table), repeating them from the default information stored in the table (see the *usrcnfg.ins* file).

Here is the body of this more efficient implementation without any hard-coding:

```
/* Filename on web page: usrcnfg2.pkg */
CREATE OR REPLACE PACKAGE BODY userconfig
IS
    g_user user_config%ROWTYPE;

    CURSOR user_cur (nm IN VARCHAR2 := NULL)
    IS
        SELECT cubicle#, max_coffee_breaks
          FROM user_config
          WHERE username = nm;

    FUNCTION cubicle# RETURN VARCHAR2 IS
    BEGIN
        RETURN g_user.cubicle#;
    END;

    FUNCTION max_coffee_breaks RETURN INTEGER IS
    BEGIN
        RETURN g_user.max_coffee_breaks;
    END;

/* Initialize Globals */
BEGIN
    /* Get user preferences for this user. */
    OPEN user_cur (USER);
    FETCH user_cur INTO g_user;
    IF user_cur%NOTFOUND
    THEN
        /* Use the defaults; user name is NULL. */
        CLOSE user_cur;
        OPEN user_cur;
        FETCH user_cur INTO g_user;
    END IF;
    CLOSE user_cur;

END userconfig;
/
```

15-30. The new SERIALLY_REUSABLE pragma offers this capability. This pragma indicates that package-level data should persist only for the duration of execution of a program in that package. Upon termination of the program, the memory is discarded. Here is an example of a package specification with this pragma:

```
CREATE OR REPLACE PACKAGE noglobal
AS
```

```
   PRAGMA SERIALLY_REUSABLE;
   right_now PLS_INTEGER := SYSDATE;
END;
/
```

Note that in this package, the noglobal.right_now is reinitialized with a call to SYSDATE every time a PL/SQL program is called from its host environment. In other words, SERIALLY_REUSABLE still allows persistence within an active PL/SQL block execution. It just removes persistence at the session or connection level (in between PL/SQL program invocations in that connection). You can examine this behavior in the *pkgser.sql* and *pkgser.tst* files on the book's web page.

16

Triggers

Beginner

16-1. A trigger is a block of code (whether in PL/SQL, Java, or C) that fires, or executes, in response to a specific event.

16-2. The statements are:

    a. True. You can create a trigger in response to most Data Manipulation Language (DML) operations.

    b. False. There is no AFTER EXECUTION.

    c. True. Oracle8*i* allows you to trap "user-level" events such as logons.

    d. True. You can create triggers that fire when Data Definition Language (DDL) statements are executed.

16-3. A trigger executes *implicitly* in response to an event, such as an update to a table. A procedure executes *explicitly* at the request of a user (or a call from another program).

16-4. A trigger can have one of two modes: ENABLED (meaning that it fires normally) and DISABLED (meaning that it does not fire, even if its triggering event occurs).

16-5. (b). A trigger that causes other triggers to fire is called a *cascade*.

16-6. Statement-level triggers fire only one time per statement, and row-level triggers fire for each row that is affected by the DML statement.

16-7. The WHEN clause causes a trigger to fire only when a specific set of user-defined conditions are met.

16-8. Trigger (b) correctly populates the employee_id column. Trigger (a), which attempts to set the sequence number using an INSERT statement, illustrates a fairly common mistake. While Trigger (a) compiles successfully, it will probably produce the following error when it's executed:

```
ORA-00036: Maximum number of recursive sql levels (50)
```

This error is generated because each execution of the trigger results in another execution of the same trigger, eventually exceeding the number of allowed recursive SQL levels. This limit was introduced to prevent such mistaken constructions from resulting in an infinite loop.

16-9. The pseudo-columns shown are:

   a. Valid

   b. Invalid

   c. Invalid

   d. Valid

   e. Valid

   f. Invalid

   g. Invalid

The OLD, NEW, and PARENT pseudo-columns can be used only in row-level triggers. PARENT, introduced in Oracle8*i*, refers to the current row of the parent table for a trigger defined on a nested table. OLD and NEW refer to the following:

- Old and new values of the current row of the relational table.

- Old and new values of the row of the nested table if the trigger is defined on a nested table (Oracle8*i*).

- For a trigger defined on an object table or view, OLD and NEW always refer to the object instances.

OLD and NEW are the default names; specifying the REFERENCING clause of the trigger can change these names.

16-10. You must have one of the following privileges:

CREATE TRIGGER

   Allows you to create a trigger in your own schema for a table or view owned by the same schema

CREATE ANY TRIGGER

   Allows you to create a trigger in any user's schema on a table owned by any schema

ADMINISTER DATABASE TRIGGER

Allows you to create database-level triggers (e.g., SERVERERROR, LOGON, LOGOFF, etc.)

16-11. The ALTER ANY TRIGGER privilege allows you only to enable/disable a trigger. The CREATE ANY TRIGGER privilege allows you to create a new trigger in any schema or recreate an existing trigger without having to explicitly drop it and then create it again.

When a trigger is created, it is compiled and stored in the database. If you want to change the text of the trigger, you cannot just "edit" a piece of code; you have to change the definition in the database. To do this, you have to either use the DROP TRIGGER and CREATE TRIGGER commands or the CREATE OR REPLACE TRIGGER command.

16-12. The error occurs in the WHEN clause; when referring to the new or old values in a WHEN clause, you must omit the colon:

```
CREATE OR REPLACE TRIGGER emp_before_ins_t
   BEFORE INSERT
   ON employee
   FOR EACH ROW
   WHEN (NEW.mgr is null)
BEGIN
   IF (:NEW.sal > 800)
   THEN
      :NEW.sal := 850;
   END IF;
END;
```

Also, note that the WHEN condition must be a SQL condition, rather than a PL/SQL condition. PL/SQL functions or methods cannot be invoked from the trigger WHEN clause.

16-13. When Oracle compiles the trigger definition, it parses the entire code and reports all the errors encountered during the compilation phase; you can see these errors by querying the trusty USER_ERRORS data dictionary view:

```
SELECT line, position, text
  FROM user_errors
 WHERE name = 'MY_TRIGGER'
   AND TYPE = 'TRIGGER'
 ORDER BY sequence
```

In SQL*Plus, you can also use the following shortcut:

```
SQL> SHOW ERRORS TRIGGER MY_TRIGGER
```

Remember that if a trigger compiles with errors, it still gets created but fails during the execution. This means that all triggering DML statements are blocked until the trigger is temporarily disabled, dropped, or replaced with the trigger version that compiles without errors.

16-14. There is only one way to explicitly recompile a trigger: execute the ALTER command with the COMPILE option:

```
ALTER TRIGGER my_trigger_name COMPILE
```

You might have to use this command because triggers, as part of the Oracle object dependency, may become invalid if an object that the trigger depends upon changes.

16-15. You might want to omit the OR REPLACE option when you first create a trigger to save yourself a headache if a trigger by that name already exists in that schema. Since you're not using the OR REPLACE option, if a trigger already exists by that name, you get the following error:

```
ORA-04081: trigger name already exists
```

16-16. The statements are:

a. Incorrect. Oracle explicitly prohibits developers from putting triggers on SYS data dictionary objects, because this could inadvertently modify the behavior of the database. If an attempt is made to create a trigger on a SYS object, Oracle generates the error:

```
ORA-04089: cannot create triggers on objects owned by SYS
```

b. Correct. See (a).

c. Incorrect. Prior to Oracle8*i*, DML events were the only events that could be trapped by triggers. Oracle8*i* introduced the ability to trap other events as well, such as database-level events (STARTUP, SHUTDOWN, etc.) and DDL events (CREATE, DROP, etc.).

16-17. The statements are:

a. False. You can create triggers only for certain types of schema objects.

b. True. Oracle7 allowed the triggers to be created at the TABLE level.

c. False. Oracle8 added the ability to define triggers for VIEWs, which opened the road to fully updateable views in Oracle.

d. Oracle8*i* introduced the triggers created on NESTED TABLE level.

e. True. As of Oracle8*i*, you can also use the ON clause to define triggers for database or schema-level events. The DATABASE keyword specifies that the trigger is defined for the entire database, and the SCHEMA keyword specifies that the trigger is defined for the current schema.

16-18. (c). Here is the required syntax:

```
CREATE OR REPLACE TRIGGER upd_employee_commision
   AFTER UPDATE OF comm
   ON emp
   FOR EACH ROW
BEGIN
   <<Trigger logic>>
END;
```

16-19. (d). The trigger already fires just once for each INSERT operation on the emp table.

16-20. The trigger fails because the statement-level trigger cannot reference a pseudo-column name such as :NEW or :OLD. This is only available for row-level triggers.

16-21. A mutating table is a table that is currently being modified by an UPDATE, DELETE, or INSERT statement, or it is a table that might need to be updated by the effects of a declarative DELETE CASCADE referential integrity constraint. The SQL statements of a trigger cannot read from (query) or modify a mutating table of the triggering statement.

Intermediate

16-22. Executing the procedure results in an error because DBMS_SQL treats :OLD and :NEW as ordinary bind variables; consequently, it complains that not all the binds have been assigned. In short, the :OLD and :NEW predicates can't be directly referenced in statements executed via dynamic SQL.

16-23. The following template shows how to raise an error when a DML statement violates a business rule:

```
/* Filename on web page: secure_del_trigger.sql */
CREATE OR REPLACE TRIGGER secure_del_trigger
   BEFORE DELETE
   ON emp
   FOR EACH ROW
DECLARE
   unauthorized_deletion EXCEPTION;
BEGIN
   IF <your business rule is violated> THEN
     RAISE unauthorized_deletion;
   END IF;
EXCEPTION
   WHEN unauthorized_deletion
   THEN
      raise_application_error (-20500,
        'This record cannot be deleted');
END;
/
```

16-24. (b). Object privileges must be granted directly by the owner and cannot be acquired through database roles.

16-25. The triggers are:

    a. Invalid. The trigger explicitly calls SQL COMMIT, which is forbidden in Oracle.

    b. Invalid. The trigger dynamically creates a sequence via the DDL statement CREATE SEQUENCE that is issuing an implicit commit. SQL DDL statements are not allowed in triggers because DDL statements issue implicit COMMITs upon completion.

    c. Valid. A system trigger is the only type of trigger that allows CREATE/ALTER/DROP TABLE statements and ALTER...COMPILE in the trigger body, despite the fact that it issues an implicit COMMIT.

16-26. No. The restriction still applies because a stored procedure, even though it's called by a trigger, still runs within the trigger's transaction context.

16-27. You can use Oracle8*i*'s autonomous transaction pragma to start a new context. The following trigger illustrates how to use dynamic SQL to execute a DDL statement, which requires an implicit commit, inside a trigger:

```
/* Filename on web page: format_table_trig.sql */
CREATE OR REPLACE TRIGGER format_table_trig
    AFTER INSERT
    ON format_table
    FOR EACH ROW
    WHEN (new.tablecode = 3334)
DECLARE
    PRAGMA AUTONOMOUS_TRANSACTION;
    seq_sql          VARCHAR(200);
    cursor_handle    INTEGER;
    execute_ddl      INTEGER;
BEGIN
    seq_sql := 'CREATE SEQUENCE ' ||
            SUBSTR (:new.table_id, 1, 21) ||
            '_SEQ START WITH 0 INCREMENT BY 1 MINVALUE 0';
    cursor_handle := DBMS_SQL.open_cursor;
    DBMS_SQL.parse (cursor_handle, seq_sql, DBMS_SQL.native);
    execute_ddl := DBMS_SQL.execute (cursor_handle);
    DBMS_SQL.close_cursor (cursor_handle);
END;
```

Prior to Oracle8*i*, you needed to use database pipes (via the DBMS_PIPE package) to achieve this sort of transaction isolation. You first wrote a program to create the sequence (or create a record into a logging table), started it in another process/session, and then used DBMS_PIPE to send it requests from inside your trigger. Since the procedure in the other session was completely isolated from the main transaction, you circumvented the restrictions on transactions inside a trigger. Of course, this method was a lot more work!

16-28. The statements are:

    a. False. A trigger can contain more than 32 lines of code.

    b. True. A trigger's size is limited to 32K.

    c. True. Only 32 triggers can cascade at one time.

    d. True. The maximum size of a string that can hold a RAW or LONG RAW is 32K.

16-29. The following SQL*Plus script enables or disables all the triggers in the current user's schema:

```
/* Filename on web page: set_trigger_status.sql */
SET VERIFY OFF;
SET SERVEROUTPUT ON;

PROMPT  Program to enable/disable user triggers
ACCEPT op PROMPT '(E - enable, D - disable): '

DECLARE
    cur INTEGER;
    done EXCEPTION;
    cnt NUMBER := 0;
BEGIN
    FOR user_trg IN (SELECT trigger_name
                       FROM user_triggers)
    LOOP
       BEGIN
          cnt := cnt + 1;
          cur := DBMS_SQL.open_cursor;

          IF UPPER ('&&op') = 'E'
          THEN
             DBMS_SQL.parse (
                cur,
                'ALTER TRIGGER ' ||
                user_trg.trigger_name ||
                ' ENABLE',
                DBMS_SQL.native
             );
          ELSIF UPPER ('&&op') = 'D'
          THEN
             DBMS_SQL.parse (
                cur,
                'ALTER TRIGGER ' ||
                user_trg.trigger_name ||
                ' DISABLE',
                DBMS_SQL.native
             );
          ELSE
             DBMS_OUTPUT.put_line (
                'Invalid input argument passed'
             );
```

```
                    DBMS_SQL.close_cursor (cur);
                    RETURN;
                END IF;

                DBMS_SQL.close_cursor (cur);
            EXCEPTION
                WHEN OTHERS
                THEN
                    DBMS_OUTPUT.put_line (
                        SQLCODE || '-' || SQLERRM
                    );
                    DBMS_SQL.close_cursor (cur);
            END;
        END LOOP;

        IF UPPER ('&&op') = 'E'
        THEN
            DBMS_OUTPUT.put_line (
                cnt || ' triggers enabled'
            );
        ELSIF UPPER ('&&op') = 'D'
        THEN
            DBMS_OUTPUT.put_line (
                cnt || ' triggers disabled'
            );
        END IF;
    END;
    /
```

Expert

16-30. Triggers of the same type fire in the order of their respective object identifiers (OIDs). OIDs, which are assigned by Oracle when the trigger is created, are beyond the designer's control. Consequently, the order of firing
triggers is not guaranteed and cannot be controlled. The best approach is
to make sure that the trigger design is independent of the order of trigger
firing.

16-31. The trigger is clearly designed to fire for DML update events and only
when the new salary doesn't equal the old salary. The way the trigger is
written at present, it fires unnecessarily across a wide range of DML events
that occur on the employee table. You can use the WHEN clause to eliminate these unnecessary executions:

```
CREATE OR REPLACE TRIGGER employee_upd_t1
    AFTER UPDATE OF salary
    ON employee
    FOR EACH ROW
    WHEN (old.salary <> new.salary)
BEGIN
    employee_pkg.update_emp (:new.employee_id, :new.salary);
END;
```

16-32. At first, you might be tempted to try something like this:

```
CREATE OR REPLACE TRIGGER employee_t1
   BEFORE DELETE
   ON employee
   FOR EACH ROW
BEGIN
  UPDATE employee
    SET mgr = null
  WHERE mgr = :new.empno;
END;
/
```

Unfortunately, this trigger results in the mutating trigger error:

```
ORA-04091 table name is mutating, trigger/function may not see it
```

You can use a combination of packaged variables and different types of triggers to solve this problem.

The first step is to create a package containing an index-by table to hold the IDs of the managers who have been deleted:

```
CREATE OR REPLACE PACKAGE mutating_table_pkg
IS
    TYPE array IS TABLE OF emp%ROWTYPE
       INDEX BY BINARY_INTEGER;

    emp_values    array;
    empty         array;
END;
/
```

The second step is to create a statement-level BEFORE DELETE trigger that fires at the beginning of the transaction; its only purpose is to initialize the emp_values table to make sure it is empty:

```
CREATE OR REPLACE TRIGGER mutating_trig_1
   BEFORE DELETE
   ON emp
BEGIN
   mutating_table_pkg.emp_values := mutating_table_pkg.empty;
END;
/
```

The third step is to create a row-level BEFORE UPDATE trigger to populate the emp_values tables with the employee numbers of the rows that are being deleted. This is the only type of processing implemented in this trigger; the UPDATE statement is intentionally removed from this trigger because it caused the "mutating table" problem in the first place:

```
CREATE OR REPLACE TRIGGER mutating_trig_2
   BEFORE DELETE
   ON emp
   FOR EACH ROW
   WHEN (old.job = 'MANAGER')
DECLARE
```

```
   i   NUMBER := mutating_table_pkg.emp_values.COUNT + 1;
BEGIN
   mutating_table_pkg.emp_values (i).empno := :old.empno;
END;
/
```

The final step is to create a statement-level AFTER DELETE that uses the array of managers to modify the employee records. At this point, the employee table is no longer a mutating table (undergoing changes), so you're free to make update statements:

```
CREATE OR REPLACE TRIGGER mut_trg_3
   AFTER DELETE
   ON emp
BEGIN
   FOR i IN 1 .. mutating_table_pkg.emp_values.COUNT
   LOOP
      UPDATE emp
         SET mgr = NULL
         WHERE mgr = mutating_table_pkg.emp_values (i).empno;
   END LOOP;
END;
/
```

16-33. As of Oracle8*i*, the only way to log in to a database that has an invalid AFTER LOGON trigger is to use a DBA utility that can CONNECT INTERNAL (e.g., Server Manager). Here's a trace of a SVRMGR session to disable the trigger:

```
SVRMGR> connect internal
Connected.
SVRMGR> ALTER TRIGGER on_logon DISABLE;
Statement processed.
```

16-34. Because the trigger is running as an autonomous transaction, the aggregate query on the emp tables doesn't see the rows inserted by the calling transaction. Consequently, the trigger doesn't correctly record the department's salary history.

16-35. The first trigger, which is governed by the local object dependency mechanism provided by Oracle, is invalidated immediately after the UPDATE_BONUS procedure is recompiled. Since it's recompiled and revalidated automatically, the next execution of the trigger fires successfully.

The second trigger, which refers to a remote procedure, is not immediately invalidated and revalidated after UPDATE_BONUS@RDB is recompiled. Consequently, the trigger produces the following stack of errors:

```
ORA-04068: existing state of packages has been discarded
ORA-04062: timestamp of procedure "UPDATE_BONUS" has been changed
ORA-06512: at "REM_PROC_TRIGGER", line 2
ORA-04088: error during execution of trigger 'REM_PROC_TRIGGER'
```

17

Calling Functions in SQL

Beginner

17-1. Generally, the answer is "Yes! You can call your own PL/SQL functions from within a SQL statement." There are, however, a number of restrictions and requirements governing how and when you can do this. The following exercises test your knowledge of these conditions.

17-2. No. When executed inside a SQL statement, your functions can operate only on individual column values within a single row.

17-3. First, here is the definition of the function:

```
CREATE OR REPLACE FUNCTION totcomp
    (sal_in IN PLS_INTEGER,
     comm_in IN NUMBER := NULL)
    RETURN NUMBER
IS
BEGIN
    RETURN (sal_in + NVL (comm_in, 0));
END;
/
```

Now you can apply that function back into the statement:

```
SELECT ename, totcomp (sal, comm) total
  FROM emp
 WHERE totcomp (sal, comm) > 1000;
```

17-4. The statements are:

a. True.

b. False. The datatypes of the parameters and the RETURN clause of the function can only be valid SQL datatypes. You cannot, for example, return an index-by table (a.k.a., PL/SQL table). You also cannot pass in a Boolean value. The Boolean datatype is not currently supported in SQL.

   c. False. That's downright silly. You can name your function whatever you want; it certainly cannot be the name of a table.

   d. False. You can only call one of your own functions if it is stored in the database; client-side functions are not accessible from within SQL.

   e. False. You can call a function in any non-DDL SQL statement, whether a query or a DML statement.

17-5. No, you cannot directly access a procedure in SQL. You can, however, build a "wrapper" or dummy function around your procedure and then call that function.

Intermediate

17-6. Prior to Oracle8*i* Release 8.1, it was necessary to add the RESTRICT_REFERENCES pragma for each function or procedure you wanted to enable for direct or indirect access from SQL. This pragma informs the compiler of how free or pure the program is from "side effects," such as modifying data in the database.

17-7. You can try to assert any combination of the following:

WNDS

    Writes no database state; no modifications made to database tables.

WNPS

    Writes no package state; no modifications made to package variables.

RNDS

    Reads no database state; no queries against database tables or other database objects.

RNPS

    Reads no package state; no read accesses of package variables.

Your program will not compile if you try to assert a purity level that is not supported by the code itself.

17-8. You must supply the name of the program and then each of the purity levels:

```
CREATE OR REPLACE PACKAGE comp
IS
    FUNCTION total
        (sal_in IN NUMBER,
         comm_in IN NUMBER := NULL)
        RETURN NUMBER;

    PRAGMA RESTRICT_REFERENCES (
```

```
        total, WNDS, WNPS, RNDS, RNPS);
END;
/
```

17-9. No program can be called directly or indirectly from SQL if it updates the database. At a minimum, you must include the following pragma to make the function usable:

```
PRAGMA RESTRICT_REFERENCES (my_function, WNDS);
```

17-10. In Oracle 8.0 and earlier, you need to assert the WNPS purity level (in addition to the WNDS level) if you want to call a function:

- In the WHERE, GROUP BY, or ORDER BY clauses of a SELECT statement

- As a remote procedure call

17-11. You can assert all the purity levels (WNDS, RNDS, WNPS, and RNPS). This function has no side effects; it simply encapsulates the formula for calculating the number of characters between start and end locations.

17-12. You can assert WNDS, WNPS, and RNPS. You may not assert RNDS, since it reads from the database.

17-13. The version:

   a. Can assert WNDS, WNPS, and RNDS, but not RNPS because it references the who_is_paying_whom.my_salary constant.

   b. Can assert only WNDS, RNDS. It both reads and writes data structures in who_is_paying_whom. You can't call this version in a WHERE clause (prior to Oracle 8.1).

17-14. The SELECT statement assumes I didn't supply a pragma for the comp. total function, and that is perfectly reasonable behavior. I didn't supply a pragma for *that* comp.total. The way I wrote the package specification reflects a common error: you have to supply a separate pragma for each overloaded program. You cannot provide one pragma and have it apply to all of them. You might not be able to assert the same purity levels for all versions of a particular named program.

17-15. First, build a function:

```
CREATE OR REPLACE FUNCTION status_string (
    hire_date_in IN DATE, eval_date_in IN DATE) RETURN VARCHAR2
IS
BEGIN
   IF hire_date_in > SYSDATE - 30
   THEN
      RETURN 'JUST HIRED';
   ELSIF eval_date_in < SYSATE - 10
   THEN
      RETURN 'NEEDS REVIEW';
```

```
    ELSE
        RETURN 'UP TO DATE';
    END IF;
END;
/
```

And then the query becomes this:

```
SELECT ename, status_string (hire_date, eval_date) status
    FROM emp;
```

Expert

17-16. You can assert only WNDS. Clearly, it reads from the database. In addition, DBMS_OUTPUT.PUT_LINE asserts only WNDS and RNDS; it does, in fact, write to the DBMS_OUTPUT buffer and also reads the values of data structures for the buffer. You can assert only the intersection of the purity levels of all referenced programs.

17-17. The following implementation of this trace function is really just a "pass-through" to DBMS_OUTPUT.PUT_LINE:

```
/* Filename on web page: traceit.sf */
CREATE OR REPLACE FUNCTION traceit (
    tab IN VARCHAR2,
    rowid_in IN ROWID)
    RETURN INTEGER
IS
BEGIN
    DBMS_OUTPUT.PUT_LINE (tab || '-' || ROWIDTOCHAR (rowid_in));
    RETURN 0;
EXCEPTION
    WHEN OTHERS
    THEN
        DBMS_OUTPUT.ENABLE (1000000);
        traceit (tab, rowid_in);
END;
/
```

I cannot call this procedure directly in SQL, so I put it inside a function that always returns 0, but in the process put information into the DBMS_OUTPUT buffer. I also added an exception section to trap and automatically correct for an error that might arise from the DBMS_OUTPUT buffer's being too small.

17-18. Here is one possible implementation:

```
CREATE OR REPLACE FUNCTION traceit (
    tab IN VARCHAR2,
    rowid_in IN ROWID)
    RETURN INTEGER
IS
    stat PLS_INTEGER;
```

```
BEGIN
   DBMS_PIPE.RESET_BUFFER;
   DBMS_PIPE.PACK_MESSAGE (tab);
   DBMS_PIPE.PACK_MESSAGE_ROWID (rowid_in);
   stat := DBMS_PIPE.SEND_MESSAGE ('SQLtrace');
   RETURN stat;
END;
/
```

You might decide to use a pipe-based trace function when you have a very long-running query. You won't see any output from the DBMS_OUTPUT version until the query finishes (and if it is a "free standing" query outside a PL/SQL block, you still have to run a PL/SQL block to flush the buffer). With DBMS_PIPE, you can check the contents of the pipe as the query continues to execute.

17-19. In Oracle 8.0, you get this error:

```
ORA-06571: Function TOTCOMP does not guarantee not to update database
```

In Oracle 8.1, you don't get an error. All the rows in emp are deleted, and then the new row is inserted. When finished, the emp table has just one row in it.

17-20. The following is an approach in "straight SQL" using a view and correlated subquery:

```
CREATE VIEW dept_salary
AS
   SELECT deptno, SUM (sal) total_salary
     FROM emp
 GROUP BY deptno;

SELECT E.deptno, ename, sal, total_salary
  FROM emp E, dept_salary DS
 WHERE E.deptno = DS.deptno
   AND sal =
     (SELECT MAX (sal)
        FROM emp E2
       WHERE E2.deptno = E.deptno)
 ORDER BY E.deptno, ename;
```

Here is another "straight SQL" using an inline view available in Oracle 7.3 and above:

```
SELECT E.deptno, ename, sal, total_salary
  FROM emp E,
       (SELECT deptno, SUM (sal) total_salary
          FROM emp
          GROUP BY deptno) DS
 WHERE E.deptno = DS.deptno
   AND sal =
     (SELECT MAX (sal)
        FROM emp E2
       WHERE E2.deptno = E.deptno)
 ORDER BY E.deptno, ename;
```

And finally, a SQL-PL/SQL implementation using a single salary statistics function:

```
SELECT deptno,
       ename,
       sal,
       salstat (deptno, 'SUM') totsal
  FROM emp
 WHERE sal = salstat (deptno, 'MAX')
 ORDER BY deptno, ename;
```

Here is the consolidated salary statistics function:

```
/* Filename on web page: salstat.sf */
CREATE OR REPLACE FUNCTION salstat
   (dept_id_in IN dept.deptno%TYPE, stat_type_in IN VARCHAR2)
   RETURN NUMBER
IS
   CURSOR stat_cur IS
     SELECT MAX (sal) max_sal, SUM (sal) sum_sal,
       FROM emp E WHERE deptno = dept_id_in;
   stat_rec stat_cur%ROWTYPE;

   return_value NUMBER;
BEGIN
   OPEN stat_cur;
   FETCH stat_cur INTO stat_rec;

   IF    stat_type_int = 'MAX' THEN return_value := stat_rec.max_sal;
   ELSIF stat_type_int = 'SUM' THEN return_value := stat_rec.sum_sal;
   END IF;

   RETURN return_value;
END sal_stat;
/
```

You can easily extend it to all the various group functions. Once you're doing one of them, there is little overhead in performing all the computations. You could also, of course, use dynamic SQL to provide one function that calculates the group function for any table-column combination (see Chapter 13, *Native Dynamic SQL*).

17-21. This solution was provided by Susan Kleinfelter and made available through the PL/SQL Pipeline:

```
SELECT func_value
  FROM (SELECT my_function(field1) AS func_value
          FROM table1)
 WHERE func_value > 3;
```

18

Character Functions

Beginner

18-1. The CONCAT function or the concatenation operator does the trick. The CONCAT function has two string arguments that it returns concatenated. The concatenation operator is specified as || and takes its arguments from its left and right sides.

You may be interested to know that || is actually a function that is itself declared in the STANDARD package:

```
DECLARE
   first_three  VARCHAR2(3) := 'ABC';
   second_three VARCHAR2(3) := 'DEF';
   third_three  VARCHAR2(3) := 'GHI';
   whole_thing  VARCHAR2(9);
BEGIN
   /*
      || The CONCAT function requires multiple steps to
      || concatenate multiple strings
   */
   whole_thing := CONCAT(first_three,second_three);
   whole_thing := CONCAT(whole_thing,third_three);
   DBMS_OUTPUT.PUT_LINE(whole_thing);
   /*
      || The concatenation operator concatenates multiple
      || very quick and easy
   */
   whole_thing := first_three || second_three || third_three;
   DBMS_OUTPUT.PUT_LINE(whole_thing);
END;
```

Note also that both functions perform an on-the-fly conversion of their arguments to VARCHAR2 datatypes:

```
SQL> EXEC DBMS_OUTPUT.PUT_LINE (CONCAT(1,2))
12
SQL> EXEC DBMS_OUTPUT.PUT_LINE (1 || 2)
12
```

Remember that if the value to be converted is of the date datatype, National Language Support (NLS) settings will affect the appearance of the resulting string.

18-2. The two words "in string" will lead you directly to the aptly named INSTR function. This function has two obvious arguments (the string to search and the string to search for). It also has two, not so obvious, but very powerful arguments (where to start and what occurrence to find):

```
DECLARE
    old_blue_eyes VARCHAR2(14) := 'do be do be do';
    v_temp VARCHAR2(10);
BEGIN
    /*
       || Find the first do three times
    */
    v_temp:= INSTR(old_blue_eyes,'do',1,1);
    v_temp:= INSTR(old_blue_eyes,'do',1);
    v_temp:= INSTR(old_blue_eyes,'do');
    /*
       || Find the second do by looking for the
       || second occurrence
    */
    v_temp := INSTR(old_blue_eyes,'do',1,2);
    /*
       || Find the second do by looking for the
       || first occurrence after the third character
    */
    v_temp := INSTR(old_blue_eyes,'do',3,1);
    /*
       || Find the very last do (twice)
    */
    v_temp := INSTR(old_blue_eyes,'do',1,3);
    v_temp := INSTR(old_blue_eyes,'do',10,1);
END;
```

The INSTR function is also quite good about converting its arguments to VARCHAR2:

```
SQL> EXEC DBMS_OUTPUT.PUT_LINE (INSTR ( 1234567890,4));
4
```

Be careful with case, though; INSTR is not so forgiving in that regard. This example forever returns a big fat zero:

```
SQL> EXEC DBMS_OUTPUT.PUT_LINE ( INSTR( 'Looter!','l'));
0
```

18-3. The REPLACE function can substitute sections of a string, or the TRANS-LATE function can substitute character by character. Both functions have the same three arguments: a string, a string to search for, and a string to replace. They work in different ways, though.

Use REPLACE when you want to substitute every occurrence of one string in another:

```
SQL> EXEC DBMS_OUTPUT.PUT_LINE
   (REPLACE ('Rain, Rain and More Rain','Rain','Sunshine'));

Sunshine, Sunshine and More Sunshine
```

Use TRANSLATE to substitute every occurrence of single characters in a string. For example, this code substitutes A for C, and C for A, to return CCCBAAA:

```
SQL> EXEC DBMS_OUTPUT.PUT_LINE(TRANSLATE('AAABCCC','AC','CA'));
CCCBAAA
```

18-4. Since the number of characters in a string is equal to its length, the LENGTH function applies here:

```
v_string_length := LENGTH(v_the_string);
```

Don't forget that a blank space is considered a character:

```
LENGTH('Hi There') <> LENGTH(' Hi There ')
```

18-5. Here's the output:

```
SQL> EXEC DBMS_OUTPUT.PUT_LINE(LENGTH(1 * 100));
3
```

3 is the number of characters in 100 (100 * 1). Note that the LENGTH function is quite gracious about converting numeric values to VARCHAR2.

18-6. Here's the code:

```
UPDATE employee
   SET last_name = UPPER(last_name)
 WHERE last_name != UPPER(last_name);
```

18-7. Why, UPPER and LOWER, of course. These functions change the case of the whole string and are useful for making case-neutral comparisons in code, for example:

```
IF UPPER('Procurement') = 'PROCUREMENT'...
```

18-8. Here's a suggested block:

```
BEGIN
   /*
      || The handy dandy SUBSTR function does the trick with
      || its last two arguments, start location and length.
      || Here we say start at the fourth character and show
      || it plus the next two.
   */
   DBMS_OUTPUT.PUT_LINE(SUBSTR('BRUSHLOTS',4,3));
END;
```

18-9. A string can be padded on the left side or the right side by LPAD and RPAD, respectively. Each of these functions returns the padded string specified by three arguments: the string to pad, the length to pad to, and the characters to pad with (a space by default).

```
DECLARE
  v_temp VARCHAR2(30);
BEGIN
  v_temp := RPAD('Pad with blanks',30);
  v_temp := RPAD('Pad with stars',30,'*');
  v_temp := RPAD('Pad with stars and tildes',30,'*~');
  v_temp := RPAD('Will be truncated at 3',3,'*');
END;
```

18-10. The INITCAP function does the trick here to change the initial letter of every word to capitals:

```
SQL> EXEC DBMS_OUTPUT.PUT_LINE(INITCAP('this is a headline'));
This Is A Headline
```

18-11. The LIKE function in SQL can eliminate the unwanted rows from the table. Then all that is required is to loop through each record in the query:

```
DECLARE
  CURSOR C1 IS SELECT * FROM EMPLOYEE WHERE UPPER(LAST_NAME) LIKE '%E%';
BEGIN
  FOR C1_REC IN C1 LOOP
    DBMS_OUTPUT.PUT_LINE(C1_REC.LAST_NAME||', '||C1_REC.FIRST_NAME);
  END LOOP;
END;
```

18-12. The INSTR function can calculate this number. Recall that one of the parameters INSTR accepts is the occurrence of the string you wish to find. By using this, you need only place a single call to INSTR to satisfy the requirement:

```
SQL> EXEC DBMS_OUTPUT.PUT_LINE (instr(upper('Steven Feuerstein'),'E', 1, 2));
5
```

18-13. Here's the block:

```
BEGIN
/*
|| Utilize the little known but very effective ability to start searching
|| from the end of the string by specifying a negative third argument for
|| the INSTR function.
||
|| I must confess that I have written many a function to do just this
|| sort of thing in the past without realizing INSTR could do it on its
|| own (DH)
*/
  DBMS_OUTPUT.PUT_LINE(INSTR(UPPER('Steven Feuerstein'),'E',-1,3));
END;
```

18-14. The LTRIM function does this nicely by specifying that all zeros be removed from the left side of the string as follows:

```
LTRIM(my_formatted_number,'0')
```

18-15. Hmm, what function is used to left-pad a string? Why, LPAD of course! And since you know that blanks are considered characters (as per a string's length), write the following:

```
/* we also know that blanks are the default padding character */
v_number_string := LPAD(v_number_string,15);
```

18-16. This does the trick:

```
DECLARE
   v_new_name VARCHAR2(50);
BEGIN
   /*
      || Because we are only replacing a single character the
      || REPLACE or TRANSLATE function will suffice
   */
   v_new_name := REPLACE('Steven Feuerstein','e','z');
   v_new_name := TRANSLATE('Steven Feuerstein','e','z');
END;
```

18-17. Here you go:

```
DECLARE
   v_new_name VARCHAR2(50);
BEGIN
   /*
      || The replace function can be used to substitute nothing
      || for a string
   */
   v_new_name := REPLACE('Steven Feuerstein','e','');
END;
```

18-18. Try this replacement:

```
v_new_string :=
   REPLACE('IF TO_DATE (my_date_str, ''MM-DD-YY'') > SYSDATE','YY','RR');
```

18-19. This code performs the replacement:

```
v_new_string := REPLACE(UPPER('IF TO_DATE (my_date_str,''MM-
DD-YY'') > TO_DATE (your_date_str,''mmddyy'')'),'YY','RR');
```

18-20. The RPAD command shown here accomplishes what you need by padding the string "-" using the option parameter to specify the pad character of "-":

```
RPAD ('-', 80, '-')
```

Intermediate

18-21. All that's displayed is "Sound effects" because RTRIM starts at the end of the string and removes all occurrences of any of the characters it is to remove, until it comes to one that is not in the list. Note that the actual length of the output is 14 (it includes a trailing blank).

18-22. This string is displayed:

```
ABCDEF
```

18-23. Here is a suggested function:

```
CREATE OR REPLACE FUNCTION ascii_converter ( p_char IN VARCHAR2 )
                  RETURN INT IS
BEGIN
   -- The ASCII function returns the numeric
   -- equivalent of a character
   RETURN(ASCII(p_char));
END;
```

18-24. Here you go:

```
CREATE OR REPLACE FUNCTION sound_the_same (
                                    p_string1 IN VARCHAR2,
                                    p_string2 VARCHAR2 )
              RETURN BOOLEAN IS

   -- always be pessimistic
   v_ret_val BOOLEAN := FALSE;

BEGIN
   -- Compare the soundex returns for the two strings
   IF SOUNDEX(p_string1) = SOUNDEX(p_string2) THEN
     v_ret_val := TRUE;
   ELSE
     v_ret_val := FALSE;
   END IF;
   RETURN(v_ret_val);
END;
```

18-25. Try this one:

```
CREATE OR REPLACE FUNCTION crlf RETURN VARCHAR2 IS
BEGIN
   -- Simply return the character associated with
   -- sequence 10 for a carriage return/line feed
   RETURN(CHR(10));
END;


CREATE OR REPLACE FUNCTION tab RETURN VARCHAR2 IS
BEGIN
   -- Simply return the character associated with
   -- sequence 10 for a carriage return/line feed
   RETURN(CHR(9));
END;
```

18-26. The REPLACE function can make the desired switch in the string:

```
DECLARE
   the_text VARCHAR2(100);
BEGIN
   -- It is important to first replace all single quotes with two quotes
   -- to include the quote in the string
   the_text :=
       'IF TO_DATE (my_date_str, ''MM-DD-YY'') >' ||
       'TO_DATE (your_date_str, ''mmddyy'')';
   DBMS_OUTPUT.PUT_LINE(REPLACE(UPPER(the_text),'YY', 'RR'));
END;
```

The TRANSLATE function cannot be used here because it replaces single letters, not patterns. This results in the following string:

```
IF TO_DATE (MR_DATE_STR, 'MM-DD-RR') > TO_DATE (ROUR_DATE_STR, 'MMDDRR')
```

Note that occurrences of a single "Y" have been changed to "R," and not only the occurrences of "YY" as was intended.

18-27. This is a suggested implementation:

```
/* Filename on web page: stripper.sf */
CREATE OR REPLACE FUNCTION NUMBER_STRIPPER ( p_string IN VARCHAR2 )
                 RETURN VARCHAR2 IS
  -- This function removes all numeric digits from the string
  -- passed in.
  v_current_element NUMBER;   -- # of elements in string being processed
  v_char_length     NUMBER;   -- length of parameter
  v_ret_val         VARCHAR2(2000);  -- return value
  v_current_char  VARCHAR2(1); -- the character being processed

BEGIN
  -- initialize the length of the parameter and the current
  -- element number
  v_char_length := LENGTH(p_string);
  v_current_element := 1;

  -- for every character in the string...
  LOOP
     -- exit when there are no more elements...
     EXIT WHEN v_current_element > v_char_length;

     -- get the value of the current character
     v_current_char := SUBSTR(p_string,v_current_element,1);

     -- if the character is not numeric then append it to the
     -- return value. I realize this is not the fastest way to
     -- check if a character is numeric but in keeping with the spirit
     -- of the exercises I did it this way.
     IF TRANSLATE(v_current_char,'1234567890','~~~~~~~~~~') != '~' OR
        v_current_char = '~' THEN
       v_ret_val := v_ret_val || v_current_char;
     END IF;

     -- get the next character in the parameter
     v_current_element := v_current_element + 1;

  END LOOP;  -- every character in the string

  RETURN(v_ret_val);

END;
```

18-28. This function returns "in" because it counts 10 characters back from the end to the "i" in "in", and returns it plus the next two characters.

18-29. This INSTR returns 2. It finds the "a" in Sandy by counting back 15 characters from the end of the string and continues towards the beginning of the string looking for the second occurrence of "a". It ignores the "a" in February because it is the first one.

18-30. CONCAT and REPLACE functions are forgiving when passed a NULL value:

```
SQL> EXEC DBMS_OUTPUT.PUT_LINE('A' || NULL || 'B');
AB
SQL> EXEC DBMS_OUTPUT.PUT_LINE(REPLACE('ABC','C',NULL));
AB
```

SUBSTR is somewhat forgiving as well:

```
SQL> EXEC DBMS_OUTPUT.PUT_LINE(SUBSTR('Big Steve and Super Dave',15,NULL));
Super Dave
```

INSTR doesn't care if NULLs are passed either. Note that this line doesn't display anything:

```
EXEC DBMS_OUTPUT.PUT_LINE(INSTR('Big Steve and Super Dave',NULL,1,1));
```

18-31. Here is a PL/SQL block that does the job:

```
BEGIN
    -- Perform a substring starting at the location of the
    -- second e plus one and going for 5 characters (the location of
    -- the fourth e minus the location of the second e minus one)
    DBMS_OUTPUT.PUT_LINE(SUBSTR('Steven Feuerstein',
        INSTR('Steven Feuerstein','e',1,2) + 1,
        INSTR('Steven Feuerstein','e',1,4) -
        INSTR('Steven Feuerstein','e',1,2) - 1));
END;
```

18-32. The winning formula is:

```
m - n + 1
```

18-33. Here is the function:

```
CREATE OR REPLACE FUNCTION betwnstr ( p_string IN VARCHAR2,
                                      p_start  IN VARCHAR2,
                                      p_end    IN VARCHAR2 )
                        RETURN VARCHAR2 IS
BEGIN
    RETURN(SUBSTR(p_string,p_start,p_end - p_start + 1));
END;
```

18-34. The PL/SQL block follows:

```
DECLARE
    -- Cursor to find all occurrences of YY
    -- in the current users source library
    CURSOR curs_find_yy IS
    SELECT *
      FROM USER_SOURCE
     WHERE INSTR(text,'YY',1,1) > 0
    ORDER BY NAME, TYPE, LINE;
```

```
BEGIN
    -- for every YY...
    FOR v_yy_rec IN curs_find_yy LOOP

        -- Display all info
        DBMS_OUTPUT.PUT_LINE(v_yy_rec.name || ' ' ||
                             v_yy_rec.type || ' ' ||
                             v_yy_rec.line);
        -- use the TAB function created earlier for distinction
        DBMS_OUTPUT.PUT_LINE(TAB || v_yy_rec.text);

    END LOOP;  -- every YY

END;
```

18-35. This function does the trick:

```
CREATE OR REPLACE FUNCTION qd ( p_string IN VARCHAR2 )
                  RETURN VARCHAR2 IS
    -- The world famous quote doubler function known
    -- the world over for; well, doubling quotes

BEGIN
    -- Simply replace all occurrences of a single
    -- quote with a single quote concatenated with
    -- another single quote
    RETURN(REPLACE(p_string,'''','!'' || ''''));
END;
```

18-36. Remove:

```
SQL> EXEC DBMS_OUTPUT.PUT_LINE(REPLACE(LTRIM(REPLACE(-
'abcabcccccI LOVE CHILIabc','abc','@'),'@'),'@','abc'));
ccccI LOVE CHILIabc
```

18-37. The statements are:

a. True.

b. False. SOUNDEX uses the first five consonants in the string to generate the return value.

c. True.

d. True.

e. Hmm. I guess we'll never really know, now will we?

f. False. Y is treated as a vowel.

18-38. For a suggested implementation, see the function in the *rplc.sf* file on the book's web page.

18-39. For a suggested implementation, see the function in the *rinstr.sf* file on the book's web page.

18-40. An easy application of RPAD does the trick:

```
/* Filename on web page: rulerstr.sf */
CREATE OR REPLACE FUNCTION rulerstr (len IN INTEGER) RETURN VARCHAR2
IS
   digits CHAR(10) := '1234567890';
BEGIN
   RETURN RPAD (digits, len, digits);
END;
/
```

Expert

18-41. Check the *center.sf* file on this book's web page for a suggested function.

18-42. Check the *betwnstr.sql* file on the book's web page for a possible solution.

18-43. Here's a suggested function:

```
/* Filename on web page: betwnstr.sql */
CREATE OR REPLACE FUNCTION betwnstr (
                        str IN VARCHAR2,
                        start_str IN VARCHAR2,
                        end_str IN VARCHAR2 := NULL )
                RETURN VARCHAR2 IS

   -- This function returns the characters in str that occur between
   -- the end of start_str and the beginning of end_str.
   --
   -- If start_str does not occur in str or it occurs after end_str
   -- then NULL will be returned.

BEGIN
   /*
      || If start_str does occur in str then perform a substring with the
      || following values :
      ||
      ||    Start Point = location of start_str + length of start_str
      ||    Length      = location of end_str - Start Point
      ||
      || Not that if end_str is NULL the natural behaviour
      || of SUBSTR will return all
      || characters after start_str
   */
   IF INSTR(str,start_str,1,1) > 0 THEN
     RETURN(SUBSTR(str,INSTR(str,start_str,1,1) + LENGTH(start_str),
          INSTR(str,end_str,1,1) -
        ( INSTR(str,start_str,1,1) + LENGTH(start_str))));
   ELSE
     RETURN(str);
   END IF;

END;
```

18-44. This function trims a pattern:

```
/* Filename on web page: trim.sf */
CREATE OR REPLACE FUNCTION PATTERN_TRIM ( p_string IN VARCHAR2,
                                          p_trim   IN VARCHAR2 )
                  RETURN VARCHAR2 IS
   /*
    || This function trims all occurrences of p_trim from the
    || start of p_string using recursion.
   */

BEGIN
   /*
    || If the first n characters of p_string are equal to p_trim
    || (where n equals the length of p_trim) then call pattern_trim
    || again with the first n characters removed from p_string otherwise
    || return p_string
   */
   IF SUBSTR(p_string,1,LENGTH(p_trim)) = p_trim THEN
      RETURN(PATTERN_TRIM(SUBSTR(p_string,LENGTH(p_trim) + 1,
                       LENGTH(p_string) - LENGTH(p_trim)),p_trim));
   ELSE
      RETURN(p_string);
   END IF;

END;
```

18-45. For a suggested implementation, see the *closet_loc.sf* file on this book's web page.

18-46. The biggest challenge in creating such a function is to come up with the most compact, yet readable (and therefore maintainable) implementation. Here is one possibility:

```
/* Filename on web page: rulerstr2.sf */
CREATE OR REPLACE FUNCTION rulerstr (
   len IN INTEGER, startat IN INTEGER := 1) RETURN VARCHAR2
IS
   digits     CONSTANT CHAR(10) := '1234567890';
   rev_digits CONSTANT CHAR(10) := '0987654321';

   v_digits CHAR(10) := digits;
   v_start INTEGER := MOD (startat, 10);
BEGIN
   IF startat < 0
   THEN
      /*
       || If negative, then switch to the reverse digits string
       || and change the start to its positive location in the string.
      */
      v_start := 11 + v_start;
      v_digits := rev_digits;

   ELSIF v_start = 0
   THEN
```

```
            /* Treat 0 same as 10: start with "0" digit. */
            v_start := 10;
        END IF;

        /* Swap the portions of the digits string to get started right. */
        v_digits := SUBSTR (v_digits, v_start) || SUBSTR (v_digits, 1, v_start-1);

        /* Use RPAD to duplicate the ruler to requested length. */
        RETURN RPAD (v_digits, len, v_digits);
    END;
    /
```

18-47. This function should work:

```
/* Filename on web page: ascii_converter.pkg */
CREATE OR REPLACE PACKAGE ascii_converter IS
    /*
        || This package converts a string into a PL/SQL
        || table containing the ASCII equivalents of each of
        || its characters.
    */

    -- a global collection for the function return type
    TYPE ascii_table_type IS TABLE OF INT
        INDEX BY BINARY_INTEGER;

    -- converion function
    FUNCTION convert ( p_string VARCHAR2 )
            RETURN ascii_table_type;

END ascii_converter;
/

CREATE OR REPLACE PACKAGE BODY ascii_converter IS

    FUNCTION convert ( p_string IN VARCHAR2 )
            RETURN ascii_table_type IS
        /*
            || This function converts p_string into a PL/SQL table
            || containing the ASCII equivalents of each character
        */
        v_ascii_table ascii_table_type;  -- local collection
        v_this_char     VARCHAR2(1);     -- current character
        v_this_counter INT := 1;         -- current character counter

    BEGIN
        -- for every character in p_string...
        v_this_char := SUBSTR(p_string,v_this_counter,1);
        LOOP

            -- exit when no more characters
            EXIT WHEN v_this_char IS NULL;

            -- put the ASCII value of the current character into the
            -- nexte element of the PL/SQL table
```

```
            v_ascii_table(v_this_counter) := ASCII(v_this_char);

            -- increment the counter and try the next character
            v_this_counter := v_this_counter + 1;
            v_this_char := SUBSTR(p_string,v_this_counter,1);

        END LOOP;   -- every character in p_string

    END convert;

END ascii_converter;
```

19

Date Functions

Beginner

19-1. Use the ADD_MONTHS function, as shown here:

```
date_plus_6 := ADD_MONTHS (my_date, 6);
```

19-2. You want to use the SYSDATE and TO_CHAR functions, along with the appropriate format mask:

```
CREATE OR REPLACE PROCEDURE show_now
IS
BEGIN
   DBMS_OUTPUT.PUT_LINE (TO_CHAR
      (SYSDATE, 'Month DDth, YYYY HH24:MI:SS'));
END;
/
```

19-3. The LAST_DAY function should do the trick:

```
SQL> EXEC DBMS_OUTPUT.PUT_LINE (LAST_DAY(SYSDATE))
31-MAR-99
```

19-4. If you don't want the time component possibly messing up your date-range computations, you can truncate the date as follows:

```
my_date := TRUNC (my_date);
```

The TRUNC function by default truncates the time component. You can use other format masks to specify different levels of truncation (day, month, week, year, etc.).

19-5. Again, TRUNC is the way to go:

```
my_date := TRUNC (my_date, 'Q');
```

19-6. The MONTHS_BETWEEN function does most of the work, but you also have to truncate the fractional component:

```
month_count := TRUNC (MONTHS_BETWEEN (start_date, end_date));
```

19-7. There is no ADD_YEARS function, so you have to do a bit of translation. Here is the code to write in a database trigger that makes sure your employees are at least 18 years old:

```
IF ADD_MONTHS (:NEW.hire_date, -1*18*12) < :NEW.date_of_birth
THEN
    DBMS_OUTPUT.PUT_LINE (
        'Too young to hire...in the US anyway.');
END IF;
```

19-8. The default time in Oracle is midnight: 12:00:00 A.M.

19-9. The easiest way to do this is to use the LAST_DAY function:

```
CREATE OR REPLACE FUNCTION days_left RETURN NUMBER
IS
BEGIN
    RETURN (LAST_DAY (SYSDATE) - SYSDATE);
END;
/
```

Intermediate

19-10. I would use a combination of TRUNC and NEXT_DAY, as shown here:

```
DECLARE
    first_monday DATE;
BEGIN
    first_monday := NEXT_DAY (
        TRUNC (SYSDATE, 'MONTH'), 'MONDAY');
    DBMS_OUTPUT.PUT_LINE (first_monday);
END;
/
```

19-11. We're talking time-zone differences, so the NEW_TIME function should work perfectly well. London is on Greenwich Mean Time, while the folks in Chicago are on Central Standard Time. Here is a function that does the conversion:

```
/* Filename on web page: chitime.sf */
CREATE OR REPLACE FUNCTION chitime RETURN DATE
IS
BEGIN
    RETURN NEW_TIME (SYSDATE, 'GMT', 'CST');
END;
/
```

19-12. TRUNC to the rescue once again:

```
CREATE OR REPLACE FUNCTION chitime RETURN DATE
IS
BEGIN
    RETURN TRUNC (SYSDATE, 'MONTH');
END;
/
```

19-13. Well, first you have to truncate the current date/time back to the beginning of the century (which also sets the time component to midnight), then move forward 25 years, make sure you're on the first day of that year, and move forward nine hours. Here goes:

```
DECLARE
    amaze_me DATE;
BEGIN
    amaze_me := TRUNC (
        ADD_MONTHS (TRUNC (SYSDATE, 'CC'), 25 * 12), 'MONTH') + 9 / 24;
    DBMS_OUTPUT.put_line (
        TO_CHAR (
            amaze_me,
            'MM/DD/YY HH24:MI:SS'
        )
    );
END;
/
```

Isn't this fun?

19-14. The four pieces of information displayed are:

```
30-JAN-99 -> 28-FEB-99
27-FEB-99 -> 27-MAR-99
31-JAN-99 -> 28-FEB-99
28-FEB-99 -> 31-MAR-99
```

19-15. Statement (b) describes accurately the behavior of ADD_MONTHS when the date you pass to it is the last day of the month. This rule can result in less than desirable behavior, as shown in the previous problem. Specifically, if the number of days in the original date is less than the number of days in the resulting month, ADD_MONTHS treats "last day in month" as a logical condition and always returns the last day in the resulting month. So:

```
ADD_MONTHS ('28-FEB_99', 1)
```

results in a date value of March 31, 1999, rather than March 28, 1999. What if you want ADD_MONTHS to always return the "physically" matching date (i.e., the same day number in the resulting month)? See the "Expert" section for such a challenge.

19-16. Here is the database trigger:

```
CREATE OR REPLACE TRIGGER for_each_new_employee
    BEFORE insert
    ON employee FOR EACH ROW
BEGIN
    :new.hiredate := ROUND (:new.hire_date, 'HH');
END;
/
```

Expert

19-17. It's a bit more complex than it sounds at first. You need to use NEXT_ DAY to obtain the nearest earlier date and nearest later date. Then, perform date arithmetic to see how far away each is from the specified date. Finally, compare the "distances" and return the appropriate date. Here is one implementation:

```
/* Filename on web page: nearday.sf */
CREATE OR REPLACE FUNCTION nearestday (
   yourdate IN DATE, dayname IN VARCHAR2)
   RETURN DATE
IS
   before_date DATE := NEXT_DAY (yourdate-7, dayname);
   after_date DATE := NEXT_DAY (yourdate, dayname);

   before_diff NUMBER;
   after_diff NUMBER;
BEGIN
   before_diff := yourdate - before_date;
   after_diff := yourdate - after_date;
   IF before_diff < after_diff
   THEN
      RETURN before_date;
   ELSE
      RETURN after_date;
   END IF;
END;
/
```

19-18. You can take one of two approaches:

- Compute the number of Saturdays and Sundays between the two dates and subtract that from the total. I'll call this the "brute-force" method.

- Execute a loop from start date to end date and keep count, ignoring the weekend. I'll call this the "smart" method.

Here is a solution following the brute-force method:

```
/* Filename on web page: bizbetwn2.sf */
CREATE OR REPLACE FUNCTION bizdays_betwn (
   ld_date1 DATE,
   ld_date2 DATE)
RETURN NUMBER AS
   ln_diff      NUMBER;
   ln_bus_days NUMBER;
   ld_date      DATE;
BEGIN
   ln_diff := ABS (TO_NUMBER (ld_date2 - ld_date1)) + 1;
   IF ld_date1 < ld_date2
   THEN
      ld_date := ld_date1;
```

```
      ELSE
         ld_date := ld_date2;
      END IF;

      ln_bus_days := ln_diff;
      FOR i IN 1 .. ln_diff
      LOOP
         IF RTRIM (UPPER (TO_CHAR (ld_date + i - 1, 'DAY'))) IN
               ('SATURDAY', 'SUNDAY')
         THEN
            ln_bus_days := ln_bus_days - 1;
         END IF;
      END LOOP;
      RETURN ln_bus_days;
   END;
   /
```

The following function implements the smart method; it is the more concise and efficient of the two and was created by Solomon Yakobson:

```
/* Filename on web page: bizbetwn.sf */
/* Provided by Solomon Yakobson */
CREATE OR REPLACE FUNCTION bizdays_between (
   start_date IN DATE, end_date IN DATE)
   RETURN INTEGER
IS
   v_sundays INTEGER :=
      NEXT_DAY (end_date - 7, 'SUNDAY') -
      NEXT_DAY (start_date - 1, 'SUNDAY');

   v_saturdays INTEGER :=
      NEXT_DAY (end_date - 7, 'SATURDAY') -
      NEXT_DAY (start_date - 1, 'SATURDAY');
BEGIN
   RETURN (
      end_date -
      start_date -
      (v_sundays + v_saturdays)/7 - 1);
END;
/
```

19-19. Here is one possible implementation, building upon the smart method (in this version, I have also isolated the common "count for day" logic into its own function):

```
/* Filename on web page: bizbetwn3.sf */
CREATE TABLE holiday (dt DATE);

CREATE OR REPLACE FUNCTION daycount (
   start_date IN DATE, end_date IN DATE, dayname IN VARCHAR2)
   RETURN INTEGER
IS
BEGIN
   RETURN (
     NEXT_DAY (end_date - 7, dayname) -
     NEXT_DAY (start_date - 1, dayname)
     );
```

```
END;
/
CREATE OR REPLACE FUNCTION bizdays_between (
   start_date IN DATE, end_date IN DATE)
   RETURN INTEGER
IS
   holiday_count INTEGER;
BEGIN
   SELECT COUNT(*) INTO holiday_count
     FROM holiday
    WHERE dt BETWEEN start_date AND end_date;

   RETURN (
      end_date -
      start_date -
      (daycount (start_date, end_date, 'SUNDAY') +
       daycount (start_date, end_date, 'SATURDAY'))/7 - 1 - holiday_count);
END;
/
```

19-20. One possible implementation is shown next. Here's one complication to keep in mind: if you start on a Monday and ask NEXT_DAY to find the next Monday, it finds it one week in the future:

```
/* Filename on web page: nthday.sf */
CREATE OR REPLACE FUNCTION nthday (
   yourdate IN DATE, dayname IN VARCHAR2, nthday IN INTEGER := 1)
   RETURN DATE
IS
   /* Start with last day of previous month. */
      retval DATE := TRUNC (yourdate, 'MONTH') - 1;
BEGIN
   /* Start search in "nth week". */
   RETURN NEXT_DAY (retval + (nthday - 1) * 7, dayname);
END;
/
```

19-21. Here is a brute force implementation I threw together:

```
/* Filename on web page: maxdt1.sql */
DECLARE
    old_date DATE;
    curr_date DATE := SYSDATE;
BEGIN
    LOOP
old_date := curr_date;
       curr_date := curr_date + 1;
     END LOOP;
EXCEPTION
    WHEN OTHERS
    THEN
        DBMS_OUTPUT.PUT_LINE (SQLERRM);
        DBMS_OUTPUT.PUT_LINE ('Last date: ' ||
           TO_CHAR (old_Date, 'MM-DD-YYYY'));
END;
/
```

A number of my readers have pointed out that this is a rather slow implementation and offered dramatically more efficient versions. Here is one:

```
/* Filename on web page: maxdt2.sql */
DECLARE
    /* Initial implementation by Eva Blinder, modified by SF. */
    curr_date DATE := SYSDATE;
    last_date DATE;
    step PLS_INTEGER := 1000;
BEGIN
    LOOP
        BEGIN
            last_date := curr_date;
            curr_date := curr_date + step;
        EXCEPTION
            WHEN OTHERS
            THEN
                IF step = 1
                THEN
                    DBMS_OUTPUT.put_line (
                        'Last date: ' ||
                        TO_CHAR (
                            last_date,
                            'Month DD, YYYY'
                        )
                    );
                    EXIT;
                ELSE
                    step := step / 2;
                    curr_date := last_date;
                END IF;
        END;
    END LOOP;
END;
/
```

In this algorithm, the potential last date is moved forward by 1,000 days at a time. When you hit an error, you go back to the last good date and step forward by half that number of days. Keep doing that (reducing your step forward by half) until the step is 1, and that means you've gone as far forward as possible.

19-22. Here is one possible implementation:

```
/* Filename on web page: addmths.sf */
CREATE OR REPLACE FUNCTION new_add_months (
    date_in IN DATE, months_shift IN NUMBER)
    RETURN DATE
IS
    retval DATE;
BEGIN
    retval := ADD_MONTHS (date_in, months_shift);
```

```
    /* Is original date the last day of its month? */
    IF date_in = LAST_DAY (date_in)
    THEN
        retval :=
            LEAST (retval,
                TO_DATE (
                    TO_CHAR (date_in, 'DD') ||
                    TO_CHAR (retval, 'MMYYYY'),
                    'DDMMYYYY'));
    END IF;

    /* Return the shifted date */
    RETURN retval;
EXCEPTION
    WHEN OTHERS THEN RETURN retval;
END new_add_months;
/
```

The core logic here says that if the date you supplied is the last day of its month, construct a "physical" last day in the resulting month. If that day number exceeds the last actual day in the month, let the exception section trap the error and return the ADD_MONTHS standard value. Otherwise, return the earliest of the ADD_MONTHS value (the last day in the month) and the date with the matching day number.

When you run the same *lastday.sql* script (saved to *lastday2*) using new_ add_months instead of ADD_MONTHS, here are the results:

```
SQL> @lastday2
30-JAN-99 -> 28-FEB-99
27-FEB-99 -> 27-MAR-99
31-JAN-99 -> 28-FEB-99
28-FEB-99 -> 28-MAR-99
```

As you can see, 28-FEB-99 now shifts to 28-MAR-99, which is the desired behavior.

19-23. One possible implementation, relying on an index-by table of formats, is in the *datemgr.pkg* file on the book's web page.

You could also store the various formats in a database table and then use a query to loop through the valid format masks. This is more flexible (change the formats through SQL or a GUI interface: no need to change the code), but much slower. A middle-ground approach is to store the formats in a table, but read them into an index-by table in the package initialization section.

20

Conversion, Numeric, and Miscellaneous Functions

Beginner

20-1. There are two related functions that accept a variable number of parameters: GREATEST and LEAST. They are used to return the greatest value in a list of values (GREATEST) or the least value in that list (LEAST).

20-2. The snippet calls for you to use the LENGTH function to compute the length of the passed string. The wrinkle, though, is that the LENGTH function returns NULL, not zero, for a NULL string. Hence, you must wrap the call inside the NVL conversion function:

```
/* Print each character in a string */
CREATE OR REPLACE PROCEDURE nvl_test
   (i_val IN VARCHAR2 DEFAULT NULL)
IS
   str_len NUMBER := NVL (LENGTH (i_val), 0);
BEGIN
   FOR i IN 1 .. str_len
   LOOP
      DBMS_OUTPUT.put_line (UPPER (SUBSTR (i_val, i, 1)));
   END LOOP;
END;
```

20-3. Use the USER function to return the current user:

```
/* Set the name of the currently connected user */
BEGIN
   v_user := USER;
```

20-4. Use the USERENV function to return a variety of environment information, such as the current session ID. The function accepts a string representing the environment variable of interest:

ENTRYID

Auditing entry identifier

LANGUAGE

Current language, territory, and character set information

SESSIONID

Auditing session ID

TERMINAL

Operating system identifier for your current terminal

Here's an example of how to display the current session ID:

```
SQL> EXEC DBMS_OUTPUT.PUT_LINE(USERENV('SESSIONID'));
```

20-5. Use the ROWIDTOCHAR function to convert a ROWID to a string. Here's an example:

```
CREATE OR REPLACE PROCEDURE rowid_to_string
IS
    CURSOR emp_cur IS
        SELECT ROWID, ename FROM scott.emp;

    row_id VARCHAR2 (50);
BEGIN
    FOR rec IN emp_cur
    LOOP
        row_id := ROWIDTOCHAR (rec.ROWID);
        DBMS_OUTPUT.put_line (row_id);
    END LOOP;
END;
```

Executing this procedure returns something like this:

```
SQL> EXEC rowid_to_string
AAAAvUAACAAACN0AAA
AAAAvUAACAAACN0AAB
AAAAvUAACAAACN0AAC
AAAAvUAACAAACN0AAD
AAAAvUAACAAACN0AAE
AAAAvUAACAAACN0AAF
AAAAvUAACAAACN0AAG
...
```

20-6. Use the TO_CHAR function with the appropriate date format mask to format SYSDATE using a four-digit year:

```
CREATE OR REPLACE FUNCTION four_digit_today
    RETURN VARCHAR2
IS
BEGIN
    RETURN TO_CHAR (SYSDATE, 'DD-MON-YYYY');
END;
```

20-7. This exercise illustrates how the RR format handles two-digit years. Since the date ("10-JAN-19") falls before the middle of the century, the format assumes it's in the 21st century and returns the year 2019.

20-8. (e). Numeric functions are built-in as part of the core PL/SQL language.

20-9. The ABS function computes the absolute value of a number. For example:

```
ABS(-10)    = 10
ABS(-55.43) = 55.43
ABS(20)     = 20
ABS(0)      = 0
```

20-10. (d). Use the ROUND function to find the nearest whole number to an arbitrary number. For example:

```
ROUND(10.55) = 11
ROUND(10.45) = 10
```

Intermediate

20-11. The following function uses the MOD function to determine whether a number is odd:

```
CREATE OR REPLACE FUNCTION is_odd (i_val IN NUMBER)
    RETURN BOOLEAN
IS
BEGIN
    RETURN MOD (i_val, 2) = 1;
END;
```

20-12. (d). The SQLERRM function returns the error code for a passed error number.

20-13. You can print a general error message (or save it to a log) by using SQL-CODE and SQLERRM in the WHEN OTHERS exception:

```
CREATE OR REPLACE PROCEDURE code_test
IS
    dummy_val VARCHAR2 (5);
BEGIN
    dummy_val := 'This string is way too big!';
EXCEPTION
    WHEN OTHERS
    THEN
        DBMS_OUTPUT.put_line (
            'Error Code (' || TO_CHAR (SQLCODE) || '):' || SQLERRM
        );
END;
```

Running this procedure in SQL*Plus generates the following output:

```
SQL> EXEC code_test
Error Code (-6502):ORA-06502: PL/SQL: numeric or value error

PL/SQL procedure successfully completed.

SQL>
```

20-14. This table shows the formats required to produce the desired dates:

Desired Date	Required Format
May 21, 1994	'Month dd, yyyy'
05/21/94	'MM/DD/YY'
The 21st of May, 1994	'"The "DDth" of "Mon", "YYYY'
Quarter 2	'"Quarter "Q'
Week 21	'"Week "WW'
Week 3 in Month 05	'"Week "W" in Month "MM'
The 3rd week in May	'"The "Wth" week in "Month"'

20-15. You can use the NVL function to rewrite the code snippet in one line:

```
name_list ( NVL(name_list.LAST,0) + 1) := next_name ;
```

20-16. The following function uses the TO_NUMBER built-in function to determine whether the passed string is a number:

```
CREATE OR REPLACE FUNCTION is_number (i_val IN VARCHAR2)
    RETURN BOOLEAN
IS
    tmp NUMBER;
BEGIN
    tmp := TO_NUMBER (i_val);
    RETURN TRUE;
EXCEPTION
    WHEN OTHERS
    THEN
        RETURN FALSE;
END;
```

20-17. Since the ABS function always returns a positive number, the program outputs: "It's positive".

20-18. The most reliable method is to add a counter variable and then use the MOD function to determine if it's a multiple of three:

```
DECLARE
    i NUMBER DEFAULT 0;

    CURSOR curs_get_numbers IS
        SELECT * FROM a_bunch_of_numbers;
BEGIN
    FOR v_number_rec IN curs_get_numbers
    LOOP
        i := i + 1;
        IF MOD (i, 3) = 0
        THEN
            DBMS_OUTPUT.put_line (v_number_rec.number_col1);
        END IF;
    END LOOP;
END;
```

20-19. The following snippet shows how you can use the TO_CHAR function to format an index into a table of quarterly totals:

```
FOR exp_rec IN exp_cur LOOP
    q_idx := TO_NUMBER (TO_CHAR (exp_rec.expense_date, 'Q'));
    quarter (q_idx) := quarter (q_idx) + exp_rec.amount;
END LOOP;
```

20-20. The procedure produces the following table of numbers:

0	10	11	11.1	11.12
0	10	11	11.1	11.13
0	10	11	11.1	11.14
0	10	11	11.2	11.15
0	10	11	11.2	11.16

Expert

20-21. Use the FM (fill mode) format mask element to suppress padding and leading zeros. FM works like a toggle: the first occurrence in the format mask turns suppression on, the second turns it off, and so on. Here is an example:

```
DECLARE
    d DATE := TO_DATE ('01-MAY-1994', 'DD-MON-YYYY');
BEGIN
    -- Normal output
    DBMS_OUTPUT.put_line (TO_CHAR (d, 'Month DD, YYYY'));
    -- Suppress padding and leading zeros
    DBMS_OUTPUT.put_line (TO_CHAR (d, 'FMMonth DD, YYYY'));
    -- Suppress padding but display leading zeros (FM is a toggle)
    DBMS_OUTPUT.put_line (TO_CHAR (d, 'FMMonth FMDD, YYYY'));
END;

SQL> /
May       01, 1994
May 1, 1994
May 01, 1994

PL/SQL procedure successfully completed.

SQL>
```

20-22. You can use the FX (format exact) format mask element to require that a date have a specific format (i.e., that it use hyphens as delimiters); the TO_CHAR function raises an exception if the string is not in the required format. If the passed string doesn't contain the correct literal characters (e.g., hypens, slashes), TO_DATE raises the exception:

```
ORA-01861: literal does not match format string
```

If the string doesn't have the expected date format (e.g., two-digit year instead of four, one-digit month instead of two, MONTH format instead of MON), TO_DATE raises the exception:

```
ORA-01862: the numeric value does not match the length of the format item

Testing exact match for FXDD-MON-YYYY
21-MAY-1999 => Format Okay
01/MAY/1999 => ORA-01861: literal does not match format string
01-MAY-99   => ORA-01862: the numeric value does not match the
   length of the format item
1-MAY-1999  => ORA-01862: the numeric value does not match the
   length of the format item
01/05/1994  => ORA-01861: literal does not match format string
01-JAN-2001 => Format Okay
```

20-23. Here is just one possible solution to the problem of converting a general string into a date. The system, which is implemented as a package, uses an index-by table to hold a number of potential date formats. The conversion function loops through each element, applying its format to the passed string:

```
/* Filename on web page: mydate.pkg */
CREATE OR REPLACE PACKAGE my_date IS
   FUNCTION get_date (dt_str IN VARCHAR2) RETURN DATE;
END;

CREATE OR REPLACE PACKAGE BODY my_date IS
   TYPE date_fmt_t IS TABLE OF VARCHAR2 (30)
      INDEX BY BINARY_INTEGER;

   target_format date_fmt_t;
   /*
   || Call the to_date function to see if the string passed matches the
   || current format. If so, return the date.  If not, trap the exception
   || and return null.
   */
   FUNCTION test_date (dt_str IN VARCHAR2, target IN VARCHAR2)
      RETURN DATE
   IS
      d DATE;
   BEGIN
      RETURN TO_DATE (dt_str, target);
   EXCEPTION
      WHEN OTHERS THEN
         RETURN NULL;
   END;

   FUNCTION get_date (dt_str IN VARCHAR2)
      RETURN DATE
   IS
      ret_val DATE DEFAULT NULL;
   BEGIN
      FOR i IN target_format.FIRST .. target_format.LAST
```

```
      LOOP
         ret_val := test_date (dt_str, target_format (i));
         EXIT WHEN ret_val IS NOT NULL;    -- exit when we find a match
      END LOOP;

      RETURN ret_val;
   END;

   -- Use the initialization section to populate the
   -- array of supported formats
   BEGIN
      target_format (1) := 'MM/DD';
      target_format (2) := 'MM/DD/YY';
      target_format (3) := 'MM/DD/YYYY';
      target_format (4) := 'DD-MON';
      target_format (5) := 'MON DD, YYYY';
      target_format (6) := 'MONTH DD, YYYY';
      target_format (7) := 'DD-MON-YY';
      target_format (8) := 'DD-MON-YYYY';
      target_format (9) := 'MON-DD-YYYY';
   END;
```

20-24. You must use the ABS function to select the columns where the difference between number_col1 and number_col2 is less than or equal to 25:

```
SELECT *
  FROM a_bunch_of_numbers
 WHERE ABS (number_col1 - number_col2) <= 25
/
```

20-25. Here's one possible solution for generating the sequence. Notice the combined use of character functions (to determine the length of the string) and numeric functions (to generate each number of the sequence):

```
/* Filename on web page: num_manip.pkg */
CREATE OR REPLACE PACKAGE BODY number_manipulation
IS
   FUNCTION gen_trial (p_number NUMBER)
      RETURN v_num_table_type
   IS
      ret_val v_num_table_type;
      n NUMBER;
      mult NUMBER := 10;
   BEGIN
      n := NVL (LENGTH (TO_CHAR (p_number)), 0);

      FOR i IN 1 .. n - 1
      LOOP
         ret_val (i) := TRUNC (p_number / mult) * mult;
         mult := mult * 10;
      END LOOP;

      RETURN ret_val;
   END;
```

```
          PROCEDURE test (i_val IN NUMBER)
          IS
             result_set v_num_table_type;
          BEGIN
             result_set := gen_trial (i_val);

             FOR i IN result_set.FIRST .. result_set.LAST
             LOOP
                DBMS_OUTPUT.put_line (result_set (i));
             END LOOP;
          END;
       END;

       SQL> EXEC number_manipulation.test(1111);
       1110
       1100
       1000

       SQL> EXEC number_manipulation.test(12345678);
       12345670
       12345600
       12345000
       12340000
       12300000
       12000000
       10000000
```

20-26. The tricky part here is to use the TRUNC function (or CEIL or FLOOR) to determine whether the number is a whole number or not:

```
SELECT number_col1 FROM a_bunch_of_numbers
   WHERE TRUNC (SQRT (number_col1)) = SQRT (number_col1);

NUMBER_COL1
-----------
          1
          4
          9
         16
         25
         36
         49
         64
         81
        100
```

21

DBMS_SQL Built-in Package

Beginner

21-1. Dynamic SQL means that the SQL string, whether it be a SELECT statement or a DDL statement like CREATE TABLE, is constructed as the program is running, rather than when it is compiled.

21-2. Dynamic PL/SQL means that the PL/SQL block of code is constructed as the program is running, rather than when it is compiled.

21-3. The four methods of dynamic SQL are:

Method 1

Non-queries (DDL and DML—inserts, updates, deletes) that do not have any placeholders (do not bind any variables from the calling program).

Method 2

Nonqueries (DDL and DML—inserts, updates, deletes) that contain a fixed (at compile time) number of placeholders.

Method 3

Queries (SELECT statements) that contain a fixed (at compile time) number of columns and placeholders.

Method 4

Queries and DML statements that contain a variable number of columns and/or placeholders. There is no way to know, in other words, until runtime just how many columns you are querying or placeholders you are binding to variables.

21-4. A placeholder is an identifier (maximum of 30 characters, must start with a letter, and then may contain letters, numbers, or any of the characters #, $ and _) preceded by a colon, appearing inside a literal string, as in:

```
'SELECT latest_excuse
   FROM pentagon
  WHERE budget_overrun > :amount'
```

In this string, ":amount" is a placeholder, which means you have to "bind" a value to that placeholder before you can execute the query. Notice that I have embedded line breaks inside the query. That doesn't cause any problems when you parse the query.

21-5. Use DBMS_SQL.OPEN_CURSOR to open a dynamic cursor.

21-6. Use DBMS_SQL.CLOSE_CURSOR to close a dynamic cursor.

21-7. Use DBMS_SQL.PARSE to parse a dynamic SQL string.

21-8. Use DBMS_SQL.EXECUTE and DBMS_SQL.EXECUTE_AND_FETCH to execute a dynamic cursor.

21-9. Use DBMS_SQL.EXECUTE_AND_FETCH (just the first row) and DBMS_SQL.FETCH_ROWS (more than one row) to fetch rows from a dynamic cursor.

21-10. Use the following programs to extract values:

DBMS_SQL.COLUMN_VALUE,
DBMS_SQL.COLUMN_VALUE_ROWID,
DBMS_SQL.VARIABLE_VALUE,
DBMS_SQL.COLUMN_VALUE_LONG,
DBMS_SQL.COLUMN_VALUE_RAW,

21-11. You can either concatenate the values into your string or bind those values. Here is an example of concatenation:

```
BEGIN
   my_query :=
     'SELECT description FROM good_deeds where type = ' || deed_type;
```

And here is that same SQL string using a placeholder (to which a value must be bound with a call to DBMS_SQL.BIND_VARIABLE) instead:

```
BEGIN
   my_query :=
     'SELECT description FROM good_deeds where type = :dtype';
```

21-12. Here is the correct order of steps needed to execute dynamic DML:

Open the cursor.
Parse the SQL statement string.
Bind any variables into place holders.
Execute the cursor.
Close the cursor.

These are the steps that are needed only for dynamic queries:

Define the type of the columns (after parse and before execute).

Fetch a row (after execute).

Extract the value from a column in the fetched row (after fetch).

21-13. The following create_index procedure handles both single and multiple column indexes:

```
/* Filename on web page: creind.sp */
CREATE OR REPLACE PROCEDURE create_index (
    index_in IN VARCHAR2,
    tab_in IN VARCHAR2,
    col_in IN VARCHAR2
    )
IS
    cur  PLS_INTEGER := DBMS_SQL.OPEN_CURSOR;
    fdbk PLS_INTEGER;
BEGIN
    DBMS_SQL.PARSE (
        cur,
        'CREATE INDEX ' || index_in ||
        ' ON ' || tab_in || ' ( ' || col_in ||')',
        DBMS_SQL.native
    );
    fdbk := DBMS_SQL.EXECUTE (cur);
    DBMS_SQL.CLOSE_CURSOR (cur);
END;
/
```

21-14. To fetch a row you call DBMS_SQL.FETCH_ROWS. If this function returns 0, you are at the end of the result set. Here's an example:

```
LOOP
    EXIT WHEN DBMS_SQL.FETCH_ROWS (cur) = 0;
    DBMS_SQL.COLUMN_VALUE (cur, 2, rec.last_name);
    DBMS_OUTPUT.PUT_LINE (rec.last_name);
END LOOP;
```

Intermediate

21-15. The steps are:

1. Open the cursor:

```
OPEN_CURSOR
```

2. Parse the SQL statement string:

```
PARSE
```

3. Define the type of each of the columns:

```
DEFINE_COLUMN
DEFINE_COLUMN_LONG
DEFINE_ARRAY
```

4. Bind any variables into placeholders:

```
BIND_VARIABLE
BIND_ARRAY
```

5. Execute the cursor:

```
EXECUTE
EXECUTE_AND_FETCH
```

6. Fetch a row:

```
FETCH_ROWS
```

7. Extract the value from a column in the fetched row (after fetch):

```
COLUMN_VALUE
COLUMN_VALUE_LONG
COLUMN_VALUE_ROWID
COLUMN_VALUE_RAW
COLUMN_VALUE_CHAR
```

8. Close the cursor:

```
CLOSE_CURSOR
```

21-16. When you fetch past the last row with DBMS_SQL.FETCH_ROWS, the PL/SQL runtime engine raises the error:

```
ORA-01002: fetch out of sequence
```

To demonstrate this behavior, run the *queens.sql* script (found on the book's web page). It creates a table named corporate_welfare_queens and then runs an infinite loop to fetch forever against that table (there might be that many corporations on the dole, but there are only three rows in the table). The result is this output:

```
McDonald's
General Electric
Boeing
Boeing
DECLARE
*
ERROR at line 1:
ORA-01002: fetch out of sequence
```

21-17. The DBMS_SQL.EXECUTE_AND_FETCH function is comparable to SELECT INTO. It executes the query and then tries to fetch the first row.

21-18. It might raise the TOO_MANY_ROWS exception (just as SELECT INTO does), or it might ignore that problem. The behavior of EXECUTE_AND_ FETCH in a "TOO MANY ROWS" situation is something you can control. The header for this function is:

```
FUNCTION DBMS_SQL.EXECUTE_AND_FETCH (
   c IN INTEGER
  ,exact IN BOOLEAN DEFAULT FALSE)
RETURN INTEGER;
```

If the second argument is FALSE (the default), TOO_MANY_ROWS isn't raised; you have not requested an exact match. If you pass TRUE for this second argument, the runtime engine raises the TOO_MANY_ROWS exception if more than one row is fetched.

21-19. In the current versions of the Oracle RDBMS, it's actually not necessary to execute the dynamic DDL statement. Up through Oracle 8.1 at least, the simple act of parsing DDL also executes that DDL and performs a COMMIT. However, Oracle warns in the DBMS_SQL specification that you should not assume this behavior; it might change in later versions. Consequently, you should always execute your DDL.

21-20. No, DBMS_SQL is smart enough to know that when it parsed the cursor, the statement was executed. When you call DBMS_SQL.EXECUTE and pass it the same cursor pointer, it ignores the request (again, that is current behavior; you should not depend on it in the future).

21-21. No, this doesn't cause any kind of problem or confusion. As you can see, the BIND_VARIABLE procedure allows you to associate a named identifier or placeholder in the string with a variable or value. There is no need for you to name your variables to match your placeholders.

21-22. Call the DBMS_SQL.IS_OPEN function, as shown here:

```
PROCEDURE exec_cursor (cur IN INTEGER)
IS
BEGIN
   IF DBMS_SQL.IS_OPEN (cur)
   THEN
```

21-23. One of the restrictions in Oracle Developer (all versions) concerning access to stored code is as follows: if you want to include a reference to a stored packaged element inside Oracle Developer's client-side PL/SQL engine, that element can be only a function or a procedure. DBMS_SQL. NATIVE is a constant and, therefore, cannot be referenced.

21-24. I have replaced any reference to the DBMS_SQL language flag constants with a literal value. How was I able to do this? I checked out the DBMS_SQL package specification source code (located in *dbmssql.sql* in the *$ORACLE_HOME/RdbmsNN/admin* directory) and found these lines:

```
--  CONSTANTS
v6 constant integer := 0;
native constant integer := 1;
v7 constant integer := 2;
```

I could then replace my reference to DBMS_SQL.NATIVE with its value. The problem with this approach is that I have now (1) exposed otherwise hidden values and (2) hardcoded those values. If Oracle ever decides to change the values, my code will no longer work properly.

How can you get around having to supply the language flag constant each time you perform a parse?

Cover it up. Here is one scenario: you want to call DBMS_SQL.PARSE from Oracle Forms, but can't reference the named constant and shouldn't put in a literal value. What to do instead? Write a "wrapper" around DBMS_SQL.PARSE as in the following:

```
CREATE OR REPLACE PROCEDURE parse_it (
   cur IN INTEGER, sqlstr IN VARCHAR2, langflag IN INTEGER := NULL)
IS
BEGIN
   DBMS_SQL.PARSE (cur, sqlstr, NVL (langflag, DBMS_SQL.NATIVE));
END;
```

Now when you call parse_it from Oracle Forms, you don't have to specify a language flag, and it automatically uses DBMS_SQL.NATIVE. And even if you are not working in Oracle Developer, this procedure can be handy since server-side developers also do not have to worry about the language flag.

21-25. Here is a reconstruction of the updnumval function that removes almost all the concatenation:

```
/* Filename on web page: bind.sp */
CREATE OR REPLACE PROCEDURE updnumval (
   col_in IN VARCHAR2,
   start_in IN DATE,
   end_in IN DATE,
   val_in IN NUMBER)
IS
   cur PLS_INTEGER := DBMS_SQL.OPEN_CURSOR;
   fdbk PLS_INTEGER;
BEGIN
   DBMS_SQL.PARSE (cur, 'UPDATE emp SET ' ||
      col_in ||
      ' = :val WHERE hiredate BETWEEN :lodate AND :hidate',
      DBMS_SQL.NATIVE);

   DBMS_SQL.BIND_VARIABLE (cur, 'val', val_in);
   DBMS_SQL.BIND_VARIABLE (cur, 'lodate', start_in);
   DBMS_SQL.BIND_VARIABLE (cur, 'hidate', end_in);

   fdbk := DBMS_SQL.EXECUTE (cur);

   DBMS_OUTPUT.PUT_LINE ('Rows updated: ' || TO_CHAR (fdbk));
   DBMS_SQL.CLOSE_CURSOR (cur);
END;
/
```

Bind in the new value, the start date, and the end date. You still concatenate the name of the column, because you can only bind variables (as the name of the procedure implies). You cannot bind structural elements of the SQL statement, such as table names, clause keywords, and so on. They can only be concatenated.

21-26. Whenever possible, you should bind instead of concatenate variables. Here are the reasons:

- If you bind, then if you need to reexecute the SQL statement with a different value, you just rebind and execute. The previously parsed version of the SQL statement is reused. If you concatenate, you must reparse and execute; this is much more expensive.

- If you bind, you let PL/SQL take care of datatype conversions, if any are necessary; generally, when you bind, you work with native datatypes. If you concatenate, you have to convert from dates to strings to dates, and so on. This is much more complicated and error-prone.

Generally, you should concatenate only when you need to place in the SQL statement string a structural element of the statement, such as the name of a table or a column, or an entire WHERE clause.

21-27. This block reflects the mistaken belief of many developers that you need to open a new cursor for each different SQL statement. Not at all. You can reuse the same dynamic SQL cursor again and again; just parse a new SQL statement to the cursor, and it is ready to meet your new requirements. So you can rewrite the previous code to:

```
DECLARE
    cur PLS_INTEGER := DBMS_SQL.OPEN_CURSOR;
BEGIN
    DBMS_SQL.PARSE (cur,
        'SELECT ename FROM emp',
        DBMS_SQL.NATIVE);

    ... execute and fetch ...

    DBMS_SQL.PARSE (cur,
        'UPDATE emp SET sal = sal * 3',
        DBMS_SQL.NATIVE);

    ... execute the update ...

    DBMS_SQL.CLOSE_CURSOR (cur);

END;
```

21-28. There are no rows in the internet_startups table. When you parse a DDL statement, it also executes and issues a COMMIT (at least through Oracle 8.1). So the deletion from internet_startups is committed, and the later ROLLBACK has no effect.

21-29. I hope you can see the pattern; the procedure simply executes a different procedure (by number) to process that specific line item number. If you isolate the line number, you're really running the same code over and over again. You can generalize the pattern into a dynamic PL/SQL block as shown in the rewrite:

```
PROCEDURE process_lineitem (line_in IN INTEGER)
IS
   cur PLS_INTEGER := DBMS_SQL.OPEN_CURSOR;
   fdbk PLS_INTEGER;
BEGIN
   DBMS_SQL.PARSE (
      cur,
      'BEGIN process_line' || line_in || '; END;',
      DBMS_SQL.NATIVE
      );

   fdbk := DBMS_SQL.EXECUTE (cur);

   DBMS_SQL.CLOSE_CURSOR (cur);
END;
```

You don't always get such dramatic improvements by moving to dynamic SQL, but when you do, they sure are easy to appreciate!

21-30. You can use DBMS_SQL.VARIABLE_VALUE to extract a value from a dynamically constructed and executed PL/SQL block, as in:

```
BEGIN
   cur := open_and_parse
      ('BEGIN get_max_sal (:deptin, :salout); END;');

   DBMS_SQL.BIND_VARIABLE (cur, 'deptin', v_deptin);
   DBMS_SQL.BIND_VARIABLE (cur, 'salout', my_salary);

   fdbk := DBMS_SQL.EXECUTE (cur);

   DBMS_SQL.VARIABLE_VALUE (cur, 'salout', my_salary);
END;
```

21-31. Here is one possible approach:

```
/* Filename on web page: updnumval.sp */
CREATE OR REPLACE PROCEDURE updnumval (
   col_in IN VARCHAR2,
   val_in IN NUMBER,
   where_in IN VARCHAR2 := NULL)
IS
   cur PLS_INTEGER := DBMS_SQL.OPEN_CURSOR;
   fdbk PLS_INTEGER;
BEGIN
   DBMS_SQL.PARSE (cur,
      'UPDATE emp SET ' || col_in || ' = :val ' ||
      NVL (where_in, 'WHERE 1=1'),
      DBMS_SQL.NATIVE);

   DBMS_SQL.BIND_VARIABLE (cur, 'val', val_in);

   fdbk := DBMS_SQL.EXECUTE (cur);
```

```
      DBMS_OUTPUT.PUT_LINE ('Rows updated: ' || TO_CHAR (fdbk));
      DBMS_SQL.CLOSE_CURSOR (cur);
   END;
   /
```

21-32. This procedure (defined in a package so that you can define a table TYPE to serve as the argument to the procedure) accepts a list of names of advertisers. For each name in the index-by table, it then deletes from the media's coverage any content that is critical of the advertiser. What? You don't think it works that way? Well, probably not with this kind of software, anyway.

In any case, the problem with this procedure is that it opens a new cursor for each advertiser (which is simply unnecessary), but it only closes the cursor after the loop finishes executing. If there are too many advertisers (that's my opinion), the session could actually hit the limit of open cursors and generate an error.

The only element of the SQL statement that changes with each iteration is the name of the advertiser. So, change the loop to execute as follows:

```
cursor_id := DBMS_SQL.OPEN_CURSOR;
LOOP
   EXIT WHEN list_row IS NULL;

   DBMS_SQL.PARSE(
      cursor_id,
      'DELETE negativity
        FROM media_coverage
        WHERE company_mentioned = :advname',
      DBMS_SQL.NATIVE);

   DBMS_SQL.BIND_VARIABLE (
      cursor_id,
      'advname',
      list(list_row));

   exec_stat := DBMS_SQL.EXECUTE(cursor_id);

   list_row := list.NEXT (list_row);
END LOOP;
DBMS_SQL.CLOSE_CURSOR(cursor_id);
```

21-33. Four cursors are opened, and only one is closed. The static cursor (all_employees) closes automatically when the PL/SQL block terminates. You don't have to include a statement such as:

```
CLOSE all_employees;
```

What other cursors are there? Two dynamic SQL cursors (I opened a cursor in the declaration section and then forgot, and did it again in the executable section) and a single packaged cursor (department_pkg.all_departments). All three are opened and not closed; all three have "global" scope. A dynamic SQL cursor only closes if you close it explicitly; the same is true for a packaged cursor.

21-34. Here is one solution:

```
/* Filename on web page: showemps.sp */
CREATE OR REPLACE PROCEDURE showemps (
    where_in IN VARCHAR2 := NULL )
IS
    cur INTEGER := DBMS_SQL.OPEN_CURSOR;
    rec employee%ROWTYPE;
    fdbk INTEGER;
BEGIN
    DBMS_SQL.PARSE
        (cur, 'SELECT employee_id, last_name FROM employee ' ||
            ' WHERE ' || NVL (where_in, '1=1'),
        DBMS_SQL.NATIVE);

    DBMS_SQL.DEFINE_COLUMN (cur, 1, 1);
    DBMS_SQL.DEFINE_COLUMN (cur, 2, user, 30);

    fdbk := DBMS_SQL.EXECUTE (cur);
    LOOP
        /* Fetch next row. Exit when done. */
        EXIT WHEN DBMS_SQL.FETCH_ROWS (cur) = 0;
        DBMS_SQL.COLUMN_VALUE (cur, 1, rec.employee_id);
        DBMS_SQL.COLUMN_VALUE (cur, 2, rec.last_name);
        DBMS_OUTPUT.PUT_LINE (TO_CHAR (rec.employee_id) ||
            '=' || rec.last_name);
    END LOOP;

    DBMS_SQL.CLOSE_CURSOR (cur);
END;
/
```

21-35. If you try to close a dynamic SQL cursor that has been previously closed, you get this error:

```
ORA-01001: invalid cursor
```

If you want to make sure you never close a cursor that has already been closed, create a wrapper around DBMS_SQL.CLOSE_CURSOR like this:

```
/* Filename on web page: closecur.sp */
CREATE OR REPLACE PROCEDURE closecur (cur_in IN INTEGER)
IS
BEGIN
    IF DBMS_SQL.IS_OPEN (cur_in);
    THEN
        DBMS_SQL.CLOSE_CURSOR (cur_in);
    END IF;
END;
/
```

21-36. What information do you need to debug the problem more effectively? You need to see the SQL statement; most of the errors you encounter in

DBMS_SQL find their origins in mistakes made constructing an often-complex string from individual pieces:

```
/* Filename on web page: dynerr.sql */
DECLARE
    cur PLS_INTEGER := DBMS_SQL.OPEN_CURSOR;
    errpos PLS_INTEGER;
    mySQL VARCHAR2(200) :=
        'SELECT ename FROM emp WHER deptno = 10';
BEGIN
    DBMS_SQL.PARSE (cur, mySQL, DBMS_SQL.NATIVE);
EXCEPTION
    WHEN OTHERS
    THEN
        errpos := DBMS_SQL.LAST_ERROR_POSITION;
        DBMS_OUTPUT.PUT_LINE (SQLERRM);
        DBMS_OUTPUT.PUT_LINE (mySQL);
        DBMS_OUTPUT.PUT_LINE (LPAD ('^', errpos, '-'));
        DBMS_SQL.CLOSE_CURSOR (cur);
        RAISE;
END;
```

If you run this block of code with the exception section, you get the following output (assuming SERVEROUTPUT is turned on):

```
ORA-00933: SQL command not properly ended
SELECT ename FROM emp WHER deptno = 10
-------------------------^
DECLARE
*
ERROR at line 1:
ORA-00933: SQL command not properly ended
ORA-06512: at line 15
```

As you can see, the SQL statement that caused the error is displayed. I have even used the LAST_ERROR_POSITION function to point to the place in the SQL string where the parser had a problem. I also make sure to close the cursor so I don't leave an open cursor "hanging" and uncloseable in my session. Finally, I reraise the exception so it stops processing in the outer block.

21-37. Call the DBMS_SQL.LAST_SQL_FUNCTION_CODE function. If you just requested a CREATE TABLE, for example, this functions returns 1. A TRUNCATE TABLE action returns a code of 85, and so on. You can find a complete list of codes in *Oracle Built-in Packages*, Chapter 2.

21-38. The DBMS_SQL.LAST_ROW_COUNT function returns the number of rows fetched at that point from the last dynamic SQL cursor. The header for this function is:

```
FUNCTION DBMS_SQL.LAST_ROW_COUNT RETURN INTEGER;
```

Notice that it does not take a cursor pointer for an argument. This function always returns information about the last dynamic SQL cursor fetched from in your session.

21-39. The following implementation executes the DDL; if there is any problem, the exception section displays the DDL string and closes the cursor:

```
/* Filename on web page: runddl.sp */
CREATE OR REPLACE PROCEDURE runddl (ddl_in in VARCHAR2)
IS
    cur INTEGER:= DBMS_SQL.OPEN_CURSOR;
    fdbk INTEGER;
BEGIN
    DBMS_SQL.PARSE (cur, ddl_in, DBMS_SQL.NATIVE);
    fdbk := DBMS_SQL.EXECUTE (cur);
    DBMS_SQL.CLOSE_CURSOR (cur);
EXCEPTION
    WHEN OTHERS
    THEN
        fdbk := DBMS_SQL.LAST_ERROR_POSITION;
        DBMS_OUTPUT.PUT_LINE (
            SQLERRM || CHR(10) ||
            ddl_in || CHR(10) ||
            LPAD ('^', fdbk, '-'));
        DBMS_SQL.CLOSE_CURSOR (cur);
        RAISE;
END;
/
```

21-40. This is a "classic" problem in the world of PL/SQL. There are two things to keep in mind:

- The PL/SQL compiler ignores privileges granted through roles; it uses only directly granted privileges.

- Stored code runs under the authority of the owner of the code, not the invoker of the code (this restriction is avoidable in Oracle 8.1 with the AUTHID feature, but holds true for all prior releases).

If SCOTT is going to take advantage of a central code repository, then that central schema, in this case allcode, needs to have all the privileges necessary to perform actions in other schemas. In other words, for SCOTT to be able to use allcode.runddl to create a table, allcode must be granted explicitly the CREATE ANY TABLE privilege.

21-41. The implementation is most easily accomplished with EXECUTE_AND_FETCH:

```
/* Filename on web page: tabcount.sf */
CREATE OR REPLACE FUNCTION tabcount (
    sch IN VARCHAR2,
    tab IN VARCHAR2)
    RETURN INTEGER
IS
```

```
    cur     INTEGER  := DBMS_SQL.OPEN_CURSOR;
    ignore  INTEGER;
    retval  INTEGER;
BEGIN
    DBMS_SQL.PARSE (cur, 'SELECT COUNT(*) FROM ' ||
        sch || '.' || tab, DBMS_SQL.NATIVE);
    DBMS_SQL.DEFINE_COLUMN (cur, 1, retval);
    ignore := DBMS_SQL.EXECUTE_AND_FETCH (cur);
    DBMS_SQL.COLUMN_VALUE (cur, 1, retval);
    DBMS_SQL.CLOSE_CURSOR (cur);
    RETURN retval;
END;
/
```

21-42. Two things to keep in mind as you extend the implementation in the *tab-count.sf* file on this book's web page (or your own):

- Provide a default value for the WHERE clause parameter so that all rows are counted if no WHERE clause is provided.

- You can use an IF clause to build the query (IF *WHERE clause* IS NULL ... ELSE) or compress the code a bit by using the NVL function, as you see in this example:

```
/* Filename on web page: tabcount2.sf */
CREATE OR REPLACE FUNCTION tabcount (
    sch IN VARCHAR2,
    tab IN VARCHAR2,
    whr IN VARCHAR2 := NULL)
    RETURN INTEGER
IS
    cur     INTEGER  := DBMS_SQL.OPEN_CURSOR;
    ignore  INTEGER;
    retval  INTEGER;
BEGIN
    DBMS_SQL.PARSE (cur,
        'SELECT COUNT(*)
            FROM ' || sch || '.' || tab ||
        ' WHERE ' || NVL (whr, '1=1'), DBMS_SQL.NATIVE);
    DBMS_SQL.DEFINE_COLUMN (cur, 1, retval);
    ignore := DBMS_SQL.EXECUTE_AND_FETCH (cur);
    DBMS_SQL.COLUMN_VALUE (cur, 1, retval);
    DBMS_SQL.CLOSE_CURSOR (cur);
    RETURN retval;
END;
/
```

Expert

21-43. You can do (a), (c), (d), and (f) with DBMS_SQL. You can't do any of the following:

b. Set a role by executing the ALTER SESSION SET ROLE DDL statement. You cannot alter a role for the current session from within a

PL/SQL stored procedure at all, either through DBMS_SQL or through a call to DBMS_SESSION.SET_ROLE (you can only call this procedure from an anonymous block!).

e. Declare a cursor variable based on a REF CURSOR type and retrieve that variable's value. You cannot declare a cursor variable and manipulate it dynamically.

g. Connect to another database session with the CONNECT statement. The CONNECT command is not a part of SQL; rather, it is a SQL*Plus command.

21-44. This functionality is similar to "indirect referencing" in Oracle Forms, where you use COPY and NAME_IN to write and read, respectively, the value of a GLOBAL variable or block's item by referencing its name. One possible solution follows: it constructs, in a straightforward manner and completely with concatenation, the assignment statement. It then executes the statement:

```
/* Filename on web page: assign.sp */
CREATE OR REPLACE PROCEDURE assign (
    val_in IN VARCHAR2, varname_in IN VARCHAR2)
IS
    cur PLS_INTEGER := DBMS_SQL.OPEN_CURSOR;
    fdbk PLS_INTEGER;
    assign_string VARCHAR2(2000) :=
        'BEGIN ' ||
        varname_in || ' := ''' ||
        val_in || '''; END;';
BEGIN
    DBMS_OUTPUT.PUT_LINE (assign_string);
    DBMS_SQL.PARSE (cur, assign_string, DBMS_SQL.NATIVE);
    fdbk := DBMS_SQL.EXECUTE (cur);
    DBMS_SQL.CLOSE_CURSOR (cur);
END;
/
```

21-45. The reason for the error is that even though you can execute a dynamic PL/SQL block within another, static block, the scope of the dynamic block is your session, not the enclosing block. From a practical standpoint, this means that the only program elements (procedures, functions, variables, etc.) your dynamic PL/SQL block can reference are those which are "globally" available in your session: standalone procedures and functions or elements defined in a package specification.

Here, for example, is a rewrite of the previous script that works just fine:

```
/* Filename on web page: greetings.sql */
CREATE OR REPLACE PACKAGE greetings
IS
    TYPE str_t IS TABLE OF VARCHAR2(100)
        INDEX BY BINARY_INTEGER;
```

```
      list str_t;
END;
/


DECLARE
   v_row PLS_INTEGER;
BEGIN
   greetings.list.DELETE;
   FOR yearnum IN 1 .. 10
   LOOP
      assign (
         ' Welcome to Year ' || TO_CHAR (yearnum),
         'greetings.list(' || TO_CHAR(yearnum) || ')',
         trc => FALSE);
   END LOOP;

   v_row := greetings.list.FIRST;
   LOOP
      EXIT WHEN v_row IS NULL;
      DBMS_OUTPUT.PUT_LINE (greetings.list(v_row));
      v_row := greetings.list.NEXT (v_row);
   END LOOP;
END;
/
```

This displays the following output:

```
Welcome to Year 1
Welcome to Year 2
Welcome to Year 3
Welcome to Year 4
Welcome to Year 5
Welcome to Year 6
Welcome to Year 7
Welcome to Year 8
Welcome to Year 9
Welcome to Year 10
```

21-46. The trick here is that you cannot pass the local variable by name. Instead, you pass in the variable itself as an IN OUT argument. The dynamic PL/SQL block executes the assignment to a placeholder/bind variable, and then you extract the value into the IN OUT argument. Here is one possible implementation:

```
/* Filename on web page: assigndt.sp */
CREATE OR REPLACE PROCEDURE assigndt (
   expr_in IN DATE,
   var_inout IN OUT DATE)
IS
   cur PLS_INTEGER := DBMS_SQL.OPEN_CURSOR;
   fdbk PLS_INTEGER;
BEGIN
   DBMS_SQL.PARSE (cur,
      'BEGIN :var := :dtval; END;', DBMS_SQL.NATIVE);
   DBMS_SQL.BIND_VARIABLE (cur, 'var', SYSDATE);
```

```
        DBMS_SQL.BIND_VARIABLE (cur, 'dtval', expr_in);
        fdbk := DBMS_SQL.EXECUTE (cur);
        DBMS_SQL.VARIABLE_VALUE (cur, 'var', var_inout);
     END;
     /
```

With this program in place, you can execute this test script successfully:

```
SQL> DECLARE
  2       dt DATE;
  3  BEGIN
  4       assigndt (SYSDATE + 10, dt);
  5       DBMS_OUTPUT.PUT_LINE (dt);
  6  END;
  7  /
08-FEB-99
```

21-47. If you are running Oracle 7.3.3 or above, you can use DEFINE_COLUMN_LONG to specify that a column in a query is LONG. Then, when you extract the value after a row is fetched, use the COLUMN_VALUE_LONG to dump "chunks" of the LONG value into a PL/SQL table of type DBMS_SQL.VARCHAR2.

21-48. Here is one possible solution:

```
/* Filename on web page: dumplong.sp */
CREATE OR REPLACE PROCEDURE dump_long (
   tab IN VARCHAR2,
   col IN VARCHAR2,
   whr IN VARCHAR2 := NULL,
   pieces IN OUT DBMS_SQL.VARCHAR2S)
IS
   cur PLS_INTEGER := DBMS_SQL.OPEN_CURSOR;
   fdbk PLS_INTEGER;

   TYPE long_rectype IS RECORD (
      piece_len PLS_INTEGER DEFAULT 2000,
      pos_in_long PLS_INTEGER DEFAULT 0,
      one_piece VARCHAR2(2000),
      one_piece_len PLS_INTEGER
      );
   rec long_rectype;
BEGIN
   DBMS_SQL.PARSE (cur,
      'SELECT ' || col || ' FROM ' || tab ||
      ' WHERE ' || NVL (whr, '1 = 1'),
      DBMS_SQL.NATIVE);

   DBMS_SQL.DEFINE_COLUMN_LONG (cur, 1);
   fdbk := DBMS_SQL.EXECUTE_AND_FETCH (cur);

   IF fdbk > 0
   THEN
      LOOP
         DBMS_SQL.COLUMN_VALUE_LONG (
```

```
            cur,
            1,
            rec.piece_len,
            rec.pos_in_long,
            rec.one_piece,
            rec.one_piece_len);
        EXIT WHEN rec.one_piece_len = 0;
        pieces (NVL (pieces.LAST, 0) + 1) := rec.one_piece;
        rec.pos_in_long :=
            rec.pos_in_long + rec.one_piece_len;
      END LOOP;
   END IF;
   DBMS_SQL.CLOSE_CURSOR (cur);
END;
/
```

21-49. Well, first of all, you can't parse it in DBMS_SQL unless you are running at least Oracle8 Release 8.0. Prior to Oracle8, the size of the largest string you can pass to DBMS_SQL.PARSE is 32K. Oracle8's DBMS_SQL offers an overloading of DBMS_SQL.PARSE that allows you to parse arbitrarily long strings. To do this, you must fill up an index-by table with "chunks" of your long string, and then pass that table (Oracle's version of an array) to DBMS_SQL.PARSE. An example of this version of PARSE put to use is in the *parslong.sp* file on the book's web page.

21-50. The DBMS_SQL.DESCRIBE_COLUMNS procedure returns column information into a PL/SQL table of type DBMS_SQL.DESC_TAB.

Here is an illustration of this procedure:

```
DECLARE
    cur PLS_INTEGER DBMS_SQL.OPEN_CURSOR;
    cols DBMS_SQL.DESC_TAB;
    ncols PLS_INTEGER;
BEGIN
    DBMS_SQL.PARSE
        (cur, 'SELECT hiredate, sal FROM emp', DBMS_SQL.NATIVE);
    DBMS_SQL.DEFINE_COLUMN (cur, 1, SYSDATE);
    DBMS_SQL.DEFINE_COLUMN (cur, 2, 1);
    DBMS_SQL.DESCRIBE_COLUMNS (cur, ncols, cols);
    FOR colind IN 1 .. ncols
    LOOP
        DBMS_OUTPUT.PUT_LINE (cols.col_name);
    END LOOP;
    DBMS_SQL.CLOSE_CURSOR (cur);
END;
/
```

21-51. Here is one possible solution:

```
/* Filename on web page: showcolinfo.sp */
CREATE OR REPLACE PROCEDURE showcolinfo (cur IN INTEGER)
IS
    cols DBMS_SQL.DESC_TAB;
```

```
      ncols PLS_INTEGER;
      nullable VARCHAR2(5) := 'TRUE';

      FUNCTION formatted (
         val1 IN VARCHAR2,
         val2 IN VARCHAR2,
         val3 IN VARCHAR2)
      RETURN VARCHAR2 S
      BEGIN
         RETURN (
            RPAD (val1, 20) ||
            RPAD (val2, 20) ||
            RPAD (val3, 20));
      END;
BEGIN
      DBMS_SQL.DESCRIBE_COLUMNS (cur, ncols, cols);

      DBMS_OUTPUT.PUT_LINE (
         formatted ('Name', 'Type', 'Nullable'));

      FOR colind IN 1 .. ncols
      LOOP
         /* This looks reversed, but it's not... */
         IF cols(colind).col_null_ok
         THEN nullable := 'FALSE';
         ELSE nullable := 'TRUE';
         END IF;

         DBMS_OUTPUT.PUT_LINE (
            formatted (
               cols(colind).col_name,
               cols(colind).col_type,
               nullable
               )
            );
      END LOOP;
END;
/
```

And here is some sample output:

```
SQL> LIST
  1  DECLARE
  2     cur INTEGER := DBMS_SQL.OPEN_CURSOR;
  3  BEGIN
  4     DBMS_SQL.PARSE (cur,
  5        'SELECT employee_id, first_name, ' ||
  6         'hire_date FROM employee',
  7         DBMS_SQL.NATIVE);
  8     showcolinfo (cur);
  9* END;
SQL> /
```

Name	Type	Nullable
EMPLOYEE_ID	2	TRUE
FIRST_NAME	1	FALSE
HIRE_DATE	12	TRUE

21-52. The ensure_minsal always keeps on truckin' until DBMS_SQL.FETCH_ ROWS returns 0. But that's not what the code says, is it? Why isn't the DBMS_SQL.LAST_ROW_COUNT stopping the loop? To understand this puzzling behavior, you must remember that the LAST functions of DBMS_ SQL always return information about the last dynamic SQL cursor executed or fetched from in your session, not in the current block. A close look at the body of the loop in ensure_minsal reveals that after FETCH_ ROWS is called, the update_salary procedure is called. This procedure executes its own dynamic SQL cursor for the update. As soon as this occurs, the value of LAST_ROW_COUNT is set to the number of rows modified by the UPDATE, in this case 1.

How can you avoid this problem? Just change one line of code and you are all set. Instead of this version:

```
EXIT WHEN DBMS_SQL.LAST_ROW_COUNT > 10 OR
        DBMS_SQL.FETCH_ROWS (cur) = 0;
```

use this version:

```
EXIT WHEN DBMS_SQL.FETCH_ROWS (cur) = 0 OR
        DBMS_SQL.LAST_ROW_COUNT > 10;
```

By changing the order in which these expressions are evaluated, LAST_ ROW_COUNT is called immediately after FETCH_ROWS, so that the row count reflects the rows queried and not the rows updated.

21-53. Oracle added the "bulk bind" feature in Oracle8. With bulk binds, you can bind an entire "array" of information (in reality, an index-by table—a.k.a., PL/SQL table) to a column or variable and also retrieve information from the SQL after it is executed.

21-54. To perform an update, you need only to bind the arrays with DBMS_SQL. BIND_ARRAY and then execute the update. Here is one possible implementation:

```
/* Filename on web page: arrayupd.sp */
CREATE OR REPLACE PROCEDURE updemps (
    enametab IN DBMS_SQL.VARCHAR2_TABLE,
    saltab IN DBMS_SQL.NUMBER_TABLE)
IS
    cur PLS_INTEGER := DBMS_SQL.OPEN_CURSOR;
    fdbk PLS_INTEGER;
BEGIN
    DBMS_SQL.PARSE (cur,
        'UPDATE emp SET sal = :salary ' ||
        'WHERE ename = :employee_name',
        DBMS_SQL.NATIVE);

    DBMS_SQL.BIND_ARRAY (cur, 'salary', saltab);
    DBMS_SQL.BIND_ARRAY (cur, 'employee_name', enametab);
```

```
        fdbk := DBMS_SQL.EXECUTE (cur);

        DBMS_OUTPUT.PUT_LINE ('Rows updated: ' || TO_CHAR (fdbk));

        DBMS_SQL.CLOSE_CURSOR (cur);
END;
/
```

21-55. Since you are going to fetch only once, you should:

- Specify in your call to DBMS_SQL.DEFINE_ARRAY that the maximum number of rows fetched at a time exceeds the total count in the table (I use 100).

- Call EXECUTE_AND_FETCH instead of FETCH_ROWS.

One possible solution is shown here:

```
/* Filename on web page: arrayqry.sp */
CREATE OR REPLACE PROCEDURE showemps (
    where_in IN VARCHAR2 := NULL
    )
IS
    cur INTEGER := DBMS_SQL.OPEN_CURSOR;
    fdbk INTEGER;

    last_name_tab DBMS_SQL.VARCHAR2_TABLE;
    hire_date_tab DBMS_SQL.DATE_TABLE;
BEGIN
    DBMS_SQL.PARSE(cur,
        'SELECT last_name, hire_date FROM employee
         WHERE ' || NVL (where_in, '1=1') ||
        'ORDER BY hire_date',
         DBMS_SQL.NATIVE);

    DBMS_SQL.DEFINE_ARRAY (cur, 1, last_name_tab, 100, 1);
    DBMS_SQL.DEFINE_ARRAY (cur, 2, hire_date_tab, 100, 1);

    fdbk := DBMS_SQL.EXECUTE_AND_FETCH (cur);

    DBMS_SQL.COLUMN_VALUE (cur, 1, last_name_tab);
    DBMS_SQL.COLUMN_VALUE (cur, 2, hire_date_tab);

    FOR rowind IN last_name_tab.FIRST .. last_name_tab.LAST
    LOOP
        DBMS_OUTPUT.PUT_LINE (
            last_name_tab(rowind) ||
            ' was hired on ' ||
            hire_date_tab(rowind));
    END LOOP;

    DBMS_SQL.CLOSE_CURSOR (cur);
END;
/
```

21-56. Here is one possible implementation:

```
/* Filename on web page: dynaggr.sf */
CREATE OR REPLACE FUNCTION dynaggr (
   tab IN VARCHAR2,
   col IN VARCHAR2,
   grpfunc IN VARCHAR2 := 'SUM',
   whr IN VARCHAR2 := NULL
   )
  RETURN NUMBER
IS
   sqlstr VARCHAR2(2000) :=
      'SELECT ' || grpfunc || '(' || col || ')
         FROM ' || tab ||
      ' WHERE ' || NVL (whr, '1=1');

   cur PLS_INTEGER := DBMS_SQL.OPEN_CURSOR;
   fdbk PLS_INTEGER;
   retval NUMBER;
BEGIN
   DBMS_SQL.PARSE (cur, sqlstr, DBMS_SQL.NATIVE);

   DBMS_SQL.DEFINE_COLUMN (cur, 1, 1);
   fdbk := DBMS_SQL.EXECUTE_AND_FETCH (cur);
   DBMS_SQL.COLUMN_VALUE (cur, 1, retval);
   DBMS_SQL.CLOSE_CURSOR (cur);

   RETURN retval;
EXCEPTION
   WHEN OTHERS
   THEN
      fdbk := DBMS_SQL.LAST_ERROR_POSITION;
      DBMS_OUTPUT.PUT_LINE (
         SQLERRM || CHR(10) ||
         sqlstr || CHR(10) ||
         LPAD ('^', fdbk, '-'));
      DBMS_SQL.CLOSE_CURSOR (cur);
      RETURN NULL;
END dynaggr;
/
```

22

DBMS_PIPE Built-in Package

Beginner

22-1. Absolutely not! That is one of the hallmarks and key advantages of DBMS_PIPE: it operates outside your session's transaction boundaries.

22-2. Here are the required steps in the proper order:

1. Pack data into the message buffer
2. Send the message

The steps in the following table aren't required; the reasons they can be skipped accompany them.

Step	Why Skip?
Check to make sure the pipe exists	If the pipe does not exist, it is created for you when you send the message.
Convert all numeric and date information to VARCHAR2 before packing it into the message buffer	You can pack dates and numbers directly into the buffer with a call to the overloaded DBMS_PIPE.PACK_MESSAGE procedure.
Create the pipe	If the pipe does not exist, it is created for you when you send the message.
Check the status of the send operation	This is a very good and recommended thing to do, but it is not required.

22-3. Here are the required steps in the proper order:

1. Receive the message
2. Unpack individual packets of data from the message buffer

The steps in the following table aren't required; the reasons they can be skipped accompany them.

Step	Why Skip?
Check to make sure the pipe exists	If the pipe does not exist, it is created for you when you send the message.
Send a "message received" confirmation message back on the same pipe	There is no requirement to respond to a message received. If you do want to reply, furthermore, you do not need to use the same pipe.
Check the status of the receive operation	This is a very good and recommended thing to do, but it is not required.

22-4. Here is one implementation; it checks to make sure the message was sent and displays a message if there was a problem:

```
/* Filename on web page: sendmsg.sp */
CREATE OR REPLACE PROCEDURE send_message (
    pipe IN VARCHAR2,
    dtval IN DATE)
IS
    stat PLS_INTEGER;
BEGIN
    DBMS_PIPE.PACK_MESSAGE (dtval);
    stat := DBMS_PIPE.SEND_MESSAGE (pipe, timeout => 60);
    IF stat != 0
    THEN
        DBMS_OUTPUT.PUT_LINE (
            'Unable to send message to ' || pipe);
    END IF;
END;
/
```

22-5. The following implementation declares a return variable as VARCHAR2(4096) because 4096 is the maximum number of bytes allowed in a DBMS_PIPE message:

```
/* Filename on web page: recvmsg.sf */
CREATE OR REPLACE FUNCTION receive_message (
    pipe IN VARCHAR2)
RETURN VARCHAR2 IS
    stat PLS_INTEGER;
    retval VARCHAR2(4096);
BEGIN
    stat := DBMS_PIPE.RECEIVE_MESSAGE (pipe, timeout => 10);
    IF stat = 0
    THEN
        DBMS_PIPE.UNPACK_MESSAGE (retval);
    END IF;
    RETURN retval;
END;
/
```

Notice the message is unpacked only if a message is successfully received.

22-6. Statements (a), (c), and (e) all describe the most useful and common applications of DBMS_PIPE:

    a. Valid.

    b. Invalid. Describes the functionality of the DBMS_JOB package.

    c. Valid, although more typical of pre-Oracle8 type containers. You no longer have to rely on DBMS_PIPE to run operating system programs since you can call an external program instead.

    d. Invalid. When the database server goes down for maintenance, the System Global Area is erased and database pipes reside in the SGA.

    e. Valid.

    f. Invalid. Describes the functionality of the DBMS_ALERT package.

    g. Invalid. Cannot be performed with DBMS_PIPE, since pipes are constrained to a single database instance and do not provide a mechanism for communicating between instances.

22-7. The DBMS_PIPE.REMOVE_PIPE procedure does the trick.

22-8. Use the DBMS_PIPE.PURGE procedure to remove left-over messages.

Intermediate

22-9. Surprisingly, your pipe name can have up to 128 characters in it. In other words, you are not constrained to the usual 30 characters. Oracle also requests that you not use/create any pipes whose names start with "ORA$".

22-10. The statements are:

    a. False. A DBMS_PIPE message consists of a single VARCHAR2 string. A message may contain any combination of packets with the following datatypes: VARCHAR2, NUMBER, DATE, RAW, and ROWID.

    b. False. The maximum size of a pipe is 2 GB. There is no maximum pipe size; the only limitation is your SGA and, by extension, the real memory of your database server.

    c. True.

    d. True.

    e. False. You can send a LONG value through a database pipe. Well, this is actually a yes and no statement. You can send a LONG value as long as it contains no more than 32 KB (i.e., it can fit into a PL/SQL VARCHAR2 variable).

    f. False. If a database pipe is "private," you must provide a password to read/write the contents of the pipe. There is no password protection for a pipe. If a pipe is private, you can read/write the pipe only if you are connected to the same schema (not session, just same schema name) as the creator of the pipe) or if you have SYSDBA privileges.

g. True.

h. True.

22-11. Use the CREATE_PIPE function to get the job done:

```
DECLARE
    stat PLS_INTEGER;
BEGIN
    stat := DBMS_PIPE.CREATE_PIPE (
        'national_security',
        2000*1024,
        private=>TRUE);
END;
/
```

22-12. Call RESET_BUFFER if you want to make sure there are no packets of information previously packed into the buffer since the last message was sent.

22-13. First of all, the error is:

```
ORA-06559: wrong datatype requested, 2, actual datatype is 12
```

And that pretty well explains the matter. You packed a date into the buffer, but tried to read that date out into a numeric variable.

22-14. Here is one possible implementation:

```
PROCEDURE analyze_assembly_data
IS
  pipe_status INTEGER;
  prod_total NUMBER;
BEGIN
  LOOP
    pipe_status :=
      DBMS_PIPE.RECEIVE_MESSAGE ('production', 10 * 60);

    IF pipe_status = 0
    THEN
      DBMS_PIPE.UNPACK_MESSAGE (prod_total);
      analyze_production (SYSDATE, prod_total);
    ELSE
      DBMS_OUTPUT.PUT_LINE (
        'Production data unavailable at ' ||
        TO_CHAR (SYSDATE, 'MM/DD/YYYY HH24:MI:SS'));
    END IF;
  END LOOP;
END;
```

22-15. First, here's the function:

```
/* Filename on web page: mkpipe.sf */
CREATE OR REPLACE FUNCTION mkpipe RETURN VARCHAR2
IS
  pipe_status INTEGER;
```

```
   pipe VARCHAR2(128) := DBMS_PIPE.UNIQUE_SESSION_NAME;
BEGIN
   pipe_status :=
      DBMS_PIPE.CREATE_PIPE (pipe, private=>TRUE);
   IF pipe_status = 0
   THEN
      RETURN pipe;
   ELSE
      RETURN NULL;
   END IF;
END;
/
```

The DBMS_PIPE.UNIQUE_SESSION_NAME function is used to automatically create a pipe name that's guaranteed unique among sessions connected to the database. Then the pipe name is returned (unless there's a problem).

Here is the script that obtains the unique pipe name (creating the private pipe at the same time) and then sends out the date/time stamp:

```
DECLARE
   pipe_status INTEGER;
   mypipe VARCHAR2(128) := mkpipe;
BEGIN
   DBMS_OUTPUT.PUT_LINE ('Write to ' || mypipe);
   DBMS_PIPE.PACK_MESSAGE (SYSDATE);
   pipe_status := DBMS_PIPE.SEND_MESSAGE (mypipe);
END;
/
```

Finally, a program to receive the message:

```
DECLARE
   pipe_status INTEGER;
   mypipe VARCHAR2(128) := DBMS_PIPE.UNIQUE_SESSION_NAME;
   myval DATE;
BEGIN
   DBMS_OUTPUT.PUT_LINE ('Read from ' || mypipe);
   pipe_status := DBMS_PIPE.RECEIVE_MESSAGE (mypipe);
   DBMS_PIPE.UNPACK_MESSAGE (myval);
   DBMS_OUTPUT.PUT_LINE (
      TO_CHAR (myval, 'MM/DD/YYYY HH24:MI:SS'));
END;
/
```

Notice mkpipe is not called again. You don't need to create the pipe, just get the pipe name. As long as this second block is executing in the same session, the UNIQUE_SESSION_NAME function always returns the same name for the pipe.

22-16. Here's one way to get the job done:

```
DECLARE
   pipe_status INTEGER;
BEGIN
```

```
    FOR days IN 1 .. 10
    LOOP
        DBMS_PIPE.PACK_MESSAGE (SYSDATE + days - 1);
    END LOOP;
    pipe_status := DBMS_PIPE.SEND_MESSAGE ('future');
END;
/
```

22-17. First of all, you should implement this function inside a package. Why? Because the function must return a record, and the record type is a programmer-defined record type, so at a minimum the record type must be defined in a package so that it can be referenced in the function's RETURN clause. Might as well put them in the same package, right?

```
/* Filename on web page: peachy.pkg */
CREATE OR REPLACE PACKAGE peachy
IS
    TYPE info_rectype IS RECORD (
        trial_began DATE,
        trial_cost NUMBER,
        house_manager VARCHAR2(100)
        );

    FUNCTION critical_info RETURN info_rectype;
END;
/
```

And here is the package body; a constant is created to contain the number of seconds in 30 days, unpack the components of the message directly into the record, and then return it. If the pipe is not read successfully, a NULL or empty record is returned:

```
CREATE OR REPLACE PACKAGE BODY peachy
IS
    thirty_days CONSTANT INTEGER := 30 * 24 * 60 * 60;

    FUNCTION critical_info RETURN info_rectype
    IS
        stat PLS_INTEGER;
        retval info_rectype;
    BEGIN
        stat :=
            DBMS_PIPE.RECEIVE_MESSAGE
                ('impeachment', timeout => thirty_days);

        IF stat = 0
        THEN
            DBMS_PIPE.UNPACK_MESSAGE (retval.trial_began);
            DBMS_PIPE.UNPACK_MESSAGE (retval.trial_cost);
            DBMS_PIPE.UNPACK_MESSAGE (retval.house_manager);
        END IF;
        RETURN retval;
    END;
END;
/
```

22-18. You need to use the special UNPACK_MESSAGE_RAW procedure to extract the raw value and then convert it using RAWTOHEX:

```
/* Filename on web page: unpackraw.sql */
DECLARE
    hex_data    VARCHAR2(12);
    raw_data    RAW(6);
    call_status INTEGER;
BEGIN
    /*
    || Receive and unpack the raw message
    */
    call_status := DBMS_PIPE.RECEIVE_MESSAGE('OPBIP_TEST_PIPE');
    DBMS_PIPE.UNPACK_MESSAGE_RAW(raw_data);

    /* Convert and display results */
    hex_data := RAWTOHEX(raw_data);
    DBMS_OUTPUT.PUT_LINE('hex of raw: '||hex_data);
END;
```

Expert

22-19. Construction of the package is straightforward; see the *invasions.pkg* file on this book's web page for the details. Here are the highlights.

First, create a named constant for the pipe name so it is not repeated throughout:

```
CREATE OR REPLACE PACKAGE BODY invpkg
IS
    pipename CONSTANT VARCHAR2(20) := 'invasions';
    stat PLS_INTEGER;
```

The sendinfo procedure makes certain to reset the buffer; error handling is left out, but you should probably check for a nonzero status and report the error:

```
PROCEDURE sendinfo (
    country IN VARCHAR2,
    date_of_invasion DATE,
    people_killed NUMBER
    )
IS
BEGIN
    DBMS_PIPE.RESET_BUFFER;
    DBMS_PIPE.PACK_MESSAGE (country);
    DBMS_PIPE.PACK_MESSAGE (date_of_invasion);
    DBMS_PIPE.PACK_MESSAGE (people_killed);
    stat := DBMS_PIPE.SEND_MESSAGE (pipename, timeout => 10);
END;
```

The record overloading simply calls the other implementation; try hard to avoid any redundant code:

```
PROCEDURE sendinfo (rec IN inv_rectype)
IS
BEGIN
   sendinfo (
      rec.country,
      rec.date_of_invasion,
      rec.people_killed);
END;
```

The nextinfo function receives and unpacks without any surprises (see the file for details). Finally, you have to deal with pipe creation. You want to make sure the pipe is created before anyone sends or receives. Since the pipe is private, the creation step must be done explicitly. The best place for this to happen is the initialization section at the bottom of the package body:

```
BEGIN
   stat := DBMS_PIPE.CREATE_PIPE (pipename, 2000 * 1024, TRUE);
END;
/
```

22-20. Sounds like a job for Super Virtual Table! You can run a query against SYS.V_$DB_PIPES as shown here:

```
SQL> SELECT * FROM SYS.V_$DB_PIPES;

  OWNERID NAME                            TYPE    PIPE_SIZE
--------- ------------------------------- ------- ---------
          WHEN                            PUBLIC       1085
       25 ORA$PIPE$000B167D0001           PRIVATE       866
          FUTURE                          PUBLIC       1087
```

22-21. You want to use the V_$DB_PIPES virtual table to obtain the names of the pipes and then apply DBMS_PIPE.PURGE or DBMS_PIPE.REMOVE_PIPE depending on the procedure. Here is one implementation:

```
/* Filename on web page: pipemnt.pkg */
CREATE OR REPLACE PACKAGE BODY pipemaint
AS
   cannot_use_pipe EXCEPTION;
   PRAGMA EXCEPTION_INIT(cannot_use_pipe,-23322);

   null_pipename EXCEPTION;
   PRAGMA EXCEPTION_INIT(null_pipename,-23321);

   /* Gets names of all specified pipes */
   CURSOR all_pipes_cur (nm IN VARCHAR2)
   IS
   SELECT name
     FROM SYS.V_$DB_PIPES
    WHERE name LIKE UPPER (nm);

   PROCEDURE purge_pipes (nm IN VARCHAR2) IS
   BEGIN
      FOR all_pipes_rec IN all_pipes_cur (nm)
```

```
        LOOP
           BEGIN
              DBMS_PIPE.PURGE (all_pipes_rec.name);
           EXCEPTION
              WHEN cannot_use_pipe THEN NULL;
              WHEN OTHERS THEN RAISE;
           END;
        END LOOP;
     END purge_pipes;

     PROCEDURE remove_pipes (nm IN VARCHAR2) IS
        stat PLS_INTEGER;
     BEGIN
        FOR all_pipes_rec IN all_pipes_cur (nm)
        LOOP
           BEGIN
           stat := DBMS_PIPE.REMOVE_PIPE (all_pipes_rec.name);
           EXCEPTION
              WHEN cannot_use_pipe OR null_pipename THEN NULL;
              WHEN OTHERS THEN RAISE;
           END;
        END LOOP;
     END remove_pipes;

  END pipemaint;
  /
```

22-22. To implement the forward procedure without an unpack and repack requires your understanding of a little known trick: it turns out that you can't simply receive and immediately send a message using DBMS_PIPE, unless you have previously called DBMS_PIPE.PACK_MESSAGE. I don't know why this is so; it just is. So you have to take the steps shown in this forward procedure:

```
/* Filename on web page: forward.sp */
CREATE OR REPLACE PROCEDURE forward
   (from_in IN VARCHAR2
   ,to_in IN VARCHAR2
   ,timeout_secs_IN IN INTEGER := 10)
IS
/* Implementation courtesy of John Beresniewicz */

   stat INTEGER;
BEGIN
   /* Initialize buffer. */
   DBMS_PIPE.RESET_BUFFER;

   /* Put some dummy information in the buffer. */
   DBMS_PIPE.PACK_MESSAGE ('bogus message');

   /* Write right over that buffer with the message to forward. */
   stat := DBMS_PIPE.RECEIVE_MESSAGE (
      from_in,
      timeout => timeout_secs_IN);
```

```
        IF stat = 0
        THEN
           stat := DBMS_PIPE.SEND_MESSAGE (
               to_in,
               timeout => timeout_secs_IN);
        END IF;

     END forward;
     /
```

22-23. The DBMS_PIPE.NEXT_ITEM_TYPE function returns the datatype of the next packet in the message buffer. Here's the function that demonstrates how this program is used:

```
CREATE OR REPLACE FUNCTION date_packet RETURN DATE
IS
    /*
    || WARNING!
    || You must have already called DBMS_PIPE.RECEIVE_MESSAGE
    || or this function will give you an ORA-06556 error!
    */
    retval DATE;
BEGIN
   IF DBMS_PIPE.NEXT_ITEM_TYPE = 12
   THEN
      DBMS_PIPE.UNPACK_MESSAGE (retval);
   END IF;
   RETURN retval;
END;
/
```

The following table shows the different return values you might get from NEXT_ITEM_TYPE.

Value	Datatype
0	No more packets
6	NUMBER
9	VARCHAR2
11	ROWID
12	DATE
23	RAW

Given this information, if you want to create a generic data structure to hold any message buffer's contents, it needs to be able to hold any of the previous datatypes. One approach you could take is to define a record TYPE with a field for each of the datatypes, and an index-by table in which each row has a record of that type—something like this, perhaps:

```
CREATE OR REPLACE PACKAGE dbpipe
IS
   TYPE message_rectype IS RECORD
```

```
(item_type   INTEGER
,Mvarchar2   VARCHAR2(4093)
,Mdate       DATE
,Mnumber     NUMBER
,Mrowid      ROWID
,Mraw        RAW(4093)
);
```

```
TYPE message_tbltype IS TABLE OF message_rectype
     INDEX BY BINARY_INTEGER;
END;
```

Notice that the record structure contains not only a field for each datatype, but also a field containing the item type. You need that information in order to know the field from which the packet value can be retrieved.

22-24. In the previous problem, you saw that NEXT_ITEM_TYPE returns one of six different integers. This can result in some very nasty code, if you hard-code "special" values in your program, as I did:

```
IF DBMS_PIPE.NEXT_ITEM_TYPE = 12
```

So the first thing to do when constructing your generic unpack procedure is to define some constants in the package specification as follows:

```
/* Datatype numbers for NEXT_ITEM_TYPE */
   c_nomore   CONSTANT INTEGER := 0;
   c_number   CONSTANT INTEGER := 6;
   c_varchar2 CONSTANT INTEGER := 9;
   c_rowid    CONSTANT INTEGER := 11;
   c_date     CONSTANT INTEGER := 12;
   c_raw      CONSTANT INTEGER := 23;
```

From there, the unpack procedure falls into place nicely:

```
/* Filename on web page: dbpipe.pkg */
PROCEDURE unpack_to_tbl (tbl_out IN OUT message_tbltype)
IS
   next_item INTEGER;
   rowindx   INTEGER := 0;

BEGIN
   /* Empty the table of any data. */
   tbl_out.DELETE;

   /* Unpack until no more items... */
   LOOP
      next_item := DBMS_PIPE.NEXT_ITEM_TYPE;
      EXIT WHEN next_item = c_nomore;

      rowindx := NVL (tbl_out.LAST, 0) + 1;

      tbl_out(rowindx).item_type := next_item;

      IF next_item = c_varchar2 THEN
         DBMS_PIPE.UNPACK_MESSAGE (
```

```
                tbl_out(rowindx).Mvarchar2);
        ELSIF next_item = c_number THEN
            DBMS_PIPE.UNPACK_MESSAGE (
                tbl_out(rowindx).Mnumber);
        ELSIF next_item = c_rowid THEN
            DBMS_PIPE.UNPACK_MESSAGE_ROWID (
                tbl_out(rowindx).Mrowid);
        ELSIF next_item = c_date THEN
            DBMS_PIPE.UNPACK_MESSAGE (
                tbl_out(rowindx).Mdate);
        ELSIF next_item = c_raw THEN
            DBMS_PIPE.UNPACK_MESSAGE_RAW (
                tbl_out(rowindx).Mraw);
        END IF;
    END LOOP;
END unpack_to_tbl;
```

22-25. Here's the solution for the string overloading of msgwith. You can check the *dbpipe.pkg* file for the other datatype implementations; they are almost exactly the same.

```
FUNCTION msgwith (
    pipename IN VARCHAR2,
    nthpacket IN INTEGER,
    matchon IN VARCHAR2)
    RETURN message_tbltype
IS
    stat PLS_INTEGER;
    retval message_tbltype;
BEGIN
    LOOP
        stat := DBMS_PIPE.RECEIVE_MESSAGE (
            pipename,
            timeout => 0);

        EXIT WHEN stat != 0;

        unpack_to_tbl (retval, stat);

        EXIT WHEN
            INSTR(retval(nthpacket).Mvarchar2, matchon) > 0;

        retval.DELETE;
    END LOOP;

    RETURN retval;
END msgwith;
```

It's a concise and readable function, precisely because I was able to leverage the unpack_to_tbl procedure. Without that, this would be a complicated and long program. Notice INSTR is used to check for the presence of the matchon value. For dates and numbers, you would probably want to do a check with equality.

To make it easier to test this program, a show_unpack procedure was added to the dbpipe package (see *dbpipe.pkg*). Here is the test script that exercises the msgwith procedure and verifies the results with show_ unpack:

```
/* Filename on web page: inpipe.tst */
DECLARE
   pipename CONSTANT VARCHAR2(30) := 'numbers_and_words';
   stat PLS_INTEGER;
   t dbpipe.message_tbltype;
BEGIN
   DBMS_PIPE.PURGE (pipename);

   FOR i IN 100 .. 110
   LOOP
      DBMS_PIPE.RESET_BUFFER;
      DBMS_PIPE.PACK_MESSAGE (sysdate+i-1);
      DBMS_PIPE.PACK_MESSAGE (to_words(i, NULL, NULL));
      DBMS_PIPE.PACK_MESSAGE (i);
      stat := DBMS_PIPE.SEND_MESSAGE (pipename);
   END LOOP;

   t := dbpipe.msgwith (pipename, 2, 'wo');

   dbpipe.show_unpack (t);
END;
/
```

where to_words is a function defined in the *towords.sf* file found on this book's web page.

23

DBMS_OUTPUT Built-in Package

Beginner

23-1. Believe it or not, early developers inserted rows of data into a database table and then used SQL to examine what had happened. Talk about crude mechanisms!

23-2. You can store up to 1 million bytes (*not* quite the same as 1 MB) in the buffer.

You can put strings, dates, and numbers into the buffer.

23-3. Use the DBMS_OUTPUT.PUT_LINE procedure:

```
CREATE OR REPLACE PROCEDURE hello_world
IS
BEGIN
   DBMS_OUTPUT.PUT_LINE ('hello world!');
END;
/
```

23-4. Call the ENABLE procedure, which also accepts as its single argument the maximum size of the buffer. In the following block, the size is set to the maximum possible:

```
BEGIN
   DBMS_OUTPUT.ENABLE (1000000);
END;
/
```

23-5. You can call DBMS_OUTPUT.ENABLE, but that won't be enough. You must use the following command:

```
SET SERVEROUTPUT ON
```

It calls DBMS_OUTPUT.ENABLE, but also tells SQL*Plus to automatically flush the contents of the DBMS_OUTPUT buffer to your screen when the block finishes executing.

23-6. What you are really doing here is *disabling* the package, so why not call:

```
BEGIN
    DBMS_OUTPUT.DISABLE;
END;
```

23-7. Just 2000 bytes. In other words, the following steps in SQL*Plus results in an error:

```
SQL> CONNECT scott/tiger
Connected.
SQL> SET SERVEROUTPUT ON
SQL> BEGIN
  2      FOR linenum IN 1 .. 25
  3      LOOP
  4          DBMS_OUTPUT.PUT_LINE (
  5              RPAD ('rich people ', 100, 'cause poverty '));
  6      END LOOP;
  7   END;
  8   /
rich people cause poverty cause poverty cause poverty...
...
rich people cause poverty cause poverty cause poverty...
BEGIN
*
ERROR at line 1:
ORA-20000: ORU-10027: buffer overflow, limit of 2000 bytes
ORA-06512: at "SYS.DBMS_OUTPUT", line 106
ORA-06512: at "SYS.DBMS_OUTPUT", line 65
ORA-06512: at line 4
```

23-8. Create a *login.sql* script with the following statement in it:

```
SET SERVEROUTPUT ON SIZE 1000000
```

This file is executed automatically when you start SQL*Plus (if the *login.sql* file is located in the working directory).

You have to reexecute this script each time you reconnect within SQL*Plus.

23-9. Here is a suggested procedure:

```
CREATE OR REPLACE PROCEDURE now_is_when
IS
BEGIN
    DBMS_OUTPUT.PUT_LINE (SYSDATE);
    DBMS_OUTPUT.PUT_LINE (TO_CHAR (SYSDATE, 'HH:MI:SS'));
END;
/
```

23-10. Here is one possible (and concise) implementation:

```
CREATE OR REPLACE PROCEDURE show_employees
IS
BEGIN
    FOR emprec IN (SELECT last_name, salary FROM employee)
    LOOP
        DBMS_OUTPUT.PUT_LINE (
            emprec.last_name || ' earns $' || emprec.salary);
    END LOOP;
END;
/
```

Intermediate

23-11. By default (i.e., the basic SET SERVEROUTPUT ON command), SQL*Plus trims leading blanks.

23-12. By default, SQL*Plus pretends you didn't ask it to display a blank line. You can override this annoying behavior with the FORMAT WRAPPED option:

```
SET SERVEROUTPUT ON SIZE 500000 FORMAT WRAPPED
```

23-13. The WORD_WRAPPED option comes in handy for this purpose:

```
SET SERVEROUTPUT ON SIZE 500000 FORMAT WORD_WRAPPED
```

23-14. The TRUNCATE option comes in handy for this purpose:

```
SET SERVEROUTPUT ON SIZE 500000 FORMAT TRUNCATE
```

23-15. You get an unhandled exception:

```
PLS-00306: wrong number or types of arguments in call to 'PUT_LINE'
```

DBMS_OUTPUT.PUT_LINE is only overloaded for VARCHAR2, DATE, and NUMBER. You cannot pass it a Boolean directly.

23-16. You get an unhandled exception:

```
ORA-06502: PL/SQL: numeric or value error
```

DBMS_OUTPUT.PUT_LINE cannot handle strings with more than 255 bytes.

23-17. You can use either DBMS_OUTPUT.GET_LINE to extract a single line or DBMS_OUTPUT.GET_LINES to dump all of the contents into an index-by table. The following procedure dumps the buffer and returns it through the parameter list:

```
PROCEDURE dump_do_buffer (buffer IN OUT DBMS_OUTPUT.CHARARR)
IS
    linenum PLS_INTEGER := 1000000;
BEGIN
    DBMS_OUTPUT.GET_LINES (buffer, linenum);
END;
```

23-18. Here is one possible implementation:

```
/* Filename on web page: putboolean.sp */
CREATE OR REPLACE PROCEDURE put_boolean (bool IN BOOLEAN)
IS
BEGIN
   IF bool
   THEN
      DBMS_OUTPUT.GET_LINES ('TRUE');
   ELSIF bool
   THEN
      DBMS_OUTPUT.GET_LINES ('FALSE');
   ELSE
   THEN
      DBMS_OUTPUT.GET_LINES ('NULL');
   END IF;
END;
/
```

23-19. Each time you connect to SQL*Plus, it resets the flag for SERVEROUTPUT. You have to remember to turn it back on each time you reestablish a connection to the database.

Expert

23-20. The most elegant (not necessarily the most efficient) solution involves recursion:

```
/* Filename on web page: println.sp */
CREATE OR REPLACE PROCEDURE println (val IN VARCHAR2)
IS
BEGIN
   /* Don't display lines longer than 80 characters;
      they are hard to read. */
   IF LENGTH (val) > 80
   THEN
      DBMS_OUTPUT.PUT_LINE (SUBSTR (val, 1, 80));
      println (SUBSTR (val, 81));
   ELSE
      DBMS_OUTPUT.PUT_LINE (val);
   END IF;
END;
/
```

23-21. To obtain this behavior, add the following exception section to the implementation of println:

```
EXCEPTION
   WHEN OTHERS
   THEN
      DBMS_OUTPUT.ENABLE (1000000);
      println (val);
END;
/
```

In other words, if any problem occurs, expand the buffer to its maximum size and then try, try again.

23-22. The most interesting aspect of the solution is the implementation of the Boolean overloading. Here is one possible approach:

```
/* Filename on web page: print.pkg */
CREATE OR REPLACE PACKAGE BODY print
IS
    PROCEDURE ln (val IN VARCHAR2)
    IS
    BEGIN
        IF LENGTH (val) > 80
        THEN
            DBMS_OUTPUT.PUT_LINE (SUBSTR (val, 1, 80));
            ln (SUBSTR (val, 81));
        ELSE
            DBMS_OUTPUT.PUT_LINE (val);
        END IF;
    EXCEPTION
        WHEN OTHERS
        THEN
            DBMS_OUTPUT.ENABLE (1000000);
            ln (val);
    END;

    PROCEDURE ln (val IN DATE) IS
    BEGIN
        ln (TO_CHAR (val, 'MM/DD/YYYY HH24:MI:SS'));
    END;

    PROCEDURE ln (val IN NUMBER) IS
    BEGIN
        ln (TO_CHAR (val));
    END;

    PROCEDURE ln (val IN BOOLEAN) IS
    BEGIN
        IF val
        THEN
            ln ('TRUE');
        ELSIF NOT val
        THEN
            ln ('FALSE');
        ELSE
            ln ('');
        END IF;
    END;
END print;
/
```

23-23. The various PUT procedures all modify the contents of the DBMS_OUTPUT buffer, which is a package variable data structure. Therefore, Oracle could not assert WNPS or RNPS on these (and any other) DBMS_OUT-PUT procedures.

23-24. Remember that the DBMS_OUTPUT buffer is only flushed to the screen by SQL*Plus when the PL/SQL block terminates. The "SELECT ... FROM emp" query executed is not a PL/SQL block, so when it finishes running, the DBMS_OUTPUT buffer is not flushed. To see the trace information, it is necessary to run some PL/SQL block after the SQL statement. This block does not need to call DBMS_OUTPUT.PUT_LINE; it only needs to complete successfully. Even if you execute a do-nothing block, as shown next, you will then see the trace information (and the new Oracle8 extended ROWID format):

```
SQL> BEGIN NULL; END;
  2  /
emp-AAAAfBAACAAAAEqAAA
...
emp-AAAAfBAACAAAAEqAAN
```

Of course, if you run this query from within a PL/SQL program, its output is displayed when the program finishes.

23-25. Row 1 is the starting point for GET_LINES.

23-26. A tricky one! Take it one step at a time:

  1. Create your own buffer (an index-by table of a type defined in DBMS_OUTPUT itself, in fact) in a PL/SQL package, let's call it xbuffer for "Expand Buffer."

  2. Build a procedure that calls DBMS_OUTPUT.GET_LINES to copy the DBMS_OUTPUT buffer contents into the xbuffer.contents.

  3. Then disable DBMS_OUTPUT to erase its buffer contents.

Here is one possible implementation:

```
/* Filename on web page: xbuff.pkg */
CREATE OR REPLACE PACKAGE xbuff
IS
    contents DBMS_OUTPUT.CHARARR;
    PROCEDURE dumpit;
END;
/
CREATE OR REPLACE PACKAGE BODY xbuff
IS
    PROCEDURE dumpit
    IS
        tempbuff DBMS_OUTPUT.CHARARR;
        linenum PLS_INTEGER := 1000;
    BEGIN
        DBMS_OUTPUT.GET_LINES (tempbuff, linenum);
        IF linenum > 0
        THEN
            linenum := tempbuff.FIRST;
```

```
        LOOP
            EXIT WHEN linenum IS NULL;
            contents (NVL (contents.LAST, 0) + 1) := tempbuff(linenum);
            linenum := tempbuff.NEXT (linenum);
        END LOOP;
    END IF;
  END;
END;
/
```

The following test script shows the storage of approximately 5 MB of data:

```
/* Filename on web page: xbuff.tst */
CONNECT scott/tiger
SET SERVEROUTPUT ON
DECLARE
    PROCEDURE fill_and_dump
    IS
    BEGIN
        /* 1000 bytes per round. */
        FOR indx IN 1 .. 50
        LOOP
            DBMS_OUTPUT.PUT_LINE ('PL/SQL and Java both');
        END LOOP;
        xbuff.dumpit;
        DBMS_OUTPUT.DISABLE;
        DBMS_OUTPUT.ENABLE (2000);
    END;
BEGIN
    /* Buffer is set to 2000. Let's fill it up,
       then dump it to my buffer, disable, re-enable,
       fill it again, dump it and see what the total
       amount is in xbuff.contents. */
    FOR oneK IN 1 .. 100
    LOOP
        fill_and_dump;
    END LOOP;
    DBMS_OUTPUT.PUT_LINE (
        xbuff.contents.COUNT * 1000 ||
        ' bytes through DBMS_OUTPUT.PUT_LINE in one block.');
END;
/
```

You'll see the following results:

```
SQL> @xbuff.tst
Connected.
5100000 bytes through DBMS_OUTPUT.PUT_LINE in one block.
```

23-27. Curious, isn't it? The error occurs because another session (A) has changed the definition of (recompiled) code that was already referenced in "your" session (B). Information about any code is cached in the session's private memory area; it is now, however, out of date, and that causes the error.

DBMS_OUTPUT.PUT_LINE displays nothing because the package has been set to "disabled." That may seem ridiculous on the face of it, since you issued a call to SET SERVEROUTPUT ON to enable the package. That was true, but take a look at the error stack information:

```
ORA-04068: existing state of packages has been discarded
```

What this is saying is that the "states" (values of data structures) of all the packages used by the session have been set back to their defaults. This includes DBMS_OUTPUT, and the default state is to be disabled.

So whenever you get this error in SQL*Plus, you should either reconnect, or run your *login.sql* script to reinitialize your settings.

24

UTL_FILE Built-in Package

Beginner

24-1. You must add one or more UTL_FILE_DIR entries to enable access to a specific directory. So unless you include an entry for your directory, you can't read/write in that location.

24-2. Entries are:

    a. Invalid. You cannot combine multiple directories onto a single line.

    b. Invalid. This set of parameters allow access to */tmp*, but not to any subdirectories of */app/datafiles/**; you cannot use wildcards in your directory specifications.

    c. Valid.

    d. Valid.

    e. Invalid. You should never append the directory delimiter (/ for Unix and \ for DOS/Windows, for example) at the end of the directory specification. You should not end your directory name with a delimiter, such as the forward slash in Unix. I even found in tests on Oracle 8.0 and 8.1 in Windows NT that if I terminated a UTL_FILE_DIR entry with a backslash, the database would not even start up!

By the way, I wasn't even certain that (d) would work, so I wrote a script to test them all. If you are interested in running this test yourself, see 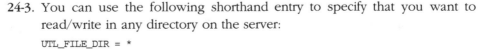 *utlfile.tst* and *utlfile.ora* on the book's web page.

24-3. You can use the following shorthand entry to specify that you want to read/write in any directory on the server:

```
UTL_FILE_DIR = *
```

This is definitely not recommended practice for any production system, since there can be serious ramifications (like writing over your database log file). It is a quick-and-dirty step appropriate for development environments only.

24-4. You can use the following shorthand entry to specify that you want to read/write in the current directory on the server:

`UTL_FILE_DIR = .`

This is also not recommended practice for any production system, since there can be serious ramifications (like writing over your database log file). It is a quick-and-dirty step appropriate for development environments only.

24-5. Generally, no. UTL_FILE allows you to perform only *server-side* I/O on files located on the same machine as your database server.

24-6. Prior to Oracle 8.05, the maximum size line you could read/write was 1023 bytes. With Oracle 8.05 and above, the limitation has been raised to 32K.

24-7. The exceptions are:

    a. Raised. UTL_FILE.INVALID_PATH is raised if you try to read from a location not specified in a UTL_FILE_DIR entry.

    b. Raised. UTL_FILE raises NO_DATA_FOUND if you try to read past the end of a file.

    c. Not raised. UTL_FILE operations never raise the TOO_MANY_ROWS exception.

    d. Not defined. UTL_FILE.FILE_ALREADY_OPEN is not defined in the UTL_FILE package.

    e. Raised. UTL_FILE.INVALID_OPERATION is a catch-all exception that is raised under many different circumstances.

24-8. Uses are:

    a. Invalid.

    b. Invalid.

    c. Valid. When you open a file, UTL_FILE returns a "handle" to the file in the form of a record of type UTL_FILE.FILE_TYPE. FOPEN takes the following three arguments: location of the file, name of the file, mode of file operation (R for read, W for write, and A for append).

    d. Valid; see (c).

    e. Invalid.

24-9. Here is one possible implementation:

```
PROCEDURE open_file (
   loc IN VARCHAR2,
   file IN VARCHAR2,
   fid IN OUT UTL_FILE.FILE_TYPE,
   opened OUT BOOLEAN
   )
IS
BEGIN
   fid := UTL_FILE.FOPEN (loc, file, 'R');
   opened := TRUE;
EXCEPTION
   WHEN OTHERS THEN opened := FALSE;
END;
```

24-10. You can close all files in your session in one of two ways:

- Call UTL_FILE.FCLOSE_ALL

- Disconnect from your session

The FCLOSE_ALL command comes in handy when you have encountered exceptions while manipulating files; and when those files were not closed, and you have "lost" the handles to those files (see the "Intermediate" section for a problem related to lost handles).

24-11. The following table explains the distinctions.

Program Name	Action Taken
UTL_FILE.PUT	Puts a string into the UTL_FILE buffer to be written to the specified file.
UTL_FILE.PUTF	Puts a formatted string into the UTL_FILE buffer to be written to the specified file. Follows the C printf conventions for formatting a string.
UTL_FILE.PUT_LINE	Puts a string followed by a newline character into the UTL_FILE buffer to be written to the specified file.
UTL_FILE.NEW_LINE	Puts a newline character into the UTL_FILE buffer to be written to the specified file.

24-12. There is only one way to read from a file using UTL_FILE: call the GET_LINE procedure to retrieve one line at a time.

Intermediate

24-13. You can do these operations:

   a. Read sequentially the contents of a server-side file.

   b. Append text to the end of an existing file.

   e. Create a new file and write text to it.

You definitely cannot do these operations:

    c. Read from a "random" location in a file.

    d. Delete a file.

You can accomplish these tasks only by reading in the complete contents of a file and then processing that text (write it to another file or to a another file in a different directory, or count the bytes):

    f. Copy a file.

    g. Move a file to a different location.

    h. Change the access privileges on a file.

    i. Obtain the number of bytes in a file without reading the entire file.

24-14. You see the following exception:

```
ORA-01403: no data found
```

This program keeps on reading forever, or until an exception is raised. UTL_FILE.GET_LINE raises the NO_DATA_FOUND exception when it reads past the end of the file, so you get an unhandled exception.

24-15. Here is one possible implementation:

```
/* Filename on web page: showfile.sp */
CREATE OR REPLACE PROCEDURE show_file (
    loc IN VARCHAR2,
    file IN VARCHAR2
    )
IS
    fid UTL_FILE.FILE_TYPE := UTL_FILE.FOPEN (loc, file, 'R');
    line VARCHAR2(2000);
BEGIN
    DBMS_OUTPUT.PUT_LINE ('Contents of ' || file);
    LOOP
        UTL_FILE.GET_LINE (fid, line);
        DBMS_OUTPUT.PUT_LINE (line);
    END LOOP;
EXCEPTION
    WHEN OTHERS THEN UTL_FILE.FCLOSE (fid);
END;
/
```

Notice that this program reads and displays the contents of the file until GET_LINE raises NO_DATA_FOUND. Then the exception handler closes the file, and you're done.

24-16. What's *right* about this code? It is a real mess! The following table shows what I found; there is probably even more.

Line	Problem
1	Nonsense keyword "PROGRAM" should be "PROCEDURE".
2	I am using %TYPE with the string_list_t, which causes a compile error. It already is a type and does not need the attribute.

Line	Problem
5	UTL_FILE.FOPEN needs both a directory location and a filename. This means there is a problem with the parameter list as well.
6 and 11	You have declared your variable to be length 100, yet the nested table contains strings of up to 255 characters. Potential VALUE_ERROR exception.
7	You're declaring the loop index (FOR linenum). This is unnecessary; PL/SQL always declares its own variable with the specified name, which can lead to errors in code.
9	The loop goes from highest to lowest, which means that it never executes the body. If you want to go from last to first, you have to write something like this: `FOR linenum IN REVERSE list.FIRST .. list.LAST`
12	When you write to a file, you must specify the file handle as the first argument.
13	You should never use the EXIT statement to terminate a FOR loop. It should be stopped only when an exception is raised or when the full set of values defined in the IN clause has been perused.
15	The file was never closed. This program leaves the file open until you disconnect or call UTL_FILE.FCLOSE_ALL out of frustration with all your locked files.
15	There is no exception section. At a minimum, you need to trap errors to close the file and reraise the error.

24-17. The following version is stripped of any unnecessary processing and also adds exception handling:

```
CREATE OR REPLACE PROCEDURE nest2file (
    loc IN VARCHAR2,
    file IN VARCHAR2,
    list IN string_list_t)
IS
    fid UTL_FILE.FILE_TYPE := UTL_FILE.FOPEN (loc, file, 'R');
BEGIN
    FOR linenum IN list.FIRST .. list.LAST
    LOOP
        UTL_FILE.WRITE_LINE (fid, line);
    END LOOP;
    UTL_FILE.FCLOSE (fid);
EXCEPTION
    WHEN OTHERS THEN UTL_FILE.FCLOSE (fid);
END;
/
```

24-18. Here is one possible implementation:

```
/* Filename on web page: dumpemps.sp */
CREATE OR REPLACE PROCEDURE emps2file (
    loc IN VARCHAR2,
    file IN VARCHAR2
    )
IS
```

```
    fid UTL_FILE.FILE_TYPE := UTL_FILE.FOPEN (loc, file, 'W');
    line VARCHAR2(2000);
BEGIN
    FOR rec IN
        (SELECT last_name, hire_date, salary FROM employee)
    LOOP
        line :=
            rec.last_name || ',' ||
            TO_CHAR (rec.hire_date, 'MM/DD/YYYY') || ',' ||
            rec.salary;
        UTL_FILE.PUT_LINE (fid, line);
    END LOOP;
    UTL_FILE.FCLOSE (fid);
EXCEPTION
    WHEN OTHERS THEN UTL_FILE.FCLOSE (fid);
END;
/
```

Notice that the file is closed both when the process completes success-fully and in case an error arises.

24-19. Unfortunately for us, the file is owned by the Oracle process. This can result in the strange situation of a user creating a file that the user cannot then delete (through the operating system).

24-20. The trick here is to use the UTL_FILE.PUTF procedure to do a formatted print:

```
/* Filename on web page: freedom.sp */
CREATE OR REPLACE PROCEDURE what_is_freedom (
    fid IN UTL_FILE.FILE_TYPE,
    it_is IN VARCHAR2)
IS
BEGIN
    UTL_FILE.PUTF (fid,
        'Freedom''s just another word \n' ||
        'for working on your %s\n-- Dave Lippman',
        it_is);
END;
/
```

With PUTF, you can specify up to five arguments that are substituted into the string at the corresponding %s delimiters. In addition, if you include the "\n" string, UTL_FILE.PUTF inserts a new line into the file.

24-21. You can call the UTL_FILE.IS_OPEN function as shown in the following sample exception section:

```
EXCEPTION
    WHEN OTHERS
    THEN
        IF UTL_FILE.IS_OPEN (fid)
        THEN
            UTL_FILE.FCLOSE (fid);
        END IF;
END;
```

24-22. You can have up to 10 files open in a given session.

24-23. Here are all the ways I can think of:

      a. `UTL_FILE.PUT_LINE ('I LUV ORACLE');`

      b. `UTL_FILE.PUT ('I LUV ORACLE');`
        `UTL_FILE.NEW_LINE;`

      c. `UTL_FILE.PUTF ('I LUV ORACLE\n');`

24-24. Here is one possible implementation:

```
/* Filename on web page: getline.sp */
CREATE OR REPLACE PROCEDURE get_line
    (file_in IN UTL_FILE.FILE_TYPE,
     line_out OUT VARCHAR2,
     eof_out OUT BOOLEAN)
IS
BEGIN
   UTL_FILE.GET_LINE (file_in, line_out);
   eof_out := FALSE;
EXCEPTION
   WHEN NO_DATA_FOUND
   THEN
      line_out := NULL;
      eof_out  := TRUE;
END;
/
```

The advantage to using get_line is that you don't have to rely on the raising of an exception to detect an end-of-file. This allows you to write code that is more readable and graceful in its file handling. Instead of writing code like this, for example, to read the contents of a file:

```
BEGIN
   LOOP
      UTL_FILE.GET_LINE (fid, line);
      process_data (line);
   END LOOP;
EXCEPTION
   WHEN NO_DATA_FOUND THEN UTL_FILE.FCLOSE (fid);
END;
```

You could write it this way:

```
BEGIN
   LOOP
      get_line (fid, line, eof);
      EXIT WHEN eof;
      process_data (line);
   END LOOP;
END;
```

Now the condition that stops the loop is explicitly referenced and is understandable.

24-25. In versions of Oracle prior to 8.1, the PL/SQL runtime engine raises a UTL_FILE.INVALID_OPERATION error. In 8.1 and above, the package behaves as you'd expect: if you cannot append, it opens the file with Write mode.

24-26. Here is an fopen function that automatically corrects for append-related errors:

```
/* Filename on web page: fopen.sf */
CREATE OR REPLACE FUNCTION fopen
    (loc_in IN VARCHAR2,
     file_in IN VARCHAR2,
     mode_in IN VARCHAR2 := 'R')
     RETURN UTL_FILE.FILE_TYPE
IS
    fID UTL_FILE.FILE_TYPE;
BEGIN
    fID := UTL_FILE.FOPEN (loc_in, file_in, mode_in);
    RETURN fid;
EXCEPTION
   WHEN UTL_FILE.INVALID_OPERATION
   THEN
      IF mode_in = 'A'
      THEN
         fID := UTL_FILE.FOPEN (loc_in, file_in, 'W');
         RETURN fid;
      ELSE
         RAISE;
      END IF;
END;
/
```

It needs to be a function so that it can return a file handle, as does the UTL_FILE.FOPEN function. If your attempt to open for append fails with the INVALID_OPERATION error, then try again for write only. If any other error occurs or if the INVALID_OPERATION error occurs for read or write modes, you propagate the exception out of the function.

24-27. Nothing happens; at least, no exception is raised. The request to close the file is ignored.

24-28. How about an fcreate procedure?

```
/* Filename on web page: fcreate.sp */
CREATE OR REPLACE PROCEDURE fcreate
    (loc_in IN VARCHAR2,
     file_in IN VARCHAR2)
IS
    fID UTL_FILE.FILE_TYPE;
BEGIN
    fID := UTL_FILE.FOPEN (loc_in, file_in, 'W');
    UTL_FILE.FCLOSE (fid);
END;
/
```

Expert

24-29. You see the following results:

```
SQL> @isopen.tst
Who closed my file?
```

In other words, even though the file is actually open, UTL_FILE acts as if it is closed. How to explain this strange behavior? Simple: the UTL_FILE.IS_OPEN function is not all that it appears to be. This program does not (as of Oracle8*i* Release 8.1, in any case) actually check with the operating system concerning the status of this file. It merely checks the value of the id field of the UTL_FILE.FILE_TYPE record (in the above block, fid); if that field is NOT NULL, the file is deemed to be open.

24-30. This is a trick, and a tricky question. There really isn't a way to get around the maximum-length limitation in UTL_FILE (1023 bytes prior to 8.0.5, 32K afterwards—at which point this idea will probably become irrelevant). Instead, you can write out chunks of the string within the allowable size, and then tack on a "continuation character" that indicates the line is continued and needs to be merged.

Here is one possible implementation that allows you to specify the continuation character and also the maximum allowable line size:

```
/* Filename on web page: putline.sp */
CREATE OR REPLACE PROCEDURE put_line
    (file_in IN UTL_FILE.FILE_TYPE,
     line_in IN VARCHAR2,
     continchar_in IN VARCHAR2 := '-',
     max_line_size_in IN INTEGER := 1023)
IS
    v_line VARCHAR2 (32767);
    v_linelen CONSTANT INTEGER := LENGTH (line);
    v_start INTEGER := 1;
    v_max CONSTANT INTEGER := max_line_size_in - 1;
BEGIN
    LOOP
        EXIT WHEN v_start > v_linelen OR v_linelen IS NULL;
        v_line := SUBSTR (line_in, v_start, v_max);
        IF v_start + v_max < v_linelen
        THEN
            v_line := v_line || continchar_in;
        END IF;
        UTL_FILE.PUT_LINE (file_in, v_line);
        v_start := v_start + v_max;
    END LOOP;
END;
/
```

Notice that it adds the continuation character only if you're not at the end of the string.

24-31. Here is one possible implementation (comments are removed for reasons of space. See the version on the web page for full documentation):

```
/*Filename on web page: infile.sf */
CREATE OR REPLACE FUNCTION infile
    (loc_in IN VARCHAR2,
     file_in IN VARCHAR2,
     text_in IN VARCHAR2,
     occurrence_in IN INTEGER := 1,
     start_line_in IN INTEGER := 1,
     end_line_in IN INTEGER := 0,
     ignore_case_in IN BOOLEAN := TRUE)
RETURN INTEGER
IS
    file_handle UTL_FILE.FILE_TYPE;
    line_of_text VARCHAR2(1000);
    text_loc INTEGER;
    found_count INTEGER := 0;
    no_more_lines BOOLEAN := FALSE;
    return_value INTEGER := 0;
BEGIN
    /* All arguments are fine. Open and read through the file. */
    file_handle := UTL_FILE.FOPEN (loc_in, file_in, 'R');
    LOOP
        /* Get next line and exit if at end of file...
           see getline.sp for implementation of this function. */
        get_line (file_handle, line_of_text, no_more_lines);
        EXIT WHEN no_more_lines;

        /* Have another line from file. */
        return_value := return_value + 1;

        /* If this line is between the search range... */
        IF (return_value BETWEEN start_line_in AND end_line_in) OR
           (return_value >= start_line_in AND end_line_in = 0)
        THEN
            /* Use INSTR to see if text is present. */
            IF ignore_case_in
            THEN
                text_loc := INSTR (line_of_text, text_in);
            ELSE
                text_loc :=
                    INSTR (UPPER (line_of_text), UPPER (text_in));
            END IF;

            /* If text location is positive, have a match. */
            IF text_loc > 0
            THEN
                /* Increment found counter. Exit if matches request. */
                found_count := found_count + 1;
                EXIT WHEN found_count = occurrence_in;
            END IF;
        END IF;
    END LOOP;
```

```
    UTL_FILE.FCLOSE (file_handle);

    RETURN return_value;
END;
/
```

24-32. This problem is a consequence of how Oracle raises exceptions in the UTL_FILE package. This package contains a series of user-defined exceptions, declared as follows:

```
invalid_path       EXCEPTION;
invalid_mode       EXCEPTION;
invalid_filehandle EXCEPTION;
invalid_operation  EXCEPTION;
read_error         EXCEPTION;
write_error        EXCEPTION;
internal_error     EXCEPTION;
```

Now, on the one hand, it is very nice that UTL_FILE gives us all these descriptive names for the errors. It does not, unfortunately, also use the PRAGMA EXCEPTION_INIT statement to assign a number to these named exceptions. Since all user-defined exceptions have a SQLCODE of 1 and a SQLERRM of "User-defined exception", we end up with lots of ambiguity when any of these UTL_FILE exceptions go unhandled.

24-33. Whenever you work with user-defined exceptions, you have to handle them by name if you are to have any hope of figuring out what went wrong. So, the first thing you want to do is add an exception section to your program. Then you include exception handlers in your program.

24-34. Here is one possible implementation:

```
/* Filename on web page: filepath.pkg */
CREATE OR REPLACE PACKAGE BODY fileIO
IS
    g_path VARCHAR2(2000);

    PROCEDURE setpath (str IN VARCHAR2) IS
    BEGIN
        g_path := str;
    END;

    FUNCTION path RETURN VARCHAR2 IS
    BEGIN
        RETURN g_path;
    END;

    FUNCTION open (file IN VARCHAR2) RETURN UTL_FILE.FILE_TYPE
    IS
        /* Location of next path separator */
        v_lastsep PLS_INTEGER := 1;

        v_sep PLS_INTEGER := INSTR (g_path, c_delim);
        v_dir VARCHAR2(500);
```

```
                    retval UTL_FILE.FILE_TYPE;
            BEGIN
               LOOP
                  BEGIN
                     IF v_sep = 0
                     THEN
                        v_dir := SUBSTR (g_path, v_lastsep);
                     ELSE
                        v_dir :=
                           SUBSTR (
                              g_path,
                              v_lastsep,
                              v_sep - v_lastsep);
                     END IF;
                     retval := UTL_FILE.FOPEN (v_dir, file, 'R');

                     -- If this far, I found the file, so stop.
                     EXIT;
                  EXCEPTION
                     WHEN OTHERS
                     THEN
                        IF v_sep = 0
                        THEN
                           /* No more dirs to try, propagate error.
                           RAISE;
                        ELSE
                           v_lastsep := v_sep + 1;
                           v_sep := INSTR (g_path, c_delim, v_sep+1);
                        END IF;
                  END;
               END LOOP;
               RETURN retval;
            END;
         END;
         /
```

24-35. Here is one possible implementation. Note the following about this implementation:

- Use a programmer-defined record to store all of the information about the log file.

- Call UTL_FILE.FFLUSH to flush each line to the file so that you can see the output immediately.

- Each time you call setfile, it closes the current log file unless the location and name match.

```
/* Filename on web page: flog.pkg */
CREATE OR REPLACE PACKAGE BODY flog
IS
   TYPE file_info_t IS RECORD (
      loc VARCHAR2(1000),
      file VARCHAR2(200),
      fid UTL_FILE.FILE_TYPE);
   file_info file_info_t;
```

```
      PROCEDURE setfile (loc IN VARCHAR2, file IN VARCHAR2)
      IS
      BEGIN
         IF UTL_FILE.IS_OPEN (file_info.fid)
         THEN
            IF file_info.file = file AND
               file_info.loc  = loc
            THEN
               UTL_FILE.FCLOSE (file_info.fid);
            END IF;
         END IF;
         file_info.loc := loc;
         file_info.file := file;
         file_info.fid :=
            UTL_FILE.FOPEN (file_info.loc, file_info.file, 'A');
      EXCEPTION
         WHEN UTL_FILE.INVALID_OPERATION
         THEN
            file_info.fID :=
               UTL_FILE.FOPEN (file_info.loc, file_info.file, 'W');
      END;

      PROCEDURE put_line (
         prog IN VARCHAR2, code IN INTEGER, msg IN VARCHAR2)
      IS
      BEGIN
         IF UTL_FILE.IS_OPEN (file_info.fid)
         THEN
            UTL_FILE.PUT_LINE (file_info.fid,
               TO_CHAR (SYSDATE, 'YYYYMMDDHH24MISS') || delim ||
               prog || delim ||
               code || delim ||
               msg || delim ||
               USER);

            UTL_FILE.FFLUSH (file_info.fid);
         END IF;
      END;

      PROCEDURE close
      IS
      BEGIN
         UTL_FILE.FCLOSE (file_info.fid);
      END;

   END flog;
   /
```

25

DBMS_JOB Built-in Package

Beginner

25-1. You need DBMS_JOB to schedule and execute PL/SQL procedures at pre-defined times or at regular intervals, such as routine maintenance procedures or developer batch jobs.

25-2. The three *INIT.ORA* parameters that affect DBMS_JOB are:

JOB_QUEUE_INTERVAL

Specifies (in seconds) how often the Oracle SNP process "wakes up" to check the job queue. Too small an interval (or too many queue processes) decreases server performance; too large an interval can cause the jobs to fall behind schedule. The recommended value for most cases is 60 seconds.

JOB_QUEUE_PROCESSES

Specifies the number of concurrent SNP background processes (i.e., how many jobs can execute in parallel). This value can range from 0 (the default) to 36. A value of 1 or 2 is usually enough for a small number of jobs.

JOB_QUEUE_KEEP_CONNECTIONS

Specifies whether database connections established by the background processes are held open during "sleep periods" (no jobs running). This value may be either TRUE, in which case the process keeps its connection, or FALSE (the default), in which case the process closes the connection and reestablishes a new one the next time it runs. While a TRUE value yields better performance, it can also interfere with the ability to shut down the database.

25-3. Since only one concurrent process is allowed, the second job must wait until the first job is complete.

25-4. No, it's not possible. Every started job establishes a lock in the V$LOCK table to prevent other processes from reexecuting the job.

25-5. DBMS_JOB has two procedures to submit a job into the queue: SUBMIT and ISUBMIT. Both procedures share the following parameters:

job A unique identifier for a particular job. You use this number, which uniquely identifies each job, to perform any operations with the job, such as querying Oracle's data dictionary about various jobs, updating the job execution interval, etc.

what
The PL/SQL block executes when the job runs (a stored procedure call is assumed to be enclosed within a BEGIN-END block).

next_date
The next date the job will execute.

interval
A date function that determines how to compute the next execution date. After a job executes successfully, the value of this function becomes the new next_date.

no_parse
A BOOLEAN flag that specifies whether you want to parse the job's *what* parameter immediately (indicated by a FALSE) or whether to wait until the first execution (indicated by a TRUE).

25-6. SUBMIT assigns a unique ID for the job automatically from the sequence SYS.JOBSEQ, and returns this number in the OUT parameter job. ISUBMIT allows you to supply your own job ID with the IN parameter job. When using ISUBMIT, you're responsible for guaranteeing a unique ID. Otherwise, you receive the following error:

```
ORA-00001: unique constraint (SYS.I_JOB_JOB) violated
```

25-7. Even though Oracle documentation states that it is not necessary, you should always issue a COMMIT after each call to SUBMIT or ISUBMIT:

```
BEGIN
    DBMS_JOB.ISUBMIT ( 33, 'calc_totals;', SYSDATE, 'SYSDATE + 1');
    COMMIT;
END;
/
```

25-8. The job never executes because the next_date parameter is set to NULL, which causes DBMS_JOB to set the next execution date to January 1, 4000 (effectively preventing the execution of the job). It allows you to submit a job, but does not yet submit it for execution.

25-9. You must remember to end your stored procedure call or anonymous block with a semicolon. Oracle doesn't do it for you.

```
DBMS_JOB.ISUBMIT (job => 33,
                  what => 'foo;',
                  next_date => NULL,
                  interval => 'SYSDATE + 1');
```

25-10. No; in fact, probably the only thing you can be sure of is it won't be 1:00 P.M.! To see why, suppose that interval is set to 60 (the default). On average, you'll have a 30-second delay every time before starting the job, resulting in a 3-hour (30 * 365 / 3600) delay per year! This cumulative shifting (i.e., later and later), or *drift*, is inherent in interval expressions such as 'SYSDATE + 1'.

To set an exact time, use the TRUNC function and date arithmetic in the INTERVAL parameter to set up the next execution time precisely:

```
DBMS_JOB.ISUBMIT (
    job => 33,
    what => 'DUMP_USERS;',
    next_date => SYSDATE,
    interval => 'TRUNC(SYSDATE) + 13/24'
);
```

The TRUNC function truncates the current date to noon, and + 13/24 means "add 13 hours from midnight" (i.e., 1:00 P.M.). Such declarations ensure that the next execution time is close to 1:00 P.M., regardless of the previous execution time. If you want to operate in minutes, not hours, use the formula 'minutes / (24 * 60)' to qualify the number of minutes you want to add.

25-11. There are two ways to temporarily stop a job (without, of course, deleting it from the queue). The first option is to use the DBMS_JOB.BROKEN procedure to set the broken flag to TRUE for the job, since broken jobs are never run:

```
DBMS_JOB.BROKEN (job => 33, broken => TRUE);
```

To return the job to its normal state, simply set the broken flag back to FALSE.

The second method is to change the next_date parameter to some date far in the future using DBMS_JOB.NEXT_DATE:

```
DBMS_JOB.NEXT_DATE (
    job => 33,
    next_date => TO_DATE ('01.01.3000', 'DD.MM.YYYY')
);
```

Better yet, you can set next_date to NULL, which, as we've already seen, will automatically set the next execution date to January 1, 4000:

```
DBMS_JOB.NEXT_DATE (job => 33, next_date => NULL);
```

25-12. Yes, you can use the DBMS_JOB.RUN procedure to run the task. This sets the broken flag to FALSE if execution was successful. So after improving and compiling the foo procedure, all you need to do is to run Job 33:

```
DBMS_JOB.RUN (job => 33);
COMMIT;
```

This way you can both return the job to the job queue and test to make sure it runs.

25-13. Submit the job with a NULL value in the interval parameter. For example, if you have a table you want to clear out three days hence, you can use the following call:

```
DBMS_JOB.ISUBMIT (
    job => 34,
    what => 'delete from CONFIDENTIAL_DOCS;',
    next_date => TRUNC (SYSDATE) + 3,
    interval => NULL
);
```

25-14. You can use the DBMS_JOB.RUN procedure to force an immediate execution. This should be done with caution, however, as there are a number of possible side effects. For example:

- Assuming that next_date follows the "SYSDATE + 1" format, rather than a "TRUNC(SYSDATE)+1" format, executing the job manually permanently changes the job's execution time. For example, if the job was originally submitted to run daily at around 12:00 A.M., and you execute it manually at 1:30 P.M., it runs in the middle of the day from then on.

- The National Language Support (NLS) settings specified when the job was originally submitted are changed to the settings of the user who reexecuted the job. If the two users have different NLS settings, this can cause problems.

- The broken flag might change.

25-15. The ALL_JOBS and DBA_JOBS data dictionary views provide you with information about all jobs in the queue. Although these views have a huge number of columns, the most interesting columns are JOB, LAST_DATE (last successful execution), NEXT_DATE (next planned execution), LOG_USER (job owner), BROKEN, INTERVAL, FAILURES (number of unsuccessful executions), and WHAT.

The DBA_JOBS_RUNNING view provides information about currently running jobs.

25-16. The following script shows the status of all the jobs in the queue:

```
ALTER SESSION SET NLS_DATE_FORMAT = 'HH24:MI DD MON';
SELECT job,
```

```
        SUBSTR (
            DECODE (
                broken, 'Y',
                'BROKEN', DECODE (
                            failures,
                            0, 'OK',
                            NULL, 'NEW ',
                            TO_CHAR (failures) || ' FAILURES'
                          )
            ),
            1,
            11
        )
            status,
        SUBSTR (log_user, 1, 15) owner,
        last_date,
        next_date,
        SUBSTR (what, 1, 20) what
  FROM dba_jobs
ORDER BY next_date;
```

This script shows NEW in the STATUS column for just-submitted jobs, OK for successful jobs, BROKEN for already broken, and number of failures otherwise. Here is sample output:

```
JOB        STATUS       OWNER            LAST_DATE      NEXT_DATE     WHAT
---------  -----------  ---------------  -------------  ------------  -----
       17  OK           PLV              19:19 07 MAR   19:20 07 MAR  test
       33  3 FAILURES   PLV                             19:26 07 MAR  AAA;
        2  OK           PLV              10:39 07 MAR   01:28 08 MAR  begin
       36  OK           PLV              15:30 07 MAR   15:30 08 MAR  NULL;
       34  NEW          PLV                             00:00 10 MAR  delete
    10000  BROKEN       PLV              00:19 05 MAR   00:00 01 JAN  update
```

25-17. This script shows the ID of the session where job is running, the user-name for this session, the job number, and the time the job was started:

```
ALTER SESSION SET NLS_DATE_FORMAT = 'HH24:MI DD MON';
SELECT r.sid,
       s.username,
       j.job,
       r.this_date,
       SUBSTR (j.what, 1, 20) what
  FROM dba_jobs_running r,
       dba_jobs j,
       v$session s
 WHERE j.job = r.job
   AND r.sid = s.sid;
```

25-18. Although doing so would be wonderful, you should not use user-defined functions (in this case, next_business_day) in the interval parameter. Although you can submit such jobs, they don't execute at the correct times. Consequently, you should use PL/SQL date functions only.

25-19. You can use the WHAT, NEXT_DATE, and INTERVAL procedures from the DBMS_JOB package. Each procedure changes the corresponding parameter. Another procedure, CHANGE, can change any or all of the parameters. For example, to change the execution interval for job #33, issue the call:

```
DBMS_JOB.INTERVAL (job => 33, interval => 'TRUNC(SYSDATE) + 7');
```

Note that you can't change the job number.

25-20. It's really easy; simply create a PL/SQL block with two commands instead of one:

```
DBMS_JOB.ISUBMIT (
      job => 36,
      what => ' BEGIN LFF; PRR; END;',
      next_date => SYSDATE,
      interval => 'SYSDATE + 1'
   );
```

25-21. You can make a job jump to the head of the queue by setting its next_date parameter to some date in the past:

```
DBMS_JOB.ISUBMIT (
      job => 58,
      what => 'URGENT_JOB;',
      next_date => TRUNC (SYSDATE) - 1,
      interval => NULL
   );
```

This works because Oracle selects jobs for execution based on the order of next_date; the new job is fetched first (assuming, of course, you have no jobs with a next_date earlier that what you set your job to).

25-22. The first way to remove the job is to use DBMS_JOB.REMOVE:

```
DBMS_JOB.REMOVE (job => 58);
```

The second way is to change the job's interval parameter to NULL:

```
DBMS_JOB.INTERVAL (job => 58, interval => NULL);
```

Note that in either case, if the job is already running when you issue the command, it is allowed to finish and then is removed from the job queue. Consequently, you can't use either method to "kill" an abnormal or long-running job.

25-23. DBMS_JOB has a special procedure for this purpose: DBMS_JOB.USER_EXPORT. Calling this procedure returns, via a VARCHAR2 OUT parameter, a string consisting of a call to DBMS_JOB.ISUBMIT. You can then execute this string in the other database to recreate the job. Remember that the other database could already have a job with the same number, so you must check this and adjust the job number if necessary. The job number can be adjusted upwards by issuing the following SELECT until it is at an appropriate value:

```
SELECT SYS.JOBSEQ.NEXTVAL FROM dual;
```

Intermediate

25-24. When the job execution fails, Oracle attempts to start it again one minute later. If it fails again, Oracle repeatedly doubles the amount of time it waits before the next execution attempt (i.e., 2, 4, 8, 16, etc., minutes), until it either exceeds the normal execution interval or fails 16 times. In this case, the job is flagged as broken.

25-25. The actual sequence is as follows:

1. Start database session with job owner's username.

2. Alter session NLS settings to those settings that were active when job was submitted.

3. Calculate next execution date using interval's formula.

4. Execute PL/SQL mentioned in the "what" parameter.

5. If block fails, increment failures number, set next execution date to one minute later if it's the first failure, double the interval otherwise.

6. If there are no errors, update next_date.

 Oracle always alters the session's NLS parameters to the ones used when the job was originally submitted. For example, if you change the NLS_DATE_FORMAT after the job was submitted, that job still uses the original NLS_DATE_FORMAT defined when you first submitted the job.

25-26. Since jobs running as background processes have no associated terminal, it's impossible to put an error message to the terminal. Consequently, to find an error that occurred during execution, you must check the log files to find the error number(s) and message(s).

To do this, check either the *RDBMSxx/TRACE* directory in the Oracle home catalog or the path defined in the BACKGROUND_DUMP_DEST parameter of the *INIT.ORA* file. While the name of the SNP's log file depends on the platform, it typically consists of a concatenation of the instance's name, the literal SNP, and the SNP process number. For example:

```
orclSNP0.TRC
orclSNP1.TRC
```

Open the file and check the last message to find the error.

Alternatively, you can force the job to run using the DBMS_JOB.RUN procedure. In this case you'll see the error messages, if any, on the screen.

25-27. There are two ways to check if a job is currently running. First, you can look in the DBA_JOBS_RUNNING view for particular job number:

```
SELECT * FROM dba_jobs_running WHERE job = 36;
```

Second, you can query the V$LOCK for a running job because Oracle establishes a special lock (lock type = 'JQ') for running jobs. The job number is defined in the ID2 column:

```
SELECT id2 "ID2->JOB#" FROM v$lock WHERE TYPE = 'JQ';
```

25-28. The following script shows the execution time (in minutes) for all current jobs:

```
SELECT r.job,
       ROUND ((SYSDATE - r.this_date) * 60 * 24) execution,
       SUBSTR (j.what, 1, 30) what
  FROM dba_jobs_running r,
       dba_jobs j
 WHERE r.job = j.job;
```

25-29. You can use any date functions. The most useful are:

ADD_MONTHS (D, n)

> Returns the date D + n months.

LAST_DAY (D)

> Returns the date of the last day of the month for the specified date.

NEXT_DAY (D, WeekDay)

> Returns the date of the first week day after the specified date D.

ROUND (D [, Fmt])

> Returns D rounded to the unit specified by the format Fmt. Fmt could be "HH24," "DD," "MM," etc. If you omit Fmt, D is rounded to the day (e.g., Fmt = 'DD').

SYSDATE

> Returns the current system date and time.

LEAST (D1, D2 [, D3 [, …]])

> Returns the least date from the list.

GREATEST (D1, D2 [, D3 [, …]])

> Returns the greatest date from the list.

TO_CHAR (D [, Fmt])

> Converts D to VARCHAR2 in the Fmt format. If you omit Fmt, NLS_DATE_FORMAT is applied.

TO_DATE (S [, Fmt])

> Converts string S in the Fmt format to date. If you omit Fmt, NLS_DATE_FORMAT is applied.

TRUNC (D [, Fmt])

Returns D with the time portion of the day truncated to the unit, specified by the Fmt format. If you omit Fmt, D is truncated to the beginning of D (e.g., Fmt = 'DD').

25-30. The interval is:

```
'SYSDATE + 1/24';
```

25-31. The interval is:

```
'SYSDATE + 1/(24*60)'
```

25-32. The interval is:

```
'SYSDATE + 1/(24*60*60)'
```

25-33. The interval is:

```
'TRUNC(SYSDATE+1) + 11/24'
```

25-34. The interval is:

```
'NEXT_DAY(TRUNC(SYSDATE), "FRIDAY") + 21/24'
```

25-35. The interval is:

```
'TRUNC(  LEAST( NEXT_DAY(SYSDATE,"SATURDAY"), ' ||
'               NEXT_DAY(SYSDATE,"SUNDAY"))) + 6/24 '
```

25-36. The interval is:

```
'LAST_DAY(SYSDATE + 1) + 23/24'
```

25-37. You can retrieve the value of a job's execution definition by including a special parameter in the job definition. The parameter must have one of the following names: job, next_date, or broken. Whenever Oracle sees one of these special names, it substitutes the corresponding value for the execution definition:

```
DBMS_JOB.ISUBMIT (
     job => 36,
     what => ' MY_PROC(job, next_date, broken_flag);',
     next_date => SYSDATE,
     interval => 'SYSDATE + 1'
  );
```

Since next_date and broken are treated as IN OUT parameters, you can allow a job to alter its schedule. For example, the job could change its next execution date regardless of interval, set itself into the broken state, or even remove itself from the job queue.

25-38. First, create a table to store the log:

```
CREATE TABLE user_log (
    tstamp    DATE,
    username  VARCHAR2(30),
    osuser    VARCHAR2(15),
    machine   VARCHAR2(64),
    program   VARCHAR2(64),
    module    VARCHAR2(48));
```

Now, write the procedure itself. Since there's a fairly complex schedule, you need to make dump_users modify its job-definition parameters:

```
CREATE OR REPLACE PROCEDURE dump_users (next_date IN OUT DATE)
IS
    d NUMBER    --detect weekday
            := TO_NUMBER (TO_CHAR (next_date, 'D')) - 1;
    h NUMBER    --detect hour
            := TO_NUMBER (TO_CHAR (next_date, 'HH24'));
BEGIN
    /*
    || Set execution schedule:
    || If day is a weekend (i.e. Sunday or Saturday) or
    || hour before 8:00 AM or after 6:00 PM, then execute hourly.
    || Otherwise, execute at 7:00 PM
    */
    IF (d IN (0, 6)) OR (h < 8 OR h > 18)
    THEN
        -- then execute every hour
        next_date := TRUNC (next_date, 'HH24') + 1 / 24;
    ELSE
        -- execute at 7 PM
        next_date := TRUNC (next_date) + 19 / 24;
    END IF;

    /*
    || Save V$SESSION information into the log table
    */
    INSERT INTO user_log
        SELECT SYSDATE,
                username,
                osuser,
                machine,
                program,
                module
          FROM v$session
         WHERE TYPE != 'BACKGROUND'
           AND username IS NOT NULL;

    COMMIT;
END;
```

Now you need to submit this job. There are two things to note. First, you need to use the special next_date parameter as part of the job definition. Second, you can use any correct nonnull interval value since you are computing the next execution date yourself:

```
DBMS_JOB.ISUBMIT (
    job => 88,
    what => 'DUMP_USERS(next_date);',
    next_date => SYSDATE,
    interval => 'SYSDATE + 1'
    );
```

Expert

25-39. As we've seen, the REMOVE procedure doesn't stop a running job; you need, instead, to use the ALTER SYSTEM KILL SESSION command, which requires two parameters: the SID of the job you want to kill and the job's serial number. You can find the SID in the DBA_JOBS_RUNNING view, and the job's serial number in the V$SESSION view:

```
SELECT r.job,
       r.sid,
       s.serial#
  FROM dba_jobs_running r,
       v$session s
 WHERE r.sid = s.sid
   AND r.job = 47;

     JOB       SID   SERIAL#
--------- --------- ---------
      47         7         3
```

The next step is to mark the job broken to prevent future execution:

```
DBMS_JOB.BROKEN( 47, TRUE);
COMMIT;
```

Finally, issue the KILL command:

```
ALTER SYSTEM KILL SESSION '7,3';
```

25-40. You'll find a suggested procedure in the *runjob.sp* file on the book's web ⊕ page.

25-41. We have:

```
next_date IN VARCHAR2,
```

in ISUBMIT and:

```
next_date IN DATE DEFAULT sysdate,
```

in SUBMIT. Since this makes no sense, it's probably just somebody's mistake during the creation of the DBMS_JOB package. What is really strange, however, is that this mistake migrates from version to version without changes, which causes two problems. The first is that since the next_date parameter doesn't have a default value, you can't omit the parameter in the ISUBMIT procedure. The second is that when you use an NLS_DATE_FORMAT different from the current default for the database instance, the ISUBMIT procedure truncates next_date to the beginning of the day. Here's an example of this:

```
SQL> ALTER SESSION SET NLS_DATE_FORMAT = 'DD.MM.YYYY';
Session altered.
SQL> EXEC DBMS_JOB.ISUBMIT(45,'NULL;',SYSDATE + 25/24,'SYSDATE + 1');
PL/SQL procedure successfully completed.
```

```
SQL> SELECT TO_CHAR(NEXT_DATE,'HH24:MI DD/MM') "WRONG!"
  2    FROM DBA_JOBS where JOB=45;
WRONG!
--------------------------------------------------------------------------
00:00 08/03
```

The only way to submit your desired next_date in this case is to do it in two steps:

```
DBMS_JOB.ISUBMIT (
    job => 46,
    what => 'NULL;',
    next_date => NULL,    -- WILL BE SET TO 01.01.4000
    interval => 'SYSDATE + 1'
);
DBMS_JOB.NEXT_DATE (job => 46,    -- SET DESIRED DATE
                    next_date => SYSDATE + 25 / 24);
COMMIT;
```

26

Using Java with PL/SQL

Beginner

26-1. (c). Oracle8*i*'s Java Virtual Machine is called Aurora (Aur-ora…get it?)

26-2. The statements are:

a. False. Java stored procedures are fundamentally different from Java applets because they are compiled and stored in the database.

b. False. Oracle8*i* allows you to call Java procedures from PL/SQL, allowing you to take advantage of the hundreds of prebuilt (and third-party) classes.

c. True. You can call Java stored procedures from SQL or PL/SQL via PL/SQL wrappers, from Java applets via JDBC or SQLJ, from Pro*C via OCI (the Oracle Call Interface), and from Visual Basic or Oracle Forms via ODBC (Open Database Connectivity).

d. False. Java is a true object-oriented language; PL/SQL, while it has some OO properties, is primarily a procedural language.

e. True. The Java foundation classes contain a rich set of operations, such as file I/O and networking, that you can exploit in your PL/SQL programs.

f. False. Java and PL/SQL are equals in the database.

g. False. Java is controlled by Javasoft, a division of Sun Microsystems. While Java is more open than PL/SQL, it is still (for now, at any rate) under the control of a single entity.

h. True. Java was designed as a "write once, run anywhere" language, so it's fairly easy to run on a variety of platforms with very little effort.

       i. False. Java programs are compiled into an intermediate form called *bytecode* that is interpreted by a Java Virtual Machine such as Aurora.

       j. True. Java, like C and C++, is case-sensitive.

26-3. (b). Java programs that are compiled and stored in the database are called Java stored procedures (JSPs).

26-4. (d). PL/SQL procedures and functions are most similar to Java methods.

26-5. (d). Compiling a Java program creates a class file that ends in *.class*.

26-6. (a). A call spec establishes a logical correspondence between a Java method and a PL/SQL procedure or function (standalone or packaged) or a member method of a SQL object type.

26-7. (b). The Java class name is the missing component in the listing; note that the Java class name is similar to a PL/SQL package name in that it identifies a group of items, such as variables and methods.

26-8. (d). The method name is the missing component in the listing. Java methods are similar to PL/SQL procedures or functions.

26-9. (b). The parameter datatype is the missing component in the listing. Like PL/SQL, Java parameters have a name and a type; unlike PL/SQL, Java parameters' datatypes are specified before their parameter names.

26-10. (e). The method return type is the missing component in the listing. All Java methods must have an associated type, even if it doesn't actually return anything (in this case, the return type is *void*, rather than a "true" type such as *int* or *double*).

26-11. (d). The function created in example (d) is a call spec, a PL/SQL function (or procedure) that maps a PL/SQL function (or procedure) onto a Java method. The call spec associates a PL/SQL function (or procedure) with a specific method within a class and defines a one-to-one mapping between the PL/SQL function's (or procedure's) parameters and the Java method's parameters.

Intermediate

26-12. These steps for accessing a Java class from PL/SQL are now in order:

       Use *javac* (or an IDE such as JDeveloper) to compile the Java code.
       Use *loadjava* to load the class into the database.
       Write PL/SQL wrappers to publish the class' methods.
       Grant the necessary privileges on the PL/SQL wrappers.
       Call the PL/SQL wrapper programs.

26-13. The operating system commands that compile and load the helloWorld class are:

```
javac helloWorld.java
loadjava "u scott/tiger "force helloWorld.class
```

26-14. The Oracle8*i* DDL command that loads the helloWorld class directly into the database is:

```
CREATE OR REPLACE JAVA SOURCE NAMED "helloWorld" AS
    public class helloWorld {
        public static void doit () {
            System.out.println("Hello World!!!");
        }
    };
```

26-15. (b). You include the LANGUAGE JAVA clause in a function or procedure header to create a call spec for a Java method.

26-16. Executing DBMS_JAVA.SET_OUTPUT (buffer size) is the equivalent of the command SET SERVEROUTPUT ON. You will not see any output from the Java's System.out or System.err until you execute this command.

26-17. (c). You should use a procedure to publish a *void* Java method.

26-18. Here is the completed table (remember that there are many Java equivalents for each PL/SQL datatype).

PL/SQL Datatype	Java Equivalent
VARCHAR2	java.lang.String
DATE	oracle.sql.DATE
NUMBER (integer)	int
NUMBER (real)	double
ROWID	java.lang.String
OBJECT	oracle.sql.STRUCT
RAW	byte[]

26-19. The call spec for the OutputTest class is:

```
CREATE OR REPLACE PROCEDURE output_test (str IN VARCHAR2)
AS LANGUAGE JAVA
NAME 'OutputTest.printIt (java.lang.String)';
```

26-20. The call spec for the Fibonacci class is:

```
CREATE OR REPLACE FUNCTION fib (n NUMBER) RETURN NUMBER
AS LANGUAGE JAVA
NAME 'Fibonacci.fib(int) return int';
```

26-21. The Java source code (the *.java* file) must have the same name as the class it contains; otherwise, you receive an error:

```
E:\JAVA>javac test.java
test.java:1: Public class helloWorld must be defined in a file called
```

```
    "helloWorld.java".
public class helloWorld {
                  ^

1 error

E:\JAVA>
```

Expert

26-22. The DDL statement to create the call spec will work fine; it won't report any creation errors. When you attempt to execute the my_hello procedure, however, you receive an error message stating that there is no method named doIt in the class. The problem is that the method's name is doit, not doIt (remember, case matters in Java!). To fix the problem, you must change the call spec to match the method name. Here's the output from SQL*Plus:

```
SQL> SET SERVEROUTPUT ON
SQL> EXEC DBMS_JAVA.SET_OUTPUT(1000);

PL/SQL procedure successfully completed.

SQL> CREATE OR REPLACE PROCEDURE my_hello
  2   AS LANGUAGE JAVA
  3   NAME 'helloWorld.doIt()';
  4  /

Procedure created.

SQL> EXEC my_hello
java.lang.NoSuchMethodException: No applicable method found


..
BEGIN my_hello; END;

*
ERROR at line 1:
ORA-29531: no method doIt in class helloWorld
ORA-06512: at "SCOTT.MY_HELLO", line 0
ORA-06512: at line 1
```

26-23. As in the previous exercise, the call spec compiles but doesn't run. The problem in this case is that you can publish only static methods. To fix the problem, add the static keyword to the definition of doit, recompile, and reload the class.

26-24. The following query displays information about the Java objects in a user schema:

```
SELECT object_name, object_type, status, timestamp
  FROM user_objects
 WHERE (object_name NOT LIKE 'SYS_%'
```

```
              AND object_name NOT LIKE 'CREATE$%'
              AND object_name NOT LIKE 'JAVA$%'
              AND object_name NOT LIKE 'LOADLOB%')
         AND object_type LIKE 'JAVA %'
      ORDER BY object_type, object_name;
```

26-25. The following procedure is an example of how to fetch the source code for a JSP into a CLOB, and then print it (note that you need a more sophisticated method to print bigger source files!):

```
/* Filename on web page: show_java_source.sp */
CREATE OR REPLACE PROCEDURE show_java_source (
   name IN VARCHAR2,
   schema IN VARCHAR2 := NULL
   )
IS
  b CLOB;
  v VARCHAR2(2000) ;
  i INTEGER ;
BEGIN
  /* Move the Java source code to a CLOB. */
  DBMS_LOB.CREATETEMPORARY (b, FALSE);
  DBMS_JAVA.EXPORT_SOURCE (name, NVL (schema, USER), b);

  /* Read the CLOB to a VARCHAR2 variable and display it. */
  i := 1000;
  DBMS_LOB.READ (b, i, 1, v);
  DBMS_OUTPUT.PUT_LINE (v); /* run pl.sp to create this procedure */
END;
/

SQL> EXEC SHOW_JAVA_SOURCE('Hello');
public class Hello {
      public static String hello() {
          return "Hello World";   } };

PL/SQL procedure successfully completed.

SQL>
```

26-26. The smallestFirst method swaps the parameter values so that the smallest one comes first. Since the parameters change, you must declare your corresponding PL/SQL parameters as IN OUT:

```
CREATE OR REPLACE PROCEDURE smallest_first
    (a IN OUT NUMBER, b IN OUT NUMBER) AS LANGUAGE JAVA
NAME 'NumberTest.smallestFirst(int[], int[])';
```

The following listing shows the results if you make the parameters IN only:

```
SQL> CREATE OR REPLACE PROCEDURE smallest_first
  2  (a IN NUMBER, b IN NUMBER)
  3  AS LANGUAGE JAVA
  4  NAME 'NumberTest.smallestFirst(int[], int[])';
  5  /
```

```
Procedure created.

SQL> declare
  2      x number := 100;
  3      y number :- 10;
  4  begin
  5      dbms_output.put_line ('X => ' || x || ', y=> ' || y);
  6      smallest_first (x,y);
  7      dbms_output.put_line ('X => ' || x || ', y=> ' || y);
  8  end;
  9  /
X => 100, y=> 10
java.lang.NullPointerException

at NumberTest.smallestFirst(NumberTest.java:3)

declare
*
ERROR at line 1:
ORA-29532: Java call terminated by uncaught Java exception:
   java.lang.NullPointerException
ORA-06512: at "SCOTT.SMALLEST_FIRST", line 0
ORA-06512: at line 6
```

26-27. The missing component is "oracle.sql.STRUCT", which passes complex Oracle object datatypes to Java.

26-28. Here is the specification for the basic file-operations package, along with the definition for the file_list_t type:

```
CREATE TYPE file_list_t IS TABLE OF VARCHAR2(2000);
/

CREATE OR REPLACE PACKAGE basic_file_ops
IS
    FUNCTION length (file IN VARCHAR2) RETURN NUMBER;
    FUNCTION delete (file IN VARCHAR2) RETURN BOOLEAN;
    PROCEDURE getDirContents (
        dir IN VARCHAR2,
        files IN OUT file_list_t);
END;
```

26-29. One of the principles of good design is to remove hardcoded values (sometimes called *magic values*) from programs by replacing them with constants or functions. This technique frees you from worrying how Java represents a Boolean true; whether the class uses a 1, −1, or even 3.1459 is not your concern. You just have to make sure your PL/SQL program interprets these values correctly.

The easiest way to do this is to store the return values of the Java "get" methods in packaged variables, which you can then use in place of literal values. First, you need three private, global variables to hold the Java literals. Second, you need three functions to return the literal values that represent true, false, and the filename delimiter. Finally, you need to use the package-initialization section to actually store the function's return value into the appropriate variable. Here's the code:

```
/*Filename on web page: basic_file_ops.pkg */
CREATE OR REPLACE PACKAGE BODY basic_file_ops
IS
    /* Used to handle conversion from number to boolean. */
    g_true INTEGER;
    g_false INTEGER;
    g_listdelim CHAR(1);

    FUNCTION tval RETURN NUMBER AS LANGUAGE JAVA
        NAME 'JFile.tVal () return int';
    FUNCTION fval RETURN NUMBER AS LANGUAGE JAVA
        NAME 'JFile.fVal () return int';
    FUNCTION delim RETURN VARCHAR2 AS LANGUAGE JAVA
        NAME 'JFile.listDelimiter () return java.lang.STring';

    -- Other procedures go here

BEGIN
    g_true := tval;
    g_false := fval;
    g_listdelim := delim;
END;
```

26-30. The easiest way to implement the delete-file function is to put a wrapper around the call spec to convert the results of the Java function into a PL/SQL Boolean value. This technique comes in handy in situations where you want to massage the results from a Java call:

```
/* Filename on web page: basic_file_ops.pkg */
    -- Here's the call spec...
    FUNCTION Idelete (file IN VARCHAR2) RETURN NUMBER
    AS LANGUAGE JAVA
        NAME 'JFile.delete (java.lang.String) return int';

    -- And here's the wrapper
    FUNCTION delete (file IN VARCHAR2) RETURN BOOLEAN
    AS
    BEGIN
        RETURN Idelete (file) = g_true;
    EXCEPTION
        WHEN OTHERS
        THEN
            DBMS_OUTPUT.PUT_LINE ('Error deleting: ' || SQLERRM);
            RETURN FALSE;
    END;
```

26-31. The function to retrieve the file's size is straightforward:

```
FUNCTION length (file IN VARCHAR2) RETURN NUMBER
    AS LANGUAGE JAVA
        NAME 'JFile.length (java.lang.String) return long';
```

26-32. As with the delete function, you implement the getDirContents file with
two procedures. The first simply retrieves the delimited string returned by
the Java function. The second parses the string and places each element
into a PL/SQL table:

```
/* Filename on web page: basic_file_ops.pkg */
FUNCTION dirContents (dir IN VARCHAR2) RETURN VARCHAR2
AS LANGUAGE JAVA
    NAME 'JFile.dirContents (java.lang.String) return java.lang.String';

PROCEDURE getDirContents (
    dir IN VARCHAR2,
    files IN OUT file_list_t)
IS
    file_list VARCHAR2(32767);
    next_delim PLS_INTEGER;
    start_pos PLS_INTEGER := 1;
BEGIN
    files.DELETE;
    file_list := dirContents (dir);
    LOOP
        next_delim :=
            INSTR (file_list, g_listdelim, start_pos);
        EXIT WHEN next_delim = 0;
        files.EXTEND;
        files(files.LAST) :=
            SUBSTR (file_list,
                start_pos,
                next_delim - start_pos);
        start_pos := next_delim + 1;
    END LOOP;
END;
```

26-33. You must grant the JAVAUSERPRIV role to a schema before it can read or
write a file. Then you must grant the JAVASYSPRIV role to create or delete
files. For example:

```
GRANT JAVAUSERPRIV TO SCOTT;
GRANT JAVASYSPRIV TO BIG_SCHEMA;
```

Finally, modify the UTL_FILE_DIR in *INIT.ORA* to specify the accessible
directories:

```
utl_file_dir = c:\temp
```

27

External Procedures

Beginner

27-1. An external procedure is an operating system file or program that can be called from within Oracle.

27-2. External procedures can be called anywhere a native PL/SQL procedure or function is called. The external procedure has a "wrapper" PL/SQL unit around it that calls the proper OS code. It can be used in situations where the programmer has implemented a program in a language other than PL/SQL but wishes to call it from within PL/SQL.

27-3. The statements are:

    a. False. Interprocess communication using external procedures requires much less complexity than using database pipes. With pipes, the programmer must set up a listener process that picks the messages off the pipe and acts on them. With external procedures, the program is executed directly on behalf of the user.

    b. False. With external procedures, communication is bidirectional. The programmer can pass information to an external procedure, and the external program can pass information back.

    c. True. With the appropriate pragmas (assuming that the PL/SQL wrapper is inside a package), calls to external procedures can be used anywhere PL/SQL stored functions can be used—for example, in SQL statements, in assignments, etc.

    d. True. The most common and well-supported language for external procedures is C (mostly because this is what Oracle is written in). The code for an external procedure can be written in any language that can be compiled into a C-callable format.

e. False. External procedures do not have to return a value but are definitely permitted to do so. If the external program returns a value, this should be mapped to a PL/SQL function, whereas a program that does not return a value should be mapped to a PL/SQL procedure.

f. False. In addition to the library itself and the PL/SQL wrapper, the DBA must also have set up an external procedure listener.

g. False. The Oracle server starts one *extproc* process for each session; they are not shared between users. For example, if user A calls an external procedure, an *extproc* process is started for that user. All subsequent calls to an external process use this *extproc* process. However, user B, connected at the same time, has her own *extproc* process.

h. False. Oracle can use only modules compiled in a shared library format as external procedures. Regular executable files cannot be used. If it's necessary to run a regular file, a shared library can be created that simply calls this file with the appropriate parameters.

i. True. The CREATE LIBRARY command provides access to the library itself and not to a particular module within that library. Therefore, the one library can access any routines inside that external library.

j. False. Oracle will raise an error if a CREATE LIBRARY statement references an external library that doesn't exist

27-4. Each external procedure to be called must have a PL/SQL program unit that provides the information needed to call the program from within Oracle. For example, if there is an external program called generate_key that resides in the library called *UTIL_LIB*, you should declare a PL/SQL "wrapper" function as follows:

```
CREATE OR REPLACE FUNCTION get_new_key
RETURN PLS_INTEGER IS EXTERNAL
LIBRARY UTIL_LIB
NAME "generate_key"
LANGUAGE C;
```

This example assumes that the library *UTIL_LIB* had been previously created using statements similar to the following:

```
CREATE LIBRARY UTIL_LIB AS '/usr/local/lib/cryptolib.sl';
```

27-5. In a Windows environment, shared libraries are generally identified by a *.DLL* (dynamic link library) extension. In Unix environments, the libraries usually have the extension *.so* (shared object) or *.sl* (shared library). These extensions are not actually what's important, however, and any file compiled in the correct format can be used, regardless of extension.

27-6. A user who wishes to create a library must have been granted the CREATE LIBRARY or CREATE ANY LIBRARY privilege by the DBA. If the appropriate privileges have not been granted, the user receives the error message:

```
ORA-01031: insufficient privileges
```

27-7. Yes, external procedures do take part in the current database transaction. This means that:

- If any uncommitted change is made in the session before calling the external procedure, it is visible.

- Any changes made in the external procedure are visible to the rest of the session.

- Changes can be rolled back.

27-8. In versions of Oracle before 8.0, the only way of establishing communications between Oracle and the operating system was to have a stored procedure send messages using a database pipe and to implement a second "listener" program written in a language supported by the operating system and Oracle (e.g., Pro*C, Pro*COBOL, Pro*PL/I). This listener program then took the messages off the pipe and processed them, calling the appropriate OS program.

This approach had several disadvantages:

- It was labor-intensive, since it required the programmer to write both a message server and a listener process.

- It required skills with multiple computer language and precompiler.

- The code had to handle concurrency if there was more than one process taking messages off the pipe.

27-9. These data dictionary views display the following information:

USER_LIBRARIES
    All libraries owned by the current user

ALL_LIBRARIES
    All libraries available to the current user

DBA_LIBRARIES
    All libraries defined in the whole database; only DBAs (or users with the DBA role) can use this view

27-10. Only operating system programs that can be compiled into a shared library can be called using the external procedures option. In a Unix environment, this is a shared object (*.sl* or *.so* file). In a Windows environment, this means a *.DLL* file. The important thing is that the format of the object be callable from C.

27-11. Deciding whether an external program should be mapped to a function or procedure is no different from using native PL/SQL. If the external process returns a value (number, string, Boolean), it should be mapped to a PL/SQL function. Conversely, if the external process does not return a value, it should be mapped to a PL/SQL procedure.

27-12. When an external procedure is called, the order of events is as follows:

> A PL/SQL application calls a special PL/SQL module body.
> PL/SQL looks for a special listener process that is running in the background.
> The listener process spawns a program called *extproc* that loads the external library.
> The code in the library returns the result back to PL/SQL.

27-13. The proper syntax to create the library is as follows:

```
CREATE LIBRARY UTIL_LIB AS 'C:\MYAPP\UTIL\APPUTIL.DLL'
```

The PL/SQL wrapper looks like this:

```
CREATE FUNCTION GET_PASSWORD
RETURN STRING IS EXTERNAL
LIBRARY UTIL_LIB
LANGUAGE C;
```

27-14. The syntax that creates the PL/SQL wrapper must be changed to include the PARAMETERS clause to specify the new parameter. The revised PL/SQL wrapper looks like this:

```
CREATE FUNCTION GET_PASSWORD
RETURN STRING IS EXTERNAL
LIBRARY UTIL_LIB
PARAMETERS (password_length INT)
LANGUAGE C;
```

There is no change required to the library since it establishes only the link to the shared library and does not contain any details about each routine inside the shared library.

27-15. With the declaration of the PL/SQL wrapper, there is an optional NAME clause. If it is not specified, Oracle assumes that the name of the routine in the external shared library is the same as the PL/SQL wrapper. If the name of the routine is different, in either case (upper or lower) or name, you can use the NAME clause to specify this name. For example, you might specify the following declaration for the function mentioned, if the actual name of the routine were Collect_Data:

```
CREATE FUNCTION COLLECT_DATA
RETURN PLS_INTEGER IS EXTERNAL
LIBRARY UTIL_LIB
NAME "Collect_Data"
LANGUAGE C;
```

27-16. The proper syntax to create a library is as follows:

```
CREATE LIBRARY library name AS 'path to library'
```

Note that some operating systems (such as Unix) are case-sensitive, and thus the following statement is not equivalent to the previous one:

```
CREATE LIBRARY MY_LIBRARY AS '/USR/LOCAL/MYLIB.SL'
```

However, on an operating system such as Windows NT which is case-insensitive, the following commands:

```
CREATE LIBRARY MY_LIBRARY AS 'c:\winnt\system32\kernal32.dll'
```

```
CREATE LIBRARY MY_LIBRARY AS 'C:\wiNnt\SysTeM32\KErnAl32.dLL'
```

are functionally identical.

The statements shown in the problems are:

a. This one is valid:

```
CREATE LIBRARY libc_l AS '/lib/libc.so'
```

b. It is possible, but unlikely, that the following example is also valid:

```
CREATE LIBRARY libc_l AS '/LIB/LIBC.SO'
```

Since it appears that the operating system is Unix, it is unlikely that directories or files are named in uppercase (remember that Unix is case-sensitive).

c. The statement:

```
CREATE LIBRARY UNIX_operating_system_c_library AS '/lib/libc.so'
```

fails because library names are subject to the usual rules for identifier names. In other words, the library name must be 30 characters or less; it must begin with a letter; and it cannot contain certain special symbols. The library name given in the example exceeds the maximum length of an identifier and fails with the error message:

```
ORA-00972: identifier is too long
```

d. This statement appears to work, but does, in fact, create an invalid library:

```
CREATE LIBRARY libc_l FOR '/lib/libc.so'
```

This can be verified by examining the USER_LIBRARIES view:

```
SQL> SELECT * FROM user_libraries;
```

```
LIBRARY_NAME          FILE_SPEC                        D STATUS
-------------------- ----------------------------- - -------
LIBC_L                                                 INVALID
```

A successfully created library has the FILE_SPEC column populated, and the status is VALID.

e. The following statement also fails for the reason described in (d):

```
CREATE LIBRARY libc_l AS /lib/libc.so
```

27-17. A library can be removed from the system by using the DROP LIBRARY command. Of course, you must have been granted the DROP LIBRARY or DROP ANY LIBRARY privilege by your DBA.

27-18. Access to the functions can be removed from Sue with no impact on other users. The most efficient way to do this would be to issue the command:

```
REVOKE EXECUTE ON util_pkg FROM sue;
```

Remember that you do not need to grant users access to the library. You simply grant EXECUTE privilege on the code that references the library. In this way, it is not an "all or nothing" approach, and access can be controlled at the routine level instead of at the library level.

27-19. When using external procedures, you must map the datatype that is being returned to the appropriate datatype in PL/SQL as shown in this table.

External Datatype	PL/SQL Datatype
int	BINARY_INTEGER, PLS_INTEGER
char * (string)	CHAR, VARCHAR2, VARCHAR (i.e., any character datatype)
double	DOUBLE PRECISION
float	FLOAT, REAL

For example, in the case of an external procedure expecting a string, passing a number generates the following number:

```
ORA-28577: argument 1 of external procedure test_proc has unsupported
           datatype OCINumber
```

Intermediate

27-20. The following table summarizes the similarities and differences between native PL/SQL procedures and external procedures.

Native PL/SQL Procedures	External Procedures
Support for all Oracle built-in and user-defined datatypes	Support for only a subset of Oracle built-in datatypes
Source code stored in database	Compiles source code into a shared library on the native operating system
Functions can be used in SQL statements	Functions in an external library cannot be used in an SQL statement
Listener isn't required	Requires a listener process to interact with the database

27-21. With the advent of external procedures comes the ability to call programs that can do things not currently supported by the PL/SQL language. Even with the large strides made in the Oracle8*i* release, there are operations that still require operating system-level programming (e.g., deleting an OS file). Programmers are no longer limited to performing tasks in PL/SQL that are directly supported. They can now write code in any Oracle-supported language and then call this code using the external procedure method.

27-22. To use an external procedure, you must follow these steps:

1. The DBA must have configured the listener to run the external program on the caller's behalf. Details of how this listener should be created, and other configuration file changes, are available in Oracle documentation (it involves changes to both the *TNSNAMES.ORA* and *LISTENER.ORA* files).

2. Create a shared library (*.so* or *.DLL* file) that is callable from C or make sure one is available on your operating system.

3. Execute a CREATE LIBRARY statement to define an alias in the data dictionary for the external shared library file. This allows the database engine to find it when it is called.

4. Create a PL/SQL program unit that references the function or procedure contained in the newly created library.

27-23. The current implementation of external procedures has the following disadvantages:

- It is single-threaded (i.e., each session currently requires its own external procedure process).

- Only scalar datatypes are supported currently; user-defined datatypes are not supported.

27-24. This error occurs when Oracle is unable to find the external procedure listener. Without this listener, Oracle cannot communicate with the OS library or shared object that contains the code for the external procedure. This is quite common if the DBA forgets to restart the external procedure listener after a system reboot (only the database listener is restarted by default).

27-25. The BY REFERENCE option in the PARAMETERS clause passes the parameter by reference (i.e., a pointer is passed to the module, and the result is changed directly by the external procedure). However, this option affects only numeric datatypes, since the other datatype (STRING) is always passed by reference.

27-26. Since Oracle uses dynamic linking, once a particular module has been loaded into memory (when the first reference to it has been made), subsequent invocations of it do not cause any further overhead. In other words, all users share the same copy of the external library code in memory. This makes the memory requirements much lower in a busy system where many users quite often call the same code. By collecting commonly used modules into their own libraries, the system load is decreased and things become more manageable.

27-27. The PL/SQL wrapper for an external procedure can be created as a stand-alone function, a standalone procedure, or a function/procedure within a package. While any of these methods works, there are several advantages to placing the wrapper inside a package:

- The details of whether or not the code is implemented as an external procedure is hidden from the caller (this may be desired to obtain a certain level of abstraction).

- By placing the wrapper in a package, a RESTRICT_REFERENCES pragma can be specified to allow a function to be used in SQL.

- Similar external procedures can be bundled together into logical groupings.

27-28. Dropping a library can be a potentially dangerous operation if you are not sure whether any stored modules are utilizing it. The easiest way to check if the library is referenced anywhere is by querying the USER_DEPENDEN-CIES view as shown here:

```
SELECT * FROM USER_DEPENDENCIES WHERE REFERENCED_NAME = 'MYLIB_NAME'
```

27-29. Logging messages to a file is often desired because of the limitations with Oracle's DBMS_OUTPUT package (e.g., output is unavailable until the program completes and is limited to 255 characters per line).

The steps in the process are listed here:

1. Ensure that the DBA for your site has properly configured an external procedure listener to handle the calls you make to OS libraries. This requires a combination of entries in both the *TNSNAMES.ORA* and *LISTENER.ORA* files.

2. Create a shared library to call the appropriate OS command to log the message. For this example, assume that the underlying operating system is Unix, and that the following code has been compiled into a shared library in the directory */usr/local/bin*:

```c
#include <stdio.h>
#include <stdlib.h>
#include <unistd.h>
#include <signal.h>

void log_text(const char * text) {
    FILE * LOGTEXT;
    char buf[80];
    sprintf(buf, "/tmp/debug.log");

    LOGTEXT = fopen (buf, "a+");

    if ( ! LOGTEXT ) {
        if ( (LOGTEXT = fopen ( buf, "w+" ) ) == NULL ) {
```

```
                    return ;
               }
          }

          fprintf (LOGTEXT,"%s\n", text);
          fclose(LOGTEXT);
     }
```

3. Create a library to reference the external code. If the name of the library is *debug_lib* and it is located in the directory */usr/local/bin*, the statement:

```
CREATE LIBRARY DEBUG_LIB AS '/usr/local/bin/debug.sl'
```

creates the Oracle library necessary to execute the program.

4. Construct a PL/SQL wrapper to call the external procedure that logs the desired text to a file. Here is a possible wrapper:

```
CREATE OR REPLACE
PACKAGE LOG_PKG IS
   PROCEDURE write_debug_message(message_in IN VARCHAR2);
END;
/

CREATE OR REPLACE
PACKAGE BODY LOG_PKG IS
   PROCEDURE write_debug_message(message_in IN VARCHAR2) IS
    external
    library debug_lib
    name "log_text"
    language c;

END;
/
```

All the pieces described must be in place before the file logging will work. If you've created all of the pieces and run without errors, but the logging still does not work, check to make sure that:

- The listener is up and listening on the appropriate port.

- The shared library has the appropriate privileges for the Oracle Unix account to read and execute it.

- The file to which the external procedure is writing (*/tmp/debug.log*) is readable and writeable by the Oracle Unix account.

Other programmers can then place calls to this procedure in their code to generate messages into the OS file. For example:

```
BEGIN
   ...
   log_pkg.write_debug_message('Attempting to add client information');
   ...
END;
```

Expert

27-30. One of the most common mistakes is forgetting to refresh the information available to the listener. If information in the *LISTENER.ORA* file is changed while the listener is up, it does not take effect until the listener is stopped and restarted. Alternatively, the *reload* command can be used to refresh the information while the listener is up.

27-31. One of the most common requests from developers or clients is to have an email message sent based on some triggering event in the database. The solution for the email-notification problem is to use an external procedure to call an operating system library to send the email. Here are the steps in the process:

1. Ensure that the DBA for your site has properly configured an external procedure listener to handle the calls you make to OS libraries. This requires a combination of entries in both the *TNSNAMES.ORA* and *LISTENER.ORA* files.

2. Create a shared library to call the appropriate OS command to send an email message. For this example, assume that the underlying operating system is Unix, and that the following code has been compiled into a shared library in the directory */usr/local/bin*:

```c
#include <stdio.h>
#include <stdlib.h>
#include <unistd.h>
#include <signal.h>

void send_email(char * address, char * message) {
  char command[256];
  FILE * PIPE;
  sprintf(command, "/usr/bin/mailx %s", address);
  PIPE = popen (command, "w");
  if (PIPE)
  {
    fprintf(PIPE, message);
    pclose(PIPE);
  }
}
```

3. Create a library to reference the OS object that contains the code that eventually sends the email message. Assuming that the name of the library is *mail_util_lib*, and it is located in the directory */usr/local/bin*, the statement:

```
CREATE LIBRARY MAIL_UTIL_LIB IS '/usr/local/bin/mail_util.sl'
```

creates the Oracle library necessary to execute the program.

4. Construct a PL/SQL wrapper to call the external procedure that sends the email. A possible wrapper is included here:

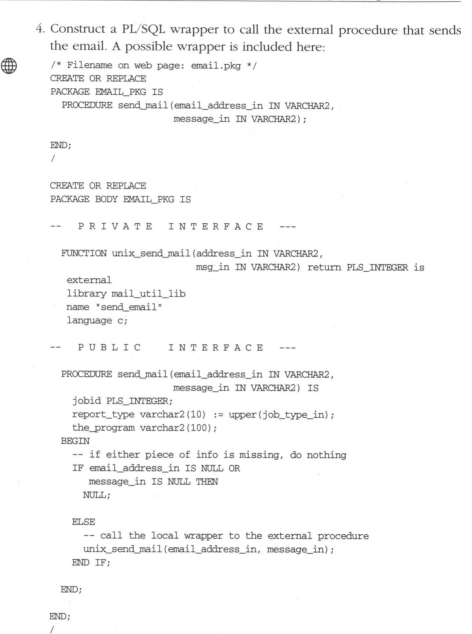

```
/* Filename on web page: email.pkg */
CREATE OR REPLACE
PACKAGE EMAIL_PKG IS
   PROCEDURE send_mail(email_address_in IN VARCHAR2,
                       message_in IN VARCHAR2);

END;
/

CREATE OR REPLACE
PACKAGE BODY EMAIL_PKG IS

--   P R I V A T E   I N T E R F A C E   ---

   FUNCTION unix_send_mail(address_in IN VARCHAR2,
                           msg_in IN VARCHAR2) return PLS_INTEGER is
    external
    library mail_util_lib
    name "send_email"
    language c;

--   P U B L I C     I N T E R F A C E   ---

   PROCEDURE send_mail(email_address_in IN VARCHAR2,
                       message_in IN VARCHAR2) IS
     jobid PLS_INTEGER;
     report_type varchar2(10) := upper(job_type_in);
     the_program varchar2(100);
   BEGIN
     -- if either piece of info is missing, do nothing
     IF email_address_in IS NULL OR
        message_in IS NULL THEN
        NULL;

     ELSE
        -- call the local wrapper to the external procedure
        unix_send_mail(email_address_in, message_in);
     END IF;

   END;

END;
/
```

5. The event that causes the email to be sent is sometimes referred to as the *triggering event*. In this case, the triggering event is the addition of a new product, or more precisely, the insertion of a row into the products table. In order to perform an action when this event occurs, create an AFTER INSERT trigger on the products table that sends an email for each row in the clients_to_notify table. This is done by call-

ing the following PL/SQL wrapper program unit (which in turn calls
the external library you have created to send the email message):

```
/* Filename on web page: notify.sql */
-- table that stores email addresses of clients that want to be notified
CREATE TABLE clients_to_notify
(email_address VARCHAR2(100))
/

-- trigger on the PRODUCTS table that will actually send the email
CREATE OR REPLACE TRIGGER email_trg
AFTER INSERT
ON products
REFERENCING NEW AS NEW OLD AS OLD
FOR EACH ROW
DECLARE
   CURSOR email_list IS
     SELECT email_address FROM clients_to_notify;
BEGIN
   -- for each email address we find in the clients_to_notify
   -- table, send a message
   FOR client IN email_list LOOP
     mail_pkg.send_mail(email_list.email_address,
                         'We have added to our product line.
                          Please come and visit us at www.widget.com');
   END LOOP;

END;
/
```

All the pieces described must be in place before the email notifications
will work. If all pieces exist and are without errors, and the email messages are still not being delivered, check to make sure that:

- The listener is up and listening on the appropriate port.

- The shared library has the appropriate privileges for the Oracle Unix
  account to read and execute it.

- The trigger is actually firing (check this by putting a debug message in
  the trigger body).

- The email server is functioning normally.

When the system is functioning, notifying a client of new products is as
easy as inserting the client's email address into the clients_to_notify table.
The email message is sent automatically by the trigger.

27-32. A single-threaded process is one that guarantees only one copy of itself is
running at any given time. Since only one *extproc* is created for each database session, you know that only one is ever running. If Oracle were to
change the implementation, you'd need to be careful that the structures or
system objects being accessed in the external procedure could handle
concurrent access. For example, if the external procedure attempted to

open and write to a file, you'd have to handle a situation in which two requests tried to open the same file at the same time. These issues are often referred to as *serialization problems*, because the requests must be "serialized" or sorted and processed in the order in which they were received.

27-33. Yes, in Oracle 8.1.5 using the DEBUG_EXTPROC package. Here is how it's done:

1. Execute DEBUG_EXTPROC.STARTUP_EXTPROC_AGENT in SQL*Plus.

2. Determine the process ID (PID) of the agent session started in the previous step.

3. Start up your debugger and load the PID identified in the previous step.

4. Set a break point on the *pextproc* function and continue the debugger.

Execute your external procedure, and the debugger should break at *pextproc*. Consult the Oracle documentation for a complete description of installing and using this package.

28

PL/SQL Web Development

Beginner

28-1. (c). HTML is most similar to a WordPerfect file because it defines the structure of a document using a relatively simple syntax composed of tags and attributes. Unlike Oracle Reports (a) or Crystal Reports (b), which are proprietary report writers, HTML is a general-purpose document format specification. ISPF is an IBM proprietary format for laying out data entry forms. A Java class file (e) is a compiled program.

28-2. (e) (None of the above). An HTML form is very different from a form created with a client-server system because HTTP, the networking protocol beneath HTML, does not maintain a persistent connection to the server. This is in direct contrast to the protocols behind client-server systems (SQL*Net, Net8, etc.). This property (called *statelessness*) has a major impact on the design of HTML-based systems.

28-3. (e) (All of the above). You can use PL/SQL in almost any web development effort, whether you are creating a user interface or not. OAS and WebDB both include architectural components and a PL/SQL toolkit you can use to develop PL/SQL web applications. Java and PL/SQL are interoperable inside the Oracle database, so you can call PL/SQL procedures from within a Java and vice versa. Oracle Forms, now completely web-enabled, uses PL/SQL as its client-side development language.

28-4. (e) (All of the above). You can use the HTP package, included in the PL/SQL toolkit, to create almost any kind of ASCII content, whether it is HTML, XML, or a delimited ASCII files. You can also generate any client-side scripting languages, such as Netscape's JavaScript or Microsoft's VBScript.

28-5. Figure 28-1 shows the major components.

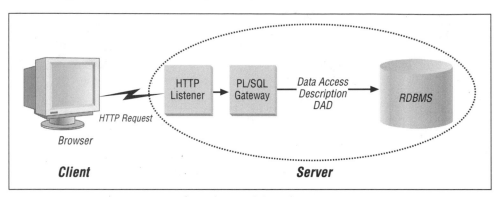

Figure 28-1. Major components of a PL/SQL web-based system

28-6. The HTTP listener (also called the web listener) is a server-side component that "listens" for requests made from a web browser. The listener
parses the request's URL to determine what to do. If the request is for a
static file, the listener simply sends the file back to the browser. If it is a
request for a PL/SQL procedure, the listener "dispatches" it to the PL/SQL
gateway.

28-7. The PL/SQL gateway is the server-side component responsible for passing
the requested PL/SQL procedure to the RDBMS. The gateway uses information in the URL or form ACTION attribute to build a PL/SQL procedure
call using the named notation format. The URL must include a virtual
mapping to the schema that owns (or can execute) the procedure, the
package and procedure name, and any required parameters.

28-8. The PL/SQL toolkit is a PL/SQL SDK (System Development Kit) for devel-
oping web applications. Its packages are HTF, HTP, OWA_COOKIE,
OWA_IMAGE, OWA_OPT_LOCK, OWA_PATTERN, OWA_SEC, OWA_
TEXT, and OWA_UTIL.

28-9. HTP. The HTP.PRINT procedure is a web-enabled version of the DBMS_
OUTPUT built-in package. A developer builds a web page by combining
HTP and other toolkit calls into a procedure a user can call from the Web.
HTF is a related package that consists of a set of functions that return syn-
tactically correct HTML strings to the procedures that call them. The
"Hello, World!" procedure is:

```
CREATE OR REPLACE procedure hello_world is
BEGIN
    HTP.PRINT('<html>');
    HTP.PRINT('<head>');
    HTP.PRINT('<title>HTP.PRINT Example...</title>');
    HTP.PRINT('</head>');
```

```
   HTP.PRINT('<body>');
   HTP.PRINT('<h1>Hello, World!<h1>');
   HTP.PRINT('</body>');
   HTP.PRINT('</html>');
END;
```

28-10. The OWA_UTIL.LIST_PRINT procedure uses dynamic SQL to automatically create a drop-down list of values (LOV). The simplest version of the procedure accepts the following parameters:

P_theQuery

> The SQL query that creates user-selectable items. The three columns in the query define the structure of the list. The first column defines the primary key for the LOV; it's the value that is returned when the user selects the item from the list. The second column defines the "real" value associated with the primary key; it's the value the user sees in the list. The third column is a flag indicating the item is the list's default selection.

P_cname

> The name given to the HTML input element.

P_nsize

> The number of rows displayed in the list. A value of 1 makes the list into a drop-down box; higher values make it into a select box.

P_multiple

> A flag that indicates that the LOV can return multiple values.

The following statement creates an LOV based on the DEPT table:

```
OWA_UTIL.LISTPRINT(
   'select deptno, dname, null from scott.dept order by dname',
   'department_number' ,1);
```

28-11. You can use the OWA_UTIL.MIME_HEADER procedure to change the default MIME header. The procedure accepts two parameters. The first parameter is for a new MIME type. The second is a flag to leave the header section open so that you can append more information.

You might use this command to redirect the output of a PL/SQL program to various programs on the user's browser. For example, you might want to create a system to download the results of a query into a spreadsheet. The following command tells the browser to launch Excel:

```
OWA_UTIL.MIME_HEADER('text/csv', false);
```

28-12. You can use the SEND command to set a cookie. However, you must be sure that you set the value inside the header section. This is done by embedding the SEND command inside the OWA_UTIL header functions. Here's an example of how to set a cookie to identify a user's session:

```
OWA_UTIL.MIME_HEADER('text/html', false);
OWA_COOKIE.SEND ('username', 'odewahn');
OWA_UTIL.HTTP_HEADER_CLOSE;
```

28-13. You can use the CHECKSUM function to compute a record's checksum value. You use this value to implement optimistic record locking in an HTML form. For example, suppose you're creating an HTML form to update a record in the SCOTT.emp table. When you first display the form, you compute a checksum value for the original record before the user makes any modifications. This value is stored in a hidden field on the form. For example:

```
csum := owa_opt_lock.checksum('SCOTT', 'emp', rec_row_id);
htp.formHidden(cname=>'old_checksum', cvalue => csum);
```

When you write the procedure to make the user's changes, you can recompute the record's checksum and compare it with the old value. If the two are equal, you can apply the user's changes. If they are not, an intervening user has made changes to the underlying record, so you must ask the user how he wants to proceed.

28-14. You can use the MATCH command to search a string for particular pattern by defining an appropriate regular expression. To determine whether S is a floating-point number you could use the command:[*]

```
OWA_PATTERN.MATCH(S,'(\+|-)?([0-9]+\.?[0-9]*\.[0-9]+)
                      ([eE](\+|-)?[0-9]+)?');
```

28-15. The three ways to call a PL/SQL procedure from a web browser are:
- Type the procedure's URL directly into the browser's address box.
- Create an anchor tag (a hyperlink) whose HREF attribute points to the procedure's URL.
- Create an HTML form whose ACTION attribute points to the procedure's URL.

28-16. The URL used to call a PL/SQL procedure uses the following basic format:

http://server:port/virtual_schema_mapping/package.procedure
http://server:port/virtual_schema_mapping/procedure

The *server* section specifies the hostname of the machine running the web server. The *port* section specifies the communication port (usually 80) on which the server's HTTP listener component is running. The *virtual_schema_mapping* section is an alias for a specific database schema; while its format varies according to your server platform (for example, in WebDB it is the name of a configured DAD), it always points to a single

---

[*] This example appeared in "Regular Expressions: Languages, Algorithms, and Software," *Dr. Dobb's Journal*, April 1999.

schema that owns (or can execute) the procedure. The *package* section is the name of the package in which the procedure resides. Finally, the *package.procedure* section specifies the actual name of the procedure to execute.

28-17. You pass parameters by appending a query string onto the URL. The query string begins with a question mark (?) and is followed by ampersand (&) delimited sets of name/value pairs. Each name/value pair consists of a parameter name, followed by an equals sign (=) and a value for the parameter. In general, the format is:

?parm1=value1&parm2=value2&parm3=value3...

28-18. For each character C in a value passed in a query string:

- If C is an alphanumeric character or an underscore, leave it alone.
- If C is a space, convert it to a plus sign (+).
- Otherwise, convert C to a percent sign (%) followed by C's hexadecimal value:
  a. Let asc2hex be the string "0123456789ABCDEF"
  b. Calculate the leading digit (LD) of the hex value with the formula LD = FLOOR(ASCII(C)/16)
  c. Calculate the trailing digit (TD) of the hex value with the formula TD = ASCII(C) - LD
  d. Calculate the coded value (CV) with the formula CV = '%' || asc2hex(LD+1) || asc2hex(TD+1)

28-19. Here is the complete table.

Character	ASCII Value	Encoded Value
The digit 9	48	9
The letter A	65	A
Space	32	+
Ampersand (&)	38	%26
Forward slash (/)	47	%2F
Right curly brace (})	125	%7D

28-20. Set the form's ACTION attribute to the procedure's URL. You pass parameters by including named input elements within the form. The name of the element must match the name of a parameter in the procedure's formal parameter list. The browser automatically encodes field values.

28-21. Here is a suggested procedure:

```
/* Filename on web page: show_emps.sp */
CREATE OR REPLACE PROCEDURE show_emps (
    i_job in VARCHAR2 default '%') as
```

```
        CURSOR emp_cur IS
            select * from scott.emp
                where job like i_job order by ename;
        emp_rec emp_cur%ROWTYPE;

    BEGIN
        HTP.PRINT ('<title>EMP table</title>');
        HTP.PRINT('<table border=1 width=100%>');
        OPEN emp_cur;
        LOOP
            FETCH emp_cur INTO emp_rec;
            EXIT WHEN emp_cur%NOTFOUND;
            HTP.PRINT('<tr>');
            HTP.PRINT('<td>' || emp_rec.ename || '</td>');
            HTP.PRINT('<td>' || emp_rec.job || '</td>');
            HTP.PRINT('<td>' || emp_rec.hiredate || '</td>');
            HTP.PRINT('<td>' || emp_rec.sal || '</td>');
            HTP.PRINT('</tr>');
        END LOOP;
        CLOSE emp_cur;
        HTP.PRINT('</table>');
    END;
```

28-22. Here's an HTML snippet that does the job:

```
<a href="http://myserver/my_agent/plsql?i_job=ANALYST">Software Analysts</a>
<a href="http://myserver/my_agent/plsql?i_job=CLERK">Clerks</a>
```

28-23. Here's another snippet:

```
<form action="http://myserver/my_agent/plsql/show_emps">
    <select name=i_job>
        <option value="ANALYST">Analyst
        <option value="CLERK">Clerk
</select>
    <input type=submit>
</form>
```

28-24. A better approach is to write a frontend to generate the lists automatically from the base tables. This guarantees that the list of links is always accurate. For example, the following example builds a hyperlink for each job in the emp table:

```
CREATE OR REPLACE PROCEDURE get_job_list IS
    CURSOR job_cur IS
        SELECT distinct_JOB FROM scott.emp ORDER BY job;
    job_rec job_cur%ROWTYPE;
    hlink VARCHAR2(1000) DEFAULT NULL;
BEGIN
    OPEN job_cur;
    LOOP
      FETCH job_cur INTO job_rec;
        EXIT when job_cur%NOTFOUND;
        hlink := '<a href=show_emps?i_job=' || job_rec.job || '>';
        hlink := hlink || job_rec.job;
        hlink := hlink || '</a>';
        HTP.PRINT (hlink);
        HTP.PRINT ('<p>');
```

```
    END loop;
    CLOSE job_cur;
END;
```

28-25. The developer has mistakenly used the field name i_emp_num when the formal parameter list requires the name i_emp_no.

Intermediate

28-26. The PL/SQL gateway uses the named notation to translate a procedure call made from the Web into a corresponding procedure call inside the RDBMS. Named notation attempts to map the names and datatypes onto a corresponding procedure. Any error, such as misspelling a parameter name or a mismatched type, results in an unhandled exception. There are three important implications for web-application development:

- The name given to a parameter in a query string or on an HTML form must exactly match the name of a corresponding formal parameter. Developing and using a best-practices naming convention can help reduce this error.

- The datatype assigned to a parameter must match the datatype assigned to the corresponding formal parameter. Declaring all parameters as VARCHAR2 helps reduce this error.

- You must supply a value for all parameters that do not have a default value. Declaring default values helps reduce this error.

28-27. You can call a procedure using just its name when you have a base URL to supply the missing server, port, and virtual schema mapping. This is called *relative URL*.

28-28. The procedure call results in an unhandled exception; it does not print "Invalid Number", even though this is clearly the intended purpose of the exception section. The flaw in the design is that, while the I_val parameter has been declared as a NUMBER, the actual value passed is a text string. When the PL/SQL gateway attempts to match the call to an existing procedure, it compares both the parameters' names *and* datatypes to the procedure's formal parameter list. Since the mismatched datatype causes the call to fail entirely, the procedure's exception section is never even reached. The following modifications make the procedure work as intended:

```
PROCEDURE val_test ( i_val IN VARCHAR2 DEFAULT NULL) is
    N NUMBER;
BEGIN
    n := TO_NUMBER(i_val);
    HTP.PRINT('The value is: ' || i_val );
```

```
EXCEPTION
   WHEN OTHERS THEN
      HTP.PRINT ('Invalid number');
END;
```

28-29. Three possible ways to maintain state in a PL/SQL web application are:

Store state information in hidden fields

A hidden field is simply an invisible input element on an HTML form:

```
<input type=hidden name=user_id value="10235">
```

To maintain a value across multiple sessions, all you need do is include the values you want to preserve as hidden fields on the form. A downside to this approach is that, for large numbers of fields, it generally results in unwieldy formal parameter lists.

Store state information in database tables

You can create a three-column table to hold the state information: one column for a unique session ID (such as the user's IP address), one column for the name of the variable, and one column for the variable's value. The downside to this approach is that it requires a database hit each time you want to add or retrieve state information.

Store state information in a cookie file

Most browsers can use a name/value pair called a *cookie* to save state information. Each cookie is saved either as a record on the user's machine or as an environment variable on the web server. In either case, it is accessible throughout (and sometimes even after) a user's session. The OWA_COOKIE package contains procedures that allow you to create, access, and even update cookies within PL/SQL.

28-30. You can use OWA_UTIL's CALENDERPRINT procedure to create the interface. Like LIST_PRINT, CALENDARPRINT creates a complex HTML structure—in this case, a monthly calendar (shown in Figure 28-2) based on a SQL statement you provide. The procedure has two parameters:

P_query

The SQL query that creates the calendar. The query must have three columns: the date of the item of interest, the text that is to be displayed for the item, and an optional hyperlink associated with the item. The procedure generates a monthly calendar for each unique month and year combination in the table.

P_mf_only

A flag that specifies whether the calendar should include only Monday through Friday. A value of "N" (the default) prints all the days of the week. A value of "Y" prints only Monday through Friday.

This procedure creates the user interface described in the problem setup:

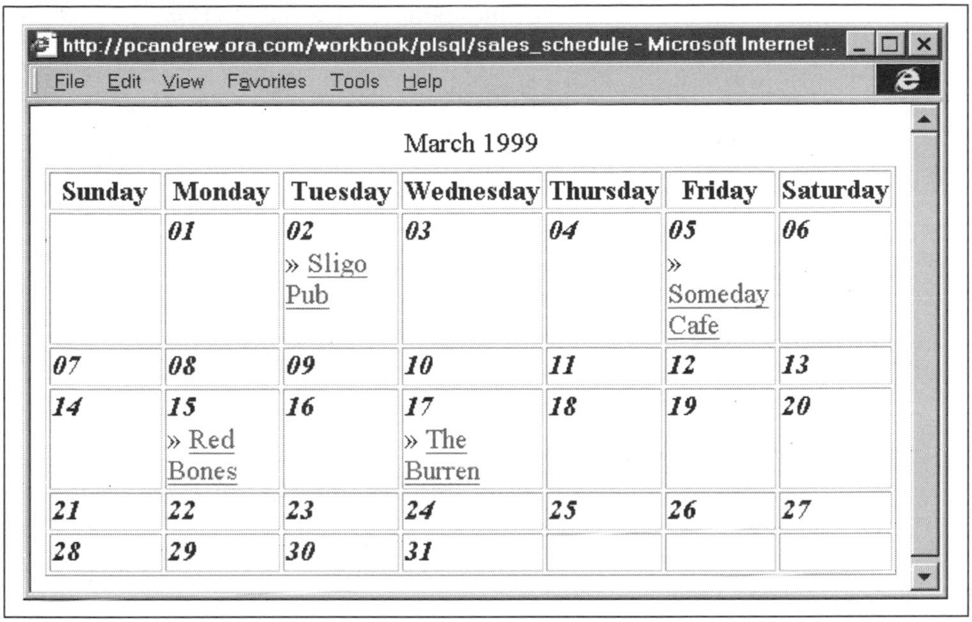

Figure 28-2. Monthly calendar produced by the CALENDARPRINT procedure

```
CREATE OR REPLACE PROCEDURE sales_schedule
   ( i_salesman_id IN VARCHAR2 DEFAULT '1') as

   qstr VARCHAR2(500) DEFAULT NULL;

BEGIN
   qstr := 'SELECT visit_date, company_name, company_url ';
   qstr := qstr || 'from onsite_schedule where ';
   qstr := qstr || 'salesman_id = ' || i_salesman_id || ' ';
   qstr := qstr || 'order by visit_date';
   OWA_UTIL.CALENDARPRINT (qstr,'N');

END;
```

28-31. The solution for this problem has several steps (see the *guestbook.sql* file for the complete solution):

Step 1

Create a table to hold the guestbook entries. You can do this with the following script:

```
CREATE TABLE guestbook_entries (
   guest_name      VARCHAR2(100),
   email_address   VARCHAR2(100),
   visit_date      DATE,
   comments        VARCHAR2(500)) ;
```

Step 2

Design the package specification. You need three procedures: one to display the main screen, one to create the data-entry form, and one to insert the entry into the guestbook_entries table. Here is a sample specification:

```
CREATE OR REPLACE PACKAGE guestbook as

    PROCEDURE main ;

    PROCEDURE show_form;

    PROCEDURE insert_entry (
        i_name in varchar2 default null,
        i_email in varchar2 default null,
        i_comments in varchar2 default null );

END;
```

Step 3

Write the main procedure in the package to generate the first screen. The procedure should create two components: an HTML form containing a single submit button, and an HTML table to display the guestbook comments:

```
PROCEDURE main IS
    CURSOR guest_cur IS
    SELECT * FROM guestbook_entries ORDER BY visit_date;
    guest_rec guest_cur%ROWTYPE;
BEGIN
    HTP.TITLE ('Employees in the EMP table');
    -- Create the button to sign the guestbook
    HTP.PRINT('<form action=guestbook.show_form>');
    HTP.PRINT('<input type=submit value="Sign the Guestbook!!!">');
    HTP.PRINT('<form>');
    -- Print the contents of the guestbook
    HTP.PRINT('<p><h1>Previous Visitors</h1><p>');
    HTP.TABLEOPEN(cattributes => 'border=1 width=100%');
    OPEN guest_cur;
    LOOP
        FETCH guest_cur INTO guest_rec;
        EXIT WHEN guest_cur%NOTFOUND;
        HTP. TABLEROWOPEN;
        HTP.TABLEDATA
          (HTF.MAILTO(guest_rec.email_address, guest_rec.guest_name));
        HTP.TABLEDATA (guest_rec.visit_date);
        HTP.TABLEDATA (guest_rec.comments);
        HTP.TABLEROWCLOSE;
    END LOOP;
    CLOSE guest_cur;
    HTP.TABLECLOSE;
END;
```

Step 4

Write the procedure in the package to generate an HTML form so that the user can leave his or her comments. The form's ACTION attribute will point to a procedure we design in the next step. Here's the proce-

dure; note the use of the more complex HTP procedures to clean up
the raw HTML tags:

```
PROCEDURE show_form IS
BEGIN
    HTP.HTMLOPEN;
    HTP.TITLE( 'Sign the guest book');
    HTP.BODYOPEN;
    HTP.FORMOPEN( curl => 'guestbook.insert_entry');
    HTP.BOLD( 'Name:');
    HTP.PRINT('<INPUT name=i_name>');
    HTP.PARA;
    HTP.BOLD( 'E-mail: ');
    HTP.PRINT('<INPUT name=i_email>');
    HTP.PARA;
    HTP.BOLD( 'Comments:');
    HTP.FORMTEXTAREAOPEN(
        cname => 'i_comments',
        nrows => '5',
        ncolumns => '40');
    HTP.FORMTEXTAREACLOSE;
    HTP.PARA;
    HTP.PRINT('<INPUT type=submit> value="Save Entry"');
    HTP.FORMCLOSE;
    HTP.BODYCLOSE;
END;
```

Step 5

Write the procedure in the package to insert the data into the underlying table. Once the record is inserted, the procedure calls MAIN to
display the main screen, which is now updated with the new entry.
Here's the code:

```
PROCEDURE insert_entry (
    i_name IN VARCHAR2 DEFAULT NULL,
    i_email IN VARCHAR2 DEFAULT NULL,
    i_comments IN VARCHAR2 DEFAULT NULL ) is
BEGIN
    INSERT INTO guestbook_entries
        (guest_name, email_address, visit_date, comments)
    VALUES
        (i_name, i_email, sysdate, i_comments);
    COMMIT;
    MAIN;
END;
```

28-32. The programmer has forgotten to encode the parameter value into the
CGI standard format. Even though the program compiles correctly, it generates syntactically incorrect hyperlinks. Since you know the format of the
data, you can use the REPLACE function to translate the offending characters (the dashes) into their coded equivalents:

```
qstr := qstr || replace (tbl_rec.todo_date,'-', '%2D');
```

Expert

28-33. The following function is a possible solution for this problem. Note the use of the SUBSTR function to perform ASCII-to-HEX conversion:

```
/* Filename on web page: cgi_encode.sf */
CREATE OR REPLACE FUNCTION cgi_encode
    (s in VARCHAR2)
RETURN VARCHAR2 is

    ret_val VARCHAR2(32762) DEFAULT NULL;
    c CHAR(1);
    ld NUMBER DEFAULT 0;
    td NUMBER DEFAULT 0;
    a2h VARCHAR2(20) := '0123456789ABCDEF';
BEGIN
    FOR i IN 1..LENGTH(s) LOOP
        c := SUBSTR(s,i,1);

        IF ((UPPER(c) >= 'A' ) and ( UPPER(c) <= 'Z')) OR
           ((c >= '0') AND (c <= '9')) OR
           (c = '_')
        THEN
            ret_val := ret_val || c;
        ELSEIF c = ' ' then
            ret_val := ret_val || '+';
        ELSE
            ld := FLOOR( ASCII ( c ) / 16 );
            td := ASCII( c ) - 16*ld;
            ret_val := ret_val || '%';
            ret_val := ret_val || SUBSTR(a2h,ld+1,1);
            ret_val := ret_val || SUBSTR(a2h,td+1,1);
        END IF;

    END LOOP;
    RETURN ret_val;
EXCEPTION
    WHEN OTHERS THEN
        RETURN 'CONVERSION+ERROR';
END;
```

28-34. The most likely cause of this problem is a buffer overflow. At the beginning of the time period, when there were just a few records, everything seemed to work fine. As more records were added, however, the system became noticeably slower. Finally, it exceeded the size of the HTML output buffer. Unfortunately, there is no PL/SQL workaround to this problem. A reasonable approach is to either break the file into sections or replace the PL/SQL procedure with a nonbuffered language such as Perl.

28-35. The original error is an infinite loop in the procedure. The much subtler error—the compiler lockup—is caused by a number of factors. In the normal flow of events, the HTTP listener passes requests for stored procedures to the PL/SQL gateway. The gateway invokes the procedure in the RDBMS and then waits for its output. When the program completes, the results are sent back through the gateway and on to the listener.

An infinite loop disrupts the process. Since the procedure never terminates, the gateway never gets the chance to send its output back to the listener. When the user presses "Stop" because he's sick of waiting, he is merely disconnecting from the HTTP listener. The gateway process, oblivious to the fact that the client has disconnected, continues trying to complete the request.

It's at this point that things get weird. Remember that the source code for a PL/SQL package or procedure is stored directly in the database. The RDBMS locks this code while a procedure executes. Since an infinite loop never terminates, the RDBMS never releases the lock on the source code. Consequently, it can't be modified until a DBA manually kills the errant gateway process with a tool like the Instance Manager of the Oracle Enterprise Manager Suite.

28-36. Here's a suggested implementation:

```
CREATE OR REPLACE PROCEDURE print_messages (
    i_thread_id IN VARCHAR2 DEFAULT NULL) as

    cursor t_cur is
        SELECT * FROM messages WHERE msg_parent = i_thread_id
            order by date_created;

    t_rec t_cur%ROWTYPE;

    link VARCHAR2(500);

BEGIN
    HTP.PRINT('<ol>');
    OPEN t_cur;
    LOOP
        FETCH t_cur INTO t_rec;
        EXIT WHEN t_cur%NOTFOUND;
        HTP.PRINT('<li>');
        link := 'print_messages?i_thread_id=' || t_rec.msg_id;
        HTP.ANCHOR (link, t_rec.msg_subject);
        HTP.ITALIC(
            '(' || t_rec.msg_author ||
            ',' || t_rec.date_created || ')');
        HTP.PRINT('</li>');
        -- Call the procedure recursively
        print_messages(t_rec.msg_id);
    END LOOP;
    HTP.PRINT('</ol>');
    CLOSE t_cur;
END;
```

29

Tuning PL/SQL

Beginner

29-1. The statements are:

a. False. A fast program that quickly reaches the wrong answer is still wrong. It's much more important that a program be correct.

b. False. There is no direct relationship between lines of code and speed (take, for instance, SELECT...INTO).

c. True. Most programs spend 80% of their time executing 20% of the code. The key to significantly improving performance is identifying that 20%.

d. False. Performance is just one property of optimal code. It's also important that the code be well-structured and readable, and that it follow best practices.

e. True. A program should both yield correct answers and perform well in production.

f. False. Since PL/SQL is stored and executed inside the Oracle database, you must take into account the fact that accessing and running that code competes with other database operations.

g. False. Tuning also involves optimizing the code itself (the algorithm) and the way that code is stored and used in memory.

h. False. There are a number of tools you can use to tune PL/SQL, such as TKPROF, the DBMS_APPLICATION_INFO built-in package, and the PL/SQL code profiler (Oracle8*i* only).

i. False. While the DBA can help optimize memory utilization or SQL performance, he or she can do almost nothing to improve the performance of a poorly designed algorithm.

29-2. (c). You can often get a big performance boost by *caching*, or saving, frequently used values (e.g., a table of status codes) as PL/SQL variables.

29-3. Check to see if Oracle has already written it! Becoming familiar with the host of procedures, functions, and packages built in to Oracle will make you a more efficient and productive developer. In addition, Oracle has tested and tuned these programs, giving you one less worry.

29-4. An algorithm is a process; a program is an implementation of an algorithm in a particular language. The classic analogy is that an algorithm is like the recipe for a cake. It tells you the steps (the algorithm) you need to follow to make a cake (the program). Unless you're very hungry, you don't eat the recipe; you eat the cake it tells you how to create (whether or not the cake is edible is a function of the skill of the cook!).

29-5. (b). Packages provide a great way to store frequently needed values. For example, you could load the contents of a lookup table into an index-by table to minimize the number of database fetches a program makes.

29-6. The following list matches the tuning tool to its description:

- 1 and d
- 2 and e
- 3 and b
- 4 and a
- 5 and c

29-7. (d). Compiled code is loaded into the System Global Area (SGA) when a PL/SQL program executes.

29-8. (b). Session data (e.g., packages, variables, cursors, etc.) are stored in the User Global Area (UGA).

29-9. (e). You can use the DBMS_SESSION package to keep a PL/SQL program in memory, particularly a frequently used package. Typically, you pin selected packages in the database startup routines.

29-10. Avoiding repetitive calculations inside a loop is a key tuning concept; the following procedure is faster because it evaluates the UPPER function (which doesn't change) only once:

```
PROCEDURE process_data (nm_in IN VARCHAR2) IS
   v_nm some_table.some_column%TYPE := UPPER (nm_in);
BEGIN
   FOR rec IN pkgd.cur
   LOOP
      process_rec (v_nm, rec.total_production);
   END LOOP;
END;
```

29-11. Oracle recommends that you avoid applying the NOT NULL constraint to a declaration, and instead check for a NULL value yourself. Therefore, the following rewrite is better:

```
DECLARE
   my_value INTEGER := 0;
BEGIN
   IF my_value IS NULL THEN /* ERROR! */
   ELSIF my_value > 0 THEN ...
END;
```

29-12. "SELECT COUNT(*) INTO emp_count" queries are inefficient and expensive ways to determine if at least one record exists in a table that meets a particular criterion (in this case, whether any employees exist for the given department). Fetching the first row and using an IF statement is a much faster way to test whether at least one row exists in a query:

```
CREATE OR REPLACE PROCEDURE drop_dept (
   deptno_in          IN NUMBER,
   reassign_deptno_in IN NUMBER
)
IS
   CURSOR my_cur IS
      SELECT COUNT (*)
        INTO temp_emp_count
        FROM emp
       WHERE deptno = deptno_in;
   cur_rec my_cur%ROWTYPE;

BEGIN
   OPEN my_cur;
   FETCH my_cur INTO cur_rec;
   IF my_cur%FOUND
   THEN
      UPDATE emp
         SET deptno = reassign_deptno_in
       WHERE deptno = deptno_in;
   END IF;

   CLOSE my_cur;

   DELETE
     FROM dept
    WHERE deptno = deptno_in;

   COMMIT;
END drop_dept;
```

Intermediate

29-13. (c). The PLS_INTEGER datatype utilizes the machine's native arithmetic functions.

29-14. Snippet (b) is faster because it exits as soon as the condition is met. In snippet (a), all 2045 conditions are always checked.

29-15. Trigger (a) is better because the WHEN and UPDATE OF clauses cause it to fire only when the desired conditions are met; Trigger (b) fires regardless of what happens. For example, suppose you update on the dept columns. Trigger (a) doesn't do anything; Trigger (b) still performs the test for each row.

29-16. One possible way to improve the code is to avoid repeating unnecessary calculations inside the loop:

```
DECLARE
    v_today CONSTANT VARCHAR2(10) := TO_CHAR (SYSDATE, 'MM/DD/YYYY');

    CURSOR emp_cur
    IS
        SELECT SUBSTR (last_name, 1, 20) last_name FROM employee;
BEGIN
    FOR rec IN emp_cur
    LOOP
        process_employee_history (rec.last_name, v_today);
    END LOOP;
END;
```

29-17. One of the best ways to simplify maintenance and minimize the number of times a SQL statement must be parsed is to replace literals with bind variables. You can almost always improve a cursor simply by replacing hardcoded values with bind variables:

```
CURSOR name_cur (dept IN INTEGER) IS
        SELECT last_name FROM employee
          WHERE department_id = dept;
BEGIN
    OPEN marketing_cur(20);
```

29-18. You can get a performance boost by replacing repetitive, cursor-based PL/SQL loops with "pure" SQL statements:

```
UPDATE emp SET sal = sal * 1.01;
```

29-19. Corrclated subqueries and complex multiple joins can result in excessive processing. You can improve the complex SQL statement by first breaking it into two cursors (using bind variables where appropriate) and then processing the cursors inside a PL/SQL procedure. Here is a rewrite of the original query:

```
CURSOR dept_cur IS
    SELECT department_id, MAX (salary) max_salary
      FROM employee E GROUP BY department_id;

CURSOR emp_cur (dept IN PLS_INTEGER,maxsal IN NUMBER) IS
    SELECT last_name || ', ' || first_name emp_name
      FROM employee
      WHERE department_id = dept AND salary = maxsal;
```

29-20. The following package uses a global package variable to cache the current user:

```
CREATE OR REPLACE PACKAGE thisuser
IS
    /* Persistent "global" variable */
    g_user VARCHAR2(30) := USER;
END;
```

29-21. Here is the implementation of the lookup package:

```
/* Filename on web page: lookup.pkg */
CREATE OR REPLACE PACKAGE te_company
IS
    FUNCTION name$val (id_in IN company.company_id%TYPE)
        RETURN company.name%TYPE;
END te_company;
/
CREATE OR REPLACE PACKAGE BODY te_company
IS
    TYPE names_tabtype IS TABLE OF company.name%TYPE
        INDEX BY BINARY_INTEGER;

    names names_tabtype;

    FUNCTION name$val (id_in IN company.company_id%TYPE)
        RETURN company.name%TYPE
    IS
        CURSOR comp_cur
        IS
            SELECT name
              FROM company
             WHERE company_id = id_in;

        retval company.name%TYPE;
    BEGIN
        IF names.EXISTS (id_in)
        THEN
            retval := names (id_in);
        ELSE
            OPEN comp_cur;
            FETCH comp_cur INTO retval;
            CLOSE comp_cur;

            IF retval IS NOT NULL
            THEN
                names (id_in) := retval;
            END IF;
        END IF;

        RETURN retval;
    END name$val;
END te_company;
/
```

29-22. Three SQL statements are parsed when the block is executed. Since the first two standalone queries are physically different, they are cached separately. The two statements inside the PL/SQL block, however, are treated as a single statement because the PL/SQL engine reformats them so that they are physically (and logically) equivalent.

29-23. You can use the Oracle8 RETURNING clause to combine the two operations into a single (faster) SQL statement:

```
BEGIN
    INSERT INTO UnionBuster VALUES (ub_seq.NEXTVAL, 'Prison', 5)
        RETURNING ub_id, hourly_wage
            INTO v_latest_bustID, v_hard_to_beat;
END;
```

29-24. If you've defined a cursor using the SELECT FOR UPDATE clause, you can use the WHERE CURRENT OF clause to speed up subsequent UPDATE or DELETE statements:

```
LOOP
    FETCH cur INTO rec;
    EXIT WHEN cur%NOTFOUND;

    UPDATE employee SET last_name = UPPER (last_name)
     WHERE CURRENT OF cur;
END LOOP;
```

29-25. You can use the Oracle8*i* FORALL statement to perform the entire operation in just one line:

```
PROCEDURE whack_emps_by_dept (deptlist dlist_t)
IS
BEGIN
    FORALL aDept IN deptlist.FIRST..deptlist.LAST
        DELETE emp WHERE deptno = deptlist(aDept);
END;
```

29-26. Here is the SQL statement that completes the program:

```
SELECT empno, ename, hiredate
    BULK COLLECT INTO enos, names, hdates
    FROM emp
    WHERE deptno = deptno_in;
```

29-27. The following script formats and displays objects that are larger than a user-supplied size:

```
SET PAGESIZE 66
COLUMN name FORMAT A30
COLUMN type FORMAT A15
COLUMN source_size FORMAT 999999
COLUMN parsed_size FORMAT 999999
COLUMN code_size FORMAT 999999
TTITLE 'Size of PL/SQL Objects > &1 KBytes'
SPOOL pssize.lis
SELECT name, type, source_size, parsed_size, code_size
  FROM user_object_size
```

```
       WHERE code_size > &1 * 1000
       ORDER BY code_size DESC
       /
       SPOOL OFF
       TTITLE OFF
```

Expert

29-28. The matches are:

- 1 and d
- 2 and b
- 3 and c
- 4 and a

29-29. There are several possible ways to improve the program. The following optimization eliminates the nested loops by accumulating the schedule in reverse, resulting in a program that is both faster and easier to understand (note that there are several versions on the book's web page):

```
/* Filename on web page: presvalue.sql */
PROCEDURE build_lease_schedule
IS
    pv_total_lease NUMBER (9) := 0;
    one_year_pv NUMBER (9) := 0;
BEGIN
    fixed_count := 0;
    var_count := 0;

    FOR year_count IN REVERSE 1 .. 20
    LOOP
       one_year_pv :=
          pv_of_fixed (year_count) +
          pv_of_variable (year_count);
       pv_total_lease :=
          pv_total_lease + one_year_pv;
       pv_table (year_count) :=
          pv_total_lease;
    END LOOP;
END;
```

29-30. You can create an anonymous PL/SQL block within an IF statement to declare and use memory only when necessary:

```
PROCEDURE only_as_needed (...) IS
BEGIN
    IF <condition>
    THEN
       DECLARE
          big_string VARCHAR2(32767) := ten_minute_lookup (...);
          big_list list_types.big_strings_tt;
       BEGIN
          use_big_string (big_string);
```

```
            Process_big_list (big_list);
          END;
      ELSE
        /* Nothing big
            going on here */
        ...
      END IF;
    END;
```

29-31. You can use native dynamic SQL to easily change the status of a trigger:

```
/* Filename on web page: settrig_status.sp */
CREATE OR REPLACE PROCEDURE settrig (tab IN VARCHAR2, action IN VARCHAR2)
IS
   v_action VARCHAR2 (10) := UPPER (action);
   v_other_action VARCHAR2 (10) := 'DISABLE';
BEGIN
   IF v_action = 'DISABLE'
   THEN
      v_other_action := 'ENABLE';
   END IF;

   FOR rec IN (SELECT trigger_name
                 FROM user_triggers
                WHERE table_owner = USER
                  AND table_name = UPPER (tab)
                  AND status = v_other_action)
   LOOP
      EXECUTE IMMEDIATE 'ALTER TRIGGER ' ||
                   rec.trigger_name ||
                   ' ' ||
                   v_action;
      DBMS_OUTPUT.put_line (
         'Set status of ' || rec.trigger_name || ' to ' || v_action
      );
   END LOOP;
END;
```

29-32. You can use DBMS_JOB to run the calc_comp procedure in parallel:

```
DECLARE
   job# PLS_INTEGER;
   PROCEDURE doit (job IN VARCHAR2) IS BEGIN
      DBMS_JOB.SUBMIT (
         job#, 'calc_comp ('' || job || '')', SYSDATE, NULL);
      COMMIT;
   END;
BEGIN
   doit ('CLERK');
   doit ('VP');
   doit ('PROGRAMMER');
END;
```

29-33. Yes, the fact that the compensation at one level is the sum of the sublevels affects your ability to run calc_comp in parallel; the processes started by DBMS_JOB must be independent (i.e., not rely on the results of a previous calculation).

29-34. Although statements (a) and (b) do the same thing (i.e., they are logically equivalent), they are structurally different (version (a) uses "2" as a multiplier, version (b) uses "2.0"). The effect of this small difference is that it prevents the PL/SQL engine from using the preparsed cursor for (a) in computing the result set of (b). In order to reuse two logically equivalent statements, they must be physically identical.

29-35. Your script must query the all_dependencies data dictionary table:

```
SELECT owner || '.' || name refs_table,
       referenced_owner || '.' || referenced_name table_referenced
  FROM all_dependencies
 WHERE TYPE IN ('PACKAGE', 'PACKAGE BODY', 'PROCEDURE', 'FUNCTION')
   AND referenced_type IN ('TABLE', 'VIEW');
```

29-36. You can use the bulk collection operations to perform this relatively complex task with a minimal amount of code:

```
FUNCTION whack_emps_by_dept (deptlist dlist_t)
    RETURN enolist_t
IS
    enolist enolist_t;
BEGIN
    FORALL aDept IN deptlist.FIRST..deptlist.LAST
        DELETE emp WHERE deptno IN deptlist(aDept)
            RETURNING empno BULK COLLECT INTO enolist;
    RETURN enolist;
END;
```

29-37. You can use packaged variables (and an anonymous PL/SQL block) to eliminate the calls to the DBMS_SQL.BIND_VARIABLES procedure:

```
CREATE OR REPLACE PACKAGE myvars
IS
    empno emp.empno%TYPE;
    deptno emp.deptno%TYPE;
    ename emp.ename%TYPE;
END;
/

CREATE OR REPLACE PROCEDURE bindnone
IS
    cur INTEGER := DBMS_SQL.OPEN_CURSOR;
    rows_inserted INTEGER;
BEGIN
    DBMS_SQL.PARSE (
        cur,
        'BEGIN
            INSERT INTO emp (empno, deptno, ename)
                VALUES (myvars.empno, myvars.deptno, myvars.ename);
         END;',
        DBMS_SQL.NATIVE
    );

    FOR rowind IN 1 .. 1000
    LOOP
```

```
      myvars.empno := rowind;
      myvars.deptno := 40;
      myvars.ename := 'Steven' || rowind;
      rows_inserted := DBMS_SQL.EXECUTE (cur);
   END LOOP;
   DBMS_SQL.CLOSE_CURSOR (cur);
END;
```

29-38. Before Oracle8, VARCHAR2 variables were treated as variable length but stored as fixed length. Hence, in an Oracle 7.3 database, this script consumes 32,767 * 32,767 bytes (approximately 1 GB!) of memory, even though each element of the array is NULL.

29-39. Pass-by-value is a problem for large collections. For example, suppose that you have a large index-by table with 50,000 elements. Passing the table as an IN OUT parameter creates another copy of the structure in memory. Additionally, any updates made to this copy must be propagated back to the original collection variables.

There are two ways to mitigate the problem. The first is to change the parameters into packaged variables. The second method, available only in Oracle8*i*, is to use the NOCOPY keyword in the parameter declaration. NOCOPY switches the parameter "more" to pass by reference.

There are several potential pitfalls with these approaches:

- Since changes take effect immediately on the variables themselves, rather than on a copy, it's impossible to "roll back" if an exception occurs.

- Global variables, unless carefully encapsulated behind a well-defined API, can create a host of maintenance problems.

- The NOCOPY keyword, like a pragma, is just a request to the compiler, not a command. For example, it's ignored when the program is called via RPC; when you pass just one element of a collection; when collection elements are constrained (i.e., NOT NULL); when parameters are records with anchored declarations; or when implicit datatypes are required.

30

PL/SQL for DBAs

Beginner

30-1. You can examine database parameters with the GET_PARAMETER_VALUE function of the DBMS_UTILITY package (Oracle 8.0.4 only).

30-2. Here's one possible implementation:

```
CREATE OR REPLACE FUNCTION get_parameter (
    p_parameter v$sysstat.name%TYPE )
RETURN v$sysstat.value%TYPE IS

    v_intval     BINARY_INTEGER;
    v_who_cares BINARY_INTEGER;
    v_ret_val    v$sysstat.value%TYPE;

BEGIN
    v_who_cares := DBMS_UTILITY.GET_PARAMETER_VALUE(p_parameter,
                                                     v_intval,
                                                     v_ret_val);

    RETURN(v_ret_val);
END get_parameter;
```

30-3. The built-in is DBMS_UTILITY.DB_VERSION, and an example follows:

```
DECLARE
    v_db_version v$version.banner%TYPE;
    v_db_compatibility v$version.banner%TYPE;

BEGIN
    DBMS_UTILITY.DB_VERSION(v_db_version,v_db_compatibility);
    DBMS_OUTPUT.PUT_LINE(v_db_version);
END;
/
```

30-4. Here's a suggested procedure:

```
CREATE OR REPLACE PROCEDURE display_db_version
  IS
  CURSOR version_cur IS
  SELECT banner
    FROM v$version
   WHERE banner LIKE 'Oracle%'
  ;
  v_db_version v$version.banner%TYPE;

BEGIN
  OPEN version_cur;
  FETCH version_cur INTO v_db_version;
  CLOSE version_cur;
  v_db_version := SUBSTR(v_db_version,INSTR(v_db_version,'Release ')+8);
  v_db_version := SUBSTR(v_db_version,1,INSTR(v_db_version,' ')-1);
  dbms_output.put_line(v_db_version);
END;
```

30-5. DBMS_SHARED_POOL maintains the SHARED_POOL.

30-6. Here's the command:

```
BEGIN
  DBMS_SHARED_POOL.KEEP('DBMS_SHARED_POOL','P');
END;
```

30-7. Packages run within the privileges of their owner, not those of the user calling them. In Oracle 8.1, this default behavior can be overridden.

Intermediate

30-8. Here's a suggested procedure:

```
/* Filename on web page: analyze_oem.sp */
CREATE OR REPLACE PROCEDURE analyze_oem IS
    -- Analyze the OEM schema. This job will be submitted
    -- every hour by DBMS_JOB.
  -- cursor to get the current hour
  CURSOR curs_get_hour IS
  SELECT TO_CHAR(SYSDATE,'HH24')
    FROM DUAL;
  v_current_hour NUMBER(2);

  -- option for analyze command
  v_method_opt VARCHAR2(15);

BEGIN
  -- get the current hour
  OPEN curs_get_hour;
  FETCH curs_get_hour INTO v_current_hour;
  CLOSE curs_get_hour;

  -- if the current hour is 1 or 2 inclusive
  -- then perform a complete analysis otherwise just do
  -- it for the indexes
```

```
        IF v_current_hour IN (1,2) THEN
          v_method_opt := NULL;
        ELSE
          v_method_opt := 'FOR ALL INDEXES';
        END IF;

        DBMS_UTILITY.ANALYZE_SCHEMA( SCHEMA      => 'OEM',
                                     METHOD      => 'COMPUTE',
                                     METHOD_OPT  => v_method_opt );
    END analyze_oem;
```

30-9. This is one possible implementation:

```
/* Filename on web page: add_trx.month.sp*/
CREATE OR REPLACE PROCEDURE add_trx_month IS
    /*
        || This function adds a new partition to the account_trx
        || table. It is to be run on the 20th of the month to
        || create a partition for the next month.
    */

    -- cursor to build date format requirements
    CURSOR curs_get_date_info IS
    SELECT '01-' || TO_CHAR(ADD_MONTHS(SYSDATE,1),'MON-YYYY') upper_bound,
           TO_CHAR(SYSDATE,'YYYYMM')                          part_name
      FROM DUAL;
    v_date_info_rec curs_get_date_info%ROWTYPE;

    -- DBMS_SQL variables
    v_stmnt VARCHAR2(2000);
    v_curs PLS_INTEGER;

BEGIN
    -- get the date information
    OPEN curs_get_date_info;
    FETCH curs_get_date_info INTO v_date_info_rec;
    CLOSE curs_get_date_info;

    -- build and execute the DDL statement to add the partition
    v_stmnt := 'ALTER TABLE account_trx ADD PARTITION trx_' ||
        v_date_info_rec.part_name ||
            ' values less than (to_date(' || '''' ||
        v_date_info_rec.upper_bound || '''' ||
            ',''DD-MON-YYYY''))';
    v_curs := DBMS_SQL.OPEN_CURSOR;
    DBMS_SQL.PARSE(v_curs,v_stmnt,DBMS_SQL.NATIVE);
    DBMS_SQL.CLOSE_CURSOR(v_curs);

END add_trx_month;
```

Expert

30-10. A good way is to use dynamic SQL, as in these examples:

```
/* DBMS_SQL version */
DECLARE
  v_curs  PLS_INTEGER;
  v_dummy INT;
BEGIN
  v_curs := DBMS_SQL.OPEN_CURSOR;
  DBMS_SQL.PARSE(v_curs,'ALTER SYSTEM SWITCH LOGFILE',DBMS_SQL.NATIVE);
  v_dummy := DBMS_SQL.EXECUTE(v_curs);
  DBMS_SQL.CLOSE_CURSOR(v_curs);
END;


/* Native Dynamic SQL (Oracle 8.1.5) version */
BEGIN
  EXECUTE IMMEDIATE 'ALTER SYSTEM SWITCH LOGFILE';
END;
```

30-11. The built-in is DBMS_UTILITY.EXEC_DDL_STATEMENT. Here's an example of its use:

```
DBMS_UTILITY.EXEC_DDL_STATEMENT('ALTER TABLESPACE USERS COALESCE')
```

30-12. Here's the CURSOR statement:

```
CURSOR cur_objects (
  p_schema VARCHAR2
  ) IS
  SELECT object_name
       , object_type
    FROM sys.dba_objects
   WHERE owner = p_schema
     AND object_type IN ('CLUSTER','TABLE')
   ORDER BY object_name
  ;
```

30-13. And here's a suggested procedure:

```
/* Filename on web page: validate_structure.sp */
CREATE OR REPLACE PROCEDURE validate_structure (
  i_schema IN VARCHAR2
  ) IS

v_sql VARCHAR2(2000);

-- From previous example.
CURSOR cur_objects (
  p_schema VARCHAR2
  ) IS
  SELECT object_name
       , object_type
    FROM sys.dba_objects
   WHERE owner = p_schema
     AND object_type IN ('CLUSTER','TABLE')
   ORDER BY object_name
  ;
```

```
a-------------------------------------------------------------------
-- Main Logic
-- Loop through the cursor to validate all objects.
-- When one fails, the procedure terminates, and
-- recovery is required for the failed object.

BEGIN
   FOR co IN cur_objects (i_schema) LOOP
      v_sql := 'ANALYZE ' || co.object_type || ' '
            || i_schema || '.' || co.object_name
            || ' VALIDATE STRUCTURE CASCADE';
      dbms_utility.exec_ddl_statement(v_sql);
      dbms_output.put_line(v_sql);
   END LOOP;
END;
```

A note on using this procedure: It can take a *long* time to execute
(hours!). This is because it completely scans all tables and clusters for the
given schema, plus any indexes on the tables and clusters. Also, the
owner of the procedure needs SELECT privilege on SYS.DBA_OBJECTS
and, if it is to analyze objects owned by other users, the ANALYZE ANY
system privilege.

30-14. Here's the CURSOR statement:

```
CURSOR cur_indexes (
   p_schema VARCHAR2
   ) IS
   SELECT segment_name
        , tablespace_name
     FROM sys.dba_extents
    WHERE owner = p_schema
      AND segment_type = 'INDEX'
   GROUP BY segment_name
        , tablespace_name
  HAVING COUNT(extent_id) > 1
    ORDER BY segment_name
   ;
```

30-15. And here is a procedure that uses it:

```
/* Filename on web page: rebuild_indexes.sp */
CREATE OR REPLACE PROCEDURE rebuild_indexes (
   i_schema IN VARCHAR2
   ) IS
v_sql VARCHAR2(2000);

-- From previous example.
CURSOR cur_indexes (
   p_schema VARCHAR2
   ) IS
   SELECT segment_name
        , tablespace_name
     FROM sys.dba_extents
    WHERE owner = p_schema
      AND segment_type = 'INDEX'
```

```
            GROUP BY segment_name
                  , tablespace_name
          HAVING COUNT(extent_id) > 1
            ORDER BY segment_name
         ;
         --  Main Logic

         --  Loop through the cursor to rebuild all indexes.
         --  When one fails, the procedure terminates.
         BEGIN
            FOR ci IN cur_indexes (i_schema) LOOP
               v_sql := 'ALTER INDEX ' || i_schema || '.' || ci.segment_name
                     || ' REBUILD TABLESPACE ' || ci.tablespace_name;
               DBMS_UTILITY.EXEC_DDL_STATEMENT(v_sql);
               DBMS_OUTPUT.PUT_LINE(ci.segment_name);
            END LOOP;
         END;
```

This procedure can also take a long time to execute. This is because it
completely rebuilds all indexes for the given schema. Also, the owner of
the procedure needs SELECT privilege on SYS.DBA_INDEXES and, if it is
to rebuild indexes owned by other users, the ALTER ANY INDEX system
privilege.

30-16. You can find out if you're working in a Parallel Server environment by
issuing this built-in:

```
         BEGIN
            IF DBMS_UTILITY.IS_PARALLEL_SERVER THEN
               DBMS_OUTPUT.PUT_LINE('Everything should be twice as nice!');
            ELSE
               DBMS_OUTPUT.PUT_LINE('You are alone in your quest for knowledge');
            END IF;
         END;
```

30-17. This procedure displays the contents of the cache:

```
         BEGIN
            DBMS_OUTPUT.ENABLE(9999999);
            FOR v_object_rec IN curs_get_counts LOOP
               OPEN curs_get_obj(v_object_rec.obj);
               FETCH curs_get_obj INTO v_obj_rec;
               DBMS_OUTPUT.PUT_LINE(RPAD(v_obj_rec.owner || '.' ||
                                      v_obj_rec.object_name,60)  || ' ' ||
                                    RPAD(v_obj_rec.object_type,20)  ||
                                    LPAD(v_object_rec.num_buffers,10));
               CLOSE curs_get_obj;
            END LOOP;
         END;
```

30-18. The procedures are shown in the *dbbc.sql* file on the web page for this
book

30-19. The package included in the *stats.sql* file on the book's web page should do the trick.

30-20. For the package body, see the *manage_constraints.sql* file on the book's web page.

30-21. Here's the detailed procedure:

```
/* Filename on web page: incremental_del.sp */
CREATE OR REPLACE PROCEDURE incremental_del
                    ( p_owner         dba_tables.owner%TYPE,
                      p_table         dba_tables.table_name%TYPE,
                      p_rows_to_del   INT := 100,
                      p_commit        BOOLEAN := FALSE ) IS
    /*
      ||
      || This function deletes records from the table identified
      || by p_owner and p_table in bunches p_rows_to_del big.
      ||
      || 15-FEB-2000 DRH Coded for workbook
      ||

    -- DBMS_SQL variables
    v_curs       PLS_INTEGER;
    v_rows_del INT;

BEGIN
    -- Create, parse and initially execute the
    -- cursor to delete records
    v_curs := DBMS_SQL.OPEN_CURSOR;
    DBMS_SQL.PARSE(v_curs,
                'DELETE ' || p_owner || '.' ||
                            p_table ||
                ' WHERE ROWNUM <= ' || p_rows_to_del,
                DBMS_SQL.NATIVE);
    v_rows_del := DBMS_SQL.EXECUTE(v_curs);

    -- Continuously execute the cursor to delete
    -- records
    LOOP

    -- stop deleting when a deletion does not actually
    -- delete any records
    EXIT WHEN NVL(v_rows_del,0) = 0;

    -- execute cursor again
    v_rows_del := DBMS_SQL.EXECUTE(v_curs);

    -- was commiting each bunch requested?
    IF p_commit THEN
      commit;
    END IF;

END LOOP;
```

```
     -- close the cursor
     DBMS_SQL.CLOSE_CURSOR(v_curs);

  END;
```

30-22. The package body is available in the *parts.sql* file on the book's web
   page.

30-23. The log_switch procedure is in the *logswtch.sp* file on the book's web
   page.

30-24. Here's a suggested CREATE PROCEDURE stub and declarative section:

```
CREATE OR REPLACE PROCEDURE estimate_tabsize (
  i_schema IN VARCHAR2
 ,i_table_name IN VARCHAR2
 ,i_rows IN NUMBER
 ,i_pctfree IN NUMBER
 ,o_initial_extent OUT NUMBER
  ) IS

c_overhead_factor NUMBER := 10;
```

30-25. Here's a suggested function:

```
/* Filename on web page: table_is_analyzed.sf */
CREATE OR REPLACE FUNCTION table_is_analyzed (
  i_schema IN VARCHAR2
 ,i_table_name IN VARCHAR2
  )
  RETURN BOOLEAN IS
  CURSOR curs_check_analyzed ( cp_schema dba_tables.owner%TYPE,
                               cp_table  dba_tables.table_name%TYPE ) IS
  SELECT last_analyzed
    FROM sys.dba_tables
   WHERE owner = cp_schema
     AND table_name = cp_table;
  v_table_is_analyzed BOOLEAN := FALSE;
  v_last_analyzed sys.dba_tables.last_analyzed%TYPE := NULL;

BEGIN
  OPEN curs_check_analyzed(i_schema,i_table_name);
  FETCH curs_check_analyzed INTO v_last_analyzed;
  IF curs_check_analyzed%FOUND THEN
    IF v_last_analyzed IS NOT NULL THEN
      v_table_is_analyzed := TRUE;
    END IF;
  END IF;
  CLOSE curs_check_analyzed;

  RETURN v_table_is_analyzed;
END;
```

There are two assumptions inherent in this script. The first is that a valid
table and owner are passed (otherwise a NO_DATA_FOUND error is
passed to the calling script). The other is that the column last_analyzed in
the DBA_TABLES view is null if the statistics are missing.

30-26. Here's the procedure:

```
CREATE OR REPLACE PROCEDURE ensure_table_analyzed (
  i_schema IN VARCHAR2
 ,i_table_name IN VARCHAR2
  ) IS

BEGIN
  IF NOT table_is_analyzed(i_schema,i_table_name) THEN
    DBMS_DDL.ANALYZE_OBJECT('TABLE',i_schema,i_table_name,'ESTIMATE');
  END IF;
END;
```

30-27. Here's the execution section of the procedure:

```
DECLARE

  CURSOR curs_get_arl ( cp_schema dba_tables.owner%TYPE,
                        cp_table_name dba_tables.table_name%TYPE ) IS
  SELECT avg_row_len
    FROM dba_tables
   WHERE owner = cp_schema
     AND table_name = cp_table_name;
  v_avg_row_len sys.dba_tables.avg_row_len%TYPE;

BEGIN
  ensure_table_analyzed(i_schema,i_table_name);

  OPEN curs_get_arl(i_schema,i_table_name);
  FETCH curs_get_arl INTO v_avg_row_len;
  CLOSE curs_get_arl;

  --  Calculation for initial extent
    o_initial_extent := i_rows *              -- Rows
            v_avg_row_len     *               -- Row Length
          (1 + (i_pctfree/100)) *             -- Add in pctfree per block
          (1 + (c_overhead_factor/100));      -- Fluff for headers, etc.


END;
```

30-28. Here's the full procedure:

```
/* Filename on web page: estimate_tabsize.sp */
CREATE OR REPLACE PROCEDURE estimate_tabsize (
  i_schema IN VARCHAR2
 ,i_table_name IN VARCHAR2
 ,i_rows IN NUMBER
 ,i_pctfree IN NUMBER
 ,o_initial_extent OUT NUMBER
  ) IS

  CURSOR curs_get_arl ( cp_schema dba_tables.owner%TYPE,
                        cp_table_name dba_tables.table_name%TYPE ) IS
  SELECT avg_row_len
    FROM dba_tables
   WHERE owner = cp_schema
     AND table_name = cp_table_name;
```

```
  c_overhead_factor NUMBER := 10;
  v_avg_row_len sys.dba_tables.avg_row_len%TYPE;

BEGIN
  ensure_table_analyzed(i_schema,i_table_name);
  OPEN curs_get_arl(i_schema,i_table_name);
  FETCH curs_get_arl INTO v_avg_row_len;
  CLOSE curs_get_arl;

--  Calculation for initial extent
  o_initial_extent := i_rows *              -- Rows
            v_avg_row_len    *              -- Row Length
            (1 + (i_pctfree/100)) *         -- Add in pctfree per block
            (1 + (c_overhead_factor/100));  -- Fluff for headers, etc.

END;
```

30-29. The DBMS_LOGMNR package provides procedures to load and unload redo log files and start and stop the mining process. The DBMS_LOGMNR_D package provides a single procedure that builds a data dictionary file. The mining process uses this dictionary file to translate the cryptic contents of the redo logs into something meaningful.

30-30. No. Log mining is done against a point-in-time snapshot of the redo logs. This snapshot is taken when the START_LOGMNR procedure is run and is removed when the END_LOGMNR procedure is called. Any changes to the redo logs in the interim aren't reflected.

30-31. Try this procedure:

```
/* Filename on web page: loadlogs1.sp */
CREATE OR REPLACE PROCEDURE load_logs IS

    -- get online redo log group numbers
    CURSOR curs_get_groups IS
    SELECT group#
      FROM v$log;

    -- get ONE member of each redo log group for loading
    CURSOR curs_get_one_member ( cp_group# v$logfile.group#%TYPE ) IS
    SELECT member
      FROM v$logfile
     WHERE group# = cp_group#;
    v_one_member v$logfile.member%TYPE;

BEGIN

    -- for every single online redo log group...
    FOR v_group_rec IN curs_get_groups LOOP

      -- get ONE member of the group
      OPEN curs_get_one_member(v_group_rec.group#);
      FETCH curs_get_one_member INTO v_one_member;
      CLOSE curs_get_one_member;
```

```
/*
    || If processing the first group and hence the first
    || log file then purge any previously loaded logfiles
    || and add the new one with the NEW constant otherwise
    || just add the new log file to the list by accepting
    || the default. Note that the default is ADDFILE.
    ||
    || The LTRIM and RTRIM are required because occasional extra
    || characters are attached to the log member name that cause
    || ADD_LOGFILE to fail.
*/
IF curs_get_groups%ROWCOUNT = 1 THEN
  DBMS_LOGMNR.ADD_LOGFILE(LTRIM(RTRIM(v_one_member)),DBMS_LOGMNR.NEW);
ELSE
  DBMS_LOGMNR.ADD_LOGFILE(LTRIM(RTRIM(v_one_member)));
END IF;

END LOOP;  -- every online redo log group

END;
```

30-32. A suggested implementation is in the *loadlogs2.sp* file on the book's web
⊕ page.

30-33. The following table details the views and their contents.

View Name	Description
V$LOGMNR_CONTENTS	Contains one row per statement including the user, operation, SQL redo, and SQL undo statements
V$LOG_CABIN	Surprisingly, this one does not exist
V$LOGMNR_DICTIONARY	Contains information about the data dictionary used in the call to START_LOGMNR
V$LOGMAJOR	If it did exist, it would sound twice as nice as Log Miner
V$LOGMNR_LOGS	Contains information about the redo logs loaded into Log Miner
V$LOGGER	I'm a lumberjack and I'm OK; I sleeps all night, and I works all day
V$LOGMNR_PARAMETERS	Records the parameters used in the call to START_LOGMNR

30-34. Enter a procedure so powerful that it warrants a package all its own:
DBMS_LOGMNR_D.BUILD! This procedure creates a Log Miner Data Dictionary that translates the redo logs contents into something readable. This
procedure relies on another built-in package, UTL_FILE, and doesn't work
unless it is installed and configured correctly. Consult Oracle's documentation for details.

BUILD has two arguments: dictionary filename and dictionary location. You can choose the filename, but the location must be a directory that UTL_FILE can access.

BUILD can be called from any SQL-compliant interface but is best run in SQL*Plus with SERVEROUTPUT enabled because it displays several status messages:

```
SQL> SET SERVEROUTPUT ON
SQL> EXEC DBMS_LOGMNR_D.BUILD('dictionary.dict','c:\plgenerator\drivers');
LogMnr Dictionary Procedure started
LogMnr Dictionary File Opened
TABLE: OBJ$ recorded in LogMnr Dictionary File
TABLE: TAB$ recorded in LogMnr Dictionary File
TABLE: COL$ recorded in LogMnr Dictionary File
TABLE: SEG$ recorded in LogMnr Dictionary File
TABLE: UNDO$ recorded in LogMnr Dictionary File
TABLE: UGROUP$ recorded in LogMnr Dictionary File
TABLE: TS$ recorded in LogMnr Dictionary File
TABLE: CLU$ recorded in LogMnr Dictionary File
TABLE: IND$ recorded in LogMnr Dictionary File
TABLE: ICOL$ recorded in LogMnr Dictionary File
TABLE: LOB$ recorded in LogMnr Dictionary File
TABLE: USER$ recorded in LogMnr Dictionary File
TABLE: FILE$ recorded in LogMnr Dictionary File
TABLE: PARTOBJ$ recorded in LogMnr Dictionary File
TABLE: PARTCOL$ recorded in LogMnr Dictionary File
TABLE: TABPART$ recorded in LogMnr Dictionary File
TABLE: INDPART$ recorded in LogMnr Dictionary File
TABLE: SUBPARTCOL$ recorded in LogMnr Dictionary File
TABLE: TABSUBPART$ recorded in LogMnr Dictionary File
TABLE: INDSUBPART$ recorded in LogMnr Dictionary File
TABLE: TABCOMPART$ recorded in LogMnr Dictionary File
TABLE: INDCOMPART$ recorded in LogMnr Dictionary File
Procedure executed successfully - LogMnr Dictionary Created

PL/SQL procedure successfully completed.
```

Now you update the call to START_LOGMNR in your procedure to use this data dictionary file as follows:

```
SYS.DBMS_LOGMNR.START_LOGMNR(
    startscn => v_min_start,
    endscn   => v_max_start,
    dictfilename => 'c:\plgenerator\drivers\dictionary.dict');
```

After executing the procedure, you see some more readable results when V$LOGMNR_CONTENTS is queried:

```
SQL> SELECT username,
  2          sql_redo,
  3          sql_undo
  4    FROM v$logmnr_contents;
```

```
USERNAME
-------------------------------
SQL_REDO
---------------------------------------------------------------------------
SQL_UNDO
---------------------------------------------------------------------------
DEPLOYER
DELETE from deployer.employee WHERE
    empno = 100 AND ROWID = 'AAANH8AAIAAAE+EAAB';
INSERT INTO deployer.employee(empno) values (100);
```

30-35. This package can be found in the *miner.sql* file on this book's web
page.

30-36. The statements are:

   a. False. The dictionary file is only up to date at the point in time it is
   created; therefore, you must recreate it after making changes to the
   database.

   b. True. All users (at least those with SELECT ANY TABLE privileges) can
   see the contents of the V$ tables.

   c. False. The Log Miner works against a point in time snapshot of the
   redo logs. Any changes made after the snapshot is taken aren't
   reflected.

30-37. The tried-and-true ANALYZE command has been used to manage statistics for years.

30-38. The ANALYZE command qualifies as a Data Definition Language (DDL)
statement so it can't be executed statically in PL/SQL. It must be wrapped
in a PL/SQL built-in or executed via native dynamic SQL. For example:

```
BEGIN
   DBMS_UTILITY.EXEC_DDL_STATEMENT('analyze table x compute statistics');
   EXECUTE IMMEDIATE 'analyze table x compute statistics';
END;
```

30-39. As an application evolves over time, there are bound to be structural
changes: a table added or removed here, an index added there. Therefore
any lists of objects to analyze must be built dynamically and what better
place to do that than in PL/SQL?

30-40. There are two key benefits:

   • The ability to gather statistics for objects whose current statistics are
   considered too "stale." Now, DBAs don't have to worry about redun-
   dantly recreating statistics for objects whose current ones are perfectly useful. It even allows them to gather a list of stale objects
   without recreating their statistics. By the way, the mighty Oracle is the
   only one that decides when statistics become stale!

- The ability to save statistics into special database tables, rather than directly into the data dictionary, and then transfer them to the data dictionary at a later date. You can now try several sets of statistics and ensure optimizer plan stability regardless of database growth.

30-41. The matching pairs are:

- 1 and b
- 2 and d
- 3 and a
- 4 and c
- 5 and e

30-42. DBMS_STATS.GATHER_DATABASE_STATS

30-43. DBMS_STATS.GATHER_SCHEMA_STATS

30-44. Here's a procedure:

```
CREATE OR REPLACE PROCEDURE analyze_table
                     ( p_owner  VARCHAR2,
                       p_table  VARCHAR2 ) IS
    /*
     || Gather statistics for the table identified
     || by p_owner and p_table.
     ||
     || Requires : ANALYZE ANY privilege
    */
BEGIN
   DBMS_STATS.GATHER_TABLE_STATS(p_owner,p_table);
END;
```

30-45. Oracle 8.1.5 introduces the MONITORING attribute for a table. It can be specified when a table is created or altered as follows:

```
CREATE TABLE x ( col1 INT ) MONITORING;
ALTER TABLE x NOMONITORING;
ALTER TABLE x MONITORING;
```

When a table is monitored, Oracle tracks the number of inserts, updates, and deletes, as well as noting whether a table has been truncated. This information can be viewed in the data dictionary table ALL_TAB_MODIFI-CATIONS. Be aware that monitoring does not occur in real time, and it may take many hours for this table to be updated.

Note that the use of the MONITORING attribute causes a table's indexes to be monitored as well.

30-46. The GATHER_SCHEMA_STATS procedure provides the functionality required via two of its parameters: options, which is where you tell it what to do, and objlist, which stores a list of affected objects. There are five possible values for the options parameter:

GATHER

Gather statistics for all objects

GATHER EMPTY

Gather statistics for objects not having any and create a list of them

GATHER STALE

Gather statistics for objects with stale statistics and create a list of them

LIST_STALE

Create a list of objects with stale statistics

LIST_EMPTY

Create a list of objects with no statistics

Since you want to gather statistics and display a list, the obvious choice is GATHER STALE. The list of objects is returned within a VARRAY typed as OBJECTTAB as defined in the DBMS_STATS package header:

```
CREATE OR REPLACE PROCEDURE analyze_schema
                ( p_owner  VARCHAR2 ) IS
    /*
      || Gather stale statistics for p_owner
      ||
      || Requires : ANALYZE ANY privilege
    */

      /* this varray will hold the list of objects that were
         found to be stale and then analysed */
    v_stale_list DBMS_STATS.OBJECTTAB := DBMS_STATS.OBJECTTAB();

  BEGIN
    DBMS_STATS.GATHER_SCHEMA_STATS(ownname => p_owner,
                                   options => 'GATHER STALE',
                                   objlist => v_stale_list);
    DBMS_OUTPUT.PUT_LINE('Stale Stats List');
    FOR counter IN 1..v_stale_list.COUNT LOOP
      DBMS_OUTPUT.PUT_LINE(v_stale_list(counter).objname);
    END LOOP;
  END;
```

30-47. There are two procedures in DBMS_STATS used to maintain these tables. CREATE_STAT_TABLE and DROP_STAT_TABLE create and drop statistic tables, respectively.

30-48. Here's a replacement procedure:

```
CREATE OR REPLACE PROCEDURE analyze_table
                ( p_owner  VARCHAR2,
                  p_table  VARCHAR2 ) IS
```

```
      /*
      || Gather statistics for the table identified
      || by p_owner and p_table. Put the stats into
      || STATS_GOD.MY_STATS
      ||
      */

      v_stale_list DBMS_STATS.OBJECTTAB;

  BEGIN
      DBMS_STATS.GATHER_TABLE_STATS(ownname => p_owner,
                                    tabname => p_table,
                                    stattab => 'my_stats',
                                    statown => 'stats_god');
  END;
```

30-49. This one is easy! They all match up: 1 with (a), 2 with (b), and so on.

30-50. The complete package is shown in the *analyzer.sql* file on the book's web
  page.

30-51. Here is a suggested exception handler:

```
      /*-----------------------------------------------*/
      PROCEDURE do_estimates ( p_stmnt VARCHAR2 ) IS
      /*-----------------------------------------------*/

         v_num_rows   NUMBER;
         v_num_bytes NUMBER;

      BEGIN
         DBMS_OLAP.ESTIMATE_SUMMARY_SIZE( stmt_id       => 'OLAPPER',
                                          select_clause -> p_stmnt,
                                          num_rows      => v_num_rows,
                                          num_bytes     => v_num_bytes );
      EXCEPTION
         WHEN OTHERS THEN
            IF SQLCODE = -30476 THEN
              RAISE_APPLICATION_ERROR(-20000,'Create Plan Table First');
            ELSIF SQLCODE = -30477 THEN
                DBMS_OUTPUT.PUT_LINE('Invalid Syntax Specified');
            ELSE
              RAISE;
            END IF;

         DBMS_OUTPUT.PUT_LINE('A Materialized View for the statement : ');
         DBMS_OUTPUT.PUT_LINE(CHR(9) || p_stmnt);
         DBMS_OUTPUT.PUT_LINE(CHR(9) || 'Is estimated to require '
            || v_num_rows || ' rows ' ||
                                        ' and ' || v_num_bytes || ' bytes.');
      END do_estimates;
```

30-52. To check this example, see the *olapper.sql* file on the web page for this
  book.

About the Authors

Steven Feuerstein is considered one of the world's leading experts on the Oracle PL/SQL language. He is the author or coauthor of *Oracle PL/SQL Programming*, *Oracle PL/SQL Programming Guide to Oracle8i Features*, *Oracle Built-in Packages*, *Advanced Oracle PL/SQL Programming with Packages*, and several pocket reference books (all from O'Reilly & Associates). Steven has been developing software since 1980 and worked for Oracle Corporation from 1987 to 1992. As Chief Technology Officer of RevealNet, Inc., he has designed several products for PL/SQL developers, including the PL/SQL Knowledge Base, PL/Vision, and PL/Generator. Steven hosts RevealNet's PL/SQL Pipeline, an online community for PL/SQL developers (*http://www.revealnet.com/plsql-pipeline*). When it comes to training and consulting, Steven is president of PL/Solutions (*http://www.plsolutions.com*). As if that weren't enough, Steven is also StarCoach (a.k.a. Chief Technology Counsel) at *Starbelly.com*.

Home is where your home is, and Steven makes his in Rogers Park, Illinois, where he shares an over-sized Georgian with his wife, Veva, his youngest son, Eli, two cats (Sister Itsacat and Moshe Jacobawitz), and Mercury, a Congo Red African Gray parrot. His older son, Chris, is busy making music and creating art nearby. Steven is a member of the Board of Directors of the Crossroads Fund, which provides grants to organizations in Chicago working for social change.

You can reach Steven via email at *feuerstein@revealnet.com, steven@starbelly.com, sfeuerstein@plsolutions.com,* or *sfinfo@stevenfeuerstein.com,* or experience the online version of Steven at *http://www.StevenFeuerstein.com.*

Andrew Odewahn is an Oracle application developer and consultant who lives in Davis Square in Somerville, Massachusetts. He is the author of O'Reilly's *Oracle Web Applications: PL/SQL Developer's Introduction*. He has a degree in computer science from the University of Alabama, where he was a fellow in the Computer-Based Honors Program. He has presented at the East Coast Oracle Developers (ECO) Conference and other Oracle events. He and his wife love the outdoors and, during the spring and summer of 1999, hiked the Appalachian Trail from Georgia to Maine.

Colophon

Our look is the result of reader comments, our own experimentation, and feedback from distribution channels. Distinctive covers complement our distinctive approach to technical topics, breathing personality and life into potentially dry subjects.

The insect on the cover of *Oracle PL/SQL Developer's Workbook* is a stag beetle (*lucanus cervus*). The stag beetle is a large, dark, tough beetle that is the largest insect in Britain. It gets its name from the male's elk-like antlers on its head, which can be as long as the body itself. These "antlers," which are actually part of the jaw and are called mandibles, are used to fight with other males, usually for a female and sometimes for food.

The stag beetle has thin, fragile wings that fold under the shell of its body. In order to fly, this shell lifts, the wings unfold, and the beetle flies awkwardly. It can also rub its wings together to make a sound that's intimidating to other insects.

Stag beetles feed on plant secretions, fruit, decaying wood, and wood sap, and thus prefer a habitat of trees and vegetation. The stag beetle is widespread in parts of England but is now far less common in Japan than it once was. This beetle's numbers are declining, and it is even on the endangered species list in some areas. Reasons for the diminishing numbers include loss of habitat, climate changes, collectors, and being killed by cars on the roads or by people stepping on them (whether accidentally or purposefully).

Mary Anne Weeks Mayo was the copyeditor and production editor for *Oracle PL/SQL Developer's Workbook*. Maureen Dempsey and Emily Quill proofread the book. Mary Sheehan, Jeff Holcomb, Melanie Wang, and Jane Ellin provided quality control. Anna Snow and Judy Hoer provided production support.

Edie Freedman designed the cover of this book, using a 19th-century engraving from the Dover Pictorial Archive. Emma Colby produced the cover layout with Quark XPress 3.3 using Adobe's ITC Garamond font. The cover layout was produced with Quark XPress 3.32 using the ITC Garamond font. Whenever possible, our books use RepKover™, a durable and flexible lay-flat binding. If the page count exceeds RepKover's limit, perfect binding is used.

The interior layouts were designed by Alicia Cech and David Futato. The text and heading fonts are ITC Garamond Light and Garamond Book. The illustrations that appear in this book were produced by Robert Romano and Rhon Porter using Macromedia Freehand 8 and Adobe Photoshop 5. This colophon was written by Nicole Arigo.